RISK MANAGEMENT HANDBOOK
for Health Care Organizations

student edition

ROBERTA L. CARROLL

EDITOR

JOSSEY-BASS
A Wiley Imprint
www.josseybass.com

Published by Jossey-Bass
A Wiley Imprint
989 Market Street, San Francisco, CA 94103-1741—www.josseybass.com

Readers should be aware that Internet Web sites offered as citations and/or sources for further information may have changed or disappeared between the time this was written and when it is read.

Limit of Liability/Disclaimer of Warranty: While the publisher and author have used their best efforts in preparing this book, they make no representations or warranties with respect to the accuracy or completeness of the contents of this book and specifically disclaim any implied warranties of merchantability or fitness for a particular purpose. No warranty may be created or extended by sales representatives or written sales materials. The advice and strategies contained herein may not be suitable for your situation. You should consult with a professional where appropriate. Neither the publisher nor author shall be liable for any loss of profit or any other commercial damages, including but not limited to special, incidental, consequential, or other damages.

Jossey-Bass books and products are available through most bookstores. To contact Jossey-Bass directly call our Customer Care Department within the U.S. at 800-956-7739, outside the U.S. at 317-572-3986, or fax 317-572-4002.

Jossey-Bass also publishes its books in a variety of electronic formats. Some content that appears in print may not be available in electronic books.

Library of Congress Cataloging-in-Publication Data

Risk management handbook for health care organizations / [edited by] Roberta L. Carroll. — Student ed.
    p. ; cm.
Includes bibliographical references and index.
ISBN 978-0-470-30017-6 (pbk.)
    1. Health facilities—Risk management. I. Carroll, Roberta.
[DNLM: 1. Health Facilities—organization & administration. 2. Risk Management.
WX 157 R59533 2009]
RA971.38.R58 2009
362.11068—dc22
      2008055679

Printed in the United States of America
STUDENT EDITION

HB Printing   10 9 8

CONTENTS

SEVEN THE RISK MANAGEMENT PROFESSIONAL AND MEDICATION SAFETY — 219

EIGHT ETHICS IN PATIENT CARE — 261

NINE DOCUMENTATION AND THE MEDICAL RECORD — 287

TEN STATUTES, STANDARDS, AND REGULATIONS — 327

EXHIBITS, FIGURES, TABLES, AND, PHOTOS

EXHIBITS

FIGURES

TABLES

PHOTOS

THE CONTRIBUTORS

ELLEN L. BARTON, JD, CPCU, DFASHRM, principal, ERM Strategies LLC, is an independent consultant. Previously, she held positions as vice president, risk management, MedStar Health, Inc., an integrated health care delivery system (1999–2000); vice president, claims and health care practice leader, Aon Risk Services, Inc., of Maryland (1998–1999); vice president, legal services for American Radiology Services, Inc. (1997–1998); and vice president and general Counsel of New American Health, Inc. (1996–1997). She served as president, Neumann Insurance Company, and director of risk management, Franciscan Health System (1987–1996). She also served as general counsel for Franciscan Health System (1993–1996) and as senior vice president, legal services (1994–1996). Barton sat on the board of directors and served as chairperson of Preferred Physicians Insurance Company, a Nebraska stock insurance company; Consolidated Catholic Casualty Risk Retention Group, Inc., a Vermont-based captive insurance company; and Alternative Insurance Management Services, Inc., a captive insurance company management firm based in Colorado. Barton also served as a member of the Trinity Health System Insurance Management Advisory Committee. She is a graduate of Rosemont College and received her JD degree from the University of Cincinnati. She is also a chartered property and casualty underwriter. Barton has conducted numerous seminars on risk management issues on a national as well as regional level and has published articles in related areas. She is admitted to the bars in Ohio, Maryland, and Pennsylvania and holds membership in the Maryland Bar Association, the Society of Chartered Property and Casualty Underwriters; the American Health Lawyers Association, in which she currently serves as chairperson of the Risk Management Affinity Group of the Hospitals and Health Systems Practice Group; the Maryland Society for Healthcare Risk Management, of which she was president in 2002–2003, and the American Society for Healthcare Risk Management, of which she was president in 1990. She is also the 1993 recipient of the Distinguished Service Award of the American Society for Healthcare Risk Management (ASHRM). In 2001, the ASHRM Modules Program, the Barton Certificate in Healthcare Risk Management, was named in her honor.

ROBERTA L. CARROLL, RN, ARM, CPCU, MBA, CPHRM, CPHQ, LHRM, HEM, DFASHRM, is senior vice president, Aon Healthcare, based in Tampa, Florida. Previously she was director of Risk Management Consulting Services and senior vice president and manager of the health care unit, Aon Risk Services of Northern California. She has held a variety of positions, including vice president of risk and insurance management for UniHealth in Burbank, California; senior vice president and manager of the health care unit for Corroon & Black of Illinois; vice president of risk management, claims, and marketing for Premier Alliance Insurance Company; trust administrator and risk manager for Premier Hospitals Alliance in Chicago; and director of risk management at Mount Sinai Medical Center, Miami Beach, Florida. Carroll served on the American Society for Healthcare Risk Management (ASHRM) board for six years and was president in 1995–1996. She was elected to the board of the Southern California Association for Healthcare Risk Management (SCAHRM) and was one of the founding members, first president, and board member of the Florida Society for Healthcare Risk Management and Patient Safety (FSHRMPS). In addition, she was one of the founders and an officer of the Florida Medical Malpractice Claims Council, Inc. (FMMCCI). She is a licensed healthcare risk manager (LHRM) in the state of Florida and faculty member for the health care risk management course at the University of South Florida (USF). Carroll is also a faculty member for the ASHRM-sponsored Barton Certificate program "Essentials" module. Previously, she was a faculty member for Module 1, "The Fundamentals of Health Care Risk Management: Constructing the Comprehensive Program," for eight years. Carroll received a bachelor of science degree in health services administration and a certificate in emergency medical services systems administration from Florida International University and a master of business degree from Nova Southeastern University. She has earned the right to use the ARM, CPCU, HEM, CPHQ, and CPHRM designations. She is editor of the *Risk Management Handbook for Health Care Organizations'* second (1997), third (2000), and fourth (2004) editions and the series editor for the fifth (2006) and student (2009) editions. Carroll has received numerous awards: in 1997, ASHRM's highest honor, the Distinguished Service Award (DSA); 1998 Distinguished Alumni Achievement Award from the School of Business and Entrepreneurship, Nova Southeastern University; Most Contributing Member to Risk Management in 1996 from the SCAHRM; and Most Valuable Contribution to the Field of Risk Management in 1993 from that same organization. She is a member of ASHRM, FSHRMPS, and the Publication Committee of the Risk Management Affinity Group (RMAG) of the American Health Lawyers Associations (AHLA). She is a well-known author, speaker, and educator in the areas of alternative risk financing, risk mitigation strategies and solutions, claims administration, early intervention programs, enterprise risk management (ERM), strategic planning, and reengineering. Her activities are on a local, state, and national level. Her professional and committee activities are numerous.

HEDY COHEN, RN, BSN, MS, vice president for the Institute for Safe Medication Practices (ISMP). She received an associate of arts degree in nursing from Bucks County Community College in Newtown, Pennsylvania; a bachelor of science in nursing from LaSalle University in Philadelphia; a master's degree in health systems administration from Rochester Institute for Technology, in Rochester, New York; and is presently a doctoral candidate in health policy at the University of the Sciences in Philadelphia. Her clinical nursing background of more than eighteen years was focused in critical care and nursing management. She is a frequent speaker for health care organizations on current issues in medication safety and has written numerous articles on improving the medication use process. She also edits ISMP's monthly newsletter, *Nurse Advise-ERR*; cowrote a handbook on high-alert drugs; and is on the national advisory board for the *Nursing Advance Journal* and *Davis's Drug Guide for Nurses*. Cohen has been appointed adjunct associate professor at Temple School of Pharmacy and faculty fellow in the Executive Patient Safety Fellowship, which is offered through Virginia Commonwealth University in Richmond. She also serves as a medication error clinical analyst for the Pennsylvania Safety Authority's reporting program.

MARK COHEN, ARM, RPLU, CPHQ, CPHRM, DFASHRM, risk management consultant, Sutter Health Risk Services. Cohen began his career in risk management in 1982 at the UCLA Medical Center and Center for the Health Sciences and was subsequently appointed director of risk management. In 1987, he moved to Sacramento to become director of risk management for the University of California, Davis Health System. Cohen joined Sutter Health as a corporate risk management consultant in 1995. He provides a broad range of risk management consultation services to Sutter Health's not-for-profit network of acute-care hospitals; physician organizations; medical research facilities; regionwide home health, hospice, and occupational health networks; and long-term care centers that serve more than one hundred Northern California communities. Cohen writes and lectures on Emergency Medical Treatment and Labor Act (EMTALA) compliance and is a member of the faculty of the California Healthcare Association's annual EMTALA seminars. He is a past president of both the Southern California Association for Healthcare Risk Management (SCAHRM) and the California Society for Healthcare Risk Management (CSHRM), and served as a member of ASHRM's board in 2002 and 2003. He currently serves on the board of the Sacramento Risk Management Forum and the South Natomas Transit Management Association. Cohen has served on the faculty of ASHRM's "Modules" and "Essentials" and CPHRM study session programs and on several ASHRM committees, most notably as longtime chair of the Online Education Committee.

DOMINIC A. COLAIZZO, MBA, is managing director of Aon's National Healthcare Alternative Risk Practice, based in Philadelphia. He is responsible for directing Aon resources for the development, implementation, and servicing of alternative risk transfer programs for the health care industry. His sixteen years of experience in health care administration and nineteen years of broking and consulting experience with Aon have provided him with a broad understanding of the issues faced by all health care providers. He had served as chief operating officer and senior vice president of a community hospital and has held various administrative positions in a major teaching hospital. He has extensive experience in developing and servicing alternative risk financing and innovative insurance programs for profit and not-for-profit health systems, health insurers, managed care organizations, extended care organizations, and physicians' groups. Colaizzo also serves as a key adviser for Aon's National Healthcare Practice.

He has earned a master of business administration for the Leonard Davis Institute for Health Economics at the Wharton School of the University of Pennsylvania. He has also earned a bachelor of arts degree in economics and mathematics from Washington and Jefferson College. Colaizzo is a diplomate of the American College of Health Care Executives and holds memberships in the American Society for Healthcare Risk Management (ASHRM), the American Hospital Association, and the Health Care Financial Association. He serves on the faculty for professional development seminars and has cowritten an article for the ASHRM Journal titled, "Integrating Quality with Risk Financing Through a Risk Retention Group."

HARLAN Y. HAMMOND JR., MBA, ARM, CPHRM, DFASHRM, assistant vice president for risk management services, Intermountain Healthcare, Salt Lake City, Utah. His responsibilities include oversight for Intermountain's risk financing, loss prevention, loss control, and claims administration efforts and safety, security, and systemwide emergency response. Hammond received his bachelor's degree in business administration from the University of Utah, followed by a master's of business administration degree from the University of Washington. Hammond has served in various capacities with ASHRM, including twice as a member of the ASHRM board of directors and as a faculty member for the Barton Certificate in Healthcare Risk Management program. He received ASHRM's Distinguished Service Award in 2000.

MONICA HANSLOVAN, JD, formerly was an associate of Horty, Springer & Mattern, PC, in Pittsburgh, Pennsylvania. She focuses her practice exclusively on hospital and health care law, with particular emphasis on medical staff matters. She advises clients on a wide range of medical staff issues, including development of, analysis of, and proposed revisions to medical staff bylaws and related documents; development of hospital and medical staff policies; and management of issues related to protection of peer review documents and sharing of confidential peer review and credentialing information. Hanslovan received her doctor of law degree magna cum laude from Widener University School of Law and her bachelor of arts with high distinction from Pennsylvania State University. She is a member of the Allegheny County, Pennsylvania, and American Bar Associations and the American Health Lawyers Association.

JUDY HART is executive vice president of Endurance Specialty Insurance, Ltd., and heads the company's health care practice. Hart has more than thirty years of experience in the insurance industry and has been dedicated to health care risk financing for the past twenty-six years. She spent most of her career at Alexander & Alexander Services, where she was a managing director and deputy national director of health care practice. During that time, she participated in the development of alternative risk financing programs for health care organizations across the United States. Before joining Endurance, she spent four years as vice president of Employers Reinsurance Corporation, where she was responsible for marketing, new product development, and the development of health care strategies and was a member of the health care senior leadership team. She is the current president of the Bermuda Society for Healthcare Risk Management. She is a frequent speaker and author on risk management issues associated with risk financing, managed care, and the evolving risks facing health care providers. She attended Southeast Missouri State University and Washington University in Saint Louis, Missouri.

PETER J. HOFFMAN, JD, is a partner of the Philadelphia law firm of McKissock & Hoffman, PC. He received his bachelor of arts degree from Washington and Jefferson College, his master of arts from the State University of New York Graduate School of Public Affairs, and his doctor of law degree cum laude from Temple University School of Law, where he was the executive editor of the Law Review. Hoffman was a member of the Pennsylvania Select Committee on Medical Malpractice from 1984 to 1986. He was a member of Governor Edward Rendell's Medical Malpractice Task Force and is currently counsel to the Commonwealth of Pennsylvania Patient Safety Authority. He is a past president of the Pennsylvania Defense Institute. He was the recipient of the Defense Research Institute's Exceptional Performance Citation in 1989 and the Fred H. Sievert Award in 1989. Hoffman was a coauthor of the book Laws and Regulations Affecting Medical Practice. He was chairman of Hearing Committee 1.15, Supreme Court of Pennsylvania Disciplinary Board, from 1993 to 1998 and serves on the faculty for the Temple University School of Law, Masters of Laws in Trial Advocacy, and Academy of Advocacy. He has been listed as a top attorney in *Philadelphia Magazine* each time the article appears and has been listed in *Best Lawyers in America* since 1995. He was cited as one of the top hundred lawyers in Pennsylvania in *Pennsylvania Super Lawyers,* 2004 and 2005. Hoffman was a member of the Temple Inns of Court. He is a member of ASHRM, a Fellow of the International Academy of Trial Lawyers, of the American College of Trial Lawyers, and of the American Board of Trial Advocates.

JOHN HORTY, JD, is the managing partner of Horty, Springer & Mattern, PC, and the editor of all HortySpringer publications. He presently serves as chair of the board and a faculty member of the Estes Park Institute in Englewood, Colorado, and president and chair of the Indigo Institute in Washington, D.C. He is an honorary fellow of the American College of Hospital Executives, a recipient of the Award of Honor of the American Hospital Association, and an Honorary Life Member of the American Hospital Association. He is a founding member of the American Academy of Hospital Attorneys; a past board member of the Hospital Association of Pennsylvania, the Health Alliance of Pennsylvania, and the Hospital Council of Western Pennsylvania; and was chair of Saint Francis Central Hospital in Pittsburgh, Pennsylvania, from 1971 to 1999.

SANDRA K. JOHNSON, RN, ARM, LHRM, FSHRM, is director of risk services for Broward Health in Fort Lauderdale, Florida. She began her career in risk management twenty-eight years ago, working for PHICO Insurance Group, Inc., in Mechanicsburg,

Pennsylvania. Past positions include director, risk and insurance, for Keystone Health System in Drexel Hill, Pennsylvania; director, risk and insurance, at Holy Cross Hospital in Fort Lauderdale, Florida; and system director of risk management at Intracoastal Health System, West Palm Beach, Florida. She has served on many ASHRM committees and as a faculty member of the 1988 annual conference and nominations committee. She has served two terms on the ASHRM board of directors. While in Philadelphia, she held various officer and committee positions with the Philadelphia Area Society for Healthcare Risk Management and the Pennsylvania Association of Health Care Risk Management. She has also been recognized on three occasions for outstanding contributions to the field of risk management by the Philadelphia Area Society for Healthcare Risk Management and the Pennsylvania Association of Health Care Risk Management. She is a past president and a board member of the Florida Society for Healthcare Risk Management and Patient Safety and was reelected as president for 2008–2009 term. Johnson is a member of the advisory board for the journal, *Healthcare Risk Management*, published by American Health Consultants, and has held positions on the Broward County Risk and Insurance Management Society board of directors. She was awarded the ARM designation in 1990 and the FASHRM designation in 1991. She is a licensed health care risk manager (LHRM) in the state of Florida.

TRISTA JOHNSON, PhD, MPH, is the director of performance measurement and analysis for Allina Hospitals and Clinics. Johnson provides coordinated, accurate analysis and results to drive organizational improvement. Previously, she served as the director of patient safety and coordinated initiatives and measurements across the eleven hospitals and forty-four clinics in the Allina system. She was involved in the creation of a standard data collection tool and taxonomy for patient safety events and continues to work with this system through analysis of the data and use of the results in safety collaboratives. A few examples of collaboratives conducted while leading patient safety include falls prevention, teamwork and patient safety, insulin safety, and the IHI trigger tool analysis. Johnson serves as a member of the Minnesota Alliance for Patient Safety (MAPS), which is involved in implementing the mandatory statewide reporting of the twenty-seven National Quality Forum events. She completed her doctoral work on the application of epidemiology to the study of medical errors.

LEILANI KICKLIGHTER, RN, ARM, MBA, CPHRM, DFASHRM, principal, the Kicklighter Group, is an independent consultant offering health care risk management, patient safety consulting, and stress management education. She serves as a risk management consultant to ambulatory surgery centers and is the course coordinator and instructor for the health care risk management online certificate course offered by the University of South Florida. This is a preparatory course laying the foundation for licensure in Florida as a health care risk manager. Most recently, she served as the corporate director of risk management services and patient safety officer for a large long-term care and skilled nursing facility. Previously, she was a health care risk management consultant with a large global insurance broker and consulted throughout the United States and internationally. Kicklighter began her career as a registered nurse. Her experience in health care risk management spans more than thirty years and has afforded her experience in a variety of health care organizational settings, including a large teaching hospital, a university medical school, a large multispecialty clinic, a for-profit community hospital, a not-for-profit integrated health care multifacility system, and a large HMO. She has been a member of the American Society for Healthcare Risk Management (ASHRM), since its inception, serving on numerous committees, the board of directors, and as president in 1997–1998. Kicklighter has been awarded the DFASHRM designation from ASHRM. She is the past president and board member of the Florida Society for Healthcare Risk Management and Patient Safety. She has a master's in business administration from Nova Southeastern University and has earned designations as an associate in risk management (ARM) and a certified professional in health care risk management (CPHRM). Kicklighter is a licensed health care risk manager (LHRM) in the state of Florida. She is a well-known author and lecturer in the fields of infection control and risk management on the local, state, national, and international levels.

JANE J. MCCAFFREY, MHSA, DFASHRM, is the director of Quality Management Services at Self Regional Healthcare in Greenwood, South Carolina. She has developed risk management programs at several South Carolina hospitals over the past twenty years. McCaffrey has served twice as president of the American Society for Healthcare Risk Management (1985 and 2003). She participates on several state-level patient safety and risk committees and was a faculty member for fundamentals of risk management for over a decade. McCaffrey received ASHRM's Distinguished Service Award in 1994. She also serves on the editorial advisory boards for ECRI's newsletter *Risk Management Reporter* and American Healthcare Consultants' *Healthcare Risk Management.* In 2005, she became a member of Health Research and Educational Trust's 2005–2006 Patient Safety Leadership Fellowship Class.

DENISE MURPHY, RN, BSN, MPH, CIC, Vice President and chief safety and quality officer at Barnes-Jewish Hospital JC Healthcare in Saint Louis. Before taking that position, she spent seven years as director of health care epidemiology and patient safety for BJC HealthCare. Murphy went to nursing school in Philadelphia, received her bachelor of science in nursing in Portland, Maine, and holds a master of public health degree from the Saint Louis University School of Public Health. Murphy's early nursing experience was in pediatric ICUs, surgical nursing, and nursing management. She entered the field of infection control in 1981, sitting for the first certification in infection control (CIC) exam in 1983. She has been an ICP in hospitals ranging from 100–1200 beds in rural and urban settings. Her presentations and publications are numerous on prevention of surgical site infections, bloodstream infections, and ventilator-associated pneumonia and on redesigning infection control services, the business of infection control, and establishment of patient safety programs. Murphy is an active member of the Association for Professionals in Infection Control and Epidemiology (APIC), the Society for Healthcare Epidemiology of America (SHEA), and the American Society for Healthcare Risk Management (ASHRM). She is a past president of the APIC Greater Saint Louis chapter and currently serves as a director on the APIC national board and chair of strategic planning. Murphy was a four-year member of the APIC annual conference task force and is currently the ICP representative on the SHEA educational conference planning committee. She graduated from the first AHA/National Patient Safety Foundation-sponsored leadership fellowship training program in 2003.

JUDITH NAPIER is corporate director, risk management and patient safety, for Allina Hospitals and Clinics in Minnesota. Before joining Allina, Napier was senior director, patient safety and risk management services, for Children's Hospitals and Clinics in Minnesota. Napier has held the position of senior vice president for MMI Companies, an international health care risk management firm, where she was responsible for an international consulting division and product innovation and customization, specifically introducing new risk management strategies and products to the health care industry. Before her work with MMI Companies, she practiced nursing in high-risk perinatal units and taught maternal child nursing in several academic accredited nursing programs at both the baccalaureate and associate degree level. Her career includes clinical practice, consultation, teaching, and more than twenty years as an executive in the health care industry. Napier holds a bachelor's degree in nursing from Niagara University and a master's degree in maternal child clinical specialty nursing from California State University at Los Angeles. She has received a certificate of completion from HRET and the Health Forum Patient Safety Leadership Fellowship. Napier has been a frequent national and international speaker in the area of patient safety, quality, and risk management.

PAMELA J. PARA, RN, MPH, CPHRM, ARM, FASHRM, is a nurse consultant for the Midwestern Consortium of the Centers for Medicare and Medicaid Services (CMS) in Chicago, Illinois. In this role, Para is responsible for the coordination of non-long-term care federal oversight functions in the Division of Survey and Certification for transplant centers, organ procurement organizations, end-stage renal dialysis centers, critical access hospitals, home care, and hospice providers. Para has served as the director of professional and technical services for the American Society for Healthcare Risk Management of the American Hospital Association in Chicago. Other experience includes evaluating a variety of health care organizations, nationwide and in Puerto Rico, for potential medical professional, general, and workers' compensation liability exposures for a major commercial insurance carrier. She has also performed medicolegal reviews of potential and litigated claims, negotiated settlements, managed workers' compensation claims, and served as adviser to risk managers and other corporate claims coordinators of various self-insured health care facilities in the metropolitan Chicago area and nationwide for a third-party claims administrator. Para has nearly twenty-five years of professional health care experience, beginning as a registered professional nurse in both civilian and military maternal-child clinical settings. She received a bachelor of science degree in nursing with a minor in Spanish from DePauw University in Greencastle, Indiana, and a master of public health degree from the University of Illinois at Chicago. She holds the designations of certified professional in health care risk management (CPHRM), associate in risk management (ARM), and Fellow of the American Society for Healthcare Risk Management (FASHRM). Para is a published author, educator, and frequent presenter on risk management and workers' compensation topics.

GINA PUGLIESE, RN, MS, vice president of the Safety Institute, Premier Inc., Chicago. She holds associate faculty appointments at the University of Illinois School of Public Health, Division of Epidemiology and Biostatistics, and Rush University College of Nursing, Chicago. Pugliese is on the editorial advisory board of the Joint Commission *Journal on Quality and Safety* and is the senior associate editor of *Infection Control and Hospital Epidemiology*. She is the codirector of the international Healthcare Epidemiology Training Program sponsored by the Society for Healthcare Epidemiology of America (SHEA) and the Centers for Disease Control and Prevention (CDC). For eight years, Pugliese was the director of safety of the American Hospital Association, Chicago. She was a founding board member and past president of the national Certification Board of Infection Control (CBIC) and has served as a board member of the national Association for Professionals in Infection Control and Epidemiology (APIC). She is the author of more than 130 publications and has served on the faculty in more than 300 educational conferences in thirteen countries and has appeared in more than thirty videotape, television, and teleconference programs. Pugliese currently serves on several national committees, including the expert panel for the CMS National Surgical Infection Prevention (SIP) and Surgical Care Improvement Projects (SCIP), AHRQ's Patient Safety Research Coordinating Center Steering Committee, and FDA's Medical Product Surveillance Network (MEDSUN) Advisory Group. Pugliese is the 2001 recipient of the APIC Carole DeMille outstanding achievement award in safety and epidemiology. In 2004, the Gina Pugliese Scholarship was established for five clinicians to attend each of the SHEA-CDC international health care epidemiology training courses, held every other year, in recognition of her contributions to health care epidemiology.

MADELYN S. QUATTRONE, JD, is a senior risk management analyst for ECRI, Plymouth Meeting, Pennsylvania. She is editor of ECRI's publication *Continuing Care Risk Management* and is a regular contributor to ECRI's *Healthcare Risk Control System*. She has been a panelist in ECRI audioconferences discussing risk management and legal issues involving the health information privacy regulations and the security regulations of the Health Insurance Portability and Accountability Act of 1996 (HIPAA). Before joining ECRI, Quattrone was a shareholder in the law firm of George, Koran, Quattrone, Blumberg & Chant, PA, in Woodbury, New Jersey, concentrating on the defense of medical malpractice cases, from 1982 to 1999. A member of the bar of the Commonwealth of Pennsylvania, New Jersey, the U.S. District Court of New Jersey, the Third Circuit Court of Appeals, and the U.S. Supreme Court, Quattrone achieved certification by the New Jersey Supreme Court as a civil trial attorney in 1990 and was selected for membership in the American Board of Trial Advocates in 1993. Quattrone has also provided risk management consultation to physicians, hospitals, and professional liability insurers and contributed to the development of a clinical-legal correspondence course for the Medical Inter-Insurance Exchange of New Jersey. She has written regularly for numerous publications, including the *Emergency Physician Legal Bulletin*, the *Emergency Nurse Legal Bulletin*, and the *Emergency Medical Technician Legal Bulletin*. For many years, Quattrone cowrote a column on legal and risk management issues affecting emergency nurses in the *Journal of Emergency Nursing*. She has developed case scenarios and participated in mock medical malpractice trials for audiences of physicians, medical students, residents, and clinical engineers and has been a frequent speaker in numerous risk management areas, including informed consent, ethical and legal issues involving human reproduction, obstetrics, the provision of emergency care, and medical record documentation. Quattrone earned a doctor of law degree from Rutgers University School of Law, Camden, New Jersey, and a bachelor of arts degree in anthropology from Temple University, Philadelphia, Pennsylvania.

MICHAEL L. RAWSON is the former corporate director of safety, security, and environmental health for Intermountain Health Care (IHC) in Salt Lake City, Utah, where he has been employed for twenty-six years. His responsibilities include management of safety, security, and environmental health issues and compliance with regulatory activities specific to these areas. Rawson holds a bachelor of science degree in sociology with a certificate in law enforcement from the University of Utah and a master's degree in administration of justice from Wichita State University. He is a certified health care safety professional (CHSP), a certified health care environmental manager (HEM), and a senior of the American Society for Healthcare Engineering (SASHE). Rawson has served on various committees with the American Society for Healthcare Engineering, the National Fire Protection Association (NFPA), the U.S. Department of Homeland Security (DHS), and the U.S. Department of Veterans Affairs–Facilities (VA) and as president of the Mountain States Society for Healthcare Engineering (MSSHE). Rawson is a faculty member for ASHE-sponsored Environment of Care Joint Committee Survey Process Preparation programs and has presented programs on hospital security, safety, and emergency preparation and management throughout the United States.

ELAINE RICHARD, RN, MS, earned a master's degree in public health at the University of Minnesota, where she served on the faculty from 1972 to 1984. During her tenure there, she pioneered one of the first post-RN and ANA-accredited geriatric nurse practitioner programs before nurse practitioner programs were recognized by the National League for Nursing. In 1977, she developed a National Institute of Occupational Safety and Health (NIOSH) graduate-level program in occupational health nursing and was subsequently promoted to associate professor. Richard later served as a NIOSH consultant reviewing university applications for occupational health training programs in the fields of medicine, nursing, safety, and industrial hygiene. She has lived in Tampa since 1984. Richard served as executive director of Saint Joseph's HealthLine and Community Care over a period of ten years. In this capacity, she planned and developed the occupational health program and clinic and corporate wellness programs. As part of the Hillsborough County initiative to serve the indigent population, she developed and implemented Saint Joseph's first off-site primary clinics to serve this population. In 1995, she became the executive director and regional vice president of EverCare, a subsidiary of United Healthcare, and implemented the EverCare Program in Florida for residents in long-term care institutions. This successful Medicare demonstration project uses geriatric nurse practitioners to bring added value to patients residing in nursing homes. Since retirement, she has worked with the University of South Florida's School of Aging Studies in the development and maintenance of the risk management course.

SHEILA HAGG-RICKERT, JD, MHA, MBA, CPCU, PHRM, DFASHRM, associate system director of risk management, CHRISTUS Health. She is responsible for oversight of CHRISTUS's loss prevention, claims management, and risk financing programs. Previously, she served as corporate risk manager for both for-profit and not-for-profit acute care and long-term care health systems, as an insurance broker, and as a health care risk management consultant. She has served on the board of directors for the American Society for Healthcare Risk Management (ASHRM) and has presented and written extensively on health care risk management and health law topics. She served as faculty for ASHRM's Advanced Forum, the third learning module in the Barton Certificate program, for more than a decade. Hagg-Rickert holds a doctor of law degree from the University of Iowa and masters degrees in both business administration and health care administration from Georgia State University. She has earned chartered property and casualty underwriter (CPCU) and certified professional in health care risk management (CPHRM) designations and is a Distinguished Fellow of the American Society of Healthcare Risk Management (DFASHRM).

FREDERICK "RICK" ROBINSON, JD, is partner in charge of the health law practice in Fulbright & Jaworski's Washington, D.C., office. His cases cover all phases of trial and appellate practice in both criminal and civil matters, including qui tam or "whistleblower" lawsuits under the federal False Claims Act. He helps health care providers create and implement corporate compliance programs and with voluntary disclosure matters. Robinson graduated with honors from Duke University School of Law in 1982 and is admitted to the bar in Maryland and the District of Columbia. He has written numerous articles and is a regular speaker at seminars and conferences regarding health care litigation and compliance matters.

JEANNIE SEDWICK, ARM, is a former health care broker for Aon Risk Services, Inc., based in Winston-Salem, North Carolina. Previously, she was director of risk management for Wake County Hospital System, Inc., in Raleigh, North Carolina, for more than twenty years. She held the position of vice president of marketing for the Medical Protective Company/Employers Reinsurance Company and was responsible for production of health care accounts for the southern United States. She served as managing director for property casualty for Insurance Resource, Inc., a division of the American Hospital Association, in Chicago, Illinois. She served on the ASHRM board for six years and was president in 1996–1997. She is a founding member of the North Carolina Chapter of ASHRM and has served as its president and board member and on many committees. She was recognized for her contributions to the North Carolina ASHRM chapter and was awarded the Distinguished Service Award in 1996. Sedwick was named to the Business Insurance Risk Manager of the Year Honor Roll in 1997 for her contributions to the field of risk management and for her achievements as risk manager at Wake County Hospital System.

KATRINA A. SHANNON, BA, JD, risk management coordinator for Barnes-Jewish Hospital in Saint Louis, and adjunct professor at Maryville University in Saint Louis. Shannon received her bachelor of arts degree in business management and her certificate in health information management from Saint Louis University. She received her doctor of law degree from Saint Louis University School of Law and a health law certificate from the Saint Louis University School of Law Center for Health Law Studies. She is licensed to practice in Missouri. Shannon is a former law clerk for the BJC Health System, Armstrong Teasdale LLP, and a former associate attorney for Lashly & Baer, PC. In these roles, Shannon practiced corporate, government, education, and health care law. Shannon is a member of the Missouri Bar Association, the Mound City Bar Association, the Saint Louis Area Health Law Association, the Saint Louis Association for Health Care Risk Managers, and the American Society for Healthcare Risk Management.

RONNI P. SOLOMON, JD, is executive vice president and general counsel at ECRI, a nonprofit health services research agency in suburban Philadelphia that focuses on the safety, quality, and cost-effectiveness of patient care. Solomon has approximately twenty years' experience in health care risk management, patient safety, law, and regulation. She works with leaders at hospitals, health systems, government agencies, continuing care organizations, and insurance providers to implement patient safety and quality assessment systems. She has published numerous articles and book chapters and has lectured frequently in the United States and abroad. Solomon serves as the center director for ECRI's Collaborating Center for the World Health Organization in patient safety, health care technology and risk management. She is a past member of ASHRM's board of directors and has served in many other leadership roles for ASHRM. She received ASHRM's first Award for Writing Excellence.

NANCY TUOHY, RN, MSN, is a medication safety specialist at ISMP. She is also the assistant editor for ISMP's *Nurse Advise-ERR* and a contributor to the other ISMP medication safety alert publications. Tuohy's interests include patient safety and health care systems analysis, including the evolution of health care informatics. Her prior work experiences cover a broad range of health care settings, including pediatrics, critical care, outpatient clinic, elementary school, pharmaceutical research, and prehospital care as an emergency medical technician. Tuohy obtained her bachelor of science in nursing degree at the University of North Carolina at Chapel Hill and her master of science in nursing degree at the University of Pennsylvania. She also holds a bachelor's degree in psychology from Wake Forest University.

JOHN C. WEST, JD, MHA, DFASHRM, is a senior health care consultant with AIG Consultants Inc., Healthcare Management Division. He holds a bachelor's degree from the University of Cincinnati, a law degree from Salmon P. Chase College of Law, and a master's degree in health services administration from Xavier University. He received the Distinguished Service Award from ASHRM in 2001, the highest honor bestowed by that society. He also received the designation of Distinguished Fellow of the American Society for Healthcare Risk Management (DFASHRM) in 1999. West has been a frequent speaker at national and regional educational programs and has published numerous articles on various aspects of health care risk management. He currently writes the "Case Law Update" column on a quarterly basis for the *Journal of Healthcare Risk Management.*

KIMBERLY M. WILLIS, CPCU, ARM, is senior vice president of Endurance U.S. Healthcare Insurance Services. In this capacity, she is responsible for developing and executing strategy for the U.S. Healthcare practice. Prior to joining Endurance, Willis served as vice president, field underwriting, for Berkley Medical Excess Underwriters. She was responsible for management of underwriting strategy, achievement of profitability and premium volume goals, and oversight of distributor relationships. Willis also served as managing director, health care syndication, for Aon Risk Services. She managed a team responsible for the design, negotiation, and broking of over $500 million in health care professional liability premiums. Willis earned her bachelor of science degree in business administration at the University of Missouri and a master of business administration degree from Maryville University. She holds the chartered property and casualty underwriter (CPCU) and associate in risk management (ARM) designations.

SHEILA COHEN ZIMMET, BSN, JD, is associate vice president for Regulatory Affairs at Georgetown University Medical Center. Previously she was associate dean, research compliance, at Weill Medical College of Cornell University, where she serves as the course director for the Tri-Institutional Responsible Conduct of Research course for Weill Cornell Medical College, Rockefeller University, and Memorial

Sloan-Kettering Institute. She previously served as Director of Research Assurance and Compliance and as senior counsel for Georgetown University Medical Center. She started her professional career as a neonatal intensive care nurse after earning her undergraduate nursing degree from Georgetown University in 1971. After she received her JD from Georgetown in 1975, Zimmet pursued a legal career with the federal government in occupational and mine safety and health. She returned to Georgetown University in 1984, where her health law practice focused on clinical, bioethical, and biomedical research issues, professional liability and risk management, and other hospital and higher education legal issues involving patients, students, faculty, and staff that are common to academic medical centers. Zimmet also serves as a member of the National Advisory Research Resources Council to the National Institutes of Health.

PREFACE

The student of risk management is entering a field in health care filled with challenges, excitement, obstacles, passion, frustration, and confusion, all combined with a strong sense of purpose and commitment. You'll either love it or be frightened by it. Risk management is not a stop on the road; it is a journey. For individuals who like a challenge, consider themselves change agents, understand organizational systems and processes, and have the ability to see the big picture and connect the dots, this is the profession for you.

The position of risk manager is an engaging one with never-ending tasks and a boredom factor of zero. You've heard the phrase "The job is what you make it." Nothing could be truer in health care risk management. The experience and expertise necessary (or as required in the job description) to carry out the assigned responsibilities and tasks are often discussed, but seldom identified are the other skills or personal attributes that are equally important if one is to succeed as a risk management professional. They include good judgment, common sense, tenacity, intuition, critical thinking skills, the ability to team well and lead well, and excellent communication skills, both verbal and written. These essential personal attributes are generally not specified in job descriptions, are hard to test, and are often difficult to assess during the interview process.

This Student Edition offers a blend of necessary technical information and guidance on how to apply that information using the personal attributes just mentioned. "What does all this mean to the risk management professional?" is a question that is answered throughout the book. The Student Edition is thus intended to be both practical and technical. It offers a wide range of expertise from twenty-nine nationally recognized experts on a variety of health care-related risk subjects.

Although the focus of responsibilities for the risk management professional has changed over time, the underlying principle of asset preservation through safe patient care has not. Nothing in risk management ever seems to go away; we keep adding to the wealth of information through new practices, procedures, protocols, systems, legislation, technological advances, value-based purchasing strategies, and so on. What has changed is how we evaluate organizational risks, the impact that one risk has on another, and our approach to eliminate or manage those risks through alternative risk financing strategies and risk control initiatives. The field of health care risk management continues to evolve, mature, and expand as the concept of enterprise risk management takes hold in health care organizations. This necessitates that the professionals responsible for managing risk also grow and change.

In today's health care environment, the risk management professional is a facilitator, mediator, negotiator, coordinator, orchestrator, and agent of change. The function has also changed, from employing tactical skills to developing and implementing strategy. Consequently, the role is becoming more proactive and less reactive. What comes to mind is a famous line from the movie *All About Eve*: "Fasten your seatbelts; it's going to be a bumpy night." The challenge for the risk management professional is how to get it all accomplished and in a timely manner given limited resources (financial, human, and time) while preserving our own quality of life.

Preparing this book for publication has required the resolve of a dedicated team. I want to express my gratitude and thanks to all the members of the Student Edition and Faculty Guide work group for their determination and commitment to this project: Kathryn Hyer, University of South Florida; Peggy Martin, Lifespan Risk Services; Glenn Troyer, Kreig DeVault, LLP; Sylvia Brown, Premier, Inc.; Ben Gonzales, Montana Health Network, Inc.; Peggy Nakamura, Adventist Health; Kathleen Shostek and Karen Holloway, ECRI; and Joe Pixler, American Society for Healthcare Risk Management.

I also extend a personal thank-you to my family for allowing me to miss many meals and stimulating conversations so that I could concentrate on getting this Student Edition ready for publication. A special thank-you goes to Terrance "Red" Carroll, my brother, who continues to support all my efforts.

We hope you find this Student Edition easy to use and a valuable resource for your reference library.

Welcome to the world of risk management!

Roberta L. Carroll, Editor

ABOUT THIS BOOK

The goal in developing the Student Edition of the *Risk Management Handbook for Health Care Organizations* was to offer students of risk management from a variety of backgrounds and settings a handbook that could be used both as a tool for study and as an authoritative reference text for later consultation. The Student Edition of the Handbook is not meant to be the final authority on any risk subject covered but rather an incitement to whet the appetite for additional reading and further learning. That being said, however, a beginning risk management professional desirous of implementing a risk management program could pick up this book and have a comprehensive road map of what to do, how to do it, and why it must be done.

The Student Edition begins by addressing basic concepts and considerations such as developing a risk management program, the risk management professional and stages in professional development, relationship with patient safety, legal concepts made easy, and the importance of effective governance. The student then progresses to recognize and understand the complexity and risks associated with medication safety, documentation, noncompliance with statutes, standards and regulations, and accreditation and licensure requirements. Basic claims administration, an introduction to risk financing and its basic principles and coverage, and the different internal and external methods used to identify organizational risks are all covered in a basic, uncomplicated manner. Ethics in patient care, risk management metrics and benchmarking, emergency management, and occupational health and safety, are discussed in terms of organizational culture and environment, organizational preparedness, and measurement.

These chapters have been carefully selected for the Student Edition from among the fifty-nine chapters in the three-volume *Risk Management Handbook for Health Care Organizations*, Fifth Edition. Consideration was given to what could reasonably be covered in a one-semester university course at either the graduate or undergraduate level. Other chapters could have been included, covering a whole host of other subjects (all equally relevant to health care risk management); however, the desire was to keep the Student Edition an introduction to the subject of risk management that can be used as a basic guide.

The design of the Student Edition also lends itself to the study of a specific topic by the nonacademic student. For anyone desiring to learn more about health care risk management or to understand a particular topic more fully, this text fits that need as well.

To facilitate the learning process, each chapter has been expanded to include learning objectives, key concepts, key terms, and acronyms. The learning objectives at the beginning of each chapter will highlight, in a concise manner, relevant questions the student should be able to answer after reading the material. The key concepts are fundamental principles of the chapter; combined with the learning objectives, they set expectations for the student reader. They identify the focus of the chapter and concepts to keep in mind as they study the material. At the back of each chapter are lists of important key terms and acronyms used in the chapter. These can serve as a quick test to see how easily students can identify their meanings.

Health care professionals speak a language of their own. To complement the Glossary at the back of the book and to assist students who do not have a clinical or medical background or may not work in a health care setting, a "Guide to Medical Terminology" has been included in the Student Edition.

This book has been developed for the academic environment; therefore, an accompanying Faculty Guide is available online. The Faculty Guide will track each chapter and offer the faculty member, teacher, or learning facilitator additional tools not offered in the Student Edition, such as chapter outlines, case scenarios, vignettes, puzzles, word games, test questions and answers, and other materials supporting specific topics. The Faculty Guide can be quickly updated and new material easily added. In this manner, the teacher can keep the course fresh and up-to-date without changing the core information in the Student Edition. It is anticipated that its shelf life will be long, making it a desirable book to own.

Roberta L. Carroll, Editor

■ ■ ■

CHAPTER

1

DEVELOPMENT OF A RISK MANAGEMENT PROGRAM

JANE J. McCAFFREY, SHEILA HAGG-RICKERT

LEARNING OBJECTIVES

- To be able to describe the key elements necessary to have a successful risk management program

- To be able to discuss three barriers for successful risk management program development and provide at least one strategy for overcoming each

- To be able to discuss one nonclinical area of related risk for a health care organization

- To be able to identify the various organizational structures that can be successful in implementing a risk management program

Organizations and individuals have always sought ways to identify and reduce the risks that threatened their existence. In primitive agrarian societies, where families and villages produced barely enough to meet their most basic needs, the loss of a year's harvest, whether to forces of nature or to the plunder of warring tribes, surely spelled disaster. The attempts of such cultures to protect their food supplies and other necessities of life from destruction by fire, flood, and theft represent history's earliest risk management efforts. As societies developed into industrialized economies, individuals and organizations continued to seek ways to understand and anticipate the risks associated with such perils in an attempt to protect valuable property from such threats, ultimately establishing mechanisms for transferring the financial consequences of such losses through policies of insurance.

Despite the age-old concern with protecting assets from the risks associated with **accidental losses, risk management** has existed for only about fifty years.[1] Health care risk management in its present form did not really begin to emerge until the **malpractice** crisis of the mid-1970s, when hospitals and other health care entities experienced rapid rises in claims costs, and subsequently insurance premiums, and witnessed the exit of several major medical professional liability insurers from the market.[2] This crisis formed the basis for health care entities to develop the first risk management programs. The **American Society for Healthcare Risk Management** (**ASHRM**; formerly known as the American Society for Hospital Risk Management) was established in 1980 in response to this developing interest in risk management among health care organizations. Over the years, health care risk management has moved from a discipline focused almost exclusively on medical professional liability issues to a profession concerned with all of the risks associated with accidental losses facing a health care organization.[3] In addition to hospitals, managed care organizations, long-term care, and **ambulatory care**, other providers of health care have come to realize the value of effective risk management and have developed formalized programs.[4] Increasingly, risk management is moving toward the concept of enterprise risk management and considering the myriad of complex legal, regulatory, political, business, and financial risks facing health care organizations. As risk management moves toward this more strategic orientation and risk management professionals prepare themselves for new roles as **chief risk officers**, such factors as diverse work experience, higher education, and broad-based business, financial, and technical skills will be valued in health care risk management professionals more than ever before.[5] Another recent development in risk management has been the return focus on **patient safety**.

The patient safety movement was prompted in large part by the 1999 publication of *To Err Is Human: Building a Safer Health System,*[6] which articulated the findings of an Institute of Medicine study of the devastating consequences of widespread medical **error** in the nation's hospitals. Risk management professionals who had long had **primary** responsibility for investigating, analyzing, and maintaining data regarding adverse patient **incidents** joined with colleagues from performance improvement, health care administration, and a variety of clinical disciplines in an attempt to systematically identify the underlying causes of medical errors in their organizations and to design and implement effective interdisciplinary organizationwide patient safety programs.

KEY CONCEPTS

- Risk management as a discipline is focused on all risks of an organization.
- An effective risk management program incorporates several building blocks, including key structural elements, sufficient scope to cover all organizational risks, appropriate risk strategies, and written policies and procedures.
- Risk management as a process uses a five-step management decision-making model.
- Risk management programs protect organizational assets through the delivery of safe patient care.
- Risk management program responsibilities vary in terms of organizational structure, size, scope of services, available resources, management commitment, and location.

RISK MANAGEMENT PROGRAM DEVELOPMENT

Whatever the health care setting or the sophistication of the risk management professional, an effective risk management program requires certain elementary building blocks: key structural elements, sufficient scope to cover all applicable categories of risk, appropriate risk strategies, and written policies and procedures. This chapter focuses on these building blocks, giving the novice risk management professional guidance in developing a comprehensive risk management program and providing the experienced risk management professional with a program overview that may be used as a self-assessment guide.

Developing a comprehensive risk management program depends on addressing several specific considerations. An effective risk management effort is built on key structural elements that enable the risk management professional to develop and enforce a risk management plan and enact the necessary changes in organizational policy. The program must include a defined scope of risks to be managed, including an examination of the risks associated with patients, medical staff, employees, governing bodies, property, automobiles, and other risks that subject the health care organization to potential liability or the threat of loss. Risk management strategies represent the mix of techniques employed to prevent or reduce potential losses and preserve the organization's assets.

The final building block is a set of written policies and procedures that ensures program uniformity and consistency and assists in communication of the program to affected parties. This chapter describes how each of these four important considerations contributes to an effective risk management program.

KEY STRUCTURAL ELEMENTS OF THE RISK MANAGEMENT PROGRAM

The exact structure of a health care organization's risk management program depends on the size and complexity of its functions and the scope of other services that it offers. Several key structural components are necessary for any health care risk management program to succeed. Whether an entity is just beginning to organize its risk management program or is seeking to revamp or expand an existing program, attention to these structural factors will help ensure that the program has a solid foundation.

Authority

The risk management professional in a health care organization must maintain sufficient authority and respect to enact the changes in clinical practice, policies and procedures, and employee and medical staff behavior that are necessary to fulfill the purpose of the risk management program. The risk manager must deal on a daily basis with highly sensitive and confidential information that directly affects the organization's public image and financial status. The risk management professional is responsible for coordinating risk management activities with members of the medical staff and outside parties and with managers and employees at all levels of the organization. For these reasons, the risk management professional's position should be relatively high in the organizational hierarchy. Ideally, the risk management professional should report directly to the CEO, or at least to another member of the senior administrative management team. Risk management professionals whose positions rank below the department manager level on the organizational chart will almost certainly face difficulty in dealing authoritatively with medical staff, nursing administration, and department managers. They may also have difficulty gaining access to senior management and representing the organization in its relations with insurers, attorneys, and other outside parties involved in the risk management process. In many nonhospital health care organizations and in smaller hospital facilities, the designated risk management professional may serve primarily as a senior manager or clinician and devote only a relatively small percentage of work time to risk management activities. Under such a model, risk finance and insurance program administration are typically handled by the organization's finance department, workers' compensation programs are managed by human resource personnel, and safety programs are developed and overseen by a facility or maintenance manager. Although this division of labor might be efficient for apportioning the workload required for a successful risk management effort, it creates special challenges when establishing ownership of the risk management function and creating an identity for those activities that comprise risk management. Such part-time risk management professionals, especially those who view their risk management responsibilities as subordinate to their other job duties, might find it difficult to acquire the wide range of expertise necessary to adequately fulfill their risk management obligations and to stay abreast of rapidly changing and often complex legal and regulatory developments affecting the field.

Visibility

The risk management professional should be highly visible in the health care organization. No one individual can perform every function of a comprehensive risk management program single-handed, even in the smallest health care facility. Therefore, it is necessary for the organization's risk management professional, through consciousness-raising, education, and communication, to foster an awareness of risk management practices and techniques among senior management and the governing body, medical staff members, and employees at all organizational levels. The risk management professional's position should be structured to enhance opportunities for interaction with others through service on appropriate committees, participation in educational activities such as employee orientation and staff in-service offerings, and access to organizationwide communication mechanisms.

Communication

As health care facilities have merged into alliances and networks and acquired physician practices, clinics, and managed care organizations to form integrated delivery systems (**IDS**s), additional issues relating to potential liability, insurance coverage, claims management, and loss control have emerged. To anticipate risk management pitfalls and opportunities in this environment, the risk management professional must be an insider who is provided with information on proposed mergers, acquisitions, and joint ventures early in the due diligence process. Equipped with such information, the risk management professional is in a position to advise senior management on the risk management implications of various new business arrangements, many of which can be substantial but are frequently overlooked by executives not attuned to risk management issues and specific insurance requirements.

Coordination

Because of the wide range of risk management functions and the diversity of activities necessary for a successful risk management program, the health care organization should establish both formal and informal mechanisms for the coordination of the risk management program with other departments and functions. To adequately integrate and coordinate risk management with other functions, the risk management professional needs to establish reporting and communication relationships with key individuals within the organization:

■ The *chief executive officer* (**CEO**) provides a vital link to the entity's governing board and medical staff and establishes the necessary support for the risk management program. The CEO serves as the key decision maker for many activities crucial to the risk management program, such as authorizing the settlement of larger claims and establishing insurance limits. Furthermore, the CEO often heads the team of senior managers responsible for the development of new business opportunities, mergers, and acquisitions.

■ The *chief financial officer* (**CFO**) may have multiple risk financing responsibilities and provides valuable information for the risk management program. These functions include establishing limits on **self-insured retentions** or trusts, monitoring the financial operations of captives, and overseeing the performance of actuarial analyses. In some organizations, the CFO is the primary purchaser of insurance coverages and must therefore rely on information provided by the risk management professional to make appropriate decisions regarding risk financing activities on behalf of the organization.

■ The *performance improvement* or *quality management director* serves as an important source of information regarding adverse clinical events occurring within the facility that have potentially serious risk management implications. The risk management standards promulgated by **The Joint Commission** (until 2007 known as the Joint Commission on Accreditation of Healthcare Organizations, or JCAHO) emphasize the interdependence of risk management and performance improvement activities.[7] Both the development of proactive patient safety initiatives and an effective root cause analysis process for post-occurrence **sentinel events** depend on the active leadership and close coordination of the risk management professional and performance improvement director. The performance improvement director may also be able to assist a risk management professional who lacks clinical training in interpreting and analyzing information contained in medical records, and in providing clinical loss prevention services.

■ The *patient safety director* or *officer* is responsible for systematically analyzing the sources of human error and systems issues that affect patient care. Patient safety directors or officers may report to the risk management professional or performance improvement director or to senior management in a health care organization. Patient safety directors or officers are very involved in the development of clinical risk management loss prevention initiatives.

■ The *compliance officer* guides the development of policy and staff education efforts related to legislative and regulatory initiatives such as **HIPAA**, Sarbanes-Oxley, and Medicare fraud and abuse prevention.[8]

■ The *infection control practitioner (ICP)* provides information on patient infections that might give rise to liability claims and can assist the risk management professional in understanding infection control protocols aimed at reducing the frequency and severity of hospital-acquired infections and establishing guidelines for coping with AIDS, tuberculosis, and other communicable diseases.

■ The *safety officer* may have primary responsibility for, or assist the risk management professional in, performing fire safety, hazardous materials management, emergency preparedness, and employee safety activities in compliance with Joint Commission standards. The safety officer usually chairs the organization's safety committee, which serves as a vital source of risk management information and organizational problem solving.

◼ The *patient representative* (or *ombudsman*) relays information regarding patient complaints and works with patients and families who have experienced difficulties with the organization or specific staff members to reach satisfactory resolutions of their concerns. Patient representatives, whether employees or volunteers, must be trained to recognize and appropriately manage risk management concerns that arise in the course of their activities and to relay information to the risk management professional.

◼ The *employee health nurse* (or *workers' compensation coordinator* or *personnel director*) may, in some organizations, manage the daily operational aspects of the facility's workers' compensation program and provide claims and injury information to the risk management professional. Often this individual is instrumental in developing transitional return-to-work and other injury management programs. The risk management professional in some health care organizations is personally responsible for the operation of workers' compensation programs but must nonetheless coordinate activities with the human resource director and various line managers.

◼ The *health information manager* (or *medical records director*) notifies the risk management professional of requests from attorneys for medical records that might signal initiation of legal proceedings or claims. The health information manager also develops policies and procedures relating to the documentation of patient care activities, patient confidentiality, and appropriate release of information and ensures the organization's compliance with HIPAA privacy requirements.

◼ The *medical director* (or *chief medical officer*) serves as a liaison between the risk management program and the medical staff and assists the risk management professional in "selling" risk management to physicians. The risk management professional must also work with the medical staff services professional to ensure that the organization's medical staff appointment, credentialing, privileging, and disciplinary procedures are conducted in accordance with sound risk management practices.

◼ The *patient accounts representative* works with the risk management professional to identify patient complaints and concerns that surface during the billing and collections process. Such concerns may be based on perceived patient care problems. They hold the potential for becoming liability claims if collection efforts are vigorously pursued.

◼ *Nursing and departmental managers* offer the risk management professional the technical and clinical expertise necessary to identify and analyze potential patient care risks and assist with the investigation of liability claims and incidents. Middle management personnel also play a crucial role in building and maintaining support for the risk management program and in educating and raising the risk management consciousness of employees within their areas of responsibility.

◼ The *education director* (or *in-service program coordinator*) assists the risk management professional in identifying staff education needs pertaining to risk management and in planning, organizing, and presenting orientation and in-service education programs.

◼ The *human resource director* maintains responsibility for developing effective job descriptions and performance appraisal processes, employee background checks and competency testing, verification of licenses and certifications, and maintenance of a drug-free workplace, all of which are crucial to the prevention and defense of medical professional liability actions. In addition, the human resource staff generally take the lead in preventing and managing claims and complaints related to issues such as alleged sexual harassment, discrimination, and wrongful termination.

Accountability

Just as risk management professionals need sufficient authority to perform assigned functions, they should be held accountable for that performance. Every health care organization's risk management professional, including those in small institutions that have job duties in addition to risk management, should have a written job description that outlines key risk management responsibilities. Annual performance appraisals assessing the risk management professional's achievement of specific, measurable risk management goals and objectives should be conducted to gauge and document the individual's effectiveness. The risk management professional should submit an annual report to senior management and the governing body that summarizes claims, insurance, and risk management program activities and documents the progress made toward the attainment of established goals.

SCOPE OF THE RISK MANAGEMENT PROGRAM

The purpose of a health care risk management program is to protect the organization against risks associated with accidental losses, regardless of the cause. One of the building blocks of an effective program is sufficient scope to cover all potential sources of risk. Although many risk management professionals focus on the medical professional liability aspects of health care risk management, the discipline extends into many other areas that are equally important to the survival of the modern health care organization. Defined broadly, health care risk management is concerned with a tremendous variety of issues and situations that hold the potential for liability or casualty losses for the organization. To be truly comprehensive, a risk management program must address the full scope of the following categories of risk:

- Patient care–related
- Medical staff–related
- Employee-related
- Property-related
- Financial
- Other

Patient Care–Related Risks

Over the course of the last several years, U.S. health care institutions and practitioners have once again experienced a "malpractice crisis" evidenced by rising jury verdicts, settlement amounts,[9] insurance premiums,[10] dwindling insurance availability due to carrier withdrawals from the medical malpractice market,[11] and the imposition of more stringent underwriting criteria.[12] The reduction in insurers' investment income resulting from the general economic downturn in the early part of the twenty-first century and the huge unanticipated insurance losses associated from the terrorist attacks of September 11, 2001, only served to exacerbate the worsening trends for health care medical professional liability insurers and their insureds.

Given the substantial proportion of total health care risk management costs associated with medical professional liability claims and insurance premiums and the current national focus on patient safety issues, it is not surprising that most health care risk management efforts begin with patient care–related issues. Patient care or clinical risk management, including information gathering, **loss control** efforts, medical professional liability risk financing, and claims management activities, forms the core of most health care risk management programs. Although most patient-related risk management activity focuses on direct clinical patient care activities and the consequences of inappropriate or incorrectly performed medical treatments, other important patient-related issues also confront the risk management professional, including the following:

- Confidentiality and appropriate release of patient medical information, especially in light of HIPAA and other privacy requirements

- Protection of patients from abuse and neglect and from assault by other patients, visitors, or staff

- Securing appropriate informed patient consent to medical treatment

- Nondiscriminatory treatment of patients, regardless of race, religion, national origin, or payment status

- Protection of patient valuables from loss or damage

- Appropriate triage, stabilization, and transfer of patients presenting to dedicated emergency departments (DEDs)

- Patient participation in research studies and the use of experimental drugs and medical procedures

- Utilization review decisions related to the timing of patient discharges and the provision of medically necessary services under various third-party managed care arrangements

- Access to care concerns

Medical Staff–Related Risks

Closely aligned with patient care–related risk management issues are those experienced by medical staff and other clinically privileged practitioners. Many, if not most, of the potentially serious occurrences related to the delivery of clinical patient care involve a facility's medical staff. It is imperative that the health care risk management professional include physicians in clinical loss prevention and claims management programs and elicit their support for overall risk management activities. Risk management concerns that stem from the unique relationship between a health care organization and its medical staff merit the risk management professional's particular attention. Of special importance are the following:

- Medical staff peer review and performance improvement activities and maintaining the confidentiality and protection of the data generated through such peer review processes

- Medical staff credentialing, appointment, and privileging processes

- Medical staff disciplinary proceedings, due process considerations, and potential allegations of antitrust and restraint of trade

- Identification and treatment of impaired physicians and other credentialed providers who pose a threat to patient or employee safety

- Business arrangements and financial incentives to physicians that might have fraud and abuse or other implications under federal Medicare regulations[13]

- Physician gatekeeper obligations and incentives under various managed care plans

In this era of expanding legal theories of corporate liability and vicarious liability, the activities of the medical staff are often deemed the activities of the health care organization. It has become increasingly difficult for defense attorneys to persuade judges and juries to distinguish between the institution and its independent contractor physicians. As physicians become business partners with health care entities and assume ownership interests in new ventures, and as hospitals and other organizations purchase or assume management of physician practices, the distinctions become even more blurred.

Employee-Related Risks

Several issues relating to the employment of personnel deserve the health care risk management professional's attention. Of obvious importance is maintaining a safe work environment for employees, reducing the risk of occupational illness and injury, and providing for the treatment and compensation of workers who suffer on-the-job injuries and work-related illnesses. In this regard, it is important that risk management professionals maintain a working knowledge of relevant state workers' compensation laws and regulations promulgated by the federal Occupational Safety and Health Administration (OSHA). Such understanding allows them to work effectively with human resource departments, employee health nurses, and designated safety officers to establish successful employee injury and management programs.

Posing particularly serious problems for today's health care organization are allegations of discrimination in recruitment, hiring, and promotion based on age, race, sex, national origin, or disability; wrongful termination; and other claims filed with the Equal Employment Opportunity Commission (**EEOC**). Claims involving alleged sexual harassment are also increasingly common.[14] The risk management professional must work closely with the facility's human resource director to help minimize such claims exposures, manage the claims that do occur, and finance the costs associated with such losses.

Property-Related Risks

Many complex health care entities have significant property assets, including large hospital and clinic structures, medical office buildings, and valuable medical and data processing equipment. It is incumbent on the risk management professional to protect these assets from risk of loss due to fires, acts of God, floods, natural disasters, and other perils that might damage or destroy such property. In addition, health care institutions typically maintain a large volume of paper and electronic records that are essential to the ongoing operations of the entity, and they must be protected from damage or destruction. Obviously, the costs associated with repairing and replacing damaged assets can be significant, and the revenues lost during the period of business interruption can have disastrous effects on the organization.

Many health care employees routinely handle cash, checks, and credit cards in the course of their job duties. Hospitals and nursing homes are often requested to safeguard cash and other valuables belonging to patients and residents. Home health workers, who function independently and without direct supervision in a client's home, are particularly vulnerable to allegations of theft. Thus it is important for the risk management professional to evaluate hiring and screening protocols for such workers, to review policies and procedures for handling cash and safeguarding valuables, and to consider various bonding and insurance alternatives to adequately protect the facility from such losses.

Financial Risks

Although the ordinary business risks associated with new ventures or services and the continued financial viability of the organization's existing operations are traditionally considered to be outside the sphere of risk management concerns, there are at least two areas of financial risk with which the risk management professional must be concerned.

First, the directors and officers of health care organizations, like those of other corporate entities, may face liability imposed by suits from shareholders or others alleging inappropriate conduct in the fulfillment of the directors' and officers' duties. Corporate charters and bylaws frequently require the entity to defend and indemnify its directors and officers against such claims. Likewise, the entity itself may be named in such actions. It is therefore important for the risk management professional to understand the corporate structure of the organization; any requirements imposed by the charter, bylaws, or other documents; and the opportunities to transfer such risks through policies of insurance, to adequately protect the organization's assets.

Second, risk management professionals who represent the interests of health care providers who contract with managed care organizations (**MCO**s) on an "at-risk" basis (typically through capitated payment arrangements) need to consider available options for limiting the financial risks inherent in such agreements. These risks may be characterized as either specific, in which case the costs associated with providing care to an individual plan subscriber greatly exceed expectations, or aggregate, in which case the total costs of providing required health care services under the plan agreement are higher than anticipated. Various options exist for contractual transfer of risks above a certain level back to the MCO or for the purchase of "stop-loss" insurance coverage.

Other Risks

There are, of course, other areas of potential concern for the health care risk management professional. Among these are property and liability losses related to the operation of automobiles, trucks, vans, and ambulances owned or leased by the organization. Many facilities also own or operate helicopters or fixed-wing air transport services or maintain heliports or helipads that pose additional liability and property risks.

Since September 11, 2001, U.S. health care institutions have become increasingly aware of their vulnerability to terrorist and bioterrorist attack. Organizations have sought to augment existing disaster and emergency preparedness plans to address scenarios in which the facility itself is the target of such an attack and those in which the institution plays a key role in triage and treatment response to an attack occurring elsewhere. Planning for such contingencies requires an analysis of patient care, employee-related and property-related risks of potentially staggering proportions, and the coordination of resources on a local, statewide, and national level.[15] (For more information on emergency management, see Chapter Sixteen.) Although typically representing a lesser proportion of the total cost of risk, hospitals and most other health care entities are accessible by the public and vulnerable to a wide variety of general liability claims stemming from visitor injuries caused by slips, falls, and other mishaps. The risk management professional must therefore be concerned with the overall maintenance of buildings, parking lots, and sidewalks and with visitor access and supervision.

Hazardous materials management is yet another area of concern for health care risk management. Ensuring that appropriate protocols are in place for the safe storage, use, and disposal of the myriad toxic chemicals and radioactive materials routinely used by health care organizations is a highly regulated and important risk management activity.[16] The implications for patients, employees, and the community at large should such materials find their way into the environment are chief considerations in managing hazardous materials programs. Proper disposal of infectious biological waste generated by hospitals and other health care entities continues to be a significant public health and environmental concern.

Special issues involving auxiliary personnel and other volunteers who may provide services at hospitals and students involved in clinical training experiences who sustain injuries in the course of their duties or may inflict harm on others also merit the risk management professional's attention. Such individuals may not be routinely covered under the organization's workers' compensation and liability insurance programs, and the risks pertaining to both groups must be specially considered by the risk management professional from both a **risk financing** and **loss prevention** perspective. Requirements for training and supervision of volunteers and students and clearly delineated duties appropriate for such nonemployees must be adequately defined.

For senior-level health care risk management professionals rising within their organizations to the level of chief risk officer (CRO), an even larger universe of potential risks merits attention. The CRO concept was developed initially in the banking and financial services industries to describe the role of a broadly experienced executive charged with responsibility for identifying and analyzing risks to an organization, whether or not insurable, developing strategies for handling such risks, and advising the governing board and senior management team. While still rare in health care settings, CROs often address issues ranging from the risk of increased market competition to the risk of regulatory sanctions if a certain course of corporate conduct is pursued and typically work closely with an organization's internal audit, legal, and finance departments to formulate risk identification, loss prevention, and risk financing strategies.

THE RISK MANAGEMENT PROCESS

Viewing risk management as a process helps the risk management professional set priorities and assists in ensuring a comprehensive risk management effort. The risk management process consists of five steps (see Figure 1.1):

1. Identify and analyze loss exposures.

2. Consider alternative risk techniques.

3. Select what appears to be the best risk management technique or combination of techniques.

4. Implement the selected techniques.

5. Monitor and improve the risk management program.[17]

The sections that follow describe how each step of the risk management process should be considered in developing a comprehensive risk management program.

FIGURE 1.1. Steps in Risk Management Decision Making

Source: George L. Head and Stephen Horn II, *Essentials of Risk Management*, 3rd ed., vol. 1 (Malvern, PA: Insurance Institute of America, 1997), p. 15. Reprinted with permission.

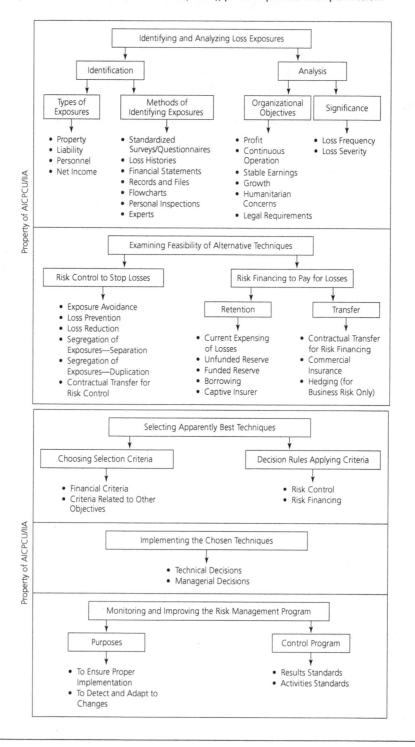

Step 1: Identify and Analyze Loss Exposures

Risk identification is the process whereby the risk management professional becomes aware of risks in the health care environment that constitute potential loss exposures for the institution. Such exposures can include loss of financial assets through liability judgments and out-of-court settlements or casualty losses to physical plant and property, human losses through death or injury of employees, and intangible losses to public image and reputation.

The risk management professional uses many information sources to identify potential risks. **Incident reporting**, in which employees report accidents and occurrences not consistent with normal operating routines or expected outcomes, is the cornerstone of most risk identification systems. Incident reporting systems range from sophisticated point-of-service electronic reporting and analysis packages to simple paper forms. Regardless of the format, incident reporting systems allow caregivers to provide the risk management department with basic early warning information about occurrences that are inconsistent with normal, expected patient care processes and that result (or have the potential to result) in injury to patients, visitors, staff, or property. Other common risk identification processes include the following:

■ *Generic occurrence screening.* Generic occurrence screening is a risk management process often performed as part of a health care organization's performance improvement program. In a generic occurrence screening process, patient records are reviewed retrospectively to determine whether the care provided meets specific predetermined criteria. Generic screening criteria of interest to the risk management professional might include "Did the patient sustain a fall during this admission?" or "Were all medications administered as ordered?" Although generic occurrence screening often provides information that duplicates that reported through incident reports, the systematic nature of the process may capture incidents that should have been reported but were not. The major disadvantages of generic occurrence screening from a risk management perspective are the time lag inherent in reviewing records retrospectively and the fact that only incidents meeting preselected criteria will be identified though the process.

■ *Patient complaints and satisfaction survey results.* Survey data tallied by patient representatives (or community relations or marketing departments) is another source of risk management information. Such survey results may provide insight into individual patient issues and may offer aggregate trend data regarding patient experiences with the health care organization.

■ *Prior medical professional liability, property and casualty, and workers' compensation claims data.* The analysis of such claims is a frequently used and valuable risk identification tool. By studying the specific services, procedures, and activities that have resulted in claims against the organization in the past, the risk management professional is in a better position to anticipate future areas of concern and take appropriate action to mitigate subsequent losses.

■ *Surveys by The Joint Commission, the National Committee on Quality Assurance (NCQA),*[18] *liability or other insurers, and risk management consultants.*

Such survey processes help the risk management professional identify sources of potential risk that might have previously been overlooked by the organization. Outside experts and consultants draw on their experience to provide insight into the risk identification process for the organization and compare the organization's performance with national standards, pointing out areas meriting the risk management professional's additional attention.

■ *State licensure surveys.* These surveys play an important role in risk identification. Although sometimes less important in hospitals and acute care settings, state surveys are an important part of risk management programs in long-term care facilities and outpatient settings. Findings from such surveys frequently identify areas of concern for risk management and performance improvement and guide loss prevention efforts.

■ *Contracts, leases, and other agreements.* A review of salient contract provisions entered into by the organization frequently reveals risk exposures that must be addressed through modification of the contract or agreement, insurance, or enhanced loss prevention activities.

■ *Information generated through the facility's infection control and performance improvement functions.* The data generated through such related functions should be routinely reviewed by the risk management professional to the extent permitted by law. (Concerns have been expressed in some jurisdictions that free access to medical staff peer review information by a risk management professional, who might use it in part to prepare for the defense of medical professional liability claims, may waive statutory protections provided under state peer review protection statutes. Seek the counsel of an attorney with expertise in this area when developing a mechanism for reviewing such information.)

■ *Informal discussions with managers and staff.* Line managers and other staff members are excellent sources of information about potential risks with which the risk management professional may previously have been unfamiliar.

Risk analysis is the process of determining the potential severity of the loss associated with an identified risk and the probability that such a loss will occur. Together, those factors establish the seriousness of a risk and guide the risk management professional's selection of an appropriate risk treatment strategy. Risk management professionals need to give priority to the areas of greatest potential risk of financial loss, such as an anesthesia or obstetrical mishap, even though claims in these areas may occur infrequently. Ordinarily, less emphasis is given to small claims that occur frequently, unless the total costs associated with a certain type of incident are especially significant. Although risk analysis is in part an art—a judgment call based on the training, experience, and instincts of the risk management professional—it is also a science in that certain data and objective sources of information are taken into consideration in evaluating a given risk. In particular, closed claims data, which reveal the frequency and severity of prior losses, should be reviewed to gain insight into the analysis of current risks. The organization's legal counsel, insurance brokers, and insurance carriers may be consulted for additional information (for more information on risk identification and analysis, see Chapter Six).

Step 2: Consider Alternative Risk Techniques

Risk management techniques or treatments refer to the range of choices available to risk management professionals for handling a given risk. Risk treatment strategies include two general categories: risk control and risk financing. Risk control involves preventing losses or mitigating the magnitude of losses, while risk financing involves paying for those losses that do occur.

Risk Control Risk control includes the following treatments or techniques:

- Exposure avoidance

- Loss prevention

- Loss reduction

- Segregation of loss exposures (separation or duplication)

- Non-insurance transfer l

Exposure Avoidance

Exposure avoidance reduces the possibility of a loss to zero. Whereas other risk control techniques will reduce the frequency or severity of a loss, avoidance is the only risk control technique to eliminate any possibility for the loss to occur. When a given risk poses a particularly serious threat that cannot be effectively reduced or transferred, think about eliminating it. For example, a hospital might elect not to provide obstetrical services, thereby avoiding the risk of a birth trauma claim. Although the strategy might be very effective in terms of controlling risk exposure, it could come at the high cost of a loss of hospital mission effectiveness, market share, revenues, patient satisfaction, and medical staff relations, which could outweigh the risk management benefit of the avoidance technique.

Loss Prevention

Loss prevention as a risk control technique reduces the likelihood of an untoward event occurring and focuses on reducing the frequency of loss. Loss prevention efforts are at the core of most health care risk management programs, are proactive, and include staff education, policy, and procedure review and revision. These interventions aim to control the number of adverse occurrences without unduly eliminating potentially risky activities.

Loss Reduction

Loss reduction or minimization involves various loss control strategies aimed at limiting the potential consequences of a given risk without totally accepting or avoiding them, thus focusing on reducing the severity of losses. Loss reduction or minimization efforts may also include risk management techniques, such as establishing and maintaining a rapport with injured patients and their families, thus limiting the severity of a loss that has already occurred. Other loss reduction treatments include prompt incident investigation, disaster and business continuity drills, written plans to support emergency management, fire drills, and building structures equipped with sprinkler and alarm systems. Also, a facility offering obstetrical services may develop a protocol to save placentas from births meeting certain criteria for pathological review. Such an examination may encourage an early settlement if the examination is unfavorable and does not support quality care. If the review does support the care rendered, the pathological findings become a defense tool in any subsequent claim against the facility or the practitioner. Although such a process does not prevent poor obstetrical outcome, it tends to reduce the potential financial consequences of such occurrences to the organization.

Accreditation agencies such as The Joint Commission have instituted formal requirements for clinical loss prevention efforts, such as prescribed root cause analysis (RCA) and failure mode and effects analysis (FMEA) processes. These analytical methodologies have long been intuitively applied by risk management professionals and are considered key patient safety and risk control activities. RCA represents a systematic approach to identifying the underlying causes of adverse occurrences so that effective steps can be taken to modify processes and prevent future losses. Through the use of FMEA, organizations analyze processes associated with high-risk procedures and clinical services so as to identify weaknesses in systems before a problem actually occurs. The processes examined need not be complex but are typically those that can have serious consequences if a systems failure occurs. The Universal Protocol, a methodology adopted by health care organizations to reduce the occurrence of wrong-site surgeries, was the result of an FMEA process.[19]

Segregation of Loss Exposures

The fourth risk control technique is segregation of loss exposures. This technique involves arranging an organization's activities and resources so that if a loss occurs, it will not affect the entire organization. Segregation of loss exposures consists of two categories: separation and duplication.

Separation Separation, when properly applied, results in the distribution of a particular activity or asset over several locations, thereby confining the extent of the loss to only a portion of the organization should a loss occur at a single location. For example, a medical supply company might distribute its inventory among multiple warehouses or purchase supplies from different vendors to reduce the potential losses associated with a warehouse or manufacturing plant fire. In a medical office, separation may be evidenced by obtaining medications from multiple suppliers and the practitioner's maintaining staff privileges at several hospitals.

Duplication Duplication results in a reserve, or substitute for a product or service, being available for use even if the primary source or activity is affected by a loss.

Keeping copies of electronic records and computer files is a form of duplication. Although duplication of records is generally a convenient method to mitigate loss, duplicate records and files should be stored off-site to prevent accidental loss.

Non-Insurance Transfer Non-insurance transfer reduces the transferor's loss exposure by contractually shifting legal responsibility for a loss through leases, contracts and agreements.

Courts often refuse to enforce non-insurance transfers which:

- Unreasonably interfere with the rights of others (against public policy); or
- Were not fairly bargained between the parties (unconscionable because they are so drastically unfair to the transferee)

Risk Financing **Risk financing** strategies include many ways to generate funds to pay for losses that risk control techniques do not entirely eliminate. These treatment techniques include both risk retention and risk transfer.

Risk Retention One strategy for managing an identified risk is risk retention. This treatment strategy involves assuming the potential losses associated with a given risk and making plans to cover the financial consequences of such losses. The retention options open to health care organizations include the current expensing of losses, using an unfunded loss reserve (an accounting entry denoting a potential liability to pay for a loss), using a funded loss reserve (a reserve backed by set-aside funds within the organization), borrowing funds to pay for losses, and providing insurance through an affiliated captive insurer.[20] Another (less thought of) form of risk retention occurs when the risk of exposure to loss is unknown and has not been identified by the organization or risk management professional, and therefore the opportunity to evaluate appropriate risk financing strategies is lost. Failure to identify a risk will result in unwitting risk retention unless insurance coverage is available under an existing policy. Risk retention is most appropriate for managing (1) risks that cannot be otherwise reduced, transferred, or avoided; (2) risks for which the probability of loss is not great and for which the potential consequences are within the institution's ability to self-fund; (3) losses that are quantifiable and predictable; and (4) small risks (such as missing dentures and eyeglasses) for which the purchase of cost-effective insurance coverage might not be feasible.

For purposes of illustration, assume that a risk management professional has identified a risk of injuries related to misdiagnosis of patients seen in the facility's emergency department. Because the hospital's governing board and administration might have identified the provision of emergency services as central to both its mission and its market-positioning strategy, the hospital is unwilling to forgo providing such services as a means of eliminating the risk. The hospital may then choose to self-insure for losses associated with injuries (retention) or perhaps purchase an insurance policy to cover such losses (a risk transfer strategy). The purchase of insurance combined with a deductible, or a program of primary self-insurance, may be a viable option to help reduce cost. Likewise, a physician's office practice in California may elect (absent any loan covenants, mortgage restrictions, or regulatory requirements to the contrary) not to purchase earthquake insurance coverage on its office building. The risk management professional may determine that the chances of the building's being seriously damaged or destroyed in an earthquake are sufficiently remote and the costs of securing such coverage are sufficiently high to merit "going bare" for the exposure. If such a risk retention strategy is selected, it may be appropriate for the risk management professional to increase loss prevention and loss reduction efforts, such as the installation of sway bracing near sprinkler heads to reduce potential water damage in the event of an earthquake. Thus risk retention, like other available risk treatment strategies, should not be viewed in isolation but rather should be regarded as part of an overall strategy for managing an identified risk.

Risk Transfer Contractual transfer techniques for risk financing involve shifting the financial obligation for a loss, but not the ultimate legal responsibilities for losses, to an outside entity through the purchase of insurance from a third-party, unaffiliated insurer or noninsurance transfer through a contract provision, commonly described as a hold-harmless agreement. Through **risk transfer**, an institution can continue to engage in a risk-producing activity while transferring the financial risk of loss to another party. For example, a hospital may purchase a medical professional liability policy to pay for any losses associated with medical malpractice, thereby transferring the financial obligation for the loss to an insurance company while remaining legally liable for patient injuries caused by the **negligence** of its staff.

Step 3: Select the Best Risk Management Techniques

Selecting the best risk management technique or treatment for a specific situation is a two-part activity. The first part requires forecasting the effects that the available risk management options are likely to have on the organization's ability to fulfill its goals. The second is defining and applying criteria that measure how well each alternative risk management technique contributes to the organization's objectives in a cost-effective way.[21] For most identified risks, the health care facility will employ a combination of risk treatment and risk financing techniques to manage a given risk. At a minimum, one risk control technique and one risk financing technique should be combined to address each significant exposure. The risk management professional may elect to employ any available combination of risk control and risk financing techniques to obtain the desired results. Typically, health care organizations accept a certain amount of patient care liability risk through an insurance deductible or self-insured retention; attempt to limit potential risk by not offering some inherently high-risk services; seek to reduce the severity of loss for incidents that have already occurred through prompt incident investigation and claim resolution; prevent future losses through in-service education, appropriate staffing, and credentialing; and transfer the remaining financial risk by purchasing insurance.

Step 4: Implement the Selected Techniques

The implementation process involves both the technical risk management decisions that must be made by risk management professionals and the related decisions that are made by other managers within the organization to implement the chosen risk management techniques. Technical expertise exercised by risk management professionals may include selecting an appropriate insurer and choosing appropriate policy limits and deductibles. In working with managers and other personnel, risk management professionals advise and influence others in implementing selected techniques that are not within their direct areas of responsibility.

Step 5: Monitor and Improve the Risk Management Program

The final step in the risk management process is to evaluate and monitor the effectiveness of the risk management program by assessing the adequacy and appropriateness of the techniques employed to identify, analyze, and treat risks. Risk management evaluation involves not only the risk management professional but also senior management, medical staff and governing board, insurers, claims managers, and legal counsel. A multidisciplinary approach to evaluating the risk management program ensures that the impact of risk management activities on various constituencies is measured accurately and that additional opportunities to improve the risk management function are fully explored. To facilitate the risk management evaluation process, the risk management professional needs to prepare a comprehensive annual report of risk management efforts, highlighting significant claims activity, new program developments, changes in insurance coverage, and contractual modifications having risk management significance. These results should be compared against clearly defined benchmarks that have been identified in advance of the review. Such benchmarks can be internal or external to the organization and may be as simple as comparing the current program results against those from the previous year. The risk management professional can also use data from independent but similar organizations against which to benchmark. Benchmarks frequently include a comparison of claims data. Claims data provide frequency and severity information for losses incurred, including the number of events reported and dollars spent to defend and settle them. (For more on benchmarking and program evaluation, see Chapter Fifteen.)

EVOLUTION OF THE RISK MANAGEMENT PROGRAM

As the delivery of health care continues to change, so must the structure of risk management programs. The existing and emerging principles that apply to risk management will need to adapt to ensure safe, cost-effective, and clinically effective care. The health care organization as it is known today will be different in the future, with multiple levels and both horizontal and vertical integration. Interdependency on organizational strategic and financial goals must be integrated into risk management program development and must meet the needs of the changing customer base and payer mix. It is possible that within one organization there will be a need to create different risk management program structures and take different steps in assessing risk management needs in the health organization's different areas.

SELECTING AN APPROPRIATE RISK MANAGEMENT PROGRAM STRUCTURE

A variety of risk management program structures can be considered, based on organizational size, scope of services and activities, available resources, and locations. Generally, acute care hospitals have preexisting systems that introduce and enhance risk management program components, whereas integrated delivery systems, long-term care settings, physician's office practices, home health care, and ambulatory care centers are less likely to have formalized risk management efforts.

The overall level of risk management responsibility can vary greatly. It can be any one of the following (or a combination, depending on organizational structure and expectations):

■ *All related risk management functions.* In a traditional model, this structure requires an experienced risk management professional and a vast array of resources that can address each type of service provided within the organization. Knowledge of and experience in clinical care delivery, plant engineering, safety, claims, and finance are particularly helpful in large, multi-institutional organizations. The newest enterprise risk management model encompasses strategic planning, marketing, and even branding components. In many situations, on-site risk management coordinators integrate activities with the corporate or home office. In many smaller organizations, all related risk management activities may be managed by one department or by one person. A physician's office practice is an example where one employee may be responsible for risk management, quality improvement, safety, medical records, disaster planning, infection control, and other functions.

■ *Responsibility for a set of defined risk management activities and services.* This structure continues to be the model of choice at community hospitals and hospitals in a system. Responsibility in this structure is spread among multiple departments. The coordination and facilitation of activities that affect risk management activities should still be managed and controlled out of a single office, preferably the risk management department. In this model, there are generally separate departments for safety, security, quality improvement, corporate compliance, education and in-service, risk financing, contract review and negotiating, claims administration, and so on. For example, the CFO may be responsible for the risk financing program, in-house legal administration may be responsible for the claims administration and contract review, or the director of the emergency department may be responsible for disaster planning. The hospital or other health care setting that is part of an organized health system also has a limit to the breadth and depth of risk management responsibility at the local level. In many cases, the corporate office mandates the risk financing program and may also manage all claims. Risk management positions at the local site generally revolve around loss control activities and are far more common than control of all risk management functions. The intent of systemwide programs is to create a general operational structure that encourages consistency and cost control while allowing for flexibility, timeliness, and accountability at the lowest possible levels.

■ *Role referred to external consultants or an outsourced professional.* At times, an organization may choose to supplement its risk management functions. Consistent with the consulting and outsourcing structure model is a process to internally manage the flow of information and facilitate communication. Consultative and outsourcing structures are commonly used during times of merger, acquisition, and divestiture, when the organization faces severe financial constraints, has a loss of key risk management personnel, or is undergoing reengineering efforts or management change. It is not unusual that in this structure the need still exists for a risk management professional. This individual then becomes the contact point between the outsourced organization or consultant and senior management, and the outsourced organization becomes the risk management "back room."

Regardless of the health care organization's choice of formal structure, its risk management program should incorporate the basic elements, components, and functions described throughout this chapter. All risk management activities require alignment with the organization's mission and strategic plan.

ASSESSING AREAS OF THE ORGANIZATION THAT NEED RISK MANAGEMENT

Assessment methodology may vary, but consistency in its application should be maintained. Assessment findings, and any improvement strategies, should be presented uniformly so that the organization and individuals maintain a clear understanding of the findings and resulting recommendations.

Any assessment can be approached in various ways, but most risk management professionals find that having written guidelines helps avoid overlooking key points. There are many tools from which to choose, one of which is the *Risk Management Self-Assessment Manual.*[22] Other sources can be found through literature searches and in outside organizations such as insurance companies, regulatory agencies, and consulting firms.

Identify the Various Areas for Assessment

Because assessments can take time, after evaluating basic organizational structures, the focus should usually start with high-risk, high-volume, and high-visibility areas. In multi-institutional organizations, assessments should be tailored so that organization-wide processes and institutional specific programs are assessed. This will allow for more comprehensive findings that reflect the organizational status.

In general, profiling the organization's current services and business relationships is important in identifying the various areas for assessment. The assessment process should include the organization on an enterprisewide basis, assessing it from an operational, clinical, and business perspective. This process could be viewed as taking inventory of activities that might have potential risk and as finding a starting point for developing or renewing the risk management program's focus. This inventory includes a systematic review of the organization's functions, data, budget, and workforce and a survey of perceptions about the effectiveness of systems and processes already in place. The assessment may reveal findings and needs that differ according to the organization's various areas. An example could be if an organization decides to institute a research department but lacks a defined and operational institutional review board, which could result in regulatory noncompliance and direct patient risk.

Analyzing Current Systems

The second phase of the assessment is to analyze systems that are already in place for minimizing risk and then determine current effectiveness. Profiles should include identification of key contacts and responsibilities, level and types of risk financing, contractual relationships, and risk management activities (including policies, orientation, job and credentialing requirements, integration into current organizational structure, and safety and quality program integration). Areas or topics to be inventoried may include these:

- Educational relationships—levels and types of agreements, formal or informal

- Staff relationships—employed, contracted, independent, network (where staff float from one entity of a large organization to another), or consulting (may involve the assessment of staff issues)

- Scope of services—not only types but also where and to what degree; might also include reporting relationships

- Subsidiaries owned, partnered, or otherwise associated with the organization

- Accreditations, licenses, certifications, or other designations in which any or all parts of the organization participate

- Human resource issues, with focus on preemployment screening, ongoing competency evaluation, and staffing

- Information management methodologies, computerized information and access, and other information issues such as retention and release

- Clinical technology issues—selection, maintenance, user training, and product and equipment problem-tracking systems—and level of support technology, such as bar coding and order entry software

- Level of consistent application of systems throughout the organization

- Assessment of the organizational core values, including philosophy and practice with regard to disclosure and nonpunitive environment

- Loss assessment data, **loss runs**, and results of inspection by regulatory agencies

- Credentialing and orientation processes for nonemployee staff, both initially and at reappointment

- Contract management protocols

- Safety and quality management program structure and its integration and effectiveness

- Emergency preparedness protocols and emergency management relationships external to the organization

Assessing Compliance

Risk management programs must meet not only organizational needs but also the requirements of outside entities that by choice or mandate make demands on the health care organization's operation. The managed care market may require not just a slate of activities and reporting provisions but also that certain accreditations be maintained. Rules set forth by regulatory agencies must also be factored into the activities and processes as the risk management program develops and expands. One should first review and analyze the most recent findings of all external reviews, inspections, and surveys and any reports from consultants. These reports and the status of the action taken in response, along with appropriate standards issued by various bodies, can be used to compile assessment tools that can assist in evaluating the risk management program and in planning for improvement. During this review of external demands, attention to the organization's ability to identify, track, and integrate external mandates should also be assessed.

Reviewing the Assessments

Assessments are often performed to identify risk management program strengths and opportunities for improvement. Analysis should include categorizing findings according to severity, frequency, effect on the organization's strategic plan, areas identified for improvement, and best practices identified. Good practice without supporting documentation should be assessed as both a practice strength and an information weakness. For example, even if it is identified that the patient care process might need no immediate attention, the recording or tracking of patient care information might require integration into a better-defined information process to substantiate practice patterns.

Setting Priorities for Program Implementation

Established risk management programs should undergo continuous reassessment, particularly as new areas are added or for those previously identified as weak. Regulations and other external mandates, along with areas of severe loss, should command the most immediate attention. Organizational emphasis (what the strategic plan and the mission support) will also need to be factored into the list of areas to be addressed first. One useful tool is to map out a strategy to take advantage of the many activities that are interdependent. Some risk management activities that might seem less important may need to be initiated to lay the groundwork for success in high-impact areas. An example might be the development of user-friendly reporting or early identification tools that are adapted for the organization's various departments and services. Such a project could be multidisciplinary and supported by various areas within the organization, which can lead to an enhanced quality-improvement database. In setting priorities for program implementation, risk management professionals should clearly define the desired **outcome**. Having done an analysis, the risk management professional should be aware of the organization's strengths and weaknesses and of improvements or expansions that need to be accomplished. Preliminary work may consist of collecting data and drafting early versions of future measurement tools. Another key item is to identify levels of understanding, not only during the assessment but also once an analysis has been formulated. The result of action or inaction must be clearly defined in relation to the direct effect on the organization.

KEY COMPONENTS FOR GETTING STARTED

For any risk management program to achieve its goals, several key components must be in place. Organizational commitment—that is, acceptance of roles and support for program aspects by the various levels of leadership, starting with the board—is a necessity. Commitment is often demonstrated through assignments of responsibility, adoption of accountability systems, approval of the program, and participation in aspects requiring support and action. The ultimate goal is to integrate risk management components, systems, and strategies into the overall organizational culture of safety.

Access to all levels of the organization, with defined accountabilities and identification of resources, is also part of the initial structure formation. No risk management program can function in isolation; its integration with other initiatives, particularly safety, is crucial to its success. By relying on already established relationships, risk management professionals can enhance programs with limited resources by strengthening operational linkages and avoiding duplication of effort. Negative perceptions about the risk management program might damage its credibility before it even gets under way. Physicians often perceive that risk management's involvement after an event has occurred only makes matters worse or that the only motivation is to minimize costs. Frequently, risk management programs are viewed as reactive to crisis rather than proactive in creating a safe culture.

Risk management activities should focus on support and service, using facilitative techniques in guiding the clinicians' understanding of the nonnegotiable forces (regulatory fines, accreditations, citations, and agency requirements) and the alternatives available. Clinical staff should have input into both the risk management process and the analysis, redesign, and monitoring stages. Most program elements that affect clinical functions require that clinical staff members become committed to risk management concepts and understand the desired outcomes. Ensuring that duplication of effort is minimized can be a key selling point to staff members in accepting their roles in the risk management effort. Simplification of any process is always welcome. A method for seeking continual staff feedback should also be developed to ensure ownership of the program by all staff.

WRITING A RISK MANAGEMENT PROGRAM PLAN

The written risk management program plan includes an overview of the purpose, structure, and process of risk management activities within the organization. Within this framework, organizational performance objectives can be developed in addition to policies and guidelines to support the identified processes that maximize achievement of the program's objectives. It is critical to maintain an integrated approach at this point of development to achieve consistency of purpose within the organization and to avoid duplication of effort. Rather than create new systems for the risk management process, the risk management professional should evaluate how best to enhance existing systems.

As with all programs that have a data collection and monitoring function, reports, memos, and minutes will be generated as communication tools. To be most effective, these tools must meet the needs of those responsible for the implementation and change of risk management and safety practices. Therefore, it is important that those served by such information have input into its ultimate design and format as a means of maximizing its usefulness. (See Appendix A for an example of a risk management program plan.)

ACHIEVING PROGRAM ACCEPTANCE

Often the quickest way to gain support for a program is to provide visibility and education on its related topics. A well-designed risk management program will not be successful unless staff members at all levels understand its purpose and methods. In some cases, the risk management professional may even provide unrelated services simply as a means to gain the acceptance and trust vital to the program's success. Often the support of an interested medical staff member serving as an advocate familiarizes others with the merits of the risk management program. The risk management program achieves visibility through participation in employee orientation and continuing education activities. A focus on the prevention aspects of risk management creates a less threatening atmosphere and aligns efforts with the increasing focus on safety. Maintaining a subject file on risk management topics such as consent, information release, falls, medication process, human factors that contribute to error-prone behavior, and credentialing allows the risk management professional to have supplemental resources when participating in education and quality and performance improvement projects. Another strategy is to become involved in the organization's efforts in responding to external initiatives or mandates such as The Joint Commission's National Patient Safety Goals, insurance carrier criteria, state licensing requirements, and conditions of participation from the Centers for Medicare and Medicaid Services.

SUMMARY

Establishing a risk management program is no simple task, particularly in today's complex health care environment. Assessment of the health care organization's internal and external relationships and forces will provide an excellent basis for the issues the risk management program must address. Establishing risk management's role in the overall safety initiatives and safety culture development must also be included in the risk management program. Obtaining commitment to the program from all levels of the organization, top to bottom, can be a slow process but must be achieved for full integration to occur. Translating a written plan into functional risk management processes requires collaboration and facilitation skills now more than ever. No matter how detailed the risk management plan may be, the program will always be evolving as it adapts to the changes in health care.

KEY TERMS

Accidental loss
Adverse occurrence
Adverse medication event
Adverse outcome
Ambulatory care
Chief risk officer
Error
Event
Exposure
Hospital-acquired infection
Incident
Incident reporting
The Joint Commission
Loss
Loss control
Loss prevention
Loss reduction
Loss run
Malpractice
Neglect
Negligence
Outcome
Patient safety
Risk analysis
Risk avoidance
Risk control techniques
Risk financing
Risk identification
Risk management
Risk reduction
Risk transfer
Sentinel event

ACRONYMS

ASHRM
CEO
CFO
CMS
CRO
DED
EEOC
FME
HIPAA
IDS
MCO
NCQA
OSHA
RCA

NOTES

1. Kuhn, A. M. "Introduction to Risk Management." In B. J. Youngberg (ed.), *The Risk Manager's Desk Reference*. Gaithersburg, Md.: Aspen, 1988.

2. Ibid., p. 1.

3. Ibid.

4. Taravella, S. "The Rise of Risk Management." *Modern Healthcare,* Oct. 8, 1990.

5. Ibid.

6. Kohn, L. T., Corrigan, J. M., and Donaldson, M. S. (eds). *To Err Is Human: Building a Safer Health System.* Washington, D.C.: National Academy Press, 1999.

7. Joint Commission on Accreditation of Healthcare Organizations. *2005 Comprehensive Accreditation Manual for Hospitals.* Oakbrook Terrace, Ill.: Joint Commission, 2004.

8. Health Insurance Portability and Accountability Act of 1996 (P.L. 104-191); 45 CFR, Parts 160 and 164 (Aug. 14, 2002); Sarbanes-Oxley Reform Act (P.L. 107-204); 116 Stat. 746, USC, Title 15, §§7201 et seq.

9. *Medical Malpractice: Verdicts, Settlements and Statistical Analysis.* Horsham, Pa.: LRP Publications, 2002.

10. "What's Ahead on the Medical Liability Front in 2002?" *Medical Liability Monitor,* Jan. 21, 2002.

11. Ibid.

12. Ibid.

13. 42 USC 1320.

14. *Laughinhouse* v. *Risser,* 786 F.Supp. 920 (Kan. 1992); *Trotta* v. *Mobil Oil Corp.,* 798 F.Supp. 1336 (D.C. N.Y. 1992); *Jewell* v. *Palmer Broadcasting Ltd.,* Iowa Dist. Ct. No. CL94-56040, Dec. 30, 1993.

15. Gamble, R. H. "The Insurance Renewal Marathon," http://businessfinancemag.com /article/insurance-renewal-marathon-0201, Feb. 1, 2002.

16. *Hazard Communication Standard: Final Rule.* Occupational Safety and Health Administration, 29 CFR 1910-1200.

17. Head, G. L., and Kwok-Sze, R. W. *Risk Management for Public Entities.* Malvern, Pa.: Center for the Advancement of Risk Management Education, 1999, pp. 4–5.

18. JCAHO, *2005 Comprehensive Accreditation Manual;* National Committee on Quality Assurance. *NCQA Standards for Accreditation* (CR 8.0, CR 13.0). Washington, D.C.: National Committee on Quality Assurance, 1995.

19. Joint Commission on Accreditation of Healthcare Organizations. *Universal Protocol for Preventing Wrong Site, Wrong Procedure, Wrong Person Surgery.* Oakbrook Terrace, Ill.: Joint Commission, 2004.

20. Head and Kwok-Sze, *Risk Management for Public Entities,* pp. 4–5.

21. Ibid.

22. American Hospital Association, *Risk Management Self-Assessment Manual.* Chicago: American Hospital Association, 2000.

SUGGESTED READING

Brown, B. L. *Risk Management for Hospitals: A Practical Approach.* Rockville, Md.: Aspen, 1979.

Healthcare Risk Control, published monthly by the Emergency Care Research Institute (ECRI), 5200 Butler Pike, Plymouth Meeting, PA 19462.

Hospital Peer Review, published monthly by American Health Consultants, Inc., 3525 Piedmont Road NE, Building 6, Suite 400, Atlanta, GA 30305.

Hospital Risk Management, published monthly by American Health Consultants, Inc., 3525 Piedmont Road NE, Building 6, Suite 400, Atlanta, GA 30305.

Jessee, W. F. *Quality of Care Issues for the Hospital Trustee: A Practical Guide to Fulfilling Trustee Responsibilities.* Chicago: Hospital Research and Educational Trust, 1984.

Joint Commission on Accreditation of Healthcare Organizations. *Hospital Patient Safety Standards: Examples of Compliance.* Chicago: Joint Commission Resources, 2002.

Journal of Healthcare Risk Management, published quarterly by the American Society for Healthcare Risk Management of the American Hospital Association, One North Franklin, Chicago, IL 60606.

Kraus, G. P. *Health Care Risk Management: Organization and Claims Administration.* Owings Mills, Md.: National Health Publishing, 1986.

Risk Management Pearls series, published by the American Society for Healthcare Risk Management of the American Hospital Association, One North Franklin, Chicago, IL 60606.

Rowland, H., and Rowland, B. *Hospital Risk Management: Forms, Checklists, and Guidelines.* Gaithersburg, Md.: Aspen, 1993.

CHAPTER

2

THE HEALTH CARE RISK MANAGEMENT PROFESSIONAL

JEANNIE SEDWICK

LEARNING OBJECTIVES

- To be able to describe six functional areas of risk management in health care settings
- To be able to describe seven health care settings in which a risk manager might function
- To be able to develop two examples of common risks associated with each setting
- To be able to identify two skill sets and two attributes required for success as a health care risk manager
- To be able to identify the major professional education programs for health care risk management professionals

Health care has changed dramatically over the past forty years, and this has led to an expansion in the role and responsibilities of health care risk management professionals. In the early years of the profession, health care risk managers focused primarily on exposures that related to general and professional liability. Today, health care risk management professionals must manage not only those exposures but also exposures that relate to managed care and capitation risks, mergers and acquisitions, employment and workers' compensation risks, and risks related to corporate compliance and organizational ethics. Despite the significant changes in health care over the past decades, the risk management process has remained virtually unchanged and continues to serve the same purpose: to maintain a safe and effective health care environment for patients, visitors, and employees, thereby preventing or reducing losses to the organization. Many risk management professionals are adopting the enterprise risk management (**ERM**) approach, described as a comprehensive process that evaluates all risk exposures confronting an organization from the top down. ERM is a discipline broad in scope and reflects an organizationwide, ongoing commitment to risk management principles. To be effective, ERM should be part of the organization's strategic plan and viewed as both a proactive and a reactive process.

This chapter provides an overview of the role of the health care risk management professional and the skills necessary for performing this function in an ever-changing health care environment. Information is provided about the educational and experiential backgrounds of risk management professionals and about commonly held designations. Educational programs for individuals who wish to enter the field or for those in the field who wish to further their education are also discussed.

KEY CONCEPTS

- Enterprise risk management is a comprehensive approach to identifying and managing all risks to an organization.

- The role of the risk management professional is influenced by an organization's size, location, structure, and risk financing program.

- The risk management professional is active in six functional areas: loss prevention and reduction, claims management, risk financing, regulatory and accreditation compliance, risk management operations, and bioethics.

- The risk management professional working with an integrated delivery system, a multifacility health system, or an academic or teaching medical center generally requires a higher level of expertise and has broader responsibilities in risk financing and claims management than would be required in the single acute care hospital.

THE RISK MANAGER'S JOB: FUNCTIONAL AREAS OF RESPONSIBILITY

The roles and responsibilities of health care risk management professionals vary widely. Risk management program components—and therefore the roles of the risk management professional—are greatly influenced by the size and structure of the organization and by the risk financing strategies it employs. The profession itself has evolved along functional needs and growing regulatory mandates, without benefit of extensive scientific study or a well-defined body of knowledge. Until recently, no attempt had been made to quantify the many activities that have come to make up the health care risk management professional's functional job responsibilities. Thus it is not possible to describe the "typical" health care risk management professional's job.

The risk management professional often performs specific duties that may result in a variety of titles for the position, including risk manager, chief risk officer, or patient safety officer, reflecting the expanding roles and responsibilities of the health care risk professional. The chief risk officer (CRO) in the health care setting is gaining more visibility in larger organizations and usually resides at the senior management level. The title of chief risk officer was first used by James Lam at GE Capital in 1993 to describe a function to manage "all aspects of risk," including risk management, back-office operations, and business and financial planning.[1] The CRO position is quickly finding a place in health care organizations to respond to increased regulatory pressures and a variety of business risks better known as ERM.

The role of the patient safety officer (**PSO**) is founded on the growth of the modern patient safety movement and new patient safety regulations and requirements. Restructuring within health care organizations so as to formalize the PSO responsibilities offers risk management professionals and others an opportunity to highlight their current contributions to patient safety, develop additional skills, and expand their profile. The job description for a patient safety officer can vary, but the basic functions are identified in Exhibit 2.1. Risk management professionals assuming the additional responsibilities of the PSO may need to enhance their job descriptions with the responsibilities at level one, two, or three as indicated in Exhibits 2.2, 2.3, and 2.4, respectively. (Additional information on the patient safety officer program can be found in Chapter Three.)

In 1999, the American Society for Healthcare Risk Management (**ASHRM**) conducted the first role delineation study in health care risk management.[2] The purpose of this study was to identify those activities that make up a health care risk management professional's job and thereby define health care risk management's body of knowledge. A list of approximately 160 task statements describing various risk management functions and activities was sent to 2,500 health care risk management professionals, who were asked to rate the importance of each task. The findings suggest that the health care risk management professional's job responsibilities can be divided

(Continued on page 50)

EXHIBIT 2.1 Patient Safety Officer Job Description

Position Summary

The Patient Safety Officer will supervise personnel responsible for the delivery of patient safety services and risk management. The Patient Safety Officer incorporates and utilizes methods to improve all aspects of patient safety, risk management, and quality. The PSO will oversee the collection, analysis and dissemination of PS data and information. The PSO will analyze clinical processes, identify potential risks for patients and employees and develop strategies to maximize safety, effectiveness and efficiency. The PSO will oversee the development and implementation of medical error reduction strategies in collaboration with all departments and patient care areas. Additionally, the Patient Safety Officer will be primarily responsible for communication and marketing related to patient safety initiatives.

Reports To: Chief Patient Safety and Quality Officer

PRINCIPAL ACCOUNTABILITIES AND ESSENTIAL DUTIES OF THE JOB

Service Excellence (100% of time)

- Provides excellent service to all customers, meeting or exceeding their needs/expectations, to ensure continuous improvement of customer-focused environment.
- Exemplifies excellent customer service towards physicians, patients, families, staff, visitors, co-workers and other departments. Shows courtesy, compassion, and respect in communication with all customers.
- Contributes to teamwork and harmonious working relationships.
- Partners with healthcare teams, patients and families to continuously solicit feedback and information to improve patient safety and quality. Actively supports patients, families and employees involved in serious PS events.

Provides clinical and operational guidance to all personnel performing patient safety and risk management duties (100% of time)

- Acts as coach and mentor to PS and Risk Management personnel, providing feedback about performance routinely.
- Performs all duties of manager at BJH including: hiring and firing, budget preparation, performance appraisals and other human resource/personnel functions.
- Assists Chief Patient Safety and Quality Officer and Chief Medical Officer with all responsibilities related to PS.

Responsible for Data Management, Analysis, and Safety Event Reporting (30% of time)

- Oversees activities related to data collection, data review, analysis and dissemination of patient safety information.
- Reviews safety event data from Safety Event Reporting databases.
- Identifies trends, clusters, and risk factors; establishes benchmarks for comparison.
- Oversees the dissemination of accurate, user-friendly PS reports in a timely fashion to key stakeholders.
- Demonstrates expertise in use of PS software and databases.

Oversee all activities related to: Risk Prevention and Medical Error Reduction (30% of time)

- Uses risk factor data to develop evidence-based PS interventions and process improvement strategies.
- Collaborates with healthcare teams to rapidly identify risk, employ prevention and risk reduction strategies.
- Demonstrates expertise and participates in PI team facilitation, leadership and membership.
- Participates in Root Cause Analysis (RCA), Failure Mode and Effects Analysis (FMEA) and cluster investigation.
- Utilizes systems thinking, human factors and complexity science, principles of epidemiology and PI improvement to prevent and mitigate risk to patients and employees.

Education, Training, and Safety Performance Maintenance (10% of time)

- Oversees the development and implementation of basic PS education and training curriculum, on-going training, employee orientation, and competency testing.
- Collaborates with clinical and administrative leaders to identify areas of educational need to enhance PS.
- Provides just-in-time education and routine PS presentations to key stakeholders.
- Actively participates in Patient Safety Council Forums and educational programs.
- Promotes a culture where errors and near-misses are openly discussed and used as learning opportunities.
- Provides education and consultation to patients, families, visitors, and healthcare teams on PS issues.

(Continued)

EXHIBIT 2.1. *(Continued)*

■ Conducts patient safety rounds to gather information and educate on routine basis.

Committee and Team Responsibilities:

■ Patient Safety and Quality Committee.

■ PI, RCA, FMEA teams.

■ Patient Safety Council.

■ May be member of policy-making committees of hospital or medical staff (e.g., Infection Control Committee, Risk Mgt. & Safety Council, Pharmacy & Therapeutics, Unit Practice Council).

Experience and Position Requirements

■ At least 10 years of clinical experience and 5 years of management experience preferred.

■ Masters in nursing, public health or other related field required.

■ Team building and budget experience required.

■ Demonstrates excellent: written and verbal communication skills, computer proficiency, relationship management and conflict negotiation problem-solving skills.

■ Use of quality improvement tools and methods preferred.

Source: Barnes Jewish Hospital, 2005. Reprinted with permission.

EXHIBIT 2.2 Risk Manager Position Description, Level One

Position Summary

The risk manager is responsible for the facility's risk management activities, which include, but may not be limited to, a general knowledge of facility insurance programs, managing claims against the facility, interfacing with defense legal counsel, administering the risk management program on a day-to-day basis, managing and analyzing risk management data, and conducting risk management educational programs, complying with risk management related standards by JCAHO and other accrediting and regulatory agencies with the objective of enhancing patient safety, promoting patient safety, quality care, and minimizing loss to protect the assets of the facility. This individual participates in formulating policy and/or organizational changes, but must seek advice and approval from higher authority. Risk management may be one of several areas of responsibility for this individual.

OPERATIONS/COMPLIANCE

Overview

The level one risk manager has specific responsibilities regarding gathering and analyzing data and preparing reports to management and outside agencies as required, which may be subject to final approval by facility management. Responsible for keeping management advised of developments in professional liability, entailing ongoing review of applicable literature. May recommend budget items to management.

Specific Activities

- Develops, coordinates, and administers facility-wide systems for risk identification, investigation, and reduction; maintains a network of informational sources and experts; performs risk surveys and inspects patient care areas; reviews facility and to assess loss potential.

- Participates on committees directed towards promoting patient safety issues.

- Maintains risk management statistics and files in compliance with JCAHO and state and federal agencies; promotes maximum confidentiality by limiting access of such information. Also strives to verify that the following information is accurate, available, and secure: includes medical records, patient billing records, policies and procedures, incident reports, medical examiners' reports (if available), as well as any other data pertinent to a particular claim.

- Collects, evaluates, and distributes relevant data concerning patient injuries: aggregate data summaries, monthly trend analyses of incidents, claims profiles, and workers' compensation trends; provides aggregate analysis of risk data; maintains statistical trending of losses and other risk management data.

- Informs directors of service and department heads regarding occurrences, issues, findings, and risk management suggestions; provides feedback to directors at all levels in the effort to eliminate risks; assists clinical chairs and department heads in designing risk management programs within their departments.

- Works with legal counsel to coordinate the investigation, processing, and defense of claims against the facility; records, collects, documents, maintains, and provides to defense attorneys any requested information and documents necessary to prepare testimony in pending litigation.

(Continued)

EXHIBIT 2.2. *(Continued)*

■ Responds to professional liability and facility liability questions posed by physicians, nurses, and other personnel.

■ May have on-call responsibility.

■ Advises security on procedures to reduce the frequency and/or minimize the severity of property loss or assets.

■ Provides assistance to departments in complying with Joint Commission or other accrediting agencies, regarding risk management related standards.

■ Recommends appropriate revisions to new or existing policies and procedures to reduce the frequency of future occurrences; recommends ways to minimize risks through system changes; reviews and revises facility policies as appropriate to maintain adherence to current standards and requirements.

LOSS PREVENTION/PATIENT SAFETY

Overview

The level one risk manager is responsible for development of loss prevention programs that may include but not limited to patient safety issues. Periodic in-services and routine orientation may be conducted for facility employees/ medical staff regarding health care risk management and related subjects. This position may utilize outside speakers and faculty for such programs, subject to the approval of management, and may coordinate such efforts with the facility's education department.

Specific Activities

■ Proactive analysis of patient safety and medical errors processes.

■ Participates in the process of disclosure for medical errors.

■ Participates in root cause analysis investigation and reporting of adverse drug events and sentinel events to the appropriate parties.

■ Maintains awareness of legislative and regulatory activities related to health care risk management.

■ Complies with various codes, laws, rules, and regulations concerning patient care, including those mandated by state and federal agencies' incident reporting. Includes investigation activities of federal, state, and local enforcement authorities.

■ Provides in-service training to medical center personnel to enhance their awareness of their role in reducing liability exposures.

- Disseminates information on claim patterns and risk control, as well as legislative and regulatory changes.
- Maintains a risk management education calendar.
- Takes steps to ascertain that risks are minimized through follow-up and actions on all regulatory/insurance survey report recommendations/deficiencies.
- Receives and investigates reports of product problems to determine appropriate response (in-house recalls, independent evaluations, etc.).
- Participates on select committees related to provision of patient care.
- Receives incident reports and other information regarding untoward occurrences in the facility, such as quality assurance outliers or variations, and collates such information systematically to permit analysis pursuant to risk management policy and procedure.
- Reviews collated data to identify trends regarding accidents or occurrences, and recommends corrective action to management, if appropriate.
- Prepares reports to management regarding trends/patterns and findings. Recommends electronic data programming initiation and improvement.

CLAIMS MANAGEMENT

Overview

The level 1 risk manager receives complaints/claims related to professional and general liability and transmits that information to the appropriate department manager, administrative representative, patient ombudsman, insurance carrier, or legal counsel. At the request of management, legal counsel, or the adjuster, participates in responding to the complaint or claim to obtain information and facilitate settlement at an early stage. Works in coordination with patient ombudsman or acts as same to resolve complaints before they develop into professional/general liability claims.

Specific Activities

Designs, implements, and maintains a direct referral system for staff to report unexpected events and potential claims against the facility through such input sources as medical records, business office, patient advocate, nursing, medical staff, quality improvement, etc.

- Investigates and analyzes actual and potential risks in the institution; assesses liability and probability of legal action for potential notification of insurance carriers.

(Continued)

EXHIBIT 2.2. *(Continued)*

- Directly refers to administration those incidents with claims potential; reports to higher authority any serious event involving actual or potential injury to patients, visitors, or employees.

- Assists in processing summons and complaints served on present and previous employees; assists defendants in completing necessary documents.

- With director of patient representatives, reviews patient complaints that may be the source of potential legal action; discusses and offers solutions when possible to resolve with patient and/or family any grievances perceived as potential liability claims.

- Participates in evaluation of claims for settlement; negotiates settlement of small claims within administrative authority; advises collection department of appropriate action for unpaid accounts involved in litigation; approves payment for or replacement of lost property after evaluating claim.

- Reviews national and local claims data; analyzes prior claims, lawsuits, and complaints against the facility.

RISK FINANCING

Overview

The level 1 risk manager has general knowledge of, and is familiar with, the facility's insurance coverage against liability and casualty loss, including self-insurance funding and budgeting for payment of deductibles, risk retention, and coinsurance. Usually participates in management reviews of insurance coverage and related issues. May prepare summaries of the facility's insurance program for management and staff.

Specific Activities

- Notifies the liability insurance carrier of all actual and potential claims, including primary and excess carriers as necessary.

- May verify with the Medical Staff Services Coordinator that each independent practitioner provides proof of adequate professional liability insurance at the time of initial credentialing and at reappointment.

- May act as liaison with the insurance carrier; completes insurance applications and responds to surveys; prepares materials necessary for renewal of primary and excess insurance policies.

- Provides insurance information to outside agencies; assists in compliance with state insurance reporting requirements.

SUGGESTED PARAMETERS FOR POSITION

- Experience is entry level, 0-3 years in risk management.
- Position title risk analysis, risk manager, patient safety coordinator, various titles reflecting combined job responsibilities i.e. QA/RM, Medical Staff Coordinator, Human Resources Manager.
- Reports to position of middle to top level management, Director of Risk Management.
- Certification/Education may include associate degree, RN, ARM, pursuing CPHRM.
- Organization size may be one facility/organization with less than 100 licensed beds.
- Key attributes: Strong written and oral communications skills, presentation skills, team player, ability to influence change without direct authority, and negotiation skills.

Source: American Society for Healthcare Risk Management. Reprinted with permission.

EXHIBIT 2.3 Risk Manager Job Description, Level Two

Position Summary

The risk manager is responsible for the facility's risk management activities, which include, but may not be limited to, coordinating insurance coverage and risk financing, managing claims against the facility, interfacing with defense legal counsel, administering the risk management program on a day-to-day basis, managing and analyzing risk management data, conducting risk management educational programs, complying with risk management related standards by JCAHO, all with the objective of maintaining patient safety, enhancing quality care, and minimizing loss to protect the assets of the facility. The level two risk manager performs these functions reporting to management at the vice-president level. This individual is responsible for reviewing and formulating policy or organizational changes and making recommendations for final approval by senior management.

OPERATION/COMPLIANCE

Overview

The level two risk manager performs the functions outlined under level one and, in addition, manages a facility department or office of risk management. Is responsible for data management, claims management, and the education components of the facility's risk

(Continued)

EXHIBIT 2.3. *(Continued)*

management program. Promotes the organizational patient safety initiatives. Develops department budget for management approval. Works directly with legal counsel as a team member in the defense of claims. Has ongoing access to facility liability defense counsel to consult regarding both preventive and corrective measures to be taken in situations having legal connotation. On request, may provide information to facility management concerning reasonableness of cost and quality of legal services.

Specific Activities

- Has full responsibility for operations of the risk management program that may include an enterprise liability approach to exposures.
- Directs loss control/loss prevention activities and reports results to senior administration.
- Supervises the statistical trending of losses and analyzes patterns.
- Designs and implements risk management surveys and studies; conducts surveys, studies, and special projects to assist in long-term planning and changes to facility policies and systems that reduce risk and losses.
- Responsible for identifying and communicating regulatory requirements.
- Leads development of organization-wide approach on disclosure of medical errors and obtains physician support.
- Designs and/or administers safety systems and procedures to minimize loss from employee casualties, and complies with OSHA regulations.
- Analyzes the risk of loss versus cost of reducing risk.
- Supervises accumulation of risk management cost data for budgetary and historical purposes: prepares budgets for departmental operations.
- Works with Medical Staff Services to develop and maintain risk management profiles on physicians and integrates that information into the credentialing process in compliance with state and federal agencies, Joint Commission and/or other accrediting bodies, and institutional requirements.
- Submits recommendations for changes in the existing risk control and risk-financing procedures based on changes in properties, operations, or activities.
- Evaluates correspondence from attorneys, patients, and other outside sources, and formulates responses, as necessary.
- Records, collects, documents, maintains, and communicates to insurance carrier and/or attorney any information necessary to prepare testimony in pending litigation.

- Directs and coordinates release of records and information in response to subpoenas, court orders, attorney requests, state and federal agency investigations, and other inquiries from outside sources.
- Maintains legal case files and strives to maintain maximum protection from discoverability of such files.
- Approves defense postures or settlement values at lower levels routinely.
- Answers medical/legal inquiries of physicians, nurses, and administrators regarding emergent patient care issues and loss control.
- Resolves treatment issues, including patient decisions made against medical advice (AMA), refusals of treatment, and consent issues; initiates court orders as appropriate via in-house and outside legal counsel.
- Reviews relevant contracts for risk exposure and insurance purposes before approval, including affiliation agreements, leases, construction agreements, and purchase orders, as appropriate.
- Maintains awareness of legislative activities that may affect risk management programs and participates in the legislative process.

LOSS PREVENTION/PATIENT SAFETY

Overview

The level two risk manager performs the functions as outlined under level one and, in addition, organizes and manages facility-wide educational programs on health care risk management and related subjects for health care practitioners. Presents such programs in conjunction with the facility's education department or other organizations. Supports the patient safety initiatives through direct participation on committees/task forces. Develops risk management budget for senior management approval.

Specific Activities

- Plans, develops, and presents educational material to administration, the medical staff, nursing personnel, and other department personnel on topics related to risk management as they affect personnel.
- Develops and implements educational programs designed to minimize the frequency and reduce the severity of actual and potential safety hazards throughout the facility.
- Leads root cause analysis and makes recommendations for improvement.
- Active participation in patient safety goals by providing data to support priorities.
- Active role in FMEA (Failure Mode and Effects Analysis).

(Continued)

EXHIBIT 2.3. *(Continued)*

- Acts as resource, internal consultant, and educator for patient safety/risk management issues.
- Complies with various codes, laws, rules and regulations concerning patient care, including those mandated by state and federal agencies, incident reporting, also includes investigative activities with federal, state, and local enforcement authorities.
- Leads investigations for adverse drug events and sentinel events.

CLAIMS MANAGEMENT

Overview

The level two risk manager performs the functions outlined under level one and, in addition, works actively with legal counsel or the adjuster in investigating claims, developing defense strategy, and evaluating the monetary value of the claim. Participates as a team member in negotiating settlements for management approval. In litigated claims, assists legal counsel in accessing facility records and personnel and may act as a corporate representative during pretrial and trial. Recommends defense strategies for approval by CEO, governing board, and legal counsel. Provides advice to senior management or the chief financial officer regarding reasonableness of expenses for claims defense.

Specific Activities

- Authority to initiate medical write-offs to mitigate potential claims.
- Oversees investigation of incidents/accidents/events that could lead to financial loss, including professional liability, general liability, and workers' compensation.
- Investigates risks involving actual or potential injury to patients, visitors, and employees; collects information necessary to prepare for the defense of claims.
- Serves as liaison to brokers and insurance company representatives in negotiating and settling specific general liability claims; directs conferences with claimants, attorneys, and insurance carriers, when applicable.
- Interacts with legal counsel, insurance carrier, and patients/families to effect timely settlement.
- Coordination of defense with co-defendants.
- Provides direction and advice to medical staff, as necessary, in connection with malpractice litigation and medicolegal matters.
- Reports patient care-related incidents to the Department of Health if required by law; directs investigation and development of corrective plans; submits required reports to state and federal agencies.

RISK FINANCING

Overview

The level two risk manager performs or coordinates the functions outlined under level one and, in addition, participates in negotiating coverage issues with carriers or trust administrators, including levels of coverage, scope of coverage, and premiums. Participates in formulating recommendations for purchase of coverage or funding of self-insurance for submission to management for final approval. Participates in preparing other financial analyses of facility's insurance program for the information of management and the governing body.

Specific Activities

- Reviews and maintains insurance policies; analyzes existing policies for coverage and exclusions; anticipates and deals with policy expirations.

- Participates in managing the facility's insurance programs and financing by preparing statistical data to support the continuation or reduction of premiums paid or reserves.

- Participates in negotiating policy provisions.

- May assess appropriate reserve funding levels, both insured and self-insured, in conjunction with an actuary.

SUGGESTED PARAMETERS FOR POSITION

- Experience is intermediate level position with 4-8 years in risk management.

- Position title may include Risk Manager, Director RM, Director Patient Safety.

- Reports to VP Risk Management, COO, CFO, or CEO.

- Certification/Education may include Bachelor Degree, RN, single risk management certification, ARM, CPHRM, **FASHRM**.

- Organization size may include 1-2 facilities, with 100-400 licensed beds.

- Key attributes: All in Level I job description, plus management of insurance portfolio and claims handling.

Source: American Society for Healthcare Risk Management. Reprinted, with permission.

EXHIBIT 2.4   **Risk Manager Position Description, Level Three**

Position Summary

The risk manager is responsible for the facility's risk management activities, which include, but may not be limited to, procurement of insurance coverage and risk financing, managing claims against the facility, interfacing with defense legal counsel, administering an enterprise risk management program on a day-to-day basis, managing and analyzing risk management data, conducting risk management educational programs, complying with risk management related standards by JCAHO other accrediting and regulatory agencies with the objective of promoting patient safety, enhancing quality care, and minimizing loss to protect the assets of the facility. While the level 3 position may be responsible for the functions in level one and two job descriptions, this position most often supervises and offers overall program direction to staff performing the task in the first two job description levels. This position reviews, formulates, and implements policy and organizational changes, performing within general programmatic authority delegated by the CEO, chief financial officer, or governing body.

OPERATIONS/COMPLIANCE

Overview

The level three risk manager performs the functions outlined under levels one and two and, in addition, oversees aspects of data management and analysis for the organization's loss control program. Establishes budget for data management and analysis aspects of loss control. Directs risk management program for a large health care system and/or multi-hospital system with facility risk managers. Works within broad guidelines established by the CEO, chief financial officer, or governing body regarding the use and integration of loss control data with other types of organizational data systems for audit and accountability purposes on a facility or system-wide basis. May serve as the organization's compliance officer. Leads patient safety initiatives in the organization. Responds to all regulatory/compliance issues and strives to incorporate processes to address the results of these surveys/requirements.

Specific Activities

- Works with senior leadership in organizational operations, quality, etc.
- May serve on subcommittees of the Board of Directors.
- Authorities to retain, direct, and approve compensation of defense counsel.
- Conducts systems analyses to uncover and identify patterns that could result in compensable events.

- Assists clinical chairs and department heads in designing risk management programs within their departments.
- Develops and implements departmental and facility policies and procedures that affect liability exposures.
- Minimizes risk by responding to all regulatory/insurance survey report recommendations/deficiencies.
- Selects and utilizes services of consulting services, brokers, carriers, etc.
- Provides board summary reports on incidents, claims, reserves, claim payments, etc.
- Works with Medical Staff Services Coordinator to provide risk management information into the credentialing process in compliance with state and federal agencies, accrediting bodies, and institutional requirements.
- Complies with various codes, laws, rules, and regulations concerning patient care/safety, including those mandated by state and federal agencies, incident reporting, also includes the investigation activities of federal, state, and local enforcement authorities.
- Implements relevant statutes and regulations, including mandated mechanisms of physician monitoring with feedback to medical staff office, reappointment process, etc.
- Assumes responsibility for contract compliance within appropriate guidelines and legal concepts; in preparing contracts for board approval, provides advice on contract language necessary to fulfill insurance and risk management requirements; evaluates each contract negotiated by the organization to verify that insurance and liability issues are adequately addressed and that risk is transferred to the other party, if feasible; establishes insurance requirements for all projects and contracts; where appropriate, negotiates changes in contracts with other parties; verifies that affiliated institutions have adequate insurance coverage.
- Reviews and approves plans and specifications for major new construction, alterations, and installation of equipment.

LOSS PREVENTION/PATIENT SAFETY

Overview

The level three risk manager performs the functions outlined under levels one and two and, in addition, develops loss control educational programs for the organization's use. This position establishes education budget, subject to approval of the CEO, chief financial officer, or governing body. May develop educational programs relative to health care risk management utilizing well known experts in the field for national or regional representation. May develop risk management educational programs with broad appeal for

(Continued)

EXHIBIT 2.4.   *(Continued)*

marketing to other organizations. May serve as Patient Safety Officer/Advocate or Sponsor.

Specific Activities

- Plans and implements a facility-system wide program for both loss prevention and loss control, and a comprehensive orientation program; those programs will be directed to all current and future employees of the board, physicians, and employees to advise them of their responsibilities, obligations, and part in the facility's risk management program.
- Participates in new business development activities by providing due diligence on new ventures/acquisitions.
- Serves as FEMA consultant/process expert.
- Directs and conducts educational sessions on risk management for medical staff and employees.
- Procures outside loss prevention services.

CLAIMS MANAGEMENT

Overview

The level three risk manager performs the functions outlined in levels one and two and, in addition has authority within broad guidelines established by the CEO, chief financial officer, or governing body to approve settlement of claims against the facility or system. Has authority to direct legal counsel and other personnel involved in claims management and to give final approval to defense strategies. Approves payment of fees of defense counsel and payment of other expenses of claims defense.

Specific Activities

- Manages the claims program, which contains the following components: reporting procedures, system maintenance, detailed claim investigations, establishment of reserves, selection and monitoring of legal counsel, conferring directly with claimants, attorneys, physicians, employees, brokers, carriers, and consultants, settlement of claims, selection and utilization of actuarial firms, as needed and/or required.
- Compliance with Medicare/Medicaid regulations as related to claims.
- Recommendations to senior management for funding requirements and necessary limits of coverage.

- Reporting claims information to senior management.
- Directs activities of investigators.
- Directs claims handling and defense preparation activities of the insurance company and defense counsel.
- Is responsible for administering claims initiated in the boiler/machinery, fire, and other loss areas.
- Projects future costs of losses, services, insurance, and other risk management expenses.
- Authority to manage and resolve claims within self-insured programs.

RISK FINANCING

Overview

The level three risk manager performs or coordinates the functions outlined under levels one and two and, in addition, manages the organization's insurance or self-insurance program within broad guidelines established by the CEO, chief financial officer, or governing body. This position has authority to finalize selection and retention of carriers or self-funding mechanisms in conjunction with the chief financial officer. Ensures the preparation of loss experience reports and summaries for the information of the CEO, chief financial officer, and governing body.

Specific Activities

- Evaluates property exposures, including new construction and renovation programs, to provide coverage and minimize risk.
- Develops familiarity with insurance markets through frequent market contact and attendance at meetings and market symposiums.
- Plans, coordinates, and administers a broad, comprehensive insurance program involving such activities as insurance purchasing, insurance consulting, administering self-insured coverage, and coordinating claims handling for all insurance lines.
- Directs and coordinates all aspects of insurance management for the institution, including developing alternatives such as self-insurance, excess insurance, and other risk-financing mechanisms.
- Develops and manages the overall risk management program, involving risks of all types, which may include using deductibles, self-insurance, captive insurance companies, financial plans, commercial insurance, and insurance/reinsurance programs.
- For property insurance, boiler and machinery insurance, crime insurance, student health insurance, automobile insurance, and all other purchased insurance coverage,

(Continued)

EXHIBIT 2.4. *(Continued)*

analyzes values and verifies that exposures are adequately insured; in the event of a loss, prepares data required by brokers and carriers and manages process through to settlement of claim.

- Prepares specifications for competitive bidding; negotiates with brokers, agents, or companies on insurance coverage, premiums, and services.

- Establishes and administers self-insurance trust funds for various types of insurance needs.

SUGGESTED PARAMETERS FOR POSITION

- Experience is senior level position with 8-10 years in risk management

- Position title may include Vice President Risk Management/ Patient Safety, Chief Risk Officer, VP Legal Services Reports to CEO, Board of Trustees/Directors

- Certification/Education may include JD, Masters Degree, multiple certifications such as ARM, CPHRM, DFASHRM, CPCU

- Organization size may include multiple facilities, IDS, with more than 400 licensed beds

- Key Attributes: Include all of those in Levels I and II, plus advanced business/health-care management skills.

Source: American Society for Healthcare Risk Management. Reprinted with permission.

(Continued from page 33)

into six major functional areas: loss prevention and reduction, claims management, risk financing, regulatory and accreditation compliance, risk management operations, and bioethics.

Loss Prevention and Reduction

This category encompasses all aspects of risk identification, loss prevention, and **loss reduction** and represents the largest functional area.

- Developing formal and informal mechanisms for risk identification, such as incident reporting, staff referrals, medical record reviews, review of patient complaints, and review of pertinent quality-improvement information

- Developing and maintaining collaborative relationships with key departments, such as quality management, nursing, medical staff, safety, security, and infection control, to enhance program effectiveness

- Developing statistical and qualitative reports on risk management trends and patterns and communicating this information effectively to appropriate audiences

- Developing root cause analysis and failure mode and effects analysis (FMEA) for incidents and potential areas of risk

- Developing policies and procedures in key areas of risk management interest, such as informed consent, product recalls, confidentiality, and handling of sentinel events

- Developing educational programs for all levels of staff on a variety of risk management topics

- Developing a program for management of exposures resulting from contracts, such as affiliation agreements, construction agreements, leases, management contracts, and purchase agreements

- Serving as a resource to organizational staff on issues related to professional liability and other risks

Claims Management

This category includes all activities associated with managing actual or potential claims, from reporting and investigation to resolution.

- Notifying carriers of actual or potential claims

- Establishing claim files and coordinating investigation

- Supervising investigators, third-party administrators (TPAs), and defense counsel

- Coordinating the organization's response to discovery requests and interrogatories

- Developing standards for the selection and evaluation of service providers

- Setting expense and indemnity reserves

- Approving and authorizing settlements

- Ensuring that the organization's senior management is kept informed of high-exposure cases and aggregate claims experience, including their effect on the risk financing program

Risk Financing

This category includes many activities associated with financing losses, whether the organization transfers or retains the risk.

- Maintaining and coordinating exposure data for the organization

- Coordinating insurance applications and renewals

- Collaborating with brokers, underwriters, actuaries, and other service providers to determine the risk financing needs of the organization

■ Evaluating coverage limits, deductibles, attachment points, and lines of coverage to ensure that all exposures are adequately covered

■ Evaluating risk financing options such as commercial insurance, retention, captives, and risk retention groups and selecting the best option based on the organization's needs

■ Monitoring and evaluating the organization's risk financing program

Regulatory and Accreditation Compliance

This category includes all activities associated with compliance with accreditation standards and with major health care regulations.

■ Promoting compliance with requirements to report specific incidents to state and federal agencies

■ Promoting compliance with regulations such as the Americans with Disabilities Act (ADA), Occupational Safety and Health Administration (OSHA), Patient Self-Determination Act (PSDA), Safe Medical Devices Act (SMDA), Emergency Medical Treatment and Labor Act (EMTALA), Health Care Quality Improvement Act (HCQIA), Health Insurance Portability and Accountability Act (HIPAA), and the patient safety initiatives prompted by the Institute of Medicine (IOM) report

■ Promoting compliance with Joint Commission requirements, including those pertaining to sentinel events and national patient safety goals and standards

■ Promoting compliance with requirements to report deaths to the medical examiner or coroner

■ Collaborating with key departments to ensure compliance with life safety codes and emergency management

■ Promoting compliance with specific regulatory initiatives and programs such as Project Lookback

Risk Management Operations

The Operations category covers activities associated with managing a risk management department.

■ Developing an organizational risk management policy statement and plan

■ Training and supervising risk management staff

■ Coordinating and administering risk management and patient safety committees

■ Developing annual goals for the risk management department

■ Evaluating the effectiveness of risk management activities

Bioethics

This category includes all activities related to issues such as do not resuscitate (DNR) orders, brain death criteria, advance directives, withdrawal of life support, and human subjects research.

- Reviewing policies and procedures related to end-of-life issues for conformance with ethical principles and adherence to applicable regulation

- Reviewing policies and procedures relating to human subjects research for adherence to applicable regulation and organizational policy

- Providing risk management consultation for specific ethical dilemmas

- Providing education for staff, patients, families, and communities on patients' rights

HEALTH CARE RISK MANAGEMENT ACROSS A SPECTRUM OF SETTINGS

As mentioned earlier in the chapter, the roles and job responsibilities of health care risk management professionals are determined by the characteristics of the organizations in which they work. The size and structure of the organization determine the needs of the organization, and this in turn influences the size, structure, and function of the risk management program. The risk financing strategies of the organization are also important determinants of risk management program structure and function.

The following sections examine the role of the risk management professional in several health care settings—the **acute care hospital** or medical center, **academic medical center**, integrated delivery system (IDS), multihospital system, ambulatory care setting, physician practices and clinics, and long-term care facility. For each setting, the relative importance of each of the six major functional areas of responsibility are examined, as are other unique characteristics of risk management programs in these settings.

The Acute Care Hospital or Medical Center

According to ASHRM's 2005 member survey, 37 percent of respondents are employed in an acute care hospital or medical center, by far the largest category.[3] (See Table 2.1 for an inventory of the type of organizations represented by respondents in the ASHRM survey.) Acute care hospitals or medical centers can range in size from fewer than one hundred licensed beds to more than five hundred. They can be classified as community hospitals, which tend to be smaller and typically do not have their own residency programs, and teaching hospitals, which tend to be larger and often have multiple residency programs.

Acute care hospitals or medical centers offer a range of services, although not all hospitals offer every type of service. Patient care services typically offered in acute care hospitals or medical centers include general medicine and surgery, medical and surgical subspecialties such as cardiology and orthopedic surgery, and primary care services such as family medicine, pediatrics, and obstetrics. Most have intensive care

TABLE 2.1. Types of Organizations

Organization	Percentage of Total
Acute Care Medical Center	32
Academic Medical Center	7
Free-Standing Community Hospital	6
Integrated Delivery System	12
Multihospital System	9
Pediatric Hospital	1
Specialty Hospital	1
Tertiary Care Facility	1
Insurance Brokerage	2
Insurance Company	9
Law Firm	1
Long-Term Care Facility	1
Managed Care Provider	1
Physician Office	1
Behavioral/Psychology Health Care Facility	1
Rehabilitation Facility	1
Risk Management Consulting Firm	2
Self-Employed	1
Other	11

Base: 911 respondents.
Source: American Society for Healthcare Risk Management, *ASHRM Membership Survey, 2005*. Reprinted with permission.

units of some type and also have emergency departments. More complex services, such as transplant surgery and advanced trauma care, are typically found in academic medical centers, which are discussed later in this section. The types of services a hospital offers are typically controlled through the state's certificate of need program.

Even within this category, risk management program structures and functions vary widely. At a small- to medium-size community hospital, it is common practice for the risk management professional to assume responsibilities for several related areas, such as quality improvement, safety and patient safety, or infection control. The limitations of the hospital's resources, together with a smaller workload, make this arrangement an attractive one for these organizations. More recently, risk management professionals in such settings have also been called on to assume the role of the corporate compliance officer, patient safety officer, or chief risk officer.

Small- to medium-size hospitals are usually commercially insured, thereby decreasing the administrative burden for the risk financing and claims management functions on the risk management department itself. Responsibilities for workers' compensation programs often rest with the human resource department. Thus the risk management professional's role in such settings often focuses on the activities associated with loss prevention and reduction: risk identification and analysis, management of serious adverse events, staff education, and policy and procedure review and development. Risk management professionals in these hospitals are also often responsible for ensuring compliance with major health care regulations and requirements and for accreditation activities. Smaller hospitals often face risks associated with access to care, specifically access to specialized or intensive care, not faced by larger hospitals. The risk management professional may also be quite involved in clinical ethics consultations, because smaller organizations typically do not have the resources to employ an ethicist or in-house counsel.

The risk management professional's role in risk financing at smaller hospitals is often limited to collecting and coordinating exposure data and managing the insurance renewal process. The chief financial officer typically assumes the burden for evaluation of carriers and insurance options, selection of new carriers, and decisions regarding risk-financing options. The risk management professional's interaction with brokers and underwriters may be limited.

When risk is transferred, responsibilities for claims management also decrease. In a smaller, commercially insured hospital, the risk management professional's role in claims management is limited to coordinating the investigation and defense activities of the investigators, adjusters, and attorneys employed or retained by the insurance carrier. In this setting, the risk management professional is not responsible for setting reserves or authorizing settlements, as this is usually the exclusive right and responsibility of the insurance carrier.

Risk management professionals in small- to medium-size community hospitals often enjoy high visibility. They are often viewed as the primary resource on a wide range of topics because the organization cannot afford to employ experts in a variety of disciplines. They very often function as the hospital's liaison to outside counsel and as such become involved in a variety of interesting legal issues. Risk management professionals in such settings have the opportunity to work and interact with nearly every health care discipline. Thus these positions offer excellent opportunities for learning and collaboration and also opportunities for advancement by assuming responsibility for related areas.

In medium to large community hospitals or medical centers, risk management professionals typically have somewhat greater and better-defined responsibilities than in smaller hospitals. They generally retain responsibility for all loss prevention and control functions but may be assisted by one or more staff members. Such staff assistants often have clinical experience or expertise that enables them to interact very effectively with patient care providers. The nature of **loss prevention** and reduction activities at such hospitals is essentially the same, though the volume tends to be greater than at smaller facilities. An enterprise risk management program is desirable, as it encourages risk management professionals to act in concert with other managers to fully evaluate the organization's exposures and promotes thinking "outside the box" for solutions. Potential partners with the risk management professional may be internal audit, treasury, security, institutional research, quality and performance improvement teams, or even individuals outside the corporate family that have a direct effect on risk, such as credit agencies, regulatory and licensing agencies, fire and rescue, and police.

Credentialing and informed consent issues assume greater significance in these settings because of the greater number of specialists on staff and the riskier nature of treatments and procedures offered.

Medium to large hospitals and medical centers usually employ a greater number of professionals specializing in a variety of disciplines, so risk management professionals in such hospitals are less likely to assume multiple job responsibilities. Usually, safety and infection control professionals are employed, and often the quality improvement function is separate from risk management. Thus the risk management professional in such settings focuses almost exclusively on risk management functions, and there is little confusion among the staff as to who the risk management professional is or what the function comprises.

Although many are commercially insured, medium to large hospitals and medical centers are often in the position to use alternative risk financing strategies. It is common for such organizations to have in place self-insured trusts, large deductibles, or captive insurance companies to finance primary liability risks. If that is the case, the risk management professional has a greater role in risk financing and claims management. The risk management professional typically works collaboratively with the chief financial officer and other executives in the development of loss exposure data, setting reserves, monitoring of program results, and evaluating existing and alternative arrangements. Claims management also becomes a higher-risk management priority in such circumstances, and the risk management professional is often responsible for directing the activities of an in-house claims staff or third-party claims administrators, investigators, and attorneys. Risk management professionals in such settings typically have a great deal of interaction with brokers, underwriters, and actuaries and may also have responsibility for self-funded workers' compensation programs.

Risk management professionals in medium to large hospitals and medical centers are often quite involved in regulatory compliance, but in many cases, there is a designated compliance officer with responsibility for the corporate compliance program. Thus the risk management professional takes a more advisory role, serving as a content expert in areas that relate to risk management. Most often risk management professionals in these settings continue to play a significant role in accreditation, but this is usually a collaborative effort with other administrators. They are involved in ethics consultations, as are their counterparts in smaller hospitals, but their role may be more advisory because larger hospitals typically have more resources devoted to their ethics programs. As the risk management department tends to be larger, the risk management professional in such a setting typically devotes more time to department administration.

Risk management professionals in medium to large hospitals and medical centers require the same skill set as those in smaller hospitals. Effective communication skills and the ability to work collaboratively in other disciplines are critical success factors in either setting. In addition, risk management professionals who work in larger and more complex settings need to develop a better understanding of more complex risks and of risk financing and claims management.

The risk management professional job descriptions for level one and level two presented in Exhibits 2.2 and 2.3 are most consistent with the functions of the risk management professional in the acute care hospital or medical center.

Academic Medical Centers

Academic medical centers pose unique risk management challenges. They tend to be large and complex organizations, and the care they provide is equally complicated. Risk management professionals and chief risk officers in these settings must deal with risks ranging from simple clinical misadventures to complicated issues involving clinical research, affiliation agreements, and academic freedom.

Academic medical centers tend to have risk management departments with several professional staff members. Some organizations may have their risk management staff or program segmented into areas of clinical risk of the medical center and the affiliated university or school risk. Most often the risk management staff for the medical center will include staff with clinical training. This is a great advantage given the complex nature of the clinical risks encountered in these settings.

Risk prevention and reduction activities in academic medical centers are made more difficult because of the many individuals involved in patient care. Unlike other hospitals, patients in academic medical centers are often cared for by students, residents, fellows, and specialists not commonly found in other settings. Because of the involvement of so many individuals in patients' care, there is a greater potential for error; thus risk is increased. In addition, staff rotations and turnover tend to be higher in academic medical centers, and there is a constant need for education and reinforcement of risk management policies and procedures, including reporting requirements.

Risk management professionals in academic medical centers often spend a great deal of time educating the staff about risk management principles and practices. They also devote a great deal of time to the investigation of incidents, because facts and circumstances tend to be more complicated and harder to discern. Credentialing and human subject research also pose special risks in academic medical centers with which the risk management professional is involved.

Academic medical centers often face unique risks that make commercial insurance vehicles unattractive. As a result, academic medical centers are often involved in alternative risk financing arrangements such as captives. The risk management professional in an academic medical center is likely to have some involvement in risk financing arrangements and must therefore have expertise and knowledge in this area. The level of the risk management professional's involvement will depend on many factors, including whether or not the organization is involved in a group risk financing arrangement, and on the culture of the organization. Often academic medical centers' risk financing functions are administered at high administrative levels, and the risk management professional's role in these functions may be limited.

Claims management in an academic medical center is usually handled within the organization rather than outsourced. Therefore, the responsible manager must have the ability to effectively investigate claims, manage the activities of defense counsel, and establish appropriate reserves. The volume of claims in an academic medical center is such that several dedicated claims professionals may be required. It is especially true if the department is expected to manage other types of claims, such as general liability, directors' and officers' liability, and property claims. (See Chapter Eleven for information on basic claims administration.)

Regulatory and corporate compliance and accreditation activities in academic medical centers are complicated and time-consuming activities usually handled by professional staff dedicated to those functions; however, the risk management professional typically serves as an adviser.

Bioethics consultation in an academic medical center is usually a collaborative effort in which the risk management professional plays an important role. Because of the strong research orientation of academic medical centers, they often have strong clinical ethics programs with dedicated staff. Risk management professionals are often members of the ethics committee and institutional review board (IRB). (See Chapter Eight for more information on ethics in patient care.)

Risk management department operations consume a great deal of time because the department tends to be larger in an academic medical center. Also, the risk management professional in an academic medical center may be expected to support the organization's teaching and research mission by accepting interns, teaching in the medical school, and assisting in risk management–related research. All of these activities increase the administrative burden of the risk management department.

The level three risk management job description presented in Exhibit 2.4 is most representative of the scope of responsibilities in an academic medical center. Depending on the organizational structure, a chief risk officer may be better suited for this position. The CRO job description in Exhibit 2.5 provides some suggestions for job responsibilities.

EXHIBIT 2.5. **Chief Risk Officer Position Description**

Position Summary

The Chief Risk Officer (CRO) has broad responsibility for the protection of the institution and its staff from fortuitous loss. The Chief Risk Officer advises and consults with senior leadership and the Board on potential sources of loss and makes decisions on how to eliminate or minimize loss.

Major Responsibilities

The following are the major areas of responsibility for the chief risk officer. These responsibilities include oversight, facilitation, coordination, supervision and technical competence in the following areas:

RISK FINANCING

Coordinates, advises and facilitates risk-financing strategy with the CFO on issues that could financially put the organization at risk.

Specific Activities

- Reviews documents and issues that impact the availability of risk financing options such as: changes to bond covenants, materials presented to bond rating agencies, all fines and sanctions levied through the OIG, FBI, CMS, and other issues of similar impact.
- Finalize the selection and retention of insurance carriers or self-funding mechanisms in conjunction with the CFO, and corporate office.
- Administer self-insurance trust funds.
- Evaluate property exposures, including new construction and renovation programs.
- Develop familiarity with insurance markets through frequent market contact and attendance at meetings and market symposiums.

- Plan, coordinate, and administer a comprehensive insurance program involving such activities as insurance purchasing, insurance consulting, claims coordination, and administration of self-insured program.
- Directs and coordinates all aspects of insurance management, including developing alternative insurance programs such as self-insurance, risk retention groups, captives, deductible programs, financial plans, reinsurance, commercial insurance, and excess insurance.

(Continued)

EXHIBIT 2.5. *(Continued)*

■ Analyze values and ensure that exposures for property insurance, boiler and machinery insurance, crime insurance, automobile insurance and all other purchased insurance are adequately insured; in the event of loss, prepare data required by brokers and carriers and manage the process through to the settlement of claim.

■ Develop familiarity with insurance markets through frequent market contact.

■ Prepare specifications for competitive bidding; negotiate with brokers, agents or companies.

CLAIMS ADMINISTRATION / EVENT REPORTING

Specific Activities

■ Approve settlement of all claims against the facility within broad guidelines established by the CEO, CFO, and/or governing body.

■ Direct legal counsel and other personnel involved in claims management and give final approval to defense strategies.

■ Approve payment of fees for defense counsel and payment of other claims defense expenses.

■ Develop and implement an "early intervention program." Include disclosure of unanticipated events, use of apology, alternate dispute resolution mechanisms, early payments strategy, lessons learned/prevention activities, and the use of employee assistance programs.

■ Ensure appropriate reporting to all required outside agencies including the NPDB and/or HIPDB.

■ Manage the claims program, which contains the following components:

  – Reporting procedures

  – System maintenance

  – Detailed claims investigations

  – Establishment of reserves

  – Use of alternative dispute resolution mechanisms

  – Monitoring of legal counsel

  – Conferring directly with claimants, attorneys, physicians, employees, brokers and consultants

  – Settlement of claims

  – Selection and utilization of actuarial firms as needed or requested

- Comply with Medicare/Medicaid regulations.
- Make recommendations to senior management regarding funding levels and coverage limits.
- Report claims to senior management and board of directors.
- Direct investigative activities.
- Procure outside loss prevention services if necessary to supplement in-house activities.
- Project future cost of losses, services, insurance, and other risk financial vehicles.

PATIENT SAFETY

Specific Activities

- Develop, implement and monitor the Patient Safety Plan.
- Coordinate all patient safety activities with other clinical loss control, quality management, performance improvement, and infection control initiatives.
- Coordinate and facilitate all initiatives to comply with the JCAHO Patient Safety Initiatives.
- Plan for creative ways to enhance patient safety by the use and support of technological advances including CPOE, bar coding, EMR, and the like.
- Monitor the Internet and professional journals and publications to remain abreast of current projects and initiatives regarding patient safety.

LOSS CONTROL (CLINICAL AND NON-CLINICAL)

Specific Activities

- Plan and implement an institution-wide program of clinical and non-clinical loss control, including a comprehensive orientation program.
- Direct and conduct educational sessions on risk management for medical staff and employees.
- Develop, implement, and manage the event reporting system.
- Conduct systems analyses to uncover and identify patterns that could result in compensable events.
- Assist clinical chiefs and department heads in the design of risk management programs specific to their department and unique risk.
- Research, write, and implement departmental and facility policies and procedures that affect liability exposures and assist in regulatory compliance.

(Continued)

EXHIBIT 2.5. *(Continued)*

- Oversee patient relations/advocate programs.

- Ensure that risks are minimized by following-up and acting on all regulatory/insurance survey report recommendations/deficiencies.

- Select and utilize all necessary outside consulting services offered insurance carriers, independent risk management consultants, and third-party administrators.

- Provide senior management and board of directors with summary reports of incidents, claims, reserves, claims payments, sentinel events, and near misses highlighting lessons learned and risk control initiatives implemented.

- Develop and maintain risk management profiles on individual physicians and ensure the integration of that information into the credentialing process in compliance with state and federal agencies, NCQA, JCAHO, and institutional requirements.

- Ensure compliance with various codes, laws, rules, and regulations concerning patient care, including those mandated by state and federal agencies, incident reporting, and investigation activities.

- Review and approve all plans and specifications for new construction, alterations, and installation of new equipment. Ensure that outside insurance carrier has signed off on plans as appropriate.

CORPORATE COUNSEL

The CRO will offer assistance to the organizations General Counsel with those legal, regulatory issues that can impact the organization from a patient safety, public relations, marketing, and risk financing standpoint. Those issues might include:

- Fraud/abuse allegations.

- Reporting to outside federal and state agencies.

- Reporting to the NPDDB, state licensing boards, CDC.

- The levying of any sanctions or fines.

- Recommendations that affect licensing and accreditation.

- Review of new and existing legislation to determine appropriate risk response.

HUMAN RESOURCES

The CRO will work with the human resource executive to identify, analyze, and manage through risk control and risk financing techniques those risks related to the workforce.

Specific Activities

- Review all employee related surveys, questionnaires, etc. that address employee morale, turnover, and the climate/culture of the organization.
- Coordinate strategy to reduce turnover, improve morale and to promote an organizational culture that support patient and employee safety.
- Identify and develop with Human Resources initiatives to improve the organizations ability to recruit all positions within the work force including physicians, and to enhance the work experience and educational level of all staff.
- Identify and develop with Human Resource methods to reduce:

  Employee fatigue

  Absenteeism/presenteeism

STRATEGIC PLANNING & MARKETING

The CRO advises senior leadership on mitigation strategy for risk inherent in the following activities:

- Advertising campaigns including all print, TV, and mixed media materials.
- Physician recruitment activities.
- Mergers, acquisitions, and divestitures.
- Joint ventures.
- New clinical programs.
- New facilities/construction.
- Clinical research.

INTERNAL AUDIT

The CRO and Internal Auditor are in a unique position to assist each other. Internal audit is charged with the identification and mitigation of the organizations exposure to loss, much like the CRO. Area of assistance and communication can be:

- Investigation of employee related crime issues, e.g., embezzlement.
- Implementation of educational initiatives for the Board of Directors on issues related to the Sarbanes-Oxley Act.
- Corporate Compliance Program.

(Continued)

EXHIBIT 2.5. *(Continued)*

CONTRACT ADMINISTRATION

Assume responsibility for contract administration to include the following components:

- Assist with the development of appropriate working guideline and legal concepts for contract review.
- Work with senior management to develop contract language to protect the institution from liability and financial loss.
- Review all contracts prior to administrative approval for compliance with written guidelines.
- Negotiate necessary changes to bring the contract into compliance with written guidelines.
- Maintain a database (or purchase software) for contract tracking.
- Assume responsibility as the central repository for all contracts.

POSITION QUALIFICATIONS

Experience

- A minimum of 10 years of progressive experience in healthcare administration with specific experience in healthcare risk management.

Education

- Bachelor degree required; master's degree preferred.
- Clinical background helpful, RN/MD.
- JD, CPCU, and/or MBA desired.
- Associate in Risk Management (ARM) desired.
- Certified Professional in Healthcare Quality (CPHQ) desired.
- Certified Professional in Healthcare Risk Management (CPHRM) desired

KNOWLEDGE AND ABILITIES

- Knowledge of NCQA, HEDIS, and JCAHO, ISMP, NPSF, Leapfrog, IHI initiative, regulations and other patient care-related initiatives to improve outcomes.
- Knowledge of regulatory codes, legal requirements, and healthcare law.
- Effective presentation skills, articulate, persuasive, and eloquent communicator both verbally and in writing.

- Self-motivated with the ability to work independently. Requires little supervision.
- Ability to manage/handle stress while under pressure from many involved parties.
- Ability to interface with a variety of professionals including members of the Board of Directors, medical staff and senior leadership, attorneys, accountants, actuaries, brokers, and the like.
- Knowledge of alternate risk financing/insurance programs.
- Demonstrated skills in strategic planning, implementing and evaluating programs.
- Knowledge of clinical and non-clinical loss control and claims administration.
- Ability to prioritize tasks and see the big picture.
- Ability to delegate and know when to ask for assistance.
- Demonstrated ability to offer creative, innovative solutions to prevent/reduce difficult risk issues.
- Ability to manage information in a confidential manner.
- Reputation and ethical conduct must be of the highest standard and beyond reproach.

POSITION RELATIONSHIPS

Member of a comprehensive healthcare team, including other healthcare providers, the patient, the patient's family and significant others. Position has managerial responsibilities within the Enterprise Risk Management Unit. The chief risk officer, if not directly responsible for the following areas, must interface with them to minimize the potential for loss:

- Emergency Management
- Process/Quality Improvement
- Medical Staff Credentialing
- Infection Control
- Workersí Compensation/Employee Health
- Environmental Health
- Patient Safety
- Risk Financing
- Claims and Litigation Management
- Risk Control (clinical and non-clinical)
- Internal Audit
- Human Resources

(Continued)

EXHIBIT 2.5. *(Continued)*

COMMITTEE RESPONSIBILITY

The Chief Risk Officer will actively participate on the enterprise risk management committee and be a permanent member on the following committees:

- Quality/Performance Improvement
- Patient Safety
- Emergency Management
- Customer Relations

The Chief Risk Officer should periodically attend or review the meeting materials/minutes of other committees such as:

- Pharmacy and Therapeutics
- Blood Utilization
- Utilization Review/Case Review
- Morbidity & Mortality
- Medical Products/Purchasing
- Credentialing Committee
- Infection Control Committee
- Surgical Case Review
- Nursing Executive Committee
- Medical Staff Departmental meetings
- Marketing and Strategy
- Human Resource

COMMUNICATION STANDARDS

Frequent contact is made with members of the senior leadership team, board of directors, medical staff leadership, and a variety of outside professionals. Position requires the ability to articulately communicate a wide variety of legal, medical, and business subjects as they relate to enterprise risk management. Promote and provide courteous and effective communication with internal and external customers. May be spokesperson for the organization in time of a crisis/disaster.

WORKING CONDITIONS

Working conditions are almost exclusively indoors in a warm, well-lit environment.

- Motor coordination and manual dexterity are frequently necessary for the coordination of eye-hand and motor function in computer and telephone use.

- Occasional inter-office or inter-campus traveling with frequent sitting.

- Requirement for periodic on-call coverage.

- Scheduling flexibility is necessary to meet early morning and evening schedules.

- Ability to handle multiple projects simultaneously, some with tight deadlines and minimal staff.

Source: Aon Healthcare. Reprinted with permission.

Integrated Delivery Systems

An **integrated delivery system** is an organization that encompasses many different types of providers under one corporate structure. An IDS often includes acute care facilities, physician group practices, multispecialty clinics, post–acute care facilities, and home care services. Providers may be employees or independent contractors, or they may be loosely affiliated with the organization. IDSs often cover broad geographical areas and can be very large and complex organizations in terms of corporate structure. In many cases, an IDS comprises facilities across several states. For all of these reasons, IDSs are particularly challenging for risk management professionals who seek to develop coordinated and consistent risk management plans and strategies.

Within the IDS, there is usually a corporate risk management professional who assumes responsibility for the IDS's overall risk management program. The corporate risk management professional is responsible for risk financing activities and has oversight responsibilities for claims management. This position is typically responsible for risk management activities only and does not assume other related responsibilities. Risk prevention and reduction activities are carried out by risk management staff at the facility level who may report to the corporate risk management professional or to the facility administrator. In many instances, the risk management function is assumed by a clinician or other facility staff member with no formal risk management training. This requires that the corporate risk management professional be an effective teacher and mentor.

The degree of integration and standardization of risk management practices and of clinical practice across the IDS is often quite variable and produces significant risk that must be managed. The corporate risk management professional establishes broad goals and objectives for the risk management program, thus providing the framework for the individual facilities to follow. These general guidelines allow individual facilities to adopt policies and practices that address issues unique to their setting. It might take time before all elements of the IDS can be successfully incorporated into a coordinated risk management program within the IDS. Very often individual facilities are permitted to remain in existing risk financing arrangements because standardization and change across the IDS is too difficult to manage. Thus the corporate risk management professional may be required to manage and oversee a complex program with many different and varied components.

In addition to the risks noted, IDSs are particularly vulnerable to the risks associated with merger and acquisition activity. Thus the corporate risk management professional's role in premerger due diligence takes on added significance within the IDS. Establishing strong relationships and being perceived as a valuable resource are essential to influence decisions and eliminate or mitigate risk before these organizational changes.

Risk identification can be accomplished in several ways in the IDS. Health plan utilization decisions that limit or deny services require a consistent approach based on currently accepted medical practices and on insuring agreements. Close study of contracts, credentialing practices, marketing and sales initiatives, capitation agreements, health benefit claims and denials, and member and patient satisfaction data are other mechanisms for identifying potential risks.

The risk management professional may oversee or be directly responsible for claims administration, including investigating, analyzing, reporting, and establishing reserves.

The corporate risk management professional in an IDS must be well versed in all aspects of risk financing and must have excellent skills in contract management. This individual must work well with other people to achieve corporate objectives, although the risk management professional exercises no control over these individuals. The level three risk management professional job description in Exhibit 2.4 most closely corresponds to this role in an IDS. The chief risk officer job description in Exhibit 2.5 also might fit this type of organization.

Multifacility Health Care Systems

Health care systems are composed of multiple facilities providing similar services owned by a single corporation or parent organization. In many ways, health care system risk management programs are similar to IDS programs. They both manage risks across discrete organizations that may have entirely different cultures and identities. However, systems do not face the same challenges that IDSs face, in that their practices and procedures tend to be standardized across the system. Thus the corporate **risk management** professional in a system is unlikely to be faced with a broad array of risk financing arrangements or facility-based practices within the system because the risk management program in a system is usually well coordinated and fairly standardized across the system.

The risk management professional in a health care system most often functions as a senior executive in the organization. Risk prevention and reduction activities are usually carried out at the facility level under the direction of the corporate office. As in the IDS, the corporate risk management professional in a system will likely be responsible for risk financing activities while using alternative risk financing strategies to control costs. Claims management activities are often centralized and handled internally by dedicated claims staff.

System risk managers usually work collaboratively with others in the organization in regulatory and accreditation compliance and bioethics and are likely to serve in a consultative capacity, or the responsibility may be delegated within the department.

The level three risk management professional or the chief risk officer job description most closely approximates the duties of the health care system risk management professional. The position requires significant risk management knowledge and experience and the ability to stay ahead of the complexities involved in a changing health care environment.

Ambulatory Care Organizations

Ambulatory care organizations (ACOs) include multispecialty clinics, freestanding surgical centers, urgent care or walk-in medical clinics, and community health or public health facilities. Physician practices may also be considered in the ACO. The organizational structure of outpatient care can be as varied as the facility itself. Some organizations may have an office manager whose job responsibilities include risk management. It is not unusual to have a physician functioning as the senior administrator to whom the office manager or risk management professional reports. Larger facilities more often have a governing body to guide the organization. As in a small hospital setting, the individual responsible for the risk management function may be responsible for several functions.

ACOs pose unique risks because of the large number of patient encounters, which increases the risk of exposure to loss. In addition, because patients generally control the progress of their health care in the ACO setting, there is a greater chance that care may be fragmented or prolonged, and a provider might not recognize changes or deterioration in a patient's condition. Finally, ACOs often do not have access, as hospitals do, to other departments that support critical risk management functions, such as safety, infection control, and biomedical engineering.

Risks in ACOs vary with the type of setting. In most ambulatory settings, the risk of "failure to follow up," either from the patient's perspective or the provider's perspective, can be a risk management concern. Also, the use and maintenance of equipment pose risk management concerns, as do concerns regarding adherence to safety standards, universal precautions, and regulatory compliance.

Outpatient surgery centers have risk issues related to appropriate discharge criteria for their patients and in maintaining practice parameters and standards of care for the many different procedures performed. Emerging risks include the performance of an expanding number and complexity of procedures, including surgery, in outpatient and office settings. Credentialing is of particular concern because of the lack of formal procedures in this area.

Incident reports and occurrence screening often provide the mechanisms for risk identification. Patient complaints also provide excellent sources of information about potential risks.

Risk financing strategies used by ACOs may vary, but rarely will an ACO be involved in a self-managed alternative risk financing arrangement. Most ACOs are commercially insured or are part of the risk financing program of a larger organization, often an IDS or system. In that case, the parent organization assumes most of the responsibility, and the ACO risk management professional plays a minor role in risk financing, usually limited to coordinating exposure data and renewals. The administrator or office manager for the stand-alone physician practice is typically more involved with risk finance decisions, claims management, quality improvement, and patient safety issues.

Most ACOs do not manage liability claims internally. Instead, this function is handled by the insurance carrier or a third-party administrator employed by the parent organization. The ACO may be called on to assist in the coordination of investigation and defense of claims but will usually not have any direct responsibility for claims management.

Risk management professionals and office managers in some ACOs do not have significant responsibilities for regulatory or accreditation issues, whereas others have complete responsibility, depending on the resources available to the organization.

The level one risk management professional job description in Exhibit 2.2 most closely corresponds to this scope of responsibility.

Physician Practices and Groups

The physician risk management professional has emerged as organizations with employed physicians, hospital-owned physician practices, and private physician groups and clinics recognize the need for a person to take responsibility for the risk management functions. Managing physician risks, similar to ACOs, include loss prevention and patient safety, claims management, and risk financing as core job functions. Among the loss exposures for physician practices are high patient visit numbers, unexpected patient outcomes, patient privacy, practice standards, federal and state regulatory requirements, and patient safety issues. The physician risk management professional, like the level one position, may have multiple responsibilities for the practice, such as being charged with handling of human resource issues, contract review, education for staff, and management of the office finances. The risk management professional is usually located in the office of the practice for stand-alone physician groups or may be located in the corporate risk management office of the health care organization for employed physician practices.

Loss prevention activities in this setting include implementing and coordinating continuing education for the staff, coordinating insurer risk assessments, or performing risk surveys for the practice. The risk management professional establishes systems for risk identification, investigation, and reductions and provides analysis of data for management review.

The risk management professional is often responsible for the development of operating standards and procedures to promote quality of care, establishing clinical workflow, procedures, quality improvement initiatives, ongoing evaluation and monitoring of clinical staff credentials, and handling patient complaints. Responsibility for claims management includes reporting claims to the insurers, to the parent organization's risk management office, or to a third-party administrator. This position supports the internal investigation of incidents and claims and may interact with legal counsel.

Risk financing responsibilities may include the coordination of medical professional liability coverage in concert with the governing board of the practice. Contract review may include negotiation of managed care contracts, employment contracts, and vendor contracts. Exhibit 2.6 provides an example of a job description for a physician risk management professional.

EXHIBIT 2.6. Physician Risk Manager Job Description

Position Summary

The Physician Risk Manager leads the risk management/quality programs for the practice. The core job functions include operations/compliance, loss prevention, claims management, and risk financing. This position develops and administers various programs that include, but are not limited to, risk management, quality improvement, patient safety, loss-prevention, and regulatory requirements. The PRM employed in a smaller physician practice may also serve as the administrative director and will often assume additional responsibilities, such as human resources, vendor relationships and managed care contracts.

Loss prevention activities include identification of risks, practice issues, quality of care and the development and implementation of employee educational programs to reduce the exposures to loss. The PRM may spend a significant amount of time developing and implementing policies and procedures/guidelines to meet regulatory and compliance issues. This position typically provides educational programs to the staff and physicians.

The risk manager ensures the reporting of incidents and claims from the staff by developing systems for gathering and tracking data. Analysis of this data is reported to upper management with recommendations for correcting or improving services.

(Continued)

EXHIBIT 2.6. *(Continued)*

The PRM is also responsible for the management/investigation of claims and risk financing. This position investigates claims and may be the initial contact for patient complaints while also serving as the liaison to attorneys, third-party administrators (TPAs), or departments who may be supervising the investigation. Claims handling may be delegated to a TPA. The PRM working with larger physician groups may be significantly involved with risk financing issues. Responsibilities include coordination with a broker to obtain insurance coverage for medical professional liability, general liability, director's and officer's liability, and property insurance. Assigned projects may include research on cost effective programs to minimize asset liability. The experienced PRM may participate in the development of major strategic initiatives such as a self-administered professional liability program that may encompass the integration of multiple practices/clinics.

Reports to: *Executive Practice Director or Administration*

Major Responsibilities

OPERATIONS/COMPLIANCE

- Maintains strictest confidentiality in all responsibilities and accountabilities.
- Establishes clinical work flow, procedures, and improvements for the practices.
- Facilitates communications with clinical staff.
- Manages projects, either self-initiated or assigned by upper administration. Develops and maintains RM Intranet site content.
- Supportive of and insures compliance with applicable organizational medical group policies.
- Interpretations and communicates current and future regulatory requirements to achieve accreditation by organizations such as OSHA, CLIA, NCQA, JCAHO, HIPPA, and other regulatory bodies.
- Presents a professional role model, exhibiting a team attitude, utilizing a positive problem solving approach with patients, physicians, and staff. Works to develop and maintain positive morale of staff.

LOSS PREVENTION

- Communicates with administration and/or Executive Practice Director to inform them of practice issues.
- Identify system concerns and make recommendations for reducing loss exposure.
- Development of operating standards and procedures to promote the quality of care, achieve licensure or accreditation with such agencies, as required, and operate within the cost constraints of the organizational budget.

- Development and implementation of required's employee-training programs required to maintain compliance with regulatory or credentialing organizations; i.e., OSHA annual in-services, ABN education, Clinical Assistant training, etc.
- Ongoing evaluation and monitoring of clinical staff credentials and skills to assure utilization of appropriate staff.
- Participation in care model development.
- Serve as a resource regarding appropriateness of services being rendered by clinical support staff to patients.
- Provides risk management training to physicians and staff.
- Maintains meaningful risk management data.

CLAIMS

- Investigates and manages professional and general liability incidents and minor claims in consultation with legal counsel.
- Responsible for all aspects of claims management, including communication with patients.
- Initiates settlements within authority level and reports to Board upon conclusion.
- Using data from claims annually identifies key areas of exposure and works with Risk Management committee to develop action plans regarding Loss Control and seeks to incorporate meaningful benchmarks where available.
- Within a hospital-based practice, may coordinate interface with organizational Risk Management by setting policy, establishing pathways for report investigation, authorizing payment subject to limit determined by the organization.

RISK FINANCING

- Participate in the budgeting process and expense management of the practice.
- Works with broker to obtain medical professional liability insurance or with organizational risk manager to ensure appropriate coverage is provided for the practice and/or the healthcare system.

KNOWLEDGE, SKILLS & ABILITIES

- Maintains current proficiency with Risk Management best practices.
- Strong communication and interpersonal skills to deal effectively with physicians, patients, and employees.
- Ability to manage and motivate employees within the environment.

(Continued)

EXHIBIT 2.6. *(Continued)*

- Strong clinical background, and understanding of medical records.

- Able to inspire confidence in physicians.

- Knowledge of risk management functions, including claims management, investigation, and resolution.

- Knowledge of management practices to direct assigned staff.

- Knowledge of Clinic's strategic business objectives and employee performance objectives.

- Skilled in exercising initiative, judgment, discretion, and decision-making to achieve organizational objectives.

- Skilled in establishing and maintaining effective working relationships with Clinic leadership, medical staffs, and support staff.

- Skilled in identifying and resolving problems. Ability to delegate responsibility and authority to staff. Ability to work creatively with management and department staff to achieve objectives.

- Ability to analyze problems and consistently follow through on solution or delegation.

- Strong analytical skills and interest in interpretation of regulatory requirements.

- Ability to generate quality management reports and documents which clearly and concisely communicates information to management.

- Detailed knowledge of regulatory requirements for clinical support staff.

SUGGESTED PARAMETERS FOR POSITION

- Bachelor's degree in a related area; MBA, MHA, JD preferred.

- Nursing degree may be preferred for smaller stand-alone practices.

- Certifications may include ARM, CPHRM, and FASHRM.

- Ten years experience as risk manager with significant management responsibility.

- One to three years practice management experience with clinical background preferred.

- Position titles may include practice administrator, risk manager, director risk management, or a combined job title with quality/peer review or patient safety.

- Organizational size may range from one physician practice, to multiple clinics/offices or may include a number of employed physicians of a healthcare organization.

Source: Everett Clinic, Everett, Wash. July 2005; Carilion Health System, Carilion Medical Group, Roanoke, Va., July 2005. Used with permission.

Long-Term Care Facilities

The organizational structure for a **long-term care** (**LTC**) facility may be as simple as a stand-alone privately owned facility or as complex as a multifacility, multistate system. Some hospital-affiliated LTC units may be housed within the acute care hospital, and others may be located separately from the hospital. LTC centers located in the hospital usually use the hospital risk management professional to manage the risk for this area, just as they would other patient care units. Some LTC facilities are independent from the affiliated organizations' management and operations and will have a separate risk management function. Risk financing most often occurs through the health care facility's insurance program. Single, privately held LTC organizations use the facility administrator to develop and oversee the risk management functions and sometimes have some owner involvement in claims management. Within the smaller setting, the quality and risk responsibilities may be combined and performed by a clinical person with direct oversight by the facility administrator.

A more complex LTC organization with multiple facilities in several states most often employs a corporate position responsible for the development of a systemwide risk management program. As in the multihospital system, the challenge is to develop standard policies and procedures and to maintain consistency in the management of claims. Loss prevention and reduction activities are usually carried out at the facility level under the direction of the system risk management professional.

LTC facilities pose unique risks because of the length of patient stays at the facility. The nature of allegations most often identified are administrative (for example, employee-related), clinical (for example, patient care-related), environmental (for example, emergency-related), provider (for example, vendor-related), and regulatory (for example, related to the Omnibus Budget Reconciliation Act). Proactive risk management and quality improvement are essential to the reduction of risk exposures to the LTC facility. Facilities specializing in the care of patients with Alzheimer's disease have specific risk exposures for wandering and elopement of residents. Employee education and training is a significant part of the risk management professional's job and is an effective loss prevention strategy for employee turnover in the LTC setting.

Risk financing strategies may include a commercially insured or self-insured alternative risk financing arrangement. In larger systems, the responsibility for insurance placement falls to the corporate risk management professional or senior management at the parent organization. The LTC risk management professional at each facility in the system plays a minor role in risk financing, often limited to coordinating exposure data. In a single facility, the responsibility for risk financing is most often assumed by the LTC administrator and may include the owner in this process. Currently, LTC facilities have been faced with a limited number of markets for professional liability coverage, which has placed much more emphasis on risk financing alternatives at the corporate level.

Risk identification occurs through incident reporting, occurrence screening, and on-site visits of licensing organizations at the state and federal levels. Patient and family complaints are often a source of information regarding potential risk exposures and claims.

Like the ACO, smaller LTC facilities do not manage their own liability claims. This function may be handled by the insurer or a third-party administrator. Larger LTC systems with self-managed programs may choose to self-administer their claims.

Bioethics issues include end-of-life decisions, such as advance directives and DNR orders. Coordinating the patient's desires and keeping the family involved are challenges in this long-term care environment and can become more complicated if the patient is taken to the acute care setting. Patient records and documents from the LTC facility are significant to the decision-making process for the patient during an unexpected hospitalization.

The level one and level two risk management professional job descriptions in Exhibits 2.2 and 2.3 are most consistent with the functions of the corporate risk management professional for a multifacility LTC system.

REQUIRED SKILLS FOR THE SUCCESSFUL HEALTH CARE RISK MANAGEMENT PROFESSIONAL

To be successful, health care risk management professionals must develop a variety of skills necessary for performing a difficult job in a complex environment. They are called on to interact with all levels of authority within the organization and with patients and other customers. They often act as the organization's "official" representative in very sensitive circumstances. This means that they must have communication skills necessary to interact effectively with many different individuals and personalities and must do so under stressful circumstances. Of primary importance is effective communication, which includes writing, listening, and speaking. Health care risk management professionals are often called on to conduct educational sessions for other health care workers, including professional and nonprofessional providers and employees. They must also frequently deliver formal presentations to management, board members, or trustees. For this reason, excellent verbal communication skills and a thorough understanding and application of effective presentation styles are of critical importance.

In addition to verbal communication, successful health care risk management professionals also must be able to communicate well in writing. They must often prepare detailed reports of individual cases, write reports of trends and patterns, and develop policies, procedures, and other guidance documents that will be used by others at all levels of the organization. For this reason, the health care risk management professional must have the ability to communicate clearly, accurately, and succinctly in writing.

Finally, the ability to listen well is an essential communication skill, especially when conducting fact-gathering following a serious event and interviewing the parties involved, carefully listening to their stories, and reconstructing the events that occurred. The health care risk management professional must also be able to glean information about risks and exposures from several sources, including committee reports and informal discussions. The successful health care risk management professional must be able to listen carefully to all information without passing judgment and to process information carefully and objectively and communicate it clearly to others. Thus the ability to listen well is a complex and indispensable skill.

Another important skill is the ability to negotiate. The health care risk management professional often serves as negotiator in different situations, such as the resolution of claims or patient complaints, securing broker services or insurance coverage, or drafting indemnification agreements or contracts. Negotiation skills are desirable and may be developed through education.

Another critical skill is the ability to remain objective despite being in an emotionally charged situation: The risk management professional is often called on to provide support and direction to individuals most closely associated with these events and must also assume responsibility for discovering the facts and determining the best course of action. To do this effectively, the health care risk management professional must have the ability to maintain objectivity and professional detachment, even in emotionally difficult situations, and to pursue the best course of action for the organization regardless of personal feelings.

Finally, a critically important skill for the health care risk management professional is the ability to maintain confidentiality. Because of the nature of their work, health care risk management professionals often encounter situations and fact patterns that might seriously harm the organization and the individuals who work there. The health care risk management professional must be able to perform the activities necessary to protect the organization and individuals while also refraining from sharing information unnecessarily, regardless of how tempting or trying the situation might be. Maintaining confidentiality is crucial not only to protect those involved in an adverse event or potentially damaging circumstance but also to gain and maintain the trust of those who might provide important information in the future.

RISK MANAGEMENT ETHICS

One hallmark of a true profession is a code of ethical conduct to which its practitioners must adhere. This is a familiar concept in health care, as medicine's own code of ethics dates back to the Hippocratic Oath. Nursing, law, and other disciplines related to health care risk management likewise have codes of ethical behavior that guide practitioners in those fields.

ASHRM's Code of Professional Ethics and Conduct articulates the standards of conduct to which its members must adhere. This code is presented in Appendix B. It provides a useful road map for health care risk management professionals who wish to maintain the highest level of professional conduct.

A PROFILE OF THE HEALTH CARE RISK MANAGEMENT PROFESSIONAL

Because of the way in which the health care risk management profession has evolved, health care risk management professionals come from many professional and educational backgrounds, including nursing, law, administration, quality assurance, and insurance. According to the results of ASHRM's 2005 member survey, presented in Table 2.2, fully 82 percent of respondents were identified as having a minimum of a bachelor's degree, and of those, 49 percent had an advanced degree.

Health care risk management professionals hold several professional designations. According to the ASHRM 2004 compensation survey, three of the top four most common professional designations were certified professional in health care risk management (CPHRM), at 26.6 percent; associate in risk management, at 20.6 percent; and certified professional in health care quality (CPHQ), at 11.9 percent.[4] Those whose highest educational level was a bachelor's degree stood at 35.1 percent, while those with an advanced degree totaled 44.1 percent. These results approximate the subsequent ASHRM member survey in 2005. Table 2.3 presents the results of the survey's findings regarding highest educational level held by health care risk management professionals.

Table 2.4 identifies the job titles as related to the job function of respondents to the ASHRM 2005 member survey. The survey classifies the respondent's job functions from senior-level to entry-level positions and includes roles dedicated to financial and claims management, compliance, legal, nursing, physician or medical director, and patient safety officer. The majority of the responses centered on some variations of the risk management professional job title.

EDUCATION AND PROFESSIONAL RECOGNITION PROGRAMS

An important characteristic that distinguishes a true professional is the desire to further develop and refine mastery of the chosen profession. One of the ways professionals pursue growth and development is by continuing their education through both formal and informal means. The profession in turn recognizes the efforts of these professionals by bestowing designations extolling their achievements. Thus continuing education and professional recognition of achievement are important components of a continuously evolving profession and important milestones for the health care risk management professional.

Academic Training

A growing number of colleges and universities either currently offer or are developing programs leading to a baccalaureate or master's degree in health care risk management. (Information about such programs is available at http://www.ashrm.org.) This trend signifies the increasing recognition of health care risk management as a

TABLE 2.2. **Level of Education**

Education	Percentage of Total
High School Graduate	1
Associate's Degree	7
Nursing Diploma	4
Bachelor's Degree	33
Master's Degree	35
Doctoral Degree	2
JD	11
MD	1
Other	6

Base: 911 respondents.
Source: American Society for Healthcare Risk Management, *ASHRM Membership Survey, 2005.* Reprinted with permission.

discipline worthy of academic attention. As the profession continues to evolve, more entrants into the field will come equipped with formal academic training rather than experiential training, as has been the case in the past. If the trend continues, it is possible that formal academic training in health care risk management will be a requirement for entry into the field. This requirement would also help provide a steady stream of new and qualified candidates for health care risk management positions; however, such programs are not yet widely available.

Continuing Professional Education

Although academic programs fulfill an important role for the profession, they might not meet the needs of practitioners who already hold academic degrees but seek further professional education in the field of health care risk management. Thus it is important that other means exist for health care professionals to obtain continuing

TABLE 2.3. **Highest Level of Educational Training.**

Designation	Percentage of Total
Bachelor's Degree	35.1
Master's Degree	25.5
MBA	7.4
JD	9.9
Associate's Degree	7.9
Doctorate	1.3
Other	10.7
None of the above	2.2

Base: 944 respondents.
Source: American Society for Healthcare Risk Management, *2004 Compensation Survey of Healthcare Risk Management Professionals.* Reprinted with permission.

TABLE 2.4. **Job Functions and Titles.**

Job Functions and Titles	Percentage of Total
Top Risk Management Officer	19
Senior Risk Manager	3
Risk Manager	16
Middle Manager Risk Management	12
Entry-Level Risk Manager	2
Top Finance/Claims Management	1

Middle Finance/Claims Management	1
Top Patient Safety Officer	2
Middle Manager Patient Safety	>1
Compliance Officer	1
Legal/Regulatory	2
Nurse Executive	1
Physician/Medical Director	>1
Third-Party Administrator	1
Consultant	6
Insurance Broker	1
Other	14
No Response	18

Base: 911 respondents.
Source: American Society for Healthcare Risk Management, *ASHRM Membership Survey 2005.* Reprinted with permission.

education in their chosen field. Fortunately, in addition to academic programs, several other avenues exist for health care risk management professionals to further their education and professional development.

The major source of professional education programs for health care risk management professionals is the American Society for Healthcare Risk Management, which has developed several educational programs that are available to both members and nonmembers. The Barton Certificate in Healthcare Risk Management program, which covers key aspects of risk management, is designed with three modules for the risk management professional. The program includes the "Essentials" module, which provides the educational foundation for new management professionals, the "Application" module, with relevant topics for those with one to five years in health care risk management, and the "Advanced Forum," for more experienced risk management individuals facing special challenges. Upon completion of all three modules, attendees are issued a certificate of completion by ASHRM. Participants may also earn undergraduate and graduate college credits and receive credit toward the ASHRM risk management certification program.

ASHRM also presents programs on more advanced topics, such as risk financing, regulatory developments, and other critical issues, throughout the year. At its annual conference, ASHRM presents programs on a wide variety of topics in the field of health care risk management and more broadly in health care. As with other offerings, attendees earn continuing education credits.

In addition to ASHRM, major health care liability insurance carriers and brokers also offer educational programs specifically designed for health care risk management professionals. Although these programs are often limited to clients or insureds, they often cover timely topics and feature nationally known speakers.

Certification

Certification provides evidence of mastery of a defined body of knowledge by requiring certificants to pass an objective test, such as a written examination. It helps set professional standards by identifying a minimum level of knowledge that all certificants must possess. It also helps ensure continued growth and development of the profession and of individuals practicing the profession by requiring recertification at predetermined intervals.

Currently, there is only one certification program specifically for health care risk management professionals in the United States. This program, administered by the American Hospital Association Certification Center (AHACC), in cooperation with ASHRM, offers the designation of *certified professional in health care risk management.* An individual who meets eligibility criteria and passes a qualifying examination becomes certified. Eligibility standards include prior work experience in addition to certain educational requirements. The CPHRM examination tests the applicant's knowledge in each of the six domain areas identified by ASHRM's role delineation study: loss prevention and reduction, claims management, risk financing, regulatory and accreditation compliance, operations, and bioethics. Certificants are required to become recertified every three years.

The Insurance Institute of America (IIA) also offers risk management education in the form of its associate in risk management (ARM) program.[5] This is a designation program consisting of three courses and accompanying examinations that focus on risk assessment (designated as ARM 54), risk control (ARM 55), and risk financing (ARM 56). Upon successful completion of the examinations, the student earns the designation *associate in risk management,* which is recognized throughout the health care and insurance industry. Although the ARM program does not focus specifically on health care risk management, it offers significant educational benefits to the individual interested in furthering education beyond the borders of health care.

Other designation programs are also offered through the Insurance Institute of America and the American Institute for Chartered Property and Casualty Underwriters, such as the associate in claims (AIC) and chartered property and casualty underwriter (CPCU). Many equate a CPCU designation to a graduate degree in insurance.[6]

Licensure

Health care risk management professionals should know and understand the specific state statutes and regulations that govern their work environment and under which their position as risk manager may be managed and controlled. For example, by Florida statute, every licensed hospital, ambulatory surgical center, nursing home, and HMO must establish an internal risk management program as part of its administrative function.[7] Every hospital, ambulatory surgical center, and HMO must hire a licensed risk manager for implementation and oversight of the facility's internal risk management program.[8] In the Florida nursing home environment, the internal risk management and quality assurance program is the responsibility of the facility administrator. The hiring of licensed risk managers is not required.

Professional Recognition Programs

Professional recognition programs serve a valuable function for a profession and the individuals practicing the profession by encouraging continued growth and development of individuals, in turn elevating standards in the profession. Such programs are typically administered by professional societies and membership organizations.

ASHRM offers the highest achievement designations for *Distinguished Fellow* (DFASHRM), which is awarded for superior achievement in the profession. The designation of *Fellow* (FASHRM) is awarded for outstanding achievement. Criteria for both designations include a combination of education, leadership, and publication experience and achievement, and designations are awarded to members who meet the criteria.

ASHRM's highest award, the Distinguished Service Award (DSA), recognizes a health care risk management professional whose efforts have advanced the profession and practice of risk management and who has made an outstanding contribution to ASHRM.

Other organizations sometimes also offer awards in recognition of superior achievement. *Business Insurance,* a nationally recognized insurance publication, offers recognition to the Risk Manager of the Year and to members of the Risk Management Honor Roll. These awards are given to winners from all industries, and health care risk management professionals have been so honored.

SUMMARY

The growth and evolution of the health care risk management profession has mirrored that of the health care industry as a whole, although its basic components and processes have not changed. The goal of an effective health care risk management program continues to be to maintain a safe and effective health care environment for patients, visitors, and employees, thereby preventing or reducing losses to the organization.

Risk management continues to compose an important part of the delivery of health care, and it has become even more important because of the greater emphasis on patient safety.

The role of the health care risk management professional continues to evolve. Loss prevention and reduction, claims management, risk financing, regulatory and accreditation compliance, risk management operations, and bioethics are the major functional areas that together compose the job description of the health care risk management professional, the chief risk officer, and the patient safety officer. The depth and breadth of these functions and their vital importance to an organization's survival have been amply demonstrated by this study.

Health care risk management professionals, chief risk officers, physician risk management professionals, and patient safety officers are a diverse group of professionals from a variety of backgrounds. Most are highly educated. They value continuing education and professional achievement as demonstrated by the demographic data obtained in the ASHRM studies.

Successful health care risk management professionals must possess certain critical skills. The ability to communicate well, negotiate effectively, remain objective, and maintain confidentiality is especially important to success.

Opportunities for health care risk management professionals to enhance their professional growth and development abound. Academic training programs in health care risk management are increasingly common, and continuing education opportunities have always been plentiful. An opportunity to enhance professional development and recognition comes with the health care risk management certification program developed by ASHRM, in conjunction with the American Hospital Association.

The continuing challenge for health care risk management professionals will be to stay abreast of developments in health care that lead to new exposures and to develop new risk financing and loss control techniques to manage those exposures. Enterprise risk management provides the tools for embedding the discussion of risk into the way an organization does business. The risk management professional who adds value to the organization by aligning risk management strategies in support of business success will not just survive but thrive in this constantly changing environment.

KEY TERMS

Academic medical center
Acute care hospital
Ambulatory care organization
Associate in claims
Bioethics
Claims management
Enterprise risk management

Integrated delivery system
The Joint Commission
Loss prevention
Loss reduction
Risk financing
Risk management ethics

ACRONYMS

ACO	CPHRM	HMO
ADA	CRO	IDS
AHACC	DFASHRM	IIA
AIC	DNR	IOM
ARM	EMTALA	LTC
ARM 54	ERM	OSHA
ARM 55	FASHRM	PSDA
ARM 56	FMEA	PSO
ASHRM	HCQIA	SMDA
CPCU	HIPAA	TPA
CPHQ		

NOTES

1. Kloman, F. H. *Risk Management Milestones, 1900–1999.* International Risk Management Institute (IRMI), March 2001, available at http://www.irmi.com

2. "ASHRM Healthcare Risk Management National Role Delineation Study," 1999, conducted by Applied Measurement Professionals, Inc., Lenexa, Kans.

3. "ASHRM Membership Survey 2005," analysis provided by Organizational Research Forum, Inc., Vernon Hills, Ill.

4. "2004 Compensation Survey of Healthcare Risk Management Professionals," American Society for Healthcare Risk Management, Chicago.

5. See American Institute for CPCU and Insurance Institute of America, Malvern, Pa., at http://www.aicpcu.org/

6. The CPCU program consists of eleven courses. You must pass eight courses to earn the CPCU designation. All candidates must complete the five foundation courses. In addition, you select either the commercial or personal insurance concentration and complete the three courses in the concentration of your choosing. You may not combine courses from both concentrations.

7. Per Florida Statutes §395.0197, §400.147, and §631.55.

8. Only organizations that have an annual premium volume of $10 million or more and that directly provide health care in a building owned or leased by the organization must hire a risk manager certified under §395.10971. Extensive qualifications for licensed risk managers are set forth in §395.10974.

SUGGESTED READING

American Hospital Association. *Mapping Your Risk Management Course in Ambulatory Care.* Chicago: American Hospital Publishing, 1995.

American Hospital Association. *Mapping Your Risk Management Course in Integrated Delivery Networks.* Chicago: American Hospital Publishing, 1995.

American Hospital Association. *Mapping Your Risk Management Course in Stand-Alone Hospitals.* Chicago: American Hospital Publishing, 1995.

American Hospital Association. *Pearls for Skilled Nursing/Long-Term Care Facilities.* Chicago: American Hospital Publishing, 2002.

American Society for Healthcare Risk Management. *The Growing Role of the Patient Safety Officer: Implications for Risk Managers.* Chicago: ASHRM, June 2004.

Berkowitz, S. L. "Enterprise Risk Management and the Healthcare Risk Manager." *Journal of Healthcare Risk Management,* Winter 2001.

Economist Intelligence Unit. *The Evolving Role of the CRO.* New York: Economist, May 2005.

Youngberg, B. J. *The Risk Manager's Desk Reference.* Rockville, Md.: Aspen, 1994.

CHAPTER

3

PATIENT SAFETY AND THE RISK MANAGEMENT PROFESSIONAL

New Challenges and Opportunities

DENISE M. MURPHY, KATRINA SHANNON, GINA PUGLIESE

LEARNING OBJECTIVES

- To be able to identify two models of accident causation from other industries that health care professionals are using to help them address medical error

- To be able to identify three steps that must be taken by any organization implementing a just culture

- To be able to identify two strategies to promote communication among health care providers

- To be able to define the role of human factors engineering and ergonomics in medical error reduction

- To be able to identify a major issue associated with the reporting of errors and describe a strategy to address this issue

Risk management has been practiced in business for more than a century, beginning with the fields of engineering and economics. In the 1960s, risk management became associated with insurance strategies aimed at minimizing or financing predictable business losses.[1] Philosophically, risk management aims to bring order from chaos and to facilitate certainty in an environment of uncertainty.

The field of health care risk management grew out of the insurance crisis of the 1970s, when professional liability premiums skyrocketed in part from the dissolution of the doctrine of charitable immunity, which once shielded a hospital's assets from malpractice lawsuits.[2]

The Joint Commission (until 2007, known as the Joint Commission on Accreditation of Healthcare Organizations, or JCAHO) defines risk management as "clinical and administrative activities undertaken to identify, evaluate, and reduce the risk of injury to patients, staff, and visitors, and the risk of loss to the organization itself."[3] Thus health care risk management is committed to reducing loss associated with patient safety–related events in health care settings.

Like the malpractice crisis of the 1970s, the patient safety movement today is forcing a great deal of change in health care risk management. One of the greatest catalysts has been the Institute of Medicine's 1999 report, *To Err Is Human: Building a Safer Health System*, known as the IOM Report,[4] which shed light on the growing problem of medical errors.

The problems exposed by the IOM Report have since given rise to mounting regulations and government scrutiny. However, despite the significant challenges, the health care industry has responded to the crisis in many innovative ways.

Most important, risk managers today must assist health care professionals in meeting an unprecedented high standard of care. Providers must prove that they acted as any other reasonably prudent provider would have acted in defending themselves in malpractice lawsuits. The evidence determining "reasonableness" now includes highly prescriptive Joint Commission standards, such as the requirement that every procedure be preceded by a "time-out." Even more challenging, to help providers implement new approaches, the risk management professional must work with other managers to transform a traditionally hierarchical health care environment into a "culture of patient safety." Risk management professionals today have additional responsibilities to help their employers satisfy patient safety reporting requirements and to stay abreast of new patient safety-related legislation such as the recent Patient Safety and Quality Improvement Act.[5]

The recent evolution fueled by the patient safety movement has also created tremendous opportunities for risk management professionals. Not only are they gaining a broader understanding of the dynamics of error from patient safety theory, but they are also learning from new tools, such as electronic incident reporting, designed to capture relevant information, help providers learn from these errors, and implement processes to prevent them in the future. Armed with additional information on the frequency and nature of errors, risk managers are in a better position to receive resources and support from organizational leaders to enhance safety programs. Health care executives also better understand why keeping patients safe from harm protects market share, reimbursement levels, organizational reputation, and accreditation status. Safety has become a top priority today in every health care organization. Most important, through patient safety efforts, the risk management professional participates in efforts that can help restore social trust in a health care system whose safety track record is being closely scrutinized by decision makers, legislators, payers, and consumers.

This chapter will discuss the scope of medical errors in health care, provide an overview of patient safety theory and related safety guidelines, and highlight strategies to leverage patient safety concepts to reduce loss and improve care.

KEY CONCEPTS

■ The "Swiss cheese model" of accident causation postulates that it may be possible to overcome one system failure. However, it is the alignment of many small system failures, as in a stack of Swiss cheese slices, that allows error to occur.

■ All professionals make errors; openness about error is highly valued; reckless behavior will not be tolerated. Team members must be encouraged to question care with which they are uncomfortable.

■ **Human factors engineering** addresses device safety through modification. **Human factors** analysis assesses the relationship between humans and devices and thus supports human factors engineering.

■ A major issue associated with error reporting is failure to report errors due to fear of consequences.

THE SCOPE OF MEDICAL ERRORS

In the IOM Report, an adverse event is defined as an injury caused by medical management rather than by the underlying disease or condition of the patient. Some but not all adverse events are the result of medical errors. The IOM Report also defines medical error as the failure of a planned action to be completed as intended or the use of a wrong plan to achieve an aim. Two studies of large samples of hospital admissions, one in New York known as the Harvard Medical Practice Study, which uses 1984 data, and another in Colorado and Utah using 1992 data, found that adverse events occurred in 2.9 and 3.7 percent of hospitalizations, respectively.[6] Data from these two studies were extrapolated in the IOM Report to the more than 33.6 million admissions to U.S. hospitals in 1997. They imply that at least 44,000 to 98,000 patients

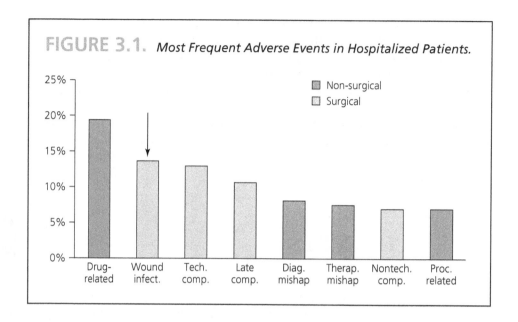

FIGURE 3.1. *Most Frequent Adverse Events in Hospitalized Patients.*

in U.S. hospitals die each year as a result of medical errors. Figure 3.1 provides details on the types of adverse events found in the Harvard Medical Practice Study among 30,000 randomly selected discharges from fifty-one randomly selected hospitals in New York.

The accuracy of the IOM's nearly 100,000 death estimate was challenged at the time it was published, but subsequent data indicate that even more deaths may be attributable to medical errors.[7] Estimates of the financial impact of medical errors are no less alarming. The Agency for Healthcare Research and Quality (AHRQ) estimates that medical errors cost a typical large hospital about $5 million per year; all told, medical errors cost the U.S. health care system between $17 billion and $29 billion per year. These costs include follow-up and additional medical treatment of any adverse outcomes and any expenses related to lost income and household productivity and potential long-term or permanent disability. Virtually none of these costs can later be recouped for proactive health initiatives.

Viewed in the larger context of medical errors, medication errors have become an increasing area of concern for risk managers. According to the IOM Report, medication errors alone, either in or outside of the hospital, have been estimated to account for over seven thousand deaths a year. Moreover, a study referenced by the IOM concluded that about two out of every one hundred admissions experience a preventable adverse drug event, resulting in average excess hospital costs of $4,700 per admission or about $2.8 million in additional costs for a typical 700-bed teaching hospital.[8] If these findings are generalizable, the IOM Report points out, the increased hospital costs alone of preventable adverse drug events affecting inpatients are $2 billion for the nation as a whole.[9]

The IOM Report enumerates and expands on the categorization of the types of medical errors that were reported by Leape and colleagues in 1993.[10] These categories are diagnostic, therapeutic, preventive, or related to failures of communication, equipment, or other systems. Diagnostic errors are further defined as those related to error or delay in diagnosis, failure to perform indicated tests, use of outmoded tests or therapy, or failure to act on results of monitoring or testing.

Treatment-related errors are defined as those that occur in performance of an operation, procedure, or test; in administering treatment; or in the dose or method of using a drug and can be the result of an avoidable delay in treatment or in responding to an abnormal test result or inappropriate (not indicated) care.

Preventive errors were found to include failure to provide prophylactic treatment or inadequate monitoring or follow-up of treatment.

According to the AHRQ, the most common adverse events that patients experience while receiving health care services include medication and transfusion errors, infections, complications of surgery (including wrong-site surgery), suicide, restraint-related injuries, falls, burns, pressure ulcers, misidentification, delays, and wrong diagnosis or treatment.

Health care-associated infections are an important patient safety issue. The Centers for Disease Control and Prevention (CDC) estimate that two million patients a year are infected in U.S. hospitals, and approximately ninety thousand die as a result of those infections. Health care–associated infections cost the U.S. health care system an estimated $6.7 billion annually (based on 2002 data).[11] In New York hospitals alone, for example, surgical site infections were found to be the second most common adverse event, according to the Harvard Medical Practice Study.[12] Recent studies have shown that up to 350,000 hospitalized patients acquire bloodstream infections each year at a minimum cost of about $38,703 per episode[13] and with a mean attributable mortality of 15 to 20 percent.[14]

Studies have shown that most medical errors occur among women and infants in hospital intensive care units, operating rooms, and emergency departments.

The health care system bears the additional costs for treatment related to medical errors. Nowhere is this more evident than in rising insurance rates and malpractice premiums. Clinicians in many parts of the country have been forced to abandon their medical practices because of increasing malpractice premiums.

Finally, two of the most overlooked effects of medical errors are the unquantifiable expense of psychological damage to patients, families, and providers and the erosion of public trust in our health care system.

SEEKING SOLUTIONS: WHAT ARE THE CAUSES OF MEDICAL ERRORS?

The financial and social implications of medical errors reveal only part of the overall problem for the health care industry. The contributing or underlying causes of medical errors must be identified if they are to be adequately addressed.

Of equal concern for risk management professionals today is an understanding of the underlying causes of medical errors. According to the AHRQ, medical errors are caused by the following:[15]

- Communication problems

- Inadequate information flow

- Human-related problems

- Patient-related issues

- Organizational transfer of knowledge

- Staffing patterns and workflow

- Technical failures

- Inadequate policies and procedures

Theories on Accident Causation

Health care professionals are reaching out to other industries to understand and address the causes of medical errors. Although there may not be total agreement on how to apply non-health care industry strategies, everyone understands that health care, like aviation, is a complex environment in which people may suffer as a result of systems failure.

Following are some of the leading theories about systems failure and how they can be applied to medical errors in a health care setting.

"Swiss Cheese Model" Two commonly used models of accident causation in the patient safety literature are found in the work of James Reason, David D. Woods, and Richard Cook. Reason's "Swiss cheese model"[16] makes it easy to visualize how complex systems fail because of the combination and timing of multiple small failures. Reason contends that any one failure or situation alone would be insufficient to cause an accident, but the combination and timing of small failures look much like the alignment of holes in a piece of Swiss cheese that has been sliced (see Figure 3.2). A practical example of this model is an ICU nurse who was "floated" to an oncology unit due to short staffing and administered a wrong dose of chemotherapy. In a subsequent review of the circumstances, it is learned that the ICU nurse failed to follow the standard protocol of having an experienced oncology nurse double-check the physician's order against the prepared medication before administering it to the patient. The experienced oncology nurse, who was anticipating being asked to assist with the double-check, was unexpectedly involved in a crisis and forgot to check in with the float nurse before the incident occurred. The holes in the Swiss cheese lined up, and the patient was harmed.

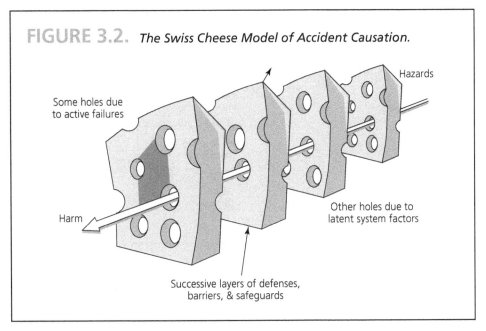

FIGURE 3.2. *The Swiss Cheese Model of Accident Causation.*

Hazards

Some holes due
to active failures

Harm

Other holes due to
latent system factors

Successive layers of defenses,
barriers, & safeguards

Source: Adapted from J. Reason, *Human Error* (Cambridge: Cambridge University Press, 1990).
Reprinted with the permission of Cambridge University Press.

Active Versus Latent Failures Following the same example, the active failure was that the nurse did not comply with the medication administration policy and therefore administered the wrong dose of a chemotherapeutic agent to the patient. Other second-layer failures, or holes in the Swiss cheese, are considered latent or hidden. For example, it is not immediately apparent in the circumstances of this error that the recent budget cut that led to the staffing shortage was responsible for the float situation in the first place. The inability of administrative staffing mechanisms to compensate for the budget cut is a good example of latent failure.

"Blunt End/Sharp End Model" Both David Woods and Richard Cook have written extensively about a second model of accident causation called the "blunt end/sharp end" model.[17] This model assumes that health care workers at the sharp end, where patient care is delivered, are affected by decisions, policies, and regulations made at the blunt end, or hospital administration side, of the system. This administrative end generates resources but also constraints and conflicts that shape the environment in which the technical work takes place and may thereby produce **latent failures** (see Figure 3.3). At the sharp end, constraints place stresses on providers, who respond with appropriate coping mechanisms, such as letting senior management know about their perception or unsafe shortcuts that increase the risk of medication error, like storing medications in their pockets as a time-saving strategy.

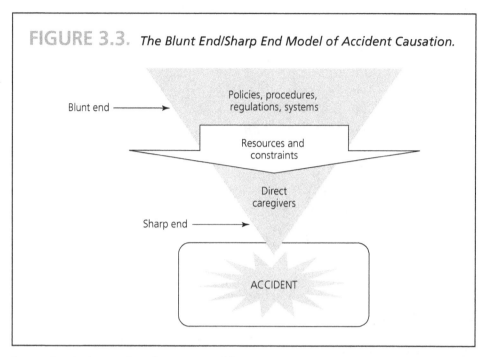

FIGURE 3.3. *The Blunt End/Sharp End Model of Accident Causation.*

Source: R. I. Cook, *How Complex Systems Fail* (Chicago: Cognitive Technologies Laboratory, 2000). Adapted from Woods, 1991.

Hindsight Bias Richard Cook, an anesthesiologist who has extensively studied causes of, and reaction to, accidents in health care, notes that investigations into accidents frequently stop with identifying the human error and designating the practitioners as the "cause" of the event. Often this determination is made without any evaluation of systems or processes that might have contributed to the error. According to Cook, this limited type of investigation can lead to solutions characterized by a phenomenon he calls "hindsight bias."[18] Such bias occurs when the investigators work backward from their knowledge of the outcome of the event. This linear analysis makes the path to failure look as though it should have been foreseeable or predictable, although this is not the case.

These theories and models raise our awareness of the complexity of the system in which patients receive care and in which providers work. They make clear that organizational leaders must become "systems thinkers" who demand in-depth analyses of safety concerns. Health care leaders must also advocate a culture of safety that replaces punitive reactions to mistakes with an open environment that encourages staff to bring errors to light so that the errors can be dissected and addressed. Only when staff members are confident that their leaders will proactively address any risks that they divulge will there be an opportunity to build safer health care organizations.

Creating a Just Culture of Safety

To envision a culture of safety, it is important to understand the concept of "organizational culture." **Organizational culture** can be described as the set of values, guiding beliefs, or ways of thinking that are shared among members of an organization. It is the feel of an organization that is quickly picked up by new members. Culture is "the way we do things around here." Culture is powerful, and is likely to become particularly visible when an organization tries to implement new strategies that are not in step with the status quo. It is human nature for people to resist changing the way they do things. Similarly, it is human nature for people to change the culture in which they live or work.

So what is the definition of a culture of safety? Tom Hellmich, a physician member of the Patient Safety Council at Children's Hospital and Clinics in Minneapolis, described it this way: "The medical culture that silently taught the ABCs as Accuse, Blame, and Criticize is fading. Rising in its place is a safety culture emphasizing blameless reporting, successful systems, knowledge, respect, confidentiality, and trust."[19]

In schools of medicine, nursing, and allied health, providers have traditionally been taught, through incident reporting procedures and behavior of other staff members, that when things go wrong, they should find out "who did it." The focus has been on individual failures. On the other hand, a safety culture asks, "What happened?" A safety culture looks at the system, the environment, the knowledge, the workflow, the tools, and other stressors that may have affected provider behavior.

When the patient safety movement began in the United States, a nonpunitive culture was seen as a solution to medical errors. This raised concerns that people who acted recklessly would not be held accountable. Lucien Leape, the Harvard surgeon who is sometimes referred to as the father of the patient safety movement, introduced the term "just culture" and noted that having a safety culture "doesn't mean there is no role for punishment. Punishment is indicated for willful misconduct, reckless behavior, and unjustified, deliberate violation of rules . . . but not for human error."[20]

David Marx, an attorney who specializes in human resources and organizational development, also differentiates between a nonpunitive and a just response to error by describing a just culture of safety in terms of a set of beliefs and a set of duties. According to Marx, providers in a just culture must recognize that professionals make mistakes, acknowledge that even professionals will use shortcuts, and support zero tolerance for reckless behaviors. Marx adds that staff members in this culture must openly admit "I have made a mistake," call out when they see risk, and participate in a learning culture, where information about mistakes and **near misses** is shared with others so they can prevent similar situations.[21]

Participants in a just safety culture are sensitive to risk, as they try to identify where and how the next mistake might occur and then work to prevent it from happening. Staff members share information about mistakes and errors to prevent them from recurring somewhere else or to someone else, and they are constantly seeking best practices. These behaviors are characteristic of a learning organization. This type of organization also values reciprocal accountability. In other words, everyone holds everyone else accountable for patient safety. Leadership can expect staff members to call out or "stop the line" when they see risk, and the staff can expect leadership to listen and act, even if that means dealing with problem professionals who display intentionally reckless behaviors. Patients and family members are respected partners and understand their own responsibility to keep themselves safe while in a health care organization. Examples of patient responsibilities include keeping written records of medications and allergies and reminding busy health care workers to perform hand hygiene.

The National Patient Safety Foundation outlines several attributes of a safety culture that all health care organizations should strive to operationalize through the implementation of strong safety management systems.[22] These include a culture that does the following:

- Encourages all workers (including frontline staff, physicians, and administrators) to accept responsibility for the safety of themselves, their coworkers, patients, and visitors

- Prioritizes safety above financial and operational goals

- Encourages and rewards the identification, reporting, and resolution of safety issues

- Provides for organizational learning from accidents

- Allocates appropriate resources, structure, and accountability to maintain effective safety systems

- Absolutely avoids reckless behaviors

In a just safety culture, top-down communication must be replaced by two-way communication that flows to the front line from leadership and back to leadership from those providing patient care on the front line. Similarly, silence about harmful events must be replaced with open, honest disclosure about serious patient safety events.

Communication and Teamwork

We know that the failure to communicate effectively is the root cause for many avoidable accidents. Dr. Peter Angood, vice president and chief patient safety officer at the Joint Commission and co-director for the Joint Commission International Center for Patient Safety told participants on a June 21, 2007 telephone conference call that while communication issues for wrong-site surgery remain high (and for the first 10 years of data tracking most of the problems were strictly related to communication), what was seen in 2006 was procedural compliance—not following the Universal

Protocol—as the main cause of these wrong site surgeries. The three components of the Universal Protocol are: pre-operative verification process, marking the surgical site, and the time out just before the performance of the procedure. Clearly, not following the Universal Protocol has a communication component as well. Many factors contribute to communication-related patient safety issues. The following are a few of the most important, accompanied by associated patient safety strategies.

Traditionally Complex Hierarchical Approach When nurses perceive that a physician or other senior clinician is using an unsafe clinical approach, they traditionally access the **chain of command** to resolve the question. In many health care organizations, the chain of command is cumbersome, and it requires the nurse to contact two or three people at minimum, based on existing reporting relationships and formal interfaces between the nursing and medical staff.

If patient safety is at stake, the most knowledgeable resolution must be achievable in a short time, and there is no time for the traditional chain of command. Many successful malpractice suits have involved circumstances in which a question about care, or need for expert intervention, was not addressed promptly.

Analogously, the aviation industry recognized that hierarchy-associated communication failures were at the root of 70 to 80 percent of all the jet transport accidents over a twenty-year period. The industry made significant improvements in its poor safety record through a strategy called **crew resource management** (CRM) training. One important tenet of this strategy is that every team member has a responsibility to point out a perceived risk. This places the pilot and crew on equal footing when the safety of the craft or passengers is in question.

Empirical proof of the value of such team training in health care has been demonstrated only in small sample studies to date, but evidence from emergency department operations and obstetric settings is proving that it reduces risk.[23] Still another strategy from outside the health care industry comes from manufacturing assembly lines. Some health care organizations have "stop the line" policies that empower everyone to respectfully call out and stop any risky process or procedure until all preventable risks are removed.[24]

Simplifying the hierarchy is a key patient safety strategy to resolving patient safety-related communication issues. Empowering charge nurses to facilitate rapid resolution of care questions is one approach that some organizations are developing.

Personal Style of Providers Hierarchy has one additional undesirable ramification; it may legitimize intimidating behavior. One Joint Commission surveyor observed, for example, that intimidation is a significant factor in wrong-site surgery. (For more information, see the discussion of the Institute of Safe Medical Practice study on intimidation in Chapter Seven.)

Solutions to address an intimidating personal style range from simple training to disciplinary action within the parameters of appropriate human resource protocols and medical staff bylaws. Long-term resolution often requires the strong support of senior administrative and clinical leaders.

At the other end of the spectrum is lack of assertiveness by frontline staff. This timidity is sometimes a response to another provider's intimidating behavior. This unassertive personal style may be equally dangerous because important issues are simply never raised. When the nurse calls a physician in the middle of the night but does not clearly explain the reason for the call, the nurse may not get the response that is needed to address the urgent clinical issue at hand.

Situational Briefing Model: SBAR One means of facilitating clear communication between providers in crisis is a standardized situational briefing model. For example, the SBAR (for situation, background, assessment, and recommendation) Communication model is an approach used increasingly in health care settings to facilitate effective communication of issues in an impending crisis by support staff to physicians.[25]

A summary of key steps in the SBAR model follows.

1. Before using SBAR Communication and calling a physician, it is important to do the following:

   - Assess the patient.

   - Review the chart to determine the appropriate physician to call.

   - Know the admitting diagnosis.

   - Read most recent progress notes and assessments from clinicians on prior shifts.

   - Have available when speaking with the physician the medical record, patient allergies, medications, IV fluids, and laboratory and other diagnostic test results.

The following are the essential components of SBAR Communication:

2. Situation

   - State your name, position, and unit.

   - Say, "I am calling about . . . " (patient name and room number).

   - Say, "The problem I am calling about is..."

3. Background

   - State the admission diagnosis and date of admission.

   - State the pertinent medical history.

   - Give a brief synopsis of the treatment to date.

4. Assessment: Begin by outlining any changes from prior assessments. Include changes in the following:

- Mental status

- Pain

- Respiratory rate or quality; retractions or use of accessory muscles

- Pulse and blood pressure rate and quality; rhythm changes

- Skin color; wound drainage

- Neurological changes

- Gastrointestinal, genitourinary, or bowel changes (nausea, vomiting, diarrhea, increased or decreased output)

- Musculoskeletal weakness, joint deformity

5. Recommendation: State clearly what you think the patient needs urgently. Examples might include the following:

- Transfer the patient to ICU or PICU.

- Come to see the patient immediately.

- Talk to the patient or family about the code status.

- Ask for a consultant to see the patient now.

- Suggest tests or laboratory studies needed (for example, chest X-ray, arterial blood gases, EKG).

If a change in treatment is ordered, ask how often vital signs should be checked and when the physician would like to be contacted again. Document any changes in patient status, what intervention was completed, and whether or not the intervention was effective. Also document any contact you have had with the physician.

Lack of Common Language Barriers to communication might stem from language, ethnic, cultural, age, and gender differences. Even among providers with similar backgrounds, there might be a lack of familiarity with terminology, including jargon and abbreviations. (See the discussion of issues surrounding unclear medication orders in Chapter Seven.) One example of a solution to standardizing communication among providers is the National Institute of Child Health and Human Development's adoption of common definitions for fetal monitor interpretation.

The Joint Commission has built several strategies to improve provider communication into its **National Patient Safety Goals** (see Exhibit 3.1). These include readbacks on verbal orders and critical lab values; identification of patients using two sources; site marking using the word *yes* on operative or procedure sites; checklists to verify correct patient, site, and procedure; and calling a time-out before procedures and operations begin to ensure that all health care team members are comfortable that safety preparations for the procedure are complete.

EXHIBIT 3.1. The 2009 National Patient Safety Goals

The 2009 National Patient Safety Goals contain improvements emanating from the Standards Improvement Initiative (SSI), including a new numbering system and minor language changes for consistency. The new numbering format was designed to enable electronic sorting (for the new electronic editions of the manual) and to accommodate the addition of new requirements. Under the new numbering system, each requirement is assigned a six-digit number that designates its place in the chapter.

The 2009 National Patient Safety Goals can be accessed online at http://www.joint commission.org/NR/rdonlyres/31666E86-E7F4-423E-9BE8-F05BD1CB0AA8/0/09_NPSG_HAP.pdf.

Chapter: National Patient Safety Goals (NPSG) 2009

Program: Hospital

Goal 1: Improve the accuracy of patient identification.

    A. Use of two patient identifiers (revised NPSG.01.01.01)

    B. Not applicable to hospital (revised NPSG.01.02.01)

    C. Eliminate transfusion errors (revised NPSG.01.03.01)

Goal 2: Improve the effectiveness of communication among caregivers.

    A. Read back verbal orders (revised NPSG.02.01.01)

    B. Create a list of abbreviations not to use (revised NPSG.02.02.01)

    C. Timely report critical tests and critical results (revised NPSG.02.03.01)

    D. Not applicable

    E. Manage hand-off communications (revised NPSG.02.05.01)

Goal 3: Improve the safety of using medications.

    A. Not applicable

    B. Not applicable

    C. Manage look-alike, sound-alike medications (revised NPSG.03.03.01)

    D. Label medications (revised NPSG.03.04.01)

    E. Reduce harm from anticoagulation therapy (revised NPSG.03.05.01)

Goal 4: Not applicable

Goal 5: Not applicable

Goal 6: Not applicable

Goal 7: Reduce the risk of health care-associated infections.

A. Meet hand hygiene guidelines (revised NPSG.07.01.01)

B. Manage deaths or major loss of function resulting from infection as sentinel events (revised NPSG.07.02.01)

C. Prevent multi-drug resistant organism infections (revised NPSG.07.03.01)

D. Prevent central-line associated bloodstream infections (revisedNPSG.07.04.01)

E. Prevent surgical site infections (revised NPSG.07.05.01)

Goal 8: Accurately and completely reconcile medications across the continuum of care.

A. Compare current and newly ordered medications (revised NPSG.08.01.01)

B. Communicate medications to the next provider (revised NPSG.08.02.01)

C. Provide a reconciled medication list to the patient (revised NPSG.08.03.01)

D. Applies to settings in which medications are minimally used (revised NPSG. 08.04.01)

Goal 9: Reduce the risk of patient harm resulting from falls.

A. Implement a fall reduction program (revised NPSG.09.02.01)

Goal 10: Reduce the risk of influenza and pneumococcal disease in institutionalized older adults.

A. Not applicable to hospital (revised NPSG.10.01.01)

B. Not applicable to hospital (revised NPSG.10.02.01)

C. Not applicable to hospital (revised NPSG.10.03.01)

Goal 11: Reduce the risk of surgical fires.

A. Not applicable to hospital (revised NPSG.11.01.01)

Goal 12: Not applicable

Goal 13: Encourage patients' active involvement in their own care as a patient safety strategy.

A. Educate patient and family on reporting of safety concerns (revised NPSG.13.01.01)

Goal 14: Prevent health care associated pressure ulcers (decubitus ulcers).

A. Not applicable to hospital (revised NPSG.14.01.01)

(Continued)

EXHIBIT 3.1. *(Continued)*

Goal 15: Identify safety risks inherent in the organization's patient population.

    A.   Identify individuals at risk for suicide (revised NPSG.15.01.01)

    B.   Not applicable to hospital (revised NPSG.15.02.01)

Goal 16: Improve recognition and response to changes in a patient's condition.

    A.   Request assistance for a patient with a worsening condition (revisedNPSG.16.01.01)

Source: ©The Joint Commission 2008. Reprinted with permission.

Other principles that can help providers avoid communication breakdowns include the following:

- The fact that one person said and understands something doesn't mean that others did.

- Communication is not accomplished unless both parties are on the same page.

- A standard method of communication gives the right amount and type of useful information that is critical to patient safety.

- Assertiveness is necessary if you have concerns about safety, because patients are counting on you.

- It is necessary to ask clarifying questions if you don't understand.

- Information about problems and mistakes must be shared appropriately to help improve systems and prevent recurrence of medical errors.

Human Factors and Patient Safety

Mistakes made by humans are reportedly responsible for most serious accidents in non-health care industries. For example, they are responsible for 80 percent of industrial and airline accidents and 50 to 70 percent of nuclear power accidents.[26]

Human factors engineering, human factors analysis, and **ergonomics** are among the disciplines developed to address risk in non-health care industries. These fields of study have much to offer patient safety initiatives.

The goal of human factors engineering (HFE) is the design of tools, machines, and systems that take into account human capabilities and limitations. To support this goal, human factors engineers research psychological, social, physical, and biological characteristics. The risk management professional and others addressing patient safety can use HFE principles to analyze the relationship between human beings and

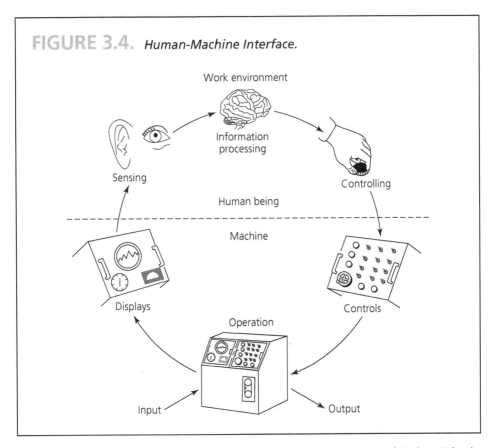

FIGURE 3.4. *Human-Machine Interface.*

Source: McCormick, E. J., and Sanders, M. S. *Human Factors in Engineering and Design,* 15th ed. (New York: McGraw-Hill, 1982), p. 14.

machines, the breakdown of which often plays a part in medical errors. Among patient safety-oriented approaches based on HFE principles are strategies that eliminate the use of dangerous shortcuts that lead to medical errors.[27] For example, staff must follow manufacturers' directions in testing defibrillators. Human factors analysis is the systematic study of the human-machine interface, with the intent of improving working conditions or operations. See Figure 3.4 for an illustration.

Ergonomics professionals study people at work and then design tasks, jobs, information, tools, equipment, facilities, and the working environment to be safe, effective, productive, and comfortable. In health care, understanding how humans interface with highly complex technology and the surrounding environment is crucial to preventing errors. For example, medication stations must have sufficient space around them for nurses to work without getting in each other's way at times that many medications are due, and there must be sufficient light for them to see what they are doing.

To evaluate the safety of a work environment and applying human factors and ergonomics principles, it is recommended that the following questions be asked:[28]

- What are the characteristics of the individual performing the work? Does the individual have the musculoskeletal, sensory, and cognitive abilities to do the required tasks? If not, can any of these gaps in ability be accommodated in the design of the task?

- What tasks are being performed, and what characteristics of those tasks might contribute to unsafe patient care? What in the nature of the tasks allows the individual to perform them safely or assume risks in the process?

- What tools and technology are being used to perform the tasks, and do they increase or decrease the likelihood of untoward events?

- Which aspects of the physical environment can be sources of error, and which promote safety? What in the environment ensures safe behavior or allows unsafe behavior to occur?

Human factors assessment should also include the following:

- Evaluating the work—what is the work-to-rest ratio?

- Evaluating the workers—what are their physical and mental capabilities?

- Evaluating the environment—are noise levels, lighting, and workflow potential barriers or facilitators to successful task completion? (See Figure 3.5.)

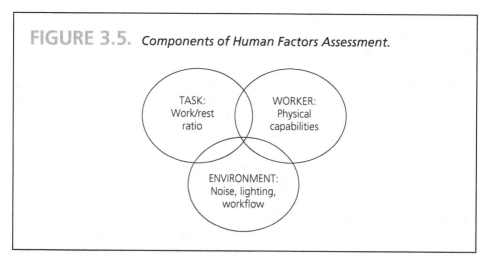

FIGURE 3.5. *Components of Human Factors Assessment.*

Source: Potter, P., and others. "Mapping the Nursing Process: A New Approach for Understanding the Work of Nursing." *Journal of Nursing Administration,* 2004, *34,* 101–109. Reprinted with permission.

Another illustration of the importance of evaluating the "human machine" is a recent study of the working memory of a nurse, which found that a nurse is thinking of an average of ten things simultaneously during a work shift.[29] It is not hard to imagine errors of omission when the typical human working memory becomes taxed if asked to hold more than a seven-digit telephone number.

The mental capabilities of health care workers should be evaluated, as should physical characteristics, such as these:

- Physical size (anthropometry)

- Endurance and fatigue (physiology)

- Force (biomechanics)

- Hand and arm coordination (kinesiology)

- Sensory characteristics (hearing, vision, touch)

Environmental issues that affect safe care delivery include the following:

- Noise, light (glare), vibration, temperature, force

- Work space or supplies layout

- Equipment-environment compatibility issues

The safety-related implications of the interface between humans and their physical environment are starkly illustrated by the potential for desensitization of the intensive care staff to the significance of one alarm in an environment in which numerous alarms are sounding all the time. This issue is clearly exacerbated by other employee-related safety issues such as fatigue. Biomedical and human factors engineers should seek solutions in each individual environment.

A simpler but equally important example of the unsafe effect that comes from ignoring human factors and ergonomics principles is the poorly designed paper towel dispenser found in many hospital bathrooms. The mechanism that holds clean towels is connected to the dirty paper towel disposal unit. This design makes it easy for freshly washed hands to be contaminated by dirty towels overflowing from the dispenser (see Photo 3.1).

Human factors and ergonomics principles can help prevent equipment-related medical errors. Proactively, these disciplines can also "mistake-proof" the environment so that providers will find it hard to do the wrong thing.

Systems Thinking

Another industrial concept useful to patient safety experts is the notion of "systems thinking." A system may be defined as a combination of elements organized in a structure to achieve goals and objectives. Systems can be seen as the interaction of many factors:

- Elements (personnel, equipment, procedures)

- Environment (physical, social, organizational)

- Inputs and outputs

- Structure

- Purpose and goals

The objectives of system evaluation must include reliability of the system and the human using it. System reliability depends on the reliability of each individual component. Components can be in series, parallel, or a combination of the two. Parallel systems are redundant and can increase reliability. Parallel redundancy is often helpful to human functions because the human component in a system is the least reliable.

The best way to assess the likelihood of human error is through a failure modes and effects analysis (FMEA). In FMEA, a team analyzes a process in detail to determine possible system failures and brainstorm solutions before the process goes into effect.[30]

Reporting

It is impossible to reduce medical errors and adverse outcomes by focusing only on any one aspect of the health care system. As Dr. Richard Cook's adaptation of David

PHOTO 3.1. *Poorly Designed Paper Towel Dispenser and Disposal Unit.*

Reprinted with permission. BJC Corporate Health Services, St. Louis, MO.

Woods's "blunt end/sharp end" model of accident causation implies, patient safety must be analyzed from the national level, where health policy and legislation are created, down to the front line of patient care delivery.

The aviation industry illustrates the positive effect of reporting on safety. In the thirty-some years since its inception in 1976 through December 2006, the Aviation Safety Reporting System (ASRS) has logged 723,427 confidential "incident reports, issued over 4,000 safety alert message and performed 60 major research studies on aviation safety. The reporting has increased 89 percent since 1988 and for calendar year 2006 the total report intake was almost 40,000 (39,964). Modeled off ASRS, the Patient Safety Reporting System was developed for the Veterans Affairs (VA) as an extension of their commitment to quality and safety.[31]

The AHRQ defines *near miss* as an event or situation that did not produce patient injury, but only because of chance.[32] " The effectiveness of a patient safety program can, to some degree, be measured by increased near-miss reporting because the data provide important insight into problems that need to be addressed.

The 2005 Patient Safety and Quality Improvement Act is a major step toward creation of a national voluntary system of incident reporting and medical error information. Key among the provisions of the act is the creation of patient safety organizations. These are responsible for developing a network of patient safety databases, which will collect and analyze voluntarily reported medical errors to use for identifying patient safety improvement strategies. The law ensures that what is reported cannot be used against the provider in court or in disciplinary proceedings. This provision is intended to encourage providers to identify and correct medical errors.

Event Reporting Systems

In addition to providing information about individual events, event reporting systems enable the organization to prioritize resources through analysis of trends. The greatest challenge has always been the fear of punishment. This single factor is often the cause of lost valuable information that could help address system problems.

It is important for the risk management professional to be aware of common **myths** or unspoken rules that staff members might use to justify not reporting. Some examples of unspoken rules include the following:[33]

"If I can make it right, it is not an error." If a dose was omitted, a nurse changes the subsequently scheduled drug administration scheduled to get back on track.

"If it's not my fault, it is not an error." Late administration or an omission occurred when the prescribed drug was not available on the unit.

"If another patient's needs are more urgent than accurate medication or treatment, it is not an error." Delayed or omitted medication delivery was caused by dealing with urgent situations arising with another patient.

"A clerical error is not a real medical error." A nurse on a previous shift failed to document drug administration or documented in the wrong section of the record.

"If my actions prevent something worse, it is not an error." Nurses know that they will be busy later due to planned admissions, discharges, and so on, and administer medication early rather than risk omitting doses.

"If everyone knows (or does it), it is not an error." Nurses sometimes give medications early or withhold medications at night so that patients suffering from sleep deprivation can rest uninterrupted for longer periods of time.

The most common barriers to reporting include lack of knowledge about what to report or how to report, lack of trust, extra work, skepticism about the likelihood that things will change, desire to forget the event, and fear of reprisal or punishment.[34]

The most important resource to counter obstacles to reporting is a just culture of safety. If providers feel confident that their senior managers will support them, they will point out risk and report medical errors. Other strategies to facilitate reporting include the following:

- New online reporting options that include telephone hotlines or that enable staff members to input medical error data more easily and facilitate analysis

- Paper reports (if they are used) that are readily accessible by all members of the health care team

- Highly effective reporting programs that keep the identity of the reporter confidential

Any risk-trending analysis must assess types of errors, people, systems, and processes involved, place and time of occurrence, and risk factors identified. This information should be shared with key stakeholders and used to drive improvements that reduce risk of harm to patients (and employees).

Joint Commission, State, and Federal Medical Error Reporting Requirements

After an adverse event occurs, the risk management professional and leadership must determine whether the event must be reported externally. The Centers for Medicaid and Medicare Services (CMS) has designated Patient Safety Indicators (for example, third-degree lacerations during a vaginal birth) as incidents that must be reported by licensed organizations receiving Medicare and Medicaid. Furthermore, organizations that are accredited by The Joint Commission must evaluate a **sentinel event** and determine whether to report it because **sentinel event reporting** to The Joint Commission is voluntary. The following are occurrences that are subject to review by the Joint Commission under the Sentinel Event Policy:[35]

- The event has resulted in an unanticipated death or major permanent loss of function, not related to the natural course of the patient's illness or underlying condition or

- The event is one of the following (even if the outcome was not death or major permanent loss of function unrelated to the natural course of the patient's illness or underlying condition):

- Suicide of any patient receiving care, treatment, and services in a staffed around-the-clock care setting or within 72 hours of discharge

- Unanticipated death of a full-term infant

- Abduction of any patient receiving care, treatment, and services

- Discharge of an infant to the wrong family

- Rape

- Hemolytic transfusion reaction involving administration of blood or blood products having major blood group incompatibilities

- Surgery on the wrong patient or wrong body part

- Unintended retention of a foreign object in a patient after surgery or other procedure

- Severe neonatal hyperbilirubinemia (bilirubin >30 milligrams/deciliter)

- Prolonged fluoroscopy with cumulative dose >1500 rads to a single field or any delivery of radiotherapy to the wrong body region or >25% above the planned radiotherapy dose[36]

In contrast, the following are examples of nonreviewable sentinel events under the Joint Commission's Sentinel Event Policy:

- Any "near miss" event

- Full or expected return of limb or bodily function to the same level as prior to the adverse event by discharge or within two weeks of the initial loss of said function

- Any sentinel event that has not affected an individual

- Medication errors that do not result in death or major permanent loss of function

- Suicide other than in an around-the-clock care setting or following elopement from such a setting

- A death or loss of function following a discharge against medical advice (AMA)

- Unsuccessful suicide attempts

- Minor degrees of hemolysis not caused by a major blood group incompatibility and with no clinical sequelae

Most health care organizations have established committees responsible for peer review that can be used if an event involves questionable practice or behavior of a licensed professional. These committees may consist of peers from medicine, nursing, pharmacy, or other allied health professions that review a case and determine the appropriateness of the provider's activities related to that case. The risk management professional should be formally accountable for referring an event to the organization's peer review committee as necessary.

State Requirements

Twenty-seven individual states have adverse **event reporting** programs, twenty-six of which are mandatory and one voluntary. Risk management professionals must stay current with the requirements of these programs and must facilitate staff members' understanding of their implications. Similarly, they must be aware of requirements and must facilitate federal reporting requirements such as those associated with the Safe Medical Devices Act (SMDA).

SUMMARY

The patient safety movement has brought numerous challenges and opportunities to risk management professionals. By collaborating with other members of the management team, risk management professionals can use these new strategies to solve the ongoing challenge of medical errors.

KEY TERMS

Active failure
Chain of command
Crew resource management
Ergonomics
Event reporting
Hospital-acquired infection
Human factors
Human factors engineering

Infection preventionist
Latent failure
National Patient Safety Goals
Near miss
Organizational culture
Sentinel event
Sentinel event reporting

ACRONYMS

AHRQ
AMA
CDC
CMS
CRM

FMEA
HFE
IOM
RCA
SBAR

NOTES

1. Orlikoff, J., W. Fifer, and H. Greeley, *Malpractice Prevention and Loss Control for Hospitals.* Chicago: American Hospital Association, 1981.

2. *Darling* v. *Charleston Community Memorial Hospital,* 33 Ill.2d 326, 211 N.E.2d 253 (1965), cert. denied, 383 U.S. 946 (1966).

3. Joint Commission Sentinel Event Glossary of Terms, 2005, http://www.joint commission.org/sentinalevents/se_glossary.htm (accessed November 11, 2008).

4. Kohn, L. T., Corrigan, J. M., and Donaldson, M. S. (eds.). *To Err Is Human: Building a Safer Health System.* Washington, D.C.: National Academy Press, 2000.

5. P.L. 109-41 (2005).

6. Leape, L. L., and others. "The Nature of Adverse Events in Hospitalized Patients: Results of the Harvard Medical Practice Study II." *New England Journal of Medicine,* 1991, *324,* 377–384; Thomas, E. J., Studdert, D. M., and Newhouse, J. P. "Costs of Medical Injuries in Utah and Colorado." *Inquiry,* 1999; *36,* 255–264.

7. Leape, L. L. "Institute of Medicine Error Figures Are Not Exaggerated." *Journal of the American Medical Association,* 2000; *284,* 95–97.

8. Bates, D. W., and others. "The Cost of Adverse Drug Events in Hospitalized Patients." *Journal of the American Medical Association,* 1997; *277,* 307–311.

9. Ibid.

10. Leape, L. L., and others. "Preventing Medical Injury." *Quality Review Bulletin,* 1993, *19,* 144–149.

11. Graves, N. "Economics and Preventing Hospital-Acquired Infection." *Emerging Infectious Diseases* [serial online], Apr. 2004, http://www.cdc.gov/ncidod/EID/vol10no4/02-0754.htm

12. Brennan, T. A., and others. "Harvard Medical Practice Study I." *Quality and Safety in Health Care,* 2004, *13,* 151–152.

13. Stone, P. W., Larson, E., and Kawar, L. N. "A Systematic Audit of Economic Evidence Linking Nosocomial Infections and Infection Control Interventions, 1990–2000." *American Journal of Infection Control,* 2002, *30,* 145–152.

14. Wenzel, R. P., and Edmond, M. B. "The Impact of Hospital-Acquired Bloodstream Infections." *Emerging Infectious Diseases,* 2001, *7,* http://www.cdc.gov/ncidod/eid/vol7no2/wenzel.htm

15. Agency for Healthcare Quality and Research. *Patient Safety Initiative: Building Foundations, Reducing Risk,* http://www.ahrq.gov/qual/pscongrpt/psini2.htm#RootCauses

16. Reason, J. "Human Error: Models and Management." *British Medical Journal,* 2000, *320,*768–770.

17. Cook, R. I., and Woods, D. D. "Operating at the Sharp End: The Complexity of Human Error." In M. S. Bogner (ed.), *Human Error in Medicine.* Hillsdale, N.J.: Erlbaum, 1994, pp 255–310, http://www.ctlab.org/documents/operatingatthesharp.pdf

18. Ibid.

19. Morath, J. Presentation at BJC Healthcare, Patient Safety Forum, Saint Louis, Mo., 2003.

20. Leape, L. L. Presentation at Missouri Hospital Association, Patient Safety Seminar, Saint Louis, Mo., 2002.

21. Marx, D. *Patient Safety and the "Just Culture": A Primer for Healthcare Executives.* New York: Columbia University, 2001, http://www.mers-tm.net/support/Marx_Primer.pdf

22. National Patient Safety Foundation. *Safety Culture,* http://search.freefind.com/find.html?id=28648537&t=s&nsb=&pageid=r&mode=ALL&s=definitions&query=Safety+Culture

23. Baker, D. P., Gustafson, S., Beaubien, J. M., Salas, E., and Barach, P. "Medical Team Training Programs in Health Care." In *2005 Advances in Patient Safety: From Research to Implementation* (Vol. 4, p. 260). Rockville, Md.: Agency for Healthcare Research and Quality, 2005, http://www.aptima.com/publications/2005_Baker_Gustafson_Beaubien_Salas_Barach.pdf

24. Ibid.

25. Kaiser Permanente's SBAR Communication model has been adapted with permission from copyrighted material of Kaiser Foundation Health Plan, Inc., California Regions.

26. Potter, P., and others. "Mapping the Nursing Process: A New Approach for Understanding the Work of Nursing." *Journal of Nursing Administration,* 2004, *34,* 101–109.

27. Gosbee, J. "Human Factors Engineering and Patient Safety." *Quality and Safety in Health Care,* 2002; *11,* 352–354, http://qhc.bmjjournals.com/cgi/content/full/11/4/353

28. Carayon, P., Alvarado, C., and Hundt, A. "Reducing Workload and Increasing Patient Safety Through Work and Workspace Design." Paper commissioned by the Institute for Medicine Commission on the Work Environment for Nurses and Patient Safety, 2003. The IOM Commission on the Work Environment for Nurses and Patient Safety, commissioned 9 separate working papers as background for the book "In Keeping Patients Safe: Transforming the Work Environment for Nurses."

29. Ibid.

30. Wolf, L. BJC HealthCare, Patient Safety Curriculum: Human Factors Module. 2004.

31. ASRS Reporting Brief. Aviation Safety Reporting System. Available at: http://asrs.arc.nasa.gov/overview/summary (accessed November 11, 2008).

32. AHRQ PSNet Patient Safety Network Glossary available at: F:\AHRQ\AHRQ Patient Safety Network Glossary.htm (accessed November 11, 2008).

33. Caleca, B. BJC HealthCare Patient Safety Curriculum: Importance of Reporting Module. 2004.

34. Leonard, M. Director of Patient Safety, Kaiser Permanente. Presentation. BJC HealthCare, Patient Safety Forum, Saint Louis, Mo. September 2002.

35. The Joint Commission. "Sentinel Event Policy, 2007," [http://www.jointcommis sion.org/NR/rdonlyres/F84F9DC6-A5DA-490F-A91F-A9FCE26347C4/0/ SE_chapter_july07.pdf]

36. Ibid.

SUGGESTED READINGS

Cook, Richard, *How Complex Systems Fail*. Cognitive Technologies Laboratory, University of Chicago, Revision D. Copyright © 1998, 1999, 2000 by R. I. Cook, MD, for CtL.

Cook, Richard; Woods, David; and Miller, Charlotte, *A Tale of Two Stories: Contrasting Views of Patient Safety*. Chicago: National Patient Safety Foundation, 1998.

Cook, Richard and Woods, David, "Operating at the Sharp End: The Complexity of Human Error," in *Human Error in Medicine*, ed., Marilyn Sue Bogner, Hillsdale, NJ: Lawrence Erlbaum Associates, 1994.

Cook, Richard; Render, Marta; and Woods, David (2000). "Gaps in the continuity of care and progress on patient safety." *British Medical Journal 320*: 791–4.

Cook, Richard (1999). *A Brief Look at the New Look in error, safety, and failure of complex systems*. (Chicago: CtL).

Woods, David and Cook, Richard (1999). "Perspectives on Human Error: Hindsight Biases and Local Rationality." In Durso, Nickerson, et al., eds., *Handbook of Applied Cognition*. (New York: Wiley) pp. 141–171.

CHAPTER

HEALTH CARE LEGAL CONCEPTS

PETER HOFFMAN

LEARNING OBJECTIVES

- To be able to describe the four basic elements of negligence
- To be able to identify the elements of attorney-client privilege and circumstances when it does not apply
- To be able to list the elements that are necessary for a consent to be "informed"
- To be able to identify two theories under which an acute care hospital can be held liable

Every person who works in the modern world of health care is likely to encounter a variety of legal concepts during his or her professional life. These might include general and professional negligence issues, contract and employment considerations, privacy concerns, and crucial questions such as when life-sustaining treatment may be withheld. The specific issues each person will face depend on his or her role in the health care field and also on the type of facility in which he or she works. Some issues that arise on a regular basis in an acute care hospital might be less or possibly more common in the context of an ambulance service, nursing home, or integrated delivery system. Given the plethora of legal concepts that routinely affect participants in the field of health care, it is useful to have at least some general knowledge of these concepts.

This chapter provides basic information about several legal concepts and describes specific issues that occur frequently in particular settings. You are encouraged to read other chapters for more detailed information about the concepts touched on here.

KEY CONCEPTS

- Negligence is the primary cause of civil action that health care providers face.

- Communication between a physician and that physician's patients are private and confidential.

- A physician's standard of care is measured by the degree of care and skill possessed by other physicians in the same or similar circumstances.

- A physician must obtain full, knowing, and voluntary general and informed consent from the patient concerning any nonemergency surgical procedure. Failure to obtain adequate informed consent can give rise to a claim, even if the procedure is performed appropriately.

- There are generally four different types of HMOs, categorized on the basis of their relationship with the medical providers. An HMO's exposure to liability depends largely on its organizational structure.

LEGAL ISSUES COMMON TO ALL HEALTH CARE PROVIDERS

There are many types of liability that affect the health care industry. We will discuss several of them here.

Negligence

Negligence is the primary civil cause of action that health care providers face. A negligence action can involve a claim of general liability or one of professional liability.

In either circumstance, there are four basic elements in any cause of action that alleges negligence.

1. *Duty:* One person must be under a **duty** to another person (or to society) before negligence becomes an issue. In the context of professional liability, duty usually applies when the provider undertakes to care for the patient.

2. *Breach of duty:* The person under the duty must **breach the duty** in some way (such as allowing a hazard to exist or failing to meet the required standard of care) to allow negligence to attach.

3. *Cause of injury:* The plaintiff must suffer an injury as a result of the defendant's breach of duty. If the injury did not arise out of the breach of the duty or the plaintiff cannot prove causation, the **cause of action** fails.

4. *Damages:* The plaintiff must be able to show legally cognizable **damages** as a result of the injury sustained. Damages typically include pain and suffering (sometimes capped by tort reform efforts), medical expenses, lost wages, emotional distress, and loss of consortium or companionship.

General Liability **General liability** issues for health care providers typically include claims that allege negligence for hazards in the environment and nonprofessional judgments and actions.[1] General liability primarily involves premises liability, as many claims entail injuries arising out of the maintenance of premises, including slips and falls, but it can also involve causes of action alleging defamation, employment issues, and slander, to name a few. Claimants asserting general liability causes of action may include patients, physicians and other providers, family members, visitors, or even trespassers.

All four basic elements apply in any claim for negligence. The only real difference between medical professional and general liability (negligence) is in the manner of proof. A claim for general negligence does not normally require that an expert witness testify as to the duty that a reasonably prudent person owes to another person or to show that a breach in that duty occurred (unless the matter is unduly technical).

Medical Professional Liability Also referred to as malpractice liability, **medical professional liability** involves claims that allege professional negligence for patient care activities. Typically, these causes of action involve allegations of negligent acts or omissions of health care providers or employees that result in injury to the patient. Patients, or their legal representatives, may allege separate theories of negligence against treating physicians, health care entities, nurses, and other employees.

To state a successful cause of action for medical negligence, a plaintiff must demonstrate all four elements of negligence. In the context of professional negligence, the duty is often referred to as the **standard of care**. Most arguments during litigation surround the proper standard of care and whether the standard was breached. Another focus is often whether the alleged substandard care was the cause of the plaintiff's injuries. Expert testimony is required to show the appropriate standard of care, to establish whether it was breached, and to show that the plaintiff's injuries were caused by the breach of the standard of care.

Concept of Standard of Care   A physician owes a duty of care to his or her patients to conform to certain standards of reasonable medical care.[2] Generally, a physician's standard of care is measured by the degree of care and skill possessed by other physicians in the same or similar circumstances.[3] The standard of care requires, among other things, that a physician remain up-to-date regarding medical developments and advancements, secure a careful history, perform a comprehensive examination, arrive at an appropriate diagnosis, recommend and implement appropriate therapies, and refer for consultation when indicated.[4]

Historically, the standard for the adequate level of care rendered by a physician was determined by the prevailing standard of care practiced by physicians in the physician's community.[5] This is known as the "locality rule."[6] Because physicians were reluctant to give expert testimony against a fellow physician in the same community, many states have modified this rule.[7] As a result, some states have implemented either the "similar locality" standard or the "national" standard.[8] Note that physicians who specialize in a particular area of medicine and who hold themselves out as specialists have been required to possess a greater level of skill in that specialty than a general practitioner would.[9]

To prevail in a medical negligence action, a plaintiff must affirmatively prove the relevant recognized standard of medical care exercised by other physicians and that the defendant physician departed from that standard when treating the plaintiff, causing the plaintiff to sustain injury or damage. Generally, it is necessary for the plaintiff to have expert witness testimony concerning the standard of care applicable to the defendant.

Expert Testimony   Some states require specific qualifications and credentials before a party can testify as an expert witness in medical malpractice cases. Generally, a person shall not give expert medical testimony unless licensed as a health professional. To determine if a witness is qualified to be an expert, the court will typically consider the witness's education and professional training, the witness's area of specialization, and the length of time the witness has been engaged in the active clinical practice or instruction of the health profession or specialty. In addition, there are two general standards, or tests, that the court will apply to consider whether an expert witness's testimony will be admissible in court: the *Daubert* standard and the *Frye* standard. In federal and many state cases, Daubert defines the standard for admitting expert scientific testimony. According to *Daubert,* the proposed testimony must be supported by appropriate validation.[10] In other states, *Frye* is the standard that applies. Under the *Frye* test, an expert's opinion is admissible if the principle or method underlying that opinion is generally accepted by scientists active in the relevant field.[11] State laws should be reviewed to determine the applicable qualifications and standard applied in the specific jurisdiction.

In any medical negligence case, physician experts must testify that their expert opinions are based on a reasonable degree of medical certainty. Expert testimony fails to meet this reasonable certainty requirement when the plaintiff's expert testifies that the alleged negligence "possibly" caused or "could have" caused the plaintiff's injury, that such negligence "could very properly account for the injury," or even that it is "very highly probable" that the defendant's negligence caused the poor result.[12]

Negligence Per Se   The court may adopt a statute as defining the standard of care in a negligence action if the court determines that the purpose of the statute was to protect the class of persons to which the plaintiff belongs from the type of risk that has ensued.[13] The violation of a statute can be treated as **negligence per se** if it is unexcused.[14] This allows the plaintiff to handily prove the existence of a duty and the breach of the duty, but the plaintiff must still prove injury and damages.

Privity   Generally, **privity** refers to a derivative interest founded on a contract or connection between two parties. It can also be thought of as a mutuality of interest. In the context of potential liability of a health care provider stemming from the care of a patient, the concept of privity usually applies when a party other than that patient—or that patient's spouse or parent (of a minor patient)—claims that the health care provider also caused that other party injury and seeks to recover for this claimed injury.

Duty of Health Care Providers to Third Parties (Nonpatients)   To sustain a professional negligence cause of action against a physician, the plaintiff must normally be a patient. A patient is defined as a natural person who receives, or should have received, health care from a licensed health care provider under a contract, express or implied.[15] Most states have implemented the general rule that a physician does not owe a professional duty to a nonpatient or a third party. Several jurisdictions have held that a hospital does not owe a duty to protect a nonpatient who is present in the emergency room from fainting[16] and that a physician does not owe a duty to a third-party nonpatient for injuries arising from the use of prescription medication by the physician's patient.[17] Some states have limited this "no duty" rule by recognizing a duty to nonpatient bystanders when the patient poses a danger of harm to an identifiable third party;[18] when the patient's behavior must be controlled to prevent a danger to a third party;[19] or when the bystander becomes a participant in the treatment of a patient—for example, being used by the medical staff to hold the patient down.[20]

In contrast, a limited number of states have held that medical professionals have a duty to third parties in two circumstances: when doctors exert control over a patient and when a doctor is aware of threats against specific, identifiable third parties. Many courts have even concluded that physicians owe a duty to injured third parties and the general public to warn their patients about side effects of prescription medication (such as drowsiness).[21]

Due to the different approaches taken by various states, it is important to review state laws to determine the approach followed by the specific jurisdiction.

Contractual Liability of Doctor to Patient An agreement to provide medical care to a patient can be expressed or implied. When a patient seeks the assistance and treatment of a physician and the physician accepts the patient, they enter into an implied contract that the physician will treat the patient. Such a contract can only be terminated by the physician when the physician gives proper notice to the patient. The patient, of course, may terminate the agreement at any time. When an implied contract is formed, the physician does not guarantee the success of treatment or that beneficial results will occur but only that the physician possesses, and will carefully apply, professional skills that are ordinarily possessed by general practitioners in the physician's locality.[22] General reassurances by the physician to the patient are considered to be an expression of opinion or hope and do not amount to an expressed contract.[23] These reassurances are considered therapeutic and do not constitute a basis for an express contract.

To be enforceable, an explicit contract must be expressed and must be supported by consideration. Physicians and patients can enter into express written contracts regarding the care provided. Such contracts are not usual but can include various treatment plans, the likelihood of success, and even the physician's promise to cure. Traditionally, courts have respected a physician's freedom to contract as the physician chooses.[24] However, once a contract is formed, a plaintiff might have a cause of action for breach of contract, in addition to other potential claims (such as medical malpractice), if the outcome of the treatment is not what was promised.

Informed Consent The physician-patient relationship is a consensual one. For more than a century, courts have required the patient's consent prior to any touching, examination, or medical procedure. Consent is traditionally defined as a person's voluntary agreement to do something proposed by another person. There are two kinds of consent: general consent (to allow touching, examination, and noninvasive procedures) and **informed consent** (to allow the performance of an invasive procedure). If the procedure is an invasive procedure that carries a material risk of harm, the patient's informed consent will probably be required. If the touching is without consent at all, the provider might be liable for battery. Generally, if the patient appropriately consents to a procedure, the patient cannot hold the physician liable unless the physician fails to perform the surgery according to the applicable medical standards (malpractice). Therefore, a physician must obtain full, knowing, and voluntary general and informed consent from the patient concerning any nonemergency surgical procedure.

Informed consent requires more from a physician than simply having the patient sign a form. Health care providers must ensure that patients are aware of the diagnosis, the benefits of the proposed treatment, the material risks of the treatment, alternative options to the proposed treatment, and possible consequences of declining the treatment. This information must be communicated to the patient so that the patient clearly understands it.[25] Once properly informed, the patient can make an intelligent decision regarding the course of treatment, regardless of whether the patient chooses rationally.

Failure to obtain adequate informed consent can give rise to a claim, even if the procedure is performed appropriately.[26] In most states, a patient's legal cause of action in a lack-of-consent case is premised on the plaintiff's ability to prove that the defendant failed to reveal a significant risk that materialized and caused the plaintiff to suffer adverse consequences[27] and that had the potential risk been disclosed, a reasonable person would not have consented to the treatment or procedure.[28] Although a physician does not generally have a duty to disclose remote risks,[29] a duty may arise if the plaintiff expressly requests that all known complications be revealed.[30]

There are three generally accepted exceptions to the rule that informed consent is required. First, health care providers may assume that informed consent would be obtained in emergency situations if the emergency did not exist.[31] This, of course, does not give the provider the right to assume consent in the face of a prior refusal. Also, traditionally, it is the treating physician, not the hospital, who has the duty to obtain informed consent.[32] However, courts have held that a hospital may be held liable when members of its staff neglect to inform the physician that the patient has withdrawn consent prior to treatment.[33] Furthermore, hospitals that sponsor or permit experimental procedures may be liable when they fail to ensure that informed consent according to the research protocol is obtained.[34]

Some parties are unable to consent. As a general rule, minors are deemed incapable of providing effective consent to medical treatment. Accordingly, the physician must obtain consent from the parent or guardian before proceeding with any examination or treatment of the minor. There are exceptions to the requirements of consent by a parent or guardian. In certain emergency situations, no consent is required prior to treatment of the minor. Medical, dental, and health services may be rendered to minors of any age without the consent of the parent or legal guardian when, in the physician's judgment, an attempt to secure consent would result in a delay of treatment that would increase the risk to the minor's life or health or when the minor is emancipated. Minors may consent to the examination or treatment of their minor children in most states.

Contractual Negotiation and Approval

Entering into a successful contract requires both parties to think about what the transaction is really about. It involves addressing many details beyond the price of a product or service. The particulars in any specific instance or facility will differ, but the material described here gives a general picture of the negotiation and approval process. As a starting point, it is helpful to ask several questions, such as these:

- Who will provide the goods or services, and who will provide payment?

- What exactly is each party required to do?

- When will each party be providing the goods or services, and when will payment be made?

- Where will the services be performed, or where will the goods be delivered?

- Why is each party performing these obligations, and why is the deal important to each party?

- How will satisfactory performance or delivery be measured?

As you begin to determine the terms of the proposed arrangement, it is often helpful to consult with your corporate counsel. Generally, most corporate counsels have developed several standard contracts that can help expedite the negotiating process while ensuring that the health care facilities' interests are effectively protected.

Typically, each party will have a starting position and an idea about what it wants to get out of the agreement. Certain points might be very important to one party and less important to the other. It is essential to negotiate a contract that clearly defines the relationship between the parties; characterizes each party's expectations, rights, and responsibilities (including payments terms, warranties, limitations on advertising, and confidentiality); and describes what should happen if something were to go wrong (for example, termination for breach, indemnification clause, insurance). These clear designations allow both parties to have an adequate understanding regarding each party's intentions, thereby allowing the parties to predict what to anticipate. This is an important element regardless of whether the contract is performed over the course of a few hours or a few years.

Health care providers and administrators should work together with corporate counsel and professional staff to draft and negotiate the agreement. Negotiating a successful contract often involves discussions within the health care facility and consultation with other departments and committees. It is essential for every member of the health care facility who negotiates a proposed contract to consider the relationship of the product to the overall strategic goal of the facility. In drafting or negotiating a contract, corporate counsel should work with management to ensure that the contractual obligations are consistent with the legal obligations of the health care facility and that the risk of liability and other legal consequences are fully understood by the key players and ultimate decision makers. In the contracting process, it is important that the anticipated benefits of the contractual relationship outweigh both the financial and legal risks to the health care facility.

All health care facilities should have an approval process, which must be followed when entering into any contractual agreement. For major contracts (in which the dollar amount is greater than $100,000), both corporate counsel and the financial department should be contacted before negotiations begin to guarantee a coordinated and prompt approach to contract review and approval.

For all purchasing contracts and agreements, the health care facility's purchasing department should be contacted before the acquisition process begins to ensure that subsequent negotiations conform with the competitive bid process and do not conflict with any new or existing agreements, contracts, or understandings. The purchasing department will also ensure that the process is consistent with the facility's commitment to group purchasing memberships and the facility's strategy.

The purpose of legal review is to provide advice and counsel concerning the proposed contract, both to ensure that the proposed terms and conditions comply with the applicable law and to identify and minimize significant legal risks.

The legal department should help negotiate and draft the contract and should identify legal issues so that the business decision makers can evaluate the risks or benefits of the arrangement to finalize the contract. Approval of a contract should be withheld only if there is a significant issue as to whether the terms and conditions of agreement comply with the law.

Most proposed contracts should also be reviewed by the health care facility's finance and administrative departments so that they can evaluate issues relating to financial liability, cash flow, and operational matters; whether the contract makes good business sense; and whether it is consistent with the facility's objectives and policies.

The finance department would generally withhold approval of the contract only if there were a significant concern about its financial liability. The purpose of an administrative review is to ensure that contracts make good business sense and are consistent with the health care facility's objectives and policies.

Once a contract has been reviewed by the appropriate departments and offices and all necessary changes and revisions have been made based on that review, the contract is ready for final approval and execution. Each of the departments and offices required to review and approve the contract should indicate final approval of the contract by signing the contract approval form. All copies of the contract should be signed and dated by the authorized health care facility representative.

Once the copies have been signed by all parties, copies of the contract should be forwarded by the originator to the appropriate authorized health care facility representatives for signature. Note that if any party makes additional changes, the contract must be reviewed again by everyone who previously had signed off. In certain cases, it may be preferable that the copies of the contract first be executed by the authorized health care facility representative and then executed by the other parties.

Once a contract has been fully executed, a copy should be forwarded by the originator to other appropriate parties, the health care facility's contract originator (or that person's department), the office of legal affairs or contract administrator (if applicable), the finance department, and the purchasing department. Fully executed contracts need to be safeguarded and maintained in accordance with the state's or the facility's records retention requirements.

When a contract comes up for renewal, the originator should contact the administrator and the purchasing department (where appropriate) at least ninety days before the expiration date, particularly if any automatic renewal rights or options are involved. In all cases, the specific contract language for renewal or termination should be reviewed to ensure compliance. All amendments, modifications, or renewals of the contract should go through the same approval process that was followed for the original contract.

If serious performance problems arise at any time during the contract term, the health care facility employees involved should immediately communicate their concerns regarding performance or termination to the contract administrator or the legal department. All performance problems and efforts to resolve these problems should be carefully documented by the health care facility employees.

Information Release: Privilege and Privacy Issues

There are several levels of information release that need to be carefully examined.

Peer Review Information Many state legislatures have agreed, at least to some extent, with the view that because the practice of medicine requires a level of expertise that can be reviewed only by other medical professionals, the medical profession should police its own activities through peer review organizations. Peer review involves the evaluation of physicians' performances by other physicians in terms of quality of care and appropriateness of decision making. Review committees are established by hospitals and used to investigate candidates for clinical privileges and to monitor the existing medical staff.

Many states have enacted statutes designed to protect the peer review process and the individuals on the peer review committee. The legislature has recognized that patients need protection from physicians who deviate from an appropriate professional standard of care. Simultaneously, the legislature has acknowledged that health care providers want limited involvement with peer review committees due to concerns that they will be held liable for the ultimate decision rendered by the board. As a result, many states have implemented peer review protections that grant immunity to members of the peer review committee and protective status to documents prepared during the peer review process. This type of legislation ensures that members of peer review organizations are at liberty to speak without restraint about controversial matters such as quality assurance, medical staff credentials, and qualifications. Review your state laws to determine the content of the statute and the extent of its protections in your specific jurisdiction.

Typically, individuals who supply information to peer review committees are protected from criminal and civil liability. This immunity, however, is not absolute. An individual will not be granted immunity if the information reported is unrelated or irrelevant to the peer review committee's purpose and scope. The individual is also not protected if the information reported was false and the individual knew or had reason to believe it was false or if the individual's appearance before the peer review board was motivated by malice.

Documents used and information recorded by peer review committees are not subject to discovery or admissible as evidence in a civil action against the health care provider if the civil action stems from a matter that is the subject of the committee's review. This protection also is not absolute. Peer review protection does not apply and the document may be disclosed in accordance with applicable law if the document used by the peer review committee can be obtained from its original source.

In addition, those testifying before a peer review committee cannot be compelled to testify at civil hearings regarding evidence that was produced or relied on at the proceedings; conversations, opinions, or evaluations discussed during the proceedings; or testimony before a peer review protection committee or opinions formed as a result of committee hearings. However, a person in attendance is not immune from testifying at other civil proceedings as to personal knowledge and information learned outside the peer review proceeding,

Generally, peer review protection is granted to the following licensed health care providers: physicians, dentists, podiatrists, chiropractors, optometrists, physiologists, pharmacists, registered nurses, practical nurses, and physical therapists. Health care facility administrators, corporations, or organizations acting as health care facilities and committees evaluating the quality of health care and credentialing are also covered.

Patient Confidentiality Communications between a physician and his or her patients are private and confidential. Individuals in need of medical attention greatly benefit from being able to discuss their medical situation with health care professionals without the concern that such information might be disclosed to others. A patient's disclosure of information pertaining to that patient's illness will help the physician provide appropriate medical treatment. Due to this benefit, most states have implemented legislation that provides protections for confidential medical information obtained by the physician.[35] This protection generally takes the form of the physician-patient privilege. This privilege creates a confidential atmosphere intended to prevent the embarrassment that patients might face upon the disclosure of their illnesses and encourages patients to disclose all possible information pertaining to their illnesses, thereby enabling the physician to render effective diagnoses and treatments for their patients.[36]

The improper disclosure of information by physicians violates state confidentiality statutes, which generally provide criminal or civil penalties or civil causes of action for the inappropriate release of a patient's confidential information. In addition, for hospitals and physicians, the improper disclosure of medical information may subject them to civil liability, including breach of contract, invasion of privacy, intentional infliction of emotional distress, breach of confidential relationship, defamation, and negligence.[37]

Under federal law, wrongful disclosure of protected health information is a federal crime. Any person who knowingly and in violation of federal law uses or causes to be used a unique health identifier, obtains individually identifiable health information relating to an individual, or discloses individually identifiable health information to another person shall be punished depending on the nature and the scope of the offense. Individually identifiable information includes any information created or received by a health care provider that relates to an individual's physical or mental health, health care, or payment for health care, and identifies or could reasonably be used to identify the individual. The penalties begin with an initial penalty of a $50,000 fine and imprisonment of not more than one year, or both. If the offense is committed under false pretenses, the fine is increased to $100,000 and imprisonment is increased to five years. If the offense is committed with the intent to sell or transfer or use the individually identifiable health information for commercial advantage, personal gain, or malicious harm, then the fine is increased to not more than $250,000 and imprisonment of not more than ten years.[38]

It should be noted that exceptions to the physician-patient relationship arise in personal injury cases and criminal cases. Where the patient is the plaintiff in a personal injury case, defense counsel is entitled to obtain the plaintiff patient's medical records and depose the patient's physicians. In criminal matters, no physician-patient privilege exists.

AIDS- and HIV-Related Issues

The testing and confidentiality issues related to AIDS (acquired immunodeficiency syndrome) and HIV (human immunodeficiency virus) are numerous. Strict adherence is necessary for patient safety and to decrease an organization's exposure to liability.

HIV Testing Generally, an HIV test cannot be performed without the patient's informed written consent. Before consent can be given, a health care provider must explain the nature of the test, including its purpose, potential uses, limitations, and meaning of the results. Pretest counseling must be made available regarding HIV prevention, exposure, and transmission.

Once results have been obtained, the physician or physician's designee must make a good faith effort to inform the patient of the test results. Medical standards may require that positive test results be confirmed before they are revealed to the patient. Upon receiving the results, the patient must be afforded the opportunity for immediate, individual, face-to-face counseling regarding the significance of the test results and measures for preventing HIV transmission. Counseling should also include the benefits of locating and counseling individuals who might have exposed the patient to HIV.

Partial waivers of the voluntary HIV testing requirements are granted in limited circumstances. In medical emergencies, when the patient is unable to grant consent, or if the patient withholds consent and the HIV-related test result is medically necessary to provide appropriate emergency care, the patient must be provided only with notice of the test results and posttest counseling. In addition, individuals who donate organs, body parts, tissues, or semen for use in medical research, therapy, transfusion, or transplantation and test negative for HIV do not need to receive notice of their test results or be given posttest counseling. However, the donor must give written consent to the test and have the opportunity to receive pretest counseling. Notice of a negative test result must also be given to any individual who asks to be provided with such results.

To protect the welfare of health care providers and those who have rendered assistance to an HIV-positive patient, various exceptions to voluntary HIV testing have been implemented. A patient's existing blood sample can be subjected to involuntary HIV-related testing to protect the welfare of health care providers and emergency medical personnel. However, health care providers who rendered care must obtain certification from a physician, other than from themselves or their employers, that they have had a significant exposure to HIV. A significant exposure is defined as the direct contact with blood or bodily fluids in a manner that according to the most current guidelines of the Centers for Disease Control and Prevention is capable of transmitting HIV. This certification must be obtained within seventy-two hours of the exposure. The certifying physician must also provide the health care provider with an opportunity to undergo voluntary HIV-related testing as outlined previously.

A copy of the written certification must be provided to the physician of the individual whose HIV test is sought or to the institutional health care provider in possession of the individual's available blood. The physician or institutional health care provider must make a good faith effort to notify the individual, or that individual's substituted decision maker, of the certification and must request consent to an HIV test within twenty-four hours of the request for HIV testing. If the individual agrees to the test, written consent must be obtained and the individual must be afforded the opportunity for pretest counseling. If the individual does not agree to an HIV test or cannot be located, an entry must be made on the individual's medical records to that effect. If the individual's blood has already been obtained, that blood may be tested, provided that the person was given the opportunity to consent or refuse to consent to the HIV test. Involuntary HIV testing will not proceed unless the health care provider requests testing and submits to baseline testing.

The patient must be given notice of the test result and the same opportunity for appropriate posttest counseling as afforded in voluntary HIV-related testing. The health care provider may be notified of the patient's test results only if the provider's own baseline HIV test is negative.

Confidentiality of HIV-Related Information

Medical records and other tests that reveal whether an individual has contracted AIDS or HIV have been the basis of considerable litigation and legislation. Many of the confidentiality issues discussed previously have arisen in the context of AIDS. Generally, physicians, their employees, and agents are required to maintain the confidentiality of all HIV-related information. This rule applies whether the information is disclosed voluntarily, involuntarily, or pursuant to a court order. Patients whose HIV or AIDS status has been improperly disclosed by health care providers have causes of action under the common law theories of breach of contract, invasion of privacy, intentional infliction of emotional distress, breach of confidential relationship, defamation, and negligence.[39]

Generally, this duty of confidentiality protects only the patient and not the treating physician. The right of privacy regarding HIV status has not been extended to treating physicians who are HIV-positive. Courts have permitted hospitals to notify patients who participated in invasive procedures that the physician involved in their care was HIV-positive.[40] This disclosure, however, is limited, as the hospital is not permitted to release the physician's name to the patients. The hospital is, however, entitled to release the physician's name and HIV status to certain colleagues with whom the infected physician might have performed surgery and to those who were in that physician's training program. It should be noted that physicians who are patients are protected by the duty of confidentiality. Courts have concluded that hospitals owe a duty of confidentiality to physicians who are patients, so hospitals must take reasonable precautions with physicians' medical records when they are being treated in the hospital. Physicians who are being treated for AIDS have an expectation of privacy that their AIDS diagnoses will not become a matter of public knowledge. This changes, however, once the physician becomes a treating physician and is performing invasive procedures on a patient.[41]

States approach confidentiality as it relates to AIDS in different ways. Some states have strict confidentiality laws to protect the privacy of HIV-infected individuals. HIV status is a private matter, and there are enforceable civil penalties for disclosure of another individual's HIV status.[42] Other states take a less rigid approach regarding confidentiality. Some require reporting of HIV status to public health authorities. This reporting includes the revelation of all new HIV diagnoses, including diagnoses involving the status of physicians.[43] Review your state laws to determine the approach taken in your jurisdiction.

Attorney-Client Privilege

This privilege is an essential component of our legal system. It promotes full communication between an attorney and a client. This assures clients that conversations with their attorneys will not be disclosed to others. The privilege belongs to the client, and the attorney must hold client communications in the strictest of confidence.

The attorney-client privilege has the following characteristics:

- The party seeking the protection of the privilege must be an actual or prospective client.

- The communication must be between a client and an attorney acting as counsel for the client.

- The communication must be made in confidence, outside the presence of third parties.

- The purpose of the communication must be to secure or provide an opinion of law or legal assistance.

- The privilege must be asserted by one holding the privilege. The privilege does not automatically attach.

- The privilege is easily lost or "waived" by improper disclosures to third parties.

The privilege does not attach to communications in furtherance of an ongoing or prospective illegal activity. In addition, the privilege does apply when attorneys defend themselves against charges of wrongful misconduct brought by clients.

Health care providers should be mindful of maintaining the attorney-client privilege in varying circumstances, including the following:

- In anticipation of potential litigation

- During the investigation of past conduct that may raise legal concerns

- Seeking advice on structuring new ventures (for example, a proposed merger)

- Peer review and risk management (such as quality improvement or malpractice defense)

- Any other sensitive issue where legal input might be helpful and confidentiality is critical

For the attorney-client privilege to protect oral communications, it is best to have an attorney participate directly in the discussion. Therefore, counsel should be present when the purpose of any meeting is to obtain or discuss legal advice or to gather information needed to obtain legal advice or assistance. Only employees who have a "need to know" should attend such meetings, and nonclient third parties should not attend. Be careful not to divulge privileged communications in meeting minutes or other memoranda. Do not discuss attorney-client information on mobile telephones or in public places (such as elevators) where you might be overheard.

The attorney-client privilege may be invoked in memoranda, correspondence, and other written communications by adhering to the following guidelines:

- Identify and assert the privilege on the document—that is, mark the document "attorney-client-privileged communication."

- Send the document to or from your attorney, and limit distribution to a need-to-know basis. Identify all recipients on the document, with no blind copies.

- Avoid the attachment of unprivileged material or written notes on the document.

- Treat the document in a confidential manner, and store it in a secure place.

- Information contained on computer disks, hard drives, and backup systems may also be protected by the attorney-client privilege.

Executives may communicate legal advice received from counsel to other executives or employees who have a need to know without destroying the privilege by identifying the communication as legal advice, limiting communication to counsel's advice, not including underlying facts, and segregating legal discussions from other topics.

When there are disclosures, take immediate action by consulting counsel, telling the recipient that disclosure was inadvertent, requesting return of any written materials, and confirming these steps in writing, if appropriate.

The attorney-client privilege can and should be invoked to safeguard the health care provider's interest whenever legal questions arise. Contact an attorney with any questions regarding the attorney-client privilege.

Employment Issues

A domain or area representing significant risks is identified as "human capital." Human capital risks are those associated with people and their employment (perceived and real) and include harassment, discrimination, practicing impaired physicians, and credentialing, to name just a few.

Respondeat Superior Liability In Latin, **respondeat superior** means "let the master answer." In the context of an acute care facility or hospital, it is a legal doctrine under which an employer may be liable for wrongful acts of an employee that are done within the scope of that employee's job. Under this theory, the hospital is vicariously liable for the actions of its employees, whom the hospital had a duty to supervise. Essentially, to bring an action under this theory, the plaintiff must establish both that the health care provider was a servant or agent of the hospital and that the act or omission of the health care provider occurred in the scope of employment. If, however, the health care provider is an independent contractor, the theory of respondeat superior is not applicable.[44]

Nondiscrimination Laws

Laws at the federal, state, and local levels prohibit discrimination against employees on the basis of race, sex, age, disability, sexual orientation, national origin, and religion. The ultimate goal of these laws is to prevent discrimination by providing equal opportunities in all facets of employment relationships. These nondiscrimination laws require that employers do not take any actions that might infringe on an employee's terms of employment based on that person's status as a member of a protected class.

Federal laws have been implemented in an attempt to rectify past discrimination and prevent future discrimination. These laws include Title VII of the Civil Rights Act of 1964, the Age Discrimination in Employment Act (ADEA), and the Americans with Disabilities Act (ADA). All health care facilities are bound by the terms of these federal laws.

Title VII of the Civil Rights Act of 1964 is the heart of antidiscrimination legislation. It prohibits harassment and discrimination of an employee based on that employee's race, gender, and national origin. Prohibitions against sexual harassment also fall under this act. Title VII applies to employers, employment agencies, and labor organizations that have fifteen or more employees during twenty or more calendar weeks in either the current or previous calendar year. It should be noted that in limited situations, Title VII allows employers to make employment decisions that are based on religion, sex, and national origin when there is a legitimate work-related requirement that is reasonably necessary for the operation of that specific industry (for example, hiring only women for the position of women's bathroom attendant).[45]

To assert a Title VII claim, plaintiffs must show that they are members of a protected class and were treated differently than similarly situated people from another class. The burden then shifts to the employer to convey a justifiable, nondiscriminatory basis for the decision that has been viewed as discriminatory. If the employer is able to articulate such grounds, the burden shifts back to the employees to establish that the employer's discriminatory reason was the primary basis for the decision made. In cases where plaintiffs assert that a particular employer engaged in the practice of discrimination against members of a protected class, the plaintiffs must prove that they were deterred from applying for a job or were not hired for a job because of the employer's discriminatory practices. Most federal courts have determined that supervisors may not be held individually liable under Title VII.[46] However, individual liability for supervisors is allowed under many states' discrimination laws. Review state laws to determine the liability laws applicable to supervisors in the specific jurisdiction.

It is an employer's legal obligation to take prompt and appropriate action in response to a complaint alleging a violation of Title VII. Managers confronted with a complaint based on race, gender, or national origin discrimination should contact human resource departments for assistance. The complaint should be investigated in a timely and thorough fashion. Every health care facility has implemented various policies regarding nondiscrimination. All individuals should familiarize themselves with the reporting and investigatory structures set forth in each policy.

The Age Discrimination in Employment Act forbids the discrimination of employees in hiring, discharging, and denying employment on the basis of an individual's age.[47] The act provides that employers who retain twenty or more employees for twenty or more workweeks are prohibited from discrimination against employees who are forty years of age or older.

Employees, applicants, and former employees may file a charge of age discrimination with one of several administrative agencies that investigate and attempt to mediate these claims. After the relevant commission has been given an opportunity to investigate the claim, the claimants may initiate legal action in either state or federal court. An employer may not defend a discrimination claim by asserting that it hired another individual in the protected age category.

Those concerned about issues of age discrimination due to the discipline or termination of an employee should contact the human resource department during the decision-making process. In addition, complaints received regarding discriminatory conduct from an employee or applicant should also be referred to the human resource department.

The Americans with Disabilities Act prohibits employment discrimination against qualified individuals on the basis of disability.[48] It requires that employers provide reasonable accommodations to qualified individuals with disabilities to help them perform the essential functions of their jobs. Although most states have laws that forbid discriminating against people with disabilities, the ADA provides uniform national protection.

Many state and local laws extend employment discrimination protection to people outside federally protected categories. Employers should consult specific state and local laws to ensure compliance. Moreover, many employers have voluntarily chosen to extend protection to certain employee groups and have added marital status and sexual orientation to their antidiscrimination policies. To be effective, any equal employment program must have support from top management and supervisors. Such policies should be put in writing and distributed to all employees and should be clearly understood and implemented by supervisors.

Sexual Harassment

Sexual harassment is prohibited by Title VII of the Civil Rights Act of 1964. Sexual harassment so severe or pervasive as to alter the conditions of the victim's employment can create an abusive working environment. This violates Title VII.[49] To be actionable under the statute, a sexually objectionable environment must be one that a reasonable person would find to be hostile or abusive and that the victim did perceive to be hostile or abusive.[50] Sporadic use of abusive language, gender-related jokes, and occasional teasing are not considered severe enough to violate Title VII.[51]

Federal courts have acknowledged two types of sexual harassment claims based on two different legal theories: **quid pro quo** harassment and hostile environment harassment. Quid pro quo harassment occurs when a superior demands sexual favors from a subordinate in exchange for continued employment or job benefits. Hostile environment harassment is a situation in which an employee's terms and conditions of employment are altered as a result of pervasive sexual conduct. This includes unwanted sexual advances, demands for sexual favors, and any conduct of a sexual nature that unreasonably interferes with an individual's work performance or creates an intimidating, hostile, or offensive working environment. In both quid pro quo and hostile environment harassment, employers can be held strictly liable for harassment by supervisors that results in tangible job actions, even if they have no knowledge of the conduct. Employees can even recover damages when no tangible job action occurs without showing that the employer was negligent or at fault for the supervisor's conduct.[52] An employer may avoid liability where no tangible job action occurs by establishing an affirmative defense showing that the employer exercised reasonable care to prevent and promptly correct sexual harassment and that the employee unreasonably failed to take advantage of any preventative or corrective opportunity provided by the employer.[53] For employers to limit potential exposure to sexual harassment claims, an employer must disseminate and enforce an effective sexual harassment policy that incorporates effective procedures for the reporting, investigation, and discipline of sexual harassment in the workplace.[54]

It is an employer's legal obligation to take prompt and appropriate action in response to a complaint of sexual harassment. It is important for a manager confronted with a sexual harassment complaint to investigate the complaint in a timely and thorough fashion, with the assistance of human resources and according to facility policy. Every health care facility must implement anti–sexual harassment policies. All individuals should familiarize themselves with the reporting and investigatory structures set forth in each policy.

Staff Credentialing Credentialing involves the careful selection, review, and evaluation of health care providers. It is a process whereby health care entities select, review, and periodically evaluate the competency of the physicians and other licensed health care practitioners in their facility. Courts have held health care institutions vicariously liable for the negligent acts of independent physicians through the doctrine of apparent agency or ostensible agency and, as noted, have imposed liability on health care entities through *respondeat superior,* for the acts of employees committed within the scope of employment.

The Joint Commission accredits and sets standards for hospitals, health systems, and home care programs to follow regarding the selection of its medical staff. The Joint Commission recommends, at a minimum, that a hospital require its medical staff to do all of the following:

- Adopt bylaws and rules and regulations, subject to approval by the governing body, that establish a framework for the conduct of the medical staff

- Make recommendations to the governing body regarding the structure of the medical staff

- Organize to accomplish their required function

- Describe and implement a process for appointment and reappointment to the medical staff

- Describe and implement a process for delineating clinical privileges and determining the appropriate qualifications required to perform these privileges

- Monitor and evaluate the quality and appropriateness of patient care

- Require members of the medical staff to participate in continuing education

Individual hospitals should be queried as to their specific requirements for their medical staff.

Impaired Professionals The American Medical Association (AMA) defines the impaired physician as one who is unable to practice medicine with reasonable skill and safety to patients because of physical or mental illness, including deterioration through the aging process or loss of motor skills or excessive use or abuse of drugs or alcohol. An institution's primary responsibility is to provide quality medical care to its patients. An impaired physician significantly deviates from this responsibility. Therefore, once the hospital becomes aware of, or has reason to be aware of, an impaired physician, it has a duty to investigate immediately and take appropriate measures in an effort to protect its patients. Efforts to rehabilitate impaired providers must be structured in such a manner that does not compromise the hospital's primary obligation.

Every institution should establish a written policy regarding how impaired physicians should be handled, and it should be properly enforced. This benefits patients by ensuring high-quality care, identifying the physician who requires assistance, and ultimately protecting the hospital from potential liability. Although hospitals implement different policies, typically a health care facility's guidelines will require that impairment be reported to the institution's in-house impairment program or to an external impaired physicians program. This report is intended to get needed help to the physician. If these reports do not help the impaired physician enter an impairment program, state law requires that the health care facility, a hospital peer, or a colleague must report the physician to the medical board. Depending on the specifics of applicable state law, a facility, peer, or colleague that fails to report an impaired physician to the medical board in such a circumstance could be fined. Upon recording suspected impairment, the medical board will assess the situation and conduct its own investigation as deemed appropriate. Any person who makes a report in good faith is immune from liability. Furthermore, some states have mandatory reporting statutes. Therefore, individual state requirements should be built into the institution's policies.

Generally, an impaired physician who has satisfactorily undergone treatment may return to practice. Certain types of accommodations might be required to help the physician return to work, as impairments may constitute a disability under the Americans with Disabilities Act. In addition, hospital administration and medical staff members involved in the credentialing process should be aware of the impaired practitioner's problem so that they can impose controls designed to prevent injury to patients that are consistent with the ADA and applicable state laws. There may be specific state-imposed requirements that affect when and under what circumstances the physician can return to practice. Generally, it is suggested that before affected practitioners are permitted to return to work, they should be required to produce satisfactory evidence of completion of a rehabilitation program; required to continue in an organized program of ongoing monitoring for a period of two to four years; agree to arrange with other physicians who will assume responsibility for the care of the affected physician's patients should the need arise; agree to submit to random substance abuse screening tests at the request of the hospital or medical staff leadership; and agree to abstain from addictive substances as a condition of continued medical staff membership and clinical privileges. These precautions are highly recommended measures designed to protect patients and reduce hospital liability. Those aware that a medical professional is impaired should follow the health care institution's guidelines and should contact the internal risk management department or legal department. Precautions should be taken by all parties to guarantee confidentiality concerning the practitioner's condition.

LEGAL ISSUES RELATED TO SPECIFIC HEALTH CARE PROVIDERS

The number of actors involved in providing health care and the intricate relationship among those actors and patients create a maze of liability for specific health care providers.

Acute-Care Hospitals

Over a lifetime, a patient may deal with different types of specific health care providers in various settings, including but not limited to acute or hospital care, long-term care, hospice care, mental and behavioral health care, and integrated delivery systems. It is important to appreciate the relationships among these providers, as several health care providers might be subject to suit under varying negligence theories when a patient sustains injury during the course of care or treatment.

Ostensible or Apparent Agency As noted previously, a hospital can be held vicariously liable for the actions of its employees under the theory of *respondeat superior,* as can any employer. A hospital may also be held vicariously liable for the acts or omissions of independent contractors who are not its employees under the theory of ostensible or apparent agency. Under this theory, a hospital may be subjected to liability if the patient looked to the institution rather than the individual physician for care, and the hospital's actions led the patient to reasonably believe that the physician was one of the hospital's employees. This theory is often used to hold the hospital liable for the acts of nonemployed physicians and other health care providers with hospital-based practices. The origin of this theory is set forth in the *Restatement (Second) of Torts* as follows:

> One who employs an independent contractor to perform services for another which are accepted under reasonable belief that the services are being rendered by the employer or by his servants, is subject to liability for physical harm caused by the negligence of the contractor in supplying such services, to the same extent as though the employer was supplying them himself or by his servants.[55]

This theory of liability is most often applied when a patient is admitted to the emergency department of a hospital and the hospital assigns a physician to the patient. If the patient subsequently alleges that the assigned physician provided negligent care or treatment, under the theory of **ostensible agency**, the patient can assert that the hospital is liable for the alleged negligent conduct. Courts have also applied ostensible agency where the conduct of hospital-based health care providers other than emergency department physicians, such as pathologists, anesthesiologists, and radiologists, is at issue.[56] Some states have even permitted an ostensible agency cause of action to be asserted against an HMO.[57] To minimize the possibility of any misconceptions that patients might have related to the legal status of independent health care providers providing care and treatment within a particular facility, many hospitals have implemented procedures to inform patients and clearly identify individuals as independent from the hospital. For example, some hospitals began noting on all literature, including admission forms, letterheads, advertisements, and billing statements, that the physicians within the facility were independent from the hospital itself. Furthermore, if the hospital provided uniforms or hospital clothing for the independent contractors, the name of the hospital did not appear on these garments. Further, upon presentation to the emergency department, all patients were given the opportunity to select their own physician or be informed that the emergency department was staffed with independent contractors.[58]

Corporate Negligence Under the theory of corporate negligence, a hospital has a nondelegable duty to the patient to ensure the patient's safety and well-being while the patient is in the hospital. The hospital is not vicariously liable for the health care provider's negligent act; rather, the hospital is liable for its own negligence in failing to ensure that a proper standard of care is upheld. To prevail under this theory, the plaintiff must prove that the hospital knew or had reason to know of a defect in its procedures and that the defect was a substantial factor in bringing about injury to the patient.[59]

Long-Term Care Liability

The aging of the baby boom generation, in the next few years, will make senior citizens the largest-growing segment in our society. It is projected that by the year 2030, there will be approximately ten million Americans eighty-five years and older.[60] As the population ages, it is likely that many more people will be living in long-term care facilities.

Types of Long-Term Care Facilities As the population ages, the services related to the senior population will expand.

Continuing Care Retirement Community

Continuing care retirement communities (CCRCs) offer a long-term contract with residents to provide housing, food, and graduated services, including nursing care, for the remainder of the resident's life. Usually, the CCRC campus consists of independent housing, personal home care services, and ultimately a nursing facility. Generally, as a resident's needs increase, the need for care increases, and the appropriate level of care is provided. Liability issues as to standard of care may vary depending on the level of care that is provided, meaning whether it is independent, personal home care services, or skilled nursing services.

Personal Care Homes

A licensed personal care home (PCH), commonly referred to as an **assisted living facility** (**ALF**), is a facility that provides food, shelter, personal assistance, and supervision for individuals who do not require the services of a licensed nursing facility but do require some assistance with activities of daily living. PCHs and ALFs are not medical facilities, although they may hire individuals with nursing backgrounds. They are often regulated by a state agency, but the level of regulation is usually far less than for a nursing home. Liability issues again depend on the level of care being administered to the patient. A common liability issue arises when the facility keeps residents who require a higher level of care than they can provide.

Nursing Homes

Nursing homes are licensed nursing facilities that provide food, shelter, nursing care, and assistance to individuals who have special needs or need assistance with multiple activities of daily living. Nursing homes are medical facilities. They employ individuals with medical or nursing training. They are either for-profit or not-for-profit. There is no practical difference between the standard of care in a for-profit and a not-for-profit facility. However, many governmentally operated nursing facilities enjoy governmental immunity for common law negligence claims, for which immunity depends entirely on state law.[61]

Regulations The **Omnibus Budget Reconciliation Act of 1987 (OBRA)** is the basis for the uniform regulations that govern the care and assessment of nursing home residents.[62] The statute established the requirements relating to the provision of care, such as assessing residents, training for nurse's aides, physician supervision, and level of nursing care. Also included in the statute are provisions for various residents' rights, such as the right to be free from physical and chemical restraints, the right to choose one's physician, and the right to confidentiality and privacy.

Included in OBRA is the Federal Nursing Home Reform Act. This establishes the standards of care for facilities receiving Medicare and Medicaid payments. The vast majority of facilities seek reimbursement through Medicare or Medicaid and are therefore subject to these requirements. Facilities that fail to comply with the regulations are subject to sanctions, the withholding of payments, and in extreme cases, termination of participation in the Medicare and Medicaid system. This statute makes it the individual state's responsibility to establish, monitor, and enforce the state's requirements for licensing and for the federal regulations.

To participate in the Medicare and Medicaid program, a nursing home must go through a survey and certification process every nine to fifteen months. Standard surveys are designed to assess whether the nursing home is in compliance with federal and state regulations. They are typically conducted without any prior notice to the facility. They cover four factors:

1. Quality of care furnished (as measured by indicators of medical, nursing, and rehabilitative care), dietary and nutrition services, activities and social participation, sanitation, infection control, and the physical environment

2. Adequacy of written plans of care

3. Accuracy of the residents' assessments

4. Compliance with residents' rights

The survey typically consists of a team of investigators from a local field office that examines records, observes care provided by the staff, interviews the staff, and interviews residents or families. If a facility is found to be out of compliance, a statement of deficiencies is filed. After this filing, the facility must submit an acceptable plan of correction, which is then followed by a revisit to ensure that the plan of correction is implemented.[63] These regulations vary by state and should be reviewed accordingly.

Types of Liability The liability issues related to health care continue to expand.

Vicarious Liability

Like hospitals and other health care providers, nursing homes and long-term care facilities can be held vicariously responsible for the actions or omissions of their employees. For example, in *Bryant* v. *Hunt,* the Court of Appeals of Michigan found that a nursing home has a responsibility to provide its residents with an "accident-free environment."[64] In this case, the patient died of asphyxiation when she became wedged between the mattress and the bed rail due to the alleged negligence of the nursing home's employees. The court found that this was an ordinary negligence claim for which the defendant nursing home could be found to be **vicariously liable**. The case was remanded to the trial court to be tried on vicarious liability

An extension of vicarious liability was created through the theory of ostensible agency. This theory holds that a nursing home could be held vicariously liable for the acts of an independent physician if the patient looks to the institution rather than the individual physician for care and the nursing home "holds out" the physician as its employee.[65] The key is whether the facility acts or fails to act in some way, which might lead the patient to a reasonable belief that the facility or one of its employees is responsible for treatment. Although not particularly common, this issue can become relevant in the case of physicians employed by or under contract to the nursing home or outsourced contractors such as occupational or physical therapists.

Corporate Liability

This theory holds that a defendant facility owes certain nondelegable duties to the resident, which, if breached, may subject it to liability for damages. In *Aptekman* v. *City of Philadelphia,* the District Court for the Eastern District of Pennsylvania declined to dismiss the suit against the defendant nursing home on the theory of corporate liability.[66] The court reasoned that although corporate liability has not yet been extended to include nursing homes, it has been expanded to include HMOs, and given the right set of circumstances, a state court may extend corporate liability to include health care organizations other than hospitals, such as nursing homes and long-term care facilities.

Claims As in other medical malpractice and medical negligence cases, plaintiffs must present an expert report or an expert witness to establish their case. In *Perdieu* v. *Blackstone Family Practice Center, Inc.,* the Supreme Court of Virginia determined that the issues surrounding treatment in a nursing home are beyond the ordinary scope of a jury's understanding; therefore, expert testimony is required.[67] The court further stated that the experts employed must be engaged in the actual performance of the procedures at issue in the case. The court therefore excluded testimony of experts who had not treated nursing home patients for more than thirty years, did not have experience in the field of nursing home care, or did not have an active clinical practice within a year of the alleged incident.

Claims against nursing homes include those for negligent hiring or firing and failure to enforce policies and procedures.[68] Statutory claims may also be brought against a nursing home or long-term care facility, such as a claim under the Unfair Trade Practices Act or Consumer Protection Law.[69] Claims for care issues can range from discrete events such as a fall or assault and battery to a course of treatment, such as wound care.

Elder Abuse One issue that has been gaining attention recently is elder abuse. Nearly one out of every three nursing homes in the United States has been cited for an abuse violation in the past few years.[70] To facilitate risk management in nursing homes, many have implemented procedures that require them to report instances of abuse to local authorities and state agencies quickly, to fully prosecute those involved if need be, and to establish safeguards to protect residents from further abuse.[71] Despite these efforts, the physical and sexual abuse of nursing home residents continues to be a rampant problem with large consequences.[72] In response, many states have adopted measures for reporting and dealing with allegations of abuse, including registries of employees who have been guilty of abusing residents.

For example, Pennsylvania law protects adults over the age of sixty who cannot perform tasks necessary for their physical or mental health. A majority of those who reside in nursing homes or long-term care facilities fall into this category. Reporting is mandatory in assisted living facilities such as nursing homes and long-term care facilities. In *Delaney* v. *Baker,* the Supreme Court of California affirmed the judgment of a lower court that awarded the plaintiff with "heightened attorney's fees" and pain and suffering damages.[73] The plaintiff sued the defendant nursing home and two administrators for damages under the theories of elder abuse, willful misconduct, negligence, neglect of an elder, and wrongful death, after the plaintiff's mother died while a resident at the home. At the time of death, the plaintiff's decedent had bedsores down to the bone.

Penalties for elder abuse are different in every state. Some states may even hold long-term care facilities and nursing homes criminally responsible for elder abuse.

Hospice Care

Hospice care differs from traditional health care treatment in its emphasis on palliative treatment for persons who are in the process of dying. In other words, unlike hospitals, where curative or restorative treatment is sought, a hospice focuses on pain management for patients facing impending death. Generally, hospice care addresses the physical, psychological, and spiritual needs of the patient. Because hospice patients are suffering from a terminal illness or disease, health care providers operating within the context of a hospice routinely encounter issues related to the Patient Self-Determination Act of 1990, advance directives, and withholding and withdrawing life-sustaining treatment.

Patient Self-Determination Act of 1990 It is imperative that all health care providers, including hospice providers, be knowledgeable regarding the statutory requirements of the **Patient Self-Determination Act (PSDA)** of 1990.[74] This federal statute prescribes that all providers subject to the act must provide each patient with written information on the patient's right under state law to accept or refuse life-sustaining treatment and to formulate advance directives (or living wills). The provider is also required to outline written policies regarding the implementation of a patient's right to refuse such treatment. The provider is further required to document in each patient's medical record whether the patient has executed an advance directive and to ensure compliance with the requirements of state law regarding advance directives. In addition, the provider is prohibited from basing the provision of care on whether or not the patient has executed an advance directive. Finally, the act requires the provider to educate its staff and the community on issues regarding advance directives.

Advance Directives An **advance directive** is a legal document that communicates an individual's medical wishes or appoints someone else to make decisions on that person's behalf should the individual become incapacitated and either permanently unconscious or terminally ill. There are two basic kinds of advance directives. Living wills are effective to communicate the patient's wishes within a period of time prior to the patient's anticipated death. Durable powers of attorney, on the other hand, usually allow a surrogate to make decisions on the patient's behalf whenever the patient is incapable of making such decisions, regardless of the imminence of death. To be effective, advance directives must comply with state statutes. State and federal governments are currently required to disseminate information about advance directives. In fact, states that fail to comply with the mandates of the 1990 PSDA risk losing Medicare and Medicaid funding.

Withholding and Withdrawing Life-Sustaining Treatment

In the absence of an advance directive, health care providers will likely encounter various legal, ethical, and moral issues related to the propriety of withholding or withdrawing life-sustaining treatment from a patient suffering from an incurable or irreversible medical condition that might lead to death. These issues can greatly complicate the decision as to whether treatment should be withheld or withdrawn, particularly when the patient can no longer communicate.

When a patient has an incurable and irreversible medical condition, the classes of treatment involved in sustaining life are typically surgery, cardiopulmonary resuscitation, antibiotic therapy, respiratory support, renal dialysis, and artificial nutrition and hydration.

Because the essence of the physician-patient relationship is consensual, continuing treatment of the type necessary to sustain life under these circumstances is nearly always invasive and would therefore constitute a battery (nonconsensual bodily invasion) if continued over the objection of a competent individual. The law is settled that such an individual has a legal right to refuse life-sustaining procedures even though refusal might shorten or terminate life. The patient's right in these circumstances is founded on a common law right to self-determination and a constitutional right to privacy. In the case of a terminally ill patient, the courts have generally held that the patient's right to self-determination and privacy outweigh the countervailing interest of the state in preserving life, preventing suicide, safeguarding the integrity of the medical profession, and protecting innocent third parties (such as minor dependents or unborn children of the patient). In general, courts considering the "right to die" issue have concluded that the state's interest weakens and the individual's right grows as the prognosis dims and the intrusiveness of the treatment increases.

The situation presented by the permanently unconscious or otherwise incompetent patient, however, is greatly complicated because the individual is not in a position to consent to or refuse continued life-sustaining treatment, even if refusal might have been the patient's preference. Under such circumstances, courts, attending physicians, and members of the patient's family usually attempt to achieve the appropriate balance among the various interests involved.

As a practical matter, in the case of the incompetent patient receiving life-sustaining treatment, the attending physician who favors withdrawal of such treatment must balance the probable but often unstated wishes of the patient against the potential of civil liability for medical malpractice, criminal liability for homicide, and professional censure for unprofessional and unethical conduct. On the other hand, continuing such treatment over the objection of the next of kin might lead ultimately to a civil lawsuit on behalf of the patient or the estate for the tort of battery. Some courts have held that the surrogate decision maker who wishes to discontinue treatment when the patient is incapable of consenting or refusing treatment may be required to prove what the patient would wish if the patient were competent through clear and convincing evidence.[75] This decision is very difficult in the case of a patient in a persistent vegetative state and even more difficult in the case of a conscious but incompetent patient. The decision can be further complicated when a patient's family members do not agree about what should be done.

The American Medical Association takes the position that in deciding whether potentially life-prolonging medical treatment is in the best interest of the incompetent patient, the physician and the surrogate decision maker should consider several factors, including the patient's values about life and the way it should be lived; the patient's attitudes toward sickness, medical procedures, and death; and the possibility for extending life under humane conditions.

The AMA maintains that it is not unethical to discontinue all means of life-prolonging treatment to a patient who is beyond doubt permanently unconscious. It is the AMA's position that medication, artificially supplied respiration, nutrition, and hydration constitute life-prolonging medical treatment. Of course, not everyone agrees with this position, and it can be difficult to achieve consensus even within the medical community as to whether a particular patient is beyond doubt permanently unconscious.

Mental and Behavioral Health Care

The unique circumstances surrounding the relationships among mental and behavioral health care providers, their patients, and third parties requires the imposition of exceptional duties on providers while simultaneously affording them immunities. It is imperative that health care providers know the law in their respective states, as these duties and immunities vary by jurisdiction.

Duty to Warn A psychiatrist or licensed psychologist cannot disclose information acquired while rendering professional services to a patient without the written consent of the patient. The protection against disclosure applies to both civil and criminal matters. However, individuals may waive this privilege by placing their psychiatric state at issue in a lawsuit. A court then has discretion to permit disclosure of the information.

Since the landmark case of *Tarasoff* v. *Regents of the University of California,* a majority of states have imposed some form of the duty to warn by statute or case law, thereby creating an exception to the physician-patient privilege.[76] In *Tarasoff,* the court held that "a psychotherapist treating a mentally ill patient has a duty to use reasonable care to give threatened persons such warnings as are essential to avert foreseeable danger arising from his patient's condition or treatment."[77] Significantly, in *Tarasoff,* the psychotherapist's efforts to contact law enforcement regarding his patient's violent threats did not satisfy his duty to warn.

In most jurisdictions, when a psychotherapist determines that a patient presents a serious danger of violence to another individual, the psychotherapist has a **"duty to warn"** or an obligation to use reasonable care to protect the intended victim against such danger. The psychotherapist does not violate the psychotherapist-patient privilege when disclosing such patient communications. However, in most jurisdictions, for this duty to warn to come into play, there must be a specific, identifiable victim and a clear means of carrying out the threat to the intended victim. In preventing the threatened danger, the psychotherapist should act in a manner that best preserves the privacy of the patient. Notably, some states have expanded the duty to warn beyond psychotherapists. In fact, the law in some states has imposed a duty to warn of an actual threat of violence on a broad range of mental health providers, including professional counselors, licensed psychiatrists, marriage and family therapists, social workers, and psychiatric and mental health nurse specialists.[78] Therefore, in an effort to avoid third-party liability, it is crucial to know the law of the state in which your particular health care facility is located.

Ambulance Services

An ambulance is defined as a vehicle that is specifically designed for transporting the sick or injured, contains certain specified equipment, and is staffed by trained personnel.[79] Ambulances must be equipped with emergency warning lights, sirens, and telecommunication equipment, including at least one two-way radio or wireless telephone as prescribed by state and local law. Further, an ambulance must also contain standard patient care equipment, including a stretcher, clean linens, first aid supplies, oxygen equipment, and such other safety and lifesaving equipment as is required by state and local authorities.[80] Generally, there are two types of ambulance vehicles, which are subject to different regulations. A basic ambulance is one that provides transportation, equipment, and staff needed for basic services, including controlling bleeding, splinting fractures, treating shock, delivering babies, and performing cardiopulmonary resuscitation.[81] The ambulance crew of a basic life support (BLS) vehicle must consist of at least two members. One of these members must be legally authorized to operate all life-sustaining equipment and be certified as an emergency medical technician (EMT) by the state or local authority. By contrast, an advanced life support (ALS) vehicle is equipped with complex specialized life-sustaining equipment and, ordinarily, equipment for radio-telephone contact with a physician or hospital. An ALS vehicle must contain two members, with at least one crew member certified as a paramedic or an EMT by state and local authority.[82]

An understanding of the distinctions between these ambulance services is important for purposes of Medicare reimbursement. Medicare requires the ambulance supplier to provide documentation that the ambulance service provider is in compliance with emergency and staff licensure and certification requirements.[83]

Integrated Delivery Systems

In recent decades, the spiraling cost of health care and health insurance premiums has contributed to the development of various types of health care delivery systems, otherwise known as integrated delivery systems (IDSs). The Clinton Health Care Reform Plan proposed in 1993 hastened this development and prompted many states to adopt their own health care reform plans.

Profile of an IDS The perceived advantage of an IDS is its economic and administrative efficiency. An IDS consolidates a variety of professional, laboratory, and technical services to control costs. For example, most IDSs contain the following cost containment features:

- Preadmission review (requires hospital admissions to be approved in advance)

- Discharge planning (establishes general guidelines for length of hospitalizations and postdischarge case management)

- Utilization review (controls the allocation of HMO resources)

- Individual case management

- Second opinions

- An appeal process (a mechanism to contest case management decisions)

Furthermore, an IDS may be set up to enter into "capitation" agreements with managed care organizations or employers. Capitation generally means that the physician or group receives a fixed monthly or annual payment for each member enrolled in the plan. The pool of proceeds available to each physician or provider diminishes with each patient referral to a nonmember physician or provider. Virtually all theories of liability asserted against an IDS stem from the competing goals of containing health care costs while maximizing health benefits.

Several theories of liability may be asserted against a particular IDS:

- *Vicarious liability:* Liability imposed on an IDS by a patient subscriber for the negligent acts of its employees

- *Direct liability:* Liability brought by a subscriber directly against an IDS for negligently selecting health care providers or managing resources; most often arises in the case of a refusal to allow services

- *Breach of contract or warranty:* Failing to honor or fulfill terms of the patient subscriber or member-physician's contract

- *Intentional misrepresentation or fraud:* Nondisclosure of material facts regarding the operation of the IDS

It is helpful to keep in mind the source of each type of liability when studying these theories. Allegations of vicarious and direct liability are vertically imposed theories that can be made only by a patient-subscriber (including parents of a minor or an estate), whereas breach-of-contract actions are horizontal and may be brought by the subscriber to the HMO or by the member-physician and provider.

It is also important to consider which type of IDS is involved, because application of these theories of liability depends largely on the particular type of IDS model present. The different IDS structures are discussed here.

Structuring an IDS The structure of an IDS is particularly important, as each IDS provides different mechanisms for balancing the competing goals of health care cost containment and maximum health care service. Each IDS creates different incentives for providers and determines the treatment available to patients.

The Health Maintenance Organization (HMO) An HMO is an IDS that provides for the financing and delivery of comprehensive health care services to participants for a prepaid fee. This is in contrast to traditional health care insurance, which reimburses the policyholder or provider for the cost of services ("fee-for-service basis"). HMOs provide services to their members through a system of prepaid physician-providers.

Common to the HMO is the primary care physician who acts as a "gatekeeper." Some critics have noted that under the traditional health care insurance model, the provider has an incentive to perform unnecessary services and thereby generate fees. The HMO model, by contrast, has no such incentive and theoretically should be more economical. However, because there is no fee for service, critics of managed care argue that there is also a disincentive to treat.

As established previously, many IDSs and HMOs have a system of capitation in which the participants' premiums are pooled. This pool is used to pay the health care providers. Typically, HMO participants are bound by the HMO to seek treatment from approved physicians. The HMO's limitation on the member's choice of physician, the right to see a specialist, and the system of capitation are the major criticisms of the HMO delivery system.

There are generally four different types of HMOs, categorized on the basis of their relationship with the medical providers. An HMO's exposure to liability depends largely on its organization.

Staff Model
The HMO directly employs staff physicians and other providers who render services only to members. This model is characterized by the employer-employee relationship

between the physician and the HMO. Staff models also occasionally own or lease their own health care facilities.

Group Model

The HMO contracts with independent medical groups or physician corporations that provide medical care to the HMO members at the group's own offices. Generally speaking, a group model pays its contract physicians a set fee per month, per covered individual. However, unlike staff model physicians, group model physicians are not restricted to treating only HMO participants.

Network

The HMO contracts with different groups of physicians who are permitted to continue to treat non-HMO patients.

Individual Practice Associations

The HMO contracts on a capitation basis with independent practice associations (IPAs), which in turn contract with individual private practice physicians to provide medical care to HMO members in their own offices. IPA physicians, like network physicians, may treat non-HMO patients.

The Preferred Provider Organization (PPO) A PPO consists of physicians, hospitals, and other medical providers who contract to provide medical care to a defined group of patients on a negotiated, discounted fee-for-service basis.

In contrast to the HMO, a PPO member may seek treatment from a nonapproved physician. Further, unlike an HMO member, the PPO member is usually not required to see a gatekeeper before seeking treatment from a specialist.

Insurance Features A patient's insurance coverage determines the amount of flexibility in choosing health care coverage. Recently, there has been an increased effort to expand the patient's choice in this area, even if it is at the expense of fewer covered benefits.

Point of Service (POS) This is a plan that combines the basic features of an HMO and PPO. Under a POS plan, the covered person may obtain treatment from an out-of-network provider, at a reduced level of benefits. The primary care physician (gatekeeper) must approve specialty and hospital services. POS organizations have been set up because HMOs are under both legal and marketing attack because of the lack of freedom of choice in selecting providers.

Exclusive Provider Organization (EPO) Similar to a PPO, an EPO consists of a group of participating providers with contractual arrangements to an insurer or other sponsoring group to provide services. Like an HMO, EPOs generally have a primary care gatekeeper, and the covered person must seek services exclusively from the participating EPO provider.

Physician-Hospital Linkages Traditional arrangements between hospitals and physicians, like those between physician and patient, are also rapidly changing throughout the country. This has produced a confusing variety of organizational alliances between physicians and hospitals. Whether this is being driven by hopes of economic survival for the hospitals, the physicians, insurance companies, or large employers is unclear. What is clear, however, is that the terrain is shifting and will continue to do so. Accordingly, it is important to understand the emerging relationships between hospitals, physicians, and insurers.

The most familiar and perhaps most interesting organization, the **physician-hospital organization (PHO)**, is a venture between one or more hospitals and one or more groups of physicians, generally the hospitals' medical staff and other ancillary providers, who have streamlined their services to act as an integrated whole. The benefits of these systems are a reduction in administrative costs and greater bargaining power in the marketplace to negotiate contracts with an IDS employer or insurance company. There are four basic models.

Traditional PHO

A traditional PHO is a joint venture between one or more hospitals and physicians. The physicians may participate in the joint venture as individuals or as an organization such as an IPA or a professional corporation. The advantage of a PHO is that it serves as the contracting agent for multiple HMOs and PPOs and for employers who fund their own benefit plans. Thus the PHO can exert greater leverage in the marketplace with health care payers. In some situations, the PHO may actually own an HMO or a PPO (or vice versa). Within the PHO, the financial and reimbursement interests of the hospital and physicians are aligned. As physicians and hospitals cooperate to achieve their common goals, they deliver care more efficiently, generating greater profitability.

Management Services Organization (MSO)

An MSO is an organization that provides management services to one or more medical practices, such as a large group, physician practice, or hospital. MSOs may assume the financial risk associated with health care management by purchasing the assets of a professional corporation and then leasing the assets back to the group. In return, they provide physicians with a full range of administrative services. The MSO can also serve to transfer hospital capital to physicians in exchange for assets, expanded clinical services, more affordable administrative systems, and comprehensive ambulatory and inpatient services.

Foundation Model

A foundation is a corporation that is organized by a hospital, a group of hospitals, or a group of nonprofit doctors with a common parent organization. The foundation provides the physical plant, administrative and marketing services, and nonmedical personnel and negotiates with managed care plans, insurers, and so on. For the most part, physicians have little control in a foundation model. Foundations grew out of the strong prohibition on hospital employment of physicians in California and other states.

Integrated Health Organization (IHO)

An IHO is an organization that requires a separate legal entity, such as a parent corporation, with at least two subsidiaries, such as a hospital and a management services organization, and often a third subsidiary, such as an educational or research foundation. The physicians are employed by the **management services corporation**, which provides coverage, the physical plant, and so on. An IHO generally sponsors its own managed care activities, such as an HMO or a PPO.

This is the most integrated of any of the PHO models. It is thought to embrace a comprehensive, community-based system of health care services, which would avoid duplication, minimize competition, and be more cost-effective.

Liability Issues Essential features common to all integrated delivery systems include strong utilization review and case management procedures and the exercise of significant control over the panel of providers. Many of the models also include some form of capitation.

As noted previously, capitation generally means that the physician or group receives a fixed monthly or annual payment for each member. This payment goes to compensate the physician or group but can also pay for referrals to specialists or entities outside the group. The press is replete with horror stories of physicians or insurers who refused to allow such referrals, even when conventional wisdom supports their medical necessity. For this reason, the capitation issue has strong emotional appeal in claims against a health care provider or an IDS.

Under traditional theories of medical malpractice, liability for negligent treatment rests with the provider. An HMO or a PPO does not technically provide medical care directly to its members. In recent years, however, liability for medical malpractice has been extended to IDSs as a result of their restrictions on their members' choice of physician, right to receive certain types of medical care, and the perceived economic disincentive to treat created by capitation.

Thus while claimants continue to pursue garden-variety professional liability claims of negligent treatment by a participating IDS physician, they may also pursue claims against an IDS on the grounds that no medical negligence would have occurred if they had had the right to seek treatment from other providers, no medical negligence would have occurred if their right to seek treatment from other providers were not restricted, or the treatment they requested was arbitrarily denied or delayed, resulting in personal injury.

These new avenues of recovery expose IDSs to significant operating risks.

Respondeat Superior As previously discussed, *respondeat superior* is a doctrine by which an employer may be held vicariously liable for the negligent acts of its employee performed in the course and scope of employment. In the context of the IDS, the master-servant or employer-employee relationship is most readily apparent in the staff model. In the staff model, an HMO's physician's negligence may be imputed to the physician's employer, the HMO, if it is established that the HMO directly controlled the physician's activities. Because staff model HMOs place tight restrictions on the scope of their physicians' practices and pay them directly, evidence of control sufficient to impose *respondeat superior* liability is relatively easy to establish.[84] Liability imputed to an IDS is not limited to the staff model. In fact, courts have extended the *respondeat superior* theory of liability to group model HMOs and even to HMOs that hire nonmember physicians to provide independent consultations.[85] Nevertheless, not all jurisdictions are uniform in their approach, and many have held that where the HMO does not directly employ its own physicians, the master-servant relationship might not exist, and therefore, no liability may be assessed against the HMO under the doctrine of *respondeat superior.*

Ostensible Agency As noted, the theory of ostensible agency is an exception to the general rule of contract law that an employer cannot be held liable for the negligent acts of an independent contractor. Under the theory of ostensible agency, an HMO can be held vicariously liable for the medical malpractice of a contracting physician in which the patient looked to the institution (the HMO) rather than the individual physician for care and the HMO "held out" the physician as its employee, thereby creating a reasonable perception in the eyes of the patient that the physician was the apparent agent or employee of the HMO. Ostensible agency is applied almost exclusively to group and IPA model HMOs. However, recent developments in federal law, particularly in the interpretation of the Employee Retirement Income Security Act (ERISA) of 1994, have questioned its continued application.[86] Increasingly, federal courts have ruled that ERISA, a federal regulatory scheme devised by Congress to control disputes related to employee benefits, may preempt state law claims against HMOs on theories of vicarious liability. The ERISA preemption is addressed later in this chapter.

Courts often look to marketing materials to see if they contain statements that imply that despite the independent contractor status of the physician, the doctor was held out as competent by the HMO or IDS. For this reason, marketing directors of health maintenance organizations need to be aware that their statements may ultimately be used to support theories of liability against HMOs. Indeed, if these and other materials suggest that the HMO held out a physician as its employee and that subscribers relied on these representations to their detriment, courts may ignore the legal distinction of independent contractor and impose liability against the HMO. A subscriber may prove reliance on the representations of an IDS by producing marketing materials that hold out the physician or provider as an employee.

Advertisements by some IDSs describing a "total care" program that not only provides payment for medical services but also "guarantees quality and service" might come back to haunt an IDS in subsequent litigation. In many plans, the subscriber-plaintiff may not see a specialist or obtain a procedure or test without prior approval or referral from the gatekeeper. This too may create an inference that the patient looked to the IDS for care and not to a specific physician.

Direct Liability or Corporate Negligence In addition to being found liable on a vicarious liability basis for the negligent acts of a third-party physician, an IDS may also be directly liable to a patient-subscriber under theories of corporate negligence, breach of contract or of warranty, or intentional misrepresentation or fraud. As applied in the managed care context, courts have upheld theories of corporate negligence against an IDS on the grounds that the IDS negligently selected its member physicians or failed to properly allocate its available resources.

Credentialing by a managed care organization of the physicians who will provide care to its participants has become an area of increasing direct liability for an IDS. Because the patient's freedom to choose a physician or specialist is generally limited by the IDS, individuals who are harmed by one of a plan's physicians may plausibly argue that they never would have been subjected to the physician's malpractice if the IDS had more carefully screened the health care providers for whose services it provides payment under the member's benefit plan.

One of the most hotly contested areas of managed care liability, responsible for producing some of the most extraordinary verdicts against health care organizations, is an IDS's system of comprehensive utilization review. In accordance with this system, decisions are made regarding to whom and on what basis treatment will be given. Liability may attach if it is determined that an IDS arbitrarily denied coverage for a given procedure or that it delayed approving a procedure, resulting in personal injury to a patient-subscriber.[87]

Employee Retirement Income Security Act of 1974 ERISA was designed by Congress to serve as a comprehensive regulatory system for resolving employee benefit disputes. To place ERISA in its proper context, it is helpful to understand the political climate that prompted its passage.

ERISA was passed in reaction to widespread concern regarding the integrity of nationwide employee benefit or pension plans. Throughout the 1960s and early 1970s, as the United States fell into recession and became less competitive in the world market, manufacturing and industrial plants started closing. One of the reasons cited for their failure was the increasingly high cost of maintaining employee benefit plans.

As a result of plant failures, senior "vested" employees, on the verge of retirement, discovered that many of their pension plans were underfunded or insolvent. Simultaneously, Congress began to question whether the Social Security system would be able to meet the demands of these future retirees. These public policy concerns prompted Congress to pass ERISA. In so doing, Congress intended to simplify the administration of pension plans by administering them under a single, cohesive federal body of law. Further, Congress sought to limit an employee's right to sue a plan for mismanagement and thereby protect the financial integrity of employee benefit plans.

As set forth more fully here, by routing litigation to the federal courts, Congress effectively nullified traditional causes of action under state law for negligence and breach of contract for mismanagement of employee benefit plans and required litigants to pursue their claims under ERISA, which permits only the recovery of benefits, not monetary damages, and attorneys' fees. This is the essence of the ERISA preemption.

Without a doubt, ERISA is the most effective tool in defending managed care liability cases. ERISA states, "Except as provided in subsection (b) of this section [the savings clause], the provisions of this subchapter and subchapter 3 of this chapter shall supersede any and all state laws insofar as they may now or hereafter relate to any employee benefit plan."[88] This is referred to as the ERISA "preemption clause."

There are only three narrow exceptions to the general rule of ERISA preemption for claims "relating to" an employee benefit plan: (1) any state law that "regulates insurance, banking, or securities,"[89] otherwise known as the "savings clause"; (2) any state cause of action that relates only tangentially to an employee benefit plan; and (3) "run-of-the-mill-type lawsuits," such as collection fee cases for unpaid rent or attorneys' fees, libel, and slander.[90]

Federal court decisions regarding the scope of ERISA preemption have varied somewhat over the years. However, most jurisdictions across the country, and in particular federal courts in Pennsylvania and New Jersey, have until recently applied the ERISA preemption broadly to prevent state lawsuits against HMOs under theories of vicarious liability, breach of contract, loss of consortium, and intentional infliction of emotional distress.

Since the Third Circuit case of *Dukes* v. *U.S. Healthcare, Inc.,*[91] courts have generally divided derivative claims into two categories: quality of care or quantity of care. Generally, courts have held that quantity-of-care claims are preempted by ERISA. In contrast, a plaintiff's claim that challenges the quality of care will not be preempted by ERISA. "In other words, if the claim involves a denial of treatment or payment pursuant to the terms of the employee benefit plan, the claim 'relates to' an ERISA plan and will be preempted." Alternatively, "if the claim relates to the quality of care received, such as a claim for physician malpractice, courts often hold that these claims do not relate to an ERISA plan and are not preempted."[92] The Third Circuit acknowledged in *Dukes* that a determination as to whether a cause of action is based on the managed care organization's quality of care or the quantity of care can be difficult because at times the two may be inextricably intertwined. Consequently, courts are apt to struggle in deciding whether ERISA is triggered by a plaintiff's claim where both quality of care and quantity of treatment may arguably be at issue.

SUMMARY

The study of potential liability and regulation in the health care field is a dynamic and expanding endeavor. Plaintiffs continue to try new theories of liability, and courts continue to recognize them. Potential liabilities and regulations relate directly to the nature of health care organizations and operations. Careful selection and management of the corporate form and operation are keys to reducing some of the liabilities inherent in health care. Understanding the legal environment in which organizations exist, once the corporate form has been selected, is the next key to controlling liability.

Although the amount of liability and regulation can be extremely frustrating at times, it is helpful to remember that people's health is typically the number one determinant of their quality of life. All the laws and regulations are merely intended to help protect this precious gift.

KEY TERMS

Advance directive
Assisted living facility
Breach of duty
Cause of action
Damages
Duty
Duty to warn
General liability
Impaired professional
Informed consent
Integrated health organization
Management services organization
Medical professional liability

Negligence
Negligence per se
Omnibus Budget Reconciliation Act of 1987
Ostensible agency doctrine
Patient Self-Determination Act
Physician-hospital organization
Privity
Quid pro quo
Respondeat superior
Standard of care
Title VII of the Civil Rights Act of 1964
Vicarious liability

ACRONYMS

ADA
ADEA
AIDS
ALF
ALS
AMA
BLS
CCRC
EPO
ERISA
HIV

HMO
IDS
IHO
LTC
MSO
OBRA
PHO
POS
PPO
PSDA

NOTES

1. *Osborne* v. *Montgomery,* 203 Wis. 223, 234 N.W. 372 (1930).

2. *Young* v. *Cerniak,* 467 N.E.2d 1045 (Ill. App. Ct., 1984).

3. *Cline* v. *William H. Friedman & Assoc.,* 882 S.W.2d 754 (Mo. Ct. App., 1994).

4. *Young* v. *Cerniak.*

5. *Logan* v. *Greenwich Hosp. Assoc.,* 191 Conn. 282, 302, 465 A.2d 294, 305 (1983); *Shilkret* v. *Annapolis Emergency Hosp. Assoc.,* 349 A.2d 245 (Md., 1975).

6. Ibid.

7. *Shilkret* v. *Annapolis*; *Pederson* v. *Dumouchel*, 72 Wash. 2d 73, 431 P.2d 973 (1967).

8. *Sheeley* v. *Memorial Hosp.*, 710 A.2d 161, 167 (R.I., 1998); Vergara v. Doan, 593 N.E.2d 185 (Ind., 1992).

9. *Williams* v. *Hotel Dieu Hosp.*, 593 So.2d 783 (La. Ct. App., 1992); *Jordan* v. *Bogner*, 844 P.2d 664 (Colo., 1993).

10. *Daubert* v. *Merrell Dow Pharmaceuticals, Inc.*, 509 U.S. 579, 590 (1993).

11. *Frye* v. *United States*, 293 F. 1013 (1923).

12. *Hreha* v. *Benscoter*, 381 Pa. Super. 556, 554 A.2d 525 (1989).

13. *Restatement (Second) of Torts*, §§ 286 and 288 (1965).

14. Ibid., §§ 288A and 288B.

15. Del. Code Ann., title 18, §6801(8).

16. *Kananen* v. *Alfred Dupont Institute of the Nemours Foundation*, 796 A.2d 1 (Del. Super., 2000); *Sacks* v. *Thomas Jefferson U. Hosp.*, 684 F.Supp. 858 (E.D.Pa., 1988); *Walters* v. *St. Francis Hosp.*, 932 P.2d 1041 (Kans. Ct. App., 1997).

17. *Webb* v. *Jarvis*, 575 N.E. 2d 992, 995 (Ind., 1991); *Conboy* v. *Mogeloff*, 567 N.Y.S.2d 960, 961 (App. Div., 1991); *Kirk* v. *Michael Reese Hosp. & Med. Ctr.*, 513 N.E. 2d 387, 395 (Ill., 1987); *Rebollal* v. *Payne*, 536 N.Y.S. 2d 147, 148 (App. Div., 1988).

18. *McElwain* v. *Van Beek*, 447 N.W.2d 442 (Minn. Ct. App., 1989).

19. Ibid.

20. *O'Hara* v. *Holy Cross Hosp.*, 561 N.E.2d 18 (Ill. Supr., 1990).

21. *Watkins* v. *United States*, 589 F.2d 214, 219 (5th Cir., 1979); *Zavalas* v. *State Dept. of Corrections*, 861 P.2d 1026, 1027 (Or. Ct. App., 1993); *Kasier* v. *Suburban Transp. Sys. Corp.* 398 P. 2d 14, 16 (Wash., 1965); *Schuster* v. *Altenberg*, 424 N. W.2d 159, 161 (Wis., 1988).

22. 61 Am. Jur. 2d, Physicians, Surgeons, and Other Healers, §186.

23. *Rogala* v. *Silva*, 305 N.E.2d 571 (Ill. App., 1973).

24. *Noel* v. *Proud*, 367 P.2d 61 (Kans., 1961); *Colvin* v. *Smith*, 92 N.Y.S. 2d 794 (1949); *Brooks* v. *Herd*, 257 P. 238 (Wash., 1927).

25. *Hudson* v. *Parvin*, 582 So.2D 403 (Miss., 1991).

26. *Gouse* v. *Casse*, 615 A.2d 331 (Pa., 1992).

27. *Corrigan* v. *Methodist Hosp.*, 869 F.Supp. 1202, 1206 (E.D. Pa., 1994).

28. *Craig* v. *Borcicky,* 557 So.2d 1253 (Ala., 1990); *Tappe* v. *Iowa Methodist Medical Ctr.,* 477 N.W.2d 396 (Iowa, 1991); *Hudson* v. *Parvin,* 582 So.2d 403 (Miss., 1991); *Roybal* v. *Bell,* 778 P.2d 108 (Wyo., 1989).

29. *Craig* v. *Borcicky; Smith* v. *Cotter,* 810 P.2d 1204 (Nev., 1991).

30. *Distefano* v. *Bell,* 544 So.2d 567 (La. Ct. App., 1989), writ denied, 550 So.2d 650 (La.., 1989).

31. *Douget* v. *Touro Infirmary,* 537 So.2d 251 (La. Ct. App., 1988).

32. *Kelley* v. *Kitahama,* 675 So.2d 1181 (La. Ct. App., 1996), writ denied, 679 So.2d 1352 (La., 1996); *Petriello* v. *Kalman,* 576 A.2d 474 (Conn., 1990); *Kershaw* v. *Reichert,* 445 N.W.2d 16 (N.D., 1989); *Johnson* v. *Sears, Roebuck & Co.,* 832 P.2d 797 (N.M. App., 2000); *Johnson* v. *St. Joseph Hosp.,* 832 P.2d 1223 (N.M., 1992); *Friter* v. *Iolab Corp.,* 607 A.2d 1111 (Pa. Super., 1992).

33. *Urban* v. *Spohn Hosp.,* 869 S.W.2d 450 (Tex. App., Corpus Christi, 1993, writ denied).

34. *Friter* v. *Iolab.*

35. 81 Am. Jur. 2d, Witnesses, §436 (1992).

36. Ibid., §441.

37. *Hammonds* v. *Aetna Casualty & Surety Co.,* 243 F.Supp. 793, 797 (N.D. Ohio, 1965); Va. Code Ann., §§32.1–36.1. (Some statutes provide the negligence standard as a basis for bringing an action for improper disclosure.)

38. Health Insurance Portability and Accountability Act of 1996 (HIPAA), P.L. 104-191, §§1171–1177.

39. *Doe* v. *Shady Grove,* 598 A.2d 507 (Md. App., 1991) (the patient brought an invasion-of-privacy action against the hospital where he was treated because employees of the hospital allegedly disclosed that he was being treated for AIDS; the patient also sought an injunction barring the hospital from publicly identifying him in court proceedings; the court held that the failure to uphold such a request would undermine the state statutes that established a presumption of confidentiality for medical records); *Estate of Behringer* v. *Med. Ctr.,* 592 A.2d 1251, 1272 (N.J. Super., 1991) (a physician was treated for AIDS at the hospital where he had staff privileges; word of his condition spread to other physicians within the hospital who were not involved in his treatment; the court found the hospital negligent for failing to protect the plaintiff's medical information from other hospital employees).

40. *In re Milton S. Hershey Med. Ctr.,* 407 Pa. Super. 565, 595 A.2d 1290 (1991), appeal granted, *Application of Milton S. Hershey Med. Ctr.,* 531 Pa. 640, 611 A.2d 712 (1992), and aff'd, *In re Milton S. Hershey Med. Ctr.,* 535 Pa. 9, 634 A.2d 159 (1992).

41. Ibid.; *Estate of Behringer* v. *Med. Ctr.,* at 1251.

42. Calif. Health and Safety Code, §120980.

43. *An Overview of 1992 State HIV/AIDS Laws* (George Washington Intergovernmental Health Policy Project, June 1992); 45 N.Y. Pub. Health Law, §2130(1). Maryland requires the Department of Health and Mental Hygiene to report HIV and CD4k counts of less than 200 mm^3.

44. *Hale* v. *Sheikholeslam,* 724 F.2d 1205 (5th Cir., 1984); *Townsend* v. *Kiracoff,* 545 F.Supp. 465 (D.Colo., 1982); *Ruane* v. *Niagara Falls Memorial Med. Ctr.,* 458 N. E.2d 1253 (N.Y., 1983); *Schloendorff* v. *Society of New York Hospitals,* 133 N. Y.S. 1143 (App. Div., 1912), aff'd, 105 N.E. 92 (1914); *Tabor* v. *Doctors Memorial Hosp.,* 563 So.2d 233 (La., 1990); *Berel* v. *HCA Health Services,* 881 S.W.2d 21, 23 (Tex. App.-Houston [1st Dist.], 1994, writ denied).

45. 29 U.S.C.A., §623(f)(1).

46. *Sheridan* v. *E. I. DuPont de Nemours & Co.,* 100 F.3d 1061, 1077–1078 (3d Cir., 1996).

47. 29 USCA 621 and 623(a)(1).

48. 42 USCA 12101.

49. *Meritor Savings Bank, FSB* v. *Vinson,* 477 U.S. 57, 67 (1986).

50. *Harris* v. *Forklift Systems, Inc.,* 510 U.S. 17, 21 (1993).

51. *Faragher* v. *City of Boca Raton,* 524 U.S. 775, 777 (1998).

52. Ibid.; *Burlington Industries Inc.,* v. *Ellerth,* 524 U.S. 742 (1998).

53. *Burlington Industries, Inc.,* v. *Ellerth,* at 807.

54. *Faragher* v. *City of Boca Raton.*

55. *Restatement (Second) of Torts,* §429 (1965).

56. *Mitchell* v. *Shepperd Memorial Hosp.,* 797 S.W.2d 144 (Tex. App. Austin, 1990, writ denied); *Pamerin* v. *Trinity Memorial Hosp.,* 423 N.W.2d 848 (Wis., 1988).

57. *Boyd* v. *Albert Einstein Med. Ctr.,* 547 A.2d 1229 (Pa. Super. Ct., 1988).

58. *1 Health L. Prac. Guide,* §2:30 (2002).

59. *Thompson* v. *Nason Hosp.,* 527 Pa. 330, 591 A.2d 703 (1991).

60. U.S. Administration on Aging, http://www.aoa.gov

61. Mundy, W. J. "Nursing Home Litigation: Defense Considerations from Initial Assessment to Discovery." Paper presented at the fourth annual Nursing Home Negligence Conference, Atlanta, 2002.

62. 42 USC 1395 and 1396.

63. *1 Health L. Prac. Guide,* §2:37 (2002).

64. *Bryant* v. *Hunt,* 2002 Mich. App. LEXIS 725 (2002).

65. *Adamski* v. *Tacoma General Hosp.,* 579 P.2d 970 (Wash. App., 1978); *Capan* v. *Divine Providence Hosp.,* 430 A.2d. 647 (Pa., 1980); *Rodebush* v. *Oklahoma Nursing Homes, Ltd.,* 867 P.2d 1241 (Okla., 1993).

66. *Aptekman* v. *City of Philadelphia,* 2001 U.S. Dist. LEXIS 19120 (E.D. Pa., 2001).

67. *Perdieu* v. *Blackstone Family Practice Center, Inc.,* 2002 W.L. 61048324 (Va., 2002).

68. *Barry by and through Cornell* v. *Manor Care Nursing Home,* 1999 U.S. Dist. LEXIS 5928 (E.D. Pa., 1999); *Ex parte McCollough,* 747 So.2d 887 (Ala., 1999). In the latter case, the plaintiff sued the defendant nursing home for a "systematic failure to enforce policies which minimize the risk of wrongdoing."

69. *Schenck* v. *Living Centers-East,* 917 F. Supp 432 (E.D. La., 1996); *White* v. *Moses Taylor Hosp.,* 763 F.Supp. 776 (M.D. Pa., 1991).

70. U.S. Administration on Aging, http://www.aoa.gov

71. U.S. General Accounting Office. "Nursing Homes: More Can Be Done to Protect Residents from Abuse." Washington, D.C.: GPO, 2002, http://www.gao.gov/new .items/d02312.pdf

72. Ibid.

73. *Delaney* v. *Baker,* 971 P.2d 986 (Calif., 1999).

74. 42 USC 1395ccc(f)(1).

75. *Conservatorship of Wendland,* 26 Calif. 4th 519, 28 P.3rd 151, 110 Calif. Rptr. 2nd 412 (Calif., 2001).

76. *Tarasoff* v. *Regents of the University of California,* 529 P.2d 553 (Calif., 1974). See also George C. Harris, "The Dangerous Patient Exception to the Psychotherapist-Patient Privilege: The *Tarasoff* Duty and the *Jaffe* Footnote." *Washington Law Review,* 1999, *74,* 47–48.

77. *Tarasoff* v. *Regents,* at 559.

78. 25 MPHYDLR 495, *Mental and Physical Disability Law Reporter,* May–June 2001.

79. 42 CFR 410.40(e).

80. 42 CFR 410.41(a)(4).

81. Irwin Cohen, *2 Health L. Prac. Guide,* §19:2 (2002).

82. 42 CFR, 410.41(b)(1)-(2).

83. Cohen, §19:2.

84. *Sloan* v. *Metropolitan Health Counsel of Indianapolis, Inc.,* 516 N.E. 2d 1104 (Ind. App., 1987), holding that where an employer-employee relationship exists, a corporation may be held vicariously liable for the malpractice of its employee-physicians.

85. *Dunn* v. *Praiss,* 256 N.J. Super. 180, 606 A.2d 862, appeal denied, 611 A.2d 657 (1992), holding that an HMO was liable under *respondeat superior* for medical malpractice committed by a urologist who was a member of a group of urologists that contracted to treat HMO subscribers. Significant to the court's finding that an employer-employee relationship existed was the fact that the group urologists were paid on a per capita as opposed to a fee-for-service basis and that they were not free to accept or reject a particular patient.

86. 29 USC 1001 et seq.

87. *Fox* v. *Health Net,* 219692 (Calif. Super. Ct., Riverside County, 1993), verdict entered against an IDS awarding $12 million in compensatory damages and $77 million in punitive damages.

88. *Pilot Life Ins. Co.* v. *Dedeaux,* 481 U.S. 41, 44–45 (1987), quoting §514(a), 29 USC 1144 (a).

89. ERISA, §514 (b)(2) (A). See *Kentucky Assoc. of Health Plans, Inc.* v. *Miller,* 538 U.S. 329 (2003).

90. *Settles* v. *Golden Rule Ins. Co.,* 927 F.2d 505 (10th Cir. 1991); *Nealy* v. *U.S. Heathcare HMO,* 844 F.Supp. 966, 971 (S.D.N.Y., 1994).

91. *Dukes* v. *U.S. Healthcare, Inc.,* 57 F.3d 350 (3rd Cir.), cert. denied, 516 U.S. 1009 (1995).

92. Bondurant, E. J., Cataland, A. K., and Dean, R. *Update on ERISA Litigation Developments.* American Law Institute, American Bar Association Continuing Legal Education, SG092 ALI-ABA 249 (2002).

CHAPTER

GOVERNANCE OF THE HEALTH CARE ORGANIZATION

JOHN HORTY, MONICA HANSLOVAN

LEARNING OBJECTIVES

- To be able to explain the importance and responsibility that governing boards have for every aspect of the organization

- To be able to recognize potential liability risks associated with not-for-profit boards

- To be able to identify the elements of risk management board education for new board members and continuing education for all board members

- To be able to submit risk management reports to the board that are meaningful yet concise

- To be able to define the two basic legal duties of a health care organization's board members

The mark of a good health care corporation, like that of any corporation, is the way it is governed. Governance determines how any organization is centered. Governance in health care is particularly important because of the responsibility of the organization to patients and to the community. Governance is the art and skill, developed over many years, of making important corporate decisions. Making decisions is the ultimate legal authority of the corporation.

The board is not passive. It makes decisions. In most instances, the corporation board should confine itself to important decisions and let management manage. However, in some situations, decisions that appear to be small or limited are (or become) important. The decisions of the board, along with the culture and values of board and management, forge the culture and values of the corporation. The culture and values of the corporation are the essence and the result of leadership—good or bad. There is no other way to govern.

The principles of corporate governance do not change. What do change are the problems that an organization faces and the decisions that it must make. All parties who support the governance of the corporation—the chief executive officer (CEO) and top management personnel, including the risk management professional—must understand the essentials of governance.

Obviously, different health care organizations face different degrees of risk. Medical groups, health care systems, long-term care organizations, insurance companies, surgical centers, and hospitals all have boards. All have the same governance responsibilities, yet the need for **risk management** in each type of organization is different. All have significant responsibilities for the care of patients. Even insurance companies (who by their actions may sometimes effectively deny care by refusing to pay for it under the terms of their policy) shoulder this responsibility.

There are several types of corporate structures, particularly in health care. Some are organized as for-profit corporations, but the majority are not-for-profit corporations. All of the health care corporations previously identified may be organized either as for-profit or not-for-profit in every state in America.

The difference between for-profit and not-for-profit corporations is in two areas. For-profit corporations have shareholders who own the corporation and hope to profit from its business. Not-for-profit corporations have no shareholders, and the people who govern them do not own the company or share in the profits. Any profits must be applied to the nonprofit purpose of the corporation.

Not-for-profit boards have a duty to the publics they serve. It is their only duty. Keeping the organization fiscally and organizationally strong is the means to that purpose. The mission of a not-for-profit corporation in the health care field is to provide quality care. In contrast, the board of a for-profit corporation (in addition to its duty to patients) owes a duty to the owners of the corporation—the shareholders—to make the business a success and to pass the profits along to the shareholders.

Although, as noted, there are many different kinds of organizations in health care, the greatest liability and risks are in hospitals. Hospitals have the largest number of employees, physicians, and other independent practitioners; have the greatest interaction with patients (by far the largest number of interactions that carry risk and potential lia-bility); and are where procedures with the greatest risk and complexity are performed.

KEY CONCEPTS

- A hospital board is responsible for ensuring that patients are safe, that the hospital is financially prudent, and that all appropriate improvements to the hospital and its products and services are made.

- A knowledgeable, committed board of directors is the strongest protector of a charitable organization's accountability to the law, its donors, the consumers of its products and services, and the public.

- Establishing and maintaining an effective compliance and ethics program is a responsibility of the health care organization's governing board.

- The purpose of the Volunteer Protection Act of 1997 is to sustain the viability of not-for-profit organizations, such as hospitals, that rely on volunteers.

- Responsibility and accountability for risk management reside with the board of directors.

ESSENTIAL RESPONSIBILITIES OF THE HOSPITAL BOARD

The essential responsibilities of the hospital board are, first and foremost, to ensure **patient safety**; second, to ensure that the hospital is financially prudent so that sufficient funds are available to accomplish its mission; and third, to ensure that appro-priate improvements to the hospital and what it does are consistently made.

Patient Safety

The foremost responsibility of any hospital board is to see that patients are safe. This is such an overriding responsibility that it almost needs no discussion. It is what every patient who enters the hospital expects and takes for granted. A board that does not see to patient safety is not doing its job. Anyone who cares for patients (physicians and others alike) must be competent and must act responsibly. The hospital must be ade-quately staffed, and equipment must be appropriately maintained and available as needed. The entire operation must put the patient first.

Finances

Hospitals (including **for-profit hospitals**) are in business to serve the patients who come to them for care. They must make enough money to do this job well, and the board is responsible to the community that it serves to ensure that the hospital has the financial resources to accomplish its mission—now and in the future. Almost all boards wisely take this financial responsibility seriously. However, patient safety must always come before profit.

Improvements

The third major responsibility of the hospital or health care board is to improve the hospital's ability to serve those who come to it as medicine changes. This responsibility has three aspects:

■ *New services.* Health care is a dynamic part of our society. Advances in technology are continuous. They allow hospitals to provide new services and new methods for the delivery of care. Further advances, such as exploration of our genetic code, will revolutionize health care in ways yet to be fully understood. A hospital board's responsibility is to weigh finances, safety, and community needs as it decides how these advances and new technologies will affect the services to provide and equipment to purchase.

■ *Better patient outcomes.* Every hospital must strive to deliver quality care and to continuously improve patient outcomes. Patient safety must always come first. By improving patient outcomes, the quality of care is enhanced and patient safety is maintained. Improved outcomes are the result of better equipment, better training of staff, and the understanding of new and better modalities of care. But equally important is the ability to measure and quantify the continuing improvements in outcomes and the changes in care that make them possible. Again, the board must make this continuous measurement of improvement a priority. Management, the medical staff, and the hospital must make it happen, but the board makes it a continuing priority and responsibility.

■ *A patient-friendly environment.* Finally, it is the responsibility of the board to set the goal of a patient-friendly hospital. This is easy to say but sometimes hard to do. Putting the hospital's patients first is a cliché, but one with real meaning. If the board does not think that this is a major goal, it won't be!

The hospital or health care board must continually strive to improve the ability to serve all who come to the hospital as medicine changes. By breaking board responsibilities into three segments, the understanding of the word *quality* is separated into three distinct and different parts: patient safety, better outcomes, and a patient-friendly environment. Clearly, the board should put patient safety first, with outcomes an important second and a friendly environment third. *Quality* has become a buzzword in this field. It often seems to be in the eye of the beholder, taken to mean whatever is being emphasized at the time. Safety, outcomes, and a friendly atmosphere are concrete and can be measured. Thus the board has a yardstick by which to measure that its responsibilities in all these areas are being met.

BASIC LEGAL DUTIES OF HEALTH CARE TRUSTEES

Two terms describe the individuals who serve on boards of corporations. For-profit corporations almost uniformly use the term ***director***. Many not-for-profit corporations use the term ***trustee*** because many early not-for-profit corporations began as charitable trusts. The term *trustee* emphasizes the duty of trust to patients and the community. In this chapter, the term *trustee* is used to refer to both trustees and directors.

Management personnel who support the governance of a health care organization must understand the two basic duties of trustees: the **duty of care** and the **duty of loyalty**. These two duties are shared by all board members of all corporations but are particularly important in the governance of a hospital or health care organization because the business of a health care corporation has immediate effects on the lives and well-being of patients.

Duty of Care

The duty of care imposed on health care board members is the duty to act in good faith, with the care that an ordinarily prudent person in a similar position would use under those circumstances and in the reasonable belief that the actions taken are in the best interest of the corporation. Courts call this the "reasonable person" standard because the action or any failure to act by the board is judged by what a reasonable person would do. Health care and hospital board members have the duty to act reasonably under the circumstances—to exercise good business judgment and to use ordinary care and prudence in fulfilling their duties. Trustees can be held liable for negligent acts or omissions in the performance of their duties and actions taken on behalf of the hospital.

Good Faith Hospital and health care trustees must act honestly and faithfully, observing reasonable commercial standards of fair dealing. It means acting without intent to defraud or to take advantage of others. It's easy to see the importance of good faith actions for any trustee, in health care or otherwise. Recent examples of the breach of this duty by some for-profit directors and executives make this painfully obvious.

Acting in the Best Interest of the Corporation This translates into a duty of reasonable care, meaning that board members have the duty to explore all options before they make an important decision—to "do their homework," so to speak. In a for-profit corporation, the duty to act in the best interest of the corporation generally means maximizing the return on the shareholders' investment. In contrast, in a nonprofit hospital or health system where no shareholders or owners exist, the board members' fiduciary duty is to act in the best interest of the people served by the organization.

Duty of Loyalty

The duty of loyalty imposed on health care board members establishes the duty not to compete with the corporation, not to disclose confidential information obtained in the performance of one's duties as a board member, not to usurp corporate opportunity, and not to gain personal enrichment at the corporation's expense.

No Competing with the Corporation Board members have a duty not to compete with the corporation they serve. A hospital or health system board would be wise to define "significant competition" in an official board policy so that it's clear to all involved exactly what this limitation means. Such a policy would give the board an objective template by which to measure any situation that occurs. For example, significant competition might mean dealings with another organization that create a net job loss for the hospital or cost the hospital 1 percent or more of its market share.

No Disclosure of Confidential Information The reasons for this duty are obvious. Any trustee (in health care or otherwise) will inevitably encounter confidential, privileged information while performing as a board member. Such information must remain confidential in all respects, meaning no idle chatter or gossip regarding the information and no deliberate release of such information.

No Usurping Corporate Opportunity In legal terms, this is known as the corporate opportunity doctrine. It means that a board member's **fiduciary duty** of loyalty prohibits the trustee from profiting from any business that properly belongs to the corporation. A hospital or health care trustee must first give the corporation ample opportunity to act before taking personal advantage of an opportunity that the corporation itself might have taken.

No Personal Enrichment at Corporate Expense Board members should not participate in any decision involving a transaction between the health care corporation and an organization in which the board members have a personal interest without disclosing this fact and obtaining board approval. A personal interest might mean that the board member would profit from the transaction, that a close family member of the board member would profit from the transaction, or that the board member serves on the board of the other corporation involved or potentially involved in the transaction.

Every hospital or health system should have a conflict-of-interest policy in place to address such situations. The board chair should see that the policy is followed when a conflict arises. Adoption of such a policy eliminates the need for the organization to have a separate "noncompete" policy.

From time to time, all board members have conflicts of interest. In almost every case, board members need not resign if they declare the conflict to the board chair and do not participate in decisions concerning these transactions.

Care and loyalty are the two basic duties shared by all trustees. Because of the nature of health care today, and because nonprofit hospital trustees are ultimately responsible for the quality of patient care, health care trustees must take these duties very seriously. Health care governance is not an easy task.

LESSONS FROM THE PANEL ON THE NONPROFIT SECTOR

In June 2005, the Panel on the Nonprofit Sector issued a report to Congress titled *Strengthening Transparency, Governance, and Accountability of Charitable Organizations.* The report made fifteen major recommendations about how nonprofit organizations should be regulated and governed. When discussing the structure, size, composition, and independence of governing boards, the report noted that "a knowledgeable, committed board of directors is the strongest protector of a charitable organization's accountability to the law, its donors, consumers of its products and services, and the public."[1] This is certainly true for those who serve on the boards of nonprofit hospitals and health care organizations. Directors of nonprofit hospitals are strong protectors of the very people the hospital serves—its patients.

Major policymakers are sitting up and taking notice of the recommendations in the report. Senator Charles Grassley, chair of the Senate Finance Committee, said, "This report… will be of great use as the Finance Committee… now begins drafting legislation. My goal is legislation that will seek to encourage more checks to charities while also ensuring that the dollars are being spent appropriately to help the community and those in need. The panel report will inform the committee and its work, particularly in the important areas of governance and transparency."[2]

Some of the report's recommendations will make it into law. And other provisions, while not becoming legislation, may well become "best practices" that nonprofit boards and managers ignore at their peril. Although the report is wide-ranging, many of its observations about governance duties and roles are quite succinct. We shall discuss three of the report's most pertinent observations and recommendations in the following pages.

"Independent" Board Members

The report defines "independent board members" as individuals (1) who have not been compensated by the organization within the past twelve months, including full-time and part-time compensation as an employee or as an independent contractor (except for "reasonable compensation" for board service); (2) whose own compensation, except for board service, is not determined by individuals who are compensated by the organization; (3) who do not receive, directly or indirectly, material financial benefits (such as service contracts, grants, or other payments) from the organization except as a member of the charitable class served by the organization; and (4) who are the spouse, sibling, parent, or child of any such individual. Nonprofit hospitals should also remember that the **Sarbanes-Oxley Act** of 2002 sets forth standards for the independence of members of board audit committees of publicly traded corporations. Although Sarbanes-Oxley generally does not apply to nonprofit corporations, it provides, with regard to director "independence," that companies registered with the New York Stock Exchange must have a majority of directors who meet the Exchange's definition of "independence."

With regard to public charities, the report recommends that at least one-third of their board members be free of the conflicts of interest that can arise when they have a personal interest in the financial transactions of the charity. Individuals who receive compensation for services or material financial benefits from the hospital (and their spouses or family members) would have inherent conflicts of interest and would not be considered independent board members.

Founders of many nonprofit hospitals probably initially turned to family members, business partners, and neighbors and friends to serve on the hospital's board. We often hear from hospitals that finding independent board members can be particularly problematic in smaller communities and rural areas. Although it can be difficult at times, hospitals should make every effort to find independent board members. The report goes so far as to state that this should be a legal requirement for public charities that are eligible to receive tax-deductible contributions on the most favorable terms.

Disqualification from Board Service

The report recommends that Congress amend the regulations to prohibit individuals who are barred from service on boards of publicly traded companies or convicted of crimes directly related to breaches of fiduciary duty in their service as an employee or board member of a charitable organization from serving on the board of a charitable organization for five years following their conviction or removal.

The Sarbanes-Oxley Act (discussed in greater detail later in this chapter) grants the Securities and Exchange Commission (**SEC**) the authority to bar individuals from serving on the boards of publicly traded companies subject to the approval of a federal judge or an SEC administrative law judge (ALJ). Currently, there is no prohibition on individuals barred by the SEC from serving on the boards of nonprofit hospitals or health care organizations. But obviously, nonprofit hospitals and other health care organizations should recognize that if someone has been barred from service on the board of a publicly traded company or convicted of a crime directly related to a breach of fiduciary duty while serving as an employee or board member of a charitable organization, this should raise serious concerns about the person's perceived ability to fulfill the fiduciary responsibilities of a board member of a nonprofit hospital.

Nonprofit hospitals should begin to ask and remind current and prospective board members about this prohibition. Ultimately, though, the responsibility for resigning or declining board service should rest with the individual who has been prohibited from such service. The report suggests that individuals who fail to inform the hospital that they are ineligible to serve should be subject to a penalty equivalent to penalties imposed on tax preparers for omission or misrepresentation of information.

Board Compensation

The report confirmed our experience that the vast majority of board members are not compensated for their services. However, charities and foundations are permitted under current law to pay "reasonable compensation" for services provided by board members. "Reasonable compensation" is defined as "the amount that would ordinarily be paid for like services by like enterprises (whether tax-exempt or taxable) under like circumstances." Federal tax laws prohibit payment of excessive compensation and contracts and transactions that provide excessive economic benefit to board members and other "disqualified persons." The report defines a "disqualified person" for public charities and also for private foundations. For public charities, a disqualified person is someone who at any time during the five-year period ending on the date of the transaction in question was "in a position to exercise substantial influence over the affairs of the organization." Any member of a disqualified person's family is considered a disqualified person, as is any entity in which one or more disqualified persons together own, directly or indirectly, more than a 35 percent interest.

The report "strongly encourages" charitable organizations to ask board members to serve on a voluntary basis. In situations where a nonprofit hospital or health care organization feels that it is necessary to compensate board members, the report recommends that there be significant disclosure requirements to detail the amount of and reasons for the compensation, including the services provided and the responsibilities of board members. Compensation for service as a board member must be "reasonable" and must be clearly differentiated from any compensation paid for services in the capacity of the staff of the organization.

In situations where the organization feels that board members should be compensated because of the complexity of the responsibility, the time commitment involved in board service, and the skills required for the particular assignment, the organization should, as a best practice, review information on compensation provided by organizations comparable in size, grantmaking or program practices, geographical scope, location, and with similar board responsibilities, to determine the "reasonableness" of any compensation provided to board members.

FEDERAL SENTENCING GUIDELINES FOR ORGANIZATIONS

Establishing and maintaining an effective compliance and **ethics** program is another responsibility of the health care organization's governing board. On November 1, 2004, the United States Sentencing Commission revised the "Federal Sentencing Guidelines for Organizations," which apply to nonprofit and for-profit organizations. The guidelines were created in 1984 to respond to a perception and some evidence (in the case of individual, not corporate, defendants) that judges in the federal circuits were adopting very different sentences for similarly situated defendants found guilty of criminal charges. Chapter 8 in the guidelines, addressing sentencing of organizations, was added in 1991.

The guidelines set a baseline range of determinate sentences for different categories of offenses; judges increase or decrease the sentence depending on enumerated circumstances listed in the guidelines (setting a culpability score from which "upward or downward departures" are made). The 2004 amendments to Chapter 8 seek to strengthen the importance of the characteristics of an effective **corporate compliance** program defined in the guidelines.

The revised guidelines broadly define the term *organization* to include "corporations, partnerships, associations, joint-stock companies, unions, trusts, pension funds, unincorporated organizations, governments and political subdivisions thereof, and non-profit organizations."[3] The guidelines also speak directly to the responsibilities placed on the board. They provide that "the organization's governing authority shall be knowledgeable about the content and operation of the compliance and ethics program and shall exercise reasonable oversight with respect to the implementation and effectiveness of the compliance and ethics program."[4] "Governing authority" is defined as the board of directors or, if the organization does not have a board of directors, the highest-level governing body of the organization.[5]

The guidelines make it very clear that for an organization to receive a reduction in fines and penalties, oversight of programs designed to prevent and detect criminal activity is the responsibility of an organization's board. The key 2004 changes to the guidelines from a board member's perspective are the following:

■ An explicit recognition of the important role ethics and culture play in ensuring effective compliance programs. The commission changed the definition of an effective program from one that provides due diligence to prevent and detect criminal violations to one that must also "promote an organizational culture that encourages ethical conduct and a commitment to compliance with the law." With this revision, the commission sought to emphasize that without ethics, compliance becomes about following a minimum set of rules and reflects the emphasis on ethics and values incorporated into recent legislative and regulatory reforms.

■ The placement of responsibility for reasonable oversight of the compliance and ethics program with the board. This means that the board must ensure that management and employees act legally and ethically to protect the company's reputation and the value that derives from that reputation.

■ A requirement that senior management "ensure" that the organization has an effective compliance and ethics program (ECEP) by working closely with senior leadership to develop a strong program.

■ A risk assessment requirement that demonstrates that the organization has identified risk areas where criminal violations may occur. This may include the use of auditing and monitoring systems to detect criminal conduct, ongoing risk assessment, and periodic evaluation of the effectiveness of the program.

■ A requirement that the organization encourage "appropriate incentives to perform in accordance with the compliance and ethics program."

■ A requirement that organizations provide employees with a means to seek guidance regarding potential or actual criminal conduct without fear of retribution. Practically, this means that boards should assess employee willingness to use the system in place in the organization.

■ Required training in relevant legal standards and obligations. It is no longer an option. The revised guidelines include a mandatory training requirement for high-level officials and for employees.

■ A requirement that compliance officers be given adequate authority and resources to carry out their responsibilities, including a direct reporting responsibility and access to the organizational leadership and the organization's board. [6]

In sum, the amendments have both raised the bar for compliance and ethics and have put responsibility for an effective compliance and ethics program in the hands of the board.

THE SARBANES-OXLEY ACT OF 2002

Even though not legally required to do so, some hospitals and health care organizations are revising their bylaws to be more consistent with the requirements of the Public Company Accounting Reform and Investor Protection Act of 2002, widely referred to as the Sarbanes-Oxley Act. Sarbanes-Oxley established new requirements for the corporate governance of issuers of securities that are regulated by the Securities and Exchange Commission. Because nonprofit hospitals and health care organizations do not issue securities that are regulated by the SEC, the act does not apply directly to these organizations.

At the same time, nonprofit boards should recognize that some of the concepts included in the act have been adopted by the Exempt Organizations Branch of the Internal Revenue Service. Nonprofit boards should also be aware that some states have been considering legislation that would impose the requirements of the Sarbanes-Oxley Act on nonprofit corporations in those states. Therefore, the boards of health care organizations are well advised to consider the concepts on which Sarbanes-Oxley was based. An open question is the extent to which the act's approach to implementing corporate accountability and other principles of governance may be applied to the nonprofit setting either through subsequent legislation or judicial review.

Although the Sarbanes-Oxley Act does not apply to nonprofit corporations, it contains certain provisions that reflect principles that directors and CEOs of nonprofit organizations have long been expected to follow. At the very least, the act is educational in that it highlights these principles and expectations. It is also possible that at some point in the future, a court would look to the act for guidance when interpreting duties of directors and CEOs of nonprofit organizations. Similarly, at some future point, legislatures may impose similar requirements on nonprofits. The following discusses the main provisions of the act that could potentially be applied to nonprofit organizations.

Accountability Just as the Sarbanes-Oxley Act is intended to make corporate executives and auditors more accountable to the shareholders of public companies and impose new obligations and restrictions on directors and senior executives of such companies, similar accountability could eventually be placed on directors and senior executives of nonprofits. For example, certain sections of the act require senior executive certification of financial reports. The act holds signing officers responsible for establishing and maintaining internal controls to ensure that material information relating to the company and its consolidated subsidiaries is made known to such officers by others within those entities. It requires the signing officers to have disclosed to the company's auditors and the board's audit committee all significant deficiencies in the design or operation of internal controls that could adversely affect the company's ability to record, process, summarize, and report financial data.

Another section of the act prohibits directors and officers of public companies from taking any action to "fraudulently influence, coerce, manipulate, or mislead" any independent public or certified accountant engaged in the performance of an audit of the company's financial statements for the purpose of rendering such financial statements materially misleading.

It's easy to see how the same technical requirements could be placed on directors and officers of nonprofits. Even though there are no shareholders in a nonprofit to bring derivative suits against corporate officers for such actions, a state attorney general could decide to look more closely into these matters.

Under Sarbanes-Oxley, the SEC is empowered to prohibit any person who violates federal securities laws, rules, or regulations from acting as an officer or director of any public company. Again, it is not a stretch to imagine that potential bars could be placed on officers and directors of nonprofits who violate certain laws, rules, or regulations, prohibiting them from serving in that capacity for any other nonprofit organization. In fact, the exclusion from Medicare of individuals convicted of certain crimes is one example of how this principle has already been applied in the nonprofit setting.

Audit Process and Oversight Sarbanes-Oxley established the Accounting Oversight Board to oversee firms that audit public companies in the United States and abroad. That board's regulations apply to the same independent auditing firms that audit nonprofits. Nonprofit boards should remember that annual external audits should be conducted and should be reviewed by the health care organization's board of directors. It is equally important for accounting firms and auditors of nonprofit health care organizations to avoid conflicts of interest and to have no business relationship with the organization outside of the auditing duties being provided.

Disclosures One significant aspect of Sarbanes-Oxley is that it requires public companies to disclose material changes in financial condition or operations on a rapid and current basis. The same "real-time disclosure" requirement could likewise be placed on nonprofits. It is foreseeable that nonprofits will be called on in the future to disclose (in plain English and on a rapid and current basis) information concerning material changes in financial condition or operations. Such a requirement would lessen or perhaps completely avoid deferral of disclosures by nonprofits.

The act similarly requires each public company to disclose in its periodic reports whether the board's audit committee has at least one member who is a "financial expert." This requirement for financial expertise on the audit committee of a nonprofit health care board seems reasonable, and it would not be a surprise if such a requirement were applied to nonprofits in the future.

Sarbanes-Oxley requires public companies to disclose whether their senior financial executives have adopted a "code of ethics." Likewise, senior financial executives of nonprofit corporations might be expected to follow this same type of code in the future (or at least to profess their allegiance to such a code to some governmental agency).

Finally, the act requires attorneys to report violations of securities laws and breaches of fiduciary duty by a public company or its agents to the chief legal counsel or CEO of the company. If the counsel or CEO does not respond appropriately, the attorney must report the evidence to the audit committee of the company's board of directors, to a committee composed entirely of outside directors, or to the board as a whole. In our estimation, it is possible that the same reporting obligations could be placed on attorneys for nonprofit corporations to report breaches of fiduciary duty by senior executives.

THE VOLUNTEER PROTECTION ACT OF 1997

One little-known but very important protection afforded to hospital trustees is the federal **Volunteer Protection Act of 1997**. This statute was passed to protect volunteers active in not-for-profit corporations such as the Boy Scouts, playgroups, Little League, and other community organizations. While not specifically incorporating trustees or hospitals, the language is broad enough to cover them.

The act defines a not-for-profit organization as "any organization which is described in section 501(c)(3) of Title 26 [of the Internal Revenue Code] and exempt from tax under section 501(a) of Title 26... or any not-for-profit organization which is organized and conducted for public benefit and operated primarily for charitable, civic, educational, religious, welfare, or health purposes."[7] Because most hospitals and health systems are tax-exempt organizations under 501(c)(3) of the Internal Revenue Code and are conducted for public benefit and operated primarily for health purposes, most hospitals easily fit within the act's definition of a not-for-profit organization.

Furthermore, trustees are specifically identified as "volunteers" under the act. The Volunteer Protection Act defines a volunteer as "an individual performing services for a non-profit organization or a governmental entity who does not receive compensation... or any other thing of value in lieu of compensation... and such term includes a volunteer serving as a director, officer, trustee, or direct service volunteer."[8]

The act specifically limits liability for volunteers such as hospital trustees. It states that "no volunteer of a non-profit organization... shall be liable for harm caused by an act or omission of the volunteer on behalf of the organization or entity if the volunteer was acting within the scope of the volunteer's responsibilities in the non-profit organization... at the time of the act or omission... if the harm was not caused by willful or criminal misconduct, gross negligence, reckless misconduct, or a conscious, flagrant indifference to the rights or safety of the individual harmed by the volunteer."[9]

Punitive damages are also limited by this act. The general rule is that "punitive damages may not be awarded against a volunteer in an action brought for harm based on the action of a volunteer acting within the scope of the volunteer's responsibilities to a non-profit organization... unless the claimant establishes by clear and convincing evidence that the harm was proximately caused by action of such volunteer which constitutes willful or criminal misconduct, or a conscious, flagrant indifference to the rights or safety of the individual harmed."[10] Although the act lists exceptions to volunteer liability protection based on certain provisions in state laws that may be applicable in some circumstances, it does limit liability for trustees of not-for-profit organizations in many circumstances.

The purpose of the Volunteer Protection Act is to sustain the viability of not-for-profit organizations (such as hospitals) that depend on volunteers. This act is an important federal law that by its very nature can limit the liability of hospital trustees should a claim be brought against them. Hospital trustees and counsel should be familiar with this protection. It is particularly valuable in this time of medical professional liability insurance crisis. Risk management professionals should be well aware of it.

RISK MANAGEMENT AND THE BOARD

A risk management professional's duty is inherent in the title of the position itself—to prevent or minimize corporate loss from legal liability. This may involve developing systems to prevent adverse events and attempting to handle events that do occur in such a manner that the organization's financial and reputation cost are minimized. For example, in the case of a sentinel event or other unexpected occurrence that could risk liability, reputation, and accreditation, the risk management professional may interview central figures to determine what went wrong, hold personal discussions with the injured party or parties, or attempt to reach a satisfactory settlement without a lawsuit.

Board accountability and responsibility for risk management and quality are not new; they have always been the duty of the health care organization governing board. This section discusses the type of relationship between the health care organization's risk management professional and its governing board that will shield the organization's losses from legal liability most effectively and efficiently.

Risk Management's Role in Educating the Board

Although it is not common for the risk management professional to report directly to the board (as will be discussed later in this chapter), the CEO and the risk management professional still need to ensure that the board is educated about the overall task of risk management and the crucial part the board itself plays in reducing potential liability by effectively discharging its risk management oversight role.

Board members must understand that they play a key part (along with the risk management professional) in preventing patient injury, preventing medical professional liability, and overseeing the corporation's prevention of loss from legal liability. This means that the board must work closely with the risk management professional and other hospital management staff, with the understanding that ineffective governance can cause harm to patients if it goes uncorrected and could also generate liability for the corporation. Board education is key, but remember that management of risk is the result of board attention to medical and other errors that harm or could harm patients and of a plan for preventing repeat errors. As previously stated, one of the most important responsibilities of the board is to see that care is taken by the hospital and physicians so that patients are not harmed.

The risk management professional and CEO should play a dual role in educating the board with regard to its risk management and oversight duties. Periodically, and for new board members, the risk management professional and CEO may conduct a "risk management orientation program." In-house counsel and medical staff leadership may also participate in this introduction or orientation to risk management. The risk management professional and hospital management can use this opportunity to ensure that the board is familiar with the following concepts:

- The relationship between the health care organization's quality improvement program and medical staff **credentialing** function and the risk management program

- The health care organization's definition of risk management and the scope of the hospital's or system's risk management program

- The role and job of the risk management professional

- The relationship between the insurance, loss of control, and claims functions and the risk management program

- How the risk management professional gathers data and identifies risks—incident reporting, occurrence reporting, generic screening, patient complaints, or other methods

- The highest-risk areas of patient injury and medical professional liability claims within the hospital and throughout the system and how they compare with national data

- Insurance coverage and costs

- The health care organization's claims history

- The part the board plays in preventing patient injury and malpractice liability and reducing overall liability exposure by effectively discharging its risk management oversight role

- The role of ineffective governance in generating liability losses[11]

Participation in such an orientation process can ensure that both new and current board members have a basic understanding of the hospital or health system's organizational structure vis-à-vis risk management and a basic understanding of the crucial role the board plays in accountability and responsibility for patient safety. The implementation of such an orientation program, however, is only the beginning of the larger role that the risk management professional (and hospital management) can play in establishing a comprehensive board orientation program.

Although an initial or periodic risk management orientation program is a good idea, it only scratches the surface of the knowledge that board members will need to effectively discharge their duties as corporate fiduciaries. The risk management professional can and should continue this educational process for the board by working with management to create a series of ongoing, well-designed activities for both new and current board members so that they are continually made aware of issues of patient safety. Such ongoing activities (as opposed to educational sessions held once or twice a year) ensure that the board's education regarding its oversight duties is not an ad hoc event but rather a continuing process.

What are the core competencies that board members should possess to keep themselves and their organizations accountable? From a risk management perspective, at least some board members should possess specific competencies in law, accounting, finance, and clinical care. It is also important for trustees to understand governance obligations, functions, processes, and best practices; the health care industry and their individual market and organization; key success factors, including strategic, financial, operational, and clinical variables; and how to read, analyze, and interpret basic financial statements.[12]

A hospital or health system board cannot effectively discharge its oversight role in patient safety until it has been properly educated. The risk management professional can play a pivotal role in ensuring that this education takes place.

Delivery of Information to the Board

Management could ask the risk management professional to report directly to the board, but this is unusual. Risk management professionals generally report to hospital management, either directly to the CEO or through a chief operating officer or senior vice president. It is not unusual for the risk management professional to report to the chief medical officer or vice president of medical affairs. Information generally comes to the board through the hospital's management. How this is accomplished is a matter to be worked out between the CEO and the board chair. Only in an extreme situation (in which the risk management professional believes that management is creating liability for the corporation and not telling the board about it) should a risk management professional bypass management and report concerns directly to the board.

Some organizations have the risk management professional report to a board committee, usually the professional affairs committee (PAC) of the board or the equivalent committee responsible for receiving and making recommendations on credentialing and peer review recommendations from the medical staff executive committee. Because the role of the PAC is generally to receive recommendations from the various medical staff committees and to make recommendations to the board regarding such things as initial appointment, reappointment, the delineation of privileges, disciplinary actions taken against medical staff appointees, bylaws, and rules and regulations of the medical staff, the PAC is an ideal committee for the risk management professional to report to in lieu of a report to the full board. This is especially true when potential liability involves a physician, as it does in almost all major cases.

Medicare and Medicaid Fraud and Abuse

The Medicare definition of fraud is "an intentional representation that an individual knows to be false or does not believe to be true and makes, knowing that the representation could result in some unauthorized benefit to himself/herself or some other person."[13] The most frequent kind of fraud arises from a false statement or misrepresentation made or caused to be made that is material to entitlement or payment under the Medicare program. The violator may be a physician or other practitioner, a hospital or other institutional provider, a clinical laboratory or other supplier, an employee of any provider, a billing service, a beneficiary, a Medicare carrier employee, or any person in a position to file a claim for Medicare benefits.

Fraud schemes that a risk management professional might become aware of could include one or more of the following: offering or accepting kickbacks; routine waiver of copayments; fraudulent diagnosis; billing for services not rendered; unbundling charges; or falsifying certificates of medical necessity, plans of treatment, and medical records to justify payment.

A risk management professional's discovery of Medicare or Medicaid fraud and abuse may sometimes represent the type of extreme situation that requires a risk management professional to bypass higher authority and go directly to the board. This would, of course, occur only if top management either were implicated or refused to take effective action.

What Should the Board Know?

What information should the hospital trustees have? First, it is very important to keep in mind that the risk management professional should couch all reports to the board in terms that maximize state peer review protection. Risk management professionals' reports should always provide a road map for peer review protection under state law. Also, it is important to strike a proper balance as to how much information to provide to the board. Nothing productive will be accomplished if trustees are overwhelmed with information. At the same time, it is essential that they be given enough information to thoroughly understand the issue. There are a few basics, however. The following should always be brought to the board's attention:

- All sentinel events and follow-up

- All lawsuits filed, the nature of claims, and what is being done to address any quality questions these raise

- All payments, settlements, and judgments

- Any quality trends

- Any questions raised by the death of a patient

There is little point in having a risk management professional if this kind of information is not given to the board.

Content and Format of Reports to the Board

It is not easy for hospital management to decide what information the board should be privy to, nor is it easy for risk management professionals to strike the difficult balance between enabling the board to thoroughly understand an issue without overwhelming it with data. In addition to the basic information just listed that the board should always be given, risk management reports should strive to provide the board with meaningful information about issues of patient safety a clear, concise, graphic format.

Information provided to the board should be in the form of a single report that is short and easy to read. Such reports (by risk management or hospital management) should state in plain English where the organization stands with respect to incidents that affect patient safety and where it strives to be.

It may also be helpful to include a "consent agenda" to streamline board meeting procedures. Consent agenda items are considered routine and noncontroversial, with documentation provided to the board that is adequate and sufficient for approval without discussion unless a board member raises a specific question. For instance, a consent agenda may routinely include such things as approval of the minutes from the last board meeting or approval of reports from the medical executive committee. The consent agenda is intended to minimize the time required for the handling of noncontroversial matters and to permit additional time to be spent on more significant matters. Any item on the consent agenda should be moved to the regular agenda at the request of any board member. Such items may also be put off to a subsequent meeting for further consideration.

Recommendations of the medical staff credentials committee regarding physician appointments and clinical privileges are usually noncontroversial and are often posted on the consent agenda. We believe that this is a bad idea. The recommendations of the credentials committee dealing with appointment and clinical privileges go directly to the most important board responsibility—the safety of patients. These recommendations must be acted on directly by the board after the board asks for and receives the assurance of the credentials committee chair that these recommendations are the result of the thoughtful work of the committee. Even though the recommendations pass through and are approved by the medical staff executive committee, they should be presented to the board by the chair of the committee that did the work. The approval may, in most cases, be pro forma, but it should be received from the committee and be endorsed by the committee chair before the board acts.

Reports to the board should include a carefully selected group of risk management indicators that show board members at a glance how well their organization is performing with respect to patient safety. Indicators might include such items as analyses of trends identified through incident reports and occurrence screens, open and closed claims, trends and costs of claims, or results of insurance audits and costs—all the while remembering that claims and their costs represent problems that need to be fixed. Board members and risk management professionals alike should not forget that the harm done to patients is more important than the insurance loss.

The report should track the organization's risk management trends over time in a graphic format and should show how the organization compares with benchmark organizations. Presenting information to boards in this way not only lays out the data for trustees but also actually helps board members interpret the data. This ensures that trustees are getting the information they need to know where their organization stands.

Moreover, when assessing the risk management status of an organization, boards will benefit by being able to see the "big picture" rather than being bogged down in data.

Risk management professionals might begin by first analyzing the most important five to ten risk management variables that the board needs to know over the course of the next year. The risk management professional, CEO, and board chair should all play a part in deciding on the crucial indicators. A chart should be prepared for each indicator containing a line or curve showing the organization's target for that indicator. Before each board meeting, management (with the risk management professional's help) plots what actually happened in a different color so that all the board members need to do is look at the chart to see if what actually happened is above or below the organization's target line.[14] Such a format facilitates quick review of the essential indicators and provides the board with the easily understood, big-picture view of the issues that it needs to govern effectively in the areas of patient safety and risk management.

How the Board Can Help Hospital Management and the Risk Management Professional

It is important for the governing board and the risk management professional of any health care organization to realize that all duties delegated to the risk management professional ultimately flow from the board through the chief executive officer. The governance of the organization should be the source of responsibilities that the risk management professional carries out. From a managerial perspective, this eases the blame or resistance to things that must be done that could potentially fall to the risk management professional should others in the organization perceive that orders are flowing from one individual alone. It must be clear that the risk management professional is carrying out delegated authority and responsibilities of the chief executive officer of the corporation.

THE MEDICAL STAFF, RISK MANAGEMENT, AND THE BOARD

The medical staff of the hospital or other health care organization is central to risk management. The most serious liability any health care organization (and particularly a hospital) faces is always at the intersection between the organization and the physicians who practice there.

The expression "medical staff" has two different meanings: one describes individual physicians who have received from the board an appointment to the hospital medical staff and treat patients in the hospital; the other refers to an organization of physicians established by the hospital board with various delegated duties pertaining to quality and the ability to act as a group to influence the hospital, its management, and its board.

How does the medical staff, both as an organization and as individuals, relate to governance? The purpose of the individual members of the medical staff is to provide top-quality medicine, whereas the purpose of the medical staff as an organization is to monitor the care provided.

The medical staff organization acts as a consultant to the hospital board. It is asked to make recommendations on quality, appointments, discipline of medical appointees, and hospital needs and procedures. Members of medical staff committees who make such recommendations must act with the same care and loyalty as board members. The medical staff is not organized for political purposes or to protect the economic interests of any or all physicians.

The hospital's relationship with members of the medical staff does not fit easily within ordinary corporate law or organization. That is why it is sometimes difficult for the risk management professional to deal with quality or liability issues that involve members of the medical staff. However, it is essential that this be done. Management, including the risk management professional, is responsible to the board for investigating all potential liability, physician-related or otherwise. The medical staff organization does not have exclusive jurisdiction over acts by physicians in the hospital.

When the Board Must Step In

The board delegates responsibility for monitoring and overseeing the quality of care to the medical staff. However, if the medical staff fails or is unable to fulfill its responsibilities in monitoring the safety and outcome of care provided by the organization, the board has the legal authority and, more important, the obligation to step in to oversee the safety and outcomes.

Medical Staff Development Plans

A medical staff development plan defines what it means to be a member of the medical staff, including sharing the hospital's vision, mission, and commitment to the community.[15] Many boards have found the development of such plans to be effective. For many hospitals, such plans have become critical to maintaining a good relationship with their medical staffs. Just going through the process of developing a plan has been helpful. Critical steps in the development of a plan follow:

Step 1: Board Adopts Resolution and Statement of Community Service Principles The board adopts a resolution that authorizes the research and analysis that lead to the plan. That resolution also establishes a staff development committee or task force composed of board members, management representatives (including the chief executive officer), and physicians. It is important that the physicians selected for this committee not be those who might be economically advantaged by its recommendations. A Statement of Community Service Principles, adopted by the board, provides the foundation for further discussions and possible actions with respect to physicians who have economic conflicts of interest.

Step 2: Communicate It is critical that physicians, especially those in leadership positions, know and understand how and why a medical staff development plan is being developed, its purpose, and its objectives. The physicians should be kept apprised of the progress of the study, and when appropriate, input from physicians should be sought and considered.

Step 3: Gather Data and Analyze Community Needs The ultimate purpose of the plan (and of the hospital itself) is to meet the needs of the community. That, obviously, is part of a hospital's charitable purposes as articulated in its Statement of Community Service Principles.

A "community needs assessment" involves collecting data regarding individuals currently practicing in the hospital; information about their practices and referral patterns, including what care is referred outside of the community and why; demographic information regarding the population served by the hospital and that population's health care needs; the study of the existing health resources in the community; and areas underserved from either a geographic, medical specialty, or income level standpoint.

Visits to the emergency department, calls from individuals seeking physicians to provide care, waiting lists for care in physician office practices, or the inability to obtain an appointment can all indicate a community need for specific services.

The task force analyzes the data collected to determine on a specialty-by-specialty basis what is necessary to meet the current and projected needs of the community.

Step 4: Communicate Again As this information is collected, it should be made available for physicians to review and comment on. Physicians should also be surveyed to gain insight into what services the hospital might offer, what services the hospital could provide better, and where efficiencies or additional progress could be achieved.

Step 5: Analyze Financial Relationships and Their Impact The task force should also analyze the financial relationships that physicians on the medical staff may have with competing entities, and how each type of financial relationship could compromise physicians' abilities to fulfill their responsibilities as members of the medical staff, or could otherwise impair the hospital's ability to fulfill its charitable mission.

Two types of physician financial relationships should be specifically analyzed: ownership or investment interests in competing facilities or services and compensation arrangements, such as employment contracts or medical directorships with competing facilities, including other hospitals or health systems. The task force's analysis should include (a) information about competing entities in the market and how those entities affect the hospital both financially and operationally; (b) disclosures from medical staff members and applicants of their financial relationships; and (c) whether the hospital can be made a more attractive location in which to practice.

Step 6: Task Force Recommends Based on its analysis of community needs and the effect of physicians' conflicting financial relationships, the task force might recommend

(a) adding, expanding, reducing, or eliminating clinical or new services; (b) recruiting new practitioners to meet clinical service needs; (c) identifying specialties which are recruitment priorities; or (d) setting organizational criteria for applicants in specialties in which applications will be accepted. Examples of such criteria may include "Potential applicants must indicate an intention to actively use the hospital's facilities to permit reasonable monitoring of their practices and to assure working familiarity with the hospital's technology, regulations, procedures, and personnel" [or] "Potential applicants must be willing to work with the medical staff and hospital to develop protocols and best practices in their specialties, to practice in accordance with such protocols or to document the reasons for variance, and to attend meetings at which such practices and protocols are reviewed and improved."

Additional organizational criteria may relate to financial concerns, including whether physicians who have conflicting financial relationships should be permitted to serve on the board or in medical staff leadership positions; should be eligible for appointment or reappointment to the medical staff or to categories of the staff that would give them the ability to participate in the governance of the staff or hospital; and should be eligible for financial relationships with, or assistance from, the hospital, for example, employment agreements, exclusive contracts, and malpractice premium assistance.

Step 7: Board Adopts Plan The board adopts a plan that is reviewed and revised on a regular basis, at least every three years.

SUMMARY

The ever-expanding responsibilities that health care organization governing boards face today make it more important than ever that individuals who support governance, such as risk management professionals, are up to the task. Health care governing boards have always been ultimately responsible for the quality of patient care provided, physician performance, risk management, and appointment and disciplining of physicians. In the future, the responsibilities of health care governing board will continue to increase.

Current media emphasis on medical errors will encourage boards to be proactive in monitoring and improving quality data, and the fallout from the recent corporate accounting scandals is certain to result in greater board responsibility for nonprofit corporate financial statements. The necessity for risk management in organizations other than the hospital is growing as lawyers for plaintiffs look for additional deep pockets to pay claims.

This will only intensify if the medical professional liability insurance crisis becomes more widespread. A strong, cooperative relationship among an organization's risk management professional, hospital management, and medical staff committees with quality responsibilities can ensure that the organization's loss from legal liability is reduced or even eliminated.

KEY TERMS

Allied health professional	For-profit hospital
Corporate compliance	Loss control
Corporate liability	Organizational culture
Credentialing	Patient safety
Director	Risk control techniques
Duty of care	Risk management
Duty of loyalty	Sarbanes-Oxley Act
Ethics	Trustee
Fiduciary duty	Volunteer Protection Act of 1997

ACRONYMS

CEO
SEC

NOTES

1. Panel on the Nonprofit Sector. Strengthening Transparency, Governance, and Accountability of Charitable Organizations: A Final Report to Congress and the Nonprofit Sector. Washington, D.C.: Panel on the Nonprofit Sector, June 2005, p. 75.

2. Sen. Charles Grassley, news conference of the Panel on the Nonprofit Sector's Final Report, June 22, 2005.

3. U.S. Sentencing Commission. "Federal Sentencing Guidelines for Organizations," §8A1.1, application note 1.

4. Ibid., §8B2.1(b)(2)(A).

5. Ibid., §8B2.1, application note 1.

6. Seidman, D. "What Every Board Member Needs to Know About Compliance." *Compliance Today*, July 2005, pp. 6, 9.

7. 42 USCA §14505(4)(A)(B).

8. Ibid., §14505(6)(A)(B).

9. Ibid., §14503(a)(1)(3).

10. Ibid., §14503(e)(1).

11. Orlikoff, J. E. "The Health Care Organization Governing Board." In R. L. Carroll (ed.), *Risk Management Handbook for Health Care Organizations*, 3rd ed. San Francisco: Jossey-Bass, 2001.

12. Mycek, S. "Accountability Stops Here: Educating the Board to Meet Its Responsibilities." *Trustee*, 2002, *55*(6), 13.

13. Centers for Medicare and Medicaid Services. "Glossary," http://www.cms.hhs.gov/apps/glossary/

14. Strenger, E. W. "The Data Game." *Trustee*, 1997, *50*(4), 28.

15. This entire section is from "Medical Staff Development Plans," *Action Kit for Hospital Trustees*, Jan.-Feb. 2004. Copyright © 2004 by Horty, Springer, & Mattern, P.C. Reprinted with permission.

CHAPTER

6

EARLY WARNING SYSTEMS FOR THE IDENTIFICATION OF ORGANIZATIONAL RISKS

ROBERTA L. CARROLL

LEARNING OBJECTIVES

- To be able to compare formal and informal methods for reporting adverse events in a health care organization
- To be able to identify why risk identification is a critical component in the risk management process
- To be able to recognize barriers to incident reporting
- To be able to identify and describe three internal and three external event reporting systems
- To be able to describe how the implementation of a risk management information system can assist in the identification and analysis of organizational risk

The effectiveness of a risk management program is commensurate with the organization's ability to identify and analyze its risk exposure. Risk management professionals use a five-step decision-making process developed by the Insurance Institute of America[1] and supported by the American Society for Healthcare Risk Management.[2] This is the foundation for health care risk management programs. Its first step is identifying and analyzing an organization's exposure to loss. This is the starting point for all risk initiatives.

The principles of risk identification and analysis can be used in all care settings and with all programs regardless of scope or size. All care settings, from an acute care hospital, home health agency, skilled nursing facility, and ambulatory surgery center to a physician group practice, find that early identification and analysis are pivotal to risk management program success.

Program scope can vary within the same type of care settings. One health care risk management program is just that: one health care risk management program. Factors on which program scope might be based include the following:

■ *Services.* Services offered are prioritized by the frequency and severity of losses or are known to be problematic in the industry. For example, most risk management professionals promote patient safety in obstetrical practices even if there have been no liability lawsuits. On the other hand, if the organization does not have a labor and delivery unit, the only aspect of obstetrical risk of concern for the risk management professional is whether or not the emergency department manages laboring patients properly under the Emergency Medical Treatment and Labor Act (EMTALA).

■ *Locale.* Several states have statutes that require the implementation of a risk management program. For example, Florida requires risk management programs in hospitals,[3] long-term care facilities,[4] and HMOs.[5] One component of these programs is the development and implementation of an incident reporting system.

■ *Skill, expertise, and interest* of the risk management professional.

■ *Organizational environment and culture.* The more caring, trusting, and open to process change an organization is, the more robust and more effective are its risk management programs.

Regardless of the setting or scope, all risk management programs must identify and analyze exposure to loss. This is the premise on which this chapter is written.

EARLY IDENTIFICATION OF EXPOSURE TO LOSS

Tactical initiatives that help an organization identify risk may be thought of as early warning systems. The risk management professional is often best positioned to implement such systems when they are based on a comprehensive assessment of organizational risk.

Health care risk management programs employ many such initiatives to identify in a timely manner the events, activities, initiatives, practices, systems, and processes that can threaten or contribute to loss. One example is the inclusion of near misses or

KEY CONCEPTS

- The effectiveness of a risk management program is directly related to the organization's ability to identify and manage its exposure to loss.

- Early warning systems alert the risk management professional to adverse events, incidents, occurrences, potentially compensable events, process and systems errors, claims, and near misses.

- The identification and analysis of risks on an enterprisewide basis encourages the risk management professional to look beyond operational or clinical risks.

- Although some states protect peer review, quality, risk, and patient safety data, information assembled from adverse event and medical error reporting systems does not enjoy federal protection.

- All employees have the responsibility to identify risks to the organization.

close calls in the reporting system of many health care organizations. In this chapter, near misses and close calls are included in the definition of an incident.

Getting Started: Risk Identification

If an organization does not identify real, threatened, or perceived exposure to loss, it will be unable to implement risk control techniques necessary to eliminate the exposure, minimize the loss, or implement financing measures to pay for losses that do occur despite best efforts. Because all other activities stem from this first step in the risk management process, it is a critical component of all risk management programs.

Assessment of organizational risk is a logical first step in program development and a useful process when evaluating the effectiveness of current programs. Identifying risk across an organization's structure or on an enterprisewide basis in what is now termed enterprise risk management allows the risk management professional to do all of the following:

- Identify all risks confronting the organization regardless of organizational setting. Risk management professionals need not act alone in this process. It is wise to engage others who have knowledge of the risks inherent in areas under their supervision. This is particularly true where the risk management professional might lack technical expertise and need the assistance of subject matter experts.

- Identify and analyze the relationship among risks. What is the synergistic relationship among risks? For example, consider how risks associated with human capital (personnel risk) such as staffing shortages, fatigue, low morale, turnover, and intimidation can increase the possibility of medical errors. Identifying risk across the organization's continuum of care will allow the risk management professional to gain a better understanding of the relationships that exist among risks.

- Understand organizational dynamics and their effect on culture and the environment.
- Corroborate the organization's mission, vision, and strategy.
- Understand the organization's structure and identify lines of business, units, divisions, and programs. Engaging staff in identifying risks in their areas of responsibility allows the risk management professional to facilitate and partake in the assessment process and empowers the staff to follow through with any recommendations. Such an approach also produces the most relevant solutions. Given the opportunity to contribute, staff who work daily in specific units or divisions are in the best position to identify areas of weakness and risk and can offer meaningful and sustainable solutions.
- Educate senior leadership in understanding the risk exposure of the organization. Risk management professionals are perfectly positioned to see risk from an organizationwide perspective—the "big picture." This understanding will support the offering of educational initiatives to the board of directors, medical staff leadership, and administrative leadership on risk issues that affect mission, vision, and strategy.
- Garner support necessary to develop and implement future solutions.
- Build credibility and promote collaboration for risk management activities.

Risk management professionals do not act alone. They engage all members of the organization in identifying and analyzing exposure to loss.

Knowledge of the organization is crucial to the success of risk management programs. The consequences of not thoroughly understanding the organization can threaten and weaken a risk management program by causing loss of trust and credibility; wasting resources (money, time, and staff support) by focusing effort in areas that do not significantly affect quality outcomes, patient safety, and fiscal strength; and diminishing the role of risk management professionals by charging them with tasks that do not reduce risk or add value to the organization's bottom line. An understanding of this last point can be reached by asking the following question: "What adds more value to the organization and promotes patient safety, a risk management professional charged with locating lost patient items (teeth, canes, glasses) or a risk management professional charged with reducing variability and risk within the labor and delivery unit?"

Although the primary business of health care is the delivery of safe and effective patient care, note that not all organizational risk management activities or programs should focus exclusively on clinical or patient-related risk. The identification and analysis of risk on an enterprisewide basis encourages the risk management professional to identify and analyze other areas of risk beyond what is referred to as operational or clinical risk. Those other areas include risks associated with the financial, human capital, legal, technological, regulatory, and hazard environments. This chapter is focused on identifying and analyzing patient-related risk.

Early Warning of Risks

Once the risk management professional understands the business of the organization and the risk inherent in its operations, the next step is to review existing early warning systems and implement new systems as necessary. Early warning systems alert the risk management professional to adverse events—preventable and unpreventable, incidents, occurrences, potentially compensable events, and claims. Systems for identifying potential risk and loss-producing incidents vary among organizations. Although risk can differ in frequency, complexity, and severity depending on the health care delivery setting (for example, the risk of pressure ulcers and elopement are greater in a long-term care setting than in an acute care hospital), the risk management process and need for a robust early warning system are the same. Internal early warning systems for the identification of risk can be formal or informal reporting and notification mechanisms. Reporting systems are used internally by the organization and externally for reporting to outside parties. Reporting systems can be mandatory or voluntary.

Formal Internal Reporting Methods

Formal risk identification systems are those that follow policies and procedures. Typically, these systems are implemented to comply with requirements by commercial insurance carriers as a requisite for coverage, alternative risk financing arrangements such as programs of self-insurance (captives, risk retention groups, trusts, and so on), compliance with state statutes and other regulatory requirements, and to meet standards such as those promulgated by **The Joint Commission**, the Utilization Review Accreditation Committee (URAC), the Commission for Accreditation of Rehabilitation Facilities (CARF), and the National Committee for Quality Assurance (NCQA).

The Incident Report Commercial insurance companies developed the **incident report** in the early 1960s as a means of event, claim, or loss notification. Most industries used incident reports to give notice to their carriers of an event that might give rise to a claim. In health care specifically, these reports were forms on which to record basic information about the patient, any other potential claimants, or third parties in the case of general liability claims. Included were name, other identifying information associated with the potential claimant, and a brief description of the incident. In addition, many forms required that follow-up information be recorded by the reporter confirming that the incident had been adequately addressed with appropriate intervention. Forms such as these were adopted for use in the majority of U.S. hospitals and other health care organizations. In fact, many insurance companies still provide the incident report forms and incident reporting protocols used in insured facilities today.

Traditionally, incident reporting has been the cornerstone of health care risk management. Generally, an incident is defined as any happening that is not consistent with the routine care of a particular patient or an event that is not consistent with the normal operations of a particular organization. Examples of incidents might include a union strike, criminal acts such as homicide or burglary, wrong-site or wrong-patient surgery, medication errors, or a physical disaster such as a hurricane, a bioterrorism threat, or the onset of mold contamination. The occurrence of an incident should trigger completion of a report sent to risk management and other necessary parties, depending on the organization's policy and, as a general rule, on a "need to know" basis. The "need to know" standard must be reviewed annually for legal requirements to ensure that the confidentiality of incident report information is maintained and the need as defined still exists.

Incident report data should be collected, coded for study, and analyzed to determine whether there are any trends that represent real or potential problems in the delivery of care or service. The results of this analysis should be distributed and discussed with the individuals and departments involved and those authorized to promote changes in protocol, policy, and procedures. The analysis may reveal positive findings, which may be disseminated to employees or members of the medical staff, and issues of concern that should be addressed in a timely manner using the committee structures, problem resolution processes, and peer review mechanisms (if applicable) at the organization.

Long-term care (LTC) facilities—including skilled nursing facilities (SNFs) and assisted living facilities (ALFs), managed care organizations (MCOs), and home health care organizations (HHCs)—have designed and implemented reporting mechanisms to capture event data necessary for risk management and loss prevention efforts. Historically, these organizations have placed less emphasis on true risk identification systems given their minimal medical professional liability experience. For example, over the past several years, the loss experience of LTC organizations has increased in terms of both frequency and severity of claims. Leading causes of loss are failure to provide adequate wound care, failure to monitor status of nutrition, elopement, pressure ulcers, abuse and neglect, and medication errors. The LTC industry has recently invested considerable time and effort in designing and implementing incident reporting systems for providers of care.

Electronic Incident Reporting

The public, including the organization's employee workforce and patient population, are in many instances experienced users of technology. Personal use of home computers, cellular phones, and personal digital assistants (PDAs) are the norm. Advances in technology, although somewhat slow in coming to health care documentation systems, are rapidly changing how and when care is delivered. Risk management professionals have increasingly embraced the computerization of risk management data. There are many commercially available prepackaged programs designed to track risk management data, including front-end reporting, statistical analysis, claims management, and insurance schedules. Database management programs can be used to customize an organization's risk management information needs.

More than two dozen risk management information systems (RMISs) are currently available to risk management professionals. As with any new system or program, implementing an RMIS is not without risk. The development of policies and procedures that specifically address the risk associated with computerized systems is a priority. Specific issues of concern include computer failures, breaches of security, unauthorized access to data, authority and access levels, pass code protection, and compliance with the Health Insurance Portability and Accountability Act of 1996 (HIPAA) for electronic data that contain protected health information.

Many RMISs promote statistical analysis and offer graphic capabilities for benchmarking, allowing risk management professionals to compare their organization with similar organizations or significant national trends. Many risk management professionals find that implementing an RMIS decreases the common problems of underreporting and lack of timeliness because those reporting are getting timely feedback through more comprehensive and understandable computer-generated reports.

An effective RMIS must have a data collection form or computer screens that allow information to be recorded accurately, quickly, and in a manner that facilitates coding and entry. For example, incident report forms should be either precoded or designed for easy coding. This will ensure fast and accurate entry and swift retrieval of information. These forms often contain check-off boxes and limited space for narrative descriptions. New technology, such as scanning software, promotes an easier means of converting paper documents to soft data, which can then be manipulated using the software.

Although a user-friendly input mechanism is vital to encourage reporting, the most important element of a successful computerized system is its ability to generate useful and readable reports. Without the capacity to produce aggregate reports and data trends, the value of a computerized system is minimal. The whole purpose of automating the data is to promote easy tracking and facilitate trend analysis, which can help the organization identify patterns and problems by comparing current data with those of last month, last year, and perhaps the past five years.

Without meaningful data, it is easy to forget that the purpose of identification and analysis of incident report data is the development and implementation of systems and processes to minimize the potential for loss while enhancing patient care. Therefore, systems that generate clear and meaningful information are essential to risk control.

Variables related to occurrences that might be analyzed (regardless of the early warning system used) include the following:

■ *Date of occurrence.* This is also sometimes called date of loss or incident or event date. This information is valuable for providing trending information to determine whether the number of occurrences has increased, decreased, or remained stable over time.

■ *Date of report.* Tracking the **date of occurrence** in relationship to the **date of report** is one metric by which risk management professionals can evaluate the effectiveness of the organization's early warning system. When a time lag in reporting is noted, systems, processes, policies, and procedures should be reviewed by the risk management professional to determine the reason for late notification. The goal is to receive few surprises in the future and for adverse events to be known at the time of their occurrence. Failure to report occurrences in a timely manner will not allow the risk management professional to implement risk control techniques to mitigate damages or to prevent future occurrences. The date of report also needs descriptors. To whom was the report sent on this date? In a large integrated system, does the date of report refer to when central risk management received the report, when the local facility risk management professional received the report, or when the insurance carrier received the first report or notice of an event? When possible, the RMIS should allow for the tracking of multiple dates in such circumstances.

■   *Date of lawsuit or notice of intent to file a lawsuit.* Tracking the filing date of a lawsuit will allow the risk management professional to further evaluate the effectiveness of the organization's early warning systems by identifying how many lawsuits were based on occurrences not previously known and reported to the risk management professional. Key metrics to monitor include time from the date of occurrence to the date of report to the date of filing suit or intent to file suit. These dates are used to evaluate the timeliness and effectiveness of the early warning system.

■   *Type of occurrence.* Looking at types of occurrences (for example, falls, medication-related errors, diagnosis-related errors, treatment-related events, and so on) and their frequency is important when trying to prioritize loss prevention activities.

■   *Location of the occurrence.* Analyzing where adverse occurrences are most likely to occur allows for targeted loss prevention activities. The effectiveness of these activities supports the generation of department-specific reports. These reports support departmental review and implementation of subsequent risk control activities.

■   *Severity of injury.* By prioritizing loss prevention activities to address occurrences with the highest likelihood of severe injury, the risk management professional can respond to possible adverse events with the greatest potential for high cost. (To review an index of categories of medical errors, see the section on NCC-MERP reporting under "Voluntary Reporting Systems" later in this chapter.)

Other elements of the occurrence that can be examined for trends include patient demographics, such as age, gender, marital status, occupation, method of payment, and diagnosis; staff characteristics, such as name, title, employment status (for example, agency versus staff nurse) of all employees involved in the occurrence or name, department, and specialty of all involved physicians; and other occurrence-related details, such as time and shift of the occurrence, physical environment at the time of the occurrence (such as wet floor or inoperative call light), location of the occurrence within the organization, or the status of family training in home-care situations.

The selection of a computerized RMIS is not an easy task. Expense, ease of use, and utility are important factors in choosing to either build or buy a system to manage reporting and data manipulation. Compatibility with the clinical and financial data systems currently in place at the organization is also a key decision element. To evaluate RMIS vendors and their products and services, risk management professionals might prepare an RMIS vendor **request for proposals (RFP)**. The RFP process takes time and can be enhanced with the assistance of others in the organization with specialized skills, such as representatives from information technology (IT), the privacy officer, finance, legal, quality improvement, and nursing. By involving these resources, the risk management professional can also ensure that needs of key risk management program stakeholders are met. Risk management professionals should plan early, as the process can take three to six months at a minimum from the development of a RFP to the selection of a vendor. In addition, visiting other organizations that use the system being considered can provide valuable information.

Contents of the Incident Report

Today's incident report forms vary in content and structure and from organization to organization throughout the continuum of care. Recent emphasis has been placed on making forms user-friendly, less cumbersome, and more likely to be used, given the time constraints and staffing shortages that affect the nursing staff, who are major contributors to reporting systems.

Although the majority of risk management programs use electronic RMISs, some reporting systems that still use a pencil-and-paper method remain effective. Not all medical errors can be captured in an electronic system, and a paper-based portable tool might identify adverse events and incidents previously unknown. Manual incident report forms can be an effective method for gathering information in some circumstances. These manual forms might have only preprinted data elements for check-off, whereas others have extensive narrative portions including description of the event, steps taken after the event, follow-up, and action plans. Regardless of format, most incident reports including the following basic information:

- Demographic information may include name, home address, and telephone number of the patient, visitor, or employee involved in the incident and medical record number, if the involved party is a patient. This information is used to identify the potential claimant and witnesses in case of litigation. Typically, most forms, particularly those in acute care settings, will have a section in which a patient's identifier "plate" can be imprinted directly on the form.

- Facility-related information, such as admission or visit date, business number (a patient's medical record number does not change; however, a different business number is generated for each admission), patient room number, and admitting diagnosis or presenting complaint. This information is used on an aggregate basis to determine whether certain units of the system are more incident-prone. Analyzing this information for trends promotes risk management interventions and action plans to manage the frequency of incidents reported.

- Socioeconomic data on the individual involved in the occurrence, such as age, gender, marital status, employment, and insurance status, help assess the severity of any potential loss. For example, collecting employment status helps the risk management professional and legal counsel determine the potential for economic damages that includes loss of wages or salary.

- Description of the incident and of the facts surrounding the event—location of the incident; type of incident (medication error, treatment error, diagnostic error, slip and fall, lost property, elopement, and so on); extent of injury incurred; pertinent environmental findings (position of bed rails, condition of floor surfaces, physical defects in equipment, and the like); and results of any physical examination of the patient, visitor, or employee by clinical staff—is often provided by the staff in the emergency department.

Staff Participation in Incident Reporting

Incident reporting is the duty and responsibility of all staff, including employed and voluntary members of the medical staff, not just the nursing department. To enhance the effectiveness of the incident report as a tool for risk management, the risk management professional should encourage physicians, residents, interns, pharmacists, laboratory personnel, and other ancillary service personnel to report incidents. Working with these practitioners to identify the types of incidents to be reported is a worthwhile exercise.

For the risk management professional in an integrated delivery system (IDS), staff participation in incident reporting presents a significant challenge. The various organizations that encompass the IDS can be geographically distant from each other; as a result, promoting the consistent and timely reporting of incidents demands effective staff education. Simplicity of the reporting system and easy accessibility to user training are especially important in encouraging staff members in widely dispersed locations to report incidents.[6] For these systems, risk management professionals should include training and development for home health care providers, private physician offices, ambulatory care centers, mobile mammogram units, and so on. Many providers have turned to the Web- or intranet-based programs to provide access to such training and development.

One of the greatest challenges risk management professionals face today is dealing with underreporting and the negative perceptions of incident reports. Although organizations are changing the work environment and culture to eliminate the punitive aspects associated with incident reporting, the negative aspects continue nonetheless. Table 6.1 lists common reasons for failing to submit incident reports.

These barriers result in no reporting or slow reporting with delayed follow-up. By providing feedback on the results of investigation and problem resolution, the risk management professional can demonstrate the value of early and timely reporting. Once staff see the value of systematically identifying and addressing problems in patient care, they often are more motivated to report incidents.

The incident report should not be used as either a punitive measure for disciplining employees or as a vehicle for airing interpersonal disagreements. The risk management professional should make every effort to ensure that incident reports are used properly. Unfortunately, if the culture of the organization is one in which these reports have been used and continue to be used as a disciplinary tool or in a punitive manner, the risk management professional will have to spend time trying to make incremental changes to the environment—no easy task. This is not to say that repeated medication errors that lead to patient injury from a single practitioner might not involve some form of discipline. Under these circumstances, the risk management professional

TABLE 6.1 Common Barriers to Incident Reporting

Staff feel overworked with not enough time to report.

Reports are viewed as a nonclinical safety function and not for clinical events.

Staff are busy at the time of the incident and then forget to file a report.

Perception is that completion of an incident report is a nursing function only.

Reporter fears embarrassment or wants to avoid embarrassing a coworker.

Reporter does not want to be considered a whistleblower or tattletale.

Routine reminders or periodic refreshers on the importance of reporting are lacking.

Individual thought someone else would complete the incident report.

Nonphysicians are uncomfortable reporting on physicians.

Person lacks the computer skills needed to complete the form online.

Confidentiality is lacking; anonymous reporting is not allowed.

Reporting is thought to be unnecessary due to lack of adverse outcome feedback or follow-up.

Person fears punishment, disciplinary action, or retribution.

Person fears a lawsuit, having to testify, or having to go to court.

The value of filing or completing incident reports is uncertain.

Administrative support is lacking.

Reporting policies and procedures are inadequate.

What constitutes a reportable incident is unclear.

Computer access is difficult or incident report forms are unavailable.

Person fears placing the facility at risk.

should keep the focus on the elements of the practitioner's performance that contributed to the error and refer to the human resource department or the practitioner's manager any necessary disciplinary action.

Incident report training should stress that the report is a factual account of what happened; no finger-pointing or accusatory language should be included. Incident reports are meant to record "just the facts," avoiding subjective, hearsay, or third-party opinions of what did or did not happen. If a grievous error was made resulting in a severe outcome for the patient, an employee might require counseling regarding the incident, and measures to prevent recurrence could be implemented. But the incident report should not be used as evidence against the employee in a disciplinary procedure and should not be placed in the personnel file.

Effectiveness of the reporting process can be enhanced by written policies and procedures that clearly define a reportable incident. Incident reports have been used to report major categories of events, including patient slips and falls, medication errors, intravenous infusion problems, and lost valuables. Effectiveness has been limited due in part to the mistaken belief that the incident report is a document prepared for the facility's environment of care or safety committee. Although events such as patient falls might occur frequently, claims studies clearly show that they are not the source of greatest payout in health care–related claims. By explaining the purpose and content of the incident report through in-service training and a clear written definition of what constitutes a reportable incident, the risk management professional can broaden the types of incidents reported to include clinically related events.

Finally, staff should be encouraged to complete incident reports promptly, accurately, and completely. Ideally, the form should be completed immediately or as soon as possible after the occurrence. Many organizations use a "twenty-four-hour rule," requiring reporting within twenty-four hours of the event or knowledge of the event. It is important that the risk management professional be aware of any legally mandated requirements that the incident report must be received within a specific time frame. For accuracy's sake, the individual who has the most knowledge about the event—that is, the employee involved in the occurrence, an employee witness, or the employee to whom it was reported—should report the incident. If the incident report requires that follow-up information be entered directly onto the form, policies should ensure that this information is transmitted rapidly, perhaps by telephone to the risk management professional, and that the completed incident report be forwarded to risk management as soon as possible. Any delay in transmitting information could prevent the risk management professional from reacting immediately to the event and following up in a timely manner. Immediacy of information and follow-up action is particularly critical in instances when the patient or other parties involved in the incident need medical attention to stabilize a condition brought on by the untoward or unanticipated event.

The analysis of incident reports will allow the risk management professional to evaluate processes, systems, protocols, and practices that give rise to losses. Efforts to mitigate loss can then be targeted and focused on areas where incidents have been frequent or losses have been severe.

When educating staff on the policies and procedures for completing an incident report, the same questions that are asked during an investigative interview are useful: What happened? How did it happen? When did the event take place? How might it be prevented in the future? Who was involved? And so on. Risk management professionals should highlight key points for participants such as members of the medical staff, office managers, and home health aides. A listing of those key points appears in Table 6.2.

TABLE 6.2. Key Points to Remember About Incident Reports

Notify risk management within twenty-four hours of an incident either in person, telephonically, or by using the formal incident reporting system.

Record only the facts related to the event.

Record the names of any witnesses and responsible parties with knowledge or involvement.

Record the time and location of the incident.

For paper-based systems, use blue- or black-ink ballpoint pens (no felt-tip pens).

Use appropriate patient descriptors such as age and sex.

Record information on the condition of the patient, resident, or client after the incident, such as "resident brought to radiology, findings negative for fracture."

Record in the patient's medical record a factual account of any unanticipated events involving patient injury.

Incident reports should go directly to risk management and not through any other department first.

Incident report forms should be received in a timely manner for review by the risk management professional. In some jurisdictions, this time is mandated by law.[a] Receipt of incident reports should not be delayed for follow-up or extra review and signatures.

(Continued)

TABLE 6.2. *(Continued)*

The clinical facts surrounding an incident should always be documented in the medical record. However, there should be no mention of the fact that a formal incident report has been completed.

Never place the incident report in the medical record. This is less of an issue as hospitals and other health care organizations move to electronic health records or use of an electronic incident reporting system. However, if the organization is using a paper-based incident report form, consider making the report form oversized, printed in another color, or printed with a colored border or strip—anything that will make it noticeable if placed inadvertently in the medical record.

The medical record and incident report are not the place for professional infighting. Do not use accusatory, threatening, or inflammatory language. Assignment of blame, liability, or fault does not belong in the medical record.

Copying the incident report for any reason should not be permitted.

[a]For example, Florida statutes require reporting an incident to the risk manager or designee within three business days.

Preserving Incident Report Confidentiality

Although completed incident reports are statements of fact and therefore contain information readily available from other sources, risk management professionals and staff should strive to maintain the confidentiality of these reports and related information. The preservation of confidentiality and any privilege that may attach. encourages accurate and frequent reporting, ensures factual information and promotes honesty of reports, prevents the perception (usually introduced by plaintiff's counsel) that something "wrong" has occurred, and supports an attorney's ability to provide for a proper defense.

Confidentiality can be invoked either under state statutes regarding quality assurance studies and peer review activities or risk management activities. Privilege will attach as work product protection in anticipation of litigation or as attorney-client privilege.

To maintain confidentiality, the original report should be sent to the risk management professional immediately upon completion. As mentioned previously, copies should never be made, and the report must never be made part of the medical record.

Frequently, a follow-up sheet is attached to the incident report form. This is usually completed by a departmental manager, the nursing supervisor, the nursing home administrator, or some other responsible party who has investigated the occurrence and, when possible, ascertained the fact pattern of events (cause) leading to the incident. It is important to protect the confidentiality of this addendum and other related information such as photographs and staffing records in addition to the actual incident report.

If managers use incident reports to support quality improvement (QI) studies or insist on having the reports for any reason, risk management professionals should suggest that managers review the originals in the risk management office. Once again, it is important to ensure that copies are not made and the originals are not removed from the file.

If the incident report is best protected through assertion of **attorney-client privilege**, the incident report should be reviewed by legal counsel in a timely fashion and maintained in specifically identified files. If report confidentiality is best achieved through statutory protection afforded to QI data and peer review activities, the reports must be reviewed through the established QI program. This review can be accomplished when there is a distinct operational link between the risk management and quality assurance (performance improvement) departments. It is best to discuss these options with legal counsel to determine the best method for preserving confidentiality, keeping in mind state statutes, regulations, and case law. Likewise, the risk management professional should consult with legal counsel regarding procedures for reviewing and maintaining the reports.

Risk management professionals and defense counsel have worked tirelessly to ensure protection of this type of information. However, recently, health care organizations have found an increasing number of challenges to this protection by plaintiffs' attorneys and the courts. So remember that while organizations work diligently to protect this information, it must be assumed that all health care information is "discoverable" and that the health care organization cannot completely rely on evidentiary protections. Given that belief, it is of the utmost importance that only facts should be recorded on incident reports—the same facts or information that could be found in other documents, including the medical record.

Risk management professionals should be aware of efforts and advances in patient safety, promotion of and requirements for the disclosure of unanticipated events, and the cultural emphasis on honesty in dealing with patients and families. Although some people, particularly patients, may perceive the practice of sequestering ("hiding") incident reports as undermining the cultural emphasis on disclosure, they must be made to understand that incident reports are business records created for a specific purpose and are not part of the patient's medical record. This should not in any way diminish efforts to deal with patients in an open and honest manner with regard to issues that arise during the course of their care and treatment.

Contrasted with traditional incident reporting, many organizations are implementing anonymous hotlines. For example, one hospital found that anonymous reporting resulted in many times the number of patient safety issues raised via the traditional incident report.[7] The risk management professional will need a clear understanding of how the organization approaches these issues before developing relevant policies and procedures for incident reporting.

Occurrence Reporting

Focused occurrence reporting gives staff clear guidelines and specific examples of reportable incidents, such as the following:

- Missed diagnoses or misdiagnoses that result in patient injury, such as failure to diagnose acute myocardial infarction, fractures, serious head trauma, or appendicitis

- Surgically related occurrences, such as the wrong patient being operated on, the wrong site operated on, the wrong procedure being performed, an incorrect instrument or sponge count, or an unplanned return to the operating room

- Treatment- or procedure-related occurrences, such as reactions to contrast material used in a diagnostic procedure, undesirable exposure to X-rays, or burns resulting from improper use of hot packs

- Blood-related occurrences, such as the wrong type of blood given to the patient, transmission of disease via infected blood, or improper use of blood or blood products

- Intravenous-related occurrences, such as the wrong solution being administered, infiltration of solution, or an incorrect infusion rate

- Medication-related occurrences

- Lack of adequate follow-up, such as failure to notify a patient of abnormal laboratory findings

- Falls

Given the attention that patient safety has been afforded via the media since the enactment of the **Patient Safety and Quality Improvement Act of 2005**, the Joint Commission International Center for Patient Safety, and The Joint Commission's National Patient Safety Goals, medication safety is at the forefront of the risk management agenda. Medication safety programs are based on adverse event reporting systems, human factor analysis, and data analysis. Medication-related claims can include the following:

- Wrong dosage

- Wrong route

- Wrong frequency (of rate for IV)

- Wrong medication

- Wrong choice of medication for condition

- Wrong time

- Wrong administration technique

- Wrong patient

- Missed dose

- Known drug interaction

- Known allergy to drug

- Wrong reason

Ideally, the organization will implement a version of the event reporting system that is specific to the clinical area to focus on this important risk management concern. Many organizations have designed specific incident report forms for each clinical and operational department. The challenge of such reporting systems is to make certain that trends that cross department lines, such as medication errors in the radiology suite and the pharmacy, are identified and assessed.

Although the majority of these examples apply to the acute care setting, many are applicable to other parts of the health care continuum. Medication-related occurrences should be reported and tracked in all health care settings, including the private office setting.

Falls, which are a prevalent cause of injury in long-term care facilities, can occur in any setting, as can the development of pressure ulcers, hospital-acquired infections, patient elopement, and failure to refer. With the elderly, the resulting injury can be severe. Finally, as more primary care is provided in alternative settings such as in the home, providers of care in these settings must design incident reporting systems that track treatment variances and equipment malfunctions that lead to patient or client injury.

To further focus the reporting process, many health care organizations define reportable occurrences by designated location, such as the emergency department (ED), surgical suite, labor and delivery room, high-risk nursery, and so on (see Table 6.3). For large integrated delivery systems and stand-alone alternative care settings, reportable occurrences are designed specifically to the type of service offered. By

TABLE 6.3 **Emergency Department Occurrence Reporting Criteria**

Any patient who leaves without being seen (LWBS)
Any patient who leaves against medical advice (AMA)
Any patient who returns to the Emergency Department without a scheduled revisit within seventy-two hours

(Continued)

TABLE 6.3. *(Continued)*

Any discrepancy in reading the initial (wet read) X-ray from the final read

Inappropriate EMTALA transfer received and transferred or discharged out

Missing or inadequate discharge instructions

Failure to deliver and act on critical test results

Failure to give patient ordered prescriptions

Any incidents of assault or violence

Patient falls

Medication errors

Any recognized failure to diagnose or misdiagnosis

Failure to use or deliver thrombolytics in a timely manner

Failure to initiate treatment in a timely manner

Failure to remove a foreign body

Inadequate staffing that affects patient care

Long wait time to be seen that affects quality of care

Misidentification of a patient

Ineffective hand-off to other personnel, unit, or area

Inadequate or missing medication reconciliation

developing lists of specific adverse outcomes or events in these high-risk areas, the clinical focus of occurrence reporting is addressed, and the incidents that need to be reported are made clear. The risk management professional receives these reports directly. Because of the highly clinical nature of these data, most facilities will share this information with quality assurance, performance improvement, or the QI committee. The data can then be peer-reviewed using root cause analyses (to be explained shortly). Action plans and incident follow-up will be implemented based on such a review. Aggregate reports of this information should be submitted to the QI and risk management committees.

Occurrence Screening

Another method that attempts to identify adverse patient occurrences in clinical areas is the **occurrence screening** process, originally developed by Joyce Craddick of Medical Management Analysis International. This system, and many others like it that followed, uses a clearly defined list of patient occurrences against which patient medical records are screened. The screeners are looking for deviations from practice, policy, and procedures. Criteria for the screens are established in areas that are considered to be high-risk, that have a high number of incidents identified as quality-of-care "red flags" to be further evaluated, or in which the effects of an untoward event might have disastrous results from an injury standpoint. In the past, most screens were centered around clinical events and related administrative occurrences, but they can just as well be used for regulatory and financial issues. Criteria are developed and exceptions are listed, if applicable. For example, in the operating room, one specific criterion that may be screened for is proper informed consent documentation. An exception to this criterion may be in a case of emergency surgery, where either the patient is unable to give consent or there is no time to obtain consent. Another criterion to screen for and evaluate, regardless of location in the health care setting, is an unexpected death. There are no exceptions to this criterion. In the emergency department, criteria may include misread X-rays or readmissions within twenty-four hours.

In an inpatient setting, all patient records are reviewed against the criteria within forty-eight to seventy-two hours of admission and every three or four days thereafter until the patient is discharged. The patient chart also is reviewed approximately two weeks after discharge to ensure that compliance with all criteria has been assessed.

Results of this screening process are prepared for each admission by trained data retrieval personnel (screeners). The abstract is then forwarded to the QI office for follow-up and data collection. When identified, serious occurrences are reported immediately by the patient care reviewers to the correct person for action. All occurrences are aggregated to aid in identifying any trends that reflect patient care problems that require remedial action.

Occurrence screening can also be effective in other settings; ambulatory care organizations (ACOs), physician group practices, and medical clinics, in particular, have found this method useful in identifying sources of risk. Using a checklist, the staff review outpatient records for items such as documentation of patient allergies, prescription refills, patient notification of test results, and telephone communications. The records are also reviewed to see whether they are sufficient for another practitioner to continue the patient's care.[8]

Although occurrence screening is an effective method for identifying adverse occurrences, its implementation in most institutions is done entirely under the QI program. The major challenge of this system is how to ensure sufficient involvement of the risk management professional. In some institutions, the risk management professional is notified by having the patient care reviewer complete a separate risk management notification form for serious adverse patient occurrences. In other instances, the risk management professional is part of the quality management team and is apprised of the results of the occurrence screening through departmental or QI committee meetings.

Regardless of the method chosen, the risk management professional should have ready access to these data for the process to be useful to the risk management program. In addition, the risk management professional should play a key role in identifying and implementing action plans relating to abnormal or increasingly negative data trends.

Failure Mode and Effects Analysis and Root Cause Analysis

Failure mode and effects analysis (FMEA) is a risk control technique used to prevent the occurrence of loss by analyzing a situation that might create risk at a later time, such as a new morphine pump that has been purchased but not been placed in use. By conducting a dry run of pump protocols, the staff can identify risk issues that require attention before the pump is used. The purpose of FMEA is to identify ways in which that process might potentially fail. The goal is to eliminate or reduce the likelihood or outcome severity of such a failure.[9] FMEA is used before an adverse event or incident occurs, and it is considered a successful technique for proactive risk management.

A root cause analysis (RCA) is a structured analytical methodology used to examine the underlying contributors to an adverse event or condition. Because RCA is implemented after an event has occurred, it is considered a reactive risk management technique.

Health care organizations accredited by The Joint Commission are required to conduct a root cause analysis in response to any sentinel event. Joint Commission standard LD.5.2 requires facilities to select at least one high-risk process for proactive risk assessment each year. This selection is to be based in part on information published periodically by The Joint Commission that identifies the most frequently occurring types of **sentinel events**. Organizations should also identify patient safety events and high-risk processes for which an FMEA would be valuable.

Informal Internal Reporting Methods

In addition to the more structured systems of risk identification, such as incident reporting, occurrence reporting, and occurrence screening and FMEA, there are many other sources of information available to the risk management professional for identifying actual loss-producing events and potential risks, including the following:

■ Committee meeting minutes, such as from those dealing with performance improvement, quality assurance, safety, patient safety, infection control, and bioethics, as well as those from departmental committees such as morbidity and mortality, tissue review, pharmacy and therapeutics, and other quality- or risk-related committees will give the risk management professional information not readily available from other sources.

■ Claims data, including a review of both the facility's loss experience over a period of time and any national or regional trends as reported in various publications will show the organizations' frequency and severity of claims as well as highlight areas for improvement. Risk management professionals will serve their organizations well by tracking regional or national loss trends even if those types of incidents have not occurred or been reported in their organization. Planning and being proactive to avoid known risks is reflective of a mature risk management program.

■ Survey reports, including those from The Joint Commission, the National Committee on Quality Assurance (NCQA), the Commission on Accreditation of Rehabilitation Facilities (CARF), the federal Occupational Safety and Health Administration (OSHA), the state fire marshal, state licensure surveys, broker or underwriter site assessments, consultant findings, and private review organization study results all offer information that will assist the risk management professional in identifying organizational risks.

■ Patient complaints and standardized patient satisfaction surveys can offer the risk management professional valuable information from the patient's perspective, a view not always ascertained in other reporting methods.

■ Risk management walking rounds and patient safety walking rounds (commonly called "rounding"), in which the risk management professional is visible and available to staff members, encourages the sharing of information that may be viewed by certain individuals as too sensitive for a written report. Having a routine presence on the units and availability in the office or by pager are important factors in the continuous effort to enhance the early reporting of incidents.

■ "Management by walking around" does not have to be a formalized scheduled process. Risk management professionals need to be visible and available. If the staff do not know who the risk managers are, where they are located, and what they do, staff members will be much less likely to call or report when they should.

Risk management professionals should contact legal counsel to determine how best to protect the confidentiality of any data collected, whether it be through **evidentiary protection**, quality improvement activity, peer review, or risk management process protections offered in some states.

Ways to Enhance Reporting Effectiveness The many ways to enhance the effectiveness of the reporting process include the following three:

■ Ensuring that departmental and medical staff are involved in development of the list of reportable occurrences so that there is agreement as to the type of occurrences to report. Physician buy-in is very important in this process.

▪ Streamlining the reporting process so that the paperwork is not burdensome and reporting is easy. Because many of the items on the list of reportable incidents occur frequently (for example, patients leaving the emergency department against medical advice), objective checklists might be more useful than lengthy narrative reports. Again, the intent is to improve reporting to improve performance. Simply increasing the number of reports is not the ultimate goal; rather receiving reports on events that require risk management review and that afford an opportunity to reduce the likelihood of legal liability is the objective.

▪ Ensuring that the results of the reporting are given to the departments involved as quickly as possible for their review and consideration, thus emphasizing the utility of identifying problems in patient care rather than the punitive aspect of potential claims.

External Reporting

Risk management professionals have a wealth of available information from which they can develop risk management activities to eliminate or reduce loss. Much of this information is generated internally and used internally. However, many groups outside the organization also need information. These outside users of an organization's internal data are as varied as is the information they need or want. Some external reports are generated to comply with legal mandates, while other information is reported voluntarily as part of collaborative efforts to enhance patient safety.

Health care organizations with collaborative ties have the benefit of identifying and analyzing adverse events and occurrences on a larger scale than is possible with data generated only internally. In many circumstances, these outside data will direct the organizations to conduct their own FMEAs or initiate other proactive measures to eliminate loss prior to an occurrence.

Let us look at a representative sampling of the external agencies and organizations with which health care organizations share data. This list is not an exhaustive and will evolve as time goes on.

The Joint Commission The Joint Commission's **sentinel event policy** is designed to encourage the self-reporting of medical errors to learn about the relative frequencies and underlying causes of sentinel events and to share "lessons learned" with other health care organizations, thereby reducing the risk of future sentinel event occurrences. Accredited organizations must update their internal reporting systems to identify these types of events.

According to The Joint Commission, a sentinel event is any unexpected occurrence that involves death or serious physical or psychological injury or the risk thereof. Serious injuries specifically include a loss of limb or function. The phrase "or the risk thereof" includes any process variation for which a recurrence would carry a significant chance of a serious adverse outcome.[10]

Whenever a sentinel event occurs, the accredited organization is expected to complete a RCA, implement improvements to reduce risk, and monitor the effectiveness of those improvements. Although the immediate cause of most sentinel events is human fallibility, the RCA is expected to dig down to underlying organizational systems and processes that can be altered to reduce the likelihood of human error in the future and to protect patients from harm when human error does occur.

Voluntary Self-Reporting of Sentinel Events

Under The Joint Commission's sentinel event policy, a defined subset of sentinel events is subject to review by The Joint Commission and may be reported on a voluntary basis. Only sentinel events that affect recipients of care (patients, clients, and residents) and that meet one of the following criteria fall into this category.[11]

- Unanticipated death or major permanent loss of function not related to the natural course of the patient's illness or underlying condition

- Suicide of any individual receiving care, treatment, or services in a staffed around-the-clock care setting or within seventy-two hours of discharge

- Unanticipated death of a full-term infant

- Abduction of any individual receiving care, treatment, or services

- Discharge of an infant to the wrong family

- Rape[12]

- Hemolytic transfusion reaction involving administration of blood or blood products having major blood group incompatibilities

- Surgery on the wrong patient or wrong body part

- Unintended retention of a foreign object in an individual after surgery or other procedure

- Severe neonatal hyperbillirubinemia (billirubin 0.30 milligrams/deciliter)

- Prolonged fluoroscopy with cumulative dose greater than 1,500 rads to a single field or any delivery of radiotherapy to the wrong body region or greater than 25 percent above the planned radiotherapy dose

Sentinel Events That Are Not Self-Reported

Each accredited health care organization is encouraged, but not required, to report to The Joint Commission any sentinel event that meets the aforementioned criteria for reviewable sentinel events. The Joint Commission may also be informed of a sentinel event by some other means, as from a patient, a family member, an employee of the organization, or the media.

Whether the organization voluntarily reports the event or The Joint Commission becomes aware of the event by some other means, there is no difference in the expected response, time frames, or review procedures.

Joint Commission Response

When The Joint Commission becomes aware by any means of a sentinel event that meets the definition of a reviewable sentinel event, the organization is required to prepare a thorough and credible RCA and action plan within forty-five calendar days of the event or of the organization's becoming aware of the event and to submit the RCA and action plan or otherwise indicate the organization's response to the sentinel event under an approved protocol, within forty-five calendar days of the known occurrence of the event.

Advantages to Reporting

There are several advantages to the organization that reports a sentinel event to The Joint Commission. First, doing so contributes to the general knowledge about sentinel events and the reduction of risk for such events in many other organizations. It also gives the organization the opportunity to consult with The Joint Commission staff while preparing the RCA and action plans. And it enhances the public perception that the organization, by collaborating and working with The Joint Commission, is doing everything possible to ensure that such an event will not happen again.

Submission of the RCA and Action Plan

The Joint Commission has several procedures to protect the confidentiality of sentinel event information submitted by accredited organizations.

For one thing, The Joint Commission advises health care organizations not to provide patient or caregiver identifiers when reporting sentinel events. An organization that experiences a sentinel event should submit two separate documents: the RCA and the action plan. The RCA will be returned to the organization once information is abstracted and entered into the Joint Commission database. If copies have been made for internal review, they will be destroyed after the review. Also, once the action plan has been implemented to the satisfaction of The Joint Commission, it will be returned to the organization.

In addition, if the organization has concerns about increased risk of legal exposure as a result of sending the root cause analysis documents to The Joint Commission, the following alternative approaches to review the organization's response to the sentinel event are acceptable.

1. An organization brings root cause analysis and action plan documents to The Joint Commission's headquarters for review and then takes the documents back on the same day.

2. A specially trained surveyor conducts an on-site visit to review the RCA and action plan.

3. A specially trained surveyor conducts an on-site visit to review the RCA and findings, without directly viewing the root cause analysis documents, through a series of interviews and review of relevant documentation.

4. Where the organization affirms that it meets specified criteria respecting the risk of waiving legal protection for RCA information shared with The Joint Commission, a specially trained surveyor conducts an on-site visit to interview the staff and review relevant documentation to obtain information about the process the organization uses in responding to sentinel events and the relevant policies and procedures preceding and following the organization's review of the specific event and the implementation thereof, sufficient to permit inferences about the adequacy of the organization's response to the sentinel event.

5. The surveyor also conducts a standards-based survey that traces the patient's care, treatment, and services and the organization's management functions relevant to the sentinel event under review.

Mandatory Reporting Systems

The reporting of adverse events by hospitals is legislated in twenty-seven states. In all but one, reporting is mandatory.[13] Many states have developed interpretive guidelines to clarify reporting requirements. States with electronic reporting guidelines may have developed Internet user guides for their systems. According to state officials, mandatory reporting systems play a vital role in hospital oversight by providing information about hospital patient safety practices. States use data to investigate individual events and ensure that corrective action is taken. Many states also share their data with other professional bodies such as licensure boards when professional standards may have been breached.[14]

Collaborative Arrangements

Publication of the 1999 Institute of Medicine report *To Err Is Human: Building a Safer Health System,* the advent of the Joint Commission–sponsored National Patient Safety Goals (NPSG) in 2003, and the prominence of organizations such as the National Patient Safety Foundation (NPSF) and the **Institute for Safe Medication Practices (ISMP)** prompted many organizations to develop complementary systems for risk identification, particularly in the area of medication errors. These complementary systems broadened traditional incident reporting to involve other professionals not previously included in the reporting and analysis hierarchy, such as the hospital pharmacist. The use of technology such as bar coding, robotics for medication dispensing and packaging, and computerized physician (provider) order entry systems (CPOE) all have the potential to lower the risk profile associated with medication administration. In many organizations, these professionals are now participating in frontline risk management activities. These complementary systems might receive near-miss and error reports before review by the risk management professional. Internal collaboration is crucial to ensure that the risk management professional is informed on a timely basis of the results and findings associated with these new systems. As noted earlier, organizational risk should be assessed on an enterprisewide basis. The risk management professional is the best person to fill that role.

FOOD AND DRUG ADMINISTRATION

The U.S. Food and Drug Administration (FDA) collects information in various categories that health care risk management professionals should be aware of and incorporate
into their reporting plans. These are the Adverse Event Reporting System (AERS), the
Vaccine Adverse Event Reporting System (VAERS), **MedWatch** Form 3500 for
reporting as mandated by the Dietary Supplement and Nonprescription Drug Consumer
Protection Act, and the Manufacturers and User Facility Device Experience (MAUDE)
database.

■   *Adverse Event Reporting System.* AERS collects information about adverse
events, medication errors, and product problems that occur after the administration of
approved drugs and therapeutic biological products. Quarterly (noncumulative) data
files since January 2004 are available for downloading on the AERS Web site (http://
www.fda.gov/cder/aers/default.htm).

■   *Vaccine Adverse Event Reporting System.* VAERS is a cooperative program
for vaccine safety of the Centers for Disease Control and Prevention (CDC) and the
FDA. VAERS collects information about adverse events that occur after the administration of U.S. licensed vaccines. (For more information, go to http://www.vaers.org.)

■   **Dietary Supplement and Nonprescription Drug Consumer Protection Act**
(Pub. L. 109-462, 120 Stat. 3469 was signed into law December 22, 2006 amending the
FD&C Act with respect to adverse event reporting and recordkeeping for dietary supplements. MedWatch Form 3500A is for use by manufacturers, packers, and distributors for
mandatory reporting of serious adverse events associated with the use of dietary supplements (http://www.cfsan.fda.gov/˜dms/dsaergui.html).

■   *Manufacturers and User Facility Device Experience Database.* Medical
device reporting (MDR) is the mechanism used by the FDA to receive significant
medical device adverse event reports from manufacturers, importers, and user facilities. Under the Safe Medical Devices Act of 1990 (SMDA), user facilities (hospitals,
nursing homes) are required to report suspected medical device–related deaths to both
the FDA and the manufacturer. User facilities report medical device–related serious
injuries only to the manufacturer unless the manufacturer is unknown, in which case
the injury is reported to the FDA. For ease of reporting, the FDA has two forms:
MedWatch 3500 for voluntary reporting (see Exhibit 6.1) and MedWatch 3500A for
mandatory reporting.[15]

MAUDE has a searchable database of all voluntary reports since June 1993, user
facility reports since 1991, distributor reports since 1993, and manufacturer reports
since August 1996 (MDR data files, 1992–1996).

In 1992, the FDA began monitoring medication error reports forwarded from several organizations, including the Institute for Safe Medication Practices and the United
States Pharmacopeia. MedWatch reports are also reviewed for possible medication
errors. Furthermore, medication errors are reported to the FDA by manufacturers with
reports for adverse events that result in serious injury and for which a medication error
may be a component.

EXHIBIT 6.1. *MedWatch Form 3500 for Voluntary Reporting and Advice About Reporting*

U.S. Department of Health and Human Services

MED WATCH

The FDA Safety Information and
Adverse Event Reporting Program

For VOLUNTARY reporting of
adverse events, product problems and
product use errors
Page ____ of ____

Form Approved: OMB No. 0910-0291, Expires: 10/31/08
See OMB statement on reverse.

FDA USE ONLY

Triage unit
sequence #

A. PATIENT INFORMATION

1. Patient Identifier	2. Age at Time of Event, or Date of Birth:	3. Sex	4. Weight
In confidence		☐ Female ☐ Male	____ lb or ____ kg

B. ADVERSE EVENT, PRODUCT PROBLEM OR ERROR

Check all that apply:

1. ☐ Adverse Event   ☐ Product Problem *(e.g., defects/malfunctions)*
   ☐ Product Use Error   ☐ Problem with Different Manufacturer of Same Medicine

2. Outcomes Attributed to Adverse Event
   (Check all that apply)

☐ Death: _____ *(mm/dd/yyyy)*   ☐ Disability or Permanent Damage
☐ Life-threatening   ☐ Congenital Anomaly/Birth Defect
☐ Hospitalization - initial or prolonged   ☐ Other Serious (Important Medical Events)
☐ Required Intervention to Prevent Permanent Impairment/Damage (Devices)

3. Date of Event *(mm/dd/yyyy)*	4. Date of this Report *(mm/dd/yyyy)*

5. Describe Event, Problem or Product Use Error

6. Relevant Tests/Laboratory Data, Including Dates

7. Other Relevant History, Including Preexisting Medical Conditions *(e.g. allergies, race, pregnancy, smoking and alcohol use, liver/kidney problems, etc.)*

PKNI KCALB ESU RO EPYT ESAEL

C. PRODUCT AVAILABILITY

Product Available for Evaluation? *(Do not send product to FDA)*

☐ Yes   ☐ No   ☐ Returned to Manufacturer on: _____ *(mm/dd/yyyy)*

D. SUSPECT PRODUCT(S)

1. Name, Strength, Manufacturer *(from product label)*

#1 _____
#2 _____

2.	Dose or Amount	Frequency	Route
#1			
#2			

3. Dates of Use *(If unknown, give duration) from/to (or best estimate)*	5. Event Abated After Use Stopped or Dose Reduced?
#1	#1 ☐ Yes ☐ No ☐ Doesn't Apply
#2	#2 ☐ Yes ☐ No ☐ Doesn't Apply

4. Diagnosis or Reason for Use *(Indication)*

#1	8. Event Reappeared After Reintroduction?
#2	#1 ☐ Yes ☐ No ☐ Doesn't Apply

6. Lot #	7. Expiration Date	#2 ☐ Yes ☐ No ☐ Doesn't Apply
#1	#1	9. NDC # or Unique ID
#2	#2	

E. SUSPECT MEDICAL DEVICE

1. Brand Name

2. Common Device Name

3. Manufacturer Name, City and State

4. Model #	Lot #	5. Operator of Device
Catalog #	Expiration Date *(mm/dd/yyyy)*	☐ Health Professional ☐ Lay User/Patient
Serial #	Other #	☐ Other:

6. If Implanted, Give Date *(mm/dd/yyyy)*	7. If Explanted, Give Date *(mm/dd/yyyy)*

8. Is this a Single-use Device that was Reprocessed and Reused on a Patient?
   ☐ Yes   ☐ No

9. If Yes to Item No. 8, Enter Name and Address of Reprocessor

F. OTHER (CONCOMITANT) MEDICAL PRODUCTS

Product names and therapy dates *(exclude treatment of event)*

G. REPORTER *(See confidentiality section on back)*

1. Name and Address

Phone #	E-mail

2. Health Professional?	3. Occupation	4. Also Reported to:
☐ Yes ☐ No		☐ Manufacturer
5. If you do NOT want your identity disclosed to the manufacturer, place an "X" in this box: ☐		☐ User Facility ☐ Distributor/Importer

FORM FDA 3500 (10/05) Submission of a report does not constitute an admission that medical personnel or the product caused or contributed to the event.

(Continued)

EXHIBIT 6.1. *(Continued)*

ADVICE ABOUT VOLUNTARY REPORTING
Detailed instructions available at: http://www.fda.gov/medwatch/report/consumer/instruct.htm

Report adverse events, product problems or product use errors with:

- Medications*(drugs or biologics)*
- Medical devices*(including in-vitro diagnostics)*
- Combination products *(medication & medical devices)*
- Human cells, tissues, and cellular and tissue-based products
- Special nutritional products *(dietary supplements, medical foods, infant formulas)*
- Cosmetics

Report product problems -quality, performance or safety concerns such as:

- Suspected counterfeit product
- Suspected contamination
- Questionable stability
- Defective components
- Poor packaging or labeling
- Therapeutic failures (product didn't work)

Report SERIOUS adverse events. An event is serious when the patient outcome is:

- Death
- Life-threatening
- Hospitalization - initial or prolonged
- Disability or permanent damage
- Congenital anomaly/birth defect
- Required intervention to prevent permanent impairment or damage
- Other serious (important medical events)

Report even if:

- You're not certain the product caused the event
- You don't have all the details

How to report:

- Just fill in the sections that apply to your report
- Use section D for all products except medical devices
- Attach additional pages if needed
- Use a separate form for each patient
- Report either to FDA or the manufacturer *(or both)*

Other methods of reporting:

- 1-800-FDA-0178 -- To FAX report
- 1-800-FDA-1088 -- To report by phone
- www.fda.gov/medwatch/report.htm -- To report online

If your report involves a serious adverse event with a device and it occurred in a facility outside a doctor's office, that facility may be legally required to report to FDA and/or the manufacturer. Please notify the person in that facility who would handle such reporting.

If your report involves a serious adverse event with a vaccine call 1-800-822-7967 *to report.*

Confidentiality: The patient's identity is held in strict confidence by FDA and protected to the fullest extent of the law. FDA will not disclose the reporter's identity in response to a request from the public, pursuant to the Freedom of Information Act. The reporter's identity, including the identity of a self-reporter, may be shared with the manufacturer unless requested otherwise.

-Fold Here-

The public reporting burden for this collection of information has been estimated to average 36 minutes per response including the time for reviewing instructions, searching existing data sources, gathering and maintaining the data needed, an completing and reviewing the collection of information. Send comments regarding this burden estimate or any other aspect o this collection of information, including suggestions for reducing this burden to:

Department of Health and Human Services	Please DO NOT	*OMB statement:*
Food and Drug Administration - MedWatch	RETURN this form	*"An agency may not conduct or sponsor, and a*
10903 New Hampshire Avenue	to this address.	*person is not required to respond to, a collection of*
Building 22, Mail Stop 4447		*information unless it displays a currently valid*
Silver Spring, MD 20993-0002		*OMB control number."*

U.S. DEPARTMENT OF HEALTH AND HUMAN SERVICES
Food and Drug Administration

FORM FDA 3500 (10/05) (Back)   *Please Use Address Provided Below -- Fold in Thirds, Tape and Mail*

INSTITUTE FOR SAFE MEDICATION PRACTICES, UNITED STATES PHARMACOPEIA, AND NATIONAL COORDINATING COUNCIL FOR MEDICATION ERROR REPORTING AND PREVENTION

Certain types of events have specific risks associated with them, due in large part to the complexity of the processes involved in delivering the care or providing the service. Medication ordering and administration is one such complex process. It involves many people, processes, and systems where failures can occur and can result in errors. Entire systems have been developed just to report, analyze, detect trends in, and ultimately reduce the occurrence of medication events. One medication-specific external event reporting system is the Medication Errors Reporting (MER) program, a voluntary

EXHIBIT 6.2. *USP Medication Errors Reporting Program Form*

MEDI-CATION ERRORS

REPORTING PROGRAM

USP MEDICATION ERRORS REPORTING PROGRAM
Presented in cooperation with the Institute for Safe Medication Practices

USP is an FDA MEDWATCH partner

Reporters should not provide any individually identifiable health information, including names of practitioners, names of patients, names of healthcare facilities, or dates of birth (age is acceptable).

Date and time of event:

Please describe the error. Include description/sequence of events, type of staff involved, and work environment (e.g., code situation, change of shift, short staffing, no 24-hr. pharmacy, floor stock). If more space is needed, please attach a separate page.

Did the error reach the patient? ☐ Yes ☐ No

Was the incorrect medication, dose, or dosage form administered to or taken by the patient? ☐ Yes ☐ No

Circle the appropriate Error Outcome Category (select one—see back for details): A   B   C   D   E   F   G   H   I

Describe the direct result of the error on the patient (e.g., death, type of harm, additional patient monitoring).

Indicate the possible error cause(s) and contributing factor(s) (e.g., abbreviation, similar names, distractions, etc.).

Indicate the location of the error (e.g., hospital, outpatient or community pharmacy, clinic, nursing home, patient's home, etc.).

What type of staff or healthcare practitioner made the initial error?

Indicate if other practitioner(s) were also involved in the error (type of staff perpetuating error).

What type of staff or healthcare practitioner discovered the error or recognized the potential for error?

How was the error (or potential for error) discovered/intercepted?

If available, provide patient age, gender, diagnosis. Do not provide any patient identifiers.

Please complete the following for the product(s) involved. (If more space is needed for additional products, please attach a separate page.)

	Product #1	Product #2
Brand/Product Name (If Applicable)		
Generic Name		
Manufacturer		
Labeler		
Dosage Form		
Strength/Concentration		
Type and Size of Container		

Reports are most useful when relevant materials such as product label, copy of prescription/order, etc., can be reviewed.

Can these materials be provided? ☐ Yes ☐ No   Please specify:

Suggest any recommendations to prevent recurrence of this error, or describe policies or procedures you instituted or plan to institute to prevent future similar errors.

Name and Title/Profession	( ) Telephone Number	( ) Fax Number

Facility/Address and Zip   E-mail

Address/Zip (where correspondence should be sent)

Your name, contact information, and a copy of this report are routinely shared with the Institute for Safe Medication Practices (ISMP). Copies of reports will be sent to third parties such as the manufacturer/labeler, and to the Food and Drug Administration (FDA). You have the option of including your name on these copies.

In addition to releasing my name and contact information to ISMP, USP may release my identity to these third parties as follows (check boxes that apply):

☐ The manufacturer and/or labeler as listed above   ☐ FDA   ☐ Other persons requesting a copy of this report   ☐ Anonymous to all third parties

Signature	Date

Return to:
USP CAPS
12601 Twinbrook Parkway
Rockville, MD 20852-1790

Submit via the Web at www.usp.org/mer
Call Toll Free: 800-23-ERROR (800-233-7767)
or FAX: 301-816-8532

Date Received by USP	File Access Number

PSF116G

WEPDF
©USPC 2003

nationwide service operated by the United States Pharmacopeia (USP) in conjunction with the Institute for Safe Medication Practices (ISMP). The MER program is designed to collect information about medication errors from physicians, pharmacists, and nurses and to share that information anonymously and develop educational services to prevent future errors. (Information about the MER program can be found at http://www.usp.org or http://www.ismp.org.)

The National Coordinating Council for Medication Error Reporting and Prevention (NCC-MERP) realized the need for a standardized categorization of errors. In 1996, the NCC-MERP adopted a "medication error index" that classifies errors according to severity of outcome. It is hoped that by creating a standardized index, health care institutions and practitioners will track medication errors in a consistent and systematic manner. The council encourages the use of the index in all health care delivery settings. Exhibit 6.2 reproduces the USP Medication Errors Reporting Program Form, Exhibit 6.3 shows the NCC-MERP Index for Categorizing Medication Errors, and Exhibit 6.4 presents the NCC-MERP Index for Categorizing Medication Errors Algorithm. (Further information is available at http://www.nccmerp.org.)

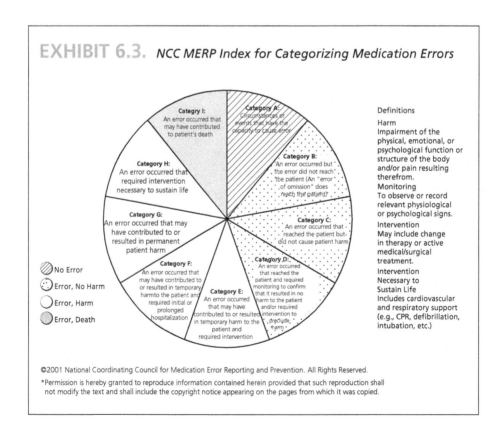

EXHIBIT 6.3. *NCC MERP Index for Categorizing Medication Errors*

©2001 National Coordinating Council for Medication Error Reporting and Prevention. All Rights Reserved.

*Permission is hereby granted to reproduce information contained herein provided that such reproduction shall not modify the text and shall include the copyright notice appearing on the pages from which it was copied.

EXHIBIT 6.4. *NCC MERP Index for Categorizing Medication Errors Algorithm*

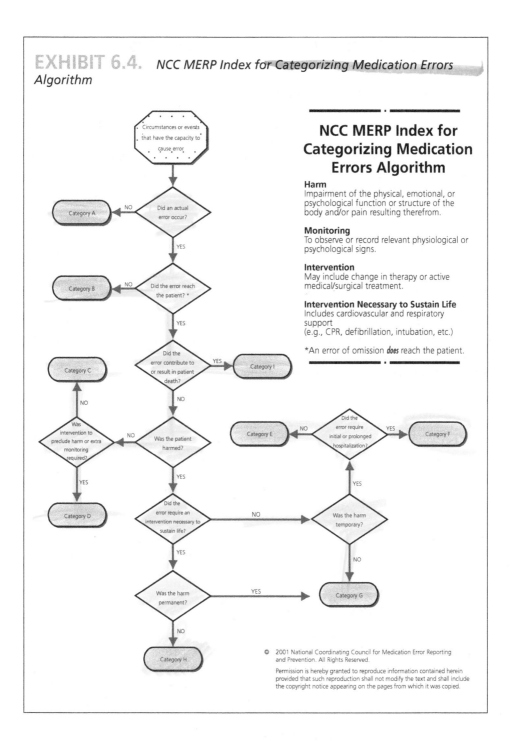

NCC MERP Index for Categorizing Medication Errors Algorithm

Harm
Impairment of the physical, emotional, or psychological function or structure of the body and/or pain resulting therefrom.

Monitoring
To observe or record relevant physiological or psychological signs.

Intervention
May include change in therapy or active medical/surgical treatment.

Intervention Necessary to Sustain Life
Includes cardiovascular and respiratory support
(e.g., CPR, defibrillation, intubation, etc.)

*An error of omission **does** reach the patient.

© 2001 National Coordinating Council for Medication Error Reporting and Prevention. All Rights Reserved.

Permission is hereby granted to reproduce information contained herein provided that such reproduction shall not modify the text and shall include the copyright notice appearing on the pages from which it was copied.

MEDICAL EVENT REPORTING SYSTEM—TRANSFUSION MEDICINE

Another example of a specialized area with complex processes involved is transfusion medicine. An online national reporting system for collecting and analyzing blood transfusion errors, adverse events, and near misses is available. The voluntary reporting system, called the Medical Event Reporting System—Transfusion Medicine (MERS-TM), is housed at Columbia University in New York City. It allows participants to report anonymously and have access to a central aggregate database for comparative purposes. (Information on MERS-TM is available at http://www.mers-tm.net.)

INTENSIVE CARE UNIT SAFETY REPORTING SYSTEM

Medical specialties are also initiating event reporting systems geared specifically to patient care issues inherent in those specialties. The Intensive Care Unit Safety Reporting System (ICUSRS), run by the Society for Critical Care Medicine and a team of investigators from Johns Hopkins University and funded by the Agency for Healthcare Research and Quality (AHRQ), is an external reporting system specifically for intensive care units. Its leaders intend to expand the program nationwide. (The ICUSRS reporting form can be viewed at http://www.icusrs.org.)

PITTSBURGH REGIONAL HEALTHCARE INITIATIVE

What began in 1997 as a consortium of Pittsburgh-area medical, business, and civic leaders concerned about health care costs has become an innovator in patient safety initiatives. The Pittsburgh Regional Healthcare Initiative (PRHI) became one of the earliest community projects to experiment with transferring ideas from industry to improve safety and quality in health care.

PRHI and its partners are now starting to prove that improving quality of care not only benefits patients but also saves money. A template is emerging that confirms one of PRHI's foundational beliefs: that quality is the business case. (For more information, go to http://www.prhi.org.)

OTHER VOLUNTARY PROGRAMS

The U.S. Department of Veterans Affairs (VA) developed in collaboration with NASA a voluntary, confidential, nonpunitive external learning system for employees in May 2000. This system, called the Patient Safety Reporting System (PSRS), was implemented departmentwide in 2002. It encourages the reporting of any issue or concern that affects patient safety. PSRS is modeled after NASA's successful and long-standing Aviation Safety Reporting System (ASRS), which it developed and has administered for the Federal Aviation Administration since 1976.

Part of the success of this program is not only the improved patient safety culture of the VA but also the legal and procedural protection afforded under Title 38 United States Code Section 5705. (For more information, visit http://www.psrs.arc.nasa.gov/flashsite/programoverview/index.html.)

STANDARDIZING A PATIENT SAFETY TAXONOMY: THE NATIONAL QUALITY FORUM

Until recently, there was no common method to classify or aggregate patient safety data because there was no standardized and consensus-driven definition of terms or language with which all institutions and providers of care could communicate effectively. In 2006, the National Quality Forum (NQF) published a consensus report called *Standardizing a Patient Safety Taxonomy.*[16] The NQF has endorsed this taxonomy and conveyed to it the special legal standing of a voluntary consensus standard. The taxonomy is not a reporting system. It is a classification methodology by which data can be organized and analyzed. It is a tool to allow providers and organizations to turn data into information from which patient safety solutions can be developed and implemented. The report presents a set of four voluntary consensus standards around a specific patient safety taxonomy, the **Patient Safety Event Taxonomy (PSET)**. It was developed by The Joint Commission with the assistance of work groups and the federal government. The effectiveness of the PSET will be its usefulness over time in providing better decision support at the point of care and with system design and policy development.

PROTECTING SENSITIVE INFORMATION

Information assembled from medical error reporting systems does not have federal protection from discovery on a global basis. Although many states offer a level of protection through peer review, quality assurance, and risk management laws, attempts to implement a federal protection have not been successful to date. Organizations also rely on attorney-client privilege and work product protections to safeguard information regarding the investigation and analysis of serious patient events or catastrophic claims. Health care organizations shield sensitive information with several acceptable methods. Organizations fear the release of information gathered from early warning systems because such information could be used against them in the court of public opinion and in a court of law.

The reporting of catastrophic events to The Joint Commission under its sentinel event policy brought this issue to the forefront. Many hospitals determined that preparing RCA reports and reporting sentinel events to The Joint Commission without explicit legal protection might place the organizations in jeopardy for the discovery of sensitive documents. The Joint Commission, sensitive to constituents' concerns, created alternative methods to comply, as discussed earlier in this chapter.

In November 2004, Florida voters passed Amendment 7 by a large majority. As Paul Barach, a professor in the Department of Anesthesiology and Medicine and associate dean for patient safety at the University of Miami Medical School, explains:

> *Amendment 7, the "Patients' Right to Know About Adverse Medical Incidents Act," allows full access to all patient records related to adverse medical events, turning back twenty years of quality assurance (QA) and peer review protection. The broad definition of the new law allowed patients, families, and their attorneys access to all records kept by a facility, including all meetings, morbidity and mortality conferences, root cause analyses, and any other professional exchange of information related to a patient's injury or death. In April 2005, the Florida legislature partly narrowed the application and interpretation of the new law, but damage to the health care system had been done. Reporting of events started to decline, and the fear of weakened peer review and QA protection had permeated the state. Anecdotal evidence suggests that morbidity and mortality conferences have either stopped or have been greatly sanitized; many now use fictitious data during case presentations. They have put a chill on the reporting of all patient events and have put a damper on patient safety and sensitive quality improvement research. The passage of Amendment 7 has led to an alarming wave of paranoia among health care providers and administration in discussing patient safety initiatives.*[17]

The developments in Florida illustrate the difficulty that health care providers have with the reporting of medical errors. A primary cause for a hospital's failure to report adverse events might be in direct relationship to its inability to ensure data confidentiality. The only way to fully protect medical error reports from legal discovery is through legislation.[18]

Patient Safety and Quality Improvement Act of 2005

The Patient Safety and Quality Improvement Act of 2005 (PSQIA), signed into law July 29, 2005, by President George W. Bush, was established to create a national database on medical errors, create and allow for the development of patient safety organizations (PSO), and provide both a privilege and confidentiality protection for certain **patient safety work products** (**PSWP**s) gathered under a **patient safety evaluation system** (**PSES**).

The U.S. Department of Health and Human Services (HHS) compiles and maintains a list of PSOs whose certification has been accepted by the HHS secretary. The first listing of 10 approved PSO's was posted to the PSO Website at AHRQ on November 5, 2008.

The final rule implementing the PSQIA has not been released. However, because of strong interest by the healthcare community and to implement the protections of the Patient Safety Act before release of the final rule, HHS has developed PSO Interim Guidance that outlines the statutory requirements and relevant sections of the proposed rule that are binding during the interim period. The *Notice of the Availability of the Interim Guidance* was announced in the Federal Register on October 14, 2008. For more information on the Interim Guidance, please see the press release "HHS Issues Interim Guidance For Patient Safety Organizations" available on the PSO Website at http://www.pso.ahrq.gov/index.html.

It is still too early to deliver concrete information about the implications and ramifications of this new law. It is hoped that over time, the language that now appears to be confusing and ambiguous will become clear. Currently, there seem to be more questions than answers:

- How will the new law interact with existing state mandatory reporting requirements for medical errors?

- How will the law interface with the Patient Safety Event Taxonomy?

- How will the law interpret the confidentiality and privilege for each state?

- How will the law further define patient safety work products and patient safety evaluation systems? Currently, those definitions are vague and ambiguous.

SUMMARY

Risk management professionals confront challenges today unheard of just a few years ago. The requirements for data collection and information reporting are staggering. The complexity of risk and development and implementation of sophisticated solutions requires continuous education. Handling risk management responsibilities and activities on a daily basis is an accomplishment in its own right. Prioritizing and simplifying activities are therefore important steps in gaining and maintaining control. Assessing the organization for its exposure to loss and the development of a robust early warning system to identify risk will enable the risk management professional to prioritize and focus efforts on risk areas of greatest frequency and severity while advancing patient safety efforts.

KEY TERMS

Attorney-client privilege
Confidentiality
Date of occurrence
Date of report
Electronic incident reporting
Failure mode and effects analysis
Incident report
Institute for Safe Medication
     Practices
The Joint Commission
MedWatch

Occurrence reporting
Occurrence screening
Patient Safety and Quality Improvement
     Act of 2005
Patient safety evaluation system
Patient Safety Event Taxonomy
Patient safety work product
Request for proposal
Root cause analysis
Sentinel event
Sentinel event policy

ACRONYMS

AERS	MER
ALF	MERS-TM
ASRS	NCC-MERP
CPOE	NQF
EMTALA	PSES
FDA	PSET
FMEA	PSQIA
HHC	PSRS
HHS	PSWP
HIPAA	RCA
HMO	RFP
ICUSRS	RMIS
ISMP	SMDA
LTC	SNF
MAUDE	USP
MCO	VAERS

NOTES

1. Information on the American Institute for Chartered Property Casualty Underwriters and the Insurance Institute of America is available at http://www.aicpcu.org.

2. Membership information available for the American Society for Healthcare Risk Management at [www.ashrm.org]

3. Florida Statute 395.0197 internal risk management programs (hospitals)

4. Florida Statute 400.147 internal risk management and quality assurance program (LTC)

5. Florida Statute 641.55(2)

6. Maley, R. A. "Building Risk Management into Integrated Healthcare Delivery Systems." *Journal of Healthcare Risk Management,* 1996, *16*(4), 31–40.

7. Gautam, N. "Ounce of Prevention: To Reduce Errors, Hospitals Prescribe Innovative Designs." *Wall Street Journal,* May 8, 2006, p. 1.

   Florida B395.0197 internal risk management programs (hospitals).

8. American Society for Healthcare Risk Management. *Mapping Your Risk Management Course in Ambulatory Care.* Chicago: American Society for Healthcare Risk Management, 1995, pp. 12–13. Information on the American Society for Healthcare Risk Management is available at http://www.ashrm.org

   Florida B400.147 internal risk management and quality assurance program (LTC).

9. Medical Risk Management Associates. "What Is the Difference Between Root Cause Analysis (RCA) and Failure Mode and Effects Analysis (FMEA)?" http://www.sentinel-event.com/rca-fmea.php

Florida §641.55 (HMO)

10 The Joint Commission online available at [www.jointcommission.org/Sentinel Events/]

11. The Joint Commission's sentinel event policy is available online at http://www.jointcommission.org/NR/rdonlyres/F84F9DC6-A5DA-490F-A91F-A9FCE26347C4/0/SE_chapter_july07.pdf

12. Ibid. Rape, as a reviewable sentinel event, is defined as unconsented sexual contact involving a patient and another patient, staff member, or other perpetrator while being treated or on the premises of the hospital, including oral, vaginal, or anal penetration or fondling of the patient's sex organ(s) by another individual's hand, sex organ, or object. One or more of the following must be present to determine reviewability:

- Any staff witnessed sexual contact as described above

- Sufficient clinical evidence obtained by the hospital to support allegations of unconsented sexual contact

- Admission by the perpetrator that sexual contact, as described above, occurred on the premises.

13. National Academy for State Health Policy, http://www.nashp.org/

14. Rosenthal J., and Booth, M. "Defining Reportable Adverse Events: A Guide for States Tracking Medical Errors," March 2003, http://www.nashp.org/Files/defining_adverse_events.pdf

15. For more information on mandatory reporting and to obtain the mandatory FDA Form 3500A, go to http://www.fda.gov/medwatch/REPORT/mtg.htm for drugs and biologicals or http://www.fda.gov.cdrh/mdr/ for devices.

16. National Quality Forum. *Standardizing a Patient Safety Taxonomy: A Consensus Report,* ed. K. W. Kizer and others. Washington, D.C.: National Quality Forum, 2006.

17. Barach, P. "The Unintended Consequences of Florida Medical Liability Legislation," Dec. 2005, http://www.webmm.ahrq.gov/perspective.aspx?perspectiveID=14

18. Medstat Group. *Implementation Planning Study for the Integration of Medical Event Reporting Input and Data Structure for Reporting to AHRQ, CDC, CMS, and FDA: Final Report*, Vol. 1. Santa Barbara, Calif.: Medstat Group, June 2002, p. 5.

CHAPTER

7

THE RISK MANAGEMENT PROFESSIONAL AND MEDICATION SAFETY

HEDY COHEN, NANCY TUOHY

LEARNING OBJECTIVES

- To be able to identify five major safety issues associated with medication preparation that result in medication errors, as well as associated risk management strategies

- To be able to identify two key safety issues associated with infusion pump use, as well as associated risk management strategies

- To be able to discuss the role of environmental stressors in medication safety

- To be able to describe two medication error prevention strategies based on education

- To be able to discuss prioritization of medication-related information as a safety strategy

- To be able to understand the role of error reporting in addressing medication errors

Before a health care culture can truly promote safety, there must first be an unquestioning acceptance, by everyone in the organization, of the premise that all practitioners make errors. There must be an appreciation by the entire staff that errors are never the result of any one isolated action or deed but rather that they result from the interaction of practitioners functioning in poorly designed systems. When an organization's leaders understand and endorse these basic principles, that organization is able to move from the pointless disciplining of individual practitioners for unintentional mistakes—a tactic that has been shown in the literature to have little effect on error reduction—to a culture of safety that is focused on identifying and addressing multifactor causes of errors. Organizations that further operationalize safety culture through strategies such as crew resource management (CRM), thereby empowering the lowest-ranking member of a team to question more senior personnel about practice concerns, and that use resources such as human factors science to facilitate safer interaction between humans and machines are well on their way to becoming what is known as "high-reliability organizations." (CRM and high-reliability organization theory are discussed in Chapter Three.)

When it comes to medication safety, health care organizations have proved to be highly unreliable. In the landmark report issued in 1999 by the Institute of Medicine, *To Err Is Human: Building a Safer Health System,* it was extrapolated that more than seven thousand hospitalized patients die each year due to preventable medication errors. Although the reason for this poor safety record is multifaceted, it is historically grounded in a culture that has focused on addressing individual practitioner errors rather than the more complex and significant role of the system in which practitioners function. Another critical influence is the ongoing demand by consumers that organizations provide more health care with less money.

This chapter will delineate key issues and suggest specific strategies to enhance medication safety. To achieve success, however, health care organizations and practitioners must first acknowledge and agree to address the many situations in wvhich frontline practitioners work with poorly designed equipment and technology, ambiguous policies and procedures, and inadequate communication between management and staff. The risk management professional's role as a facilitator of senior-level commitment, as a teacher of the importance of systems—rather than individual-focused issues analysis—and as a partner to clinicians who are seeking to implement new approaches is essential and exciting.

LATENT AND ACTIVE FAILURES

The Institute for Safe Medication Practices (ISMP), a nonprofit organization dedicated to medication safety, recognizes that each unintentional medication error has its roots in multiple system failures. Although all errors are the result of **active failures** (which occur at the level of the frontline practitioner, with effects that are felt almost immediately), **latent failures** (weaknesses in the organization whose effects are usually delayed) are often the most challenging causes of medical error.[1] Active failures are sometimes characterized as **"sharp-end"** and latent failures denoted as

> ## KEY CONCEPTS
>
> ■ All practitioners make errors. Most are due to poorly designed systems or processes. How an organization responds to errors highlights its culture for patient safety.
>
> ■ Organizations addressing medication safety need to embrace systems thinking and understand how processes interrelate; the failure of one part can affect the whole process.
>
> ■ The Joint Commission standards and National Patient Safety Goals requiring medication reconciliation are meant to address systems issues during transitions in care.
>
> ■ **Computerized provider order entry systems**, in addition to documenting and transferring orders, are intended to verify appropriateness for treatment, to identify potential drug interactions and allergies, and possibly to make the ordering practitioner aware of any issues that may prevent completion of the order.
>
> ■ Interruptions during any step in the medication process can have devastating consequences. Prescribers, pharmacists, and nurses must never order, dispense, or administer any medication with which they are not totally familiar.

"**blunt-end.**" To illustrate the interaction of active and latent failures in the context of a medication error, consider the following example (active failures are underlined, and the latent failures appear in *italics*).

It is important that risk management professionals focus their energies on the role of latent failure to prevent other such heartbreaking outcomes from occurring. Because the medication administration process is in reality a complex system with parameters usually outside the control of the individual practitioner, most errors are rarely the fault of one individual. Providing an optimal level of medication safety therefore requires that organizations proactively recognize and correct underlying system failures before injuries to patients occur. This requires a shift in focus beyond "naming, blaming, shaming, and training" of individuals.

SYSTEMS THINKING

Based on the foregoing discussion, in addition to committing to a culture of patient safety and aspiring to become high-reliability operations, organizations addressing medication safety must also embrace systems thinking. This approach assesses how individual processes interrelate. Most important, it helps us understand how individual flaws in a complex system like medication use can cause a serious error. As illustrated by Photo 7.1, we are vulnerable to system failures in our everyday life. In this example, we see how poor design may impede the process of entering a building. You want

CASE STUDY 7.1

An infant was born to a mother with a prior history of syphilis. Despite having incomplete patient information about the mother's past treatment for syphilis and current medical status of both the mother and child, a decision was made to treat the infant for congenital syphilis. After consultation with infectious disease specialists and the health department, an order was written for one dose of "Benzathine Pen (penicillin) G 150,000U IM."

The physicians, nurses, and pharmacists, unfamiliar with the treatment of congenital syphilis, also had limited knowledge about this drug, which was not in their formulary. The pharmacist consulted both the infant's progress notes and Drug Facts and Comparisons[2] to determine the usual dose of penicillin G benzathine for an infant. However, she misread the dose in both sources as 500,000 units/kg, a typical adult dose, instead of 50,000 units/kg. Due to lack of a pharmacy procedure for independent double checking, the error was not detected. Because a unit dose system was not used in the nursery, the pharmacy dispensed a tenfold overdose in a plastic bag containing two full syringes of Permapen 1.2 million units/2mL each, with green stickers on the plungers reminding the provider to "note dosage strength." A pharmacy label on the bag indicated that 2.5 mL of medication was to be administered IM, to equal a dose of 1,500,000 units.

After glancing at the medication, the infant's primary care nurse was concerned about the number of injections it would be necessary to give. (Because 0.5 mL is the maximum that providers are allowed to administer intramuscularly to an infant, a 1,500,000-unit dose would require five injections.) Anxious to prevent any unnecessary pain to the infant, the nurse involved two advanced-level colleagues, a neonatal nurse practitioner and an advanced-level nursery nurse, who decided to investigate the possibility of administering the medication IV instead of IM.

NeoFax[3] was consulted to determine if penicillin G benzathine could be administered IV. The NeoFax monograph on penicillin G did not specifically mention penicillin G benzathine; instead it described the treatment for congenital syphilis with aqueous crystalline penicillin G, IV slow push, or penicillin G procaine IM. Nowhere in the two-page monograph was penicillin G benzathine mentioned, and no specific warnings that penicillin G procaine and penicillin G benzathine were to be given "IM only" were present.

Unfamiliar with the various forms of penicillin G, the nurse practitioner believed that "benzathine" was a brand name for penicillin G. This misconception was reinforced by the physician's method of writing the drug order, written with "benzathine" capitalized and placed on a line *above "penicillin G" rather than after it on the same line* (see Figure 7.1). It is noteworthy that many texts use ambiguous synonyms when referring to various forms of penicillin. For example, penicillin G benzathine is frequently mentioned near or directly associated with the terms "crystalline penicillin" and "aqueous suspension." *Believing that aqueous crystalline penicillin G and penicillin G benzathine were the same drug, the nurse practitioner con-*

clarity, the neonatal nurse practitioner assumed that she was operating under a national protocol, which allowed neonatal nurse practitioners to plan, direct, implement, and change drug therapy. Consequently, the nurse practitioner *made a decision to administer the drug IV.* The primary care nurse, who was not certified to administer IV medication to infants, transferred care of the infant to the advanced-level nursery RN and the nurse practitioner.

FIGURE 7.1. *Entry for Benzathine on the Patient's Chart.*

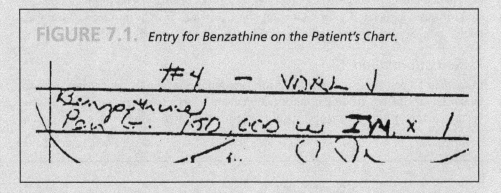

---

cluded that the drug could safely be administered IV. While the nurse practitioner had been taught in school that only clear liquids could be injected IV, she had learned through practical experience that certain milky white substances, such as IV lipids and other lipid-based drug products, can indeed be given IV. Therefore, *she did not recognize the problem of giving penicillin G benzathine, a milky white substance, through an IV.*

Complicating matters further in this example, hospital policies and practices did not clearly define the prescriptive authority of nonphysicians. Partly as a result of this lack of

As they prepared for drug administration, *neither of these providers noticed the tenfold overdose or that the syringe was labeled by the manufacturer "IM use only."* The manufacturer's warning was not prominently placed. The syringe needed to be rotated 180 degrees away from the name before the warning could be seen. The nurse *began to administer the first syringe of Permapen slow IV push.* After about 1.8 mL was administered, the infant became unresponsive, and resuscitation efforts were unsuccessful.

to open a door that has a pull handle. You pull the door toward you to open it, but the door does not budge.

You pull again with no success. Then you realize that the door is to be opened by pushing rather than pulling. Your expectation was that a door designed with a pull handle is supposed to be pulled, not pushed. This same type of misperception can occur when a nurse obtains a medication from an automated dispensing machine. When the medication bin is labeled with the name of a specific drug, the nurse assumes that the correct drug is in that bin. If, however, the wrong drug was inadvertently placed in the bin, an error can easily occur.

To facilitate understanding of the complex processes that interact to cause medication errors, ISMP identified twelve safety-critical components of the medication use system and categorized numerous reported errors accordingly. The following discussion of issues associated with each component provides insight into medication use–related risk. Specific risk reduction strategies are also presented.

Patient Information

More than 18 percent of prescribing errors are due to inadequate patient information. Of particular concern are lack of information about allergies and comorbidities such as hepatic function and pregnancy status.[4] A critical related issue is that key patient

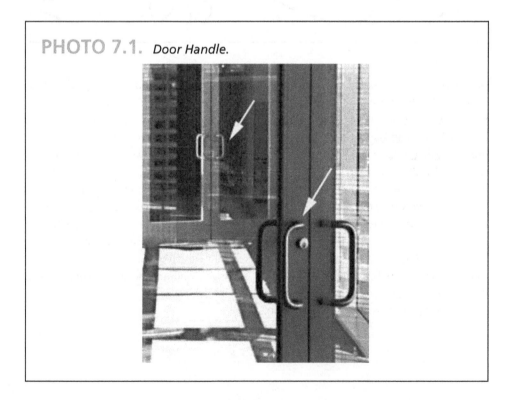

PHOTO 7.1. *Door Handle.*

information (see Table 7.1) is often unavailable to pharmacy and nursing staff prior to dispensing or administering drugs for new admissions.

When drugs are dispensed or administered without adequate patient information such as laboratory values or key patient comorbidities, critical data that should be double-checked is omitted, and risk potentially increases. For example, warfarin, an anticoagulant, is ordered on admission, but the provider ordering warfarin is unaware that the patient's international normalized ratio (INR) is elevated. (The INR is a standardized measure of clotting time.) In another hypothetical situation, a prescriber might order a standard dosage of aminoglycide, which is contraindicated, for an end-stage renal patient, because there is no available documentation of the patient's condition. Barring an emergency situation, drugs should never be dispensed unless specific clinical information has been reviewed during the ordering process. Clearly, health care practitioners must identify effective ways to facilitate the presence of key clinical information at this critical point in the patient's care.

A real-life example of an error due to lack of information about comorbidities involved an eighty-four-year-old woman who was transferred from a nursing home to a hospital for a coronary artery bypass graft. After surgery, her platelet count dropped by 50 percent. A hematologist was consulted, who determined that the patient was suffering from heparin-induced thrombocytopenia. Although the physician documented this diagnosis in his consultation report, it was not written elsewhere in the patient's chart, and the pharmacy was not notified. As a result, two days later, when the patient was transferred to a surgical unit, nurses, unaware of the patient's comorbid diagnosis of heparin-induced thrombocytopenia, flushed her IV lines with heparin. The patient

TABLE 7.1. **Essential Patient Information**

Allergies
Diagnosis and comorbid conditions
Renal and hepatic function
Pregnancy and lactation status
Age, weight, height
Full medication history (over-the-counter, herbals, cultural)
Laboratory and other diagnostic results
Clinical observations (vital signs, mentation)
Demographics

suffered a stroke six hours later and died. Although her death was probably due to the surgery, the illicit heparin administration was likely a contributing factor.

Another error that resulted from inadequate patient information occurred when a double-strength concentration of a potentially dangerous or "high-alert" drug was ordered for a cardiac patient in the intensive care unit (ICU). A nurse called the pharmacy and inadvertently requested that an infusion of regular insulin be prepared, at twice normal strength. In carrying out this erroneous verbal order, the pharmacist failed to notice in the order entry system that diabetes mellitus was not documented as a patient diagnosis. Then, without seeing a copy of the written order, he prepared and delivered the insulin infusion. Subsequently, during ICU pharmacy rounds, he failed to obtain a copy of the physician's order or review the patient's chart to verify hyperglycemia. Without an independent double check, the nurse hung the double-strength regular insulin infusion. As a result, the patient suffered permanent central nervous system impairment.

Information that is of obvious and closely related concern is the patient's identity. The Joint Commission requires that staff use two patient-specific identifiers before administering any medication. These are likely to include patient name and birth date. But accurate and complete validation of patient identification for purposes of medication administration cannot occur without comparing the patient identification to the **medication administration record** (**MAR**). Staff members should also encourage patients to state their name and show their identification bracelet before accepting any medications.

Further illustrating the importance of patient identification, medication errors also occur due to order sheets without a name. In one case, a potentially serious error occurred when an order for high-dose cytabarine, a chemotherapy agent, was written on a blank order sheet that contained no patient identification. The order sheet was then accidentally stamped by the unit clerk with the wrong patient's name and faxed to the pharmacy. Luckily, the patient's diagnosis of hairy cell leukemia was in the pharmacy's computer system. The error was averted when an oncology pharmacy specialist, scanning patient demographics before entering the order, realized that the high-dose cytabarine was totally inappropriate for the patient.

To enhance the collection of key patient data, all medication forms, including prescriber order forms, the MAR, and the pharmacy profile, should contain a designated area with pertinent prompts and sufficient space to document essential patient information. Such approaches should make it easy to capture issues such as weight fluctuation and new allergies. Health care organizations must educate all staff on the importance of obtaining accurate inpatient and outpatient information. Ideally, an electronic medical record (EMR) or other form of computer technology should integrate all collected data, including outpatient information.

As another safeguard, the organization should have policies and procedures in place that prevent medication orders from being profiled in the pharmacy without basic clinical and demographic information. It is also important that high-alert nonprofiled medications available from unit stock be independently double-checked before administration, except in emergency situations. An independent double check is effective only if done in the following way. The first practitioner completes the task (calculation, pump programming, syringe verification, and so on) without sharing methods with the checking practitioner. The second checking practitioner completes the task again, without help or hints from the first. The second practitioner then compares the results of both practitioners against the original order for accuracy.

Still other preventive strategies include the following. The pharmacy information system and computerized provider order entry (CPOE) should be kept up to date as drugs are added to the formulary. Furthermore, all systems should contain alerts for allergies, cross-sensitivities, weight and age restrictions, and drug duplications when new medications are added to a patient's profile.

Drug Information

In recent years, there has been an explosion of new medications and innovative uses of older drugs. Keeping abreast of all this constantly evolving information is a daunting, if not impossible, task. It has been noted that most medication errors occur during the prescribing and administration stages because up-to-date drug information is not available at the point of care.[5] In addition, many health care organizations do not have pharmacists readily available to interact, face to face, with practitioners on patient care units.[6]

Because many medication errors occur due to lack of essential drug information, ongoing staff education regarding the appropriate uses, dosages, side effects, and interactions of drugs is crucial. For example, the use of the cancer chemotherapeutic agent methotrexate is well established in the oncology setting. Recently, providers have begun to prescribe this medication in low doses for rheumatoid arthritis, asthma, psoriasis, inflammatory bowel disease, myasthenia gravis, and inflammatory myositis. When used for these chronic diseases, such doses are administered weekly or sometimes twice a week. However, because relatively few medications are dosed on a weekly basis, practitioners who are unfamiliar with this new clinical approach make mistakes related to frequency of administration and to the novel dosage. In one reported case, a seventy-nine-year-old patient was to receive methotrexate for a nononcology indication. The prescription was erroneously written and dispensed as methotrexate four times daily. This patient died after receiving nine doses of the medication in a seventy-two-hour period.

Prescribers, pharmacists, and nurses must never order, dispense, or administer any medication with which they are not totally familiar. Although this might be challenging for organizations that face demands for efficiency, it is essential to provide practitioners with a workload that allows adequate time to learn about their patients' medications. In yet another example of an error, a cardiac patient was admitted from the ED as an "overflow" patient to a surgical ICU unit where the staff was unfamiliar with the administration of thrombolytics. The cardiologist mistakenly ordered a loading dose of epifibatide (used to inhibit platelet aggregation) as 180 mcg, not as 180 mcg/kg. The pharmacy was particularly busy, and the pharmacist, who was unfamiliar with epifibatide dosing, did not read the package insert or verify the dose with the prescriber. The surgical ICU nurse, who had never administered this drug before, compounded the error when she misread the prescriber's order as 180 mg. She initiated the loading dose by giving 75 mg over one hour, planning to call the pharmacy for the remainder of the dose. As the infusion was ending, another pharmacist discovered the error, and the infusion was discontinued. Fortunately, the patient suffered no permanent harm.

Strategies to make drug information available at the point of care include the use of rule-based computerized provider order entry systems that provide drug information, warnings, and alerts during order input. If CPOE is not available in the organization, the use of a sound, user-friendly computerized drug information system such as Formulary Advisor® and Clinical Xpert part of the Micromedex Healthcare Series offered through Thomson Reuter's[7] or up-to-date drug information books can provide valuable current drug information. The pharmacy computer system should also give specific warnings for drugs that have unusual dosing schedules, such as weekly or monthly, and alerts for cumulative drug dosing. Another effective strategy is to move the pharmacist, an expert in the clinical uses of medication, from the centralized pharmacy into satellite pharmacies within patient care areas. This allows the pharmacist to establish a close working relationship with the practitioners and patients, follow the patients' clinical courses, and consult regularly with the professional staff about appropriate drug selection, dosing, and administration. It has been shown that when the pharmacist is close to the point of care, patient outcomes are improved and errors and drug costs are significantly reduced.[8] If pharmacists are not already in place in patient care units, organizations can take a first step toward this model of care by having pharmacists make daily rounds of patient care units or enter medication orders directly at the computer terminals in patient care units. The next logical step in integrating pharmacists more closely with the care team should be to prioritize implementation of unit-based pharmacy support in key areas, such as the intensive care unit, the pediatrics or oncology units, the operating room, and the emergency department.

Communication of Information

Organizational barriers to communicating essential clinical patient and drug information effectively include drug information systems that do not interface with other vital patient information systems, such as the electronic medical record and the laboratory system. Such disconnects clearly hamper the practitioner's access to information essential for safe administration, such as allergies and pertinent test results. Another closely related obstacle is the absence of computer order entry systems. Without such systems, there is increased risk of order-related error due to illegible handwriting, missing or ambiguous information, nonconventional abbreviations, and unclear documentation of dosage.

Another barrier is a provider's flawed communication style. Of particular concern is intimidation, which contributes to about 10 percent of the serious errors that occur during administration. In fact, ISMP receives many reports of lethal errors in which orders were questioned but not changed. In one ISMP survey, almost half (49 percent) of all respondents related that their past experiences with intimidation had altered the way they handle order clarification or questions about medication orders. At least once during the previous year, about 40 percent of respondents did not act on concerns about a medication order or ask another professional to talk to the prescriber, rather than interact with a particularly intimidating prescriber. Three-quarters (75 percent) had asked colleagues to help them interpret an order or validate its safety so that they did not have to interact with an intimidating prescriber. Also, 34 percent reported that they had found the prescriber's stellar reputation intimidating and had not questioned an order about which they had concerns. When the prescriber had been questioned about the safety of an order and refused to change it, 31 percent of respondents suggested that the physician administer the drug or simply allowed the physician to give the medication himself, and almost half (49 percent) felt pressured to accept the order, dispense a product, or administer a medication despite their concerns. As a result, 7 percent of respondents reported that they had been involved in a medication error during the previous year, in which intimidation clearly played a role.[9]

To address flawed communication style, many health care organizations are using established protocols, consistent with human resource protocols and medical staff bylaws, to follow up with providers who are perceived to be intimidating. Appropriate strategies in this regard may include the use of incident or event reports, objectively completed, to document clinically pertinent events. Of great assistance in improving communication housewide is a crew resource management approach, in which a team member with minimal stature is empowered to question team leaders. Recognize that effective implementation of such strategies cannot occur without senior administrative and clinical leadership endorsement.

Another key communication issue involves verbal orders. Such orders, whether spoken in person or over the telephone, are inherently problematic because they can easily be misheard or misinterpreted. For example, there have been error reports in which verbal orders for "Celebrex 100 mg PO" were misheard to be for "Cerebyx 100 mg PO." Drug names are not the only verbal information prone to misinterpretation. Numbers are also problematic. For example, an emergency room physician verbally ordered "morphine 2 mg IV," but the nurse heard "morphine 10 mg IV," and the patient subsequently received a 10-mg infusion that caused respiratory arrest. In another situation, a physician called in an order for "15 mg of hydralazine" to be given IV every two hours. The nurse, thinking that he had said "50 mg," administered an overdose to the patient, who developed tachycardia and had a significant drop in blood pressure.

To reduce the frequency of verbal orders, some organizations have instituted the use of fax machines to communicate orders. However, fax machines are connected to telephone lines, and significant line noise can result in the loss of important information, such as portions of a drug name or even the dose. For example, the order shown in

Figure 7.2 was mistaken as Flagyl 250 mg instead of Flagyl 500 mg. A related problem occurs when prescribers write on the very edge of the order form, making it impossible for some fax machines and scanners to read the entire order. Thus an order for "Lomotil QID PRN" may appear as "Lomotil QID," as if the "PRN" were never written.

Verbal orders must be eliminated, except in emergency and sterile situations. Such orders are especially inappropriate when potentially lethal drugs, such as chemotherapy agents, are prescribed. To further decrease the risk of verbal order–related errors, health care organizations should adopt yet another crew resource management principle. This particular strategy concerns the standardization of communication. Here are approaches that might help achieve standardization of verbal orders:

- When verbal orders are allowed, prescribers must enunciate the order clearly and the receiver should always repeat the order to the prescriber to avoid misinterpretation.

- As an extra check, either the prescriber or receiver should spell unfamiliar drug names, using "T as in Tom," "C as in Charley," and so forth. Pronounce each numerical digit separately, saying for example, "one six" instead of "sixteen" to avoid confusion with "sixty."

- The receiver must ensure that the verbal order makes sense when considered in conjunction with the patient's diagnosis.

- The verbal order must be immediately recorded on an order sheet in the patient's chart, whenever possible.

- For telephone orders, the recipient must obtain a telephone number in case it is necessary to call back with follow-up questions.

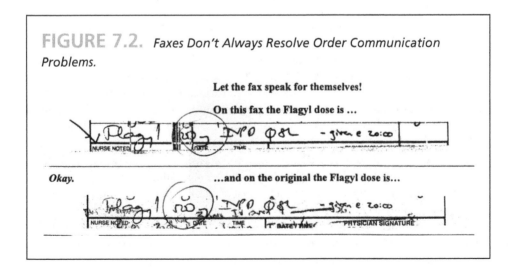

FIGURE 7.2. *Faxes Don't Always Resolve Order Communication Problems.*

- Limit verbal orders to formulary drugs, as staff members are more likely to misunderstand drug names and dosages with which they are unfamiliar.

- Limit the number of personnel who routinely receive telephone orders, to reduce the potential for unauthorized orders.

Still another issue is poor communication of medical information at care transition points. According to the Institute for Healthcare Improvement (IHI), miscommunication when the patient moves from one care environment to another is responsible for about 50 percent of all medication errors and up to 20 percent of adverse drug events, in numerous health care organizations across the country.[10] One illustration of this type of error involved a patient who was transferred from one hospital to another and received a duplicate dose of insulin because the receiving nurse did not know that the medication had been given before transfer. In another case, enalapril 2.5 mg IV was administered to a patient after transfer from a critical care unit to a medical unit. The drug had been discontinued upon transfer, but the orders had not yet been transcribed. Yet another error occurred when, before discharge, the patient's Lexapro was increased to 10 mg daily, but the discharge instructions erroneously called for 5 mg daily. When the error was noticed, a pharmacist called the patient and learned that she had been cutting her newly prescribed 10 mg tablets in half.

Joint Commission standards now require that health care organizations address medication reconciliation. Particularly helpful is documentation of this process, which assesses and addresses medication duplications and incompatibilities at vulnerable points of transition, such as admission, transfers between care settings, and at discharge.

Finally, to facilitate communication about medication orders, it is of great importance that written and computerized medication orders include the generic and brand names of the medication, without abbreviations. There are literally thousands of drug pair names that sound and look similar, so detailed information helps prevent these medications from being mistaken for one another. In addition, medication should never be prescribed by volume, number of vials, or ampoules. When such orders are received, the staff should seek clarification immediately.

Labeling, Packaging, and Drug Nomenclature

Improper hospital drug labeling and failing to keep drugs in packaging until administering them contribute to medication errors. Furthermore, the pharmaceutical industry has sometimes unwittingly undermined the safe use of medication by marketing drugs under names that look alike and sound alike, using confusing labeling, or providing drugs to health care organizations in nondistinctive or ambiguously marked packages. In reports submitted to MEDMARX (a subscription-based reporting program sponsored by the United States Pharmacopeia), nearly 32,000 medication errors over a thirty-nine-month period occurred among look-alike or sound-alike drugs due to packaging or labeling. Approximately 2.6 percent of these errors were classified as harmful.[11]

Labeling Confusing labeling, sometimes associated with manufacturers' use of similar colors, font sizes, and layout to achieve a product image, can result in errors.

For example, the drug Temodar (temozolomide) has reportedly been the subject of numerous dispensing and administration errors because labeling leads staff members to misinterpret capsule strength. This alkylating agent is available in 5, 20, 100, and 250 mg capsules. The strength is stated directly beside the quantity of capsules (see Photo 7.2). Someone who reads the number of capsules right next to the strength, as in "20 capsules 100 mg," might conclude that the total number of capsules in the bottle adds up to the strength, for example, "twenty capsules of 5 mg each equal 100 mg," rather than "twenty capsules of 100 mg each." Adding to the confusion is similarity between the strength of the dosage and the number of capsules in the bottle. Capsules in strengths of 5 mg and 20 mg are often dispensed in packages that contain either five or twenty capsules. The Food and Drug Administration (FDA) pointed out that this confusing packaging and labeling can lead to serious and even fatal errors.[12]

Recently, an error was reported in which a prescription for oral Temodar 60 mg daily was written for a patient with a brain tumor. The pharmacist dispensed the dosage from a 100-mg bottle containing twenty capsules and simply misread the label. The pharmacist was under the impression that twenty capsules were equal to 100 mg, so he concluded that each capsule contained 5 mg and dispensed twelve capsules to make up a 60-mg dose. Fortunately, the patient's mother caught the error when she was filling the patient's pillbox before any of the medication was given.

To address these issues, the manufacturer submitted a redesigned label to the FDA for approval.

To proactively address label confusion like this, organizations may affix "name and strength alert" stickers on products that have potentially confusing labels and highlight

PHOTO 7.2. *Capsule Quantity Is Often Mistaken for Product Strength.*

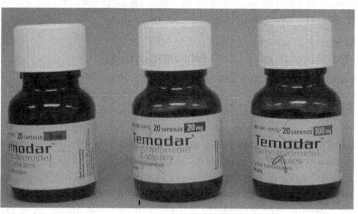

the differences with a pen or highlighter. The staff should also employ at least two independent checks in the dispensing and administration processes for these medications. Organizations might also consider implementation of point-of-care bar coding technology, which, for example, requires the provider to scan the patient's name band with the drug package before administering the drug. Other valuable devices are "smart" infusion pumps that contain drug libraries to further enhance safe administration of such drugs.

Packaging Like confusing dose information, look-alike packaging is of great concern. Related errors generally involve assumptions by staff members that a medication that sounds similar to the one they are ordered to give is appropriate, or they pick up a wrong vial or other dispensing device because it looks like the medication they are ordered to give. In one example, a woman who was thirty-one weeks pregnant received Methergine (methylergonovine) instead of Brethine (terbutaline), which resulted in the emergency premature C-section delivery of her baby. Similar-sounding names and similar-looking packaging contributed to the error (see Photo 7.3). Fortunately, mother and child were unharmed.

Another look-alike medication issue involves respiratory therapy inhalation drugs, such as ipratropium (Atrovent) and levalbuterol (Xopenex), which are packaged in disposable, clear plastic containers with raised, embossed labels that are difficult to

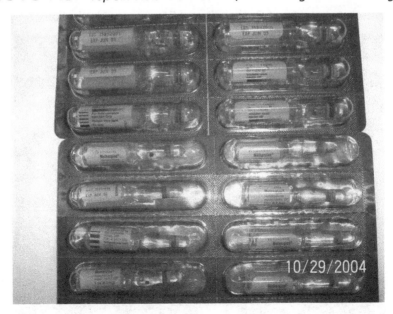

PHOTO 7.3. *Top Six Vials Are Brethine; Bottom Eight Are Methergine.*

read. Compounding the risk, respiratory therapists often pocket several of each of these medications, to be more efficient. Of additional concern, other products, such as opthalmic solutions and preservative-free medications, like xylocaine, are also illegibly packaged in small plastic vials (see Photo 7.4).

To minimize confusion associated with look-alike packaging, health care organizations should, whenever possible, consider using equivalent products from different manufacturers. Organizations should also avoid storing look-alike products near one another in unit stock and automated dispensing cabinets.

Applying auxiliary labels might help distinguish similar-looking packages. In addition, the use of "tall-man" lettering might visually differentiate drug names on similar-looking packages. Tall-man lettering uses capital letters within a drug name to highlight the letters that differentiate two similar names: for instance, "hydrALA-ZINE" and "hydrOXYzine." In 2001, the FDA's Office of Generic Drugs requested manufacturers of sixteen look-alike name pairs to reformat the appearance of these drug names on their packaging, and tall-man lettering was used extensively in this effort (the list can be viewed at http://www.fda.gov/cder/drug/MedErrors/nameDiff.htm). This was a voluntary program, and not all manufacturers complied. Facilities, however, may choose to employ tall-man lettering on auxiliary labels, shelf and bin labels, or medication administration records.

Yet another packaging-related issue that contributes to errors involves the removal or discarding of packaging before the drug is administered. Although most drugs are

PHOTO 7.4. *Mix of Opthalmic and Respiratory Medications.*

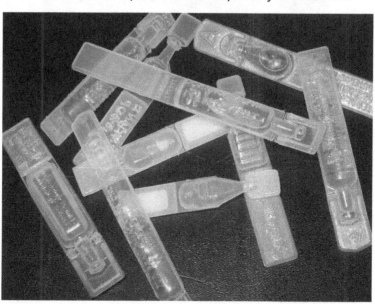

packaged as unit doses, this does not ensure that medications will remain labeled until they reach the patient's bedside. Often nurses prepare drugs at a central location, removing pharmacy or manufacturer drug packaging and labeling and placing the open medication in cups for administration. Thus the chance for errors, especially administering a medication to the wrong patient, is greatly increased. Institutions should require that the drug remain labeled throughout the drug use process, up to the point of administration. Using bar code technology might make this easier. Until this technology is instituted nationwide, however, it might be valuable to convene staff focus groups to identify and address the reasons that providers remove drug packaging and labels before administering drugs.

Nomenclature Errors in identifying medication sometimes occur when providers refer to medication by a shorter name. Other reasons for misidentification include confusion due to the indiscriminate use of brand and generic names, in combination and separately, in written and computerized orders. Sometimes confusion results from a "line extension," when the manufacturer substantively changes the drug but changes only the suffix of the name, to facilitate marketing of the progeny of a successful pharmaceutical. To address such confusion, ISMP recommends that both brand and generic names be documented (if appropriate) in ordering and transcribing, with the indication for the medication.

One example of potential omission related to nomenclature was generated by a mix-up between the sound-alike medications Cerebyx and Celebrex. In this case, Cerebyx (fosphenytoin) 100 mg IV TID, an anticonvulsant, was listed on a patient's medication administration record from a transferring hospital. The admitting cardiologist at the receiving hospital was unfamiliar with Cerebyx and misread the drug as Celebrex (celecoxib), a pain medication, even though he knew it was not available in a parenteral form. He did not order the drug because the patient was not having pain. When a pharmacist reviewed the orders along with the old MAR and investigated, he was able to correct the order, thus preventing an omission error. Although often not considered as serious a potential threat to patient safety, patients can be harmed as much by the omission of a drug as from an erroneous dose.

In another issue related to nomenclature, Pamelor (nortriptyline), an antidepressant, was misheard as Tambocor (flecainide), an antiarrhythmic, and the prescription was dispensed as such. Although the patient took this erroneous medication for one month and experienced fatigue, he fortunately suffered no cardiovascular symptoms.

In yet another example, a pharmacist received an order for Gabitril (tiagabine), which is used for seizure disorders. He entered the order correctly, but the patient still received the wrong drug because the pharmacy mistakenly dispensed Zanaflex (tizanidine), a drug used for muscle spasticity. Tiagabine and tizanidine were stored alphabetically by generic name in the pharmacy, separated by only one space on the shelves. Both drugs are also available in 2-mg and 4-mg strengths. The error occurred despite a bright-orange warning sticker stating "Name Alert" on the tizanidine supply. The potential for error was increased because the hospital had repackaged the drugs in unit doses using only the generic names. Fortunately, in this case, a nurse detected the difference before administering the drug.

Recent discussion of nomenclature-related safety issues has taken place at the United States Pharmacopeia (USP), resulting in adoption of a resolution to encourage the use of generic names alone for new single-active-ingredient products marketed after January 1, 2006. However, a single drug name—generic or brand—would not prevent all such mix-ups. Examination of the drug pairs delineated in the Joint Commission National Patient Safety Goals, requiring accredited entities to review a list of pertinent look- and sound-alike drugs annually, reveals that nine of ten problem pairs are similar generic names.[13]

Trademark extensions are another risk issue. There are no standard meanings for various suffixes such as "XL," "ER," and "SR" following drug names. The line of Wellbutrin (bupropion) products has been of particular concern in this regard. Twice in one week, a hospital psychiatrist ordered Wellbutrin XL 300 mg, but two tablets of Wellbutrin SR 150 mg were dispensed. The pharmacists filling the orders were unaware of the new XL formulation, and poor physician handwriting made it difficult to discern the XL portion of the drug name. In another reported case, a prescriber wrote Wellbutrin "XR" (instead of either XL or SR) 150 mg daily. The pharmacist could have looked at the once-daily frequency and concluded that it must be the XL product. However, he reviewed the profile and found that the patient had in fact been taking Wellbutrin SR daily, so that is what he dispensed. Unfortunately, the physician actually meant to prescribe the XL formulation.

Different forms of a drug can also be confused. For example, significant harm can occur when liposomal and conventional products are mixed up. In one case, liposomal doxorubicin (Doxil) and conventional doxorubicin (brand names include Adriamycin and Rubex), both packaged in 20-mg vials, were stored together in the same drawer in a pharmacy refrigerator. Although both drugs are chemotherapeutic agents, their mode of action is very different. The patient involved received an IV push injection of 75 mg of Doxil, rather than the conventional doxorubicin that was intended. The patient's reaction was not serious, but other reports of similar incidents have resulted in severe side effects and even death.

To reduce drug mix-ups related to nomenclature, it is important that providers seek clarification if the drug being ordered does not seem to match the patient's condition. Furthermore, institutions should require both the brand and generic names in all documentation, including orders, and on pharmacy labels.

Drug Storage, Stocking, and Standardization

The traditional model of medication storage and stocking has been phased out in most U.S. hospitals. Formerly, a nearly complete pharmacy was maintained on every unit in a hospital or nursing home, which increased the probability of errors. Acting alone, the nurse typically interpreted and transcribed a physician's order, chose the proper container from hundreds available on the shelves, prepared the correct amount, placed the dose in a syringe or cup, labeled it, took it to the patient, administered it, and verified that the dose had been administered. The obvious lack of check systems has led to the elimination of this medication administration model in most organizations.

Errors are still likely to occur, however, in organizations that employ a modified floor stock model on nursing units, even if there are just a few "stock bottles" for nurses to manage. The chance of error under these circumstances increases if drugs are stored by alphabetical name on units (or in the pharmacy) or the unit fails to sequester high-alert drugs (such as neuromuscular blockers).

Technological solutions are helpful only to a point. For example, even when unit stock is placed in automated dispensing machines, problems might still occur if there are not enough machines or if poor workspace planning results in nurses' crowding the machines at times when many patients require medications simultaneously. Under such circumstances, staff members often try to circumvent an inefficient work environment by storing medications in their pockets. Also of concern is the partial implementation of technological solutions—for example, the pertinent technology does not integrate with other in-house documentation systems or fails to encompass safety features such as patient profiling and on-screen alerts.

Indeed, if automated dispensing cabinets (ADCs) store a wide assortment of medications or excessive quantities of a single medication but do not interface with the pharmacy's computer-based profiling system, the risk of error actually increases. Pharmacy profiling allows a pharmacist to review each medication order and screen it for safety before the drug can be removed from the cabinet. Without this safeguard, nurses might not be alerted to unsafe doses, potential allergic reactions, duplicate therapy, contraindications, drug interactions, or other important information that could make the drug, dose, or route of administration unsafe. In addition, medications in ADCs are not always limited to the dosage that is necessary for a patient. Also, manufacturer-generated unit dose medication is not often labeled with the individual patient's dose. These issues resulted in a serious error when a patient died after receiving 10 mg of colchicine IV. The physician had prescribed "colchicine 1.0 mg IV now," but the decimal point was hidden on the line of the order form, and the use of an unnecessary trailing zero led to misinterpretation. However, the error reached the patient primarily because there was an excessive quantity of colchicine in the ADC. Ten ampoules of colchicine (1 mg each) were available in the ADC; thus the nurse had enough ampoules to prepare the overdose.

Safety procedures for **automated dispensing technology** are essential error prevention tools. For example, without a protocol that addresses proper storage, drugs can erroneously be placed in compartments of a cabinet that has been labeled for other medications. Procedures should also require that no medication be routinely available for administering to patients without appropriate order screening by the pharmacist. This includes initial doses of medication. Particularly dangerous drugs should be dispensed directly only from the pharmacy.

Device Acquisition, Use, and Monitoring

Practitioners involved in the medication-use process often employ one or more devices to administer a specific drug. Historically, many devices, such as infusion pumps, were designed without the benefit of human factors engineering. Human factors engineering and human factors ergonomics are the "scientific disciplines concerned with the understanding of interactions among humans and other elements of a system, and the profession that applies theory, principles, data, and other methods to design in order to optimize human well-being and overall system performance."[14] This definition was adopted by the International Ergonomics Association in 2000. Failure to take human factors principles into consideration while designing medication delivery devices can contribute to patient harm.

For example, the misuse of infusion pumps and other parenteral device systems is the second leading cause of serious errors during drug administration.[15] A classic human factors–related problem that involves infusion pumps is the free flow of medication into a patient due to the lack of free-flow protection on intravenous (IV) pumps. Before The Joint Commission standard that required free-flow protection on pumps, such errors occurred when practitioners forgot to slide the clamping mechanism closed when they removed the infusion tubing sets from pumps. As the issues associated with infusion pumps illustrate, reliance on human vigilance is inherently prone to error. All devices should be designed to compensate for normal error-causing human behavior, such as momentary lapses in attention and fatigue.

Even with more recent equipment, errors may still occur. For example, the design of infusion pump keypads makes it easy for tenfold dosing errors to occur. Specifically, the close proximity of the zero and decimal point keys on some IV pumps, and multiple-function keys, such as an up arrow that also serves as an enter key, has led nurses to misprogram pumps with rates that can cause overdose. The newest pumps, called smart pumps, may include a computerized drug library of preset dose limits that alert nurses to programming errors, but many older pumps without such features remain in use.

Other problems involving IV infusion pumps include the following:

- Infusion pumps being turned off accidentally by users or when physically bumped against other objects

- Lack of visible or audible warning alarms when the syringe or cassette is not properly loaded, resulting in overdosing or underdosing of medication

- Confusing tubing on pumps where multiple lines are used

- The inadvertent setting of a drug or solution at the primary IV rate instead of at the intended secondary rate

- Decimal point errors, such as keying in the infusion rate at ten times the intended rate (for example, 44.5 mL/h instead of 4.5 mL/h or 88 mL/h instead of 8 mL/h)

- Dosage calculation errors

- Keying in the volume of the drug to be infused as the infusion rate (for example, a volume of 500 mL heparin mistakenly entered as rate of 500 mL/h)

Special precautions are needed with **patient-controlled analgesia** (PCA) pumps. When used as intended, PCA reduces the risk of oversedation by allowing patients to self-administer more frequent but smaller doses of analgesia through an infusion pump. However, because this therapeutic intervention combines inherently error-prone devices, and narcotics, serious unintended outcomes have frequently occurred.

Fortunately, by identifying specific issues, risks associated with this technology can be reduced. Table 7.2 summarizes some of the issues surrounding the use of PCA pumps and appropriate solutions.

TABLE 7.2. **Patient-Controlled Analgesia (PCA) Problems and Safety Recommendations.**

Problem	Description	Safety Recommendations
PCA by proxy	When another person (health professional, family member) administers a dose of medication instead of the patient's dosing themselves. Can lead to oversedation, respiratory depression, and death. Patients must control the PCA, but a sedated patient cannot press the button, thereby overdosing.	Warn patients, family members, and visitors about the dangers of PCA by proxy. Place warning labels on activation buttons that state "FOR PATIENT USE ONLY." Keep PCA flowsheets at the bedside to document PCA doses and patient monitoring.
Improper patient selection and education	Only patients who have the mental alertness and sufficient cognitive, physical, and psychological ability should use a PCA pump Can lead to inadequate pain control or oversedation. Teaching patients during the immediate postoperative period is ineffective if the patient is too groggy to understand. This has often led to poor pain control in the first twelve hours following surgery.	Check patient allergies, which should be visible on the MAR, before initiating PCA. Educate patients preoperatively about PCA use. Establish patient selection criteria. In general, infants, young children, and confused patients are not suitable candidates to use a PCA pump.

(Continued)

TABLE 7.2. *(Continued)*

Problem	Description	Safety Recommendations
Inadequate patient monitoring	Patients using a PCA pump must be frequently and appropriately monitored. The level of consciousness achieved from physical stimulus is only a temporary way to monitor for toxicity.	Ensure that nurses recognize the signs and symptoms of opiate toxicity. Have oxygen and naloxone readily available. Teach the need to assess using minimal verbal or tactile stimulation.
	When the physical stimulus is removed, patients can quickly fall back into an oversedated state. Pulse oximetery alone can give a false sense of security because oxygen saturation is usually maintained even at low respiratory rates.	Establish a standard pain assessment scale. At minimum, evaluate pain, alertness, and vital signs, including rate and quality of respirations, every four hours. More frequent monitoring should be done in the first twenty-four hours and at night, when hypoventilation and nocturnal hypoxia may occur. Keep PCA flowsheets at the bedside to document PCA doses and patient monitoring. Monitor the use of naloxone to identify adverse events related to PCA.
Drug product mix-ups	Many opiates used for PCA have similar names and packaging, leading to selection errors. Morphine and meperidine have been packaged in similar boxes. Use of floor stock of opiates in PCA pumps has led to significant overdoses.	Require independent double checks for patient identification, drug and concentration, pump settings, and the line attachment. Establish one concentration for each opiate used for PCA. Store hydromorphone and morphine separately. Affix prominent warning labels on nonstandard concentrations. Use commercially prefilled syringes, bags, and cassettes. Require pharmacy review of all PCA orders before initiation. Alert all clinicians to drug shortages, and provide clear alternative dosing instructions.

Practice-related problems	Misprogramming the PCA pump is the most frequently reported practice-related issue.	Require independent double checks for patient identification, drug and concentration, pump settings, and the line attachment.
	Other problems include incorrect transcription of orders, miscalculation of dose or rate of infusion, and IV admixture errors.	Limit PCA pumps to a single model to promote proficiency. Provide laminated instructions attached to each pump. Program pumps to require a review of settings before infusing.
Device design flaws	Many PCAs are not intuitive in their design, making programming problematic. Many PCAs have default programming for medication concentrations, such as 0.1 mg/mL or 1 mg/mL, but a higher concentration may be used in the device, leading to overdoses and deaths. Other drug delivery problems include failure to review programming before starting the infusion and free flow of medication as a result of syringe or cassette breakage. Patients may also confuse the PCA button with the nurse call button, resulting in overdosing and frustration.	Establish default settings of zero for all opiates. Connect the PCA pump to a port close to the patient (to avoid dead space), and prominently label the infusion line to avoid mix-ups. Require pumps to be programmed in mg/mL and mcg/mL, not just mL. Program pumps to alert users and stop PCA if a syringe or bag is empty or damaged. Limit PCA pumps to a single model to promote proficiency. Provide visual and auditory feedback to patients when the button is pressed.
Inadequate staff training	Nurses may not receive effective training or may not retain proficiency when PCA pumps are used infrequently or if multiple types of devices are in use.	Ensure that training is timely and comprehensive and that annual competency testing is required. Require independent double checks for patient identification, drug and concentration, pump settings, and the line attachment.

(Continued)

TABLE 7.2. *(Continued)*

Problem	Description	Safety Recommendations
	Prescribers may not undergo verification of proficiency with this form of pain management, resulting in improper medications and dosing.	Limit PCA pumps to a single model to promote proficiency. Provide laminated instructions attached to each pump.
Order communication errors	Mistakes are made in converting an oral opiate dose to the IV route. Most problematic is hydromorphone. Concurrent orders for other opiates while a PCA pump is in use have resulted in opiate toxicity.	Design standard order sets to guide drug selection, doses, and lockout periods; patient monitoring; and precautions such as avoiding concomitant analgesics. Limit verbal orders to dose changes only. Require independent double checks for patient identification, drug and concentration, pump settings, and the line attachment. Use morphine as the opiate of choice; use hydromorphone for patients needing very high doses; reserve meperidine for patients allergic to morphine and hydromorphone.

PCA Problems and Safety Recommendations

Nursing staff, biomedical engineers, and others should plan and monitor the effectiveness of infusion pump deployment. A first step is to provide nursing and other users with input into selection of all new pumps. All IV pumps should be tested for free-flow protection, and any that fail (medication flows freely from the tubing as the set is removed) should be removed from service. By limiting standard hospital IV pumps to a single model, and limiting specialty pumps, such as syringe and PCA pumps, to clinical areas where the staff are fully competent in their use, the proficiency of all nurses using these devices can be maximized. Attaching laminated instructions and a safety checklist to each pump raises awareness and reinforces key safety measures. Each provider who uses a pump should also be required to label all tubing and have a partner assist with independent double checks for patient identification, drug and concentration, pump settings, and line attachment.

Above all, an independent double check that verifies dose and rate settings is indispensable. This is because the settings on PCA pumps often default to a standard concentration, which requires the operator to change the settings if a nonstandard concentration is used. Even when the staff have expertise in the proper use of these drug delivery devices, serious dosing errors have been associated with improper flow rate settings. PCA pump settings should therefore be programmed by one individual and checked independently by another before administering. Settings at the time of administration should be documented, based on this independent check.

Other medication administration devices can also cause errors in a health care setting. For example, the wrong reservoir in implantable medication delivery devices has reportedly been filled with medication, causing patient death. Also, patients are often admitted to the hospital with implantable devices, such as insulin pumps, yet no instructions are available to assist nurses with the use of these devices.

Additional misuses of medication-related devices, with often serious outcomes, include the inadvertent connection of intravenous tubing to devices not intended for medication delivery. In one case, a nurse accidentally connected the blood pressure monitor tubing to a needleless IV port. Propofol, which is white and opaque, had been infusing through the patient's IV line. Thus the IV tubing and its port looked very similar to the white length of tubing and connector on the BP cuff (see Photo 7.5). In a similar case, an agitated patient died when he removed the tubing from his BP cuff and attached it to his IV line.

PHOTO 7.5. *Tubing Lines.*

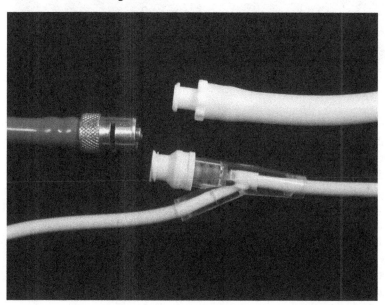

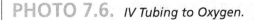

PHOTO 7.6. *IV Tubing to Oxygen.*

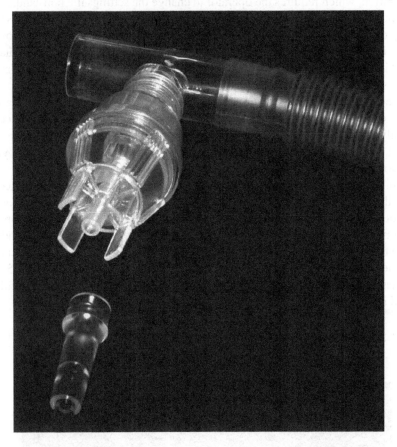

In another tubing-related event, a young child died when her oxygen tubing was mistakenly connected to her IV line. The child had been receiving medication via a nebulizer to treat asthma. While still attached to a wall outlet, the oxygen tubing became disconnected from the nebulizer fluid chamber (see Photo 7.6).

The situation worsened when the staff member who discovered the disconnected oxygen tubing accidentally reconnected it to the injection port on a Baxter Clearlink Needleless Access System IV tubing Y-site. Although oxygen tubing does not have a Luer connector, the staff member managed to make the connection with Baxter's Clearlink valve work by applying considerable force (see Photo 7.7). The oxygen tubing disconnected from the IV tubing in seconds, but not before the pressure of the compressed oxygen supply forced the needleless valve open and allowed air into the tubing. The child died instantly.

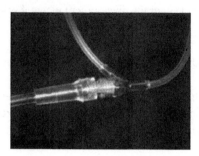

PHOTO 7.7: *IV Misconnection*

Similar issues have occurred when medications have inadvertently been delivered into the balloon inflation ports of endotracheal tubes, gastrostomy tubes, and Foley catheters, instead of into the intended IV catheter. In each case, the balloon expanded when the medication was injected, causing harm to the patient.[16]

Health care organizations should review existing medical equipment used in their facilities to identify the potential for misconnection. Each practitioner who connects or reconnects tubing should be required by policy to completely trace the tube from the patient to the point of origin before beginning. Appropriately labeled IV lines help alert the staff that they may be about to access the incorrect line accidentally. In addition, before introducing new tubes, catheters, and connectors, an interdisciplinary team should use **failure mode and effect analysis** (**FMEA**) to identify potential issues related to connectivity with other medical equipment.

As previously noted, medication safety is enhanced when health care organizations involve end users in the product selection process. Building on this principle by using a standardized evaluation process for devices and looking for areas of potential failure, before the device is acquired, might help the organization avoid future errors. A suggested approach for evaluating infusion pumps is identified in Table 7.3. The same process can be adapted for use with any new medical device.

TABLE 7.3: **Using Failure Mode and Effect Analysis to Predict Failures with Infusion Pumps**

Basic Functionality: How Well Does the Pump Perform the Required Task?
Is this the correct pump to perform the desired task?
Can the pump deliver the volume or increments needed under the correct pressure?

(Continued)

TABLE 7.3: *(Continued)*

Are any features incompatible with the environment where it will be used (size, weight, number of channels)?

Will the pump deliver medications in the concentrations most typically used?

What tubing and other supplies are required for the pump to perform effectively and safely? Are they interchangeable with other pumps? Could interchangeable tubing be used for this pump, rendering it unsafe?

Are users alerted to pump-setting errors? Wrong-patient errors? Wrong-channel errors? Wrong-medication or wrong-solution errors? Mechanical failure?

Does the pump have memory functions for settings and alarms with an easily retrievable log? If the pump is turned off, does it retain settings for a period of time?

User-Machine Interface: How Easy and Intuitive Is It for People to Use the Pump?

What functionalities do users expect the pump to have?

Is the number of steps for programming minimal?

Are the touch buttons used for programming clearly labeled, logically positioned, and the proper size?

Are the screens readable with proper font size, lighting, contrast, and other cues to enhance performance?

Do the units of medication delivery (mcg/kg, mcg/kg/min) match current practices?

Do the medications, units of delivery, and strengths appear in a logical sequence for selection?

Is there any information that defaults to a predetermined value? If yes, is it safe?

Is it easy to install and prime administration sets and to remove air in the line?

Are any special features, such as drug or dose calculations and dose alerts, helpful and easy to use?

Are the screens free of abbreviations, trailing zeros (as in 1.0 mg), and naked decimal points (.1mg)?

Do the alarms clearly guide staff to the problems? Is it possible to disable audible alarms permanently or to set them too low to be heard?

If the infusion rate is changed but not confirmed, does the device continuously alert the user that the solution is infusing at the old rate?

Could the administration sets be mispositioned during installation or accidentally dislodged, separated, or removed by patients?

Does the administration set prevent gravity free-flow of the solution when it is removed from the pump?

Is the device tamper-resistant?

Does the pump fit into the typical workflow?

How does the pump compare to the pumps now in use?

Patient Monitoring

Connected to each medical device or piece of equipment is a patient. For therapeutic interventions to succeed, practitioners must continually assess their effectiveness by monitoring the patient, based on predetermined parameters such as vital signs, including criteria for neurological assessment, quality of respirations, and lab results. In addition to proactively defining key parameters as part of established protocols, order sets, and flowsheets, health care providers might also need to incorporate them in computerized monitoring systems.

Documentation of monitoring is critical, and all associated forms (for example, diabetic flowsheets, PCA flowsheets, and sedation flowsheets) should be used at the bedside, and the information should remain there for quick reference. This is the case whether documentation is entered on paper or into a computerized record. Appropriate antidotes and resuscitation equipment should also be readily available at the bedside, and their presence should be noted in the record. Subsequent chart audits should contrast documentation of patient monitoring with outcomes to identify patterns in untoward care results and opportunities for improvement.

Environmental Stressors

In an ideal health care setting, medications would be prescribed, transcribed, prepared, and administered in an environment free of distractions, with comfortable surroundings, adequate physical space, and lighting. Practitioners would come to work rested and could take rest and meal breaks to maintain focus and attention. In reality, hospital workers are constantly exposed to noise, interruptions, and nonstop activity. The process of order transcription is particularly vulnerable to distraction, as it usually occurs in an environment where unit secretaries, nurses, and pharmacy personnel are answering telephones and talking with other providers and patients. A study confirms that simple slips due to distractions are responsible for almost three-quarters of all transcription errors.[17] Some strategies that might minimize such distractions include overlapping of staffing coverage during peak activity times and encouraging fax or e-mail communications to the nursing station instead of telephone calls.

Interruptions during any step in the medication-use process can have devastating consequences. In one example, an emergency department patient died after receiving a 10-mg dose of hydromorphone when morphine 10 mg was ordered. As the ED nurse was selecting the drug, she was temporarily distracted by another of her patients who was attempting to climb off the end of the stretcher. She quickly placed a vial of hydromorphone in her pocket while she attended to the second patient, interrupting her normal routine of checking the medication and documenting the signout on the narcotic record. After settling the agitated patient, she resumed medication administration to the first patient, inadvertently omitting the step of signing out the narcotic. After receiving 10 mg of hydromorphone, when 2 mg is the usual intramuscular dose, the patient was discharged. He subsequently suffered a respiratory arrest in the family car and could not be resuscitated.

Fatigue, too, can contribute to medication errors. Research conducted by the Anesthesia Patient Safety Foundation documented anesthesiologists' performance failures when fatigued.[18] One group of researchers observed in a study of anesthesiologists the incidence of a phenomenon called "micro-sleeps." Micro-sleeps are intermittent lapses in consciousness, lasting seconds to minutes. The person's eyes are open, but the person is not cognizant of surroundings, cannot process information, and once fully conscious again, is unaware that the lapse has even occurred![19] In videotapes of surgical procedures, the researchers identified behaviors indicative of micro-sleeps 30 percent of the time in a four-hour case.[20]

Research has also shown that the risk of nurses making medication-related errors is increased significantly when they work longer than twelve hours in a shift, when working overtime, or when working greater than forty hours in one week.[21] Performance of a fatigued health care worker has been shown to equal that of a person with a blood alcohol level of 0.1 percent—over the legal limit for driving in many states.[22] See Table 7.4 for a list of the effects of fatigue.

Addressing safety issues associated with fatigue requires that the institution support a culture in which admission of fatigue is accepted and rewarded. To achieve this environment, management and staff must be educated about the risks associated with fatigue and research-based approaches to optimize performance in the face of fatigue, especially with regard to night-shift workers. Based on organizational commitment to address this important problem, health care organizations should examine staffing patterns to ensure adequate rest and recovery opportunities for their employees. Contingency plans should be developed to manage staffing needs if personnel appear

TABLE 7.4. Effects of Fatigue

Slowed reaction time

Reduced accuracy

Diminished ability to recognize significant but subtle changes in a patient's health

Inability to deal with the unexpected

Lapses of attention and inability to stay focused

Omissions and neglect of nonessential activities

Compromised problem solving and decision making

Impaired communication skills

Inability to recall

Short-term memory lapses

Reduced motivation

Irritability or hostility

Indifference and loss of empathy

Intrusion of sleep into wakefulness

Decreased energy for successful completion of required tasks

Decreased learning of new activities

Reduced hand-eye coordination

Sources: M. Gillberg, G. Kecklund, and T. Akerstedt, "Relations Between Performance and Subjective Ratings of Sleepiness During a Night Awake," *Sleep,* 1994, *17,* 236–241; L. M. Linde and M. Bergstrom, "The Effect of One Night Without Sleep on Problem-Solving and Immediate Recall," *Psychological Research,* 1992, *54,* 127–136; S. Howard, "Fatigue and the Practice of Medicine," *Anesthesia Patient Safety Foundation Newsletter,* Spring 2005, *20,* 1–4.

to be or consider themselves too fatigued to work safely. It is important to ensure that staff members can take fifteen- to thirty-minute rest breaks away from the work area and a meal break during each shift. Other interventions to consider are providing for short planned naps in the workplace and offering light therapy to reduce the effects of fatiguing schedules and disrupted circadian rhythms.[23]

To address all of these environmental impediments to medication safety, organizational leaders should aim to foster a "sterile cockpit" similar to the one used by the airline industry to promote safety. In a sterile-cockpit environment, pilots and flight crew members are specifically prohibited from participating in distracting activities while performing critical duties. The Federal Aviation Administration's written policies (14 CFR 121.542) state:

> (a) No certificate holder shall require, nor may any flight crewmember perform, any duties during a critical phase of flight except those duties required for the safe operation of the aircraft. Duties such as company required calls made for such non-safety related purposes as ordering galley supplies and confirming passenger connections, announcements made to passengers promoting the air carrier or pointing out sights of interest, and filling out company payroll and related records are not required for the safe operation of the aircraft.
>
> (b) No flight crewmember may engage in, nor may any pilot in command permit, any activity during a critical phase of flight which could distract any flight crewmember from the performance of his or her duties or which could interfere in any way with the proper conduct of those duties. Activities such as eating meals, engaging in nonessential conversations within the cockpit and nonessential communications between the cabin and cockpit crews, and reading publications not related to the proper conduct of the flight are not required for the safe operation of the aircraft.
>
> (c) For the purposes of this section, critical phases of flight includes all ground operations involving taxi, takeoff and landing, and all other flight operations conducted below 10,000 feet, except cruise flight.

Because a failure in any step of the complex medication use process could lead to a medication error and patient harm, every step equates to an aircraft's "critical phase of flight." Distractions, interruptions, and competing activities should be eliminated or minimized. Managers and staff members should focus on creating and supporting an environment that allows concentration on the critical task at hand.

Competency and Staff Education

Many practitioners have limited awareness of error-prone situations, even those that are well documented in their own organization or published in professional literature. Without this information, these staff members are likely to make similar errors. With the information, staff members can help the organization identify ways to prevent such errors from occurring. Upon hire or joining the medical staff and regularly thereafter, staff members should be provided with current information about errors that have occurred within the organization and those that occur elsewhere. Health care organizations should also develop a "medication safety" test for providers who will administer medications. Included should be questions that address problem-prone areas such as morphine and insulin dosing and the use of cross-allergenic medications such as Toradol and aspirin.

Medication Competency Tests

Anecdotal evidence from ISMP shows that many medication competency tests currently in use are outdated. For example, the questions on such tests often contain, and thus legitimize, dangerous abbreviations and dose designations. They also test obsolete approaches such as conversion from apothecary units (formally eliminated in 2001 by the American Society of Health-System Pharmacists) to metric units.

In addition to updating the content, it is crucial that such tests go beyond mere calculation and memorization of drugs and doses to encourage critical thinking. Medication competency tests should incorporate questions about safety issues, such as laboratory values associated with drug use, appropriate monitoring of patients, and correct patient identification procedures. They should address such issues as identifying high-alert medications and the special precautions that these drugs require. It is, of course, important to have staff members explain the correct procedure for an independent double-check, and they should also be able to describe appropriate and inappropriate therapy for patients, based on medical history.

When administering a medication competency test, allow the practitioner who is unsure of an answer to use medication resources (books, Internet or intranet, other practitioners). With this approach, all questions should be answered correctly, and any wrong response should be thoroughly followed up with the test taker.

Staff education, vitally important, cannot be successful as a singular safety strategy; it must be provided in conjunction with other approaches. One case that illustrates the importance of this principle involved a nurse who successfully completed her medication competency test but later administered a dose of pronestyl after checking the pronestyl level but not the NAPA level. (NAPA is a metabolite of pronestyl that has the same pharmaceutical effect as pronestyl.) The NAPA level was elevated. Therefore, the medication should have been held and the prescriber contacted. The nurse was unaware of the need to check the NAPA level before administration of this drug.

Simply drafting a policy or including a question on a competency exam about NAPA levels and pronestyl administration is likely to be ineffective in addressing this situation without the accompanying use of such resources as auxiliary warnings printed on MARs to check NAPA levels, warnings, and hard stops. A hard stop prevents the practitioner from proceeding with an order unless a current lab value or other patient data (weight, allergy status, and so on) are entered. In this case, a hard stop would probably take the form of a note that appears on the provider order entry screen, requiring the user to check or enter the NAPA lab result before administration. A hard stop requiring lab value entry could also be implemented in bedside bar code drug administration software. Tools like these compensate for natural lapses in human concentration and memory in ways that education alone cannot.

Patient Education

An alert and knowledgeable patient can serve as the last line of defense in preventing medication errors. For example, patients who have been educated about the need for proper identification prior to procedures or medication can alert staff members when their armband has not been checked. Also, when patients are aware of the usual times for drug administration, they can remind staff members that their medication is due, to prevent drug omission errors. To fulfill this role in preventing errors, patients must receive ongoing education by physicians, pharmacists, and nurses about drug brand and generic names, indications, usual and actual doses, expected and possible adverse effects, drug or food interactions, and how to protect themselves from errors. Although this education takes additional staff time, it can pay significant dividends in patient safety.

Even patients who have merely been encouraged to ask questions and seek satisfactory answers can play a vital role in preventing medication errors. A tragic example of a case in which a staff member did not heed the patient's questions involved an informed patient at the Dana Farber Cancer Institute who told her health care practitioners that she felt that something was wrong after two days of cancer chemotherapy. Numerous times, both the patient and her husband requested that the staff check her chemotherapy orders for accuracy because she was experiencing different side effects from her previous courses of therapy. Without a thorough investigation of their concerns, the patient's practitioners reassured the patient and her husband that the medication she was receiving was correct. Unfortunately, she received an entire course of chemotherapy every day for four days. It is impossible to say whether the patient would have survived if the error had been detected earlier, but there is no doubt that those four days of chemotherapy were the direct cause of her death.

The way in which patients are educated about their medication is also critical. Simply handing a drug information sheet to a patient is often not sufficient, as patients might misunderstand or be frightened by the information concerning the risk of taking the medication. Also, one study claims that 36 percent of the population has either basic or below basic health literary skills. Among adults who receive Medicare and Medicaid, 27 percent and 30 percent respectively had below basic health literacy.[24] Thus practitioners need to assess whether patients fully understand their medications by asking what they are taking and why these medications are being given. For patients receiving multiple drugs or receiving medications with a narrow therapeutic index, the health care organization should consider involving a pharmacist in patient education during admission and at discharge.

RISK MANAGEMENT: A PRIORITIZING APPROACH

To help the organization address risk and improve safety of medication use, it is crucial that the risk management professional be aware of strategies for prioritizing issues and interventions.

Some medication safety strategies are more effective, or have more leverage, than others. Actions that produce an output more powerful than the input are considered to possess high leverage and thus are more effective in producing change. Leverage is

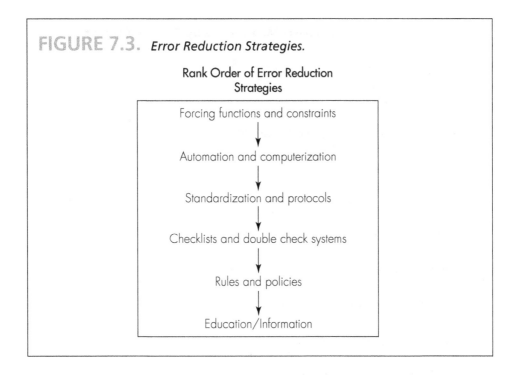

FIGURE 7.3. *Error Reduction Strategies.*

Rank Order of Error Reduction Strategies

Forcing functions and constraints

↓

Automation and computerization

↓

Standardization and protocols

↓

Checklists and double check systems

↓

Rules and policies

↓

Education/Information

considered to be highest when it meets ISMP's first principle of error reduction: lessening or eliminating the possibility of errors. The second principle of error reduction, possessing moderate leverage, is to make errors visible. The third is to minimize the consequences of errors after their occurrence. These principles provide a framework for developing error reduction strategies. The error reduction strategies in Figure 7.3 are presented in order of leverage, from highest to lowest.

An example of a constraint is purchasing epidural tubing without any ports that might allow accidental injection of intravenous drugs. Forcing functions are strategies that do not allow an action to occur unless certain conditions are met, potentially preventing an error. (The terms *forcing function* and *hard stop* are often used interchangeably.) Computerized or automated devices can act as forcing functions—for example, the provider might be prevented from entering a drug order unless patient weight is entered or might be unable to access an automated dispensing drawer unless the drug in that drawer is in the patient's pharmacy profile.

Automated devices may also alert the user in the event of a negative outcome, thereby making an error visible (for example, alarms on infusion pumps, patient monitors). Although the result might be after the fact and therefore lower in leverage, automated alerts can also prompt drug orders for antidotes and reversal agents, thereby minimizing the consequences of an error. Rules, policies, and education are important components of error reduction strategies but have very limited leverage in creating real change.

TABLE 7.5.   **High-Alert Medications by Class or Category**

adrenergic agonists, IV

adrenergic antagonists, IV

anesthetic agents, general, inhaled, and IV

cardioplegic solutions

chemotherapeutic agents

dextrose, hypertonic

dialysis solutions

epidural or intrathecal medications

glycoprotein IIb/IIIa inhibitors

hypoglycemics, oral and insulin

inotropic medications, IV

liposomal forms of drugs

moderate sedation agents

narcotics/opiates, IV and oral

neuromuscular blocking agents

radiocontrast agents, IV

thrombolytics/fibrinolytics

total parenteral nutrition

Another important prioritizing strategy is to categorize certain medications and patient populations as "high-alert" or "high-risk." Medications considered high-alert are those that pose the greatest risk of causing significant harm when misused (see Tables 7.5 and 7.6). High-risk patients are those at risk of suffering significant harm if

TABLE 7.6. **Specific High-Alert Medications**

amiodarone, IV
colchicine injection
heparin, low molecular weight, injection
heparin, unfractionated, IV
insulin, subcutaneous and IV
lidocaine, IV
magnesium sulfate injection
methotrexate, oral, nononcologic use
nesiritide
nitroprusside, sodium, for injection
potassium chloride for injection concentrate
potassium phosphates injection
sodium chloride injection, hypertonic
warfarin

they experience a medication error (see Table 7.7). "High-alert" and "high-risk" do not mean that errors occur more frequently with these medications or to these patients; it simply means that the resulting harm is more difficult to ameliorate. Such categories help the health care organization properly prioritize error reduction efforts.

Because risk reduction efforts must begin at the highest leverage point, where the most effectiveness can be gained from minimal actions, prioritization is crucial to maximize the organization's resources, including staff time.

Furthermore, certain subprocesses in the medication-use process may be considered more error-prone than others (see Table 7.8). These processes should be examined in detail, with attention to various ways that things could go wrong at each step

TABLE 7.7.   **High-Risk Patient Populations**

Patients with renal or liver impairment
Pregnant or breast-feeding patients
Neonates
Elderly or chronically ill patients
Patients on multiple medications
Oncology patients

TABLE 7.8.   **Error-Prone Processes**

Patient-controlled analgesia; epidural analgesia
Use of automated dispensing equipment
Preparation of complex products in the pharmacy with automated compounders
Administration of enteral feedings in patients with IV catheters in place
Obtaining accurate allergy information

and the potential for patient harm that might result from a failure at each process step. A more formalized examination entails a failure mode effects analysis (http://www.ismp.org/profdevelopment/pcamonograph.pdf).

Yet another high-priority activity that often involves the risk management professional is due diligence regarding a new clinical development. In some settings, competition with other organizations is resulting in rapidly expanding services. Neonatal intensive care, organ transplants, open-heart surgery, home care infusion, and oncology units are but a few examples of the areas currently experiencing growth. Often in such situations, there has been little time to properly prepare for the new activity by reorganizing workflow and providing staff education.

It is essential that appropriate planning take place and that medication use issues be given high priority. In one unfortunate situation, soon after a hospital established a new pediatric emergency service, a pharmacist was called to supply the unit with ketamine injection to sedate children during procedures in the ED. Ketamine is available in vials with concentrations of 10 mg/mL, 50 mg/mL, and 100 mg/mL. The pharmacy sent five 100-mg/mL vials to the unit. Before long, a four-year-old patient came to the ED for suturing of a wound. A physician who was accustomed to using vials of ketamine 10 mg/mL did not notice the 100 mg/mL concentration and inadvertently administered the total content of the 500-mg vial instead of the 50-mg pediatric dose. The child suffered a respiratory arrest but was successfully resuscitated. During review of the error, the pharmacy staff readily admitted that they were not well informed about the use of ketamine for ambulatory sedation in pediatric patients and were therefore unsure about which concentration to supply. It was also determined that no one in the pharmacy department had prior pediatric care experience.

When a new service or expansion of an existing department is contemplated, senior management must ensure that all staff members are provided with timely communication. A failure mode and effect analysis should take place to uncover potential areas of weakness and explore steps that are needed to promote safety. Staff orientation and proper education for new services must be planned as early as possible, but close enough to the start of the new service to maintain an appropriate skill level. In addition, consideration must be given to staffing levels, which might need to be increased (perhaps temporarily) in proportion to the new workload. The risk management professional can play a valuable role in facilitating senior administrative support of necessary planning.

Error Reporting and Follow-Up

Each individual practitioner must firmly believe that errors may be reported without disciplinary action and that the organization will use the incident report to evaluate the medication delivery system. In one case, a nurse was afraid to report a serious medication error to her manager because of her concern that this would blemish her record. She feared that the next time she committed an error, she might be suspended or even fired. The nurse contacted ISMP because she was afraid to ask anyone at work if her patient, who was scheduled for an invasive procedure later that day, could be adversely affected by an inadvertent overdose of heparin. Although it seemed unlikely that the increased amount of heparin would have an effect several hours later, ISMP encouraged her to report the error because the physician might choose to postpone the procedure as a precaution. It was later learned that because of her fears, she did not inform anyone of the incident. Therefore, any opportunity for preventing patient harm or addressing the system issues that caused this error was lost.

Although no one would condone this nurse's decision, it is easy to understand the mind-set behind it. If practitioners do not see any benefit associated with reporting, there is no incentive to report. If they perceive a danger to themselves, they will be discouraged from reporting and may even discourage others.

Patient safety cannot be promoted in any organization without open communication about errors. Risk management professionals have the opportunity to encourage such openness and maximize the value of reporting. Practitioners can be motivated to report if they are clear that the purpose of reporting is proactively aimed at protecting their patients from future harm.

SUMMARY

It is fundamental that risk management professionals and the multidisciplinary team they are part of accept ownership of the medication-use process and enthusiastically embrace the opportunity to improve patient safety. While they may celebrate a "safety week" or "safety month," organizational leaders must also demonstrate around-the-clock commitment to medication safety. Risk management professionals can facilitate senior management support of the financial commitment and time required to train staff members in communication skills and maintain a physical environment that promotes safe and effective medication-use processes. Critical to achievement of this goal is a thorough understanding of exactly how each component of these processes interacts, taking into account the varied perspectives of practitioners and the complexity of their patients.

KEY TERMS

Active failure	High-alert medications
Automated dispensing cabinet	High-reliability organizations
Blunt-end	High-risk patients
Computerized physician-provider order entry	Latent failure
	Medication administration record
Crew resource management	Patient-controlled analgesia
Failure mode effects analysis	Sharp-end

ACRONYMS

ADC	INR
CPOE	ISMP
FDA	IV
FMEA	MAR
ICU	PCA

NOTES

1. Reason, J. *Managing the Risks of Organization Accidents.* Aldershot, England: Ashgate, 1990.

2. *Drug Facts and Comparisons.* Saint Louis, Mo.: Facts and Comparisons.

3. *NeoFax.* Raleigh, N.C.: Acorn Publishing, 1995.

4. Leape, L. L., and others. "Systems Analysis of Adverse Drug Events." *Journal of the American Medical Association,* 1995, *274,* 35–43.

5. Ibid.

6. Institute for Safe Medication Practices. *2004 ISMP Medication Safety Self-Assessment for Hospitals.* Huntingdon Valley, Pa.: Institute for Safe Medication Practices; 2004.

7. Thomson Reuter's Micromedex Healthcare Series, Clinical Xpert and Formulary Advisor®® online database at http://www.micromedex.com/products/clinic alxpert

8. Leape, L. L., and others. "Pharmacist Participation on Physician Rounds and Adverse Drug Events in the Intensive Care Unit." *Journal of the American Medical Association,* 1999, *282,* 267–270.

9. Institute for Safe Medication Practices. "Intimidation: Practitioners Speak Up About This Unresolved Problem (Part I)." ISMP Medication Safety Alert! 2004, 9(5). Available at: https://www.ismp.org/Newsletters/acutecare/articles/20040311_ 2.asp Survey results available at https://www.ismp.org/Survey/surveyResults/ Survey0311.asp (accessed November 10, 2008).

   "Intimidation: Mapping a Plan for Cultural Change in Healthcare (Part II)." *ISMP Medication Safety Alert!* 2004, *9*(6). Available at: https://www.ismp.org/ Newsletters/acutecare/articles/20040325.asp (accessed November 10, 2008).

10. Institute for Healthcare Improvement. "Reconcile Medications at All Transition Points," http://www.ihi.org/IHI/Topics/PatientSafety/MedicationSystems/ Changes/Reconcile+Medications+at+All+Transition+Points.htm

11. "Look-Alike/Sound-Alike Drug Products Affect Cognition." USP CAPSLink, May 2004, pp. 1–5, http://www.usp.org/pdf/EN/patientSafety/capsLink2004-05-01.pdf

12. Holquist, C., and Phillips, J. "Fatal Medication Errors Associated with Temodar." *Drug Topics,* 2003, *7,* 42.

13. The current Joint Commission NPSG for look-alike and sound-alike drug names can be found at http://www.jointcommission.org/NR/rdonlyres/C92AAB3F- A9BD-431C-8628-11DD2D1D53CC/0/LASA.pdf

14. International Ergonomics Association. "What Is Ergonomics?" http://www.iea.cc/ browse.php?contID=what_is_ergonomics

15. Ibid.; Leape and others, "Systems Analysis."

16. Institute for Safe Medication Practices Canada. "Devices with Inflation Ports: Risk for Medication Error–Induced Injuries." *ISMP Canada Safety Bulletin,* 2004, *4*(5), http://www.ismp-canada.org/download/ISMPCSB2004-05.pdf

17. Leape and others, "Systems Analysis."

18. Howard, S. K. "Fatigue and the Practice of Medicine." *Anesthesia Patient Safety Foundation Newsletter,* Spring 2005 *20,* 1–24.

19. Rosekind, M. R., and others. "Crew Factors in Flight Operations: Alertness Management in Flight Operations." *NASA Technical Memorandum No. 1999-208780.* Moffett Field, Calif.: National Aeronautic and Space Agency; 1999.

20. Howard, S. K., and others. "Simulation Study of Rested Versus Sleep-Deprived Anesthesiologists." *Anesthesiology,* 2003, *98,* 1345–1355, discussion A.

21. Rogers, A. E., Hwang, W.-T., Scott, L. D., Aiken, L. H., and Dinges, D. F. "Hospital Staff Nurse Work and Patient Safety." *Health Affairs,* 2004, *23,* 1–11.

22. Dawson, D., and Reid, K. "Fatigue, Alcohol and Performance Impairment." *Nature,* 1997, *388,* 235.

23. Howard, "Fatigue and the Practice of Medicine."

24. Kutner, M., Greenberg, E., Jin,Y., and Paulsen, C. (2006). *The Health Literacy of America's Adults: Results from the 2003 National Assessment of Adult Literacy (NCES 2006–483).* U.S.Department of Education, Washington, DC: National Center for Education Statistics, pp. v and 17.

CHAPTER

ETHICS IN PATIENT CARE

SHEILA COHEN ZIMMET

LEARNING OBJECTIVES

- To be able to describe the ethical principles of patient autonomy
- To be able to discuss the principles in the Belmont Report in assessing biomedical and behavioral research principles
- To be able to operationalize research principles into policies for institutional review boards based on protecting the safety of human subjects
- To be able to recognize the obligations and rights of patients for treatment and refusal of treatment
- To be able to describe the functions of institutional review boards

This chapter is intended to provide an understanding of the ethics and law affecting everyday patient care issues, particularly those that are the most difficult to resolve—decisions to withhold or withdraw medical treatment and experimentation on human subjects. It is hoped that an understanding of the relevant bioethical and legal principles will assist the risk management professional in reducing legal exposures by promoting communication among health care providers, patients, and their families as to available treatment options and the benefits and burdens of each. All too often risk management issues arise because patients, their family members or surrogates[1] are uncomfortable about treatment decisions that have been made either with or without their participation. They feel they have been the subject of experimentation without their knowledge, or they simply are not comfortable deciding to forgo further treatment because they think it might not be the "right" thing to do.

If the families or surrogates of patients with terminal, incurable illnesses were counseled, understood the benefits and burdens of treatment, and understood that it is ethically permissible, or perhaps preferable, to withhold futile care when the burdens of treatment outweighed the benefits of that treatment, there would be far less suspicion and even hostility in intensive care units. It is important that patients and their families understand and believe that treatment recommendations are made on the basis of burdens and benefits to the patient, not to the managed care system. It is the rare family dispute or stalemate over a terminally ill patient's treatment options that cannot be resolved by having health care providers, family members or other surrogates, and religious and ethics consultants together in one room, openly discussing the ethically permissible options, including the option of no further treatment.

KEY CONCEPTS

- The success of medical research depends on trust between the scientific enterprise and the public, trust in the integrity of the discovery process, and especially trust in the safety of patients and healthy volunteers who participate.

- The role of the industrial review board is to safeguard that trust and to assess research in terms of risks and benefits, the adequacy of informed consent, the adequacy of safeguards to protect the privacy and confidentiality of subjects, and the equitable selection of subjects.

- It is ethically appropriate to reject treatment when the burdens of treatment outweigh the benefits of treatment or when treatment is deemed to be futile.

- Basic ethical principles most relevant to clinical bioethics are beneficence, autonomy, nonmaleficence, and justice.

The reading selections and Web sites listed at the end of this chapter consist of basic ethics and regulatory documents that are useful reference tools for the risk management professional. The emphasis is on ethics because ethical principles, along with constitutional interpretation, are the source of the law that has developed in this area. The legal concept of patient self-determination that is recognized in judicial opinions and codified into law derives from the ethical principle of respect for autonomy (defined further on), as does the law applicable to research on human subjects.

ETHICAL PRINCIPLES AND MORAL OBLIGATIONS

The relationships between health care providers and their patients and families are guided by certain basic ethical principles and the morally binding obligations that are derived from those principles. The basic ethical principles that are most relevant to clinical bioethics are the following:

- *Beneficence,* which creates an obligation to benefit patients and other people and to further their welfare and interests

- Respect for patients' *autonomy*[2]

- *Nonmaleficence,* which asserts an obligation to prevent harm or, if risks of harm must be taken, to minimize those risks

- *Justice,* which is relevant to fairness of access to health care and to issues of rationing at the bedside

The morally binding obligations between patient and clinician or other health care provider that derive from these principles are these:

- To respect the patient's privacy and maintain a process that protects confidentiality

- To communicate honestly about all aspects of the patient's diagnosis, treatment, and prognosis

- To determine whether the patient is capable of sharing in decision making

- To conduct an ethically valid process of **informed consent** throughout the relationship

The concepts of doing good (**beneficence**), avoiding harm (**nonmaleficence**), privacy, confidentiality, and **justice** that are central to these ethical principles and moral obligations are recognized in the **Oath of Hippocrates**.[3]

RESEARCH

In 1990, Dr. Marcia Angell, the *New England Journal of Medicine's* executive editor, reiterated the journal's position that only research conducted in accordance with the rights of human subjects would be published. The results of unethical research would not be published, regardless of scientific merit.

There are three reasons for our position. First, the policy of publishing only ethical research, if generally applied, would deter unethical work.... Furthermore, any other policy would tend to lead to more unethical work.... Second, denying publication even when the ethical violations are minor protects the principle of the primacy of the research subject. If small lapses were permitted we would become inured to them, and this would lead to larger violations. And finally, refusal to publish unethical work serves notice to society at large that even scientists do not consider science the primary measure of a civilization. Knowledge, although important, may be less important to a decent society than the way it is obtained.[4]

The primacy of the human subject of which Angell wrote is the central concept of the modern system of human subject protection in biomedical research. It has its roots in the basic ethical principles of respect for people, beneficence, and justice, the hallmarks of the National Commission for the Protection of Human Subjects in Biomedical and Behavioral Research's Belmont Report (1979).[5] The Belmont Report described the basic ethical principles on which all biomedical and behavioral research should be based.

The Belmont Report was not the first to address these important concepts in the context of human research. In developing its report, the National Commission looked to the principles enunciated in the **Nuremberg Code**, developed during the Nuremberg war crimes trials. These principles were used as a set of standards to judge the conduct of physicians and scientists who had conducted biomedical research on imprisoned populations and for whom the results of that research took priority over the human subjects themselves.[6] The commission also looked to the **Declaration of Helsinki**, first adopted by the World Medical Assembly in 1964, as recommendations to guide medical doctors in biomedical research involving human subjects. The Declaration of Helsinki provides the accepted ethical standards for international human subject research.[7]

The three basic ethical concepts of the Belmont Report, in addition to the current regulations governing research on human subjects, are defined in the report as follows:

- Respect for persons: a recognition of the personal dignity and autonomy of individuals and special protection of persons with diminished autonomy; an affirmative obligation to protect vulnerable populations

- Beneficence: an obligation to maximize benefits and minimize risks of harm (nonmaleficence)

- Justice: a fair distribution of the benefits and burdens of research

Adherence to these basic ethical concepts ensures that the disadvantaged are not used as research subjects for the benefit of the advantaged and that social progress resulting from human research does not justify overriding the rights of the individual subject.[8]

The Belmont Report distinguished between research and practice in discussing which activities require special review. Practice includes interventions that are designed to enhance the well-being of a patient through either diagnosis or treatment and have a reasonable expectation of success. Per the Belmont Report, research was defined as an activity designed to test a hypothesis, permit conclusions to be drawn, and thereby to develop or contribute to generalizable knowledge (expressed, for example, in theories, principles, and statements of relationships). A departure from standard practice or the institution of a new treatment was not viewed as research. However, the commission recommended that new procedures should first be made part of formal research protocols, to evaluate safety and efficacy.

Following publication of the Belmont Report, both the Department of Health, Education and Welfare, now known as the Department of Health and Human Services (HHS), and the Food and Drug Administration (FDA) strengthened their human subject protections, increasing but not altering the role of the **institutional review boards** (IRBs). The HHS human research regulations, including IRB requirements, are codified in the Code of Federal Regulations, Title 45, part 46 (including the federal policy or "Common Rule," followed by all federal agencies that sponsor research). FDA regulations on human research are codified in CFR Title 21, parts 50 (on informed consent), 56 (on institutional review boards), 312 (on investigational new drug applications), 812 (on investigational device exemptions), and 860 (on medical device classification procedures).

Each health care institution that receives federal funding for human research from a department or agency covered by the federal policy or Common Rule or that is subject to FDA regulation must have one or more IRBs with authority to prospectively review, require modification of, approve, or disapprove the research. The IRB may be established by the institution or, less often, may be an independent entity under contract to the institution to provide IRB services. A document ensuring compliance with human subject protections must be negotiated between the institution and HHS before HHS-funded research may be conducted. The document, known as an assurance, may be for a single project or, more often, may be what is known as a federalwide assurance (FWA).

Applicable regulations are codified at 45 CFR 46.103. The HHS and FDA have the authority to conduct compliance inspections of institutions engaged in research, including the activities of IRBs, and to halt or restrict federally funded research if institutions are found to be out of compliance with human subject protections. For example, an institution found to be out of compliance may have its assurance restricted or revoked.

Inspections by the FDA and the Office for Human Research Protections (OHRP) may be routine, not-for-cause inspections or may be performed in response to a complaint. In an "open letter to the human research community," dated April 17, 2002, Dr. Greg Koski, director of OHRP, announced a new quality improvement program that focuses on institutional self-assessment with follow-up "collegial and constructive" on-site consultation visits by OHRP staff. OHRP's Division of Assurances and

Quality Improvement (DAQI) would not "ordinarily" share information obtained by OHRP pursuant to voluntary QI evaluations with its Division of Compliance Oversight.[9]

In another open letter, dated September 12, 2002, Koski renewed OHRP's invitation for institutions to participate in the QI program and noted that OHRP will defer not-for-cause evaluations of an institution that has participated in or is scheduling a QI consultation. In other words, health care organizations are more likely to be subject to a not-for-cause inspection if they do not voluntarily participate in the QI program.

The federal research requirements are founded on respect for the autonomy of the research subject, evidenced by stringent informed consent requirements; the protection of vulnerable populations; the absence of coercion; and the reasonable balance of benefits and burdens of the proposed research for the individual subject, not for society at large. An individual's decision not to participate in research may not in any way affect the ability of the individual to receive medical care or other benefits to which the individual would otherwise be entitled. It is the role of the IRBs to review and monitor the conduct of research and to educate the research community about the proper conduct of research. A discussion of the role of the IRBs and recent regulatory activity in this area follows.

INSTITUTIONAL REVIEW BOARDS

For Dr. Gary B. Ellis, former director of the Office for Protection from Research Risks (OPRR),[10] the relationship between subject and researcher is based on trust, and that trust must be respected:

> In the final analysis, research investigators, research institutions, and federal regulators are stewards of a trust agreement with the people who are research subjects. For research subjects who are safeguarded by the federal regulations, we have a system in place that (1) minimizes the potential for harm, (2) enables and protects individual, autonomous choice, and (3) promotes the pursuit of new knowledge. By doing so, we protect the rights and welfare of our fellow citizens who make a remarkable contribution to the common good by participating in research studies. We owe them our best effort.[11]

To Dr. Jordan Cohen of the Association of American Medical Colleges, the successful conduct of medical research in a free society depends on trust between the scientific enterprise and the public, trust in the integrity of the discovery process, and especially trust in the safety of patients and healthy volunteers who participate in the process.[12]

It is the role of the IRBs to safeguard that trust and to assess research, in terms of risks and benefits, the adequacy of informed consent, the adequacy of safeguards to protect the privacy and confidentiality of subjects,[13] and the equitable selection of subjects (for example, is inclusion of vulnerable populations appropriate? Are minorities and women of childbearing potential adequately represented, or is a clear and compelling reason for their exclusion provided?). The IRB must (1) identify risks of the research, (2) determine that the risks will be minimized to the extent possible, (3) identify probable benefits of the research, (4) determine that the risks are reasonable in relation to the benefits to the subject and the knowledge to be gained, (5) ensure that research subjects are provided with an accurate and fair description of the risks, discomforts, and anticipated benefits, (6) ensure that research subjects are offered the opportunity to voluntarily accept or reject participation in the research or discontinue participation without coercion or fear of reprisal or deprivation of treatment to which the patient is otherwise entitled,[14] and (7) determine intervals of periodic review and, when necessary, determine the adequacy of mechanisms for monitoring data collection.

Maintaining strong safeguards for the safety of human subjects in medical research is a paramount obligation of clinical investigators and their institutions. Institutional review boards are the heart of the protection regime; they are responsible for reviewing all clinical and translational research conducted at their respective institutions and for making ethical determinations that risks to human subjects have been minimized to the greatest extent possible; that risks are reasonable in relation to anticipated benefits, if any; and that the risks, benefits, and alternative options are clearly communicated to the potential participants in the informed consent process.

In a time of declining clinical revenue, there may be increased pressure from principal investigators and administrators to cut corners and speed up the approval process for sponsored research. Such an approach places the welfare of the researcher and the research institution ahead of the welfare of the subject and is inconsistent with the ethical foundation of biomedical research and the derivative regulatory framework. The results of research, whether in terms of scientific recognition or of financial reward, may never take priority over the research subject. Furthermore, compliance activities of federal regulatory bodies have shown that an approach to research that minimizes protection of the subject can ultimately prove to be very costly, in both revenue and reputation.

At the 2002 Fraud and Compliance Forum sponsored by the American Health Lawyers Association and the Health Care Compliance Association, Dr. Melody Lin of the OHRP Office of Research Compliance identified common findings and deficiencies associated with compliance oversight activities:

Initial and continuing review issues

- Inadequate IRB review, particularly with respect to issues affecting vulnerable populations
- IRB review without sufficient information
- Contingent approval with no system for follow-up
- Inadequate continuing annual review, including failure to review at least once per year

Informed consent and informed consent documentation issues

- Language that is too complex
- Use of impermissible exculpatory language
- Standard consent forms inadequate for certain procedures
- Reliance on standard surgical consent form to collect tissue samples
- Inappropriate boilerplates
- Failure to minimize possibility of coercion or undue influence

IRB membership and expertise issues

- Lack of researcher diversity
- Lack of IRB expertise for research
- Lack of IRB expertise for research involving children and prisoners
- Lack of sufficient understanding of regulations
- Designation of an additional IRB without OHRP approval

Documentation of IRB activities

- Inappropriate application of exemption (not in six categories)
- Inappropriate use of expedited approvals
- Failure to document consideration of additional safeguards
- Inadequate minutes (meaning votes not recorded, no summary of important issues, inability to reconstruct what was approved)
- Poorly maintained files

IRB convened without a quorum

- Nonscientist absent
- Majority not present

Conflict-of-interest issues

- IRB members
- Office of sponsored research
- Institutional officials
- Inappropriate waiver of informed consent

Lack of written standard operating procedures

Failure to report unanticipated problems to OHRP

Inadequate IRB resources and overburdened IRBs, which is considered the primary problem

Government oversight compliance activities have increased significantly since 1999 and are expected to gain momentum, signaling an increase in public interest in the ethical and procedural propriety of biomedical research. OHRP posts its compliance activities on its Web site, including the text of determination letters sent to research institutions operating under OHRP assurances. Risk management professionals will find it useful to review the letters posted there to determine OHRP compliance priorities.[15]

A review of determination letters posted on the OHRP Web site reveals a similar pattern of common deficiencies: (1) consent form deficiencies such as language not understandable to the public, inadequate explanation of potential risks, failure to address all required elements of informed consent, and failure to describe all research procedures; (2) IRB procedural and process deficiencies, such as inadequate written policies and procedures; improper use of expedited review for research not within permissible categories; inadequate information considered by the IRB to make required risk and benefit determinations, particularly with respect to research involving pediatric subjects for which specific documented findings are required; substantive changes to protocols and consent forms without full board re-review; failure of documentation of IRB actions, including attendance, specific votes on actions taken, and summary of IRB discussions; (3) lapsed IRB approval—IRB approval expires after one year, and the study administratively terminates; all research activity must stop unless the IRB specifically finds that it is in the best interest of subjects already enrolled to continue research activities, 4) failure to report to OHRP unanticipated problems involving risks to subjects, serious or continuing noncompliance, suspensions, and terminations.

The risk management professional should review the OHRP determination letters, informed consent checklist, guidance documents, and decision charts at the OHRP Web site (http://www.hhs.gov/ohrp/) for a more detailed analysis of and useful tools for compliance with the IRB's obligations in each of these areas. Comprehensive, mistake-proof IRB application forms, consent form templates, and IRB reviewer forms that elicit all required information, address all necessary informed consent elements, and contain required IRB findings are important tools for maximizing the safety of human subjects and minimizing institutional liability.

The failure of some IRBs to consider whether the investigator has a potential conflict of interest and to determine how to manage or eliminate that conflict, along with the failure to inform the subject of potential conflicts of interest of the investigator or the institution, has resulted in significant public condemnation and increased regulatory scrutiny. It is essential that each research institution establish its own policies and procedures for the reporting and managing of investigator and institutional conflicts of interest. Does an investigator, for example, have an impermissible financial conflict of interest because of a paid consultancy or an equity interest in the sponsor? Can the conflict be managed with an independent oversight committee to verify the integrity of the data?[16]

It is also the responsibility of each research institution and its IRB to educate investigators to monitor the conduct of research and to ensure that the IRB members themselves are adequately and continually trained in human research protection. Ultimately, the expectation is for increasing institutional support for the research compliance infrastructure, including adequate staff resources that incorporate a research compliance officer function for implementation and monitoring of research activities and for management of research funds.

Gene or Recombinant DNA Research

Research involving recombinant DNA or gene therapy that has any federal funding requires additional levels of review and approval at the institutional level (Institutional Biosafety Committee) and at the federal level (Recombinant DNA Advisory Committee [RAC] of the Office of Biotechnology Activities [OBA]). The RAC was established to respond to public concerns about the safety of research that involves gene manipulation.[17]

Risk Management Implications

Each research institution should review its own policies and procedures and its IRB records for compliance with federal regulations to determine whether it is vulnerable to an adverse action on the basis of the mentioned criteria. For example, does the institution have an internal for-cause and random monitoring or auditing system to verify that investigators are complying with research protocols? Do all subjects sign consent forms? Do IRB policies and procedures satisfy federal requirements? Are minutes of IRB meetings adequate? Does training of IRB members and investigators meet the regulatory compliance emphasis on education? The risk management professional should assess whether and how to assist the institution in meeting its obligations in the area of human biomedical research or how a research compliance officer or similar official could do it. The risk management professional should also assess coordination of the activities of its research regulatory bodies—the IRB, the institutional biosafety committee (for recombinant DNA and biohazards), and the radiation safety committee (for radiological safety; radiation safety review and approval are required under the institution's Nuclear Regulatory Commission license).

If compliance is not adequate, the loss to the institution, in terms of funding and reputation, could be enormous. Institutions must be vigilant in their review and monitoring of the activities of the IRB and investigators and mindful of their own institutional financial conflicts of interest and those of their researchers. If they are not, they can expect that federal oversight, investigative, or prosecutorial bodies will be.

Risk management professionals should also be mindful of the potential for costly civil and criminal litigation growing out of regulatory noncompliance. Numerous well-publicized instances of death or serious injury to human subjects in clinical trials have given rise to costly litigation against institutions, investigators, and individual IRB members. In virtually all instances, civil litigants have cited nondisclosure of prior adverse effects experienced by research subjects or nondisclosure of conflicts of interest as a basis of their causes of action. It is advised that the risk management professional ensure that IRB procedures and audit mechanisms provide for full disclosure to the IRB and research subjects of all potential risks and complications and all conflicts of interest associated with the research. It is further advised that the risk management professional investigate whether coverage for personal injury and death arising out of administrative actions (such as actions of IRB chairs and members) is included in the institution's insurance portfolio, whether through its professional and general liability coverage or its directors' and officers' (D&O) insurance. Keep in mind that D&O policies traditionally do not include coverage for personal injury and death.

An additional area of potential risk arising out of regulatory noncompliance relates to enforcement activities of the HHS Office of the Inspector General (OIG) and the U.S. Department of Justice. The risk management professional should be aware that obtaining federal funds in a fraudulent manner, for instance, through billing of the federal government for health care services provided pursuant to a clinical trial for which billing is not permitted; engaging in scientific misconduct in a federally funded research proposal; or improper time and effort and cost reporting in federally funded grants can all serve as the basis for both civil and criminal charges under the federal fraud and abuse laws, including the False Claims Act. In the civil context, the government is entitled to treble damages for successful prosecution. Federal prosecutors have indicated that noncompliance with IRB requirements such as false information or a failure to provide required information to the IRB regarding adverse events can serve as a basis for prosecution under the fraud and abuse laws.

Federal enforcement of regulatory requirements as they apply to research has been and will continue to be aggressive, whether through agency enforcement activities or application of civil or criminal penalties (or both). The cost of noncompliance to the institutions and its employees and agents could be high.

Medical Record Privacy

Under the Common Rule, the IRB must consider whether there are adequate provisions to protect the confidentiality of human subjects. There are additional regulatory requirements for protection of **protected health information (PHI)**, under the privacy provisions of the **Health Insurance Portability and Accountability Act (HIPAA)** that apply to research.[18] These privacy protections became effective April 14, 2003, and are enforceable by HHS through both civil and criminal penalties. The discussion here will focus only on HIPAA and research.[19]

Use and Disclosure of Protected Health Information for Research Purposes

In general, PHI may be used or disclosed by a covered entity for research purposes under the following circumstances:

1. If the covered entity obtains an authorization from the individual to use the individual's PHI

2. If an IRB or privacy board has approved a waiver of the need for an individual authorization based on specific criteria set forth in the regulations

3. If the researcher reviews the data "preparatory to research" and does not remove the data from the premises

4. If there is a "data use agreement" between the covered entity and the researcher to obtain a "limited data set" of data that is facially deidentified

Individually identifiable health information relating to either living or deceased persons that is transmitted or maintained by covered entities in any form or medium is considered PHI and is subject to HIPAA protection. However, under the Common Rule, a human subject is defined as "a living individual" about whom an investigator obtains data through intervention or interaction or obtains identifiable private information. Accordingly, under HIPAA, the IRB or privacy board must review and approve the confidentiality provisions of research and must require authorizations or waive the requirement for authorizations for research involving PHI of deceased persons that would not have been reviewed by the IRB under the Common Rule. Risk management professionals should note that the definition of PHI includes the requirement that the information be identifiable. Accordingly, information is not PHI if all identifiers are removed as specified in the privacy regulations or if an expert certifies that the information used alone or in combination with other available information could not identify the individual.

Notwithstanding strong objection from the research community, the final rule issued by HHS retained the requirements that for information to be deidentified, all of the following information must be removed:

Names

Geographical subdivisions smaller than a state except for the first three digits of the ZIP code

All elements of dates (except year) for subjects eighty-nine years of age or under

Telephone numbers

Fax numbers

E-mail addresses

Social Security numbers

Medical record numbers

Health plan beneficiary numbers

Account numbers

Certificate or license numbers

Vehicle identifiers and serial numbers, including license plate numbers

Device identifiers and serial numbers

World Wide Web universal resource locators (URLs)

Internet protocol (IP) addresses

Biometric identifiers, including fingerprints and voice prints

Full-face photographic images and any comparable images

Any other unique identifying number, characteristic, or code, with some exceptions

The rules permit use and disclosure of PHI without an authorization for treatment, payment, and health care operations. But, because research is not considered a health care operation, disclosure without an authorization for research purposes is not permitted, with limited exceptions (for example, research on decedents under certain specified circumstances, reviews preparatory to research, and research using a limited data set).

Authorization for Use and Disclosure of Protected Health Information for Research Purposes

To be valid, an authorization for research must include (1) a description of the PHI to be used or disclosed (and this must be the minimum necessary for the research); (2) the person or class of persons who may use or disclose PHI and to whom use or disclosure may be made; (3) the purposes of the use or disclosure; (4) the possibility of redisclosure; (5) an expiration date (end of research study or "none"); (6) signature and date; and (7) a right to revoke. Note also that although research may be conditioned on the subject executing an authorization to use and disclose protected health information for research purposes, treatment may not be conditioned on a subject's agreement to participate in research. Refusal to provide treatment if a subject refused to agree to participate in research would be viewed as impermissible coercion.

Exceptions from the Authorization Requirements

If a researcher requests that authorization be waived for a particular research proposal, the IRB or privacy board may waive the authorization only with the following findings:

- The use or disclosure involves no more than minimal risk to the individual's privacy, based on a plan to protect identifiers or a plan to destroy identifiers as soon as possible unless there are research or legal reasons not to do so.

- Assurance is provided that the PHI will not be reused or disclosed to any other person except as required by the research or law.

■ The research could not practicably be conducted without the waiver.

■ The research could not practicably be conducted without the PHI.

Risk management professionals should note that this analysis is very similar to the analysis currently employed by IRBs when determining whether subject consent for research may be waived. IRB templates can be modified to accommodate the new requirements.

A covered entity may allow access to the PHI of a deceased individual without an authorization or waiver if the researcher represents that the information is sought solely for research on the PHI of decedents. If requested, the researcher provides documentation of the death of the individuals and documentation that PHI is necessary for research purposes.

A covered entity may allow use or disclosure of PHI without an authorization or a waiver for reviews preparatory to research if the researcher represents that (1) the use or disclosure is solely to prepare a research protocol or otherwise preparatory to research, (2) no PHI will be removed from the covered entity, and (3) the PHI is necessary for research purposes.

Compilation of research databases or manipulation of PHI to create a database or to bank tissue also requires an authorization or waiver by an IRB or privacy board. This waiver does not eliminate the requirement for either an authorization to use the data in research or a waiver. An authorization or waiver is required for referral of a patient to a researcher or for a researcher to contact a patient directly. The PHI that the researcher may use or disclose must be defined in the authorization, or if by waiver, the researcher must specify the minimum information necessary to accomplish the research.

Researchers are not considered business associates under the privacy rules and would not be required to execute business associate agreements with the covered entity to access PHI. The authorization for access to PHI for research must describe the research for which the PHI is to be used. "Future research," although currently a common description used in consent forms, is not an adequate description under HIPAA. Of course, the IRB may waive authorization based on the criteria previously mentioned.

Record-Keeping

If PHI is accessed pursuant to an authorization, the institution is not required to keep a record of that disclosure. If PHI is disclosed pursuant to a waiver, a review preparatory to research or research on decedents, the covered entity must keep a record of disclosures and must provide an accounting when requested. This may be accomplished either through an annotation of the record, which is then provided to the subject, or by providing the subject a list of protocols for which waivers have been granted during the time period involved.

Summary

HIPAA is one more regulatory burden that potentially could delay the review and approval process for research, to the chagrin of researchers and research institutions.

However, once it is determined whether the institution will rely on the IRB to make privacy decisions or whether a separate privacy board will make such determinations, templates can be developed to facilitate the process and prevent regulatory mistakes.

Risk management professionals should be aware that the 2005 work plan of the HHS Office of the Inspector General indicated an intent to conduct an assessment of the policies and procedures of colleges and universities for protecting the privacy of medical records of people participating in NIH-funded clinical trials and other research, in compliance with the HIPAA privacy standards.

PATIENT SELF-DETERMINATION ACT

The federal **Patient Self-Determination Act** of 1990 (PSDA) requires institutional health care providers who receive federal funds, such as hospitals, nursing homes, hospices, and home health agencies, to inform patients of their right to make health care decisions.[20] This includes the right to accept or refuse treatment and the right to formulate **advance directives** (commonly referred to as living wills and durable powers of attorney).

The law requires hospitals to provide written information to each adult patient at the time of admission concerning the institution's policies for implementing the patient's right to make health care decisions. Advance directives are documents formulated in advance of a period of incapacity in which individuals executing the documents set forth their wishes with respect to treatment options or delineate who should serve as surrogate decision makers in the event that the individuals become unable to express their own wishes.

The PSDA sets forth a mechanism for educating patients about their constitutional right to self-determination that was recognized by the U.S. Supreme Court in its first "right to die" case, *Cruzan* v. *Director, Missouri Department of Health*.[21] In *Cruzan*, the Court held that the due process clause of the Fourteenth Amendment to the U.S. Constitution gives to each person a constitutionally protected liberty interest in refusing unwanted medical treatment, thereby giving constitutional status to the ethical principle of respect for patients' autonomy. In this context, the right of autonomy and the right of self-determination are synonymous.

If a person is incapacitated and hence unable to make or express an informed and voluntary choice to accept or refuse treatment, that patient does not lose the right. Rather, the individual's right to make the treatment choices must be exercised by a surrogate. The durable power of attorney for health care is the mechanism by which an individual designates who will serve in that surrogate role.[22]

The PSDA focuses on the right of competent patients to determine and direct the future course of their medical treatment. The act seeks to avoid a situation in which the wishes of a patient are not clearly known or there is no legally valid surrogate decision maker available to advise the health care provider what the patient would want under the circumstances. The PSDA does not alter the common law concept of next of kin, nor does it affect substantive state law regarding surrogate decision making. It sets forth a mechanism whereby patients learn about their rights under state law to make treatment decisions and execute advance directives and are offered the opportunity to take advantage of those rights. Under the PSDA, health care institutions must do the following:

- Provide written information to all adult patients upon admission or initial receipt of care about their rights to make decisions, including the right to accept or refuse treatment and to execute advance directives, and the written policies of the institution that respect these rights

- Comply with state law regarding the rights of patients to make treatment decisions and execute advance directives

- Educate the staff and the community about these issues

- Document in the patient's medical records whether the individual has executed an advance directive[23]

- Not require the execution of an advance directive as a precondition to the provision of care

Even when an individual has executed an advance directive that sets forth the individual's wishes regarding the acceptance or refusal of treatment, including life-sustaining treatment, it is not always clear to the health care provider or the surrogate what the individual intended under particular clinical circumstances. For example, did the individual who specified that life-sustaining treatment be withdrawn "in the event of a terminal, incurable disease or persistent vegetative state" intend that mechanical ventilation and artificial hydration and nutrition be withheld or just the respirator? If the individual did not address a persistent vegetative state but addressed only a terminal, incurable disease, did that individual intend the treatment choice to be applied to the former, and would state law permit the withdrawal of treatment under these circumstances? State laws differ on the interpretation of when a person is in a terminal, incurable condition so as to invoke the terms of an advance directive. State law may require that an advance directive specify its applicability to a persistent vegetative state for the treatment options to apply. Advance directives should be drafted that specifically address treatment options under these different clinical presentations.

In light of court decisions upholding the rights of pregnant women to refuse invasive medical treatment regardless of the gestational age of the fetus, whether or not the treatment is deemed lifesaving or otherwise beneficial,[24] advance directives that address the treatment wishes of pregnant patients should be considered, particularly for institutions providing tertiary maternal-fetal medicine or perinatology services. The directive should address the provision of life-sustaining treatments for the mother, including artificial hydration, nutrition, and CPR, both before and after birth of the fetus, and whether or not the patient authorizes a cesarean section if it is deemed to be in the best interest of the unborn child. The directive should provide for authorization or refusal of these treatments and should specify that failure to provide the treatments may result in harm to or death of the baby.

"DO NOT RESUSCITATE": WITHHOLDING OR WITHDRAWING TREATMENT

It has been said that the paradox of modern medicine is that treatment intended to save life often ends up prolonging the agony of dying.[25] Whether it is due to the clinician's or family's refusal to accept defeat, the mistaken belief that the **withholding or withdrawing of treatment** is ethically abhorrent, or the simple discomfort that accompanies a discussion of the inevitability of death, this issue continues to be one of the most difficult and most frequent ethical dilemmas health care providers face. It is not a new issue. In his treatise *The Art,* Hippocrates' definition of the purpose of medicine included "to do away with the sufferings of the sick, to lessen the violence of their diseases, and to refuse to treat those who are over-mastered by their diseases, realizing in such cases that medicine is powerless.... Whenever therefore a man suffers an illness which is too strong for the means at the disposal of medicine, he surely must not expect that it can be overcome by medicine."[26]

It is clear from the prior discussions of patient autonomy and self-determination that there is a constitutionally protected and ethically sanctioned right to refuse treatment, including life-sustaining treatment. It is important to understand, and to put into practice, a process to determine and implement the treatment decision when the patient cannot make or communicate the choice. Frameworks for decision making can be found in the President's Commission for the Study of Ethical Problems in Medicine and Biomedical and Behavioral Research report titled *Deciding to Forgo Life-Sustaining Treatment* (1983)[27] and in the Hastings Center's *Guidelines on the Termination of Life-Sustaining Treatment and the Care of the Dying* (1987).[28]

Health care providers should understand that their patients have the right to make health care decisions based on their own values and experiences and to have their decisions respected. The first step is determining the appropriate decision maker. Competent adult patients who can understand the significance of their decisions and can communicate those decisions effectively have the right to make the decisions. Patients have the right to balance benefits and burdens and decide whether to proceed with treatment, based on their own values and personal preferences. As the President's Commission noted, "The moral claim of autonomy supports acting in accord with the patient's preference."[29] It is ethically appropriate to reject treatment when the burdens of treatment outweigh the benefits of treatment or when treatment is deemed to be futile.

If the patient cannot make or communicate the decision, it is the role of the appropriate surrogate decision maker to advise the health care provider what the patient would want. This is known as the "substituted judgment test." It is not the role of the surrogate to make an independent judgment of what is in the best interest of the patient (the "best interest test") unless a decision could not otherwise be reached, as is the case when the patient has never had the capacity to form a judgment (such as a new-born). In general, unless the health care provider has reason to believe that the treatment choice of a legally valid surrogate is inconsistent with what the patient would make or has set forth in an advance directive, the decision of the surrogate should prevail.

In the event of a disagreement between clinician and surrogate as to the appropriate course of action, internal mechanisms to resolve the matter, including ethics committee consultation, should be attempted. Resorting to a judicial forum to resolve disagreements between health care providers and decision makers regarding the appropriate course of treatment for an incapacitated patient is generally unproductive. "Decision-making about life-sustaining care is rarely improved by resort to the courts."[30] It is not the role of the court to substitute its own judgment for the informed substituted judgment of the surrogate, nor will it substitute its own best-interest determination for that of the surrogate. Unless the health care provider can establish that the decision of a surrogate to either require or refuse medical treatment, including a **"do not resuscitate"** (**DNR**) order, constitutes either neglect or abuse, thereby invoking the authority of the state to protect innocent third parties,[31] courts will not override the decisions of legally valid surrogates.

Another example is *In re Baby K,* in which an appeals court affirmed the district court ruling requiring the hospital to provide full pulmonary resuscitation for an anencephalic infant when requested by the mother, even though the care was deemed futile and outside the scope of the standard of care.[32] The court of appeals held that a refusal by emergency room personnel to provide stabilizing resuscitative measures to the infant, if brought to the emergency department in respiratory distress, would constitute a violation of the requirements of the Emergency Medical Treatment and Labor Act (EMTALA),[33] which provides that all persons seeking emergency medical treatment receive an appropriate medical screening and stabilizing treatment. The lower court ruling that it could not substitute its judgment for the judgment of the mother, who was the legally valid surrogate, was affirmed. The court also stated, with respect to the moral dilemma facing the health care providers who thought the provision of futile care to Baby K was inappropriate "to the extent that [Virginia law] exempts treating physicians in participating hospitals from providing care they consider medically or ethically inappropriate, it is preempted…it does not allow the physicians treating Baby K to refuse to provide her with respiratory support."

In a decision by the District of Columbia Court of Appeals, the court recognized that parents have a fundamental constitutional right to the care, custody, and management of their child that is not absolute but must yield to the best interest and well-being of the child. In the case of *In re K.I.,* the parents disagreed as to the appropriateness of resuscitation for their terminally ill child.[34] The medical evidence established that resuscitation would be futile and would result only in pain and discomfort. The lower court concluded that the mother's refusal to consent to the issuance of the

DNR order was unreasonably contrary to the child's well-being. In affirming the lower court ruling that a DNR order should be entered, the court of appeals held that "in cases involving minor respondents who have lacked, and will forever lack, the ability to express a preference regarding their course of medical treatment . . . and where the parents do not speak with the same voice but disagree as to the proper course of action, the best interests of the child standard shall be applied to determine whether to issue a DNR."[35]

In a case that reached national prominence and involved state and federal government intervention, the husband of a patient determined to be in a persistent vegetative state sought to have life-prolonging procedures terminated, over the objection of her parents. Michael Schiavo, the husband of Terri Schiavo, petitioned the guardianship court in Florida to authorize termination of artificial hydration and nutrition. The court found by clear and convincing evidence that Terri Schiavo was in a persistent vegetative state and that she would elect to cease life-prolonging procedures if she were competent to make her own decision. The decisions of the state and federal courts that heard and reviewed this case ultimately supported Terri Schiavo's constitutional liberty interest to accept or refuse treatment, without interference by the legislative and executive branches of government. There were numerous court proceedings related to this matter.[36]

SUMMARY

It is recommended that risk management professionals become familiar with the ethical issues discussed in this chapter and promote their dissemination to the health care providers who deal with these difficult issues on a regular basis. An ethics consultation mechanism should be made available anytime it is needed to assist health care providers, patients, and their families reach health care decisions that can be implemented with the knowledge that all parties are comfortable with the decision.[37]

KEY TERMS

Advance directive

Autonomy

Belmont Report

Beneficence

Declaration of Helsinki

Do not resuscitate

Ethics committee

Health Insurance Portability and
    Accountability Act

Informed consent

Institutional review board

Justice

Nonmaleficence

Nuremberg Code

Oath of Hippocrates

Patient Self-Determination Act

Privacy

Protected health information

Withholding or withdrawing treatment

ACRONYMS

DNR	OBA
FDA	OHRP
HHS	PHI
HIPAA	PSDA
IRB	RAC

NOTES

1. A surrogate is an individual who is legally authorized to make health care decisions on behalf of a patient who cannot make or communicate decisions due to incapacity. The surrogate may be the common-law next-of-kin or an individual designated by the patient in a durable power of attorney for health care to make health care decisions for the patient in the event of temporary or permanent incapacity.

2. Fletcher, J. C., and others. "Clinical Ethics: History, Content, and Resources." In J. C. Fletcher, *Introduction to Clinical Ethics*. Hagerstown, Md.: University Publishing Group, 1995, pp. 3–17. The term *autonomy* derives from the Greek *autos,* meaning "self," and *nomos,* meaning "rule." The concept of *autonomy* ("self-rule") is associated with privacy, free choice, and personal responsibility for one's choices. Beauchamp, T. L., and L. Walters. *Contemporary Issues in Bioethics*. Belmont, Calif.: Wadsworth, 1994, p. 22.

3. The Hippocratic Oath is available from the National Library of Medicine at http://www.nlm.nih.gov/hmd/greek/greek_oath.html

4. Angell, M. "The Nazi Hypothermia Experiments and Unethical Research Today." *New England Journal of Medicine,* 1990, *322,* 1462–1464.

5. The Belmont Report is available from the National Institutes of Health at http://ohsr.od.nih.gov/guidelines/belmont.html

6. The Nuremberg Code is available from the National Institutes of Health at http://ohsr.od.nih.gov/guidelines/nuremberg.html

7. The Declaration of Helsinki is available from the National Institutes of Health at http://history.nih.gov/laws/pdf/helsinki.pdf

8. Jonsen, A. R. "The Ethics of Research with Human Subjects: A Short History." In A. R. Jonsen, R. M. Veatch, and L. Walters. *Source Book in Bioethics*. Washington, D.C.: Georgetown University Press, 1998, pp. 5–9.

9. For more information, see the open letter, program description, and self-assessment tool on the OHRP Web site at http://www.hhs.gov/ohrp/qi/

10. OPRR is the former federal office with human subject research oversight authority. The office relocated from the National Institutes of Health (NIH) to the Office of Public Health and Science within HHS and is now called the Office for Human Research Protection (OHRP). The move was generally accepted as a means of increasing the visibility of federal oversight of human subject protection and access to the secretary of HHS.

11. Ellis, G. "Protecting the Rights and Welfare of Human Research Subjects." *Academic Medicine*, 1999, *74*, 1008–1009.

12. Cohen, J. J., and Siegel, E. K. "Academic Medical Centers and Medical Research." *Journal of the American Medical Association*, 2005, *294*, 1369.

13. For particularly sensitive research, such as genetic research when there is a concern that the release of information regarding the research results could lead to discrimination in the workplace or in the ability of individuals who are found to be carriers of genetic diseases to obtain life or health insurance, there is a mechanism for protection of data. The secretary of HHS, or the secretary's designee, may issue a Certificate of Confidentiality "to protect the privacy of research subjects by withholding their identities from all persons not connected with the research.... Persons so authorized to protect the privacy of such individuals may not be compelled in any Federal, State, or local civil, criminal, administrative, legislative, or other proceedings to identify such individuals." 42 USC 241(d) and Public Health Service Act, sec. 301(d). For further information, call the National Institutes of Health at (301) 402-7221.

14. For example, is the amount of compensation offered so excessive as to be coercive? Is the subject compensated only at the end of a six-month clinical trial so that the subject cannot withdraw during the trial without loss of all compensation? Or is the compensation prorated for the amount of time the subject participated?

15. Office for Human Research Protections, "Determination Letters," http://www.hhs.gov/ohrp/compliance/letters/index.html

16. For more information, go to http://grants1.nih.gov/grants/policy/coi/index.htm and http://www.aamc.org/research/coi/start.htm

17. See "Frequently Asked Questions" at the OBA Web site at http://www4.od.nih.gov/oba/RAC/RAC_FAQs.htm

18. See 45 CFR 160 and 164.

19. On December 4, 2002, the HHS Office for Civil Rights issued the comprehensive "Guidance on the National Standards to Protect the Privacy of Personal Health Information." It can be found at http://www.hhs.gov/ocr/hipaa; the section on research is on pages 85–98 of the document.

20. Public Law 101-508, codified at 42 USC 1395(c)(c) and 1396(a)(a), and §4206 of the Omnibus Reconciliation Act of 1990. Subsequent to enactment of the PSDA, which is enforceable only against institutions that participate in the Medicare and Medicaid programs, The Joint Commission amended its accreditation standards to require all of its health care organizations to maintain mechanisms for informing patients about their rights to self-determination and honoring those rights.

21. *Cruzan v. Director, Missouri Department of Health,* 497 U.S. 261, 110 S.Ct. 2841, 111 L.Ed. 2nd 224, 58 USLW 4916 (1990).

22. This chapter focuses on the rights of patients and their surrogates to make treatment decisions. It is important for the risk management professional to understand that the law presumes consent for medically necessary medical treatment in a medical emergency when consent of the patient cannot be obtained and a surrogate is not available. If the patient's life or future health may be jeopardized if treatment is not instituted immediately and the treatment has not been refused by the patient, consent will be presumed.

23. Although not specified in the law, institutional policies should include a mechanism by which the patient's advance directive is included in the medical record so that it is readily available and known to the clinicians before implementation is needed. An advance directive in a safe at the bank or in a drawer at home is not helpful to the health care provider when a decision must be made immediately.

24. See *Baby Boy Doe v. Mother Doe,* 260 Ill. App. 3d 392, 632 N.E. 2d 326 (Ill. App. 1994); *In re A.C.,* 573 A. 2d 1235 (D.C. App. 1990).

25. Hite, C. A., and others. "Death and Dying." In J. C. Fletcher and others, *Introduction to Clinical Ethics,* pp. 115–138.

26. Hippocrates. *The Art.* In *Hippocrates,* vol. 2, W. H. S. Jones (trans.). Cambridge, Mass.: Harvard University Press, 1967, p. 193.

27. President's Commission for the Study of Ethical Problems in Medicine and Biomedical Research. *Deciding to Forgo Life-Sustaining Treatment: A Report on the Ethical, Medical, and Legal Issues in Treatment Decisions.* Washington, D.C.: U.S. Government Printing Office, 1983. Many of the developments during the decade subsequent to the issuance of this report that shape the law and ethics of patient self-determination, as it is understood today, grew out of the commission's recommendations—for example, state enactment of legislation providing for advance directives and the growth of institutional ethics committees to provide consultation to clinicians and patients and their families on issues that have life-or-death consequences for patients.

28. Hastings Center. *Guidelines on the Termination of Life-Sustaining Treatment and the Care of the Dying.* Indianapolis: Indiana University Press, 1987. An excellent

summary of the decision-making process described in the ethics literature, including reference to the reports by the President's Commission and the Hastings Center, can be found in Carol Taylor's article "Ethics in Health Care and Medical Technologies." *Theoretical Medicine,* 1990, *11,* 111–124.

29. President's Commission, *Deciding,* p. 245.

30. Ibid., p. 247.

31. For example, courts have traditionally ordered medically necessary and appropriate treatment of children over parental objections. See *In the matter of Adam L.,* 111 Wash. L. Rep. 25 (D.C. Sup. Ct. 1983). However, in instances when treatment is not likely to preserve life or is itself highly risky, judges generally will not substitute their judgment for the judgment of patients or their legal decision makers.

32. *In re Baby K,* 16 F. 3d 590 (4th Cir. 1994).

33. 42 USC 1395(d)(d).

34. *In re K.I.,* 98-FS-1683 and 98-FS-1767, 1700–1742 (D.C. App. 1999).

35. The standard for deciding whether and under what circumstances it is legally permissible to forgo life-sustaining treatment for critically ill or handicapped newborns is set forth in the 1984 amendments to the Child Abuse Prevention and Treatment and Adoption Reform Act of 1974 (42 USCA 5102 (3)(A) and (3)(B). Regulations are found at 45 CFR., part 1340. In general, it is not permissible to withhold medically indicated treatment except under certain specified conditions:

- The infant is chronically and irreversibly comatose.

- The provision of such treatment would merely prolong dying.

- Treatment would not be effective in ameliorating or correcting all of the infant's life threatening conditions.

- Treatment would otherwise be futile in terms of the survival of the infant.

- Treatment would be virtually futile in terms of the survival of the infant and the treatment itself would be inhumane.

- To the extent that the law prohibits the withholding of artificial hydration and nutrition from these infants, that portion of the law is inconsistent with the Supreme Court holding in *Cruzan* that affords constitutional status to the right to withhold medical treatment, including artificial hydration and nutrition, which was the medical treatment at issue in that case.

36. See, in particular, *Jeb Bush* v. *Michael Schiavo,* SC 04-925 (Sup. Ct. Fla. 2004). After fifteen years in a persistent vegetative state, Terri Schiavo lived another two weeks after life support was removed under the court order.

37. Whether an ethics consult note should be entered in the patient record and what its contents should be are the subject of ongoing debate in the ethics literature. I generally favor a consult note placed in the chart that outlines the ethical dilemma and sets forth the recommendations regarding whether the various treatment options that are available to the practitioner and the patient or surrogate are ethically or morally permissible under the clinical circumstances but does not dictate treatment decisions. A record of the consult must be maintained and, in the event of litigation, it is discoverable whether it is in the patient chart or in the records of the consult service. In other words, the content of the note (in terms of objectivity and recognition that the ultimate decision makers are the physician and the physician's patient and surrogate) is more important than its location.

SUGGESTED READING AND RECOMMENDED WEB SITES

American Council on Education. HIPAA information: http://www.acenet.edu/washington/policyanalysis/HIPAA.pdf

American Medical Association. "Current Opinions of the Council on Ethical and Judicial Affairs": http://www.ama-assn.org/ama/pub/category/2503.html

American Medical Association. "Principles of Medical Ethics": http://www.ama-assn.org/ama/pub/category/2512.html

American Nurses Association. "Code for Nurses with Interpretive Statements," "Position Statement on Forgoing Artificial Nutrition and Hydration," "Position Statement on Nursing and the Patient Self-Determination Act," "Position Statement on Nursing Care and Do-Not-Resuscitate Decisions": http://www.NursingWorld.org

Association of American Medical Colleges. Task force recommendations: http://www.aamc.org

Common Rule: http://www.hss.gov/ohrp/humansubjects/guidance/45cfr46htm

Electronic investigator training programs: http://cme.nci.nih.gov and http://ohrp.osophs.dhhs.gov/humansubjects/guidance/local.htm

Food and Drug Administration. "Guidance for Institutional Review Boards and Clinical Investigators": http://www.fda.gov/oc/ohrt/irbs/default.htm

Hastings Center. *Guidelines on the Termination of Life-Sustaining Treatment and the Care of the Dying.* Indianapolis: Indiana University Press, 1987.

Investigator 101 (human subject protection training program CD-ROM) can be obtained from Public Responsibility in Medicine and Research at http://www.PRIMR.org and distributed by OHRP to institutions with federal assurances.

National Institutes of Health, Office of Extramural Research. "Conflict of Interest Information Resources Available on the Web": http://grants1.nih.gov/grants/policy/coi/resources.htm

Office of Human Research Protection. "Institutional Review Board Guidebook": http://ohrp.osophs.dhhs.gov/irb/irb-guidebook.htm

Office for Protection from Research Risks. "Human and Animal Protection": http:// grants.nih.gov/grants/oprr/oprr.htm

President's Commission for the Study of Ethical Problems in Medicine and Biomedical and Behavioral Research. *Deciding to Forgo Life-Sustaining Treatment: A Report on the Ethical, Medical, and Legal Issues in Treatment Decisions.* Washington, D.C.: U.S. Government Printing Office, March 1983.

Recombinant DNA and gene therapy research information: http://www4.od.nih.gov/ oba/RAC/RAC_FAQs.htm

U.S. Agency for International Development. "Protection of Human Subjects in Research Supported by USAID": http://www.info.usaid.gov/policy/ads/200/ 200mbe.pdf

U.S. Department of Energy, Office of Science, Office of Biological and Environmental Research. "Protecting Human Subjects.": http://www.science.doe.gov/production/ ober/humsubj

CHAPTER

DOCUMENTATION AND THE MEDICAL RECORD

SANDRA K. JOHNSON, LEILANI KICKLIGHTER, PAMELA J. PARA

LEARNING OBJECTIVES

- To be able to define the purposes of documentation
- To be able to describe at least four documentation models
- To be able to identify three sources of rules that govern documentation and medical record management
- To be able to describe the process and procedure for documenting a medical error
- To be able to list five documentation dos and don'ts and explain why they are listed

The medical record is important as a tool of effective communication. It facilitates continuous performance improvement, supports reimbursement of services provided, and supplies clinical data for research and education. The purpose of a medical record is to document the course of a patient's care and treatment. Documentation is the essence of the medical record, and risk management professionals have a vested interest in preserving the record and in enhancing the quality of documentation.

Medical records can take many forms, including paper, electronic, microfiche, and fax, depending on the setting and culture of the organization. The health care industry's move to electronic medical records is generating new risks. For example, computer physician order entry (**CPOE**) has created challenges related to documentation and efficiency during conversions from paper-based systems to CPOE systems. The health care risk management professional's organizational risk assessment should identify the methods by which patient care is documented throughout the health care system.

It is important for the health care risk management professional to remember that although the medical record is the central repository for the documentation of all health care delivery segments, it is not the only important business document. The business aspects of health care require the same recordkeeping and documentation as other businesses. Retention and easy retrieval of any business document is important.

Medical records also take various forms in different types of health care settings (acute care, long-term care, ambulatory care). Depending on the environment, regulatory and accreditation requirements may specify the contents of the medical records as well as retention and other requirements. Table 9.1 lists the contents of a typical medical record.

TABLE 9.1. **What Constitutes a Medical Record?**

Standard Medical Record Components	Other Components (Depending on the Circumstances)
Admission, identification, or face sheet	Electrocardiogram
Vital signs and graphics sheet	Imaging and X-ray reports
Physicians' orders	Lab reports
Medical, surgical, and health history and physical condition	Emergency department record
Problem list	Operative report
Medication record	Consultation reports
Progress notes	Autopsy report
Discharge notes or summary	Transfer records

Authorization forms (consents for admission, treatment, surgery, and release of medical records)	Anesthesia record
	Recovery room record
	Labor and delivery record
	Fetal monitoring strips
	Non–stress test reports

While there are several types of documents with which health care risk management professionals should be aware, the purpose of this chapter is to emphasize and reinforce the role of risk management in the need for proper systems and processes for documentation and maintenance of the medical record. The medical record is a well-established communication link benefiting both patients and health care providers in any health care setting. For a sampling of documents of interest to the risk management professional, see Table 9.2.

TABLE 9.2. Types of Documents of Interest to Health Care Risk Managers

Medical records	Financial records
Employee health records	Billing records
Corporate and organizational policies and procedures	Minutes of board and committee meetings
Licenses, certificates, and permits	Personnel files (including documentation of competencies and job descriptions)
Incident and occurrence reports	OSHA records
Electronic correspondence and backup tapes	Insurance policies
Contracts and agreements	Fetal monitoring strips
Electrocardiogram reports	Radiology films (X-ray, CT, MRI)
Patient logs (surgery, labor and delivery, emergency department)	Accreditation and other inspection reports

(Continued)

TABLE 9.2. *(Continued)*

Patient transfer forms	Consultation reports
Lab reports	Autopsy reports
Credentialing files	Claims files and legal records
Advance directives	Consent forms
Medical staff bylaws	Equipment maintenance records
Patient education materials	Staff training manuals and records
Record of patient's valuables	Discharge reports and forms (with patient's signed understanding of any discharge instructions provided; AMA forms)
Checklists (regarding falls, restraints, activity, dietary, preoperative, sponge and needle counts)	Non–stress test results
Care plan	Medication administration record

KEY CONCEPTS

- The risk management professional should be vigilant in assessing the quality of medical record documentation, looking for opportunities to enhance the value and quality of the medical record.

- The medical record may be the organization's best defense in claims alleging medical negligence.

- The medical record contents, supporting policies, procedures and practices, and regulatory requirements differ by health care setting.

- Patient care can be compromised by inadequate, incomplete, missing, or illegible record keeping.

- Advances in health care technology have affected all aspects of medical record documentation and patient care. However, technological advances are not without risk. The risk management professional should be conversant with all aspects of the organization's practices and policies as they relate to documentation as well as legal, regulatory, accreditation, and billing rules.

DOCUMENTATION

Documentation may be defined as the recording of pertinent facts and observations about an individual's health history, including past and present illnesses, tests, treatments, and outcomes. Documentation is the basis for reimbursement, establishes a medical history, and creates a legal record in the event of a claim. Other purposes of documentation include but are not limited to the following:

- Chronologically documenting the care rendered
- Planning and evaluating the patient's treatment
- Facilitating communication among all caregivers
- Providing continuity of care for the patient
- Providing evidence of care and treatment in legal actions and for reimbursement purposes
- Meeting the standard of care
- Meeting accreditation and licensure requirements

The challenge of using documentation as a tool of communication across different types of health care settings is to connect all entities in an efficient way.

Accreditation, Licensure, and Regulatory Requirements

Health care is a highly regulated business that requires documentation to support compliance. Federal regulations affecting documentation, maintenance, and release of health information include the Health Insurance Portability and Accountability Act of 1996 (**HIPAA**). HIPAA affects confidentiality and authorized access to protected health information (**PHI**).

The rules that govern documentation and medical record management come from several sources:

Federal requirements: The Centers for Medicare and Medicaid Services (**CMS**) documentation requires the following:

- Records of a physical examination, including a health history, performed no more than seven days before admission or within forty-eight hours after admission
- Admitting diagnosis
- Results of consultative evaluations of the patient and appropriate findings by clinical and other staff involved in the patient's care
- Documentation of complications, hospital-acquired infections, and adverse reactions to drugs and anesthesia
- Properly executed informed consent forms for procedures and treatments specified by the medical staff, or by federal or state law, if applicable, to acquire patient consent

- All practitioners' orders; nursing notes; medication records; radiology, treatment, and laboratory reports; and vital signs and other information necessary to monitor the patient's condition

- Discharge summary with outcome of hospitalization, disposition of care, and provisions for follow-up care

- Final diagnosis with completion of medical records within thirty days following discharge

State statutes and licensure requirements: These vary from state to state and address such things as content, timeliness, retention procedures, maintenance, destruction, and signing of medical records.

Professional practice standards: Organizations such as the American Nurses Association (**ANA**), American Health Information Management Association (**AHIMA**), Health Information Management Systems Society (**HIMSS**), Health Insurance Association of America (**HIAA**), and American Medical Association (**AMA**) have specific standards for documentation. The ANA offers a tool to streamline the documentation process for nurses.[1]

Specific health care facility protocols: Although not laws, these protocols can be used as evidence in civil litigation to establish the facility's acceptable standard of practice.

Insurance companies, managed care organizations, and other third-party organizations: These parties may refuse to pay claims if the care rendered is not properly or thoroughly documented.

The Joint Commission: The Joint Commission's information management (**IM**) standards focus on hospitalwide information planning and management processes to meet the hospital's internal and external information needs. The Joint Commission standards are designed to be compatible with paper-based, electronic, and hybrid systems. These standards specify the following elements of documentation:[2]

- The hospital has a complete and accurate medical record for every individual assessed, cared for, treated, or served.

- The medical record thoroughly documents operative or other high-risk procedures and the use of moderate or deep sedation or anesthesia.

- For patients receiving continuing ambulatory care services, the medical record contains a summary list of all significant diagnoses, procedures, drug allergies, and medications.

- Designated qualified personnel accept and transcribe verbal orders from authorized individuals.

- The hospital can provide access to all relevant information from a patient's record when needed for use in patient care, treatment, and services.

Annually, The Joint Commission collects data on accredited organizations' compliance with published accreditation standards and the **National Patient Safety Goals**. For calendar year 2007, the following were the non-compliance rates for hospitals[3]:

Goal 2B: Standardize a list of abbreviations, acronyms, symbols, and dose designations that are not to be used throughout the organization. 25 percent of the hospitals non-compliant

MM3.20: Medication orders are written clearly and transcribed accurately. 20 percent of hospitals non-compliant

IM.6.10: The hospital has complete and accurate medical records for patients assessed, cared for, treated, or served. 26 percent of hospitals non-compliant

IM 6.50: Designated qualified staff accept and transcribe verbal or telephone orders from authorized individuals. 25 percent of hospitals non-compliant

Documentation may also be used to demonstrate compliance with The Joint Commission's National Patient Safety Goals (NPSG) for handoffs through a continuity of care record.

- Individual state nursing practice acts
- Textbooks and articles

Charting and Documentation Models

Organizational policy should specify the charting style and documentation model to meet the specific needs of the particular environment. However, some standard charting components apply throughout the health care industry.

Essential Charting Components Joint Commission Standard IM.6.20 specifies that each medical record should contain, as applicable, the following clinical and case information:

- Emergency care, treatment, and services provided to the patient before the patient's arrival, if any
- Documentation and findings of assessments
- Conclusions or impressions drawn from medical history and physical examination
- Diagnosis, diagnostic impression, or conditions
- Reasons for admission or care, treatment, and services
- Goals of the treatment and treatment plan
- Diagnostic and therapeutic orders
- All diagnostic and therapeutic procedures, tests, and results

- Progress notes made by authorized individuals

- All reassessments and plan of care revisions, when indicated

- Relevant observations

- The response to care, treatment, and services provided

- Consultation reports

- Allergies to foods and medicines

- Every medication ordered or prescribed

- Every dose of medication administered, including the strength, dose, or rate of administration, administration devices used, access site or route, known drug allergies, and any adverse drug reaction

- Every medication dispensed or prescribed on discharge

- All relevant diagnoses or conditions established during the course of care, treatment, and services[4]

Each medical record contains, as applicable, the following demographic information:

- The patient's name, sex, address, date of birth, and authorized representative, if any

- Legal status of patients receiving behavioral health care services

Each medical record contains, as applicable, the following information:

- Evidence of known advance directives

- Evidence of informed consent patient care

- Records of communication with patient regarding care, treatment, and services (for example, telephone calls or e-mail), if applicable

- Patient-generated information (for example, information entered into the record over the Web or in previsit computer systems), if applicable

For patients receiving continuing ambulatory care services, the medical record contains a summary list including the following information:

- Known significant medical diagnoses and conditions

- Known significant operative and invasive procedures

- Known adverse and allergic drug reactions

- Known long-term medications, including current prescriptions, over-the-counter drugs, and herbal preparations[5]

Documentation requirements will differ, depending on the setting—hospital, nursing home, home health care agency, or other community facility. For example, perioperative, critical, and emergency care areas have specialized criteria and forms for documenting nursing care. In addition, requirements may change with the patient population (for example, requirements in obstetric settings differ from those in geriatric settings).

Documentation Models There are quite a few documentation models that can be used, depending on the culture and needs of the organization.

Charting by Exception

Charting by exception encourages documentation of only abnormal findings, significant changes, and unusual occurrences. Although originally intended to reduce the length and repetitiveness of the narrative note, it creates the perception that care proceeded from one bad event to another.[6] Documentation sources have cited *Lama* v. *Borras* (1994), a case in which the court stated that there was evidence to suggest that charting by exception did not regularly record information important to an infection diagnosis, such as the changing characteristics of the surgical wound and the patient's complaints of postoperative pain. One of the attending nurses conceded that under the charting-by-exception policy, she would not report a patient's pain if she did not administer medicine or if she gave the patient only over-the-counter-type medication. The court also concluded that the intermittent charting of possible signs of infection failed to record the sort of continuous danger signals that would most likely spur early intervention by a doctor.[7]

Narrative Charting

Narrative charting involves a chronological account of the patient's status, the interventions performed, and the patient's responses.[8] Handwritten or computer-generated narrative notes summarize information obtained by general observation, the health history interview, and a physical examination. The current trend in hospitals and home care agencies is to avoid writing long narrative note entries.[9] Because nursing documentation is judged more for quality than quantity, the narrative note should be concise, pertinent, and relevant, based on patient evaluation. If it is too lengthy, it will interfere with efficient data retrieval.

Assessment-Intervention-Response (AIR)

This is a narrative charting format that synthesizes major nursing events while avoiding repetition of information found elsewhere in the medical record.[10]

Flowsheets

Also called abbreviated progress notes, flowsheets have vertical or horizontal columns for recording dates, times, and interventions. Data can be inserted quickly and concisely, preferably at the time care is given or when a change in the patient's condition is observed. An advantage of this model is that all members of the health care team can compare data and assess the patient's progress over time. However, using flowsheets does not exempt an organization from narrative charting to describe observations, patient teaching, patient responses, detailed interventions, and unusual circumstances.

Checklists

Tasks that need to be accomplished by the staff member or the patient are recorded on checklists.

Computerized Charting System

This consists of a complex, interconnected set of software applications that process and transport data input by the health care team; categorizes the patient's data and stores the health care history, including inpatient and outpatient records from various facilities; and helps guide the health care team in providing care and identifying patient education needs.[11] An effective computerized documentation system must have the capacity to record and send data to the appropriate departments, adapt easily to the health care facility's needs, display highly selective information on command, and provide easy storage access and retrieval for all trained personnel while maintaining the highest standards of patient confidentiality.[12]

Focus Charting

Based on patient-centered problems, focus charting tends to rely only on individual occurrences or significant changes. This often eliminates positive notes that are useful in documenting care that is outcome-based; it works best in acute care settings and on units where the same care and procedures are repeated frequently.[13]

Problem-Oriented Medical Record System (POMR)

The **POMR** describes specific patient problems in multidisciplinary progress notes. It is most effective in acute care and long-term care settings.[14]

Problem, Interventions, and Evaluations of Interventions (PIE)

This approach organizes information according to patients' problems and integrates a plan of care into the nurses' progress notes.[15]

FACT

FACT consists of *flowsheets* individualized to specific services; *assessment* features standardized with baseline parameters; *concise,* integrated progress notes and flowsheets documenting the patient's condition and responses; and *timely* entries recorded when care is given. FACT documents only exceptions to the norm or significant information about the patient and so incorporates charting-by-exception principles. It was developed to help caregivers avoid documentation of irrelevant data, repetitive notes, and inconsistencies among departments and to reduce the amount of time spent charting.[16]

Core Approach

The core approach focuses on the nursing process; it is most useful in acute care and long-term care facilities.[17]

Critical Pathway Approach

The critical pathway approach features an interdisciplinary care plan that describes assessment criteria, interventions, treatments, and outcomes for specific health-related conditions (usually based on a DRG) across a designated timeline; the pathway is usually organized by categories, such as activity, diet, treatments, medications, patient teaching, and discharge planning.[18]

SOAP

A popular method of charting, this method of documentation originated in the 1960s from a problem-oriented medical record format. SOAP is now used in acute care, long-term care, home care, and ambulatory clinic settings. The problem-oriented medical record defines and follows each clinical problem individually and organizes it for solutions. The SOAP model is used for the progress notes section of this type of medical record and take the form of either SOAP or SOAPIER:

S = Subjective: Principal complaint or history, symptoms, in the patient's own words whenever possible

O = Objective: Measurable, observable, what the provider observes and inspects; may include a physical exam, diagnostic test results, and so on

A = Assessment: Diagnostic; includes determination of the problem, interpretation or impression of the current condition, and what the provider thinks is going on based on the data

P = Plan: Plan of action for each problem

I + E = Interventions and Evaluation: Specific interventions implemented and patient's response to them

R = Revision: Any changes from the original care plan (interventions, outcomes, or target dates)

Table 9.3 lists the advantages and disadvantages of using the SOAP model of documentation.

Many health care facilities have adapted the source-oriented or problem-oriented method to meet their documentation needs. In the home health care setting, for example, nurses have created many documentation forms, including the initial assessment form, problem list, day-visit sheet, and discharge summary, to better reflect the services and essential aspects of care they provide. Whichever documentation model is selected, policies and procedures should determine the approved method for the individual health care organization or system. The use of checklists and flowsheets also needs to

TABLE 9.3. **Advantages and Disadvantages of the SOAP Model of Documentation.**

Advantages	Disadvantages
All of a patient's problems are considered in total context	Requires training and commitment of entire professional staff
The record clearly indicates the goals and methods of the patient's treatment	If not implemented in its pure form, format modifications can diminish the original goal of structured and logical entries
Facilitates interdisciplinary communication	Potential redundancy among flowsheets, care plans, and SOAP(IER) notes
Easier to track corrective actions for purposes of quality improvement monitoring	Charting may not meet the needs of organizations that are searching for a less time-consuming method of documentation
Structure: each entry contains information in a predetermined format, which lends consistency to the documentation of patient care	May meet resistance from other health care professionals
Reflects the nursing process by encompassing assessment, nursing diagnosis, planning, interventions, and evaluation of nursing care	Routine care may remain undocumented
Can be used effectively with standard care plans	Need to make sure to resolve the problems if the format is truly problem-oriented
Can be incorporated into integrated medical record documentation to foster collaboration and enhance communication among health care professionals	
Organizes problems into specific categories	
Promotes continuity of care	
Minimizes nonessential data	

Advantages	Disadvantages
Is factual	
Facilitates follow-up care	
Complies with recognized standards and accepted formats	

be described in written policies and procedures. Policies and procedures set minimum requirements that can be used as a guideline for quality improvement criteria. The chosen documentation model must meet documentation needs while complying with organizational policies, state and federal laws, and other regulations or accreditation requirements. Compliance and consistency are paramount, and staff education is key.

Documentation Techniques and Considerations

Risk management strategies include several documentation techniques and thought processes that can facilitate accurate communication and support the core purposes of the medical record.

Correcting Errors in the Medical Record The acceptable method for correcting an error is to draw one line through the entry, initial or sign it, date it, and place the correct information above the drawn-through entry. If space is not available or if the corrected information is too lengthy to place adjacent to the incorrect entry, the corrected note should be placed in the appropriate place on the record (progress notes, nursing notes, and so on), and it should be contemporaneous with that date's notes. It should be dated and signed with the reason for the correction noted. Incorrect entries should not be obliterated, erased, or "whited out," as these correction methods may appear to be attempts to conceal the original entry. It is recommended that any medical record documentation not contemporaneous with current care or while a patient is still hospitalized be thoughtfully reviewed prior to adding any note. This is particularly true when adding documentation after the patient has experienced an adverse event or complained or after a request for medical records has been received from plaintiff's counsel. These notes will be viewed as self-serving and could possibly be considered as record tampering.

Hearsay The risk management professional should advise staff that hearsay, statements made by persons other than the author of the entry should not be documented as if the statements were fact. Instead, how and when the author of the entry heard the statement and the fact that it came from a different source should be recorded, with the statement itself enclosed in quotation marks.

Telephone Calls and Telephone Advice in Physician Office Practices It is recommended that medical advice not be given over the phone unless the identity of the receiving party is known. However, this is a common occurrence for physicians who receive calls from patients. All health care organizations should have clearly stated policies governing who other than the physician may give what type of advice over the phone. In instances when medical advice is provided, documentation is imperative. This requirement should be emphasized particularly in organizations or areas that are more prone to receive patient calls, such as outpatient clinics, physician offices, home health agencies, and emergency departments.

Patients often call their physicians' offices during the day or after hours. A duplicate phone message pad (even at the bedside at home) is one way to keep a backup log of who called, the date and time, and the reason. In the clinic or office, the original copy should go to the physician to return the call, and the conversation should be added to the note for filing in the patient's medical record. Such documentation should reflect the initial reason for the call, the further description of the problem as described to the physician, and the physician's response or recommendation. Documentation of this information can prove valuable if the quality of care is ever called into question. At a minimum, the date, time, and content of the discussion should be documented. All telephone messages must be filed in the medical record in chronological order.

Physician Notification The date and time of every call to a physician should be carefully recorded. The record of the conversation itself should include the date and time if different from the call and should describe the conversation's content, including the exact signs and symptoms, lab results, and other details conveyed to the physician and the response, including additional information requested and given to the physician. Responses from the physician need to be similarly recorded. If the situation is serious and the physician has not responded in a timely manner, the nurse must follow the chain of command and contact the nursing supervisor or other appropriate person, according to facility procedures. In addition, the chief of the physician's specialty should be notified. Regardless of setting or reason, when patient care staff needs to make contact with a physician, especially in acute care high-risk units, time is of the essence. Each health care setting should have policies governing expected response time and steps to take if response is not received within policy parameters.

Many physicians use an answering service to take calls. The service then pages the physician. The answering service should keep a log of the time the call was received for the physician and the time the physician returned the call to the service. Staff who reach an answering service when calling a physician should record the name of the person taking the call and the phone number of the answering service for future reference.

Countersignatures Countersignatures imply that the health care provider has done more than just read and sign an entry or order. The countersignature connotes that the health care provider agrees with the patient care described or transcribed. Whenever a health care provider signs an entry in a medical record, the provider is responsible for whatever is contained in the entry.

History and physical (H&P) records, operative notes, admission notes, and discharge summaries are often dictated and transcribed. When completing charts, the physician signs these transcribed documents, authenticating the contents. As often as possible, the risk management professional should emphasize to the medical staff the significance of reading, verifying, and correcting transcribed notes before authenticating them with their signatures.

Users of electronic medical records should be assigned electronic signatures, which should never be given to anyone else to use; for instance, the radiologist should not give the electronic signature to the radiology transcriptionist to bypass verifying and authenticating the transcription. In some states, this could be construed as fraud, which is an offense reportable to the state licensing board.

CMS requires that documentation of verbal orders or entries requiring countersignatures be signed as soon as possible. One physician cannot sign for another unless they have joint responsibility. Facility policies and medical staff bylaws should define whether documentation by house staff and allied health professionals requires countersignatures. In some instances, this is governed by state law.

Medical students' and nursing students' documentation should be countersigned by a supervisor. Check state statutes for specifics.

Abbreviations Abbreviations save time; however, they may easily be misinterpreted and are a leading cause of medication errors. Health care providers should have policies and procedures documenting which abbreviations, acronyms, symbols and dose designations to avoid using as unsafe practice. This do-not-use list should be circulated to all staff and compliance monitored. Both The Joint Commission and the Institute for Safe Medication Practices (ISMP) promulgate do-not-use listings that are available on their respective Web sites. Medical abbreviations acceptable for use within the organization should be standardized, universally accepted and approved by the individual health care facility. Abbreviations can vary by setting. Special consideration should be taken to ensure that health care providers not employed by the organization and who may practice at multiple facilities know what abbreviations are acceptable for use and what are not. This group may include locum tenens (temporary replacement staff), traveling nurses, physicians, and agency nurses. The Joint Commission's Sentinel Event Alert 23 and National Patient Safety Goals have addressed the use of abbreviations to prevent medication errors.

Authentication The Joint Commission requires that entries in medical records be made only by individuals explicitly given that right in written facility policies and procedures and medical staff bylaws. All entries should be dated, timed, and signed by the author. In addition to the full name, the professional title should be indicated (MD for medical doctor, PA for physician's assistant, APRN for advanced practice registered nurse, RN for registered nurse, and so on). It is suggested that policies, procedures, and bylaws be reviewed to ensure that there is no conflict among them. The Joint Commission will survey a facility's performance against its own guidelines, and discrepancies can result in conditional or preliminary denial of accreditation.

Documentation of Termination of Care When dealing with noncompliant patients and families (those who fail to follow instructions on diet, medications, or use of safety devices or who tamper with medical equipment), the risk management professional should advise staff to thoroughly document these issues objectively, including all education and reinforcement provided. If it becomes necessary to "administratively or permanently discharge" or refuse further care, the usual practice is to advise the patient and family of the intent to do so orally, followed immediately by written notice, sent by certified mail with return receipt requested. This written notice should set out a time frame (usually thirty days) for continued care (sometimes limited to emergency care during the notice period). Included should be either prescriptions for the notice period or a reference that if a refill prescription is needed during the notice period, it will be provided. It should also include referrals for continued care, such as several names and phone numbers of physicians in the same specialty and the names and phone numbers of the local or regional medical and osteopathy societies. A copy of correspondence with the patient should be maintained in office files and in the medical record. It is recommended that the risk management professional check with legal counsel to verify that such a termination process complies with specific state statutes and case law. Prior to termination, consider the health literacy of the patient. Many patients who are considered noncompliant have limited or low health literacy skills. This at-risk population could benefit from educational intervention and support systems.

Documentation Challenges

It is the responsibility of each health care professional to comply with the facility's documentation policies and procedures. Documentation must be objective and free of speculation.

Verbiage

Plaintiffs' attorneys look for gaps in documentation and flow and inappropriate language to discredit or cast doubt on the credibility of medical records. Terms such as *unintentionally, inadvertently,* and *unexpectedly* are not appropriate because they reflect a judgment that something untoward happened. Words such as *appeared, apparently,* and *seems to be* are not specific and can be used by plaintiffs' attorneys to cast doubt. In addition, many words can have different meanings or interpretations, and misuse could leave the author open to criticism or question. If it is necessary to use ambiguous words, supplemental information is needed to provide clarity.

It is also important not to imply, either inadvertently or intentionally, that a fellow provider was negligent. Here are some ways to avoid raising a "red flag" that might make you the target of a lawsuit by another provider:

- Do not place blame for an unsatisfactory outcome.

- Empathize, don't apologize.

- Do not comment before having all the facts.

- Don't write in the medical record that someone was negligent.

- Do not prematurely document a corrective action plan.

- Discuss differences of opinion in a private environment away from patients.[19]

Legibility The biggest documentation challenge is legibility. Records should be able to be read without requiring deciphering. In a legal proceeding, jury members will need to make a determination based on their interpretation of what they see. Poor handwriting leads to misunderstandings among health professionals and patients. Studies report that illegible notes also lead to poor communication among specialties.

In 1994, the American Medical Association reported that medication error resulting from misinterpreted physicians' prescriptions was the second most prevalent and expensive claim in ninety thousand malpractice claims over a period of seven years. In 1994, the average indemnity payment for the 393 most recent medication error claims was $120,722, with a range of $5,000 to $2.2 million per claim.[20]

Legibility has likewise affected litigation. In a widely publicized 1999 case in Odessa, Texas, a jury awarded $450,000 to the widow and children of a patient who died after a pharmacist dispensed the wrong drug after misreading the physician's handwriting.[21] Half of the judgment was assigned to the pharmacy, leaving the physician responsible for paying the other half. The defense attorney believes that the jury was trying to send a message to the medical community that in the computer age, there is no reason for doctors to create the potential for error by writing out their prescriptions instead of typing or printing them out. On August 12, 2004, a forty-one-year-old man in Redwood City, California, received a lethal chemotherapy overdose, ten times the proper dosage, allegedly attributed to the doctor's illegible handwritten prescription. The family asked the county counsel's office for $1 million and a written apology.[22]

There may be regulatory and accreditation implications to illegible handwriting. The federal Conditions of Participation for Hospitals: Medical Record Services state that "all entries must be legible and complete, and must be authenticated and dated promptly by the person (identified by name and discipline) who is responsible for ordering, providing, or evaluating the service furnished."[23] Criteria for quality medical records at the state level are commonly addressed in state licensing acts. Additional sources of handwriting legibility compliance can be found in The Joint Commission's Medical Staff Standards, Management of Information Standards, and Performance

Improvement Standards. It is incumbent on the risk management professional to be familiar with associated regulatory and accreditation requirements and to facilitate compliance throughout the health care organization.

In consideration of the real and potential threats to patient safety posed by illegible medical records, experts predict that Joint Commission surveyors will check medical records more thoroughly for compliance with pertinent Joint Commission standards and requirements. During a Joint Commission survey, a hospital in Kentucky received a citation for illegible handwriting primarily because "neither the surveyor nor anyone in the room could determine [whether] the order for a medication was for 50 mg or 5.0 mg," according to the hospital's director of performance improvement.

Poor handwriting has been attributed to time pressure. Another reason is that handwriting instruction in Europe and in the United States has used models and teaching methods that do not hold up under any degree of speed.[24]

Three solutions for the problem of illegibility have been proposed. The medical staff of Cedars-Sinai Medical Center decided to offer a special class in handwriting for members of the medical staff, which they speculated would be "raising the bar for other medical institutions."[25] Salem Hospital held a handwriting class for area medical professionals by instructors who teach penmanship to doctors and nurses around the world, because "improving handwriting among medical professionals can greatly reduce the risk of medical errors."[26] Second, studies reveal that transcription services are not only faster than writing but also improve physician productivity, satisfaction, and legibility of medical records.[27] Finally, computers already play a major role in solving handwriting problems. To minimize the potential for adverse drug reactions and miscommunicated orders, many hospitals are using computers for decision support and to order medications. Computers also note potential drug interactions, allergies, and side effects and suggest dosage adjustments based on patient data such as age, weight, and height. These systems can also provide detailed therapy recommendations from a database of commonly prescribed drugs.[28]

Whereas one of the numerous goals for converting to an electronic medical record is to resolve legibility issues, the acute care setting is probably further along in the conversion process. Long-term care facilities, home health agencies, outpatient clinics, physician offices, and other health care settings may not be as far along in that process because it is costly, in terms of both financial and human resources.

Reimbursement Today's health care system includes multiple, complex structures with multiple, complex requirements for reimbursement. Caregivers and health care organizations are accountable not only to internal quality management teams, case managers, and required reimbursement structures but also to federal and state agencies, **HMO**s, preferred provider organizations (PPOs), and independent practice associations (IPAs), among others. Documentation is scrutinized by Medicare, Medicaid, and insurance company reviewers, among others, for quality of care, patient outcomes, and need for continued treatment. Reviewers from these groups examine the medical record for discrepancies. They look for differences in the treatment ordered and the treatment provided. If a discrepancy cannot be explained satisfactorily or reconciled reasonably, payment may be denied.

Payments by Medicare and Medicaid are sources of operating revenue for the health care organization. Although both Medicare and Medicaid were established in 1965 under the Social Security Act, the two organizations differ in their reimbursement policies, regulations, and documentation guidelines. Under Medicare, documentation is required to support the need for skilled medical and nursing care and its delivery. For example, a record for a Medicare Part A skilled facility resident must support not only the direct skilled services provided but also the assessment and oversight that skilled services require. In the home care setting, Medicare has tied reimbursement to Outcome Assessment Instrument Set (OASIS) regulations that require that nurses complete an assessment and that agencies transmit the assessment and other data within strict time frames. Under Medicaid, documentation is required to ensure payment, but essential content varies according to setting. Lack of documentation as to the medical necessity of a test, procedure, or service could prove troublesome should a claim arise in which this issue is in question.

Besides a lack of documentation, especially in the long-term care environment, there needs to be congruence among the various documents within the medical record, without which the credibility of the care might be compromised, not to mention cause for suspicion of fraud and abuse.

Documentation discrepancies identified by reviewers can also be red flags if the medical record becomes evidence in litigation. Inconsistencies in documentation leave both the caregiver and the health care organization open to accusations of incompetence and financial irresponsibility. Ultimately, a medical record containing inconsistencies can be difficult or impossible to defend in court. Risk and health information management professionals must establish a partnership to communicate such findings and act on them in an expedient manner.

Documenting a Medical Error Documentation of patient care and events in the medical record is mandated by state and federal laws, accrediting organizations, professional organizations, and clinical standards of practice. Medical records may be used for legal proceedings, including state board disciplinary proceedings and negligence actions filed against the facility or specific health care providers when a patient injury or death occurs. The assumption is that the testimony following such an event will be based on factual documentation in the medical record.[29]

Although it is not appropriate to make the incident report itself a part of the medical record, the facts about the incident and how it was resolved should be documented. Neither the completion of an incident report nor reference to risk management should be referenced in the medical record because it is considered confidential and privileged under many state laws and might unnecessarily raise a red flag. Here are some tips for health care professionals who need to document a medical error:

■ Refer to organizational policy about what is classified as a medical error.

■ Document the actual time of the event.

- Do not refer to the event as a "medical error."

- Objectively document what happened in the accepted charting model for the organization.

- Document who was notified.

- Document the response received to notifications and any other interventions.

- Document the patient's, resident's, and family's understanding of the event and how questions were answered.

- Document the outcome and treatment plan as indicated.

- Document the disclosure discussion.

Physician and Allied Health Chart Completion Issues Not only do delinquent or incomplete medical records compromise reimbursement, but they are also an obstacle to providing quality care. The standard is that records are to be completed within thirty days after discharge. If the period of completion is longer, those numbers count against the facility when surveyed by The Joint Commission, and the physician is not in compliance with the medical staff bylaws and risks being suspended from admitting privileges. In addition, should the record be requested by an outside party, such as a third-party payer or an attorney, issues could arise from sending an incomplete record, especially if additions or changes are made to the record when the chart is finally completed.

Dictated notes reflect the date and often the time of dictation and of transcription. It is preferable to time the dictation as close as possible to the date of the action (surgical procedure, consultation, history, physical). Dictations dated after the date of a request from a third party can be regarded with suspicion.

Physicians and others who dictate reports or notes should be reminded that their signature is evidence that they have read and agreed that the transcription is correct, thereby authenticating the note or report. Notes and reports sometimes have references to the wrong side or wrong site, to an antibiotic or other medication that sounds alike but is incorrect because the physician did not spell the name of the drug. Further, there might be blanks in the transcription because the transcriber could not understand a particular word. Sometimes a physician whose first language is not English can dictate with an accent that results in transcription errors. In such cases, physicians should take extra care to review their transcribed reports and summaries. When physicians sign a report or summary that contain blanks or errors, they are confirming that the contents are correct; it exposes both physician and institution to great risk of liability if inaccuracies in the files are raised as an issue in a deposition or other legal proceeding.

Because turnaround time of the transcribed reports and summaries can be a deterrent to timely chart completion, risk management should work closely with health information management to monitor controls. Strategies for encouraging chart completion include the suspension of privileges and imposition of fines.

Risk management professionals need to work with organizational and medical staff leaders to prepare a fair procedure for enforcing compliance with timely and appropriate chart completion.

Medical Record Alterations If the medical record is altered, intentionally or unintentionally, it can be misleading to others, and documentation as to the actual care provided may be disputed. In *Pyle* v. *Morrison* (1986), a malpractice suit was brought against doctors for their treatment of a child's fractured arm. The jury decided in favor of the plaintiffs—$400,000 for the child and $15,000 for the father. The deciding factor was the testimony of a nurse who said that she thought a portion of the medical record had been altered after the child's surgery.[30] Tampering with the medical record is both unethical and illegal. Falsification, including alteration of medical records, can also be grounds for a criminal indictment or a civil claim for damages. Even with the best of intentions, changing inaccurate information, filling in omissions, altering dates and times, rewriting text, destroying records, adding to someone else's notes, or correcting or amending notes in violation of the facility's policy can be construed as "tampering with medical records." This can expose the health care organization and health care provider to many different types of claims, raise many other issues, and may even result in the loss of affirmative defenses in a negligence claim. Furthermore, tampering may be reportable to external agencies and professional licensing boards. All known cases of tampering should be reported to the corporate compliance officer.

In the state of Florida, the Agency for Health Care Administration makes the requirements explicit: "The Board of Nursing shall impose disciplinary penalties upon a determination that a licensee . . . (d) Has falsely represented the patient's chart, patient flow sheets, narcotic records, or nursing progress records, or otherwise misrepresented the facts on records relating directly to the patient."[31] Although this illustrates a specific state's handling of this issue, risk management professionals should be thoroughly familiar with their respective states' disciplinary rules, promulgated by professional regulatory and licensing boards.

The risk management professional should be notified and should assist in the investigation whenever it is suspected or determined that a record has been altered. Reports should be filed with the external licensing board as appropriate. In addition, the risk management professional can assist in the preservation of records and deter alterations. Having a policy and procedure on the early sequestering of medical records after a significant incident will decrease the probability that the records will be released and altered.

If a patient experiences a poor or unexpected outcome, the urge to alter the record to make the care appear more appropriate can be overwhelming. With this in mind, the risk management professional should rely on established policy and procedures (developed in conjunction with legal counsel and the medical records department) to preserve the current record. Table 9.4 lists some documentation "dos" and "don'ts."

One effective way to decrease alterations is to copy the current record that discusses the poor outcome for the medical record file and put the original in the "legal file" under the care and control of the medical records director. The copy on the shelf is available for patient care reference. Should the original need to be reviewed or completed, a representative of the medical records department should sit with the individual to prevent alterations. It is the medical records department personnel who must testify or sign affidavits to the effect that the original record has been in their care, control, and custody. Should the original record be sent to risk management or legal counsel for safekeeping, the medical records department personnel would not be able to make such statements. If this policy is consistently followed for potentially serious incidents and events, the likelihood of alterations should be prevented because no one would have unfettered access to the original record. Usually, when a serious incident has occurred, the risk management professional asks for a copy to begin an early investigation, which would be another copy available for comparison should alterations after the fact be suspected.

TABLE 9.4. Documentation Dos and Don'ts

Do:	Don't:
Complete the record as soon as possible	Use vague, ambiguous, or subjective terms
Use a ballpoint pen, not pencil or a felt-tip pen	Make statements against a colleague
Be neat and write legibly	Change a record, postdate an entry, or record false information
Record date and time, and sign each entry with full name and professional designation	Use correction fluid or erase an entry
Document facts, observations, patient's condition, and complications	Skip lines or leave blank spaces between entries
Show thought process—know what you plan to do and why	Use unapproved abbreviations or ones that may offend or may be misunderstood
Be accurate—use clear and concise language that can be explained later	Criticize another practitioner's judgment or recommendations
Chart both positive and negative findings	Refer to incident reports, errors or to risk management, quality assurance, and peer review activities or meetings

Correct errors by lining through them once, initialing, and writing in the corrected word or statement	Release the original copy of the medical record
Give all information on drugs—name, dosage and strength, route, time	Alter, destroy, or otherwise tamper with a medical record
Chart anything unusual or unexpected	Include subjective statements, other than those quoted directly from a patient or resident
Follow an established, accepted method of charting	
Use only standard abbreviations	
Make sure the patient's name is at the top of each new page	
Use clear and concise language; avoid ambiguous terms and phrases	
Make sure that verbal orders are documented and cosigned according to hospital policy	
Record pertinent laboratory results	
Record patient responses to medication and treatment	
Avoid improper corrections, erasures, or obliterations	
Avoid accusatory language	
Avoid time gaps and omissions	
Follow protocol for late entries	
Document patient and family education	

Omissions Entries with the distinction of being the most frequently omitted might be some of the most important to the overall record. For example, some of the most frequently omitted entries in the long-term care setting are resident and family education, conversations with family, and cues and redirection of the resident.[32]

RECORD RETENTION

How long a record should be kept depends on factors such as statutes of limitations, individual state statutes, and various standards and regulations, including the following:[33]

■ The Joint Commission

■ Centers for Medicare and Medicaid Services (CMS): for hospitals, home health agencies, state and long-term care facilities, comprehensive outpatient rehabilitation, organ procurement, rural primary care

■ Occupational Safety and Health Administration (**OSHA**)

■ The Public Health Services Act: Immunization Program and National Childhood Vaccine Injury Act

■ The National Commission on Correctional Health Care for Health Services in Jails and Prisons

■ Federal reimbursement requirement guidelines

■ Institutional record retention policies

Clear and complete recordkeeping guidelines must be developed and implemented for every health care organization. Although most records are maintained in one location, recordkeeping guidelines should also address all departments that maintain separate files. In addition, recordkeeping guidelines must address the review of all medical records shortly after the patient or resident is discharged, to ensure that the record is complete. Records that are involved in pending or threatened legal action should be segregated.

Destruction of patient health information is carried out in accordance with federal and state law and pursuant to a proper written retention schedule and destruction policy approved by the health information manager, chief executive officer, medical staff, and legal counsel. Records involved in any open investigation, audit, or litigation should not be destroyed.[34]

RELEASE OF RECORDS

Records should be released only as authorized by state and federal laws and by the organization's policies and procedures. Policies and procedures for the release of medical records should address all of the following matters:

■ Who may request and secure a copy of a patient's medical record (in the acute care setting, it is most often the patient or an authorized representative who requests the record; in the long-term care setting, it is more often the resident's guardian, surrogate, or holder of power of attorney)

- Who is authorized to release records and to whom (such as patients, another staff member, attorneys, insurance company representatives)

- How access to medical records is monitored and documented (who checks out and returns records and when)

- Appropriate mechanisms to protect sensitive patient and employee health information (such as information related to HIV results, lifestyle, substance abuse, psychological profiles, or behavioral health records)

Failure to follow proper release procedures can result in significant liability. To minimize opportunities for liability, records should not be removed from the central location. Alternatively, only a copy of the record should be released so that the original records are always present in the records retention area.

The American Health Information Management Association has defined the legal health record for disclosure purposes.[35] The legal health record is generated at or for a health care organization as its business record, and it is the record that will be disclosed upon request. It does not affect discoverability of other information held by the organization. It is imperative that health care organizations define their legal health records, because the content is governed by laws and regulations that vary by practice setting and state.

OWNERSHIP OF MEDICAL RECORDS

The medical record is an unusual type of property, as both the patient and the health care facility or provider have an ownership interest. The health care facility or provider owns the actual record, but the patient owns the information contained therein. The record must remain in the facility or doctor's office; therefore, the facility or office has the responsibility to exercise control in the release of the document itself or the information contained therein. Patients and others who have a vested interest have a right to access the information contained in the record; but there are limitations on this right, which vary by state.

In today's environment, medical record ownership issues arise relative to mergers, acquisitions, divestitures, and HMO provider contracts. This is illustrated by a case from the Florida Fourth District Court of Appeals in *Humana Medical Plan* v. *Fischman,* decided in December 1999. Humana terminated an agreement with a physician provider. This decision was based on a contract provision, which stipulated that the medical records relating to Humana members, during the term of their enrollment, would be the property of Humana. Despite many requests, the physician provided only those records for which he had received prior written consent from his patients. The physician argued that according to Florida Statute 455.667, governing the disclosure of patient medical records, Humana did not qualify as the "owner" of the records.

Humana conceded that F.S. 455.667 did not authorize it to obtain these records and admitted it did not obtain written authorization from the insured in advance. The Florida Appeals Court upheld the lower court's decision in favor of the physician. Cases such as this demonstrate the importance of reviewing contract language, in advance, regarding the issue of ownership of the medical record.

For records that are stored in the medical records department, it is prudent to have a policy and procedure on the release or availability of records to requesting parties. Depending on the status of an identified event (incident, notice of intent to sue, claim being made, lawsuit, and so on), the record could be sequestered with the original not being made available unless under direct supervision. This policy will prevent the inadvertent alterations or misplacement of the record (see Appendix B).

MEDICAL RECORD AUDITS

Compliance with documentation standards and expectations can be verified through regular medical record audits. Typical questions to be answered with a medical record audit are presented in Exhibit 9.1. Medical records may be audited by asking questions regarding organizational processes:

- Is the reason for the patient encounter documented?

- Is there a process to verify that services that are provided are documented?

EXHIBIT 9.1   *Questions for medical record review*

- If the patient alleged some deficiently in patient care, could the record negate the patient's story?

- Is there a logical process presented in the record for coming to a decision about the course of treatment?

- Would any reasonable physician be likely to come to the same conclusion?

- Were the appropriate tests ordered in a timely manner?

- Do test results verify the course of treatment?

- Was appropriate consultation obtained?

- Do the consultants' reports agree with the course of treatment?

- If not, were the differences clearly explained and justified in the record?

- Did the physician comment on the interventions and results of treatments provided by other professionals (e.g., nurses and therapists) that may have affected the condition of the patient or the treatment regimen?

- Does the record clearly explain why support services, procedures, and supplies were provided?

- Is the assessment of the patient's condition apparent in the record?

- Does the record contain information on the patient's progress and on the results of treatment?

- Does the record include a plan for care?

- Does the information in the record describing the patient's condition provide reasonable medical rationale for the services?

- Does the information in the record support the care given in case another health care professional must assume care or perform medical review?

- Is the documentation in compliance with established policies and procedures with and local, state, and federal requirements?

DOCUMENTATION AND RISK MANAGEMENT

The medical record has historically been a tool of risk management. Appropriate documentation promotes quality of care, preserves the financial integrity of the organization, and maintains competitiveness in the marketplace. Documentation is multidisciplinary and a way for all members of the patient care team to work together for the patient's benefit.

- Do the progress notes indicate that the patient knew about the benefits and reasonably expected risks and alternatives before giving consent to high-risk or invasive procedures?

- Are the entries accurately timed, dated, signed, and above all, legible?

- Do they reflect professionalism (for example, no evidence of infighting with other members of the care team)?

- Is there any evidence of alteration of the record? (Even if this was done innocently, juries frown on even the appearance of fraud or cover-up.)
  a) Looked at in its entirety, does the medical record present a complete picture of the care provided with no ambiguity, no unexplainable gaps in time for treatments or medications, no illegible entries, and so on?

Liability Exposures

A discussion of legal considerations pertaining to documentation must reflect the changing demands of the health care environment. More elderly people are receiving medical care, and medical conditions are more acute. New procedures, drugs, and equipment to provide medical care are constantly being introduced. There is more emphasis on consumers' rights, and the media's heightened interest attracts even further attention and scrutiny of the provision and quality of health care services.

One only needs to attend a professional liability trial or read a malpractice case transcript to realize how much a jury relies on documentation. What the providers document or fail to document will certainly influence the outcome of any case.

Plaintiffs' attorneys have erroneously promoted that an action that is not documented is not performed. Health care providers know that this contention is incorrect, as much patient care is rendered that is never documented. However, documentation is especially significant in cases of informed consent, medication, treatment entries, and also "routine" observations. Table 9.5 provides a listing of what plaintiffs' attorneys look for in the medical record.

TABLE 9.5.   What Plaintiffs' Attorneys Look for in the Medical Record

Vague, ambiguous, or contradictory statements open to interpretation
Incomplete or sparse records that fail to demonstrate consistent, attentive care
Failure to address discrepancies in observations made by other clinicians
Failure to follow up on recommendations made by other clinicians
Failure to address signs or complaints of distress
Criticisms of the care rendered or perceived mistakes made by other practitioners
References to incident reports, risk management activities, quality assurance meetings, or peer review procedures
Omissions, including missing laboratory test results, radiology results, and EKG strips
Erasures, use of correction fluid, or any other attempt to alter the record

Inaccuracies or inconsistencies that can be used to infer substandard care

Words and phrases with multiple meanings or interpretations

Any loose ends that can be used to imply negligence or substandard care

Lack of supervision

Alterations

Lack of informed consent documentation

Lack of patient education documentation

Illegible entries or signatures

Time delays and unexpected time gaps

When a continuous record of the patient's status is lacking and deterioration occurs, absence of documentation will be used to support a claim of negligence. Other ways that medical records can be used adversely in the event of a claim include these:

- A series of events leading up to a patient's injury in the hospital

- Failure of the staff to use information available in the patient's record

- Failure to impart important information from one department to another

- Failure to write legible medical orders

One way for health care providers to evaluate their charting is to view it through an attorney's eyes, asking themselves, if this were presented as evidence to a jury, would it be thorough and convincing?

Liability issues specifically concerning medical records include the following:

- Record authentication

- Record retention

- Record destruction

- Access to medical records

- Release of confidential information

- Release of information in litigation

- Electronic record security

Documentation issues that help jurors make decisions about cases include these:

- What is reasonably expected of the health care professional's peers?

- What is in accordance with the standard of care?

- How does it reflect on the quality of care provided?

A medical record that can be used in the affirmative defense of a claim meets the following criteria:

- It documents all relevant medical information.

- It substantiates the rationale for care provided or not provided.

- It highlights the interaction between professionals.

- It presents a timeline for care rendered.

- It documents the psychosocial needs and concerns of the patient and relevant others.

- It preserves the medical history of patient care.

- It is more reliable than personal recollection.

- It demonstrates good communication.

- It demonstrates quality medical care.

Protecting Privileged Information

Documents that can remain protected from discovery in legal proceedings are defined by each individual state. Risk management professionals should explore state statutes for particular information about which documents are considered privileged, confidential, or protected by attorney client privilege or attorney work-product information. The following records may be privileged, along with others:

- Incident reports

- Risk and quality management committee minutes

- Incident investigations

- Peer review proceeding

- Corrective action plans

- Root cause analyses

The specifics of whether or not a particular document remains privileged or confidential should also be explored. For example, if the document is typically protected from discovery but is shared with a third party, the privilege or confidentiality may be waived. Risk management professionals and medical records personnel should coordinate efforts to ensure that the proper protections are effective and in compliance with federal and state statutes.

Forensic Documentation Examination

For many years, forensic documentation techniques have been used to analyze handwriting, signatures, and chronology of entries. The techniques have not changed, but the scope of the analysis has broadened. The following is a brief list of such forensic methods, which can be used in support or defense of a claim. For more information, a knowledgeable defense attorney should be contacted.

- *Electrostatic Detection Apparatus.* This equipment can detect latent impressions on the underlying pages of a document that have been amended. The advantage is that it provides a hard copy; the disadvantage is that the equipment is not portable.

- *Ink Analysis.* This technique can be used if there is a possibility that the medical record was altered. It is the only method to establish identifiers of the ink type used for entry. The advantage is that it may provide conclusive evidence of fabrication if the ink contains certain markers; the disadvantage is that because tiny ink samples are lifted from the original document, damage does occur. Many types of ink have not been tagged, and there is no standardization.

- *Infrared Exams.* Infrared tools are used to identify ink types but cannot prove that inks are the same. The advantage is that they do not destroy the document. The disadvantages are that the equipment is not transportable, so original documents must go to a laboratory, and the exams cannot distinguish among all ink types.

- *Identification of Date Markers.* Date markers can identify most paper copy machines, printers, and typewriter ribbons. An advantage is that they are objective and reliable; however, the analysis is very time-consuming.

- *Handwriting Analysis.* If an expert handwriting analysis is undertaken, risk management professionals must ensure the integrity of the chain of custody of evidence. Often this requires hand-carrying the original medical record or documents to the analyst and remaining with them until they are returned to the original custodian. The custodian may be called on to testify to the maintenance of this chain of custody of evidence.

Documentation and Litigation

The medical record is a crucial legal document. In a malpractice lawsuit, the patient's medical record demonstrates the quality of care provided. It describes (or fails to describe) acts, events, conditions, diagnoses, and opinions at or near the time of the alleged malpractice event. The following cases illustrate the medical record's importance in the courtroom.

- In *Cruz* v. *West Volusia Hospital Authority d/b/a West Volusia Memorial Hospital,* Volusia County, Florida Circuit Court No. 95–10313 (1997), the nurse failed to inform the obstetrician of fetal distress or document it. As a result, the baby suffered hypoxic ischemic encephalopathy. The parties reached an out-of-court settlement for $2,425,000.[36]

- In *Cloughly* v. *St Paul Fire and Marine Insurance Company,* Washington County, Arkansas Circuit Court, Case No. C1V95–996 (1997), neither the hospital nor the nurse documented how a portable ventilator was set up, and there was no record that oxygen saturation readings had been taken. A $2,125,000 settlement was reached before trial.[37]

- In *Toinkham, Administrator of Estate of Muncey* v. *Mount Carmel Health d/b/a Mt. Carmel East Hospital,* Franklin County, Ohio, Court of Common Pleas, Case No. 94CVA-09–6736 (1997), the plaintiff's attorney alleged that the nurses did not properly assess, monitor, and care for the patient before and after the injection of morphine because these actions were not documented in the medical record. The patient was later found in total cardiac arrest and could not be revived. A $433,415 verdict was returned at trial.[38]

Table 9.6 identifies chart components that may be of interest when evaluating liability.

TABLE 9.6. **Essential Charting Components of Interest to the Health Care Risk Management Professional**

Nursing observations and assessments	General demeanor or affect
Appearance	Activity and restrictions
Height and weight	Vital signs
General physical condition	Mental state
History of past hospitalizations	Medication administration record (MAR)
History of past surgery, anesthesia, and any complications	Discharge plan

Allergies	Dietary restrictions
Reason for admission or presenting complaint	Physical or cultural disabilities
Preferred language	Skin condition
Instruction provided to patient, resident, and family (including opportunities for them to ask questions, return demonstrations, any specific instructional materials provided)	Discharge instructions: diet, activity, medications, skin care and hygiene, specific treatments indicated, referrals, follow-up appointments
Problem list	Consents
Physicians' orders	Ancillary provider notes and consultation reports
Relevant health risk factors	Patient's progress, including response to treatment, change in treatment, change in diagnosis, and patient noncompliance
Intake and output	

In Anticipation of Legal Action

The following tips may be useful if legal action is anticipated.

- Follow the organization's claim reporting procedures.

- Secure all pertinent records.

- Release a copy of the record only after receiving a written request and signed authorization, in accordance with organizational policy.

- Before releasing the medical record, seek to obtain the specific components of the medical record that are needed by the requester, and release only those portions that are requested.

- Never change a record in any way once a copy has been released.

Amendments to the **Federal Rules of Civil Procedure** (**FRCP**) went into effect in December 2006. Most medical professional liability suits are brought in state court, which are not obligated to follow the FRCP. However, most state courts are adopting new rules of civil procedure, many of which are modeled on the FRCP. It is imperative that the risk management professional, along with legal counsel and the organization's health information officer, review and revise as appropriate all policies, procedures, protocols, and practices that relate to records (hard copy or electronic) that could be requested in civil proceedings. [39]

EMERGING RISK EXPOSURES

Although the basic principles of documentation remain the same, new forms of documentation require an examination of related risk exposures.

Electronic Recordkeeping

President Bush, in his State of the Union Address on January 20, 2004, outlined a program whereby most Americans would have electronic health records within the next ten years. This commitment was also reflected when Department of Health and Human Services Secretary Mike Leavitt told the House Appropriations Committee that he "sees a day when every American can have access to an electronic health record."[40]

Electronic medical records reduce costs and improve care. Electronic databases can eliminate the need for physicians to repeat certain tests and allow them to find out which medications a patient is taking. Nevertheless, hospitals face the challenge of making the transition. Cedars-Sinai Medical Center in Los Angeles shelved its $34 million computerized physician-order entry (CPOE) system after three months, following "full-blown staff rebellion in the fall of 2002." Complaints included poor technology ("clunky and slow"), insufficient training, resistance to change, and the fact that only a few of the two thousand doctors with privileges at the hospital were involved in developing the system.[41]

With the advent of electronic medical records, policies and procedures need to be reviewed to accommodate new considerations, such as corrections in the medical record. Hospitals must be able to strike a balance between the benefits of the technology and the method and pace of implementation, always with an eye on safety.

Computerized Physician Order Entry

In 2005, about 6 percent of hospitals nationwide had computerized systems for doctors' orders.[42] According to the CPOE Digest 2008 from KLAS, (an impartial health-care technology vendor performance firm based in Orem, Utah) that percentage increased in 2008 to 17.5. Hospitals that are complying with the Leapfrog Group's recommendation that hospitals issue voluntary reports on progress in implementing computerized physician order entry (CPOE) systems and other measures to improve safety have reported that they have eliminated virtually all transcription errors by going to electronic physician ordering.[43]

However, more than 90 percent of prescriptions are still written by hand, and researchers have found that computer systems are prone to make twenty-two types of medication errors (for example, selecting the wrong patient file because names and drugs are similar or because patients' names do not appear on the screen; different doctors using the same terminal, so if one fails to log off, a prescription could go to the wrong patient).[44]

A study that analyzed the effect of computerized order entry systems on medical errors at the Veterans Administration Medical Center in Salt Lake City found that the VA's CPOE system was able to eliminate mistakes from illegible handwriting and could offer simple advice, such as avoiding drug interactions, but it was not "designed to provide more sophisticated advice on drugs, dosages and patient-monitoring strategies that might have averted harm." Another study at the University of Pennsylvania hospital corroborated these findings. The studies highlighted "strikingly high numbers of adverse drug events" and "many potential glitches" in a CPOE system.[45]

Risk management professionals are cautioned to carefully evaluate the risks and flaws of any CPOE system and encouraged to contribute to contingency solutions.

Medical Record Database Privacy Issues

In May 2005, California health officials notified 21,600 Medi-Cal beneficiaries that a laptop containing their personal information had been stolen. In response, state Sen. Jackie Speier (D) vowed to introduce a bill that would require California agencies and contractors to encrypt all personal information stored in laptops.[46] By August 11, 2005, the California Department of Health (CDHS) had successfully encrypted 1,700 laptops with Encryption Plus Hard Disk positioning the department as a compliance model for other state agencies.

THE RISK MANAGEMENT PROFESSIONAL'S ROLE

The risk management professional should be vigilant in assessing the quality of medical record documentation, looking for opportunities to enhance the value and quality of the medical record.

The following are some suggestions to the risk management professional for addressing documentation issues:

- Review incident patterns and trends for documentation issues and problems throughout the organization.

- Evaluate on a regular basis the effectiveness of the organization's documentation style and format.

- Review annually all forms, policies, procedures, protocols, and standards relating to documentation in the medical record.

- Review the minutes of the medical records committee and closed records review proceedings to assess the response to previously identified concerns.

■ Contact defense counsel for advice on documentation issues that have been identified in claims, and obtain a copy of pertinent documentation case law.

■ Review the protocol for handling inappropriate documentation.

■ Familiarize yourself with current federal and state statutes, Medicare Conditions of Participation, and other standards regarding documentation.

■ Develop a collaborative relationship with the medical records department personnel responsible for coding medical records and for responding to subpoenas and requests for records.

■ Incorporate risk management and documentation issues as part of the general orientation for all new employees.

■ Conduct random audits of medical records to identify documentation issues.

■ Develop a collaborative relationship with transcription services and include them in the auditing process.

With the increased pressure to be cost-efficient, the necessity for real-time access to information, the advent of telemedicine, and the development of the electronic medical record, all coupled with an increasing array of delivery sites, the risk management professional is required to maintain an understanding of evolving documentation risks and challenges.

SUMMARY

As one of many health care business documents, the medical record can be the organization's strongest ally in providing quality care. It can also be its worst enemy if improperly prepared or maintained. Ensuring the appropriateness, thoroughness, and timeliness of medical record documentation is a significant loss prevention activity that should be undertaken by the risk management professional. The medical record is the one lasting documentation of patient care. It is the primary document in which health care information about a patient is recorded.

Proper documentation enhances good health outcomes. Patients and residents receive quality nursing and medical care based on a documented assessment of their needs. Medical records can be more than the sum of their parts.

KEY TERMS

Abbreviations	Federal Rules of Civil Procedure
Alterations	Forensic documentation examination
Authentication	Hearsay
Computerized physician order entry system	Legibility
	National Patient Safety Goals
Countersignatures	Reimbursement

ACRONYMS

AHIMA	IM
ANA	NPSG
CMS	OSHA
CPOE	PIE
FACT	PHI
HIAA	POMR
HIMSS	SOAP
HIPAA	SOAPIER
HMO	

NOTES

1. American Nurses Association. *Principles for Documentation.* Silver Spring, Md.: American Nurses Association, 2005.

2. Joint Commission. *Hospital Accreditation Standards.* Oakbrook Terrace, Ill.: Joint Commission Resources, published annually.

3. *2007 Most Challenging Standards.* The Joint Commission. *This Month,* September 2008

4. Joint Commission. *Hospital Accreditation Standards,* 2005 ed., I.M.6.20.

5. Ibid., Standards IM.6.10, IM.6.20, IM.6.30, IM.6.40, IM.6.50, and IM.6.60.

6. Beicher, T. *Defensive Documentation for Long-Term Care: Strategies for Creating a More Lawsuit-Proof Resident Record.* Marblehead, Mass.: HCPro, 2003, p. 10.

7. Beverage, D., and others. *Charting Made Incredibly Easy,* 3rd ed. Philadelphia: Lippincott Williams & Wilkins, 2006, p. 137.

8. Holmes, H. N., and others. *Documentation,* 2nd ed. Philadelphia: Springhouse, 1999, p. 67.

9. Ibid., p. 107.

10. Ibid., p. 70.

11. Beverage and others, *Charting,* p. 97.

12. Holmes and others, *Documentation,* p. 11.

13. Beverage and others, *Charting,* p. 70.

14. Ibid., p. 63.

15. Holmes and others, *Documentation,* p. 74.

16. Beverage and others, *Charting,* p. 81.

17. Ibid., p. 85.

18. Ibid., p. 50.

19. Worsley, B. "Pointing Fingers Is Risky Business." *Medical Liability Monitor,* 2004, *29*(11), 8.

20. Cabral, J. D. "Poor Physician Penmanship." *Journal of the American Medical Association,* 1997, *278,* 1116–1117.

21. *Vasquez et al.* v. *Kolluru,* A-103 Tex. 042 (2000).

22. Friedland, N. "Chemo Overdose Result of Illegible Prescription." *San Francisco Examiner,* April 26, 2005. The case was eventually settled for $160,000. Durand, M. "Chemo Death Case Settled." *San Mateo Daily Journal,* Dec. 20, 2006.

23. 42 CFR 482.24(c)[1].

24. "Back to the Blackboard: Physicians Must Improve Handwriting Skills." HCPro, 2002, http://www.msleader.com

25. "Handwriting Challenged' Doctors to Take Penmanship Class at Cedars-Sinai Medical Center." *Science Daily Magazine,* Apr. 27, 2000, http://www.science daily.com/releases/2000/04/000426155803.htm

26. Monaghan, M. "Physicians Get Help with Poor Pen Skills." *Statesman Journal,* Mar. 16, 2005.

27. "Back to the Blackboard."

28. Cabral, "Poor Physician Penmanship."

29. Brent, N. J. "How Should I Document a Med Error?" *Nursing Spectrum—Career Fitness Online,* Mar. 3, 2005.

30. *Pyle* v. *Morrison,* 716 S.W. 2d 930 (Tenn. Ct. App. 1986).

31. Florida Administrative Code 59S-8.005.

32. Beicher, T. "Common Medical Record Omissions and Pitfalls of the Pen." In *Defensive Documentation,* pp. 81–94.

33. Fletcher, D. M., and Rhodes, H. B. *Retention of Health Information* (Updated). American Health Information Management Association, 2002, http://library. ahima.org/xpedio/groups/public/documents/ahima/bok1_012545.hcsp?dDoc Name=bok1_012545

34. Ibid.

35. AHIMA e-HIM Work Group on the Legal Health Record. *Update: Guidelines for Defining the Legal Health Record for Disclosure Purposes.* American Health

Information Management Association, 2005, http://library.ahima.org/xpedio/groups/public/documents/ahima/bok1_027921.hcsp

36. *Cruz* v. *West Volusia Hospital Authority d/b/a West Volusia Memorial Hospital,* Volusia Co., Fla. Circ. Ct. 95-10313 (1997).

37. *Cloughly* v. *Saint Paul Fire and Marine Insurance Company,* Washington Co., Ark. Circ. Ct. C1V95-996 (1997).

38. *Toinkham, Administrator of Estate of Muncey,* v. *Mt. Carmel Health d/b/a Mt. Carmel East Hospital,* Franklin Co., Ohio, Ct. of Common Pleas 94CVA-09-6736 (1997).

39. Amendments to the Federal Rules of Civil Procedure available at [http://www.uscourts.gov/rules/EDiscovery_w_Notes.pdf]

40. "E-Health:Health." *National Journal*, Mar. 3, 2005, [http://www.nationaljournal.com/pubs/techdaily/pmedition/2005/tp050303.htm]

41. "HHS Secretary Touts EHRs, Telemedicine." California HealthCare Foundation, Mar. 4, 2005, http://www.ihealthbeat.org/index.cfm?Action5dspItem&itemID5 10941442.

42. Connolly, C. "Cedars-Sinai Doctors Cling to Pen and Paper." *Washington Post,* Mar. 21, 2005.

43. Ibid.

44. Ritter, J. "Docs' Scrawl Can Endanger Patients." *Chicago Sun-Times*, May 8, 2005.

45. "*Wall Street Journal* Examines Impact of Computerized Physician Order Entry Systems on Medical Error Rate." Henry J. Kaiser Family Foundation, Daily Reports, June 1, 2005, http://www.kaisernetwork.org/daily_reports/rep_index .cfm?DR_ID530456

46. "Stolen Laptop Contains Information on Medi-Cal Beneficiaries." California Healthline, California Healthcare Foundation, May 31, 2005, http://www.califor niahealthline.org/articles/2005/5/31/Stolen-Laptop-Contains-Information-for-MediCal-Beneficiaries.aspx?topicID=40

SUGGESTED READING AND RECOMMENDED WEB SITES

American Health Information Management Association: http://www.ahima.org

American Hospital Association: http://www.aha.org

American Medical Association: http://www.ama-assn.org

American Nurses Association: http://www.nursingworld.org

Beicher, T. *Defensive Documentation for Long-Term Care: Strategies for Creating a More Lawsuit-Proof Resident Record*. Marblehead, Mass.: HCPro, 2003.

Beverage, D., and others. *Charting Made Incredibly Easy,* 3rd ed. Philadelphia: Lippincott Williams & Wilkins, 2006.

Centers for Medicare and Medicaid Services: http://www.cms.hhs.gov/default.asp

Getty, B., and others. "Rx for Handwriting Success: A Handwriting Seminar for Medical Professionals," http://www.handwritingsuccess.com

Health Insurance Association of America: http://www.hiaa.org

Holmes, H. N., and others. *Documentation,* 2nd ed. Philadelphia: Springhouse, 1999.

Institute for Safe Medication Practice: http://www.ismp.org

The Joint Commission: http://www.jointcommission.org

NSO Risk Advisor: http://www.nso.com

Office of Inspector General: http://www.oig.gov

CHAPTER

10

STATUTES, STANDARDS, AND REGULATIONS

MARK COHEN

LEARNING OBJECTIVES

■ To be able to identify critical laws and regulations that require close monitoring for changes or interpretations

■ To be able to describe risk management techniques to reduce exposure to loss due to noncompliance

■ To be able to recognize resources to enhance or acquire relevant knowledge of statutes, standards, and regulations that affect health care organizations

■ To be able to develop policies, procedures, protocols, and guidelines to assist in organizational compliance with statutes, standards, and regulations

> *It will be of little avail to the people . . . if the laws be so voluminous that they cannot be read, or so incoherent that they cannot be understood; if they be repealed or revised before they are promulgated, or undergo such incessant changes that no (one) who knows what the law is today can guess what it will be tomorrow.*

JAMES MADISON, *FEDERALIST*, No. 62 (1788)

It should not be much of a surprise to risk management professionals that health care is one of the most heavily regulated of all sectors of commerce. Much of these regulations, such as federal and state laws, are legislative mandates; others reflect regulatory requirements imposed by government-sponsored programs—Medicare chief among them. Others are more or less self-imposed to conform with other government and private initiatives. Irrespective of the source, the number and variety of rules that govern how health care is delivered are staggering. Because of the broad civil liability, and criminal and administrative sanctions that may result from deliberate or accidental violations, risk management professionals should familiarize themselves with at least the basic elements of key statutes and regulations. Keeping up to date on a regular basis will help the risk management professional identify and, if necessary, correct defects in compliance. Use of available resources (including corporate counsel, compliance officers, federal and state agency representatives, and professional journals) will help broaden the risk management professional's understanding of both the letter and the spirit of the law.

Space permits a brief review of a small fraction of the laws, regulations, and rules that affect health care delivery. The discussions in this chapter are meant to provide an introductory overview of selected laws and regulations only and should not be considered a comprehensive review of the entire scope of the law or the final word on compliance. As laws, regulations, and regulatory guidance are subject to amendment, revision, court interpretation, suspension, or repeal at any time, the reader is cautioned to refer always to the most current version of the law.

Note that for the sake of brevity, the word *law* may be used to refer collectively to statutory laws, regulations, interpretive guidelines, **conditions of participation**, and other stipulations, even though the matter being addressed may not actually be a law per se. In addition, references to a "patient" include any lawful surrogate decision makers, conservators, guardians, agents under a power of attorney for health care, advance health care directives, and similar parties.

PATIENT CARE

The following laws relate to various aspects of direct patient care. Readers are strongly advised to familiarize themselves with these and related laws that may be found in their own state's body of statutes and regulations.

> ## KEY CONCEPTS
>
> ■ Health care is one of the most highly regulated sectors of commerce.
>
> ■ Accidental or intentional violations or failure to comply with legislative mandates, governmental program requirements, accreditation standards, and enrollment in voluntary programs may result in civil and criminal actions, sanctions and fines, loss of provider status, loss of licensure, loss of accreditation, reduced reimbursement, diminished quality of outcomes, and loss of reputation.
>
> ■ The risk management professional must develop a process for disseminating information regarding changes to existing statutes, standards, or regulations or the imposition of new ones in a timely manner.
>
> ■ Identification, analysis, and compliance with applicable rules, regulations, statutes, and standards should be conducted on an enterprisewide risk management basis.

Emergency Medical Treatment and Labor Act

The **Emergency Medical Treatment and Labor Act** (**EMTALA**),[1] once referred to as **COBRA** or the **"antidumping law,"** is one of many pieces of legislation contained in the Consolidated Omnibus Budget Reconciliation Act of 1986. EMTALA is essentially a nondiscrimination statute, enacted in response to the then common practice among hospital emergency departments to refuse service to patients who lacked the ability to pay. These patients were often transferred or referred ("dumped") to already crowded public hospitals for care. At the time EMTALA was enacted, such dumping was legal in about half the states, often causing or contributing to patient injury or death. In response, California Representative Pete Stark drafted this law, cosponsored in the Senate by Kansas Senator Bob Dole.

EMTALA, compliance with which is a condition of a hospital's Medicare "supplier agreement," provides that people who come to a hospital seeking assessment or treatment for what they believe may be a medical condition must be provided all available diagnostic and therapeutic services necessary to (1) determine if an "emergency medical condition" exists; (2) clinically stabilize any medical condition that poses an immediate threat to the health of the patient, subject to the availability of resources; and (3) if the necessary clinical resources are not available, be transferred to a hospital that has them. Everything in this law serves to support these few basic requirements. To be certain that patients understand their rights, hospitals are required to post EMTALA information signs "conspicuously...in a place or places likely to be noticed by all individuals entering."[2]

Although patients are guaranteed access to screening and stabilizing services without first having to establish their ability to pay, hospitals and their treating physicians are fully entitled to bill patients, or their health plan, for any care provided. The law does not provide for free care, just unimpeded access to a rather narrowly defined level of care. Financial screening is permitted if it does not delay the medical examination or access to other services. Some state laws may be more restrictive as to when financial screening can take place, so you should consult your state's statutes for clarification. In response to "prior authorization" requirements of some managed care organizations, the **Centers for Medicare and Medicaid Services (CMS)** made it clear in a Special Advisory Bulletin that a hospital should not attempt to obtain treatment authorization from the patient's primary caregiver or health plan before providing a **medical screening examination (MSE)**, any needed "stabilizing" treatment, or arranging an EMTALA transfer to a higher level of care.[3]

Patients who require specialized treatment or resources that the hospital does not have must be transferred without delay to someplace that does. However, under no circumstances may such transfers be based on financial considerations alone. Patient consent, hospital notification, transfer certification, and other elements of the transfer process are defined in the regulations and interpretive guidelines.

Hospitals must keep a "central log" of everyone who comes to the facility and requests assessment and care.[4] Logs must also be maintained by departments, whether on or off the premises, that offer nonscheduled primary care access, such as labor and delivery units that provide walk-in labor checks, psychiatric departments, and urgent or primary care clinics, if they meet any one of the three criteria for a **dedicated emergency department (DED)**: (1) it is licensed as an emergency department, (2) it advertises itself as providing emergency care, or (3) one-third or more of its walk-in patients are seen for conditions that meet the threshold of an "emergency medical condition" as defined by the statute.

Emergency departments must also keep a roster of physician specialists and subspecialists who are available "on call" to provide consultation or care for EMTALA patients who need their special expertise.[5] Although round-the-clock on-call coverage for every service represented by the medical staff would be ideal, CMS recognizes that this is neither realistic nor required. If full-time on-call coverage is not possible, hospitals must make, and document, efforts to arrange for such coverage to the best of their ability—for example, through transfer agreements or contracts with specialty medical groups. Medical staff bylaws or rules and regulations must reflect the obligations of medical staff to participate in the on-call rotation and to provide time frames within which the physicians serving on call must respond to consultation requests. The Final Rule for FY 2009 Inpatient Prospective Payment System released on July 31, 2008 by CMS allows hospitals to meet their EMTALA on-call obligations through participation in a "community-call plan". It is thought that these plans, through the pooling of resources within a community, will ease the burden on hospitals to provide round-the-clock physician on-call coverage. So while the on-call mandate (with civil monetary penalties of up to $50,000 per violation, as well as loss or suspension of Medicare or Medicaid provider status[6]) remains unpopular among physicians it is anticipated that the potential for penalties on noncompliant physicians will be reduced with approval of these plans.

EMTALA also requires hospitals to make every reasonable effort to advise patients about the medical risks of leaving before completing their screening assessment or treatment. Efforts must be documented, and whenever possible, the patient should be asked to sign a form that confirms any decision to leave "against medical advice."

Risk Management Implications

Noncompliance with just about any element of EMTALA may result in investigation by the state licensing authority (SA), state quality improvement organization (**QIO**), CMS, the **Office of the Inspector General** (**OIG**), and when discrimination is alleged, the **Office of Civil Rights** (**OCR**). In addition to the prospect of steep civil monetary penalties, the financial consequences of forfeiting one's Medicare provider agreement should make a believer of everyone. Further adding to the cost of noncompliance is the often large legal expense incurred when responding to EMTALA investigations. Embedded in the law is a self-policing mandate imposed on hospitals, which requires them to report other hospitals (and in narrowly prescribed circumstances, physicians) that they suspect of having violated provisions of the law, either to their state licensing authority or directly to the CMS regional office. Failure to file such a required report can itself result in the assessment of fines of up to $50,000 per violation. These penalties also apply to individuals or organizations that retaliate against (1) a physician or other "qualified" individual who refused to authorize an unsafe or other improper transfer or (2) anyone who reported a suspected EMTALA violation to the SA or CMS.

Many hospitals continue to struggle with EMTALA compliance. The U.S. Supreme Court has ventured into this arena only once,[7] but the primary issue under review (a requirement found in some jurisdictions that a so-called improper motive was necessary to establish an EMTALA violation) was dismissed. Under provisions of the Public Health Security and Bioterrorism Preparedness and Response Act of 2002, and the Inpatient Prospective Payment Systems Final Rules for FY 2008 and 2009, the Department of Health and Human Services (HHS) may waive certain elements of EMTALA during emergency situations.

Hospitals and physicians must remember that this law is primarily process-oriented, not outcome-oriented. EMTALA is not a malpractice statute. This point has been restated in numerous court decisions. However, regulators do focus on whether the hospital has complied with the individual mandates of the law in a uniform, non-discriminatory manner. If a hospital focuses on doing what's right for its emergency patients clinically and upholds the administrative requirements of the law, compliance will be easy to achieve.

MEDICARE MODERNIZATION ACT

Section 1011 ("Federal Reimbursement of Emergency Health Services Furnished to Undocumented Aliens") of the Medicare Prescription Drug Improvement and Modernization Act of 2003, commonly known as the **Medicare Modernization Act** (**MMA**), established the government's first program to compensate hospitals for providing services under EMTALA.[8] The provisions require the development of new policies and processes for the business office and the registration staff to pursue these funds. A fund of $250 million was set aside for this purpose through 2008, two-thirds divided among all fifty states and the remaining third divided among the six states with the estimated largest number of undocumented aliens. Allotted funds are paid directly to eligible providers of EMTALA-related services. However, to be eligible for reimbursement, a provider must first exhaust efforts to obtain payment from any other sources, including the patient, state, county, and municipal alternative payment plans, low-income health care insurance programs, and emergency services funds.

Reimbursement may be obtained for services provided to (1) undocumented aliens; (2) aliens who have been paroled, that is, granted special permission by the secretary of the Department of Homeland Security to enter the United States for humanitarian or "public benefit" purposes; and (3) Mexican citizens who enter the United States under a restricted "laser visa." Eligible providers must first submit a "provider enrollment application" to the designated contractor retained by the CMS to administer the enrollment and payment process. Other forms are designed to submit requests for reimbursement to the contractor and help determine whether a patient meets the criteria that will allow the provider to receive payments from the fund.

Risk Management Implications

Although the prospect of "free" money is attractive, the devil is in the details. The section stresses the need for providers to identify undocumented aliens and other qualified individuals without giving the appearance of discrimination. This process must be undertaken by trained staff so as to avoid unintentionally discouraging the patient from being seen, which, if this should occur, would represent a violation of EMTALA. If considering participation, based on best "guesstimates," try to determine approximately how many individuals representing the identified groups have been seen recently for emergency services. If you see a sizable number and other funding is absolutely not available, consider enrolling in the program. If the numbers are relatively low or if state or regional funding already exists for reimbursing providers for uncompensated care, weigh the possibly limited financial benefits against the cost in time, energy, and labor in developing detailed policies and procedures and the staff training needed to implement this program. The choice is yours.

MEDICAL STAFF

The **Health Care Quality Improvement Act (HCQIA)**[9] went into effect on November 14, 1986. Congress enacted the law in response to a variety of areas of concern, including a nationwide upward trend in the number of medical malpractice claims, an apparent need to improve the overall quality of care provided through effective peer review, and the lack of any nationwide infrastructure within which to track the movement of inept physicians from state to state without discovery or disclosure of their track record of negligence or incompetence.

Health Care Quality Improvement Act of 1986: Peer Review

The HCQIA encourages hospitals, state licensing boards, and professional societies to identify and discipline physicians, dentists, and other health care providers who, after adequate, nondiscriminatory peer review, were found to have engaged in negligent or unprofessional conduct. In support of these objectives, Congress established a broad legal immunity from civil liability to physicians and others who actively engage in or contribute to the peer review process, provided that the review was performed to further high-quality health care, after a reasonable effort had been made to establish the facts of the matter, after required "notice" and "fair-hearing" opportunities have been provided, and in the reasonable belief that the action is supported by the facts. This element of the law was enacted in part in response to the "malicious" peer review memorialized in the landmark *Patrick* v. *Burget* decision.[10] The court found that efforts by Columbia Memorial Hospital's peer review committee to drive Dr. Patrick off of the medical staff constituted a violation of the Sherman Antitrust Act. The damages awarded by the jury trebled as a consequence.

Risk Management Implications

The peer review process also had its basis in other well-publicized court decisions from the 1970s and 1980s. Typical of these findings was that in the case of *Elam* v. *College Park Hospital,* in which the court found that "a hospital is accountable, under the doctrine of corporate negligence, for negligently screening the competency of its medical staff to insure the adequacy of care rendered to its patients. Furthermore the hospital itself had a direct and independent responsibility to its patients of insuring the quality of care provided."[11] The objective of peer review is to promote patient safety through the continual monitoring of physician performance. This obligation is generally vested in an organization's board of directors, which in turn delegates operational elements to the medical staff. To encourage physician involvement in this process, several states have enacted laws that provide protection from civil liability for individuals who participate in peer review activities. At the federal level, the HCQIA provides similar protections.

Sometimes confidentiality is provided through the application of a legal privilege to committee records. In others, protection is afforded by way of immunity from discovery arising out of civil litigation. Consequently, both hospital and medical staff should be reminded periodically that such protections are important in preserving the integrity of the peer review process and that these often fragile, narrowly defined safeguards may be relinquished if the protected information is accidentally (or deliberately) waived through improper release or when used for purposes for which it was not intended. Depending on the nature of the applicable state laws, consider having peer review participants sign a confidentiality statement. Doing so will help reinforce the confidentiality provisions of the process and provide some measure of liability protection.

National Practitioner Data Bank

The HCQIA also established the **National Practitioner Data Bank (NPDB)** for the reporting of adverse actions against physicians and other health care

NPDB

practitioners—commonly known as simply the Data Bank. The Data Bank acquires information from several sources in connection with claims of professional negligence that were resolved with either a judgment found against the practitioner or a settlement made on his or her behalf, regardless of the amount.

Hospitals must report to their state board of medical examiners or state licensing board any action taken that (1) adversely affects a practitioner's medical staff membership or clinical privileges for a period exceeding thirty days or (2) a physician's voluntary relinquishment of medical staff privileges (or an application for such privileges) submitted to avoid disciplinary action. Health care entities may also report actions taken against other health care practitioners (such as nurse midwives) but are not required to do so. The board of medical examiners or state licensing board must in turn report to the Data Bank any actions taken against a practitioner's license. Time frames within which reports must be made to the Data Bank are specifically defined by the law and must be adhered to.

Hospitals are required to query the Data Bank about all applicants for medical staff membership and at least once every two years thereafter in connection with the renewal of their clinical privileges. A hospital may voluntarily query the Data Bank at any time in support of its peer review activities. Although there is no provision for imposing civil monetary penalties against facilities that fail to query the Data Bank as required, hospitals that do not do so put the confidentiality of the Data Bank records of their medical staff at risk by providing an opportunity for access to them by plaintiffs' attorneys.

Physicians, dentists, and other practitioners may query the Data Bank about themselves at any time. However, the Data Bank is prohibited from disclosing information to a medical malpractice insurer, defense attorney, or member of the general public. Nonetheless, as noted previously, if a plaintiff's attorney can establish that the hospital failed to query the Data Bank as required by law, the attorney can gain access to otherwise confidential Data Bank information about the defendant physician.

The Healthcare Integrity and Protection Data Bank

The **Healthcare Integrity and Protection Data Bank** (**HIPDB**) was established by the Health Insurance Portability and Accountability Act of 1996 (**HIPAA**) as a clearinghouse for the reporting and disclosure of certain final "adverse actions" taken against health care practitioners, suppliers, and other providers. To avoid duplication of effort for entities that must report to or query both the HIPDB and NPDB, the Integrated Querying and Reporting System (IQRS) was established to allow simultaneous reporting to and querying of both systems.

Risk Management Implications

Complying with the reporting and Data Bank inquiry elements of this law is essential. The immunity provisions of this law support peer review by providing desirable protection for participants in the process. The confidentiality provisions of the law must also be observed closely, as civil monetary penalties of up to $11,000 may be levied for improper disclosure of confidential information obtained from the Data Bank. Penalties of up to $11,000 may also be imposed for the failure to report to the Data Bank any judgments and settlement dollars paid on behalf of a practitioner.

The Bureau of Health Professions of the Health Resources Service Administration (HRSA) believes that hospitals significantly underreport to the Data Bank. Unfortunately, there is probably a strong basis for such suspicions. Consequently, the HRSA has advocated for increasing penalties for violators. At the state level, for example, California has significantly increased the penalties levied against hospitals for not filing required reports. Make every effort to ensure that your organization remains compliant with all HCQIA requirements.

Patient Self-Determination Act of 1990

The **Patient Self-Determination Act (PSDA)** was enacted as part of the Omnibus Budget Reconciliation Act of 1990. Even though the PSDA was effective December 1, 1991, final regulations were not released until July 27, 1995.[12] The tragic case of accident victim Nancy Cruzan and the exhaustive efforts of her parents to gain the right to make end-of-life decisions on her behalf spurred Congress to address these issues in this landmark statute. More recently, the controversy surrounding the decision by Terri Schiavo's husband to discontinue her nutrition and hydration once again riveted the public's attention on this sensitive and highly personal topic. The PSDA establishes the right of competent patients to make binding, legally enforceable decisions about their health care preferences that are to be followed should they later become unable to express them. The law imposes compliance on a broad range of providers: hospitals, skilled nursing facilities (**SNF**s), home health care or personal care services, hospice programs, and health maintenance organizations (HMOs). Freestanding outpatient clinics and private physicians' offices are not covered by the law. Obligated providers must furnish their patients, clients, or insurance plan enrollees with written information about their right to prepare an advance directive and also, where required, inquire whether the patient has completed one.

The law defines an advance directive as a lawful written instruction, such as a living will, power of attorney for health care, or advance health care directive that describes an individual's preferences for health care should that individual become unable to express them later on. By requiring health care providers to furnish information about "self-determination" to their patients, it was hoped that more people would be encouraged to consider their options in this regard.

Risk Management Implications

Develop, implement, and monitor compliance with policies and procedures that address each element of the law. It's a good idea to retain copies of advisory materials distributed to patients for later reference, if necessary to help establish compliance. Familiarize yourself with the specifics of your own state's laws, if any, relating to advance directives. Responding to critical clinical and end-of-life treatment issues for patients who have left neither directions nor evidence of treatment preferences can be a highly charged and very difficult emotional and legal process for everyone involved. Although advance directives are a good idea and their use should be encouraged, patients are not required to complete them, nor should access to care be withheld because they have not done so.

Patients' Rights

This Medicare **condition of participation** (**CoP**) for hospitals was proposed as a rule in 1997 and enacted in 1999.[13] It establishes six standards relating to patients' rights issues that must be complied with by acute care hospitals, psychiatric treatment units within acute care hospitals, psychiatric hospitals, and skilled nursing facilities.

Notice of Rights Hospitals must inform each patient or, when applicable, the patient's representative, of that patient's rights "in advance of furnishing or discontinuing patient care whenever possible." As CMS has not specified precisely how to accomplish this, a compliant policy should reflect at a minimum how, when, and where to provide patients with this information. Hospitals are also directed to establish a formal process for investigating and resolving patient grievances. The law delegates to the hospital's governing body the responsibility of overseeing this process, although the responsibility may be redelegated to an individual or to a committee established for this purpose. Upon completion of grievance review, patients must be provided with a written notice of its findings, including (1) the name of the hospital contact person, (2) the steps taken to investigate the complaint, (3) the actual results or findings, and (4) the date of completion. CMS also expects that issues of consequence that arise during the investigation be referred to the applicable quality improvement, utilization, or peer review groups. CMS has also not defined the term *grievance*, nor has it made a distinction between a "grievance" and a "complaint" (if in fact one exists). Thus each facility must develop a reasonable means of compliance of its own.

Exercise of Rights Patients must be advised of their rights to (1) participate in developing and implementing their plan of care, (2) make informed decisions regarding their course of treatment, (3) be continually informed of the status of their health by their providers, and (4) formulate advance directives and have them complied with.

Privacy and Safety Patients are entitled to personal privacy and to receive care in a safe environment without the threat of harm, abuse, or harassment.

Confidentiality of Patient Records This standard reiterates patients' rights reflected within both the federal HIPAA statutes and state law. These requirements were developed in response to concerns that patient confidentiality protections were steadily eroding as a result of the increasing volume of personal health care information (PHI) available electronically to a broad range of individuals and organizations allowed access to it. The HIPAA privacy rule was subsequently enacted to further strengthen these confidentiality provisions and should be referred to for compliance guidance. This CoP also entitles patients to have access to their medical records in a reasonable period of time. As there might be some restrictions imposed on such access, the records should be reviewed carefully, before they are released, by qualified health information management staff.

Restraints in Acute Medical and Surgical Care This is the first of two standards relating to the use of restraints. This standard defines what constitutes a restraint and the conditions under which its use is permitted. The standard generally, but not exclusively, applies to the acute care and surgical settings. Hospitals are required to provide ongoing staff education regarding restraint use. Don't forget to keep the attendance sheets in case you are ever asked to show evidence of compliance with the training requirements.

Seclusion and Restraint for Behavior Management This second restraint standard was enacted in response to a series of articles published in 1998 in the Connecticut's *Hartford Courant* about injuries and deaths occurring in psychiatric care settings and resulting from apparent misuse and sometimes abuse of restraints and seclusion. Requirements relating to issuing and monitoring restraint orders are specified, including requiring a "licensed independent practitioner" to see the patient in person and evaluate the need for continued restraint or seclusion within one hour after initiating its use. Risk management professionals are advised to see the one-hour issue as only one element of the standard and remember to comply with the remainder. Finally, patient deaths occurring in conjunction with the use of restraints or seclusion must be reported to CMS prior to the close of business on the business day following the day of the patient's death.

Risk Management Implications

To be confident that everyone is aware of and compliant with the rules, the principles of this CoP should be reinforced periodically with the entire staff. Federal and state-mandated patients' rights must be posted conspicuously in specified public areas or made available to patients as otherwise required. As there are often many different (and sometimes redundant) rights prescribed by law, be sure to address them all. For the sake of convenience, consider developing a consolidated list of patients' rights—each right with its corresponding citation—in a single posting. Check with legal counsel and the state licensing authority to see if this is permissible (it generally is). Implement a policy that addresses posting and other means of notifying patients of their rights.

Medicare Conditions of Participation

The three distinct sets of CoPs found within these Medicare regulations apply to home health agencies (42 CFR 484), comprehensive outpatient rehabilitation facilities (CORFs, 42 CFR 485), and hospitals (42 CFR 482). These regulations are precisely what they are labeled as: conditions that must be met by service "suppliers" to bill for services to Medicare enrollees. Although space precludes an in-depth review of all of the CoPs, two have been selected from those covering acute care hospitals for purposes of illustration.

Infection Control This CoP (42 CFR 482.42) establishes a mandate for hospital infection control programs, specific requirements of which include (1) the designation of an infection control officer and development of relevant policies that address the identification and control of infections and communicable diseases, (2) the development and maintenance of a log system to track such conditions, and (3) the imposition of responsibility and accountability onto the hospital CEO, the medical staff, and director of nursing services for ensuring that hospitalwide quality improvement and training programs are implemented to address issues identified by the infection control officer and implementing corrective action plans in problem areas.

Nursing Services This one (42 CFR 482.23) defines the operational elements of a nursing service. Among the issues covered are requirements governing staffing and staff supervision, the development and implementation of nursing care plans, staff competency assessment, medication administration, and reporting blood transfusion reactions, adverse drug reactions, and medication errors.

It is strongly recommended that you familiarize yourself with the requirements of each of the other hospital CoPs; providing emergency services at nonparticipating hospitals (482.2), compliance (482.11), obligations of the governing body (482.12), quality assessment and performance improvement (482.21), medical staff (482.22), medical records (482.24), pharmacy services (482.25), radiology (482.26), laboratory services (482.27), food and dietetic services (482.28), utilization review (482.30), physical environment (482.41), discharge planning (482.43), organ, tissue, and eye procurement (482.45), surgical services (482.51), anesthesia services (482.52), nuclear medicine (482.53), outpatient services (482.54), emergency services (482.55), rehabilitation services (482.56), respiratory care (482.57), "swing-bed" requirements for long-term care providers (482.66), and, for psychiatric hospitals alone, special conditions (482.60), medical records (482.61), and staff requirements (482.62).

Many other conditions of participation and **conditions for coverage** (CfCs) exist for a broad range of entities and programs. Space precludes a detailed analysis or even a listing of all of them. However, one list that risk management professionals should be certain to review is found at 42 CFR 410—Supplementary Medical Insurance Benefits. A sampling of some of its requirements are included in the following abbreviated list. Look for sections that might apply to you, and become familiar with their requirements.

Advance Directives (42 CFR 489.102)

Ambulatory Surgery Services (42 CFR 416.40–49)

Comprehensive Outpatient Rehabilitation Facilities (CORFs) (42 CFR 485.50–74)

Critical Access Hospitals (42 CFR 485.601–645)

Diabetes Self-Management Training (42 CFR 410.10–146)

Durable Medical Equipment (42 CFR 410.38)

End-Stage Renal Disease Services (42 CFR 405.2100–2184)

Home Health Services (42 CFR 484.10–55)

Hospice Care (42 CFR 418.50–100)

Immunization Standards for Hospitals, Long-Term Care Facilities, and Home Health Agencies (42 CFR 482.22, 483.40, and 484.18)

Intermediate Care Facilities for the Mentally Retarded (42 CFR 483.400–480)

Long-Term Care Facilities (42 CFR 483.1–75)

Managed Care (42 CFR 417.400–418)

Medical Nutrition Therapy (42 CFR 410.130–134)

Medicare Advantage (42 CFR 422.100–132 and 152–158)

Organ Procurement and Transplantation (42 CFR 405)

Outpatient Physical Therapy (42 CFR 485.701–729, 486.150–163)

Programs for All-Inclusive Care for the Elderly (42 CFR 460.60–140)

Psychiatric Hospitals and Units (42 CFR 482.60–62, 42 CFR 412.20–30)

Rehabilitation Hospitals and Units (42 CFR 482.56)

Religious Nonmedical Health Care Institutions (42 CFR 403.730–746)

Rural Health Clinics and Federally Qualified Health Centers (42 CFR 491.1–11)

Telemedicine 42 CFR 410.78

Risk Management Implications

Although nothing can substitute for a complete review of each CoP and CfC, the size of such an undertaking is likely more than most risk management professionals can possibly accommodate. However, it is of genuine benefit to at least familiarize yourself with their key measures. Remember, ignorance of the law remains no defense for noncompliance. The CMS and OIG have left the development of the means of meeting these requirements mostly up to program participants, so home health agencies, **CORF**s, long-term care, hospitals, and other providers have much leeway to develop compliance measures that will work best for them. Due to the unclear and occasionally ambiguous nature of some of the CoP and CfC standards, advice from legal counsel regarding interpretation and application is strongly suggested. Full compliance with all applicable CoPs and CfCs is essential, as failure to do so could result in termination of the facility's Medicare provider agreement.

Safe Medical Devices Act of 1990

The objective of the federal Food and Drug Administration (FDA) is to protect the public health by regulating commerce that involves food, drugs, medical devices, and the like. As part of the **Safe Medical Devices Act** of 1990 (**SMDA**), Medical Device Amendments of 1992,[14] the FDA is authorized to gather information regarding the safety of medical devices, including adverse incidents attributed to their use. In 1984, under authority granted by the federal Food, Drug and Cosmetic Act of 1938 and the 1976 Medical Device Amendments, the FDA issued reporting regulations for medical device manufacturers. Subsequently, the agency determined that the number of device-related incidents that resulted in injury or death was underreported, especially incidents that occurred in hospitals. In response, the FDA sought congressional support for a more stringent set of reporting requirements. As a result of the enactment of the SMDA, final device-tracking regulations went into effect on August 16, 1993, with final reporting regulations following in 1996. An excellent overview of the reporting requirements ("Reporting Problems with Medical Devices") is available through the Office of Surveillance and Biometrics of the FDA's Center for Devices and Radiological Health (**CDRH**) and can be found on its Web site (http://www.fda.gov/cdrh). This law applies to hospitals, ambulatory surgical facilities, nursing homes, home health care agencies, ambulance providers, rescue squads, rehabilitation facilities, psychiatric facilities, and all outpatient diagnostic and treatment facilities that are not physicians' offices. Physicians, chiropractors, optometrists, nurse practitioners, employee health clinics, dental offices, and freestanding care units are exempt from these reporting requirements.

To preserve any confidentiality or immunity protections that may be afforded by state law, investigations that involve potential SMDA reportable events should occur under the auspices of a protected peer review, quality improvement, or other related program. The team of investigators may be brought together on an ad hoc basis to conduct the investigation; prepare (or direct the preparation of) a report to the FDA, if one is warranted; and submit their findings to their board or other responsible body through their primary committee.

Reporting Using the MedWatch form, device users must notify manufacturers (or the FDA if the manufacturer's identity is not known) within ten days of becoming aware of an event involving a serious patient injury or death (the FDA-sponsored MedWatch form is shown in Exhibit 10.1). The FDA must also be notified in the same time frame in cases where a death is involved. A facility "becomes aware" when clinical personnel employed by or affiliated with a user facility learn that a potentially reportable event has occurred. In addition, facilities are required to report to the FDA on January 1 of each year a summary of MDR reports made during the previous year. Report forms, instructions, and event code books are available from the FDA. Online submissions also are acceptable with prior approval from the agency. Although facilities are obligated to maintain copies of these reports for a minimum of two years, risk management professionals are advised to keep them for at least five years (or longer) in recognition

EXHIBIT 10.1. *MedWatch Form for Reporting Serious Patient Injury or Death*

U.S. Department of Health and Human Services

Form Approved: OMB No. 0910-0291, Expires: 03/31/05
See OMB statement on reverse.

MEDWATCH

For VOLUNTARY reporting of
adverse events and product problems

The FDA Safety Information and
Adverse Event Reporting Program

Page ____ of ____

FDA USE ONLY

Triage unit
sequence #

PLEASE TYPE OR USE BLACK INK

A. PATIENT INFORMATION

1. Patient Identifier	2. Age at Time of Event:	3. Sex	4. Weight
	or _____	☐ Female	_____ lbs
	Date of Birth:	☐ Male	or
In confidence			_____ kgs

B. ADVERSE EVENT OR PRODUCT PROBLEM

1. ☐ Adverse Event   and/or   ☐ Product Problem *(e.g., defects/malfunctions)*

2. Outcomes Attributed to Adverse Event
(Check all that apply)
☐ Death: _____ *(mo/day/yr)*
☐ Life-threatening
☐ Hospitalization - initial or prolonged
☐ Disability
☐ Congenital Anomaly
☐ Required Intervention to Prevent Permanent Impairment/Damage
☐ Other: _____

3. Date of Event *(mo/day/year)*

4. Date of This Report *(mo/day/year)*

5. Describe Event or Problem

6. Relevant Tests/Laboratory Data, Including Dates

7. Other Relevant History, Including Preexisting Medical Conditions *(e.g., allergies, race, pregnancy, smoking and alcohol use, hepatic/renal dysfunction, etc.)*

C. SUSPECT MEDICATION(S)

1. Name *(Give labeled strength & mfr/labeler, if known)*
#1
#2

2. Dose, Frequency & Route Used	3. Therapy Dates *(If unknown, give duration) from/to (or best estimate)*
#1	#1
#2	#2

4. Diagnosis for Use *(Indication)*
#1
#2

5. Event Abated After Use Stopped or Dose Reduced?
#1 ☐ Yes ☐ No ☐ Doesn't Apply
#2 ☐ Yes ☐ No ☐ Doesn't Apply

6. Lot # *(if known)*	7. Exp. Date *(if known)*
#1	#1
#2	#2

8. Event Reappeared After Reintroduction?
#1 ☐ Yes ☐ No ☐ Doesn't Apply
#2 ☐ Yes ☐ No ☐ Doesn't Apply

9. NDC# *(For product problems only)*
____ - ____ - ____

10. Concomitant Medical Products and Therapy Dates *(Exclude treatment of event)*

D. SUSPECT MEDICAL DEVICE

1. Brand Name

2. Type of Device

3. Manufacturer Name, City and State

4. Model #	Lot #	5. Operator of Device
Catalog #	Expiration Date *(mo/day/yr)*	☐ Health Professional
Serial #	Other #	☐ Lay User/Patient
		☐ Other:

6. If Implanted, Give Date *(mo/day/yr)*	7. If Explanted, Give Date *(mo/day/yr)*

8. Is this a Single-use Device that was Reprocessed and Reused on a Patient?
☐ Yes   ☐ No

9. If Yes to Item No. 8, Enter Name and Address of Reprocessor

10. Device Available for Evaluation? *(Do not send to FDA)*
☐ Yes   ☐ No   ☐ Returned to Manufacturer on: _____ *(mo/day/yr)*

11. Concomitant Medical Products and Therapy Dates *(Exclude treatment of event)*

E. REPORTER *(See confidentiality section on back)*

1. Name and Address	Phone #

2. Health Professional?	3. Occupation	4. Also Reported to:
☐ Yes ☐ No		☐ Manufacturer
5. If you do NOT want your identity disclosed to the manufacturer, place an "X" in this box: ☐		☐ User Facility
		☐ Distributor/Importer

Mail to: **MEDWATCH**   -or-   FAX to:
5600 Fishers Lane   1-800-FDA-0178
Rockville, MD 20852-9787

FORM FDA 3500 (12/03)   Submission of a report does not constitute an admission that medical personnel or the product caused or contributed to the event.

of statute of limitations and related liability and compliance provisions. Consult legal counsel, your insurer, and the state hospital association for further guidance. Upon learning of a "reportable" incident that involves the use of their product or device, manufacturers are also required to submit an MDR to the FDA. At the FDA's request, a "five-day" report must be submitted by a manufacturer when the FDA believes that immediate intervention is necessary to prevent risk of harm to the public health.

Medical Device Tracking Rules The SMDA was amended in 1993 to require device manufacturers to track products that are (1) permanently implantable, (2) life-sustaining or life-supporting and intended to be used outside of device user facilities, or (3) otherwise designated by the FDA. A complete list of these devices can be found in 42 CFR 821.20. These tracking requirements were later expanded by the FDA Modernization Act of 1997, with new rules adopted in 2002.

As a requirement of the device tracking protocol, the final distributor (such as the hospital) is required to collect the personal identifying information of each patient who receives a tracked device and to submit this information to the manufacturer. New rules that went into effect in May 2002 revised the scope of the regulation and added certain patient confidentiality requirements. Patients who fall under the new rules may refuse to release identifying information such as Social Security number, name, address, and telephone number to manufacturers. When faced with such a refusal, the provider should counsel the patients about the risk they face of not being contacted by the manufacturer if problems with the device are identified, or a recall is initiated, later on. This discussion, as usual, should be documented in the patient's record.

Reusable Single-Use Devices On August 14, 2000, the FDA issued "Guidance on Enforcement Priorities for Single-Use Devices Reprocessed by Third Parties and Hospitals."[15] This Guidance was published in response to earlier FDA efforts to map out a strategy for addressing the reprocessing of single-use devices (**SUDs**), items characterized by their manufacturers as being intended for single use only. The new requirements were established to be phased in over time and include the following:

- *Registering and listing the devices.* Companies that reprocess SUDs must register with the FDA and submit a list of the devices they reprocess.

- *Medical device reporting and tracking requirements.* Hospitals and independent reprocessors are instructed to adhere to the same device tracking requirements as the manufacturers.

- *Device corrections and removals.* The FDA requires that a report be submitted about specified types of device repairs, modifications, or recalls, if the purpose of the "correction" or "removal" was to reduce a health risk posed by the device or to correct violations of the act.

- *Quality system regulations.* These regulations govern oversight of the methods and controls used in the design, manufacture, packaging, labeling, storage, installation, and servicing of devices. These requirements, known collectively as good manufacturing practices (**GMPs**), must be followed closely.

■ *Labeling.* These requirements mandate that device packages bear the name of the product, the manufacturer, the place of manufacture, and directions for use.

■ *Premarket requirements.* The FDA has specified three classes of SUDs. Depending on the classification of the device, a premarket notification is required to be submitted to the FDA to allow it to assess whether the device is safe and effective as a legally marketed "predicate device," that is, the original device from which the SUD is derived or patterned. Upon completion of the assessment, marketing clearance will be either approved or rejected.

Risk Management Implications

Identifying factors that directly or indirectly contribute to patient endangerment is a fundamental objective of health care risk management. Complying with the reporting requirements of this law compels providers to actively participate in an important oversight process. The **Manufacturers and User Facility Device Experience** (**MAUDE**) database (http://www.fda.gov/cdrh/maude.html) is an excellent source of information relating to the FDA's adverse event tracking efforts. From a Medicare compliance standpoint, each facility must carefully consider how to develop a reasonable cost process when using SUDs in combination with new devices. The compliance officer should be consulted to discuss how such charges can be properly reflected in cost reports.

Mammography Quality Standards Act of 1992

The **Mammography Quality Standards Act** of 1992 (**MQSA**)[16] was later amended by Congress with the Mammography Quality Standards Reauthorization Acts of 1998 and 2004 (**MQSRA**).[17] Enacted in response to the public's increasing awareness and concern about breast cancer screening and treatment, the law focuses primarily on issues related to improving the diagnostic and technical standards of mammography, although the proper reporting of study results to referring practitioners and their patients also is addressed. More than ten thousand facilities in the United States and its territories are certified under the act to provide mammography services. If an organization is certified or intends to become certified, a close review of this complex law is necessary.

The act applies to facilities, practitioners, and specified personnel involved in providing breast cancer screening, diagnosis, and treatment and covers a variety of areas, including the following:

■ Ensuring the competency and qualifications of interpreting physicians, medical physicists, and radiological technicians

■ Maintaining facility accreditation in connection with annual facility compliance inspections performed by the FDA or any one of five FDA-approved accrediting bodies[18]

- Adhering to specified equipment testing and maintenance protocols

- Developing and implementing quality assurance and quality control programs

- Reporting mammogram results to the referring health care provider and to the patient in a prescribed manner

Risk Management Implications

The FDA has published an MQSA guidance document that is an excellent resource for facilities and practitioners in understanding the many facets of this complex law.[19] As is the case with virtually every law, the risk management professional is not expected to be an expert on each of its constituent elements but rather to understand its basic tenets, including the penalties or other risks of not complying. If the facility falls within the application of this law, an in-depth review of all required elements of compliance should be carried out, including ongoing review to identify additions or other changes.

The Newborns' and Mothers' Health Protection Act of 1996

In the face of the increasing incidence of "drive-through" short-stay deliveries, Congress enacted the Newborns' and Mothers' Health Protection Act of 1996.[20] The law provides protections for mothers and their newborns from restrictions that may be imposed by managed care organizations (**MCO**s) and health plans on hospital lengths of stay permitted following childbirth.

The law applies to group health plans, other health insurance issuers in the group and individual markets, obstetricians, and facilities that provide obstetrical services. In a nutshell, health plans and health insurance issuers may not restrict covered hospital benefits for a mother and her newborn to less than forty-eight hours following a vaginal delivery or ninety-six hours following a cesarean section. Although discharging a patient within a shorter period of time provided for by this law is permitted only with the mutual agreement of the attending provider and mother, a group health plan or other health insurance issuer is not required to extend coverage for these time periods if the attending provider, after speaking with the patient, determines that it is safe to discharge either the mother or the infant earlier.

Health plans and other insurers are prohibited from coercing or otherwise pressuring a mother, or her health care provider, to agree to an early discharge. In addition, providers are not required to obtain prior authorization for these prescribed lengths of stay. State laws that address this issue may supersede this federal statute if they meet one or more of the following requirements:

- Minimum allowable lengths of stay meet or exceed the forty-eight- or ninety-six-hour requirements.

- Coverage provided by health plans and insurers complies with guidelines established by the American College of Obstetricians and Gynecologists, the American Academy of Pediatrics, or any other established professional medical association.

■ Although decisions regarding the postpartum length of stay are left exclusively up to the provider in consultation with the mother, insurance coverage may not be extended for such care based on the assessment of need by the attending provider.

Risk Management Implications

Violation of these requirements might result in the suspension or termination of a health plan or health insurer's license. Physicians, nurse midwives, or other licensed providers who fail to comply with this law run the risk of being accused of unprofessional conduct, fraud, or professional negligence. Hospitals, insurance companies, and HMOs are not considered "providers" under this act.

Organ Transplantation

Before the enactment of the **National Organ Transplant Act** of 1984 (**NOTA**), the system for allocating and distributing organs for transplant in the United States was fragmented. With the enactment of NOTA, Congress established a set of unified standards to be followed by organ procurement organizations (**OPO**s) throughout the country. To implement the act, the **Organ Procurement Transplant Network (OPTN)** was established and is currently operated under contract with the Division of Transplantation of the Health Resources and Services Administration (HRSA) by the **United Network for Organ Sharing (UNOS)**.[21] In 1997, the National Organ and Tissue Donation Initiative was also launched in support of this general program. CMS later enacted regulations that require hospitals to work collaboratively with local OPOs to improve access to potential donors. Amendments to the Final Rule relating to the management and oversight of the OPTN were released by the HHS on October 20, 1999.[22] These amendments were the result of a study performed by the National Academy of Science's Institute of Medicine (IOM). The amendments established greater accountability of the OPTN to develop and implement improved criteria for organ allocation, mandated the establishment of an advisory committee on organ transplantation, revised and clarified oversight responsibility for program enforcement, developed specific performance criteria, and made changes with respect to the composition of the OPTN board of directors.

This law (42 CFR 482.45), a Medicare CoP, applies to hospitals, transplant centers, and organ procurement organizations. Member hospitals of the OPTN and eye and tissue banks are required to do the following:

■ Implement a working agreement with the OPO by which it will notify them of individuals either whose deaths are imminent or who have died. Responsibility for determining whether a patient is a suitable donor candidate rests with the OPO, not the hospital.

■ Develop a similar agreement with at least one tissue bank and one eye bank.

■ Collaborate with the OPO to inform families of potential donors of their options with respect to organ donation. Although this activity is mandated to hospitals by law, it should always be carried out in a manner that is sensitive to the circumstances and to the cultural or religious beliefs of the family.

■ Work with the OPO to educate the hospital staff on identifying and reporting potential donors, tissue testing, and so on.

Risk Management Implications

As noted, these regulations are conditions of participation in Medicare. Noncompliance might result not only in loss of the facility's Medicare or Medicaid provider agreement but in loss of participation in the OPTN as well.

The Clinical Laboratory Improvement Amendments of 1988

Congress enacted the **Clinical Laboratory Improvement Amendments (CLIA)** to establish quality standards for clinical laboratories.[23] Among the driving concerns behind the law were increasing reports of misread Pap smears, the absence of workload limits for technologists, and an apparent proliferation of unregulated laboratories. As the act's regulations undergo continual revision and updating, risk management professionals are advised to keep abreast of changes by referring to the Centers for Disease Control and Prevention's Division of Laboratory Systems Web site (http://www.phppo.cdc.gov/dls/default.asp). This law established three categories of covered tests: waived complexity, moderate complexity, and high complexity. In effect, the more complicated the test, the more stringent the CLIA requirements. CLIA specifies quality standards for proficiency testing (PT), patient test management, quality control, personnel qualifications, and quality assurance for laboratories that perform moderate- or high-complexity tests. Recently enacted regulations require laboratories that perform gynecological cytology testing to ensure that each cytotechnologist or pathologist who participates in such screening must enroll annually in a CMS-approved cytology PT program. The CMS, the Centers for Disease Control and Prevention (CDC), and the FDA have responsibility for overseeing compliance with different elements of CLIA. To enroll in the CLIA program, laboratories must register by completing an application, paying the required fees, undergoing a survey, and, if applicable, completing the certification.

Risk Management Implications

Data released by the CMS indicates that quality deficiencies decreased approximately 40 percent from their first laboratory survey to their second and even further on subsequent surveys.[24] Given risk management's efforts at promoting patient safety, the apparent successes of the CLIA program dovetails perfectly with this objective.

Human Research Subjects

Protection of Human Subjects regulations (45 CFR 46 et seq.) set the groundwork for human subject protections by defining the interrelationship between researchers, the institution's research oversight committee, the sponsoring organization, and the research subject.

Institutional Review Board The institutional review board (**IRB**) is required to review proposed research at formal meetings of the board where the majority of members are present. Approval of research may occur only with the authorization of the majority of the IRB members present. Each IRB must have at least five members, one of whom must be an individual "whose primary concerns are in nonscientific areas" and another "who is not otherwise affiliated with the institution and who is not part of the immediate family of a person who is affiliated with the institution." The characteristics of the membership must reflect expertise, experience, and diversity. Outside experts may be called on by the IRB for consultation and advice, but they have no vote in the proceedings.

Sponsoring Institution Research approved by the IRB may be subject to further review and approval—or disapproval—by the "officials of the institution." Institutions may not, on their own, approve research; that authority rests exclusively with the IRB.

Informed Consent No investigator may engage the participation of an individual in research without having obtained, in advance, the person's informed consent. The basic elements of such consent include (1) a statement that the study involves research and an explanation of the purpose and anticipated duration of the study; (2) a description of the study, specifically identifying those elements that are experimental; (3) a description of reasonably foreseeable risks or discomforts; (4) an explanation of the anticipated benefits to the subject or others that might reasonably be expected from the research; (5) disclosure of alternative procedures or courses of treatment, if any, that may be available; (6) a statement that reflects the confidentiality provisions of the research records; (7) for research involving more than minimal risk, an explanation of whether compensation or medical treatment may be provided in the presence of injury occurs; (8) identification of whom to contact if questions about the study or the subject's rights later arise; and (9) a statement that participation is voluntary and that refusal to participate will not result in penalties or loss of benefits to which the subject is otherwise entitled. Other disclosures are also required under circumstances that are defined in the regulation. These additional disclosure requirements should be reviewed to ensure that they are applied as circumstances dictate. Requirements that govern the content and timing of the informed consent disclosure may, under narrowly defined circumstances, be suspended in whole or in part.

Consent Documentation Consent must be documented in writing and signed by the subject or the subject's legally authorized representative, and a copy of the form must be given to the person who signed it. Subjects or their representatives must be given adequate opportunity to read the form before it is signed. Under narrowly defined circumstances that relate to either a potential breach of confidentiality or the absence of any notable risk to the subject, the requirement for obtaining a signed consent form may be waived.

The **Office for Human Research Protections (OHRP)** of HHS has primary oversight responsibility for human subject research-related programs and activities. The OHRP's Division of Assurances and Quality Improvement provides liaison, guidance, and regulatory interpretation to researchers, the federal government, and the public. The division operates and maintains a registration system for IRBs and performs a variety of related oversight and education services. The OHRP's Division of

Policy Planning and Special Projects develops and publishes guidance regarding regulatory and ethical issues for biomedical and behavioral research, provides staff support to both the National Human Research Protections Advisory Committee and the Human Subjects Research Subcommittee, and coordinates responses to requests for information from both inside and outside the government.

Additional regulations (21 CFR 50, 56, 312, and 812) address issues relating primarily to research performed under the guidance of the FDA. Among the many issues addressed are those relating to obtaining a research subject's informed consent, mandatory reporting of known or suspected procedural violations, the investigational use of new drugs and devices, and a delineation of penalties that may be imposed for failing to comply with the law, including disqualification of the IRB from further FDA-approved research activities and exposure of both the research investigator and the research institution to civil liability.

Risk Management Implications

Because liability issues related to human subject research activities are wide-ranging and complex, the prudent risk management professional must remain on the lookout for changes in regulations and developments in case law. Risk management professionals of facilities that carry out research protocols must become familiar with these regulations, as they may be asked to serve on or consult with IRBs. Members of IRBs should also develop an in-depth understanding of human subject informed consent and research-related recordkeeping requirements. Risk and liability issues commonly associated with human subject research include research performed without proper IRB review and approval, inadequate IRB review of proposed research, inadequate continuing review, conflicts of interest among members of the IRB panel, and general noncompliance with administrative procedures. (See Chapter 8 on ethics in patient care for more information on clinical research.)

Medicare Regulations for Long-Term Care Facilities

Since the original legislation and regulations[25] were enacted, long-term care has received increasing attention from federal and state authorities. In 1998, CMS's Office of the Inspector General (OIG) published "Quality of Care in Nursing Homes: An Overview,"[26] which reflected that although the overall number of deficiencies found during nursing facility surveys was decreasing, the number of "quality of care" and other serious deficiencies was increasing. Long-term care facilities, along with the rest of the health care industry, came under increasing surveillance by the OIG with respect to allegations of Medicare billing irregularities. The OIG's "Compliance Program Guidance for Nursing Facilities" delineates expectations with respect to efforts by facilities to curb fraud and abuse.[27] The CMS has called upon states to crack down on facilities that are found to have repeatedly violated health and safety requirements. The CMS Web site (http://www.cms.hhs.gov) provides consumers with information regarding residents' health status (including the prevalence of bedsores, incontinence, and other conditions) at every Medicare- or Medicaid-certified nursing facility.

In brief, nursing facilities have been ordered as a condition of maintaining their Medicare provider agreements to (1) develop initiatives to improve the overall level of care provided (including special focus on reducing the use of restraints whenever possible), (2) reduce the incidence of bedsores and malnutrition, and (3) ensure that all rights entitled to by patients are recognized and supported in practice and not just relegated to a sign posted in the front office. Among the rights afforded to patients are the following:

- Information about their physical condition, medical benefits, and the costs of treatment

- Access to a physician and the identity, specialty, and means of contacting that individual

- Obtaining copies of their medical records

- Active participation in their own treatment decisions, including refusal of recommended treatment and the right to prepare advance directives

- Freedom from physical restraints and psychoactive drugs that are not required as part of the medical plan of care

- The ability to file formal complaints about suspected infractions of any of these rights

The rules also impose staffing requirements on facilities, such as nursing coverage, physician examinations, and follow-up visits. Facilities are required to provide formal training and certification of nursing assistants. To extend relief to understaffed facilities, regulations were enacted in 2003 that permit providers to employ "feeding assistants" to help patients with eating and drinking. In response to a series of tragic nursing home fires in 2003, CMS has ordered that nursing homes that do not have sprinkler systems or hard-wired smoke detectors must install battery-operated smoke detectors in all patient rooms and public areas. Facilities are also directed to establish a quality assurance committee that meets at least quarterly.

Implementing a comprehensive compliance program that addresses identification and prevention of fraud should be a key priority.

Risk Management Implications

Recent enforcement actions have made headlines across the country. Enforcement regulations enacted in 1995 empower survey agencies (either state agencies or the CMS) to impose a wide range of sanctions on noncompliant providers, including civil monetary penalties or fines of up to $10,000 per day, denial of payment for new admissions, and termination from the Medicare program. Sanctions imposed by the regulators depend on how the agency characterizes the level and pervasiveness of harm. As not all survey actions are subject to appeal, it is important for providers of long-term care services and their risk management professionals to (1) understand the regulations, (2) participate actively in the survey process, and (3) maintain an ongoing dialogue with reviewers.

Above all, providers must be prepared. State inspectors, employing up-to-date inspection protocols, have been told by the CMS that they must stagger surveys and conduct visits on weekends, in the early morning, and in the evening, times when quality, safety, and staffing problems are most likely to be apparent.

Risk managers should become familiar with The Joint Commission's current standards as reflected in the *Comprehensive Accreditation Manual for Long-Term Care* (CAMLTC).[28] Although all elements of the standards are important, risk management professionals should focus on the sections that reflect the "dimensions of performance"— that is, the nature and extent of services provided residents and the effectiveness of service delivery. Credentialing practices associated with all licensed "independent practitioners" should also be reviewed to ensure that they are carried out thoroughly and consistently. Finally, allegations of elder abuse and neglect, especially with respect to the development of pressure ulcers, has led to a notable increase in civil litigation and occasionally even criminal prosecution filed against nursing facilities. Risk management professionals should ensure that effective treatment protocols for the protection of the elderly are in place and closely adhered to.

LIFE SAFETY CODE

The **Life Safety Code** (**LSC**) (29 CFR 1910.35) is a compilation of fire safety requirements established by the National Fire Protection Association (NFPA) and adopted in part by CMS. Compliance with the 2000 edition of the NFPA's Life Safety Code is required under the final rule adopted by the CMS in 2003 of all Medicare-participating facilities, unless granted a waiver. The LSC is a dominant component of the overall "environment of care" standards established by The Joint Commission and other accrediting organizations. The NPFA recognizes and permits the use of alcohol-based hand rub (ABHR) solutions in patient rooms, corridors, and suites of healthcare facilities through amendment of the 2000 and 2003 editions of the life safety codes (LSC). As there were significant other changes made as well with the new amendment, it is crucial to understand these changes, which govern such things as emergency alarm systems, standards for rooftop heliports, and emergency lighting. Also important are other provisions of the final rule that provide for case-by-case program waivers, and clarification of the application of LSC, to ambulatory surgery centers and hospices.

A statement of conditions (SOC) must be completed for all buildings that contain housing or treatment facilities, with the exception of specified "business occupancies" defined in the code. Completing an SOC, seen by The Joint Commission as an ongoing activity, is an involved, cumbersome process that must be overseen by someone with an in-depth understanding of the LSC and the organization's buildings. This process is generally a team effort delegated among the facility's engineers, safety officer, and others.

Basic building information (BBI) forms must be completed for each building that provides the designated patient or resident services. Current floor plans or layouts of each story must be attached to the BBI. A life safety assessment (LSA) should be carried out on an ongoing basis to identify any LSC deficiencies (violations). For deficiencies that can't be promptly corrected, plans for improvement (PFIs) must be developed that contain (1) a description of the deficiencies, (2) actions undertaken to correct them, (3) identification of funding sources for the corrections, and (4) a schedule of the correction actions. PFI forms, whether the short or long versions (depending on the nature and scope of the deficiencies), are reviewable by surveyors. If an organization fails to make sufficient progress in complying with the corrective actions that it establishes for itself, the surveyor may recommend conditional accreditation. The Building Maintenance Program allows for establishing routine maintenance schedules to deal with some types of LSC deficiencies instead of placing them on PFIs. This program extends only to hospitals and long-term care facilities. Examples of building maintenance items that can be included in this program are specified door latches and closing devices, exit signs, and maintenance of certain grease control and disposal systems.

Risk Management Implications

Although oversight of compliance with the LSC is generally the responsibility of the organization's engineers, safety officers, and others, the foundation of the LSC is an example of the basic principles of risk management at work, an ongoing process of risk identification and control, loss prevention, and follow-up assessment. Evidence of LSC compliance may be looked for by the organization's property insurance administrators, real estate and leasing services, and property insurance underwriters.

Nuclear Regulatory Commission

Established under the auspices of the Atomic Energy Act of 1954, the federal Nuclear Regulatory Commission (NRC) established rules and NRC oversight authority for handling, storage, and use of radioactive substances.[29] A detailed set of instructions is provided for the management of such material.[30] Types of medical use of nuclear materials regulated by the NRC include (1) radioactive uptake, dilution, excretion, imaging, or local diagnostic clinical or research procedures; (2) the delivery of palliative or therapeutic doses to specific tissues or anatomical areas; and (3) research involving human subjects.

Among the many issues covered by the regulations are mandatory reporting to the local NRC regional office within fifteen days of discovery of any misadministration of nuclear by-product material, extensive staff training requirements, the establishment of a quality management program, and the provision of penalties for violations. The role of the facility's radiation safety officer is defined, as is the facility's detailed recordkeeping responsibilities. Due to the enormous risk attendant to these services, continual monitoring of these services is essential.

Risk Management Implications

Risk management professionals of facilities that provide diagnostic or therapeutic services that use radioactive substances are advised to familiarize themselves with the basics of the applicable regulations. The rigorous monitoring and reporting requirements in the regulations must be adhered to, or the facility might face the loss of its NRC license.

Violations of the regulations generally invite a quick response by the NRC. In 1999, a facility in Michigan was the focus of an NRC investigation arising from the misadministration of iodine-131 used in the treatment of a patient with thyroid carcinoma. Instead of receiving 150 millicuries as ordered, the patient was administered 100 millicuries. After realizing his mistake, the technician deliberately altered the prescribing physician's written order to cover up the error. Subsequently, the physician discovered the alteration and notified the hospital administration, which in turn notified the NRC's regional office as required by regulation. The NRC's Office of Investigations responded within two weeks and found that the technician had committed deliberate misconduct. In another instance, a nuclear medicine technologist was found to have administered technetium-99, an NRC-licensed material, to a relative without a doctor's order. During the ensuing investigation, the NRC also determined that NRC-mandated training was out of compliance with the regulations. Although no civil fines were assessed in this case, the hospital was let off with a warning to get its compliance program into shape. Finally, the NRC found a deliberate failure by a hospital's chief nuclear medicine technologist to obtain confirmation of a dosage of I-131, which resulted in the administration of 6.6 millicuries for the patient's thyroid scan, an amount significantly greater that the 100 microcuries ordered. Civil fines were imposed in this situation because the technologist had deliberately refused to engage in basic patient safety protections—and as this individual was also the hospital's radiation safety officer, he should have known better.

Child Abuse and Neglect

According to the HHS's report from the Administration for Children and Families titled "Child Maltreatment 2006" children were abuses or neglected at a rate of 12.1 per thousand children in the population resulting in an estimated 905,000 victims. The rate and number of children who received an investigation or assessment was 47.8 children per thousand in the population resulting in estimated 3,573,999 children. During federal fiscal year 2006, 3.3 million referrals concerning the welfare of approximately 6 million children were made to **Child Protective Service** (**CPS**) agencies throughout the United States. Professionals such as physicians, teachers, police officers, social service staff, and lawyers made 56.3 percent of all reports made. Nationally 905,000 victims were identified characterized by neglect (64.2 percent), physical abuse (16 percent), sexual abuse (8.8 percent), and psychological maltreatment (6.6 percent). Nearly 80 (79.9 percent) percent of perpetrators were parents. For 2006, it is estimated that 1,530 died of abuse or neglect. More than three quarters (78 percent) of the victims were under four years old, with infant boys (under 1 year of age) representing the highest rate of fatalities with 18.5 deaths per 100,000 boys followed closely by infant girls (under 1 year of age) with 14.7 deaths per 100,000 girls. For the sake of perspective, the overall death rate among children in general during 2006 was 2.04 deaths per 100,000 children in the national population.[31]

The key federal initiatives in this area are the 1974 **Child Abuse Prevention and Treatment Act** (**CAPTA**), subsequent amendments,[32] and the Keeping Children and Families Safe Act of 2003, which defined child abuse and neglect as any recent act or failure to act on the part of a parent or caretaker that results in death, serious physical or emotional harm, sexual abuse, or exploitation or any act or failure to act that presents an imminent risk of serious harm.[33] Every state has enacted, to one degree or another, mandatory reporting requirements relating to suspected child abuse and neglect. Although state statutes often differ in their definition of terms, most define abuse as representing harm or threatened harm to a child's health or welfare. Abuse is characterized as four major types: neglect, physical abuse, sexual abuse, and emotional abuse. Neglect is generally defined in terms of the deprivation of adequate food, clothing, shelter, or medical care. Exceptions to such reporting do exist and often, but not always, relate to children who are under treatment by spiritual means.

Elder Abuse

The National Elder Abuse Incidence Study, conducted in 1996 by the National Center on Elder Abuse, and the discussion sponsored by Attorney General Janet Reno in 2000 titled "Elder Justice Roundtable: Medical Forensic Issues Concerning Abuse and Neglect,"[34] explored a wide range of issues relating to elder abuse and neglect in this country. Because the legislative mandate limited the incidence study to the assessment and preservation of violence in domestic settings only, elders living in nursing homes, assisted living facilities, and other institutional or group facilities were not included in the study. Information on substantiated cases of abuse or neglect was gathered from Adult Protective Service (APS) agencies and other sources from twenty counties in fifteen states. The study confirmed that reported cases of abuse and neglect (including self-neglect) represent only the tip of the iceberg. An estimated 551,000 elderly persons, aged sixty years and over, were the victims of abuse or neglect in domestic settings in 1996. The study further estimated that only approximately 21 percent of these cases were ever reported and substantiated by state APS agencies.

Elder abuse is often categorized according to the following major types: physical abuse; sexual abuse; psychological or emotional abuse; neglect; financial exploitation; abandonment; self-neglect, or the intentional decision by a competent individual to refuse or fail to obtain adequate food, water, clothing, shelter or who engages in acts that threaten his or her own welfare; and abduction by family members. The National Center on Elder Abuse (http://www.elderabusecenter.org) is one of several excellent resources for information about the incidence of elder abuse in the nation and about the efforts under way to engage the general population in learning how to identify and report suspected cases.

Risk Management Implications

Risk management professionals must become familiar with all mandatory reporting requirements, including permitted statutory exceptions relating to child, elder, and dependent adult abuse and neglect. Hospital staffs, including medical staffs, must be advised (and reminded periodically) of their individual reporting obligations under state laws. To encourage reporting, many states have enacted immunity provisions that protect reporters from civil liability. Even the laws that regulate disclosure of patients' records related to federally funded substance abuse treatment programs expressly permit reporting suspected child abuse to state agencies. Significant penalties up to and including the loss of licensure, allegations of unprofessional conduct, and exposure to civil litigation are possible for individuals or facilities that fail to comply with these important reporting obligations.

FEDERAL HEALTH INSURANCE LAWS AND REGULATIONS

Risk management professionals should be thoroughly familiar with the risk implications of federal Medicare, Medicaid, and Employee Retirement and Income Security Act regulations.

Medicare

Medicare is the nation's largest health insurance program. It provides benefits for more than forty-two million enrollees with an additional forty-three million covered under Medicaid (including about six million covered under both programs) and more than six million children covered under the State Children's Health Insurance Program (**SCHIP**). The Centers for Medicare and Medicaid Services of the Department of Health and Human Services administers this program and works in partnership with the states to provide Medicaid and SCHIP benefits. The Congressional Budget Office (CBO) estimates outlays for FY 2008 at $1.1 billion.[35] Enacted in 1965 under Title 18 of the Social Security Act, Medicare was originally established to provide access to health services for the elderly, a segment of society that was considered vulnerable and often least able to afford necessary care. In 1972, Medicare eligibility was extended to individuals under age sixty-five with specified long-term disabilities or who had end-stage renal disease. The fee-for-service Medicare program consists of two parts: hospital insurance, also known as Part A, covers inpatient hospital services, short-term care in skilled nursing facilities, home health care, and hospice care, and supplementary medical insurance, known as Part B, covers outpatient services, physician services, home health care not covered under Part A, durable medical equipment, ambulance, and a variety of other medical services. The CMS contracts with private companies, known as fiscal intermediaries, to administer payments to hospitals, skilled nursing facilities, certain home health services, and hospices for their Part A and some Part B bills. A carrier is a private company that is likewise contracted to CMS to provide similar services to physicians and others for their Part B bills. In 1983, the Inpatient Prospective Payment System (**IPPS**) was introduced, in which a predetermined rate was applied for services provided to inpatients with similar diagnoses. This method of reimbursement, called a diagnosis related group (DRG), replaced the fee-for-service system of reimbursement that had been the standard of the Medicare payment model since its inception. Although the transition to this payment system was difficult for hospitals, the new method was so successful in reducing Medicare program costs that Congress demanded similar cost-saving initiatives in the outpatient setting. In May 2000, Medicare, through the Outpatient Prospective Payment System (**OPPS**), adopted a new, fixed reimbursement amount that, like the DRG model, is based on groupings of outpatient health care services with similar cost and clinical characteristics. This new "unit of payment," called ambulatory payment classifications (APCs), is only one element of a complex system of reimbursement enacted by the CMS. The 2003 Medicare Modernization Act made sweeping changes to the program. The MMA created a discount drug card until a new Part D outpatient prescription drug benefit went into effect in 2006. In addition, the MMA replaced the old Medicare+Choice program under Part C with Medicare Advantage. Another element of the MMA provides for payment for EMTALA-related care provided to undocumented aliens and a select few others, as noted earlier in this chapter.

Limitations preclude an in-depth review of all aspects of the enormously complex and ever-changing Medicare program. However, risk management professionals are advised to familiarize themselves with the program's basic structure, as noncompliance can result in civil monetary sanctions being levied or, in a worst-case scenario, disenrollment from the program altogether. Increasingly, individuals are being held criminally liable for misappropriation of Medicare funds, with jail time and hefty financial penalties being assessed. With the addition of new programs and other changes in the system actively under way, "situational awareness" is strongly advised.

Compliance oversight of Medicare programs rests with the CMS and is delegated to the CMS's nine regional offices. The hands-on certification survey process is delegated to state licensing and regulatory agencies. To ensure a reasonable standard for these state agencies throughout the nation, the CMS developed the *State Operations Manual* (SOM), a massive, detailed guide to all aspects of Medicare program compliance.[36] Risk management professionals are strongly encouraged to identify the applicable sections of the SOM, especially the surveyor guidance in its appendixes. Deficiencies (violations) of program compliance are identified by the regional offices in conjunction with the state agency surveyors and are submitted to the institution on a "statement of deficiency" form (CMS-2567). The facility is given ten days to develop and submit a credible plan of correction (**PoC**) for each identified deficiency. The "statement of deficiency" form, including the accepted PoC, is accessible to the public under the federal Freedom of Information Act.

Medicaid

Medicaid was established in 1965 as a jointly funded program whereby the federal government matches state spending for medical services for qualified enrollees. Medicaid programs provide coverage to individuals who fall into one or more of twenty-five different eligibility categories, including pregnant women, children, the elderly, and individuals who are disabled or blind. The contribution by CMS to each state's program is called the federal medical assistance percentage. It is reassessed annually using a standard formula. Because states are given broad latitude on how to organize their programs, determine eligibility standards, set payment rates, and so on, there is considerable variability in program content from state to state. Medicare beneficiaries who have limited income or resources may apply for supplemental coverage from their state's Medicaid program for services and for supplies that are available through the program.

Employee Retirement Income Security Act

Risk management professionals with responsibility for managed care–related risks or employee benefit programs should become intimately familiar with this 1974 federal statute, the Employee Retirement Income Security Act (**ERISA**).[37] Although the purpose of ERISA was to establish a nationwide standard for administrative functions of employee welfare benefit plans, ERISA also established a federal preemption of state laws that cover plan benefits. The practical effect of the ERISA preemption was the removal of lawsuits filed in connection with the provision of plan benefits from state courts to federal courts, thereby limiting the few remedies available to plaintiffs under this law. Although there have been several high-profile, high-dollar lawsuits involving managed care plans, they have usually involved health plan enrollees who were employees of governmental agencies, whose health care plans are not covered under ERISA. However, several important court decisions throughout the United States have eroded some of the MCOs' protections afforded by ERISA. Texas and California are among a growing number of states that have enacted legislation that now permits health plan enrollees to sue their MCOs, in defiance of the ERISA preemption. Although court challenges have been filed to overturn some of these new laws, it appears that MCOs may find themselves more accountable for treatment decisions than ever before as the plaintiffs' attorneys try out new theories of liability to penetrate the shield of the ERISA preemption.

Risk Management Implications

Although health plans may deny payment for services, they are not in a position to actually deny a patient access to the service itself. To help lessen an organization's liability exposure in this area of law, ensure that the staff understand their independent duty of care to patients as health care providers and patient advocates. A misunderstanding of this issue has been the source of innumerable violations of EMTALA when patients have been denied access to services based on insurance considerations. The staff should document all their efforts in contesting what they reasonably believe to be improper treatment denials. Such documentation should include a description of the information provided to support the appeal and the subsequent response by the MCO or plan representative. The staff must advise patients of treatment denials made by their health plans and review reasonable alternative courses of treatment that might be available, irrespective of whether the health plan may cover the treatment. Again, these discussions should be thoroughly documented in the patient record.

TORT REFORM

Since the professional liability insurance crisis of the 1970s, malpractice litigation has proliferated. In fact, the genesis of today's health care risk management profession can be traced directly to industry efforts to address the alarming rise in the frequency (number) and severity (cost) of hospital and professional liability lawsuits. From the beginning, risk management professionals, insurers, and health care industry leaders have tried to control the growth of this litigation. These efforts have generally taken the form of statutory controls. California's landmark **Medical Injury Compensation Reform Act (MICRA)** has served as a benchmark for other states' tort reform efforts. Enacted in 1975 as emergency legislation, MICRA established several basic tenets that influenced similar efforts throughout the country: (1) a cap (limit) of $250,000 was set for noneconomic ("pain and suffering") damages; (2) periodic payments of future damages in excess of $50,000 were permitted to ensure that a steady source of money remained in place to cover costs over time; (3) juries were allowed to have information on collateral sources of payment made to the patient or plaintiff to ensure that the plaintiff did not benefit from excessive financial remuneration from multiple sources; and (4) the rates of attorneys' contingency fees were fixed by statute to ensure that plaintiffs were not taken advantage of by unscrupulous lawyers. Many states have established tort reforms based on this model. A 2003 report by the Government Accountability Office found that insurance premiums for certain medical specialties, such as surgery, obstetrics and gynecology, and internal medicine, rose by an average of 15 percent during 2001 and 2002, and in some cases by 100 percent.

Risk Management Implications

The road to meaningful tort reform has been a rocky one. Several state courts have overturned or curtailed all or part of many tort reform efforts. However, the tort reform movement has been picking up steam, with increasing numbers of state legislatures tackling the issue.

Risk managers should become familiar with tort reform initiatives in their states. To further the objective of reducing the costs associated with runaway litigation, risk management professionals should support efforts to establish reasonable and balanced means of dispute resolution, such as mediation, arbitration, and private judicial review. Sound risk management loss control techniques demand that institutions and providers work closely with injured patients and their representatives to reach an equitable and mutually satisfactory resolution to disputes whenever possible. Although nonmeritorious lawsuits should be defended whenever necessary, the many claims that reflect gray areas of liability should be addressed proactively and creatively. By so doing, the risk management professional contributes to the successful loss control efforts of the program.

Professional Practice Acts

Risk managers are often called on during an investigation to consider "scope of practice" issues. For example, a question might arise as to whether a nurse, therapist, or other licensed health care professional performed an act that, under state statute, was outside the scope of professional practice as defined by the particular licensing board or agency. The state's pertinent professional practice act should be reviewed under such circumstances. From an insurance standpoint, coverage determinations are often dependent on such findings. For each group of health care professionals licensed by the state, laws and regulations define the scope of practice and outline the oversight authority vested in their professional regulatory boards. Professional practice regulatory boards are established by statute. Specific requirements regarding professional practice are generally found in state laws and regulations. They detail the process of licensure, including the state's requirements, if any, for mandatory continuing education, the definition of "unprofessional conduct" (such as unlawful use of controlled substances), and mandatory reporting requirements. For example, many states require a medical professional to report a colleague to the licensing board if there is a reasonable belief that the public welfare might be compromised as a result of the colleague's substance abuse.

Risk Management Implications

A risk management professional cannot completely assess the full extent of regulatory compliance or professional liability exposure without understanding the standards of professional practice that might apply. From a regulatory standpoint, an example of a federal standard of practice is the authority granted to nonphysician "qualified medical personnel" involved in performing medical screening examinations pursuant to the Emergency Medical Treatment and Labor Act. An understanding of professional practices is a key element of the review of professional liability exposures, as it relates to the establishment of so-called standards of care. Identifying such standards, which can vary on a case-by-case basis, remains a primary focus of malpractice litigation. In addition, knowledge of such standards is crucial in controlling risk during the development and implementation of new and alternative treatment regimens. From an employment liability standpoint, state-imposed disciplinary and licensure mandates should be clearly understood by risk management professionals and human resource personnel alike.

Risk Management Regulation

Risk managers in a few states have their professional practice regulated under specific risk management laws. In 1987, the American Society for Healthcare Risk Management (ASHRM) developed and published a model risk management program. Although ASHRM does not endorse a state legislative scheme for health care risk management, its model prescribes the elements of an acceptable health care risk management program. Those elements include a system for identifying, evaluating, and handling risk exposures; employment of a qualified risk management professional; data sharing and continuing education; and most important, commitment from the governing body to the risk management effort. (A board resolution example is presented in Exhibit 10.2.) In addition, ASHRM developed sample statutory language for confidentiality of all risk management–related documents and immunity for participants in risk management activities. As the states overhaul their medical malpractice statutory schemes, these concepts are gradually being incorporated into state code books.

EXHIBIT 10.2. **Sample Board Resolution**

Mt. St. Elsewhere Medical Center

RESOLUTION

WHEREAS, The Board of Directors of [name of facility] acknowledges its responsibility to provide for the safe and professional care of patients and the safety of the organization's employees, visitors and affiliated personnel, and furthermore, the Board of Directors recognizes that the organization's future fiscal strength will be greatly enhanced by its ability to minimize its risks and liabilities across the entire spectrum of its services and operations,

NOW THEREFORE, be it resolved:

1. That in accordance with the ongoing commitment to provide for the safe and professional care of all patients, visitors, and affiliated personnel, The Board of Directors directs the Chief Executive Officer to take appropriate action necessary in accordance with the organization's established Bylaws, Rules and Regulations, to support a comprehensive Risk Management Program to include, but not be limited to, all initiatives and activities necessary to identify and reduce the possibility, and extent of, unintended loss to the entire organization.

2. That this resolution shall go into full force and effect from the date of its passage.

Passed on this _____ day of _____, 2009.

_____

Chair—Board of Directors

POLICY AND PROCEDURE MANUALS

Policy and procedures establish an organization's internal regulatory practices. They are viewed by regulatory and accreditation agencies as evidence of the organization's acknowledgment of and compliance with established standards. Plaintiffs' attorneys routinely demand access to individual policies and procedures to assess whether professional or operational standards were breached. Unfortunately for many organizations, policies, procedures, medical staff bylaws, best-practice guidelines, and other such measures are often neglected. Out-of-date policies or those that no longer comply with changes in the law serve little practical purpose from an operational standpoint and pose a significant risk to the organization. Policies must be reviewed periodically to ensure that they reflect key regulatory and practice requirements. Individual departments should be given the flexibility to establish and modify guidelines and procedures on an ongoing basis to ensure that they represent current practices. As the function of such manuals is to provide a resource to optimize the quality of care and operations of the facility, attention should be paid to their development and ongoing review and maintenance.

Risk Management Implications

Policies, procedures, and guidelines must remain "works in progress" and consequently be subject to change as circumstances dictate. Input from risk management professionals and legal counsel during the creation and review of such manuals is encouraged so that reasonable and achievable standards are developed.

Risk managers should recognize the value of maintaining obsolete policies, manuals, and similar materials. This effort has significant risk management implications as it allows the organization to establish what its standard of care was at a given time, should it become an issue during litigation. Whether in paper form or online, modified policies and protocols should be afforded the same consideration as any noncurrent business records. Store them so that they can be accessed should the need arise.

CASE LAW

Statutes and regulations enacted by Congress and the states do not address every possible situation in which they might apply. Under certain circumstances, litigants may ask appellate courts at both the state and federal level to review unfavorable decisions. When a court renders a decision in the form of a written opinion, the opinion becomes part of the body of law and should be recognized and given the same consideration as enacted legislation. Decisions by these courts should be routinely monitored by risk management professionals. Several resources are available to help risk management professionals achieve this objective—for example, regulatory updates published by state health care organizations, law firm advisories, the courts' own Web pages, and the American Society for Healthcare Risk Management. Exhibit 10.3 presents an example of an internal legislative update.

EXHIBIT 10.3. Sample Legislative Update

{PRIVATE}   LEGISLATIVE UPDATE

SUTTER HEALTH RISK SERVICES DEPARTMENT

Office of the General Counsel

Prepared by Mark Cohen, ARM, RPLU, CPHQ, CPHRM, DFASHRM

Risk Management Consultant

{PRIVATE}

December, 2002

SB 1301: Reproductive Privacy Act

SUMMARY: This bill, sponsored by Planned Parenthood, replaces California's 35-year old Therapeutic Abortion Act and the many conflicting and outdated elements of that law that have remained on the books since it was enacted. The original Act has long been superseded by newer legislation and case law, including the United States Supreme Court's 1973 opinion in *Roe v. Wade*. Passages deleted from the original law include those that stipulated that abortions may only be performed with the pre-approval of a medical staff committee, specific gestational time frames within which abortions may or may not be performed, i.e. ". . . after the 20th week of pregnancy" and all abortions must be reported to the state.

In their place, the Reproductive Privacy Act (the Act) establishes a new set of provisions governing women's reproductive rights. The foundation of the Act is defined within the following State public policy positions:

1. Every individual has the fundamental right to choose or refuse birth control.

2. Every woman has the fundamental right to choose to bear a child or choose to obtain an abortion, except as specifically prohibited.

3. The state shall not deny or interfere with a woman's fundamental right to choose to bear a child, or to choose and obtain an abortion prior to the viability of the fetus, or when the abortion is necessary to protect the life or health of the woman.

COMMENT: *Minors*. Although statutory language remains that requires the written permission of a parent or legal guardian before an abortion may be performed upon an *unemancipated* minor, an Appellate court concluded, in the 1997 case *American Academy of Pediatrics, et al v. Lundgren,* that this requirement violated the privacy rights of pregnant minors. Consequently, parental consent is no longer required.

Limitation on when abortions may be performed: Abortions may not be performed if, in the good faith medical judgment of the physician, 1) the fetus is viable and 2) continuation of the pregnancy poses no risk to the life or health of the pregnant woman. "Viability" is defined as ". . . on the particular facts of the case before [the] physician, there is reasonable likelihood of the fetus's sustained survival outside the uterus without the application of extraordinary medical measures."

COMMENT: The previous "20-week" rule has been replaced by the more subjective "good faith judgement of the physician" and "viability" standards which now become the new legal benchmarks in these cases.

Who may participate in the abortion process: Previous law provided that only

(Continued)

EXHIBIT 10.3. *(Continued)*

physicians were authorized to perform an abortion or aid or assist in the process. The new Act removes this restriction and permits the active involvement of nurses and physicians assistants with a ". . . valid, unrevoked, and unsuspended license or certificate obtained in accordance with some other provision of law that authorizes him or her to perform the functions necessary [to assist in performing either a surgical or non-surgical (i.e. pharmacological) abortion]."

COMMENT: The new Act does not revoke existing law that permits physicians, nurses, and other staff to refuse—without fear of discipline or penalty—to participate in an abortion if they have *filed a written statement with their employer* that establishes ". . . a moral, ethical, or religious basis for such refusal."

WHO NEEDS TO KNOW: Administrator, Patient Care Executives, Chief of Staff, Obstetrics Department medical staff, Family Practice medical staff, Labor and Delivery Manager, Social Services Manager, Human Resources Director, Bioethics Committee.

WHAT NEEDS TO BE DONE: Revise present policies relating to the provision of abortions to eliminate references to any deleted elements of the law, and re-define all relevant clinical elements, including guidelines reflecting the physician's authority to establish fetal viability. NOTE: With the new authority given physicians to exercise their discretion when assessing fetal viability, medical staffs may wish to consider adopting guidelines to ensure the application of recognized clinical standards in this regards.

As nurses, physician's assistants, and other specified licensed personnel may now actively participate in this procedure—as provided for under the law and subject only to any limitations that may imposed under their license—a review of current practice is suggested to provide an opportunity to update job descriptions and functions. Be certain to thoroughly educate all L&D, OB/Gyn, Family Practice, and other involved clinical and non-clinical staff alike, on the new parameters of the law. Doing so will help minimize any confusion or questions that may arise about the revised law, as well as ensure that advice given patients is accurate.

To access the complete bill on the internet, go to *www.leginfo.ca.gov/bilinfo. html* and enter the requested information. This bill was passed during last year's legislative session.

SUMMARY

Risk managers should be prepared to help their organizations understand and comply with the entire spectrum of laws and regulations. If the issue at hand is beyond their expertise, risk management professionals should be able at the least to identify the required resources. As regulatory noncompliance exposes both the organization and, in some cases, individuals to a wide range of financial or criminal penalties, persistent efforts by risk management professionals in providing guidance to constituents is essential. Complying with laws and regulations is somewhat like playing a game whose rules are constantly changing. Ideally, subscribing to newsletters or other resources will help identify issues in the ever-changing legal and regulatory landscape. As virtually all federal and state regulatory agencies are well represented on the Internet, risk management professionals should develop the habit of periodically reviewing these Web sites for news of upcoming changes in rules or regulations or important guidance information. Web sites of law firms that specialize in health law are another promising resource, as they are often among the first to publish assessments of new or pending legislation, regulations, and case law. Ensure that everyone in the organization with a need to know is apprised of additions or significant modifications of the law.

KEY TERMS

Centers for Medicare and Medicaid Services

Child Abuse Prevention and Treatment Act

Child Protective Service agencies

Civil monetary penalties

Clinical Laboratory Improvement Amendments

Conditions for coverage

Conditions of participation

Consolidated Omnibus Budget Reconciliation Act

Dedicated emergency department

Emergency Medical Treatment and Labor Act

Employee Retirement and Income Security Act

Healthcare Integrity and Protection Data Bank

Health Care Quality Improvement Act

Institutional review board

Life Safety Code

Mammography Quality Standards Act

Manufacturers and User Facility Device Experience database

Medical screening exam

Medicare Modernization Act

Medical Injury Compensation Reform Act

National Organ Transplant Act

National Practitioner Data Bank

Organ Procurement Transplant Network

Office for Human Research Protections

Office of Civil Rights

Office of Inspector General

Patient Self-Determination Act

Safe Medical Device Act

Single-use device

United Network for Organ Sharing

ACRONYMS

CAPTA

CDC

CDRH

CfC

COBRA

CoP

CORF	MQSRA
CLIA	MSE
CMS	NOTA
CPS	NPDB
DED	OCR
EMTALA	OHRP
ERISA	OIG
FDA	OPO
GMPs	OPPS
HCQIA	OPTN
HIPAA	PoC
HIPDB	PSDA
IPPS	QIO
IRB	SCHIP
LSC	SMDA
MAUDE	SNF
MCO	SOM
MICRA	SUD
MMA	UNOS
MQSA	

NOTES

1. Social Security Act of 1867, codified as 42 USC 1395dd, 42 CFR 489, and others.

2. 42 CFR 489.20.q.(1–2).

3. Department of Health and Human Services, Office of the Inspector General and the Health Care Financing Administration. "EMTALA Special Advisory Bulletin," 1998, http://www.emtala.com/oblig.txt

4. 42 CFR 489.20.r(3).

5. 42 CFR 489.20.

6. 42 USC 1395dd(d)(1).

7. *Roberts* v. *Galen of Virginia, Inc.*, 525 U.S. 249 (1999).

8. "Federal Reimbursement of Emergency Health Services Furnished to Undocumented Aliens," http://www.cms.hhs.gov/providers/section1011/

9. 42 USC 42, 11101; 45 CFR 60, P.L. 99-660.

10. *Patrick* v. *Burget*, 486 U.S. 94, 96 (Ore. 1988).

11. *Elam* v. *College Park Hosp.*, 132 Cal. App. 3d 332, 183 Cal. Rptr. 156, 164 (1982).

12. 42 USC 1395cc.

13. 42 CFR 482.13.

14. 21 USC 360i(a); 21 CFR 803.

15. Available at the CDRH Reuse of Single-Use Devices home page, http://www.fda.gov/cdrh/reuse.

16. 42 USC 263b; 21 CFR 16, 900, 1308, and 1312; 42 CFR 498.

17. P.L. 105-248.

18. The American College of Radiology and designated state agencies under contract with the FDA are the Arkansas Department of Health, Iowa Department of Health, and Texas Department of Health.

19. "The Mammography Quality Standards Act Final Regulations, Modifications and Additions to Policy Guidance Help System No. 5: Guidance for Industry and FDA," July 2000, http://www.fda.gov/cdrh/mammography/index.html

20. 42 USC 300gg–63, 91, and 92; 42 CFR 144.101 and 146.130.

21. See the United Network for Organ Sharing home page, http://www.unos.org

22. 42 CFR 21; see Organ Procurement and Transplantation Network, http://www.unos.org.pdf

23. PL 100-578.

24. For details, see the Centers for Medicare and Medicaid Services' CLIA General Program Description, http://www.cms.hhs.gov/clia/progdesc.asp

25. 42 CFR 483 and 488; 42 USC 1395i-3.

26. Department of Health and Human Services, Office of the Inspector General. "Quality of Care in Nursing Homes: An Overview," 1999, http://www.oig.hhs.gov/oei/reports/oei-02-99-00060.pdf

27. "Compliance Program Guidance for Nursing Facilities," *Federal Register,* vol. 65, no. 52, Thursday, March 16, 2000, notices page 14289. http://www.oig.hhs.gov/authorities/docs/cpgnf.pdf

28. Joint Commission. *Comprehensive Accreditation Manual for Long-Term Care.* Oakbrook Terrace, Ill.: Joint Commission, published annually.

29. 42 USC 2011 et seq.; 10 CFR 35.

30. 10 CFR 35.

31. U.S. Department of Health and Human Services. Administration on Children, Youth and Families. *Child Maltreatment 2006* (Washington, DC: U.S. Government Printing Office, 2008) Available at: http://www.acf.hhs.gov/programs/cb/pubs/cm06/cm06.pdf

32. PL 93-247, amended by P.L. 104-235.

33. PL 108-36.

34. National Institute of Justice. "Elder Justice Roundtable: Medical Forensic Issues Concerning Abuse and Neglect," 2000, http://www.ojp.usdoj.gov/nij/topics/crime/elder-abuse/roundtable/welcome.htm

35. CBO Estimates of Medicare, Medicaid, and SCHIP Extension Act of 2007 (GOE07D03) available at: http://www.cbo.gov/ftpdocs/88xx/doc8898/SFC_MMS_ExtensionGOE07D03.pdf.

36. Available from http://www.cms.hhs.gov/Manuals

37. Employee Retirement Income Security Act (29 USC 1001), http://www.dol.gov/dol/topic/health-plans/erisa.htm

CHAPTER

11

BASIC CLAIMS ADMINISTRATION

ELLEN L. BARTON

LEARNING OBJECTIVES

- To be able to understand the current claims environment and its impact on the health care industry
- To be able to describe the essential claims management functions
- To be able to identify the steps in the claim process and explain the importance of each
- To be able to outline the risk management professional's responsibilities
- To be able to define alternative dispute resolution mechanisms

"There is always a great deal at stake in a health care professional liability claim: large sums of money, of course, but also professional reputations and even individual careers. With the crisis in medical malpractice and health care liability growing more severe daily, the stakes have never been higher and the need for professionalism in claim management has never been greater."[1]

Given this environment, it is incumbent on new risk management professionals to understand basic claims administration, because they are likely to be involved, at least to some degree, in the process. The purpose of this chapter is to introduce the principles of claims administration and highlight best practices for risk managers new to the process.

KEY CONCEPTS

- Although the health care industry is working hard to ensure the delivery of safe care, we must continue to deal with claims of patient injury due to the alleged negligence of a health care provider or delivery system.

- When a facility is commercially insured for medical professional and general liability, the insurance company generally provides complete claims management services.

- When a facility is self-insured for health care professional and general liability, it is the facility's responsibility to provide the services necessary to manage such claims.

- The first step in the claims process is a coverage determination.

- The risk management professional's responsibilities in managing claims will depend on a variety of factors, including whether the facility is commercially insured or self-insured, whether the facility chooses to outsource the claims management function, or whether the facility has assigned responsibility for the claims process to the legal department.

THE CLAIMS ENVIRONMENT

One has only to read the local newspaper on a regular basis to understand that our society has adopted what some would call a "lottery mentality." Some buy lottery tickets in hopes of winning big money, and others sue whomever they can for whatever "wrong" they have incurred in hopes of winning big money. Unfortunately, the latter behavior dramatically affects the health care industry. Although the industry is working hard to ensure the delivery of safe care (see Chapter 3), we must continue to deal with claims of patient injury due to the alleged negligence of a health care provider or delivery system.

Commercial Insurance

When a facility is commercially insured for medical professional and general liability, the insurance company ordinarily provides complete claims management services. Such services may include claims investigation, assignment of a claims adjuster, medical records production, claims management (including the strategy for handling a claim), setting reserves, assignment of legal counsel, settlement discussions, and litigation management (if, after suit has been filed, a decision is made to defend the claim). Even if the company retains an outside claims service, it is still the company's responsibility to provide these services. Although it is likely that the risk management professional will be involved in various aspects of the process, the insurance company manages the process.

Self-Insurance

When a facility is self-insured for health care professional and general liability, it is the facility's responsibility to provide the services necessary to manage such claims. The facility may decide to retain a **third-party administrator (TPA)** to perform some or all of a set of identified services. For instance, the facility may decide to hire a TPA to investigate and manage the claim, including settlement discussions until a lawsuit is filed. Then the facility may assign the case to legal counsel with the TPA having no further responsibility. TPAs generally employ trained individuals who are qualified to investigate claims, review medical records, engage in settlement discussions, and maintain appropriate documentation. Another facility may decide to outsource the entire claims process to a law firm or TPA, and yet another facility may decide to manage the entire claims process internally with appropriately trained personnel. Whatever approach is adopted, it is important for the facility to employ effective claims management practices.

THE CLAIMS PROCESS

The first step in the claims process is a **coverage determination**. Just as the owner of a new automobile buys an auto insurance policy to provide coverage for accidents involving injuries to third parties, a health care organization buys medical professional and general liability insurance to provide coverage for medical incidents involving injuries to patients. However, after an auto accident, a determination must be made that the auto accident was indeed covered under the policy. Likewise, when a patient is injured at a health care facility and a claim is reported, it is first necessary to determine that there is coverage. If the facility is **commercially insured**, the insurance company will make the determination. If the facility is self-insured (through a trust fund, a captive insurance company, or designated operating funds), an appropriately designated individual will determine coverage in accordance with the facility's policies and procedures. Coverage determinations are important for several reasons: first, to ensure the integrity of the policy language (commercial insurance or captive insurance company), the trust document (self-insurance), or other specified parameters when operating funds are used; and second, to comply with the terms of the facility's or insurance company's excess carriers or reinsurers (see Chapter 12). It cannot be emphasized enough that understanding coverage and reporting requirements is crucial to a successful claims management program. The following questions must be answered to determine whether a loss is covered:

■ *Is the person involved covered?* Is the physician employed and thus covered under the facility's medical professional liability policy, or is the nurse working for an agency whose contract requires the agency to provide coverage?

■ *Is the time of the loss within the policy period?* This is particularly critical with "claims-made" professional liability policies, especially where the policy requires that the date when the loss occurred and the date when the claim was made fall within a particular time period for coverage to apply. (For further discussion on coverage forms, see Chapter 13.)

■ *Is the cause of the loss covered?* For instance, was the injury caused by medical negligence (a "covered loss") or assault and battery, an intentional tort excluded from coverage?

■ *Are the types and amounts of damages covered?* This specifically refers to compensatory and punitive damages. Many insurance policies exclude punitive damages. Others are silent on the issue, thus allowing state law to allow or deny punitive damage coverage. Compensatory damages are those that compensate claimants for injuries and might include such items as lost wages, medical bills, expected future medical costs, and pain and suffering. The policy, however, will not pay more than the stated limit under any circumstance.

■ *Is the location covered?* Most medical professional liability policies will provide coverage anywhere in the world as long as the activities of the covered individuals are within the scope of their employment. However, there might be situations where an employed resident physician moonlights at a nonaffiliated, competing hospital in a neighboring community and the policy does not extend coverage to such situations.

■ *Do any exclusions apply?* For example, most if not all professional liability insurance policies exclude assault and battery as mentioned previously, sexual abuse (or even allegations of sexual abuse), and other defined causes of loss.

■ *Is there other insurance that would apply to the loss?*[2] This question is important to answer because many health care professionals purchase their own medical professional liability insurance regardless of their employment situation. Nurses often subscribe through a state or national association program for medical professional liability coverage and might have limits of coverage available separate and apart from the facility's policy. Because of potential coverage conflicts, it is "best practice" for a risk management professional to review specific medical professional liability policy and coverage language with respect to the section on other insurance. In most instances, this section will dictate how other policies or coverages will be treated for the claim in question. Risk management professionals should develop a complementary policy and procedure addressing how such personal (other) coverage will be treated. Within the facility, the primary question to answer is, "Will the personal coverage be considered primary or excess to the facility's coverage, or will both carriers share in the loss proportionally?" The thought of having additional limits available to pay the claim might be appealing to the risk management professional, but senior management needs to make this clarification known to avoid causing a serious employee relations issue. The facility's policy on personal coverage should be clearly articulated to avoid any misunderstanding or potential conflicts in the management of the claim.

If a facility is commercially insured and the insurer makes a preliminary determination that there is likely no coverage, the carrier will often undertake to investigate and defend the claim but issue a "**reservation of rights**" letter in an attempt to preserve the company's right to deny coverage at a later date.

THE RISK MANAGEMENT PROFESSIONAL'S RESPONSIBILITIES

The risk management professional's responsibilities in managing claims will depend on a variety of factors, including whether the facility is commercially insured or self-insured, whether the facility chooses to outsource the claims management function, or whether the facility has assigned responsibility for the claims process to the legal department. Regardless of the specific responsibilities, the risk management professional should have a thorough understanding of the entire process to ensure that claims are resolved appropriately. The risk management professional therefore needs to ensure that the following five functions are appropriately performed:

1. Claims reporting
   - Primary insurer, if commercially insured
   - Internal mechanism, if self-insured
   - Excess carrier or reinsurer, if applicable

2. Claims investigation
   - Medical record review
   - Interviews (coordinate with legal counsel to interview patient, health care provider, witness, and others)
   - Expert review of case
   - Initial assessment
   - Reserve setting

3. Claims management strategy
   - Liability determination
   - Decision to settle or defend

■   Claims committee review (such review can serve as a quality control mechanism to be certain that the liability determination is accurate and that the decision to settle or defend is prudent)

4. Settlement

■   Documentation (supporting the payment amount)

■   Documentation that the approval process was followed

5. Litigation

■   Pretrial and trial strategy

■   Coordination on public relations concerns

■   Witness preparation

■   Decisions and information exchanged during trial

■   Posttrial strategy

Claims Adjuster's Responsibilities

Just as risk management professionals' responsibilities vary, so do claims adjusters' responsibilities, depending on the service agreement between the adjusters and either the insurance company or the health care facility. In most cases, however, if claims adjusters have been assigned to handle claims, their responsibilities will include the same five functions just outlined.

Claims Identification and Investigation

The organization's risk management plan will include mechanisms to identify and report potential and actual claims and a method as to how those claims will be investigated and managed. Identification mechanisms include formal systems such as the **incident reporting system** or informal mechanisms such as information received from surveys, questionnaires, and other sources. The initial **investigation** is an important aspect of claims handling. Regardless of the risk financing mechanism chosen, the risk management professional plays an important role in the investigative process.

Reporting of Claims The **reporting of claims** is the single most important step in the process of ensuring coverage for any payments that may be required. This reporting happens on multiple levels. First, there is the report of a potential claim from within the facility to the risk management professional. Next, if the facility is commercially insured, there is the report from the facility to its insurance carrier. This reporting requirement and its timing are critical to ensure compliance with the terms and conditions of the insurance policy. Similarly, there may also be instances when reporting to excess carriers or reinsurers (for captive insurance companies) is necessary. Risk management professionals must first understand the facility's risk financing program and then design a process that facilitates the facility's ability to adhere to various reporting requirements. Insurance policies specify the circumstances that require reporting. Unfortunately, the policy wording in the insurance policy that specifies the circumstances for which reporting is required is not always clear or easy to understand. Therefore, the risk management professional, in conjunction with the insurance agent or broker, should clarify the reporting requirements to avoid situations that could result in a lack of coverage for failure to report or late reporting. Finally, there is the reporting of a claim that is in the form of a written demand for compensation from a claimant or the claimant's attorney. To avoid these surprises, the facility needs an **early warning claim reporting system** that provides the risk management professional with immediate information regarding facts and circumstances that have caused or are likely to cause injury to a patient and may likely lead to payment of money. A facility's incident reporting system may also serve as the claims reporting system. (For more information, see Chapter 6). The best results occur when the risk management professional has the trust and confidence of the health care facility and its medical staff and employees regardless of the reporting system. It is generally a phone call or e-mail from within the facility that will signal the need for a formal investigation. Regardless of how the information is relayed, the key is to establish a communication link with the medical and nursing staff and all ancillary personnel. Once the risk management professional has been alerted to an incident or a situation that needs further attention, there is a need for a greater formality in communication.

Initial Investigation If the risk management professional is going to conduct the initial investigation, it is important for any such investigation to be done at legal counsel's direction in order to provide the greatest protection possible for the information gathered. Generally, TPAs working either for insurance companies or for health care facilities will instruct claims adjusters to operate under the direction of legal counsel to gain protection afforded by the attorney-client privilege. Initial investigations play a critical role in determining liability and the anticipated amount of damages. Such investigations should be done as soon as practicable after notice of an occurrence or a claim. That is when the most information will be available regarding the facts and circumstances surrounding the injury or potential for injury. This reinforces the importance of timely internal notice—notice simultaneous with the occurrence itself, which will provide the best opportunity for a thorough investigation. Witnesses, patients, the medical records, and other necessary documentation are more likely to be available near the time of the occurrence rather than days, months, or even years later.

Interviews and Evidence "Investigation means assembling, with maximum accuracy and minimum effort, the information and evidence on which the insurer (commercial company or self-insurance trust fund) can determine the position it should take in respect to its legal obligation—or to put it in practical terms, whether to settle, compromise, or deny the claim."[3]

Probably the most common technique to gather information and evidence is interviewing, a skill that can be learned. It is incumbent on the risk management professional to learn it well, given what is at stake for those involved in the claim. All witnesses—meaning all who are in a position to provide information that is both relevant and material to the claim—should be interviewed. Thus the first task is to identify all possible witnesses and obtain contact information. Contact information should include name, address, age, sex, name and address of an emergency contact (someone who will always know the witness's whereabouts), nationality, phone number, Social Security number, occupation, and current employment. It is also best practice to inform witnesses who are also insureds as to the status of the coverage determination and their rights and responsibilities as insureds. Finally, all insureds should be cautioned not to discuss the facts and circumstances of the case with anyone without prior authorization from the risk management professional or legal counsel. Because a claim's life is generally at least several years, it is also best practice to update the involved parties as to the status of the case on a regular basis. Doing so also allows the risk management professional or claims adjuster to update contact information that might be needed later.

If an interview is undertaken at the direction of legal counsel, it is important to preserve the information in the most authentic manner possible. The use of an outline or guidelines on questions to ask may prove helpful. The use of signed or recorded statements, routine in adjusting auto claims, is rare in the context of health care professional liability claims. In interviewing witnesses, the goal is to understand what happened from the witness's perspective. When documenting an interview, it is important for the risk management professional or adjuster to document the witness's view as objectively as possible and without drawing conclusions. This is particularly important because negligence in a health care setting involves the applicability of various standards of care that are usually determined by expert testimony. When interviewing witnesses, the risk management professional or adjuster can take witnesses through the preliminary information by asking a series of questions. Then the interviewer should allow the witness to tell what happened in the witness's own words. As the witness relates the information, the interviewer can clarify various aspects by asking "why" questions. For example, if the claim involves a medication overdose and the nurse who administered the overdose is being interviewed, it is important to understand why the nurse failed to adhere to the appropriate protocol. The gentle use of "why" questions is the best method for getting the full explanation. Often initial interviews in health care professional liability claims are not documented simply because many defense attorneys do not want to create a record at this time. Thus documentation should be undertaken carefully.

Evidence generally refers to medical records, pathology slides, X-rays, and other radiographic images. It would also include photographs, diaries or journals, employment records, income tax returns, and physical objects (such as the piece of equipment that is suspected of having malfunctioned). Gathering evidence is particularly important for several reasons: it will help determine liability, it may also help evaluate damages, and it will provide the basis for an **expert opinion**. All evidence in a medical professional liability claim should be sequestered by the risk management professional and accessed only by authorized personnel. Although interviews with the claimant will produce information regarding the injury (and hence damages), it will also be necessary to have medical reports written by care providers that define in more objective terms the extent and permanency of injuries and what, if any, additional treatment might be necessary.

Should a lawsuit be filed involving a claim that was previously filed, reported, and investigated, it is incumbent on those supervising the claims management process to give all appropriate materials from the initial investigation to defense counsel so that duplication of effort is avoided and conflicting information does not impede the evaluation of the claim.

Claims File Management

Regardless of whether a health care organization is commercially insured or self-insured, it is important for the organization to maintain a claims file. If the organization is commercially insured, there should be agreements about what documents will be kept in which file. For example, if a case is in litigation, the decision might be that all depositions will be maintained by defense counsel and copies of deposition summaries will be maintained by the risk management professional and the insurance company. There should be a system for naming and numbering the files for easy access for several reasons, including claim audits and auditors' reports.

Contents It will be helpful to maintain a sense of order in the file. Regardless of how the claims file is organized, there are distinct general categories of materials that should be maintained, as follows:

- Correspondence
- Investigation documentation
- Medical records
- Expert reports
- Medical research
- Damages
- Legal papers
- Expenses
- Reserve history

The manner in which the materials are filed should be consistent for all claims files, to facilitate retrieval and review. In addition, it might be helpful to prepare a cover sheet for each claim that contains up-to-date information regarding what the claim is about, the status of the claim or litigation, and expense and indemnity history, including payouts, remaining reserves, and reserve dollar change with dates.

Documentation

All documentation maintained in a claim file should be legible and clearly identified. If a risk management professional is uncertain about exactly what materials should be maintained in the claim file, a review with defense counsel should provide the necessary guidance.

Claims Reserving

A **loss reserve** is simply an estimate of how much it will cost to pay the claim. In addition, reserves need to be calculated for loss adjustment expenses (LAE)—the amount of money it will cost to "adjust the claim," conduct the investigation, review medical records, hire a TPA, pay legal fees, and so on. There is no real science to reserving, and although many insurance companies and TPAs have developed worksheets in an attempt to make the process somewhat objective, there is no definitive method to reserving losses. Most often health care facilities use the individual case method: the claims adjuster, insurance company, or risk management professional sets a dollar amount based on the facts and circumstances of the particular claim. In such cases, the following should be considered:

- *Demographics:* What is the claimant's age, gender, occupation, level of education, number of dependents?

- *Nature and extent of injury:* Is it permanent? Was there significant pain and suffering?

- *Damages:* What are the total medical bills? What type of care or treatment might be needed in the future? Were there any lost wages?

- *Representation:* Is the claimant represented by legal counsel? Does the attorney have a good reputation?

- *Liability factors:* Was the standard of care breached? If so, do the actions go beyond negligence? Would the facts support a claim for punitive damages? Did the claimant contribute to the injury?

- *Precedents:* Have any comparable verdicts been handed down? Are there any legal limits to recovery, such as a cap on pain and suffering?[4]

Obviously, it is important to place some monetary value on a claim so as to reserve those funds for when payment is due. However, there is another equally important reason to reserve claims: to allow actuaries for both the commercially insured and the self-insured to predict losses into the future and thereby set premiums or funding contributions for alternative risk financing arrangements.

"**Stair stepping**" is a practice in which **loss reserves** are periodically increased by set amounts in the absence of any circumstance that would support such an increase. This practice should be discouraged because it might improperly inflate not only individual case reserves but also aggregate reserves and "**incurred but not reported**" (**IBNR**) reserves—amounts set aside for claims that have occurred but have not yet been reported.

Claims Management Strategy

Although a health care facility may be commercially insured, it is just as important for the risk management professional to be involved in claim management strategy in those situations as when the facility is self-insured because, quite simply, no matter who pays the claim, the loss history belongs to the facility. So while a commercial insurance company might argue that a good business decision might involve paying a nominal amount of money to settle the claim, a risk management professional might argue that the good reputation of the facility is worth defending the claim.

Settlement

There is general agreement that when a determination of liability has been made (that is, a duty to adhere to a standard of care existed, the duty was breached, and damages resulted directly from the breach of the duty), it is far better for all parties to reach a settlement agreement. This generally includes paying money, providing additional treatment, and having the claimant sign a release of future liability. It is in everyone's best interest to settle legitimate claims as soon as possible. This generally follows a thorough investigation and appropriate communication with the involved health care professionals, the facility's senior management, and any insurance carrier involved. It is equally important to defend claims that are found to be baseless. This approach supports the integrity of the facility and of the health care professionals who practice in it. Unfortunately, even though there might be a determination of liability, the parties may not agree on the amount of damages and thus may be unable to reach settlement.

Alternative Dispute Resolution

When settlement between or among the parties is not reached through informal discussions, a variety of mechanisms are available to facilitate resolution of the claim before filing suit and using the legal system. Among the alternative dispute resolution mechanisms are the following:

- Mediation
- Arbitration
- Private judging
- Neutral fact finding
- Ombudsman
- Minitrial
- Summary jury trial
- Moderated settlement

These mechanisms may be binding or nonbinding, and some may in fact be prescribed by state law as part of tort reform legislation. Remember that using any of these alternative dispute resolution mechanisms is more likely to provide a satisfactory conclusion than litigation would.

The Legal System

The use of the legal system as a claims management strategy should be reserved for cases in which suit has been filed and the health care facility has made a determination that it has no legal liability for the injuries claimed. Defending such cases sends an important message to the plaintiff's bar and supports the integrity of the claims management process.

REGULATORY REPORTING OF CLAIMS

Health care professionals are under enormous scrutiny in the practice of medicine and the delivery of health care. In addition to a facility's peer review and quality improvement committees, there are other entities that are entitled to information regarding the quality of a health care professional's practice.

National Practitioner Data Bank

Organizations and insurance companies who pay money on behalf of a health care provider (physicians, dentists, or other licensed practitioners, such as nurses or nurse midwives) for injuries sustained by a patient during the course of medical treatment are required to report such information to the National Practitioner Data Bank (see Chapter 10).

Governmental Agencies

The National Practitioner Data Bank also requires those payments to be reported to the appropriate state licensing agency within thirty days of the date the payment was made. Patients can also file claims against physicians through the state medical or nursing board. Such claims are taken very seriously and are generally investigated by members of the medical or nursing board in a manner similar to a peer review process.

SUMMARY

Once a claim is resolved, it is important to review the various aspects of the case with the involved individuals and others (such as members of a claims committee or patient safety committee) to identify whatever risk management issues might be the basis of future educational sessions, new or revised policies and procedures, or significant systemic change. Thus risk management professionals' roles in claims administration becomes a necessary component of their responsibilities to promote practices that support patient safety. Health care providers are trained to learn from their mistakes, and the risk management professional can play a vital role in assessing the systems that support the practice of medicine and ensure that an atmosphere of continuous quality management with a focus on safe patient care prevails.

KEY TERMS

Claims investigation	Investigation
Commercial insurance	Loss adjustment expense
Coverage determination	Loss reserve
Early warning claims reporting system	Reporting of claims
Evidence	Reservation of rights
Expert opinion	Stairstepping
Incident reporting system	Third-party administrator

ACRONYMS

LAE	SIR
IBNR	TPA

NOTES

1. Cambridge *Professional Liability Brochure,* 2004, http://www.cambridgeintegrated.com/claims_svcs/files/CISG_ProfLiab.pdf, p. 17.

2. Hoopes, D. *The Claims Environment* (2nd ed.). Malvern, Pa.: American Institute for Chartered Property Casualty Underwriters/Insurance Institute of America, 2000, p. 2.8.

3. Johns, C. T. *An Introduction to Liability Claims Adjusting* (2nd ed.). Cincinnati: National Underwriting Co., 1972, p. 111.

4. Hoopes, D., *Claims Environment,* p. 2.18.

SUGGESTED READING

Hoopes, D. *The Claims Environment* (2nd ed.). Malvern, Pa.: American Institute for Chartered Property Casualty Underwriters/Insurance Institute of America, 2000.

Johns, C. T. *An Introduction to Liability Claims Adjusting* (2nd ed.). Cincinnati: National Underwriting Co., 1972.

CHAPTER

INTRODUCTION TO RISK FINANCING

DOMINIC A. COLAIZZO

LEARNING OBJECTIVES

- To be able to identify basic elements of risk financing
- To be able to discuss the criteria by which a risk financing option is chosen
- To be able to recognize the difference between risk retention and risk transfer and to identify key factors in electing one option over another
- To be able to identify the four types of insurance coverage and give examples of each

Chinese merchants were among the earliest known businesspeople to use risk financing in the conduct of trade and commerce. Merchants who shipped their goods on the Yangtze River could never be sure that their goods would arrive safely at the trading centers downriver. It was not unusual for a merchant boat to sink, losing both the boat and its cargo, because some sections of the river were treacherous and difficult to navigate. To avoid total loss, merchants would coordinate their shipping activities and distribute their cargo among several ships. If a boat and its cargo were destroyed during its voyage, an individual merchant suffered only a partial loss instead of a disastrous total loss. By pooling their interests, these merchants had greater assurance that all would not be lost.

In the late 1600s, individuals interested in investing or financially participating in shipping and trade ventures would gather at Edward Lloyd's Coffee House in London. Notices of trade voyages would be posted that identified the type of ship and its cargo, destination, crew, and captain. Individuals would write their names under these notices with the amount of liability that they would assume in the event of a loss at sea. Each underwriter pledged his personal assets to cover his percentage of the loss in return for a premium for taking the risk. When the notice or slip was fully subscribed, the contract was complete.

Throughout history, close-knit communities have practiced risk financing in an informal way by pooling their resources. In central Pennsylvania, Amish tradition provided for the entire community to help rebuild a barn or house devastated by fire or storm. In return for each member's pledge and resources to participate in the rebuilding effort, the risk of disaster was transferred and distributed to everyone in the community.

In recent years, health care institutions have faced aggressive audits and investigations of their billing practices under the Medicare program by the Centers for Medicare and Medicaid Services (**CMS**) and the Office of the Inspector General (**OIG**). As billing practices were found to be in noncompliance with the government's interpretation of the reimbursement regulations, many providers were (and still are) faced with the repayment of large amounts to Medicare plus fines and penalties. Most providers never anticipated or funded for these business losses, which have had a material negative effect on the financial solvency of their institutions. Traditional insurance for such losses is for the most part unavailable. To finance these payments, some providers entered into contracts with insurers that indemnified the provider for the full loss in the year of payment in return for a full repayment of the **insurance** proceeds, plus the insurer's expenses, over a designated time period. Although this transaction had all the characteristics of a loan, it was structured as an insurance transaction, allowing the provider to spread the financial impact of this loss over several years.

In the examples mentioned, the Chinese, English, and Amish entrepreneurs and the health care executives all used some form of **risk financing** to deal with the potential for financial loss associated with adverse events. The basics of risk financing for a trip down the Yangtze River or to address Medicare fraud and abuse are essentially the same, including some or all of the following:

- The need to anticipate the risks of the group's operations
- A plan or means to financially deal with a loss if it occurred
- The pooling of resources to finance risk

- Transferring risk to others

- Spreading the risk among others with similar risks

- Risk retention

- Written contracts to substantiate financing arrangements in the event of a loss

- Identifying the simplest, least expensive, and most creative way to finance loss without jeopardizing the financial integrity of the group's operations

- The motivation to prevent the loss in the first place

Today, risk financing is viewed as a complicated subject involving legal contracts, sophisticated accounting, and myriad government regulations. All sorts of risk financing structures are available: an **indemnification** clause in a contract, an insurance policy that transfers the risk for a given exposure for a given price, the use of a **captive insurance company** for self-insurance, or a risk securitization plan that uses corporate bonds triggered by preestablished loss criteria. The types of exposures and losses faced by health care institutions for which a planned approach of risk financing is needed are also numerous and complex. Examples include a slip and fall in the parking lot, failure to properly diagnose a patient's condition, water damage to facilities as a result of severe weather, employee injuries while at work, a reduction of an institution's financial assets as a result of poor investment performance, the loss of key management individuals to the competition, the business risks of capitated reimbursement, Medicare fraud and abuse, and even acts of terrorism.

This chapter will introduce you to the concepts of risk financing within the overall context of the risk management process. It will establish the principles and foundation for structuring and implementing the various risk financing techniques. Further discussion on this topic can be found in Chapter 13.

KEY CONCEPTS

- Risk financing structures vary in complexity from programs offering guaranteed cost coverage on a primary basis to more complex and sophisticated retention programs involving captives and other alternative arrangements.

- If an organization's exposure to loss cannot be significantly reduced or eliminated through risk control measures, plans must be made to finance for losses that do occur despite best efforts.

- The most common forms of retention are the self-insurance trust and a captive insurance company.

- The prerequisite for risk retention is an effective risk management program, which includes management support, access to sound risk information, loss control strategies, and robust claims and litigation management practices.

RISK FINANCING IN THE CONTEXT OF THE RISK MANAGEMENT PROCESS

The risk management process involves two major areas that are intricately tied to each other—the identification and analysis of exposures and treating the exposures through some form of risk management technique. Figure 12.1 delineates the structure of this process and its key elements.

If we cannot treat these exposures in a manner that significantly eliminates the potential for loss through loss control, we must plan for their treatment through some form of risk financing.

The focus of this chapter is on the risk financing techniques and methods for generating funds to finance losses that risk control could not avoid. In some cases, the potential for loss was not identified or anticipated to allow for risk treatment. As Figure 12.1 shows, risk can be financed through risk retention or transfer to an outside party.

The decision to use a specific method to treat your organization's risk should be based on cost efficiency, financial stability and security, and the control over program administration that each method affords your organization.

RISK RETENTION

Risk retention techniques can vary from the unplanned payment of a loss from operating funds to a more planned approach such as the use of a captive insurance company. Basically, there are four methods organizations employ for the financing of loss through retention.

Use of Available Cash

Losses can be paid out of available cash from operations. Neither loss reserves nor funds have been established or designated for these payments. For example, institutions typically pay the deductible for an automobile or property loss out of available operating cash. These deductible payments are typically treated as unplanned expenditures from operations.

From a risk financing perspective, this technique is acceptable for losses that are small and occur infrequently. However, this is not an acceptable technique for financing medical professional liability exposures that tend to be both significant and frequent for most health care organizations. Unplanned or unfunded payments for this exposure could affect the financial stability of the organization at any given time.

Establishment of Loss Reserves

A **loss reserve** can be established for the potential liability of payment for losses. The reserve is typically based on expected losses and is treated as an accounting entry that identifies the potential liability on the organization's financial statements. Cash, securities, or other liquid assets can be earmarked to fund this liability. This technique recognizes that a potential for loss exists. It can go as far as setting aside assets

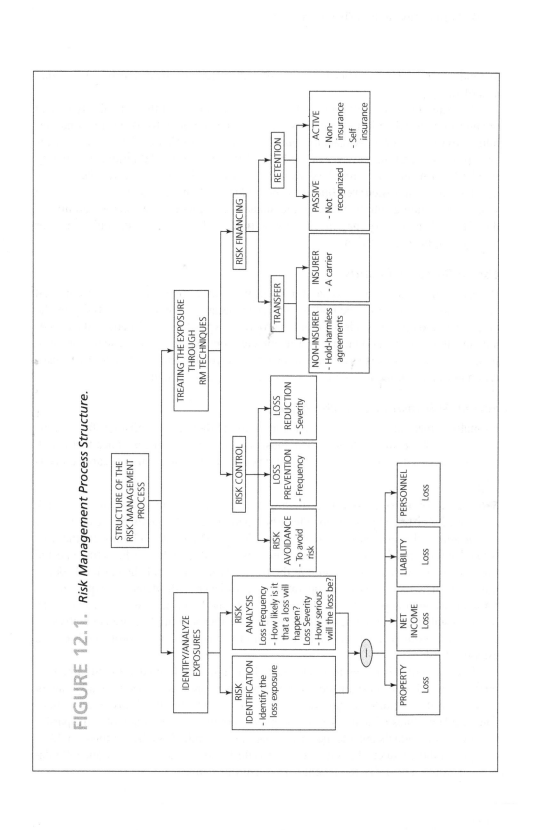

FIGURE 12.1. *Risk Management Process Structure.*

to fund potential losses. This is the significant difference from the first technique described.

An example of the use of this technique is the treatment of the tail liability that an organization has when it uses a claims-made insurance policy for its professional liability exposures. (For a discussion of *tail liability*, refer to Chapter Thirteen on insurance principles and the glossary at the back of this book for a definition. Accounting standards for health care providers require them to "book" or account for the liability they have for claims **incurred but not reported** (**IBNR**) at the end of each accounting year. An accounting entry is made on the financial statements to reflect the liability for this IBNR. This liability may or may not be funded, depending on the philosophy or resources of the organization.

Use of Borrowed Funds

Borrowed funds can be used to pay for losses when they come due. For the traditional health care provider, this method is inefficient because it reduces the ability of the organization to borrow funds for more appropriate expenditures. Moreover, the cost of unplanned borrowing is typically inefficient and more expensive. The use of borrowed funds to pay for losses is essentially a means of borrowing time. Ultimately, the institution must pay for the loss with its own earnings or other resources.

Formal Self-Insurance Techniques

Formalized methods of self-insurance can be used when an organization finances its losses through a planned strategy. The most typical form of self-insurance that health care institutions use today is the self-insurance trust or some form of a captive insurance company.

Self-Insurance Trust A trust is a funding vehicle that, in simplest terms, is a bank account administered by an independent third party (trustee). The funds are designated for the sole and restricted purpose of paying losses. The trustee administers the trust through a formalized agreement and a statement of coverage that outlines the type and limits of losses to be paid. Funding in the trust is typically established at levels determined by an actuarial study and operated in accordance with Medicare requirements. From an accounting perspective, the trust's assets and liabilities are recognized on the financial statements, and a description of the liabilities and funding are generally disclosed in a footnote to those statements. Both profit and not-for-profit entities can establish trusts.

Because a trust is not an insurance vehicle, it is strictly limited to the funding purposes for which it was established. For not-for-profit entities, a trust typically cannot be used for its for-profit subsidiaries. Also, a **trust** lacks the flexibility to accommodate regulated lines of insurance and cannot accommodate the risks of third parties (entities or individuals outside the parent's economic family). Such activities would be considered the conduct of insurance and would be subject to state insurance regulations or would jeopardize the parent's not-for-profit status.

The trust was once the most common vehicle for self-insurance of the primary professional and general liability exposures of a health care provider. Over time, trusts were replaced by captive insurance companies because these vehicles are more flexible in accommodating the various exposures and risk financing needs that a health care institution faces in today's environment. Recent hard market conditions for professional liability are once again elevating this risk financing option for consideration, especially for smaller not-for-profit providers whose financial resources are limited and whose risk financing priorities are not driven by the need to accommodate other lines of coverage or the risks of third parties. Many providers are now combining the use of trusts and captives to take advantage of the benefits that each vehicle has to offer.

Captive Insurance Company A captive is a closely held insurance company whose insurance business is primarily supplied by and controlled by its owners and in which the original insureds are the principal beneficiaries. Simply stated, a captive is a corporation for which the product is the payment of losses and the revenue is premium payments. Because a captive is an insurance vehicle and can be structured in many ways, it has great flexibility to accommodate the numerous and varied risk financing needs of organizations such as third-party businesses, for-profit entities, and multiple lines of coverage. It is a more formalized method of self-insurance in that it has separate financial statements and is regulated in the domicile in which it is established. This vehicle elevates the risk management function in an organization as its separate financial statements are scrutinized by board members typically drawn from the senior ranks of management and the parent's board. Because of a captive's visibility, there is a greater emphasis on controlling losses, the primary driver of costs for any program.

The form, structure, and ownership of captives can be established in different ways and combinations to meet the ownership, control, and coverage goals of their insureds.

Note that the use of captive insurance companies, trusts, and other forms of **self-insurance**—often referred to as the **alternative risk transfer** (**ART**) marketplace— has grown significantly in recent years. According to A. M. Best, a leading provider of ratings, news and financial data for the insurance industry worldwide, ART now accounts for over 50 percent of the commercial insurance marketplace in the United States. For health care institutions, this percentage is much higher because of the nature and volatility of the risks that must be dealt with in the context of a limited standard insurance marketplace. For financing of all types of risk, ART can no longer be referred to as the "alternative," as it has become a standard approach by which institutional insureds finance their risks.

Risk Transfer

When an outside party pays for losses when they occur, some form of **risk transfer** agreement is used. The most common method of risk transfer is the purchase of commercial insurance. Risk transfer can also be accomplished through noninsurance techniques, such as the use of an indemnification provision in a contract. Indemnification is the process by which one is restored or reimbursed to the extent of the loss ("made whole again").

Insurance is a contractual relationship that exists when one party (the insurer) for consideration (premium) agrees to reimburse or pay for another party's (insured) fortuitous loss caused by a predefined event (peril). Risk is shifted to others and spread among many parties. In general terms, covering the risks of unrelated parties by a company owned by multiple owners will constitute insurance.

From a practical view, insurance will nearly always involve some form of risk retention on a planned or unplanned basis. The use of a deductible would be an example of a planned retention. Denial of coverage as a result of an adverse policy coverage interpretation by the commercial insurer would certainly be an unplanned retention. The insurance policy, therefore, should never be viewed as a complete transfer of risk.

There are many forms and types of insurance that are generally classified in four areas as defined and illustrated in Table 12.1. Chapter 13 will provide a more detailed discussion of these coverages. Remember the principles and practices of these coverages as you apply them in a risk financing program.

The other method of risk transfer, the use of indemnification provisions in a contract, can be an effective tool to lower the overall cost of risk. A **hold-harmless agreement** is an agreement between two or more parties that defines an obligation or duty resting on one party to make good the liability, loss, or damage that the other party has incurred or may incur. Hold-harmless indemnification provisions can vary significantly. A common type of mutual indemnification clause may read as follows:

Provider agrees to indemnify and hold harmless the managed care organization (MCO) against any negligent act or claim made with respect to items or services provided by Provider under this Agreement to the extent that the negligent act or claim is attributable to any person or activity for which Provider is solely responsible or which arises in connection with the use or maintenance of property, equipment, or facilities under the direction or control of Provider. MCO agrees to indemnify and hold harmless Provider against any negligent act or claim made with respect to items or services provided under this Agreement to the extent that the negligent act or claim is attributable to any person or activity for which MCO is solely responsible or otherwise arises from duties or obligations that are solely the responsibility of MCO under this Agreement.

This clause states that each of the parties to the agreement will be responsible for indemnifying the other party for loss caused due to that party's negligence. This method of risk transfer is practical in certain situations, such as the execution of construction or supply contracts, but not in others, such as for the professional liability risks of providing care to patients. Patients are unlikely to sign a hold-harmless agreement before consenting to admission to the hospital for care. (Consent-to-treat agreements that patients are asked to sign before surgery or other invasive treatment are not intended to transfer risk but rather to authorize the particular treatment being proposed.)

TABLE 12.1. Types of Insurance

Type of Insurance	Definition	Examples
First-party	Provides coverage for the insured's own property or person. Is intended to indemnify and restore the insured to the same financial position existing prior to the loss.	Fire/property Business interruption Boiler and machinery Builder's risk Flood Earthquake Crime HMO/Capitation stop-loss
Third-party/liability insurance	Provides coverage to a party other than the insured. Coverage is intended to indemnify the third party for loss or injury caused by the insured. Involves three parties: (1) the insured who caused the harm or damage, (2) the party who is harmed, and (3) the insurer.	Professional liability General liability (Premises liability) Excess/Umbrella liability Employers' liability Auto liability Directors' and officers' liability Management errors and omissions Environmental impairment
Health and welfare insurance (benefits)	Provides coverage for an insured's employees. Coverage is intended to indemnify the employee by restoring his or her health and earnings to the level prior to the loss.	Workers' compensation Health benefits Long-term disability Short-term disability Dental/Vision/Life
Financial guarantees (sureties/bonds)	Provides a guarantee that specific obligations of a contract or performance will be fulfilled. Contracts of suretyship differ from traditional insurance in that assets are pledged for the full amount of risk transferred.	Sureties/Bonds Public official bonds Judicial bonds Contract/Performance bonds License and permit bonds

As with any risk financing technique, indemnification provisions need to be evaluated for the cost efficiency, financial security, and control that they afford in the risk transfer process. Therefore, these agreements need to be supported by the financial resources of the contracting party or some form of insurance or surety. They also need to be written or supported in such a way as to clearly define each party's rights and obligations in the event of a loss. In any event, given the legal uncertainties in enforcing hold-harmless agreements, they should never be relied on exclusively to accomplish risk transfer.

Risk Retention Versus Risk Transfer

The decision to transfer or retain risk will depend on many factors, including the following:

- The size and type of the organization and its operations

- The financial strength and resources of the organization

- The type of risk to be treated

- The organization's risk-taking philosophy

- The organization's future goals and objectives

- The overall effectiveness of the risk management and loss control programs

Risk financing can be viewed as a continuum between total risk transfer to total retention. Figure 12.2 provides a framework for evaluating the cost efficiency and cost certainty that each technique provides. Total risk transfer through insurance will fix costs with certainty, but cost efficiencies are sacrificed as a result of the insurance company's charges for taking on the full risk. The opposite is true for self-insurance of total exposures.

For example, if you purchased insurance for the first dollar of loss for your professional liability exposures, your financing costs for a given period of time would be fixed, providing you with the highest level of cost certainty. Theoretically, it could also be the most costly approach, as your premium would cover all of the following items:

- The insurance company's profit and overhead

- Estimated losses to be paid under the policy

- Charges for use of the policy form and administration of the insurance program (claims handling, loss control, and other policy services)

- Reinsurance

- A charge for the risk the company is assuming for this exposure

- Charges to reflect adverse loss development of other insureds and hard market conditions

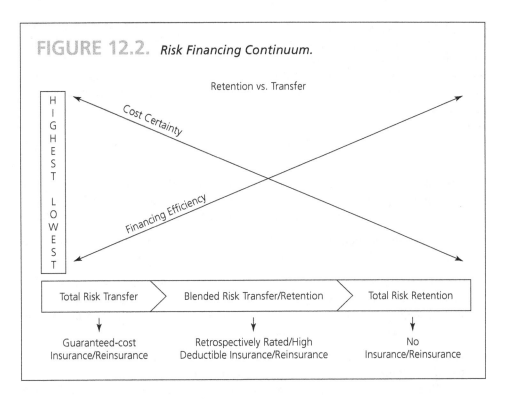

FIGURE 12.2. *Risk Financing Continuum.*

Because the insurance company is taking the risk, it will want to retain control over most or all major decisions involving the coverage. This might be the best risk financing technique for a small organization with limited assets and resources in which maximum cost certainty is important for financial well-being. It might also be a better technique for financing miscellaneous exposures for which the frequency or severity of loss cannot be reasonably predicted. These exposures can usually be insured at a reasonable price.

At the other end of the continuum, you could choose to retain all the risk for your professional liability exposures through some method of self-insurance. The cost of financing the risk would be most uncertain and would vary significantly with the frequency and severity of losses. Your cost efficiency would be at a high level because you would not pay an insurer for profit, overhead, and program service administration charges and because you would retain control over all aspects of the risk financing program. This approach might make sense for very large organizations that have the resources to manage all aspects of their risk management programs in an effective manner and have sufficient assets to accommodate the volatility of loss payments without impairing the financial strength of the organization.

Typically, risk managers use a combination of risk transfer and risk retention for professional liability exposures, whereby the predicable layer of loss is retained while the unpredictable, catastrophic loss is transferred. This approach strikes a balance between cost efficiency and certainty. By retaining the predictable loss layer, insurance company profit and overhead and other charges are minimized. Transferring the unpredictable, more volatile catastrophic losses to an insurer at a reasonable premium prevents significant swings in overall program costs and promotes financial stability over the long term, a key objective of any well-run organization. Program control is also balanced in a more effective and appropriate manner between the organization and the insurer.

As you chose between risk transfer and retention, consider the following guidance:

- The risk-taking philosophy of your organization affects the goals of the risk financing program. Define the risk you are willing to take versus what you can afford. Senior management needs to be involved in establishing the philosophy.

- Self-insure the predictable layer of loss where possible. To do otherwise would be trading dollars with an insurer with a loss of control over your program.

- Transfer the unpredictable or catastrophic layers of potential loss at limits sufficient to protect the assets of your organization. Excess coverage at sufficient limits is usually available at reasonable prices. Self-insuring this exposure to loss would be risking a lot to save a little.

- If you retain risk, you should have an effective risk management program in place to control or minimize loss. Sound risk information, loss control, claims handling, and litigation management systems are prerequisites. You also need to involve senior management and all your insureds in the process. An effective program will also make your organization an attractive risk for insurance purposes as you purchase coverage for catastrophic exposures. Keep in mind that risk retention through some form of self-insurance is not a cure for poor loss experience.

- Always take a long-term view of your risk transfer versus retention strategy. In a soft marketplace, you might be able to purchase insurance at a cost that is lower than expected losses. What effect does this have on your long-term costs and control over the program? Will the purchase of insurance take focus away from loss control efforts?

- Be prudent and conservative in funding for your self-insurance program. You can always fund less in the future if your loss experience develops better than expected. You always need a buffer to accommodate adverse loss experience in any program.

- When purchasing insurance, know your carrier better than it knows itself. Make sure it has the financial security, stable management, and policy services to be a good partner. Investigate its track record for paying claims and honoring its commitments. Do you have a relationship with your insurer to resolve gray areas of coverage?

■ Choose your risk financing consultants, brokers, actuaries, legal advisers, defense counsel, and auditors carefully. They need to be your partners and advocates in safeguarding your organization's assets and reputation. They not only have to be qualified through education and experience but also need the integrity to have your total interest at heart. Make sure they can work together as a team to make your program as effective as possible.

SUMMARY

The financing of losses that occur despite your best risk control efforts may come from the unstructured payment of losses from operating funds, from the application of the indemnification provision of a contract, or from the structured terms of a formal captive insurance company. The best and most effective method for your organization will depend on many factors, including the type of risk, its predictability for loss, the financial effect on your organization, your risk-taking philosophy, the sophistication of your risk management program, the degree of control you desire over program services, and the availability and affordability of insurance coverages.

As a risk management professional, it is your responsibility to guide your organization in making the best choice in meeting the overall mission and objectives of the organization. A sound risk financing program is important in protecting the assets of your organization and ultimately its reputation and ability to serve its customers and patients.

KEY TERMS

Captive insurance company	Loss reserve
Hold harmless	Risk financing
Incurred but not reported	Risk transfer
Indemnification	Trust
Insurance	

ACRONYMS

ART	IBNR
CMS	OIG

SUGGESTED READING

Best's Review, published monthly by A. M. Best Co.

Captive Insurance Company Reports, published monthly by the International Risk Management Institute.

Elliot, M. W. *Risk Financing*. Malvern, Pa.: Insurance Institute of America, 2000.

Krauss, G. E. *Essentials of Property and Casualty Insurance: A Complete Guide to the Pennsylvania Licensure* (11th ed.). Pittsburgh: Magellan Group, 2002.

Rejda, G., and Elliott, M. W. *Insurance Perspectives*. Malvern, Pa.: American Institute for Chartered Property Casualty Underwriters, 1994.

Society of Chartered Property and Casualty Underwriters, Georgia Chapter. *The Hold Harmless Agreement: A Management Guide to Evaluation and Control* (4th ed.). Cincinnati: National Underwriter Co., 1987.

CHAPTER

13

INSURANCE: BASIC PRINCIPLES AND COVERAGES

KIMBERLY WILLIS, JUDY HART

LEARNING OBJECTIVES

- To be able to identify key criteria when choosing an insurance carrier
- To be able to describe how insurance is purchased and regulated
- To be able to identify and describe the four standard elements in an insurance policy
- To be able to describe the difference between claims-made and occurrence coverage
- To be able to describe what is meant by a "hard market" and the role of the risk management professional

This chapter presents insurance principles and practices that apply to the health care industry. There are two main themes in this chapter. The first is a discussion of the basic concepts of insurance and how it is purchased and regulated, and the second is a review of the major types of insurance purchased by health care organizations.

The most common method of transferring or financing risk is to purchase insurance. Unfortunately, many individuals charged with health care risk management duties and assigned responsibility for the purchase of insurance have limited knowledge of its nuances. Many health care risk management professionals seek an insurance product that is a comprehensive and cost-effective method of transferring unwanted risk to an insurer. This dictates a need to understand the nature of insurance, know how to read an insurance policy, understand traditional coverages applicable to health care, and have an ability to determine when changes are necessary. Insurance alone cannot prevent risk, but it can provide financial security against loss.

KEY CONCEPTS

- To manage a risk financing program effectively, the risk management professional must understand the concept of risk transfer, know how to read and interpret policy language, understand the insurance market, understand traditional coverage, and have the ability to determine when changes are necessary.

- An insurance policy is a legal contract that creates obligations for both the insured (health care organization transferring the risk of financial loss) and the insurer (company that for a premium or consideration accepts the transferred risk).

- The policy's limits of liability state the maximum financial obligation of the insurer. The limits are frequently quoted on a per-occurrence and annual aggregate basis. Defense cost can be included in the limit of liability or be in addition to the stated limit.

- There are four general categories of insurance offered by the insurance industry: first-party coverage, third-party or liability coverage, health and welfare coverages, and financial guarantees.

DEFINITION OF INSURANCE

Insurance is "a system by which a risk is transferred by a person, business, or organization to an insurance company, which reimburses the insured for covered losses and provides for sharing of costs or losses among all insureds. Risk, transfer, and sharing are vital elements of insurance."[1] **Risk**, or the possibility of loss, creates the need for insurance. An organization can retain risk or transfer its risk to another organization.

Risk is commonly transferred to an insurance company. By accepting and sharing in the risk of many organizations, the insurance company can statistically calculate the likelihood that losses will or will not occur. It can also calculate their likely severity. This calculation permits establishment of a premium that the organization wishing to transfer its risk is charged. If the method of premium calculation is sound, the insurer should be able to pay the claims that are incurred and still earn a profit.

An insurance policy is a legal contract that creates obligations for both the insured (the individual organization wishing to transfer risk) and the insurer (the insurance company accepting the risk). Under this contract, the insurer promises to pay certain amounts if defined events take place. For example, the insuring agreement of a **medical professional liability** policy obligates the insurer to pay on behalf of the insured sums that the insured shall become legally obligated to pay as damages for the rendering or failure to render professional health care services. This obligation is modified by various other clauses, coverage terms, exclusions, and definitions in the insurance contract. The obligations of the insured vary, but most frequently they are required to pay a premium, report claims or likely losses in a speedy manner, and minimize the likelihood for loss. Insured losses must usually be fortuitous events—sudden and accidental. Intentional acts that result in loss are generally not covered by the insurance contract.

Although insurance contracts vary, they usually contain four standard elements: the declarations page, insuring agreement, conditions of the policy, and exclusions.

The declarations page identifies the named insured and describes the property or activity to be insured. Components of the page include the policy number, coverage inception and expiration dates, retroactive date, insured address, policy limit, applicable deductibles, insurer, and premium. The declarations page may also identify the various forms or endorsements to be attached to the policy.

The insuring agreement states the insurer's obligations under the terms of the contract. In general, the insuring agreement is often broadly stated but later narrowed by additional wording elsewhere in the policy. The insuring agreement contains conditional promises to pay. For example, if the policy states that the insurer will pay sums related to the rendering of or failure to render "professional services," the meaning of "professional services" is defined elsewhere in the policy. If the claim does not fall within this definition, it will not be covered. When interpreting the policy, the insured should remember that the insuring agreement is subject to the declarations, conditions, exclusions, and definitions contained elsewhere in the policy.

The conditions of the policy spell out many of the obligations of the insured and the insurer. Here are some examples of important conditions that may be included:

- The insured's obligation to provide prompt notice of loss
- The insured's obligation to cooperate with the insurer in investigation and settlement of a loss
- The insured's obligation to pay the premium in a timely manner
- The conditions under which the policy may be canceled or not renewed

- The insurer's right to inspect the premises

- The coverage territory of the policy

- The applicability of limits, deductibles, and defense expenses

Failure of an insured to adhere to the policy's conditions could result in the insurer's refusal to honor a claim.

Exclusions refer to policy provisions that eliminate or minimize coverage that the insurer does not intend to provide. Exclusions are usually identified in a specific section of the policy; however, additional exclusions may be dispersed throughout the insurance contract. In some cases, exclusions are added by endorsements attached to the main policy form. Although exclusions may seem punitive, they might not be. In some cases, an exclusion may be added to eliminate the potential for duplicate coverage or coverage not needed by a typical insured. Under other circumstances, an insurer may add an exclusion for its own benefit. Such is the case when the carrier is trying to limit risks it considers undesirable, a morale hazard, or outside its reinsurance arrangements. Typical exclusions include intentional acts, war, pollution or nuclear energy, terrorism, mold, and criminal acts. Many liability policies also exclude or minimize coverage provided for sexual misconduct, antitrust, punitive damages, and discrimination.

Insureds should work closely with the broker, agent, consultant, or carrier to make certain their insurance policies provide comprehensive, cost-effective, and financially secure transfer of risk.

How Insurance Is Regulated

Insurance is a highly regulated industry. Most regulation is mandated at the state level. The rules and regulations vary by state. Nearly all states give their insurance departments the power to regulate rates, to license insurers and insurance company representatives, to approve policy forms, and to respond to consumer complaints.

Insurance brokers and agents must be licensed in their states of operation. This usually involves a state examination and continuing education requirements.

Most insurance carriers must apply and financially qualify in every state in which they wish to solicit or conduct business. Once a carrier is approved by the state, it is considered admitted. As an **admitted insurer**, the carrier must obey all state laws regulating the operation of an insurance company. In addition, it must file its current policy forms, any changes in forms, and any premium rate increases or decreases with the state for approval by the insurance department. Most states have established guaranty funds to protect insureds from the insolvency of admitted carriers. These funds are typically financed by assessments against those insurers.

For various reasons, some carriers operate as **nonadmitted** or "surplus line" carriers in a state. These companies are exempt from rigorous state regulations. Neither their premium rates nor the contents of their policies are subject to regulation and review. Because these carriers are exempt from various state regulations, they are not allowed to participate in the **guaranty fund**. Most states require that insureds who purchase coverage from a surplus lines carrier pay taxes or other fees on the premium. These taxes are usually in addition to the annual premium quoted by the carrier.

Insurance Company Financial Security

The financial stability of an insurance carrier should be a key consideration in an insured's decision to transfer risk. If an admitted carrier fails, its insureds may have access to the state guaranty fund. Unfortunately, the protection offered by these funds is limited. Not all state funds cover all policies or claims. For example, some guaranty funds exclude medical professional liability policies. Others limit the time in which a claim can be reported to the fund. The duration may be shorter than the time provided under the original insurance policy. In some cases, the limits of liability provided by the fund are lower than the limits the defunct insurance carrier provided. For example, the fund may pay 33 cents on each dollar of the policy limit, or it may provide only a $100,000 limit. Under this scenario, the insured is responsible for the remainder of any claim.

It is critical that insureds carefully evaluate the financial position of their insurance carriers. To assist insureds and others with this evaluation, a rating system has been developed to categorize the financial condition of carriers. The most frequently cited rating resource for insurance companies is A. M. Best Co. (http://www.ambest .com). Best performs a comprehensive quantitative and qualitative analysis of each company's balance sheet strength, operating performance, and business profile.

Financial Strength and Size

Best's reviews include an evaluation of the company's spread of risk exposures, appropriateness of reinsurance, quality and diversification of assets, adequacy of loss reserves, adequacy of surplus, capital structure, management experience, market presence, and policyholders' confidence. These tests primarily focus on profitability, leverage and capitalization, and liquidity. Each carrier's financial performance is examined, and more than one hundred financial tests are performed. Based on the ratios, Best assigns a value from A++ (superior) to F (in liquidation).

Companies that receive a letter rating from Best are further evaluated as to their financial size and placed in a financial size class (FSC) category. Policyholder surplus and other conditional or technical reserve funds are the basis for this rating. The rating is expressed in roman numerals, from the smallest FSC, I, to the highest, XV. Most insured will purchase insurance coverage from insurers that they feel can best provide adequate limits to cover their risk.

An insured can obtain an insurer's A. M. Best rating by asking the insurance carrier, agent, or broker for a copy of the current report. In addition, Best manuals are usually available at large public or university libraries. (For more information on A. M. Best, go to the Web site.) Other sources of financial information are Standard & Poor's and Moody's rating agencies.

Health care risk management professionals should inquire as to the financial rating of their current and past insurance carriers. Health care medical professional liability is a long-tail exposure. Although some claims are reported promptly and paid quickly, other claims might not be known or paid until years into the future. When the policy is purchased, a carrier may be financially sound, but over time, the carrier's financial strength could weaken to the point of insolvency.

How Insurance Is Purchased

Most health care risk management professionals gain access to the commercial insurance market by using an insurance broker or independent agent.

Traditionally, brokers are independent insurance professionals who represent the insurance buyer to the insurance company. In this role, they participate in the evaluation of risk potential, gathering of exposure and loss information, presentation of the data to the insurance community, negotiation of coverage terms and premium pricing, and evaluation of quotations. Brokers may also provide assistance in loss mitigation, with alternative means of financing risk. Historically, agents have legally and contractually represented the interests of the insurance carrier, not the insured. An agent may represent one or many insurance carriers. In practice, the line between a broker and an agent has blurred. Both act as facilitators for the evaluation and purchase of insurance.

Brokers and agents are often compensated on a commission basis. The amount of commission varies by line of coverage and carrier. Brokers are frequently willing to accept compensation on a flat-fee basis. This removes any bias the broker might have regarding its commission level with a particular carrier. Some brokers are willing to work on a fee-plus-incentive basis. Regardless of the method of compensation, your broker or agent should be willing to discuss and disclose all methods of compensation received from placing coverage.

Drafting Coverage Specifications

Risk management professionals often have the responsibility of securing cost-efficient, comprehensive insurance coverage. This is not an easy task. The process should begin at least six months before policy inception. The first step is an evaluation of exposures and the insurance products available to cover them. Once the exposures to be transferred are identified, an application for coverage is prepared. This application is often called an **underwriting** submission. The submission serves as a tool to present your organization's business strategies, risk exposures, and insurance desires to the insurance marketplace.

Some carriers will allow the insured to develop its own application for coverage. Others require that the submission be prepared based on a standard format developed by the carrier. The submission is then submitted to the carrier's underwriting department. A quotation is developed. The insured, the broker or agent, and the insurer then negotiate through coverage terms, services, and pricing considerations. Upon agreement, the coverage is bound. The underwriting submission frequently includes the following components:

- A description of operations and organizational chart

- Listing of named insureds and additional insureds

- Retroactive dates (if the coverage is on a **claims-made basis**)

- Location listing
- Current and historical exposure information
- Currently valued historical loss experience (five to twenty years of loss experience)
- Large loss detail for any claim over $100,000
- Signed application (as requested by the carrier)
- Current annual report or other financial statements
- Description of risk management department procedures, including loss prevention, quality improvement, patient safety initiatives, and claims management
- Current actuarial report
- Trust, captive, or underlying coverage document
- Joint Commission or other accreditation report
- Description of desired coverage—limits, deductible, coverage extensions, underlying coverages, pricing guidelines, policy period, key coverage terms, services, and so on

Identifying the carriers who are interested in assuming your risk is the next step. Since 2000, various carriers have been liquidated, and others have voluntarily left the market. Some carriers have refocused their health care initiatives, and new entrants have entered the marketplace. Following are some key criteria to consider when selecting a carrier:

- Does the purchase of this policy support the short-term or long-term objectives of the health care organization and risk management department?
- Is the insurance carrier financially secure? What is its financial rating according to A. M. Best or other rating organizations?
- Is the carrier knowledgeable in health care operations?
- Is the carrier flexible?
- Is the pricing competitive?
- How will future pricing be affected by your organization's favorable or unfavorable loss experience?
- How will future pricing be affected by losses within the health care industry or outside the health care industry?
- Is the carrier capable of meeting the claims administration, loss prevention, clinical risk management, risk management information systems (**RMIS**), and educational needs of your facility?
- How long has this carrier been offering this type of coverage? What is its past history in the marketplace? Is it a long-term option?

- What is the carrier's claims-handling philosophy? Will it allow input from your organization?

- What firms are on the carrier's legal defense panel? Does the insured have a choice of counsel? Can a firm or individual attorney be easily added to the insurer's defense legal panel?

Once quotations are received, they must be analyzed for price, terms, services, and other qualitative issues. Insurance policies vary in terms and conditions, but key coverage considerations should include the following:

- Is the quotation based on complete and accurate exposure and loss information? If the information is not complete, could the pricing change according to outstanding data?

- What are the limits of the policy? How do they apply?

- Is there a deductible or retention, and how does it apply?

- Does the policy include a coinsurance provision?

- What are the policy period, effective date, and expiration date of coverage?

- What is the premium? Is there a minimum premium? Is the premium flat, assessable, or auditable?

- Is coverage claims-made or occurrence?

- If coverage is claims-made, what is the retroactive date?

- What is the intent of coverage? Has the carrier released sample forms and endorsements?

- What are the key exclusions? Are these common? Can they be amended?

- Who is covered by the policy—organizations in addition to individuals?

- What is the coverage territory?

- What is the procedure for reporting claims?

- What is the definition of a claim?

- What is the time frame within which claims must be reported? Is there a prescribed format for reporting? Who must report claims?

- Does the application become a warranty to the policy?

- How are defense costs handled? Are they included within the limit or retention or exclusive outside the limit or retention?

- Are there provisions for adding or deleting exposures during the policy period?

- Under what circumstances can the insured and insurer cancel or non-renew the policy?

Once coverage has been bound, the broker or carrier will issue a binder of insurance evidencing that coverage was purchased. Once the actual policy is issued, the binder is no longer needed. It might also be helpful to have your broker or agent prepare an insurance summary. This tool emphasizes key components of your insurance policy. The summary will often include a description of the type of policy purchased, policy numbers, policy period, limits of coverage, deductibles, premiums, a coverage overview, and major exclusions.

Another helpful tool that is often prepared by your broker or agent is a schedule of insurance. This schedule is a condensed version of all insurance coverage placed and serves as a quick reference or guide. Many risk management professionals have this schedule readily available as an aid in answering questions. The schedule of insurance generally covers much the same material as a policy summary, except that the coverage overview and narrative description of policy type are not included and all lines of coverage are included.

The Hard and Soft Market

The insurance industry is cyclical. It is characterized by periods of low premiums, flexible terms, and generous capacity followed by periods of escalating premiums, strict underwriting procedures, and limited availability of coverage. The periods of flexible pricing and terms are known as "soft" markets. Once pricing and terms become more limited, the market is said to be in a "hard" cycle. The cycles usually last five to seven years. Although no one can predict a turn in the market or the best position to take in a **hard insurance market**, considerations such as these should be evaluated:

- What is the overall business strategy of the carrier?

- Has it historically been committed to the health care industry?

- Is it committed to your organization?

- How has the carrier reacted to other pricing cycles?

- What is the financial status of the carrier?

- What is the carrier's loss ratio for similar accounts? Is the exposure profitable for the carrier?

- Does it make sense to place all the organization's exposures with one carrier and hope that the economies of scale prove beneficial, or is it better to disperse the exposures throughout the marketplace and establish numerous relationships?

The potential for a hard market also dictates that a health care organization reevaluate its current risk financing program. Analysis should include the following activities:

- Review of limits purchased: Are they enough? Should they be reduced, increased, or restructured?

- Review of retentions: Should they be restructured?

- Should the organization continue to transfer this risk? Could the risk be better managed by the use of an alternative risk financing vehicle or retention of the risk?

- Review of the organization's risk and claims management programs: Are they in order?

Throughout the course of their professional careers, risk management professionals will have to deal with hard markets. Because of this certainty, health care risk management professionals should constantly be reviewing their risk financing vehicles for short-term and long-term benefits. They must also evaluate the best method and technique for presenting their risk to the insurance marketplace. Without proper planning, coverage may not be available at any cost. A hard market cycle dictates that the risk management professional take the following actions:

- Consider alternative program structures. This might include considering higher deductibles, purchasing lower limits, going without coverage, and establishing a captive or trust in addition to other finite risk vehicles.

- Start the process of securing coverage six months before inception of the policy. This will allow time for adequate planning, preparation of the submission, presentation of the risk, and evaluation of alternatives.

- Develop a timeline for each viable alternative. Identify critical dates.

- Engage senior management in the process. In a hard market, senior management might find its insurance budget woefully inadequate. Premiums could escalate.

- Rely on experts to assist in the process. Consultants or knowledgeable health care brokers can provide assistance as to the marketplace and presenting the risk, but actuaries, accountants, legal firms, clinical risk and claims specialists, and other experts may be needed if the organization is considering increasing retentions significantly through a trust, captive, or other alternative financing arrangements.

- Recognize that **underwriters** view certain risk areas more or less favorably. For example, certain carriers are comfortable with physician exposures, whereas others are not and prefer to focus primarily on hospital exposures.

- Present the risk in a way that appeals to the carrier. Each carrier's appetite for risk is different. Research each carrier's senior management and risk philosophy. Present your risk in a way that differentiates it in the marketplace. Be concise. Minimize the difficult areas of your risk picture, and maximize the positives. Present a complete and accurate loss picture, and identify steps that have been taken to reduce the likelihood of future occurrences.

A Discussion of Claims-Made Versus Occurrence Policies

Certain health care–related policies are written on a claims-made basis. Examples include directors' and officers' liability and managed care errors and omissions. Other policies are offered on an occurrence basis. Automobile, property, and workers' compensation policies are usually written on an occurrence form. Still other coverages, such as medical professional liability, can be written on either a claims-made or an occurrence basis.

An occurrence policy covers an insured for incidents that occur while the policy is in effect, regardless of when the incident is reported to the insurer. Unlike claims-made, there is no need for an insured to obtain an additional policy endorsement or extension when the insured wishes to move to a new insurer. The date the claim or incident is filed has no effect on the applicable policy period. The date that the claim occurred determines the applicable policy period.

A claims-made policy covers an insured for incidents that both occur and are reported to the insurer while the policy is in force. This method of tracking claims can be burdensome because claims or incidents might occur during one policy period but are not reported until after the policy period has ended. If this happens, coverage might not apply for the claim. This potential gap in coverage can be minimized through the maintenance of the original retroactive date (**nose**) or the purchase of a policy endorsement for an extended reporting period (**tail**).

For coverage under a claims-made policy to apply, the incident or claim must have occurred after the retroactive date of the policy. The retroactive date is usually the first date that the insured purchased claims-made coverage. Under most circumstances, the retroactive date should be maintained on all subsequent policies.

For example, assume that a physician purchases a first claims-made policy on July 1, 2008, from XYZ Insurance. The policy will cover claims that are incurred and reported from July 1, 2008, to June 30, 2009. Because this is the first claims-made policy the physician has purchased, it will have a July 1, 2008, retroactive date. Now assume that three years pass and the physician has maintained claims-made coverage with XYZ for the entire three-year period. In addition, the original retroactive date of July 1, 2008, has been maintained. Unknown to the physician, an incident occurred on August 1, 2008, but was not known to the physician until the current policy period (July 1, 2010, to June 30, 2011). Even though the claim occurred on August 1, 2008, it will be paid under the current claims-made policy rather than the original July 1, 2008, to June 30, 2009, policy. This is because the physician has maintained the retroactive date of July 1, 2008, on the current policy. The current policy covers claims incurred and reported for the current policy period (July 1, 2010, through June 30, 2011) and that occurred subsequent to July 1, 2008, and reported during the current policy period. The current policy, however, would not cover any claim that occurred prior to the retroactive date of July 1, 2008, or any claim reported in a previous policy period. If the physician failed to maintain the July 1, 2008, retroactive date, the claim would not have been covered by either the July 1, 2008, to June 30, 2009, policy (in place at the time of the event) or the July 1, 2010, to June 30, 2011, policy (in place at the time of the report). In contrast, if the physician had purchased **occurrence coverage**, the claim would have been paid under the July 1, 2008, to June 30, 2009, occurrence policy.

Nose

Under the claims-made form, the nose is the period of time between an insured's retroactive date and the commencement date of the current policy period. In the example just given, the nose is the period July 1, 2008, through June 30, 2010. The policy will respond to claims that have been incurred during the period July 1, 2008, through June 30, 2010, but are not reported until the July 1, 2010, to June 30, 2011, policy year. In addition, the July 1, 2010, to June 30, 2011, policy will also provide protection for claims incurred and reported during the July 1, 2010, to June 30, 2011, policy year.

Tail

A tail is also known as an **extended reporting period** (**ERP**). Various scenarios create the need for an ERP, but the most common scenario is when an insured changes carriers. The ERP essentially converts a claims-made policy to an occurrence policy by extending coverage to all claims that arise from care rendered during the policy period (and nose period, if applicable), regardless of when the claim is reported.

ERPs can be limited in time and in the limits of liability that they offer. An unlimited time for the extended reporting period is preferred, but some carriers limit the ERP to twelve months, thirty-six months, or some other specific period of time. The limits of liability purchased with an ERP also can vary. They can simply be an extension of the policy limits remaining and available from the last or expiring policy period, a new set of limits identical to the limits on the expiring policy, or some other negotiated limit. Remember that the limits of liability for the ERP are available for the payment of claims only if the limits have not been exhausted by payment of previous claims. Should the limits be exhausted through the payment of reported claims, many carriers will allow the insured to purchase an additional set of limits for a premium. This is called "reinstating the limits."

The carrier will charge an additional premium for the ERP. The additional premium is generally 100 percent to 200 percent of the annual premium for the current policy period. During a soft market cycle, carriers might be more willing to offer this extension at a more reasonable price. An ERP can be purchased from the expiring carrier or the new carrier. Generally, using the new carrier is the more cost-effective option.

An additional item to consider when purchasing claims-made coverage is the definition of a claim. Most claims-made policies define a claim as "a lawsuit or an incident likely to result in a lawsuit." This allows the insured to report incidents that it feels could give rise to a lawsuit and have any subsequent lawsuits covered under the current policy regardless of when the claim is made. This definition minimizes the likelihood of a gap in coverage. Some policies, however, define a claim as only a written demand for compensation or a filed lawsuit. Care must be taken when moving from one claims-made insurance carrier to another. Even if the new carrier agrees to maintain the insured's original retroactive date, it is possible for a gap in coverage to result if each carrier defines a claim in different terms.

How Much to Purchase

Health care risk management professionals often wonder about the appropriate amount of insurance coverage to purchase. This question is not easily answered. Guidelines are provided by reviewing the limits historically purchased by the organization, the loss history of the organization, analysis of the regulatory and legal climate, evaluation of exposures created by the organization's business strategies, and benchmarking these factors against other similar organizations. Included in this analysis is a review of what limits are being purchased and of risk retained through a deductible or self-insured retention.

Limits of Liability

The policy limits of liability state the maximum obligation of the insurer. Limits are frequently quoted on a per-occurrence and annual aggregate basis. For example, coverage might be purchased to provide $1 million per claim with a $3 million annual aggregate. These limits are commonly represented as "$1 million to $3 million." Under this scenario, the most the carrier will pay is $1 million for a claim during the policy year. In addition, the most the carrier will pay for all claims in the policy year is $3 million regardless of the number of claims filed.

How defense cost will be treated is a key coverage condition. Defense cost can be inclusive or exclusive. Inclusive defense cost means that the costs to defend the case are part of the limits of liability (included) and erode the limits as costs are paid. This treatment diminishes the limits available (amount of money) to pay for any subsequent awards, judgments, or settlements. Under these circumstances, the maximum amount of money the carrier will pay out on behalf of the insured is $1 million. This is the less desirable method. Defense costs that are exclusive do not erode the limits of liability and are paid in addition to the available limits remaining on the policy. It is preferable to have defense costs outside the policy limits. Under these circumstances, the carrier will pay up to $1 million plus all defense costs.

The treatment of defense cost also has a direct effect on the calculation of premiums. Policies that offer defense costs inclusive of the limits of liability are generally less expensive than policies under which defense costs are exclusive or in addition to the limits. Limits of liability for policies that provide for inclusive defense cost will erode faster than policies with defense cost excluded. Once the insurer has paid out the limits of liability on a defense-included policy, its responsibility ends. Coverage for policies with defense costs exclusive or outside the limits of liability will have a higher premium cost because the possibility exists that the insurer will have to pay out more money—not only the limits of liability but also the cost of defense for each claim. It is understandable that the insurer would charge more for policies that offer defense costs exclusive of the limits of liability.

In addition to per-claim and aggregate limits, some policies contain sublimits. A sublimit caps the most the policy will pay for a particular peril. This limit is usually within the limits provided by the policy; it is seldom in addition to the policy limit.

Deductibles or self-insured retentions (**SIR**s) state the amounts the insured has agreed to retain. Deductibles or SIRs may apply to each claim, each occurrence, or in aggregate for all losses for the policy period. Both serve to reduce premiums. Under a deductible, claims handling usually remains within the authority and responsibility of the insurance carrier. The actual limit provided by the policy is usually the per-claim limit minus the deductible. Thus if the policy contains a $1 million limit and a $100,000 deductible, the most the policy will actually pay is $900,000. In most cases, the insurer will pay the total cost of the claim and request reimbursement from the insured for the insured's deductible. In contrast, if the policy includes a SIR, the policy will pay the full limit described in excess of the insured's SIR. The SIR obligates the insured to pay the first $100,000, after which the carrier will pay up to $1 million. SIRs usually allow the insured influence or control over the claims administration process.

SPECIFIC TYPES OF INSURANCE FOR THE HEALTH CARE INDUSTRY

Several broad categories of insurance are offered by the insurance industry. These types of coverage are categorized by the kinds of losses they insure against. The most common types of coverage relating to losses inherent in the health care industry are **first-party coverage**, **third-party** or liability **coverage**, health and welfare insurance, and financial guarantees provided by carriers in various forms of bonds such as **surety bonds**.

First-Party Insurance

First-party insurance provides financial reimbursement as the result of damage or destruction to the insured's own property. This type of insurance is also called "direct damage" coverage.

A significant exposure faced by a health care organization is direct damage to property it owns, operates, controls, or is under the obligation to insure for physical loss or damage and the loss of income should all or a portion of its property be unusable as the result of a loss. Such losses can result from fire and lightning, windstorm, hail, explosion, smoke, impact from aircraft and vehicles, objects falling from aircraft, strike, riot, civil commotion, vandalism, theft or attempted theft, sprinkler leakage, collapse of buildings, and other perils.

The common risk treatment for property losses is the purchase of commercial insurance. Property insurance for health care organizations has traditionally been readily available in the insurance market because of the positive nature of health care industry property risks. Most health care property is classified as highly protected risk (HPR), meaning that the risk is adequately protected and that management has a proactive attitude toward loss avoidance and life safety. Health care property risks are considered well below the national average.

The property insurance marketplace for health care risks is cyclical, based on the overall insurance market cycle and on natural and man-made events that can have a catastrophic effect on the industry. According to the National Hurricane Division of the Atlantic Oceanographic and Meteorological Laboratory, the four hurricanes to hit the state of Florida in 2004 resulted in an estimated loss of more than $45 billion and the 2005 hurricane season faired no better with losses estimated at $115.4 billion. The 2005 hurricane season encompassed five hurricanes, three of which are well known due to their significant damages: Katrina with cost estimates at $81 billion; Wilma at $20.6 billion; and Rita at $10 billion.[2] Current estimates for hurricane Ike in September 2008 could exceed costs related to the entire 2004 season or Hurricane Katrina. These estimates are catastrophic in terms of both dollars and people. The magnitude of the losses resulting from the September 11, 2001, terrorist attacks affected every insurance product and the risk appetite of every insurance carrier. Those effects are still being felt in the industry, particularly in the availability of terrorism insurance. Counting the value of lives lost as well as property damage and lost production of goods and services, losses already exceed $100 billion,[3] making this the costliest disaster in U.S. history. In spite of that, the health care property market has not been severely affected by the loss of capacity. Adequate capacity remains available in the market at attractive terms; however, certain catastrophic exposures in high-risk areas are more difficult to place. In certain coastal areas, coverage can be acquired only through government-sponsored insurance programs such as the National Flood Program and catastrophic wind pools formed in some coastal states.

Many property carriers provide loss prevention services to their policyholders. These value-added services can assist the risk management professional in maintaining the status of the current facilities and can provide input on new construction. Generally, these carriers provide inspections and recommendations on an ongoing basis. The benefits of complying with the insurers' recommendations should be measured against the cost of compliance.

The majority of property policies available to the health care industry are **comprehensive** in form. A single policy can incorporate coverages such as the following:

- Physical damage to real and business personal property

- Time element coverage

- Boiler and machinery

- Transit coverage

- Automatic builder's risk protection

- Fine arts coverage

- Valuable papers and records

- Electronic data processing (EDP)

- Accounts receivable

Property policies specify the exact property and business personal property to be covered, the dollar amount of coverage afforded, and the types of losses covered under the policy. Property insurance may protect any covered person or organization that has an **insurable interest** in the property.

Property coverage can be written on an **actual cash value** (**ACV**) basis or **replacement cost** basis. Actual cash value is the replacement value of the property at the time and place of the loss or damage, minus deductions for depreciation. Under a property policy written on a replacement cost basis, claim payments will be based on the cost to repair or replace the property without any deduction for depreciation. Because this preferred option requires that the insured carry enough coverage to replace damaged or destroyed property, it is very important to determine the correct property limit. Most replacement cost policies contain a coinsurance provision. This provision requires the insured to carry insurance equal to a specified percentage of the replacement cost of the value of the property covered. If the amount of coverage is inadequate, a coinsurance penalty is assessed at the time of loss. This may result in reimbursement for loss that is less than the replacement cost or cost to repair.

Named Peril Versus All-Risk Coverage Insurance to protect against direct damage losses can be purchased on a **named peril** or **all-risk** basis. Under a named peril policy, only losses due to the specific perils named in the policy are covered. The burden is on the insured to prove that there has been a loss. The preferred form of coverage is the all-risk form. Its broad, blanket-insuring agreement covers all losses that are not specifically excluded. In the all-risk form, the burden of proof is on the insurance carrier to prove that a loss is not covered.

Even with comprehensive all-risk forms, several perils are difficult or impossible to insure. These include earthquake, landslide, mudflow, subsidence, flood, nuclear reaction or contamination, volcanic eruption, war and terrorism, intentional losses, normal expected wear and tear, and business perils such as marketing and political risk.

Where significant exposure exists for perils such as earthquake, wind, and flood, carriers may provide sublimits of coverage or exclude coverage all together. In such instances, excess or wrap-around coverage can be provided by purchasing a difference in conditions (**DIC**) policy. In these policies, the definition of earthquake includes landslide, quake, and other similar movements. The definition of flood includes surface water, tidal or seismic sea wave, rising or overflowing of any body of water, and seepage or influx of water from natural underground sources into basements or other floors.

Time Element Coverage In addition to direct damage losses, a health care organization faces the peril of losing revenues as a result of an insured loss. Coverage for this kind of loss is provided by consequential loss or time element insurance.

Major wind damage, fire, or flood could result in either a partial or total shutdown of a hospital's operations. During the shutdown, revenues generated by those operations are lost, and there would probably be additional expenses in attempting to continue as nearly as possible the normal conduct of business. **Business interruption**, a time element coverage, pays for the loss of earnings and continuing expenses resulting from a covered loss. These expenses can include ordinary payroll if included in the limit determination. The insurer will also reimburse the insured for extra expenses incurred to keep a facility operating while repairs are being made or to mitigate further damage. These so-called extraordinary expenses are those considered above and beyond the insured's ordinary operating expenses from the time ordinary operations are interrupted to the time they are resumed. Examples include the expense of transferring patients to another facility and the loss of income as the result of closing the emergency room or operating room while repairs are being made.

Time element claims are some of the most difficult to adjust. Potential disputes relating to lost revenue and expenses can be avoided by providing the insurance carrier with a thoroughly completed business interruption worksheet each year. The worksheet will identify continuing expenses and loss of income that the insured will experience if an insured claim results in a total or partial facility closure.

This coverage can provide a contribution clause that operates much like a coinsurance clause. To ensure that the limit of coverage applicable to the risk meets the policy's requirements, limits should be reviewed annually with the insurance carrier or broker. The deductible for this form of insurance is typically stated as a specified number of hours or days following the actual loss.

Boiler and Machinery **Boiler and machinery insurance** provides insurance for mechanical and electrical breakdown of equipment and can extend to cover such exposures as ammonia contamination, hazardous substances, water damage, and the drying out of electrical equipment. Equipment covered can extend to pressure vessels, refrigeration equipment, heating and air-conditioning systems, and pumps and compressors. The policy covers owned property and resulting damage to other property, including property in "your care, custody, and control for which you are liable." Accidents to boilers and machinery are in most instances directly related to the energy inherent in their operations, such as heat, pressure, electrical energy, centrifugal force, and reciprocating motion.

Standard property policies cover losses to boilers and machinery and to other property when caused by perils insured against in the policy. However, these forms do not cover damage to boilers and machinery or anything else when the loss is caused by uninsured or excluded perils. These might include explosions or other sudden breakdowns in the boilers and machinery. Where such losses are excluded, a separate boiler and machinery policy is necessary. Many of the newer "comprehensive" property policies have limited boiler and machinery exclusions, eliminating the need to carry separate coverage.

Builder's Risk Property risk associated with new construction is typically covered under a builder's risk policy. Buildings under construction face unique hazards. Building materials on the premises are subject to theft or destruction. Because fire protection systems, such as sprinkler systems, might not be fully installed and operational, the risk characteristics for a loss are modified.

A builder's risk policy may be issued to cover the interests of the building owner, the contractor, or both jointly as their interests may appear. A separate builder's risk policy may be provided by the contractor or purchased by the health care organization. Under a comprehensive policy, automatic **builder's risk coverage** is generally extended to construction on any existing premises. Coverage can be added to cover exposure at an off-site location, subject to carrier notification and acceptance.

Electronic Data Processing and Media Coverage Electronic data processing (EDP) equipment is subject to loss from all the perils to which other equipment is exposed (fire, windstorm, and so on) and is sensitive to perils that have little effect on other property. These include dust, temperature, and humidity changes that can affect the equipment enough to result in an actual loss. Recorded media data are vulnerable to the same losses, including magnetic storms. They can also be lost, stolen, erased, or tampered with.

In addition to direct loss, the temporary loss of data processing facilities could result in a serious interruption to the organization. The extra expense coverage in an EDP policy could reimburse for equipment rental or use of time-sharing facilities, additional payroll, temporary office equipment, or temporary help.

Separate EDP policies or an EDP extension on a standard property policy provide protection for the added risks associated with these exposures. Standard property policies pay for the loss of media but not the loss of information. EDP coverage will pay for replacement of information displayed on cards, disks, drums, or tapes.

Commercial Crime Insurance and Employee Dishonesty **Crime insurance** covers two broad categories of risk—crimes committed by outsiders and crimes committed by employees. Because crime-related losses are not typically covered under property insurance policies, crime insurance is an important coverage in a health care organization's insurance portfolio.

Crime insurance can cover money and securities against burglary, robbery, theft, destruction, disappearance, and employee dishonesty.

Crime insurance also covers property other than money and securities against loss due to specified crime perils such as burglary, robbery, theft, computer fraud, extortion, and employee dishonesty. Crime coverage also extends to loss as the result of property damaged but not stolen by burglars or robbers.

Probably the most significant financial risk for health care providers is employee dishonesty. This can include embezzlement, the theft of drugs or other hospital supplies, or the alteration of financial records for personal gain. Along with the rapid growth in technology has come a new opportunity for criminal losses. Computer fraud is at an all-time high and is rapidly increasing. Computer crime includes electronic theft of money and securities, embezzlement, fraud, or erased or modified information.

Third-Party Insurance

Third-party insurance provides coverage to pay on behalf of the insured or reimburse the insured for bodily injury, personal injury, or property damage loss due to negligence caused by an insured. It involves three parties—the party who is harmed, the insurer, and the insured party who caused the harm or damage. Unlike first-party coverage, the named insured is never a direct recipient of the payment for loss responded to by a liability policy. The following are the most common third-party coverages applicable to a health care organization:

- Medical professional liability

- General liability (premises liability, personal injury, products or completed operations, independent contractor's liability, and contractual liability)

- Umbrella excess liability

- Employment practices liability

- Automobile liability

- Directors' and officers' liability

- Miscellaneous errors and omissions, including managed care errors and omissions

- Environmental impairment liability

- Fiduciary liability

- Heliport and nonowned aircraft liability

Medical Professional Liability Medical professional liability insurance provides coverage for claims arising from the rendering of or failure to render medical, surgical, dental, X-ray, or other imaging or nursing service or treatment or the furnishing of food or beverages in connection therewith; furnishing or dispensing of drugs or medical, dental, or surgical supplies or appliances; postmortem handling of human bodies; and service by any persons as members of a formal accreditation, standards review, or similar professional board or committee, as a person charged with executing the directives of such board or committee.

The named insured should be broad enough to cover all corporate entities, the insureds' interest in joint ventures, the board of directors or trustees, members of committees, employees, students, volunteer workers, and members of religious congregations acting at the request or behest of the named insured. If interns, residents, fellows, or employed or contracted physicians and surgeons are to be covered for their personal interests, basic policy wording requires modification. The basic policy form should also be reviewed to ensure that physicians are covered for administrative responsibilities without a requirement to specifically extend the coverage to include that exposure. Coverage extended to employees that include physicians and surgeons typically extends to negligent acts occurring within the scope of their duties on behalf of the named insured. Even though several insureds are covered under the policy, the limit of liability applicable to each medical incident applies on a per-incident or per-occurrence basis. The aggregate limit on the policy is the maximum amount of losses to be paid in any particular year.

Health care entity employees, particularly nurses, frequently ask the risk management professional whether they should carry their own insurance. In responding to that question, the risk management professional should inform employees whom and what the entity's policy covers. The risk management professional should also review the other insurance provisions of the organization's medical professional liability policy to see how the coverage would respond if an employee carries individual coverage. In some instances, the policy would be excess over and above the employee's personal insurance; in other instances, the policy would contribute to the claim proportionately with the employee's carrier, based on the limits of each policy. The entity's policy will usually cover employees for negligent acts and omissions within the scope of their employment. Coverage would not extend to a second job or moonlighting activities. If those activities exist, a separate policy should be purchased. Furthermore, the risk management professional should remind employees that although the entity's policy protects them from the costs of defense and indemnity, they will have no decision-making authority over how their defense is conducted—something they may have with their own policy.

Most hospital bylaws require all voluntary attending physicians to carry their own medical professional liability coverage at stated minimum limits. If the physician and health care entity are found to be negligent, the entity may be held financially liable for the inadequacy of the physician's limits under the theory of joint and several liability. Where physicians have challenged the entity's ability to impose minimum insurance requirements as a condition of staff membership, the courts have said the entity may do so if the requirement is not applied arbitrarily or capriciously.

Medical professional liability insurance is considered a "specialty coverage." Most carriers have developed customized policy forms, many of which differ in terms and conditions. It is critical that the risk management professional perform a thorough evaluation and comparison of coverage terms and conditions when selecting a medical professional liability carrier. A broker, agent, or insurance company representative can be very helpful in this process. In addition to the product itself, most carriers provide a portfolio of risk management services that are available to assist risk management professionals in meeting their risk management objectives. These services should be evaluated on their perceived effectiveness and their ability to meet the risk management professional's needs.

Two forms of medical professional liability coverage are available in the industry: claims-made and occurrence. In purchasing this coverage, it is critical that the risk management professional be knowledgeable about the differences in the forms, ensuring that all claims—those reported and those that have occurred but are not yet reported—are covered by a single policy or by continuous policies. (Claims-made and occurrence policies were discussed at greater length earlier in this chapter.)

The delivery of health care services in an integrated setting has presented additional exposures that the health care risk management professional must address. Basic medical professional liability policies need to be reviewed to ensure that they extend coverage to new exposures, including these:

- Miscellaneous errors and omissions (E&O) coverage, such as data processing E&O, employed attorney's E&O, and hospital or physician management E&O

- Contractual liability as it relates to professional liability assumed on behalf of others if liability would not have been present in the absence of the agreement

- Utilization management and review, particularly as it relates to liability assumed on behalf of a health maintenance organization (HMO)

- Marketing, advertising, and Internet exposures

- Confidentiality issues

- Credentialing of physicians and allied health care providers for others

- Antitrust or restraint of trade

- Third-party claims administration and claims management for others

- Enterprise liability and vicarious liability for all aspects of delivery in an integrated network

- Coverage for day care centers, special health care events, and volunteer activities

- Architects' or builders' legal liability

- Telemedicine and the associated licensing issues

- Medicare billing errors and Medicare fraud and abuse issues

Commercial General Liability Most medical professional liability policies cover all injuries to patients on or about the premises for the purpose of receiving medical treatment. A health care provider is subject to third-party claims from members of the public other than patients for injury as the result of negligence in connection with the nonmedical aspects of its premises. This would include non-medical-related contractual obligations, injury to visitors, product liability, independent contractors' liability, advertising liability, and personal injury allegations such as libel, slander, false arrest, or defamation of character.

Commercial general liability protects the named insured against financial losses resulting from liability to third parties arising out of the premises owned or occupied, acts of independent contractors hired, products sold that leave the premises, and liability assumed under contract, subject to the exclusions in the policy. Coverage applies to bodily injury, property damage, and personal injury allegations.

The same insurer that provides the **medical professional liability** coverage to the health care entity usually provides **general liability coverage**. Those two types of protection are frequently combined in a single policy, avoiding the gray area of determining what is a professional versus a general liability claim. Where coverage is purchased separately, the general liability carrier will include an amendment excluding injury to patients. This limitation will typically read something like this: "Coverage is excluded for bodily injury to any person who is in your building or on your premises for the purpose of receiving any type of medical evaluation, care, or treatment." In some instances, the coverage can be modified with the following additional language: ". . . except for injuries caused by windstorm or fire, including any injury from smoke, fumes, or panic, earthquake, lightning, or explosion." This extension of coverage provides additional protection in the event of a catastrophic loss injuring patients as well as visitors.

Additional commercial general liability exposures can exist for organizations with child care centers. These exposures may include corporal punishment, sexual molestation, or failure to maintain sanitary conditions resulting in the spread of disease.

In addition, many health care entities are affiliated with academic universities that require special protection for claims that might arise out of an educational setting. Examples of those claims are failure to educate, wrongful suspension from a program, or inadequate supervision. Commercial general liability policies should be reviewed to make certain that coverage is included for these exposures, or a separate policy must be purchased.

The risk management professional is challenged to stay informed about the health care entity's activities, to ensure that the policy is broad enough to cover new ventures and operations. Common areas of concern are increased advertising (including e-marketing), **environmental impairment** or hazardous waste disposal exposure, asbestos removal, and the general liability exposures applicable to patient-owned premises in home health operations.

Managed Care E&O Coverage The emergence of managed care has significantly increased the need to purchase **managed care E&O coverage**. Managed care entities such as preferred provider organizations (PPOs), management service organizations (**MSO**s), physician-hospital organizations (PHOs), HMOs, independent practice associations (IPAs), and foundations have presented new exposures that health care risk management professionals must address. As stated earlier, a medical professional liability policy responds to bodily injury allegations as the result of the delivery of or failure to deliver medical services. However, it may not respond to allegations for "wrongful acts" in the design and administration of a managed care plan. These allegations may involve economic loss rather than bodily injury.

Allegations of negligence against managed care organizations may include the following:

- Improper design or administration of cost control systems

- Physician incentive agreements

- Breach of patient confidentiality

- Employee Retirement Income Security Act of 1974 (**ERISA**) violations

- Antitrust

- Economic credentialing

- Denial of benefits or services

- Failure to refer, delay in referral

- Discrimination

- Violation of state insurance regulations

- Invasion of privacy

- Insolvency or bankruptcy

The insurance industry has responded to this risk with separate managed care E&O policy forms. Some forms will include coverage for the administrative risk associated with managed care and extend to provide direct medical professional liability coverage for employed providers. Other forms are intended to cover the administrative risk associated with managed care and provide vicarious liability coverage for the organization facilitating the delivery of health care services. The typical insuring agreement of these policies covers damages because of personal injury in the performance of professional services, including utilization review, peer review, claims processing, enrollment, and marketing of services.

Managed care E&O policy forms contain several exclusions or coverage limitations applicable to the risk associated with managed care contracting and health care delivery. It is important that the risk management professional review these restrictions to have a clear understanding of what portion of the risk is insurable and what portion is not.

Excess Umbrella Liability Catastrophic losses can have a major effect on the bottom line of a health care entity, threatening its long-term financial viability. Excess **umbrella liability coverage** can be purchased to provide coverage after the first layer—the primary layer—of liability coverage has been exhausted. The primary layer is typically considered a minimum $1 million per claim and $3 million annual aggregate. The excess policy picks up over and above the primary limits afforded per claim and, if so written will drop down to effect coverage in the event of aggregate exhaustion of the underlying coverage. Umbrella excess liability coverage is a comprehensive form of excess liability coverage, providing coverage excess of several third-party exposures such as medical professional liability, commercial general liability, automobile liability, **employer's liability**, nonowned aircraft, and heliport liability. It can normally be extended to cover managed care E&O.

To maintain concurrency (avoid gaps in coverage), primary and excess insurance policies should maintain the same effective date. If the coverage is claims-made, policies should also maintain the same retroactive date. In addition, it is important that primary and umbrella excess medical professional and commercial general liability coverage be written on concurrent coverage forms. If the primary is claims-made, the excess coverage should be claims-made to avoid gaps and overlaps in coverage. If the primary is written or self-funded on an occurrence basis, the excess should be maintained on an occurrence basis. If primary coverage is afforded on an occurrence basis and the excess coverage is written on a claims-made basis, it is necessary for the risk management professional to maintain two sets of loss data, one on an occurrence basis as required by the primary carrier and one on a claims-made basis to meet the requirements of the claims-made excess carrier.

As with primary medical professional liability policies, all umbrella excess liability carriers have customized policy forms. Most of these forms are "stand-alone" and do not necessarily follow the form of the primary policies or self-insured documents that they sit over. It is important that the risk management professional conduct a thorough evaluation of policy forms to make certain that continuity of coverage exists.

Although the frequency of losses has remained stable over the past few years, loss severity has continued to increase. In view of this, it is important that the risk management professional continually review the limits of liability insurance purchased, making certain that the assets of the organization are adequately protected.

Automobile Liability Health care entities are exposed to liability as the result of owned or leased automobiles and nonowned and hired automobiles. In addition, automobile exposures can exist from the operation of parking garages, including valet parking. A **commercial automobile policy** protects against loss arising out of the ownership, maintenance, or use of automobiles and their equipment. It extends to vehicles "you own, hire, or borrow and those you do not own but may be responsible for," such as the personal car of an employee used in a home health operation. Coverage provided for vehicles not owned is excess over any coverage the owner may have.

Uninsured motorists (**UM**) coverage and personal injury protection (**PIP**) are also included subject to limits required by each state. These cover bodily injury in most states. Repairs for physical damage to the vehicle caused by an uninsured driver are not covered. The policy should provide automatic coverage for newly acquired or leased vehicles, including those used for emergency or patient transport. Automobile physical damage—comprehensive and collision coverage—should be considered for owned and long-term-leased vehicles.

Insurers determine rates for automobile coverage based on loss experience, territory of operation, location of the vehicle while garaged, and type and use of the vehicle. Loss prevention activities such as safe driver programs and insurance requirements for individuals using their personal vehicles on behalf of the organization are taken into consideration in the final pricing determination.

The risk associated with employees using their personal vehicles associated with home health organizations has materialized into a major exposure for many health care risk management professionals. In some instances, automobile carriers are adding premium surcharges to accounts with this exposure. It is important that health care organizations maintain liability insurance requirements for all individuals using their personal vehicles in business at an adequate level of liability coverage. Certificates of insurance should be required and maintained on a current basis for all drivers. It is also recommended that each driver participate in a safe-driving course at least every two years. Updated motor vehicle records (**MVR**s) should be obtained on each driver annually.

Garage Liability Exposure Some health care organizations provide valet parking for emergency room patients and visiting family members. Two significant exposures are created by this service. A third-party liability exposure develops when hospital employees operate the vehicles. The hospital can also be held responsible for damage to patient vehicles while parked in hospital-owned or -operated parking garages. While difficult to quantify, this ultimate exposure can be determined by the maximum value of all vehicles parked in the garage. Protection for this risk can be found in both automobile and commercial general liability policies. The risk management professional should review commercial general liability and automobile policies before purchasing a separate **garage liability policy**.

Most general liability policies respond to garage operations as the result of damages such as a parking garage entrance arm malfunction that causes damage to a third-party vehicle. It also responds to injury due to the "existence" exposure of the premises, such as a visitor slip and fall in the parking garage. An automobile policy can protect the insured for the ownership, maintenance, and use of any vehicle. A garagekeeper's legal liability policy provides coverage for physical damage (comprehensive and collision) for automobiles in the care, custody, and control of the insured. The basic coverage in this form applies to damages for which an insured is legally liable. The policy can be endorsed to include "goodwill" coverage, providing reimbursement for damages where there is a question of legal negligence. This can be used as a public relations tool for the risk management professional. The coverage can be modified to respond on either a primary or excess basis. If written on a primary basis, coverage for damage to the third-party vehicle is provided automatically regardless of any other insurance. Coverage on an excess basis only provides payment in excess of the owner's automobile coverage.

The risk management professional can take several steps to reduce the probability of loss. Garage security and a system to provide vehicle key protection should minimize vandalism and theft. A driver-recruiting program, including MVR verification for all employees driving third-party automobiles, may reduce exposures. Outsourcing the garage operations to a third party by contract will shift the majority of the exposure to the garage management company.

Directors' and Officers' Liability Decisions made by directors, officers, trustees, and other key executives have a significant effect on the financial health and daily operations of a health care entity. It is essential that they have the freedom to make wise, responsible, and sometimes difficult decisions without risk to their personal assets.

The board delegates authority to conduct affairs on a day-to-day basis to administrative and medical staff officers. However, the board is ultimately responsible for the establishment and maintenance of appropriate standards relating to all activities associated with the delivery of health care services. This governance responsibility cannot be delegated. The purpose of **directors' and officers' (D&O) insurance** is to protect directors, officers, trustees, and key executives in the event of personal liability litigation or to insure the health care entity's obligation to provide indemnity from such litigation.

Staff-related issues are becoming a more significant exposure for directors and officers, who are being held increasingly accountable for medical staff decisions related to staff credentialing and privileging. In making these decisions, they may be accused of lack of due process or interference with a person's right to practice a profession. What were once routine denials of staff privileges can now give rise to antitrust allegations with charges of restraint of trade by denying an individual the right to practice a profession or by favoring one group of competing interests over another.

Statutory immunity laws have been enacted in several states that grant immunity from personal liability to directors of not-for-profit health care facilities. However, this relief does not guarantee immunity from being sued. Also, state laws provide no protection from legal actions under federal statutes involving for example, antitrust, discrimination, and environmental protection.

Changes in the health care industry have opened new areas of risk for health care executives. Integrated delivery networks are engaged in joint ventures with physicians, private enterprises, and other health care providers. These alliances hold a strong potential for antitrust allegations from excluded providers or suppliers who claim that a cooperative arrangement restricts their ability to compete in the community. Heightened competition for patients, managed care contracts, and other revenue sources present a restraint of trade exposure.

Mergers, acquisitions, and divestiture activities among hospitals and physicians is another area of concern. Companies involved in these ventures experience a significantly heightened frequency and severity of D&O claims.

Another source of exposure is third-party contractual relationships. As health care organizations increasingly take advantage of opportunities to deliver care on an outpatient basis, it is often difficult to maintain the same quality standards across their owned and managed facilities and their off-site delivery facilities, such as surgical centers and home health operations.

There are several ways to manage this risk. Most organizations purchase D&O liability insurance, including employment practices liability insurance coverage from the commercial insurance market. Others are now assuming this risk in their alternative risk financing vehicles, such as a captive insurance company.

The D&O liability policy, typically written on a claims-made form, pays on behalf of the organization all losses for which the organization grants indemnification to the insured persons and for which the insured persons have become legally obligated to pay on account of any claim for a wrongful act. A wrongful act means any error, misstatement, misleading statement, act, omission, neglect, or breach of duty.

D&O liability insurance policies typically have three distinct insuring agreements. The first pays on behalf of the individual insureds' claims for wrongful acts, which are nonindemnifiable events under the organization's bylaws indemnification agreement. The second reimburses the entity for wrongful acts on the part of individual insureds who can be indemnified under the corporate bylaws. These insuring agreements are considered "individual" coverage (Part A) and "corporate reimbursement" (Part B). "Entity" coverage (Part C) can be purchased to provide coverage for the entity if it is held legally responsible for wrongful acts covered in the individual coverage sections of the policy.

Employment Practices Liability Employment practices liability (EPL) coverage can be included in the D&O policy by endorsement or purchased as a separate policy. The risk management professional should evaluate this risk and determine if a combined D&O approach is appropriate or if separate coverage should be purchased.

The EPL policy is designed to reimburse an organization for alleged negligence in the selection and hiring of employees and other employment issues associated with all current health care personnel. Recent legislative changes and increased public awareness have expanded liability risk for employment-related claims, making it easier to file claims and secure greater compensation. Some of these exposures are discrimination, sexual harassment, hostile work environment, wrongful termination, and violation of the Americans with Disabilities Act (ADA).

Fiduciary Liability The need for insurance protection for individuals who exercise management or administrative responsibilities for employee benefit plans was redefined by the **Employee Retirement Income Security Act** of 1974 (ERISA). ERISA defines the principal responsibilities for individuals who are fiduciaries of employee benefit plans while making the fiduciaries personally responsible for their actions. Employers with more than twenty-five employees are subject to ERISA, with limited exceptions. Two of these exceptions are plans providing government-sponsored benefits (including Medicare) and some plans sponsored by religious organizations.

Every plan subject to ERISA must have a written document that defines the benefits provided to eligible participants, their vesting rights, and how claims will be handled. In addition, the plan document must identify by name the individuals responsible for management of the plan. An annual update to plan participants is required.

Fiduciaries are defined by ERISA as individuals named as fiduciaries in the plan documents and any other persons or organizations responsible for administering benefits or claims or collecting or handling funds relating to the plan. **Fiduciary liability** insurance covers the alleged breach of a fiduciary's responsibility under common law or ERISA for directors and administrators of the plans.

Employee Benefit Legal Insurance In addition to management responsibilities, individuals with duties relating to the administration of employee benefit plans can create situations in which they or their employees might become liable for misadministration of an employee benefit program.

Administrative risk arising from **workers' compensation**, Social Security, unemployment compensation, or statutorily required nonoccupational disability benefit programs exists even though these programs do not fall under the ERISA regulations.

Insurance protection against this administrative risk is called employee benefit liability. This coverage is usually endorsed onto a commercial general liability policy.

Environmental Impairment Liability Insureds are more aware and concerned than ever over the extent of potential liabilities related to the transfer of properties that might be contaminated.

Exposures include the particularly serious cases of gradual pollution that can occur in the course of normal operations of a hospital entity and liability for sudden and accidental exposure. Impairment is considered to have occurred when substances (shock, noise, pressure, radiation, gases, vapors, heat, or other phenomena such as light) propagate or spread through soil, air, or water. Examples in the hospital environment include underground storage tanks, hazardous waste incinerators, and radioactive, hazardous, medical, pathological, and infectious wastes.

Since 1973, most commercial general liability policies have excluded contamination and pollution except when sudden and accidental. This exclusion created a gap in basic liability coverage that very few insurers have filled, even under specialty coverage or in the excess and surplus lines marketplace. Certain specialty underwriters, however, have developed **environmental impairment liability** coverage, which insures liability for environmental impairment, including cleanup costs. "Sudden and accidental" contamination or pollution is excluded unless the insured cannot obtain such coverage under the commercial general liability policy.

Aviation Coverage: Non-owned Aircraft and Heliport Coverage Many health care facilities have sites available for helicopter landings. A separate heliport liability policy should be purchased if such a site is designated as a helipad for use by life-flight operators or other emergency helicopter landings. The exposures associated with this risk depend on the hospital's role in the operation and use of the heliport premises along with any contractual obligation it assumes as the result of operation of the heliport.

Heliport liability policies cover bodily injury and physical damage arising out of the use, ownership, or operation of a helipad, including slips and falls that occur during the loading and unloading of patients, bodily injury to bystanders, and damage to the property of others. Operation and use of the helipad is excluded from a commercial general liability policy.

Non-owned aircraft liability policies cover bodily injury and property damage caused by an accident involving a nonowned helicopter or one involving a nonowned aircraft for which the organization is responsible.

The frequency of air travel by employees and health care executives should be evaluated to determine the need for this type of coverage. Claims have been made against corporate entities arising out of their sponsorship of meetings in connection with which employees became victims of commercial air disasters or chartered aircraft crashes. Risk management professionals should also evaluate the adequacy of insurance provided by charter companies and helicopter services.

Health and Welfare Insurance: Employee Benefit Insurance Although most employee benefit insurance plans are coordinated by human resource departments, it is important for risk management professionals to be familiar with the types of plans provided by their employers. Some risk management professionals may have responsibility for coordinating such programs or be involved in the decision-making process for carrier selection. These coverages can include long- and short-term disability, life, health, accident, dental, and vision insurance.

Workers' Compensation All states create a statutory obligation on the part of employers to provide compensation to employees for injuries arising out of and in the course of their employment. All employers are subject to the applicable workers' compensation laws of the states in which they operate and under appropriate circumstances to federal statutes. Failure to comply with these laws can result in fines and penalties, one of which is statutory removal of the employer's defense to suit by employees alleging injury as a result of their work. Workers' compensation insurance is a pure form of no-fault insurance. Adherence to the workers' compensation statute is governed by each state's division of workers' compensation.

Employers who fall under the workers' compensation statutes are required to purchase insurance, qualify as a self-insured, or reject the act, which is permissible in some states. Workers' compensation insurance provides statutory benefit coverage with virtually unlimited medical benefits to work accident victims. It also replaces a portion of lost wages defined as indemnity payments. Employer's liability, part of the standard workers' compensation policy, protects employers from suits brought by injured employees to recover monetary damages separate and distinct from claims for statutory benefits. Employer's liability claims can arise from the following sources:

- Employees who reject the act (possible in some states)

- Injuries not covered by the act (questionable claims relating to scope of employment)

- Suits by a spouse for loss of consortium or companionship

- Suit by a third party that has been held liable for the injury and seeks reimbursement from the employer

The premium for workers' compensation insurance is based on the application of rates established on a state-by-state basis to employee remuneration. The rates are based on classifications determined by the risk associated with the responsibilities of the employee. Individual claims history is used to modify the ultimate premium, based on experience rating models for each classification of employee. Risk management professionals should work closely with the human resource and employee health departments in identifying, measuring, and addressing workers' compensation risks.

Financial Guarantees

Surety bonds are frequently required to comply with laws associated with several health care exposures. In a **surety** contract, one party (the surety) agrees to be bound, along with the principal, to a third party in the same agreement. The surety and the principal on the bond become the promisor to a third-party promisee. The third party would be able to collect the obligation from the surety if the principal cannot meet the financial responsibility. If the surety is called on to meet the obligations under the bond, it attempts to collect the obligation (seek reimbursement) from the principal. This is the major difference in financial guarantee insurance versus other insurance contracts.

Health care organizations are required to post surety bonds to comply with laws in a number of areas, including the following:

- Patients' valuables

- Durable medical equipment

- Home health bonds
- Liquor bonds
- Residents' funds bonds
- Performance and payment bonds for construction projects
- License bonds
- Various court bonds such as appeal bonds
- Notary bonds
- Pharmacy bonds

Provider Stop-Loss Coverage **Provider stop-loss coverage** may be needed by organizations that have agreed in advance to bear financial risk for the provision of health care services under full or partial capitated managed care contracts. Provider stop-loss coverage reimburses a health care provider, subject to daily limitations and coinsurance requirements, for losses in excess of a stipulated amount per member per year.

There are two avenues for the risk management professional to consider in purchasing such coverage. Some managed care organizations are willing to include a certain amount of stop-loss protection in the provider's capitated agreement. The coverage can also be purchased from the commercial insurance industry.

Risk management professionals should evaluate both options to ensure that the avenue selected provides maximum protection for the financial performance of their organizations.

SUMMARY

Insurance is only one of the many tools available to the health care risk management professional to manage the financial aspects of risk. The risk management professional's primary insurance responsibility is to identify the organization's risk exposures and determine whether the transfer of risk to an insurance company is the appropriate method of treatment of that risk. Using insurance products for risk treatment requires the risk management professional to develop a level of insurance knowledge and a good working relationship with agents or brokers and with the insurance industry. The risk management professional's role should also include the preparation of statistical risk data, including rating data and up-to-date historical loss data for use by the carriers in determining the appropriate premium. The risk management professional should also be familiar with the resources external to the organization, such as **brokers**, agents, and consultants, who are available to help place coverage, the analysis of carriers, and the proposals submitted by those carriers.

KEY TERMS

Actual cash value
Admitted insurer
All-risk coverage
Auto liability insurance
Aviation coverage
Boiler and machinery coverage
Broker
Builder's risk coverage
Business interruption coverage
Claims-made coverage
Commercial auto coverage
Commercial general liability
Crime coverage
Directors' and officers' insurance coverage
Electronic data processing coverage
Employer's liability
Employment practices liability
Employment Retirement Income Security Act
Environmental impairment liability
Exposure
Extended reporting period
Fiduciary liability
Financial guarantees
First-party coverage

Garage liability policy
General liability insurance
Guarantee fund
Hard insurance market
Managed care E&O liability
Medical professional liability
Named peril coverage
Nonadmitted insurer
Nose coverage (prior acts coverage)
Occurrence insurance
Professional liability insurance
Property coverage
Provider stop-loss coverage
Replacement cost
Risk
Surety
Surety bond
Tail coverage
Third-party coverage
Umbrella coverage
Underwriter
Underwriting
Workers' compensation

ACRONYMS

ACV
ADA
DIC
EDP
EPL
ERISA

ERP
MSO
MVR
RMIS
SIR
UM

NOTE

1. Smith, B. D. *How Insurance Works: An Introduction to Property and Liability Insurance*. Malvern, Pa.: Insurance Institute of America, 1984, p. 4.

2. Hurricane Research Division, Atlantic Oceanographic and Meteorological laboratory, National Oceanic and Atmospheric Administration, US Department of Commerce, site accessed 11.07.8 [http://www.aoml.noaa.gov]

3. "How much did the September 11 terrorist attach cost America?" Institute for Analysis of Global Security site accessed 11/07/08 [http://www.iags.org/costof 911.html]

SUGGESTED READING

Best's Insurance Reports. Oldwick, N.J.: A. M. Best Co., updated annually.

Head, G. L., Elliot, M. W., and Blinn, J. D. *Essentials of Risk Financing* (3rd ed.). Malvern, Pa.: Insurance Institute of America, 1996.

MacDonald, M. G., Meyer, K. C., and Essig, B. *Health Care Law: A Practical Guide.* New York: Bender, 1987.

Malecki, D. S., Horn, R. C., Wiening, E. A., and Donaldson, J. H. *Commercial Liability Risk Management and Insurance* (2nd ed.). Malvern, Pa.: American Institute for Property and Liability Underwriters, 1986.

Rodda, W. H., Trieschmann, J. S., Wiening, E. A., and Hedges, B. A. *Commercial Property Risk Management and Insurance* (3rd ed.). Malvern, Pa.: American Institute for Property and Liability Underwriters, 1988.

Smith, B. D., Trieschmann, J. S., and Wiening, E. A. *Property and Liability Insurance Principles* (2nd ed.). Malvern, Pa.: Insurance Institute of America 1994.

Troyer, G., and Salman, S. *Handbook of Health Care Risk Management.* Rockville, Md.: Aspen, 1986.

CHAPTER

14

INFORMATION TECHNOLOGIES AND RISK MANAGEMENT

RONNI P. SOLOMON, MADELYN S. QUATTRONE

LEARNING OBJECTIVES

- To be able to identify examples of computerized clinical applications
- To be able to identify ways in which health information technology can integrate risk management, patient safety, and quality improvement initiatives
- To be able to list examples of the types of information that are reported, tracked, and trended through electronic reporting systems
- To be able to describe security risks and identify strategies to reduce risks associated with information technologies commonly used in health care organizations

Health care risk management professionals are witnessing a revolution in health information technology that is expected to transform the delivery of health care and the work processes of health care risk management professionals.

As the patient safety movement gained momentum, the 2001 Institute of Medicine (IOM) report *Crossing the Quality Chasm* recognized that information technology must play a central role in the redesign of the health care system to support substantial improvements in quality and patient safety. "Many medical errors, ubiquitous throughout the health care system, could be prevented if only clinical data were accessible and readable, and prescriptions were entered into automated order entry systems with built-in logic to check for errors and oversights in drug selection and dosing," the report stated.[1] Although it was not the first organization to call for greater automation of clinical data, the IOM recommended national health information infrastructure to establish what it called the "rules for the road" for distributing health care data.

Three years later, in the spring of 2004, President George W. Bush, calling for an **electronic health record** (EHR) for most Americans within a decade, established within the U.S. Department of Health and Human Services (**HHS**) the **Office of the National Coordinator for Health Information Technology** (ONC) to coordinate and promote health information technology. Headed by David J. Brailer, MD, PhD, national coordinator for health information technology, the office identified four goals and twelve strategies to guide the adoption of **information technology** (**IT**) in the nation's private and public health care sectors. The goals are (1) the adoption of electronic health records, (2) the development of a secure national health information network to permit the exchange of health information among clinicians, (3) the use of personal health records, and (4) the improvement of public health through quality measurement, research, and dissemination of evidence. Indeed, HHS envisions the years ahead as "the decade of health information technology."[2]

In 2005, the **Government Accountability Office** (**GAO**) reported on HHS's efforts to develop a national health IT strategy and to identify lessons learned from the Department of Defense (**DOD**), Department of Veterans Affairs (VA), and other nations' experiences in implementing health care IT. States are also beginning the process of building health IT networks to share health information statewide, raising concern that different health IT systems in different states and in different hospitals may not be able to "talk to each other." The following month, a bipartisan legislative initiative, Senate Bill 1262, known as the Health Technology to Enhance Quality Act of 2005, was sponsored by Senators Bill Frist and Hillary Rodham Clinton to spur the development of national health IT standards for the electronic exchange of health information. The bill would also provide financial grants to measure the quality of care provided to patients and to develop the infrastructure of health IT systems.

Industry standards for EHR systems are in need of development and should be adopted so as to allow data to be shared as envisioned by the IOM. Indeed, electronic data storage that employs uniform data standards will enable health care organizations to comply more readily with federal, state, and private reporting requirements, including those that support patient safety and disease surveillance.

To encourage the implementation of EHRs among physicians participating in the Medicare program, the Centers for Medicare and Medicaid Services (CMS) announced that as of August 2005, it would offer participating physicians, free of charge, a simplified version of EHR software that has been used by the VA for two decades. CMS estimates that by choosing Medicare software, a typical five-physician office practice could save more than $100,000 annually. High start-up costs for purchasing and installing software are frequently cited as a major reason for physician practices' relatively slow adoption of EHRs.

Digitally transforming hospitals, health care services, and physician office practices raises complex issues. IT managers, users, and even IT staff become prophets of the doctrine of unanticipated consequences. Risk management professionals should become familiar with health IT generally and should prepare thoughtfully for the benefits and risks of electronic technology, whether related to clinical information systems, electronic incident reporting systems, or other health IT applications. Artful risk management professionals will embrace and benefit from the new information technologies while helping their organizations set and maintain the standards that govern their use.

This chapter will inform risk management professionals about current and emerging health IT applications and will look at health IT from three perspectives: (1) ways in which risk management professionals themselves might use IT, (2) ways in which clinical staff might use IT to improve safety and reduce loss, and (3) general risk management issues that are raised as organizations switch to an electronic environment.

KEY CONCEPTS

- Risk management programs today require more data more frequently and from more sources than ever before.

- The core need of the risk management professional is to review the right information at the right time to make the best decision.

- The risk management professionals needs tools to automate common processes, a knowledge bank of credible information on which sound risk reduction strategies can be based, and ways to automate the gathering of intelligence for in-depth analysis in real time.

- Many health information systems have been shown to reduce errors and thereby have a positive effect on quality of care, patient safety initiatives, and medical professional liability.

RISK MANAGEMENT INFORMATION NEEDS

Today's risk management programs require more data more frequently and from more sources than ever before. They require creating new loss prevention and control programs for various care settings and liability exposures. To be effective, these programs must be alert to the ever-increasing and fast-changing laws, regulations, clinical practice guidelines, best practices, and evidence-based safety recommendations that ultimately bear on the organizationwide risk management program and its liability exposure. Whatever IT system or programs are used in risk management, the goal should be to turn data into meaningful information that supports the risk management program through effective risk management action.

As health care risk management expands its reach, the number of risk management staff is likely to remain the same or even decrease in some organizations. Risk management professionals will have to broaden their base of knowledge, understand various health IT applications, and develop new approaches to risk management that foster collaboration with patient safety, quality assurance, performance improvement, legal and regulatory compliance, and other relevant departments and programs within their organizations. As a result, risk management professionals have a need for automated programs and systems that not only capture data from multiple sources but also produce meaningful and timely reports. Indeed, the failure to adopt new systems might reduce the value—real and perceived—that risk management brings to the organization. Unlike electronic incident reporting systems, manual systems are typically incapable of decreasing time lag, making it difficult to implement a rapid-response program. The time lag that occurs when manual systems are used can inhibit timely data analysis and trending, loss control initiatives, and decision making. Ultimately, the use of manual risk management systems might make it impossible to demonstrate reduction in the overall cost of risk.

Health care risk management professionals have many IT needs. The core need is to review the right information at the right time to make the best decisions. Risk management professionals also need tools that automate various risk management processes, such as identifying and analyzing incident and loss information, and performing organizational risk assessments, a knowledge bank of credible information that underpins risk reduction strategies and helps to promote risk management and patient safety initiatives to others, and automated ways of gathering the intelligence that will enable a shift from general risk management assessments and evaluations to more focused and in-depth analyses of specific areas of risk that have high payback potential.

Information technologies, many with Web-enabled modules, can support these risk management needs. Computer technologies can also help spot problems that were previously unidentifiable and can facilitate efforts to improve the quality and safety of patient care. For example, in performance measurement, automated assessment provides significant advantages over manual review of medical records. Electronic review of EHRs has also been shown to be more accurate, systematic, and efficient than manual review of paper medical records. Automated review systems also eliminate human error caused by fatigue, inattention, difficult-to-read handwriting, buried information, missing data, and the like. Electronic systems have the power to assess archived data quickly and within minutes assess data and information that would take weeks or even months to review by nonautomated means.

Computer automation is a key to effective risk management. Automated tracking and trending, filing and retrieving information, performing statistical analysis of data, performing risk assessment surveys, electronic claims management, tapping into electronic libraries, and communication with peers through computer electronic mailing lists, e-mail, and discussion forums are critical tools for today's risk management professional. It can be expected that risk management IT applications will have a significant payoff. Real-time electronic reporting of "near misses," for example, might trigger timely proactive risk assessment and result in the prevention of losses.

RISK MANAGEMENT INFORMATION SYSTEMS

Many health care facilities use some form of **risk management information system** (**RMIS**) that automates many aspects of record keeping. Mergers, acquisitions, and joint ventures have increased the need for RMISs, particularly ones with network capabilities that serve multiple sites and locations. These software systems are indispensable for corporate risk management professionals who have responsibilities for multiple institutions.

RMISs consist of computerized databases that, simply put, are comprehensive collections of information. Risk management data might include incident and occurrence reports, claims tracking and claims administration data (for workers' compensation, professional liability, general liability, directors' and officers' liability, and other claims information), insurance policy information, reserve data, regulatory compliance information, survey reports, patient complaints, and litigation management information. Basic RMISs typically have the capability of data collection and consolidation, data analysis, data reporting, and report circulation and may permit remote access.

Off-the-shelf and customizable RMISs are available from software vendors or can be developed to meet an organization's specific needs by in-house IT staff. Some insurance carriers, brokers, third-party administrators, and management service organizations also offer specialized RMISs. Regardless of the source of the system that is used, risk management professionals should work closely with IT staff in reviewing or developing software specifications, ongoing support services, data entry and maintenance requirements, Web interfaces, and other key characteristics. Special needs and expectations are best discussed before purchasing software and at the outset of a development project.

Computerized and Web-based incident management systems that provide real-time access to incident data and reports are used in many health care organizations. Web-based systems allow for quick "point and click" entry using standard browser technology at any computer site in the organization. Reporting forms often consist of highly categorized fields using check boxes or drop-down menus. Once a report is entered, the data are immediately available to the organization's management and leadership. Access to information is by authorization and typically varies by job duty: only frontline staff will have the ability to access the reporting form and enter data; department managers might have access to individual and aggregate information on reports filed by that department and be able to enter or update information; risk management professionals would likely have full access to all reporting information and the analytics.

Paper incident reports may take months and even years to reach the risk management professional's office and get logged into a system. In contrast, online reports facilitate immediate action and investigation and daily review of reports. Standardization and taxonomy provide better, more accurate data that lead to better analysis. From a security and confidentiality perspective, online reporting permits limitations on who can view, who can print, and who can enter or update data. It also offers better controls on the circulation of reports. System controls also prevent others from deleting or changing data or "losing" a report.

Interactive Web-based assessment tools are available to help with proactive analysis, often in high-risk or specialized areas. These tools may include questionnaires along with the evidence base that would support the optimal answer. Benchmarking of results may be available if many organizations participate in the assessment program. When assessment results are automated into a computerized database, new benefits arise. A key advantage is the ability to integrate and sort information located in different parts of the overall data collection. This helps transform risk management data into risk management information. A database system has the capability to retrieve and display records, to extract subsets of data, and to produce formatted reports. Each use, however, must be carefully planned to ensure that it will generate accurate, useful, and effective reports.

USING INFORMATION SYSTEMS TO GENERATE REPORTS

When envisioning reports, risk management professionals should consider who should be authorized to receive them, how they will be used, and how often they will be produced. With these facts in mind, they can decide what sources of data should be used and how best to present data (in graphic or narrative form).

Risk management professionals should consider what factors should be tracked and analyzed. These will vary, depending on whether it is an incident reporting, claims management, risk assessment, or other type of system. The list of elements that can be captured by electronic information systems is endless. The following are some examples of the types of information that electronic systems typically report:

- Insurance policies and coverage limits
- Newly reported losses or incidents
- Losses or incidents by department or service
- Losses or incidents by date reported
- Losses or incidents by date of occurrence
- Loss costs by accident type or part of body

- Current status of open claims

- Incident frequency by job and location

- Number of employee injuries or patient incidents

- Types of employee injuries or patient incidents

- Lost work time

- Actual medical costs versus average costs

- Most frequent and most expensive causes of loss

- Reserves

- Allegations

- Staff involved in incident or claim

- Patient characteristics

- Names of attorneys

- Names and contact information for witnesses

- Insurance carriers

- Status of claim

- Actions taken

INTEGRATING RISK MANAGEMENT, QUALITY ASSURANCE, AND PATIENT SAFETY

Risk management professionals, patient safety officers, and others involved in quality assurance (QA) should recognize the capabilities of EHR systems to facilitate better and safer patient care and should work together to develop strategies that will take advantage of the technologic capability of EHRs. Interoperable electronic information technology allows different systems to "communicate" with each other. **QA** information that is captured electronically from routines in daily practice, rather than from reports generated by reviewing medical records, can be referred to risk management and patient safety systems. The transfer of information among risk management, patient safety, and QA systems helps foster effective follow-up on patient safety issues and facilitates proactive risk assessment.

Certain indicators that are tracked for safety and QA purposes should be referred to the RMIS (for example, dental injuries or ocular injuries in the operating room). This information could indicate the need for risk management investigation or for setting up a potential claim file. Conversely, risk management incident trending reports can be incorporated into the QA and patient safety systems. Reports can be coded numerically with selected factors, such as date, location, individual who assessed the patient, and follow-up information.

ELECTRONIC MAIL

The use of electronic mail (e-mail) has burgeoned over the past decade. Few risk management professionals today can envision working without it. The use of e-mail, a means of communication by and between health care providers, patients, health care organizations, and staff, is a revolutionary cultural change. An increasing number of hospitals and physician practices have public Web sites that facilitate direct e-mail communication with staff. Through e-mail, individual providers interact with patients, communicate with pharmacies and hospitals, and consult with colleagues and subspecialty physicians across the globe. A nationwide telephone survey conducted in April 2005 by a marketing information firm revealed that about 31 percent of all practicing pediatricians were using e-mail to communicate with their patients' parents.[3]

E-mail has many advantages over traditional paper-based mail and voice messaging. E-mail messages can be sent at any time, and recipients can collect their e-mail when they want, from wherever they are. It is easier than writing, printing, proofing, addressing, and stamping a letter. In contrast to voice messages, which typically contain brief contact information, e-mail facilitates communication of detailed messages and makes it easy for recipients to reply to the sender and to forward the message or reply to others. Because of its unique characteristics, e-mail communication between health care providers and patients raises risk management, legal, and regulatory concerns about confidentiality, privacy, and medical record documentation.

For example, although the details of what is communicated by telephone between physicians and patients are rarely recorded and preserved, e-mail communication between the patient and a health care provider can be saved electronically and preserved in paper form by sender and recipient alike. Because e-mail can be intercepted or inadvertently sent to persons not intended to receive it, confidentiality and privacy of e-mail health communication might be jeopardized without appropriate safeguards. The timeliness of replies to e-mail communication requiring a rapid response can be delayed if e-mail systems go down or if messages are delayed by heavy Internet traffic. Written policies and procedures are needed to facilitate compliance with applicable federal and state laws and regulations concerning the privacy, security, and confidentiality of individually identifiable health information communicated by e-mail.

Risk management professionals should participate in drafting and updating their institutions' e-mail policies and procedures, noting guidelines such as those of the American Medical Association (AMA) for physician-patient e-mail, and applicable federal and state law and regulatory mandates concerning health information privacy and security. Policy should require that e-mail concerning a patient's health care be preserved electronically or printed in hard copy if paper medical records are maintained and made a part of the patient's medical record in accordance with sound documentation and recordkeeping practice.

INTERNET- AND WEB-BASED TECHNOLOGY

The Web is rapidly transforming the way clinicians communicate, document, treat, and diagnose. Physicians can get online access from their homes or offices to laboratory and radiology results, pharmaceutical profiles, clinical pathways, and medical references. A system that permits patients with implantable cardiac devices to send clinical information to their physicians over the Internet can result in more timely and efficient monitoring, thus potentially improving patient care. The technology is made up of a handheld monitor that patients hold against their chest to capture electronic signals from the implanted device. The monitor is connected to a small console that resembles an external modem from a personal computer. The console automatically downloads the data from the implanted device and transmits it over a standard telephone line directly to a secure server. The system has two secure Web sites, one for physicians and one for patients, where clinical information can be accessed.

Health care information technology is poised to play a major role in advancing communication of health information between patients and their health care providers. Until recently, the paper medical record was rarely shared freely with patients. Now large health systems and health maintenance organizations (**HMO**s) are taking steps to implement EHR systems that will make patient records available to physicians and patients via the Internet.

PERSONAL HEALTH RECORD

Most people who maintain a **personal health record** (**PHR**) create paper records or establish electronic ones by typing or scanning their personal health information into software applications and storing the information on personal computers. Newer, more sophisticated Web-based services now allow individuals to maintain their health information in online accounts that include e-mail, document sharing, videoconferencing capability, and access to the individual's health information from Internet-connected devices. Some applications give individuals the option of allowing their health care providers and hospital emergency departments access to their electronic PHR, which may include information that is not otherwise readily available, such as end-of-life advance directives. Some systems would also allow providers to enter health care data directly into the PHR. These and similar products are being made available to the public by several entities, such as the AMA-affiliated Medem organization and the American Health Information Management Association (**AHIMA**).

In the near future, technology solutions will allow seamless integration of health information between EHRs and PHRs. Information such as test results could be directly entered into PHRs from EHRs, and communication via the Internet and e-mail might become a preferred means of discourse between patient and provider about certain medical conditions. Policies and procedures for dissemination of health information to PHRs will be needed to ensure that clinicians have had the opportunity to review critical test results and confer with patients before results make their way into PHRs.

Although the PHR and EHR may one day be integrated, the PHR will not replace the medical record that must be maintained by health care providers. Risk management professionals should keep up-to-date on developments in this area as technology-savvy patients begin to use electronic, interoperable PHRs.

ELECTRONIC HEALTH RECORDS AND SYSTEMS

An electronic medical record is generally defined as a longitudinal collection of health information that is made accessible in electronic form to authorized users.[4] In addition to patient information and billing applications, EHR systems may include knowledge and active clinical decision support tools to enhance patient safety, health care quality, and operational efficiency.

Interactive EHR systems can prompt clinicians automatically with reminders about care and can flag potentially adverse outcomes. In place of time-consuming manual reviews of paper medical records, EHR systems can provide automated assessments of performance measurement, such as adherence to clinical guidelines. In a pilot demonstration of a national health information infrastructure, known as the eHealth Initiative, participating hospitals provide continuous, real-time electronic data about performance directly to CMS via a secure Internet connection.[5]

EHRs are expected to help provide an effective means of implementing institutional policy and procedures and related accreditation requirements. Because EHRs store and share information such as medication history, laboratory results, allergies, test results, and other pertinent health data, they support and facilitate patient safety initiatives and facilitate compliance with related policies and procedures.

Innovative comprehensive EHR systems in development in several large health systems may serve as bellwethers for health care organizations nationwide. An EHR system recently put into place by Sutter Health, a large California system, allows affiliated physicians to view comprehensive patient data beginning with an office visit, an emergency department visit, or a hospital admission. Lab test results, medication histories, and physician notes are available as real-time data. Patients have access to the system using the Internet to schedule physician appointments, view their personal health history, send e-mail to their physicians, and access health information related to their diagnoses. The EHR system also includes numerous patient safety functions, such as alerts to potential drug interactions and reminders about relevant clinical guidelines.

Few facilities currently employ electronic charting, which typically uses templates for clinician documentation. And although significant advances have been made in voice recognition technology, clinicians in many health care organizations continue to dictate patient information. Many EHR systems store health information that has been dictated and transcribed, often by transcribers in foreign countries who can transmit the transcribed information to providers over the Internet. To ensure legal and regulatory compliance, health care risk management professionals in organizations that outsource transcription of health care information should be aware of the numerous federal and state laws and regulations that apply to their situation. Contracts with transcription vendors should also adequately address related risks.

Health care risk management professionals should champion their organization's transition from paper-based health records to EHR systems while remaining aware of risks to patient safety during the transition. Risk to the quality and safety of patient care can arise during the significant process and cultural changes that occur during transition. For example, whereas laboratory results, X-ray interpretations, and physician progress notes may be available electronically, other vital patient information may remain on paper or be maintained in other media.

Risk management professionals must keep their focus on the end result—safer and better patient care. They can support their organization's transition to EHRs by developing policies and procedures that support the organization's strategic plan for switching to an EHR environment and by developing policies and procedures pertinent to an electronic environment. AHIMA's practice briefs provide a resource for risk management professionals and others in health care facilities who are switching to the electronic environment.

CLINICAL INFORMATION SYSTEMS AND "SMART" TECHNOLOGIES

Many health information systems have been shown to reduce errors and thereby have a positive effect on quality of care, patient safety initiatives, and medical professional liability. Hospitals and health care organizations are moving incrementally toward the use of electronic information into the clinical aspects of health care delivery. Although risk management professionals are not the primary users of these systems, they should become educated about them and consider their applications to risk management and patient safety programs. Risk management professionals who are equipped with an understanding of clinical information systems can more effectively take steps to identify and reduce risks as facilities evolve from paper-based organizations to integrated digital organizations.

A **computerized provider order entry system** (**CPOE**) is a networked system that allows users to electronically enter specific diagnostic orders, such as laboratory tests and radiology exams; medication orders, for which users can maintain an online **medication administration record** (**MAR**); nursing orders; and special orders. Data can be accessed from the full range of orders found in a paper-based environment, including medication orders. These systems also provide online clinical decision support and safety alerts. Authorized users have access—from a single workstation or remote location—to clinical data from multiple sources. This data include patient medical information from workstations within the facility and from physician offices or workstations in physicians' homes. CPOE systems replacing paper-based systems are intended to achieve specific objectives:

- Reduce misinterpretation of handwritten or oral orders

- Eliminate the use of paper documents

- Reduce the number of inputs to generate orders and execute them

- Provide rules-based clinical decision support through embedded clinical guidelines (such as dosage calculations and suggestions for alternate therapy)

■   Enhance patient safety by alerting clinicians to certain occurrences, such as an unsafe order (for example, the prescription of a drug to which the patient is allergic or the prescription of a drug that interacts adversely with another prescribed medication) or the completion of an order (such as notification that laboratory results have been returned)

■   Generate a reliable electronic health record

Although hospitals have been slow to adopt the technology, hospitals and health systems in the United States are increasingly investing in CPOEs that include hazard alerts for cautions, contraindications, and drug interactions. However, many clinicians who use such systems lack knowledge about the range of patient safety features that exist on their clinical computer systems. A study reported in 2005 in the journal *Quality and Safety in Health Care* discussed the experience of physicians in the United Kingdom, where 90 percent of physicians in general practice regularly use advanced computer systems to assist directly in providing patient care. The study showed that only 25 percent of the physicians received formal training in the use of the patient safety features available on their systems and that many physicians made erroneous assumptions about the safety features' warning functions.[6] The importance of raising clinicians' awareness of patient safety features on their clinical IT systems and ensuring that appropriate training is available should be on the agenda of health care risk management professionals in all organizations that have implemented CPOEs or plan to implement them.

Laboratory information systems are widely used to improve the flow of information inside and outside of clinical laboratories. These systems are designed to order tests, create bench worklists, verify specimens, report results, collate patient demographics with results for reports, and process or transfer billing information. Some systems also integrate with EHR systems.

Automated anesthesia recordkeeping systems not only interface with anesthesia gas machines and patient monitoring equipment but also document drug administration, timing, and patient response more accurately and completely than manual recordkeeping. Indeed, the automated record might help defend against charges of anesthesia professional liability.

Some emergency departments (**EDs**) use clinical support systems to enhance physician decision making about whether to admit a patient for a cardiac workup. Artificial intelligence technology estimates the probability of an acute myocardial infarction based on patient history and EKG findings. This technology might help reduce the frequency of inappropriate defensive medicine practices and the frequency and severity of medical professional liability claims that allege failures in diagnosing and treating acute myocardial infarctions.

A number of pharmacy applications help reduce the risk of errors. Examples include automated drug dispensing systems, drug interaction programs, drug allergy warnings, dosage crosschecking, side effect data, and drug and food interaction warnings.

Bar coding, a technology that has been used for years in the retail industry, has the potential for numerous applications in health care. The VA hospital system has been a leader in employing the technology in medication ordering and administration to verify that the right patient gets the correct drug, dose, and route at the correct time. A bar code representing the patient identification number is scanned, and the computer displays the medications that are due. Alerts and pop-up boxes display discrepancies and potential problems. Before administering medications, nurses use retail store–type scanners to compare bar codes embedded in patient identification bracelets against the labels on the medications.

Computer-assisted protocols that are used for antibiotic therapy employ real-time patient data to calculate antibiotic dose, duration of therapy, and cost-effective choices. These systems can pull patient information directly from bedside monitors in intensive care units (**ICUs**).

Radiology systems are linked to remote viewing units, such as the ICU and off-site physician practices, thereby reducing film retrieval time from a typical twelve hours to less than one minute. All of these applications have the potential to reduce medical professional liability.

Other examples of computerized clinical applications include the following:

- Automated dispensing systems

- Drug interaction programs

- Triage documentation, discharge instructions, and prescriptions

- Tickler systems for physician office visits and periodic screening examinations

- Patient tracking systems

- Bed tracking systems

- Medical device tracking systems

- Medical equipment control programs

- Health hazard appraisal systems

The list grows daily. Risk management professionals should view computerized clinical applications as potential clinical risk management tools that might help reduce loss exposures in certain practice settings. At the same time, they can champion the adoption of appropriate technologies and encourage the necessary cultural change that must occur as health care organizations switch from manual to digital systems. Risk management professionals must continue to help develop and maintain policies and procedures that protect the security and confidentiality of electronic data and that encourage proactive risk assessment to identify risk-prone systems and processes that might benefit from the application of newer computerized health information technology.

INFRASTRUCTURE TECHNOLOGY

Risk management professionals and their organizations will also need to ensure that there are backups to their electronic health information system so that ongoing operations and patient care are not affected when a system goes down. Redundancy, failover,[7] and disaster recovery protection features are necessary to avoid downtime that can paralyze an institution, resulting in patient harm and financial loss. Risk management professionals and regulatory compliance officers should work with their organization's IT department to ensure compliance with federal and state laws and regulations addressing the security of electronic health information.

Everything from infusion pumps to magnetic resonance imaging (**MRI**) scanners is now controlled by computers; hence medical device security should also rank among important risk management, legal, and regulatory compliance concerns. Health care risk management professionals should become familiar with risks that might threaten the security of computer-based medical devices that generate, store, and transmit patient health data and should champion strategies for risk reduction and legal and regulatory compliance. The modernization of medical equipment has seen a proliferation in the number of computer-based devices, which are vulnerable to viruses and other malicious programs that target computers.

Many medical devices are networked for data exchange or Internet access. Most hospitals currently use technical solutions such as firewalls to isolate the internal hospital network from the outside world. While this usually blocks outside threats, computer viruses could enter a network through an internal device, thereby bypassing the firewall protection. In traditional local area network (**LAN**) architecture, all of a hospital's devices are connected in a single network, thus allowing a virus that infects the LAN to access all of the devices in a hospital. Because some medical device suppliers do not take an active role in maintaining the security of their devices in the field, health care organizations must be vigilant in ensuring that device security is regularly updated, as with any other device on the hospital's network. Health care organizations' IT staff, clinical engineers, and risk management professionals should combine their expertise in a team effort to identify and resolve risks to the security of their institutions' computer-based medical devices. Exhibit 14.1 provides a security checklist for information technologies.

EXHIBIT 14.1. Security Checklist for Information Technologies

- Develop and strictly enforce policies against disclosing or sharing passwords, access codes, key cards, and other means of access to the system.
- Develop policies and procedures for the assignment of passwords, as well as for their deactivation should an employee leave.

- Institute a time-out on computer terminals; that is, program terminals should have screens go blank after a certain period (for example, three minutes) of inactivity following the display of a patient record.

- Establish audit trails so that access to each record is tracked by the system.

- Sharply limit access to sensitive records or portions of records (for example, HIV-antibody test results).

- Protect against mass access and extraction of information.

- Educate staff about the importance of privacy and the problems that arise from sharing passwords.

- Ask medical staff members to sign confidentiality statements.

- Hold physicians liable for any entries to a record made by nurses or assistants using the physician's password.

- Provide 24-hour assistance to authorized users who forget their access codes or to persons who legitimately need one-time access.

- Provide mechanisms for minimizing human error, such as review of input data for accuracy. If bar codes or other programmed codes are used to record clinical observations, there should be a mechanism for visual confirmation or other verification of entries. Document accuracy reviews.

- To the extent possible, limit connections to, and electronic data sharing with, outside computer systems.

- Use disks from reputable software vendors only.

- Obtain antivirus software to protect against computer viruses.

- Require software vendors to indemnify against all damages and costs arising from viruses, bombs, and similar sabotage inserted into the software by the vendor or its agents.

- Explore the feasibility of using optical disk "write-once, read many" (WORM) technology; although it is considered antiquated for other industries, it may be ideal for hospitals because records cannot be altered after they are initially recorded in this form.

- Properly maintain hardware, and thoroughly debug and maintain software.

- Include performance standards in any lease or contract with a vendor, as well as guarantees of reliability and ongoing maintenance support.

- Have adequate backup and emergency capability. (For example, frequent backup of databases; off-site as well as on-site computer tape storage; and emergency data processing capability are essential, as is electrical power during power outages.)

- Routinely monitor available security systems and ensure that existing measures are reasonable by current standards.

POINT-OF-CARE TECHNOLOGY

Current and emerging health information technologies hold the promise of increasing patient safety at the point of care and should become an integral part of risk management programs in health care organizations.

Medical "smart cards" are designed to improve patient care and reduce medical and administrative errors by storing patient data that are accessible at several points of care. The small plastic cards are embedded with microchips that can process information and store numerous pages of a patient's vital health and demographic information, making it easier for patients to interact with the health care system. Smart cards have numerous capabilities. Card readers installed in the emergency department, for example, allow for rapid access to potentially lifesaving information about a patient, such as allergies to medications and chronic medical conditions. Patient information can be updated during physician office visits. Patients can view their **medical information** and obtain a printed copy of the smart card record. Information stored in the card is encrypted for security purposes, and each card contains a confidential code that is required for decrypting the text. Patients use personal identification numbers to access their information, and unauthorized or questionable use of the smart card automatically deactivates it.

Radio-frequency identification (RFID) tags store identifying information and hold promise for various applications in health care, including reducing the risk of elopement by mentally incompetent patients and infant abduction. RFID tags may be attached to patients at the wrist or ankle and can be used to track patients' whereabouts as they move, for example, from the emergency department to the operating room to the recovery room and then to a bed on a surgical unit. RFIDs are used for tracking and matching blood for transfusion and tracking inventory. The market for RFID tags and systems in healthcare will rise rapidly from $90 million in 2006 to $2.1 billion in 2016. Primarily, this will be because of item level tagging of drugs and Real Time Locating Systems (RTLS) for staff, patients and assets to improve efficiency, safety and availability and to reduce losses.[8]

TELEMEDICINE

Telemedicine is the use of telecommunication technology for medical diagnosis and patient care for sites that are at a distance from the provider. Thus telemedicine permits care to be provided without moving the patient. Several technologies are employed in telemedicine. Typically, digital images are transferred from one location to another, and two-way interactive television is used for real-time videoconferencing.

This technology has a wide range of applications. Telepathology involves rendering diagnostic opinions on specimens at remote locations. Teleradiology is the electronic transmission of radiological images from one location to another for interpretation or consultation. Radiologists who are continents away from the patient can provide "digital readings" of radiology images, transmitting their preliminary interpretations to clinicians in a timelier manner than could otherwise be achieved. The technology also allows clinicians to make virtual house calls to patients in remote locations and permits a surgeon in one location to remotely control a robotic arm for surgery on a patient in another location.

Several hospitals, including Johns Hopkins Hospital in Baltimore, employ robotic technology for making patient rounds within the hospital. Equipped with video camera and microphones, "robo-docs" permit virtual "telerounds" of hospitalized patients by electronically linking the robot to a physician at a remote location, giving the live physician a remote presence in the hospital. Viewing a computer monitor, the physician directing the robot near the patient sees and hears what the robot "sees" and "hears." Patients can see the physician's face displayed on a flat screen on the robot's shoulders and can talk with the physician. The system uses the Internet and a wireless network.

Other uses exist and undoubtedly will evolve as states, such as New Mexico, with its large rural area, establish telemedicine systems and provide funding for telemedicine projects. Although improvements in technology have led to a revitalization of interest in telemedicine, its viability will be shaped by insurance reimbursement policies adopted by public and private payers.

Telemedicine carries a host of risk management, legal, and regulatory issues that must be identified and resolved. One of the first hurdles is the state-based physician licensure system, which runs counter to telemedicine's "virtual" boundaries. The rules for licensure by endorsement and out-of-state consultations vary among the states and pose barriers to development of interstate systems. Risk management professionals should be aware of telemedicine initiatives on the state and national levels. A related problem that must be addressed is credentialing of physicians who would need to be granted telemedicine privileges.

Medical professional liability issues for telemedicine practitioners also evolve over time. Telemedicine networks may cross state lines and international boundaries, raising uncertainty about the jurisdiction in which a malpractice suit may be filed and what state or nation's law should apply. These issues are important for several reasons. For example, different statutes of limitations and different statutory limitations on the amount of financial compensation that can be awarded to successful plaintiffs may apply. What is the standard of care for a telemedicine practitioner in a particular specialty? Who is legally responsible for the quality of telemedicine equipment? In addition to these legal and risk concerns, measures must be taken to address applicable federal and state laws and regulations affecting the privacy and security of patient health information for information that is electronic and networked to remote locations via modem, telephone lines, satellite, and other communication technology.

SUMMARY

The Internet and the application of associated computer and digital technologies in health care are revolutionizing the delivery of health care services and the role of the health care risk management professional. Health information technologies will continue to promote collaboration, increase the knowledge base, enhance the quality of health care, and improve patient safety, thus reducing the risk of harm to patients and losses to the organization. Risk management professionals who champion their facilities' transition to an electronic environment will be poised to be key players in ensuring that these changes are in the best interest of the organization and the patients that they serve. Risk management professionals will face many challenges as they adapt health IT risk management functions, collaborate with patient safety and quality assurance to identify the benefits and risks of new technology applications, and develop policies and procedures to reduce the risk of harm and ensure legal and regulatory compliance.

KEY TERMS

Computerized provider order entry
Electronic health record
Government Accountability Office
Information technology
Office of National Coordinator for
Health Information Technology

Medication administration record
Personal health record
Radio frequency identification
Risk management information system
Telemedicine

ACRONYMS

AHIMA
CMS
CPOE
DOD
ED
EHR
GAO
HHS
HMO
ICU

IT
LAN
MAR
MRI
ONC
PHR
QA
RFID
RMIS

NOTES

1. Institute of Medicine. *Crossing the Quality Chasm: A New Health System for the 21st Century.* Washington, D.C.: National Academies Press, 2001, p.176.

2. Government Accountability Office. *Health Information Technology: HHS Is Taking Steps to Develop a National Strategy.* GAO-05-628. Washington, D.C.: Government Accountability Office, May 27, 2005, p 32, 37.

3. Payne, J. W. "E-Mailed Parents Feel Better." *Washington Post,* June 7, 2005, p. HE1.

4. Government Accountability Office. *Efforts to Promote Health Information Technology and Legal Barriers to Its Adoption.* GAO-04-991R. Washington, D. C.: Government Accountability Office, August 13, 2004.

5. Visit the eHealth Initiative Web site at http://www.ehealthinitiative.org

6. Morris, C. J., and others. "Patient Safety Features of Clinical Computer Systems: Questionnaire Survey of GP Views." *Quality and Safety in Health Care,* 2005, *14,* 164–168.

7. Failover is the capability to switch over automatically to a redundant or standby computer server, system, or network upon the failure or abnormal termination of the previously active server, system, or network. Failover happens without human intervention and generally without warning, unlike switchover.

8. *Rapid Adoption of RFID in Healthcare,* May 8, 2006. IDTechEx. Available at: http://www.idtechex.com/research/articles/rapid_adoption_of_rfid_in_health care_00000470.asp (accessed November 11, 2008).

SUGGESTED READING

ECRI, a nonprofit health care research services agency, is the source of numerous publications and programs, including *Healthcare Control System, Health Technology Forecast, Health Devices, Health Care Standards Directory Online,* and *Information Security for Biomedical Technology: A HIPAA Compliance Guide.* For more information, go to the ECRI Web site at http://www.ecri.org

APPENDIX 14.1

IT GLOSSARY FOR RISK MANAGERS

@ (*at* symbol) Separates the specific user ID and domain name of an Internet address.

Access The ability to use a computer or program to store or retrieve information.

Address A unique identification assigned to a specific computer. To send e-mail, the sender needs the Internet address. Usually consists of a user ID, the @ symbol, and a domain name and can use or include numbers as well as words.

Anonymous FTP A public file transfer protocol (FTP) file archive that is made available for Internet users to access.

Application program A program designed to carry out specific tasks for the user. Such programs may be purchased from commercial software companies or written by computer staff.

Application service provider (ASP) A company that offers individuals or enterprises access over the Internet to applications and related services that would otherwise have to be located in their own personal or enterprise computers.

Archie An Internet search tool used to locate files on anonymous FTP sites.

ASCII American Standard Code for Information Interchange, a standard code used in computer telecommunication that allows computers to exchange text-based files.

Bandwidth The volume of data that a particular transmission channel can carry at once. There are several media for transmission; two types are twisted-pair telephone wires and fiber optics.

Bits per second (bps) Transmission rate; the higher the rate, the more data can be transmitted.

Browser Software that enables users to move around the World Wide Web to explore Web sites. Examples are Netscape and Internet Explorer.

Bug An error that occurs in a computer program.

Bulletin board system (BBS) Software that allows messages to be left on a computer from a remote computer.

Chat A real-time typed conversation between two or more people over the Internet or a proprietary computer network such as America Online or CompuServe.

.com A commercial organization's domain designation.

CPR Computerized patient record.

Database An entire collection of stored data.

Domain The name of the computer that is connected to the Internet. Computers are uniquely identified by a series of numbers. The domain name system translates those numbers into a name to which users can relate.

Download To transfer or capture data files from a database to the user's computer storage area; to retrieve files from an external computer to one's own computer.

.edu An educational institution's domain designation.

Electronic data processing (EDP) The automation of a routine manual clerical activity (for example, an association membership list).

Electronic signature A feature that allows a physician to sign off on a report through the information system by using a special password, logging off, or some other means that does not require signing a hard copy.

EPR Electronic patient record.

FAQ Frequently asked questions; a file that contains questions and answers about specific topics.

Field Specific pieces of data that will be coded as a sequence of characters. Each field is given a name (incident type, incident location, date, shift).

File A subset of the database that is stored and used as a unit.

File transfer protocol (FTP) A service that supports file transfers between local and remote computers.

Gateway A hardware and software interface system that links two different types of computer systems, such as a mainframe and a LAN.

Gopher A search tool that displays information through a system of menus and menu choices.

.gov A government agency's domain designation.

Hardware The pieces of equipment used by the system.

Home page A location on the World Wide Web that identifies an individual or organization, generally used to refer to the first screen at a site. A home page welcomes visitors and points them to other information available at the Web site.

HTML Hypertext markup language, the standard format for documents on the World Wide Web.

http Hypertext transfer protocol, used by the World Wide Web for transmitting Web pages and other hypertext-linked files over the Internet.

Hypertext Text that has contextual links to other related text. For example, if a document uses a term that is defined or explained in depth somewhere else, a hypertext document would include a link from that term to the related text.

Internet An interconnected collection of computer networks.

Internet relay chat (IRC) Software that allows real-time typed conversations between two or more people over the Internet.

Listserv Trademarked name for an electronic mailing list used to transmit an electronic newsletter to all its subscribers or to facilitate a discussion of a special-interest group. All e-mail sent to the Listserv is sent to everyone on the list.

Mailing list A group discussion distributed through e-mail.

Management information system (MIS) System, generally for middle and operating management, that integrates data from several functional areas and produces much of its output on an on-demand basis.

.mil A military organization's domain designation.

Modem A modulator/demodulator, an electronic device that translates computer signals into a form suitable for long-distance transmission, usually by telephone; the hardware that translates between analog and digital so that a digital computer can communicate over an analog telephone line.

.net An Internet organization's domain designation.

Newsgroup A discussion group on Usenet. Each newsgroup covers a specific topic. Within a newsgroup, there are initial postings listed by subject and subsequent response postings. Newsgroups are not real-time conversations; the postings are stored and forwarded and often last for weeks or months.

Node Any single computer connected to a network.

.org A not-for-profit organization's domain designation.

Packet A unit of data sent across a packet-switching network.

Prompt An on-screen instruction.

Protocol A set of rules governing communication between computers on the Internet.

Record A collection of related fields describing an entity.

Software The programs required for the computer to perform desired operations.

Systems software Software that makes the entire computer system operate. It is provided by the manufacturer.

TCP/IP Transmission control protocol/Internet protocol, the standardized set of computer guidelines that allow different types of machines to talk with each other and exchange information over the Internet.

Telnet A terminal emulation protocol that allows Internet users to log into a host computer from a remote location using a Telnet program.

Upload To transfer information or data files from a user's computer to another computer.

URL The uniform (or universal) resource locator, a unique identifier that points to a specific site on the World Wide Web.

Usenet A collection of discussion areas (bulletin boards) known as newsgroups on the Internet.

Virus Software designed to cause damage to computers or files. Viruses generally enter a computer system via files received on floppy disk or over networks.

Web site An organization's or individual's Web pages, the first of which is called the home page.

CHAPTER

15

RISK MANAGEMENT METRICS

JUDITH NAPIER, TRISTA JOHNSON

LEARNING OBJECTIVES

- To be able to describe the specific steps for successful performance improvement
- To be able to articulate how key process measures are defined
- To be able to identify the seven pillars of quality in health care
- To be able to define five characteristics identified with good measures

This chapter defines metrics that are useful when measuring the success of a risk management program. Risk management professionals need to determine how risk management is defined in the organization, the essential components to be measured, to whom the measurements will be provided, and how success will be determined. This chapter focuses on traditional measurements and provides information to assist organizations that are linking patient safety and risk management processes.

Risk management is defined in several ways. Broadly defined, "risk management includes any activity, process or policy to reduce liability exposure. From both a patient safety and a financial perspective, it is vital that health centers conduct risk management activities aimed at preventing harm to patients and reducing medical malpractice claims."[1]

It is sometimes considered in processes related to adverse outcomes and claims handling when litigation occurs. Unless the risk management process is clearly defined in an organization, it is difficult to determine the appropriate measurements to apply. Also, consideration should be given as to whether one is describing risk prevention or

KEY CONCEPTS

- High-reliability research has focused on the fundamental principles that need to be in place for an organization to develop predictable processes producing dependable outcomes.

- Benchmarking involves uncovering best practices wherever they exist.

- A "total cost of risk" report provides a financial snapshot of the cost to the organization of the risk management program across all lines of insurance and operating business units.

- The "plan, do, check, act" (PDCA) cycle offers health care systems a simple yet effective way to measure and modify change based on the effect on the quality outcome of the change they are attempting to achieve.

- In most health care organizations, potential accidents are rarely reported through traditional safety event or incident reporting systems.

- The most useful metrics support strategic goals of the health care organization and the risk management program and produce actionable information for use by the governing body, medical staff, risk management professional, or other stakeholders.

The authors thank Marva West Tan, associate director, Quality Initiative, State of Maryland, Department of Health and Mental Hygiene, for her research assistance in developing this chapter.

risk mitigation after an event has occurred. Risk prevention activities are proactive and risk mitigation are reactive initiatives. Each would have different descriptions, expectations, and processes.

Risk analysis is also a process described in multiple ways. Risk analysis may involve a review of data, a process, or a situation to learn and apply the information for trends or patterns. Risk analysis is sometimes used to quantify risk **frequency** or severity or to describe the magnitude of potential risk. This would suggest that there is a screening process or severity rating applicable to the events, which can be used to establish priorities of risk mitigation efforts. Another definition of risk analysis equates to the liability assessment used to determine the legal liability exposure of a specific event and the subsequently assigning of a value to the potential financial loss.

The terms *risk management* and *risk analysis* are often used interchangeably, yet they are not synonymous. Risk analysis is part of the risk management process. Before measuring the success of a facility's risk management program, the risk management professional needs to establish what the terms mean to the various stakeholders in the organization.

BENCHMARKING DEFINED

The American Productivity and Quality Center (**APQC**) defines benchmarking as "the process of identifying, learning, and adapting outstanding practices and processes from any organization, anywhere in the world, to help an organization improve its performance. Benchmarking gathers the tacit knowledge—the know-how, judgments, and enablers—that explicit knowledge often misses."[2]

Another well-known expert in the area of benchmarking, Robert C. Camp, has described benchmarking as "the search for industry best practices that lead to superior performances."[3]

Background

The Xerox Corporation was one of the first companies in America to develop and use benchmarking as a method to understand its competition. In 1976, after the Japanese excelled in the office copier market, Xerox recognized the need to do things differently. In 1979, Xerox introduced benchmarking methods as a means to study its competitors' products and to compare to and contrast its own products and processes.

When Xerox first applied benchmarking principles to the manufacturing of its products, significant changes were made to the processes that led to incorporating the best features of the competitors' products. Success in manufacturing led to implementation of benchmarking principles in other parts of the organization, including maintenance, warehousing, distribution, and billing. Xerox quickly found that the principles applied to all aspects of the company.

Many tools are now available to assist organizations in benchmarking. In 1994, the U.S. Department of Defense produced a document that establishes a framework for managing process improvement using benchmarking as a process.[4] The tool introduced specific steps for successful performance improvement:

■ Establishing a strong foundation by selecting an improvement project, analyzing the process, and calculating metrics and gaps in performance

■ Selecting benchmark partners with "best in class" processes to form a benchmark team. Planning for productive sessions with tight agendas, trained personnel, and defined responsibilities

■ Establishing an appropriate benchmark through site visits, data gathering, interviews, and questionnaires

■ Analyzing the results and planning to make changes to achieve a best-in-class model

The key process measures are defined in this tool in the following categories:

■ *Fitness for purpose (FFP):* These measures record how well the process is satisfying the stakeholders' interests, requirements, and desires. They define effectiveness measures.

■ *Conformance to standard (CTS):* These measures record how well the process is conforming to rules, regulations, standards, requirements, and specifications. These are quality measures.

■ *Cycle time (CT):* These measures record how responsive the process is. They are considered efficiency measures.

■ *Process cost (PC):* These measures record the fixed or investment costs associated with the process. They are overhead measures.

Currently, benchmarking in risk management relies on national data such as average cost of claims, average verdict data, and number of staff in risk management departments, so as to compare results to other health care risk management departments. The Risk and Insurance Management Society (http://www.rims.org) produces an annual benchmark survey that reviews the overall cost of risk for many different types of organizations. Health care has been adapting these tools to measure the effectiveness of risk management programs in the hospital and health care settings. The information compares an organization's cost of risk against industry competitors to gauge the cost of effectiveness of risk management departments.

However, "benchmarking involves uncovering best practices where ever they exist."[5] Thus it is important to compare not only data but also processes. Benchmarking suggests that the risk management professional looks at the processes that are used to achieve results and then modifies internal processes to gain better results with the benchmark. Instead, the data are often used as a gauge to establish what is an acceptable range of results, and therefore, the organization is able to stay the course. However, an organization should evaluate internal processes affecting the numbers and define, measure, and monitor the processes that affect the data.

True benchmarking through the sharing of lessons learned in system changes and system failures is a new direction. Using process improvement measures in risk management raises the issues of linkages between patient safety, quality, and risk management efforts. Deciding whether these disciplines fit together suggests that the information collected in each of these disciplines has connectivity. The health care industry is trying to understand what the data mean across the enterprise, rather than in each distinct discipline.

With the advent of the 1999 IOM report *To Err Is Human: Building a Safer Health System,* and the follow-up report, *Crossing the Quality Chasm: A New Health Care System for the 21st Century*, the bar was raised for health care to look at its systems in a new way.[6] The industry shifted focus to the patient and asked whether this is the best that health care has to offer our communities. In many cases, the answer was a resounding no, and so began the patient safety movement.

Avedis Donabedian, widely acknowledged as the father of health systems research, introduced a model in which he identified the "seven pillars" of quality in health care:[7]

1. Efficacy—improving a patient's well-being

2. Efficiency—obtaining the greatest improvement at the lowest cost

3. Optimality—balancing costs and benefits

4. Acceptability—adapting care to the wishes, expectations, and values of the patient

5. Legitimacy—providing care acceptable to society at large

6. Equity—distributing care fairly

7. Cost—providing the greatest benefit at the lowest cost while optimizing the cost-benefit ratio.

Donabedian built his premises on these pillars—that health problems are not a collection of unrelated events but rather a complex process that follows general principles. This breakthrough thinking in his initial work is accepted today as a fundamental principle. The patient safety movement and the body of work that has begun to reflect the science of safety clearly recognizes the complexity in health care systems. High-reliability research has focused on the fundamental principles that need to be in place for an organization to develop predictable processes that produce dependable outcomes. Such principles include a just culture, open reporting systems, and teamwork and communication across multiple disciplines.

In a just culture, everyone speaks up. The current model of reporting incidents, which risk management has relied on for several years, is based on a voluntary system. Unfortunately, the feedback loop has often resulted in the disciplining of the individual who was involved in the event. To break that cycle, risk management needs to team with patient safety to create a just culture for reporting events, to streamline the reporting process, to decrease the time needed to complete reports, and to develop essential feedback loops to caregivers when system failures are reported. If the health care facility begins to shape its efforts around these foundations, the work focuses on the patient rather than on the organization. This makes the risk management program a multidimensional part of the health care organization, rather than a one-dimensional function managing after-the-fact investigations and litigation.

Traditional risk management measures continue to be important cornerstones in program evaluation, but they are not the only focus for an organization interested in making significant improvements in safety. Traditional measures will be described, along with how they are typically collected and analyzed.

CLAIMS

Risk management professionals often choose medical professional liability claims as an area to benchmark because claims represents measurable outcomes, claims data is readily available, and a clear baseline can be established.

Total Number of Claims

Most health care risk management professionals track the number of claims that the organization is involved with at any given time. The total number of claims represents, arguably, high-level results of the safety and risk program at a facility. The measurement is attained by counting the total number of claims for a given time period and can be tracked in a line graph plotting the monthly, quarterly, or annual number of claims. The advantage of this measure is that it provides a baseline of the volume of claims against the organization in several areas. The disadvantage is that the numbers are often too small to be statistically significant, and the claims that are currently active in an organization reflect events that occurred months or even years before the report.

Just as the organization has to define risk management and risk analysis, it also has to define what constitutes a claim. Many organizations identify a claim as any event that the risk management professional thinks could give rise to compensation or a formal demand for compensation, be it a letter or filed lawsuit. Other organizations define a claim as a filed lawsuit. It is important that the organization define how it will use the term *claim* and then consistently apply that definition.

Total Number of Potential Claims

Many health care risk management programs track potential claims, such as events that involve identifiable patient harm or events where there is no legal activity or demand for compensation but the risk management professional determines that there is potential for an assertion. These potential claims provide a sense of the volume of potentially compensable events that the organization is experiencing, allowing for early intervention and disposition.

Cost to the Organization for Claims

The total claims costs, along with the claims volume, are good basic measurements of a traditional risk management program. Total claims costs include expense and indemnity dollars, both reserved and paid. Expense dollars generally include the cost to defend or settle a claim, along with the cost of investigation, medical record copying fees, deposition cost, expert witness fees, attorneys' fees, and the like. Indemnity costs include the dollars necessary to settle the case with the plaintiff and can represent medical cost (past, present, and future), lost wages, pain and suffering, and so on. The advantage of this cost measurement is that it provides a direct measure of financial obligation, but the disadvantage is that the values are quite variable.

Potential Claims by Event Type or Cause

Risk management professionals can isolate, per specialty, the number and severity of cases so as to implement specific risk prevention strategies. However, the breakdown of claims into subgroups by event type or cause often results in such small numbers in the subgroups that they cannot be used effectively for tracking purposes.

Total Cost of Risk

The total-cost-of-risk report is a means of capturing multiple data sets to describe the risk management structure and services so as to focus on the issues relative to the financial measurement of risk. Taking a snapshot in time allows the organization to look at the insurance program structure (limits, coverage, and premium costs); expenses to run the program, including salaries of risk and claims staff; funding of the self-insured retention or deductible; claims adjusting costs if an outside TPA is used; medical bill write-offs; and costs to defend or manage claims. The administrative expenses, including the costs related to risk management and loss control, audit fees, actuary fees, and the like, should be factored into the total cost of risk.

A total-cost-of-risk report provides a financial snapshot of the cost to the organization of the risk management program across all lines of insurance and operating business units. An example is provided in Exhibit 15.1.

Qualitative Measurements of Risk Management Programs

Many organizations track broad process measures that indicate that the structure of a risk management program has been implemented. These measures are most important in an organization where the risk management program is relatively new. They include the creation of policies and procedures to document the risk management program or the communication of risk management issues to senior leadership or the board of directors. Although these measurements indicate whether a basic risk management infrastructure has been established, they do not reflect how successful the organization has been in reducing risk exposures. The disadvantage of traditional measurements for risk management is they do not provide data that can be acted on in any meaningful way because the data reflect financial risks for events that occurred in the distant past.

EXHIBIT 15.1. Total Cost of Risk Report

Provides a snapshot in time used to summarize, inform, and improve the health care system's total cost of risk by using data to identify risk trends for the health system and individual business units

	YEARS FOR COMPARISONS			
	2005	2004	2003	2002
Premium Expense				
• Gross premiums				
• Broker fees				
• State fees				
• Bonds/Securities				
• Other				
• Excess (state-related)				
Subtotal				
Loss Expenses				
• Funded losses				
• Claims adjusting—TPA (insourced)				
• Medical/Rehab (insourced)				
• Deductible retained				
• Investigation (business unit claims and litigation)				
Subtotal				
Administrative Expenses				
• Department costs related to risk				
• Loss control: System				
Local				
Outsourced				
• Audit Fees				
• Actuary Fees				
Subtotal				
GRAND TOTAL				

A method often used in the past is to benchmark the number (frequency) of claims in a particular area against the cost or severity of those cases. For instance, tracking the number of neonatal injury cases and the average cost of those cases in various parts of the country is one method risk management has used to provide a focus to one clinical area. Defense costs and the average cost to defend certain claims are calculated and tracked over time. This might be relevant information; however, it only identifies a potential problem. To address the problem and move toward resolution, it is necessary to apply process improvement in a quantifiable way to compare a facility's processes against other facilities that might have better results.

Other measurement tools for performance and process improvements have been proposed by W. Edwards Deming and Joseph Juran. Their work is viewed as fundamental for quality improvement principles and tools for industry and health care.[8]

Deming focused on the theoretical aspects for managing organizations and emphasized systems effect on outcomes. His work to define systems and understand variation in practice supported much of the early work in health care quality.

Juran had a more practical approach to managing quality in organizations. He used principles to implement strategic quality processes to manage quality functions in organizations. Quality improvement, quality planning, and quality controls were touted as the means to affect the strategic quality planning for organizations.

Together, these two giants established the premise that top management needs to be the driver for long-term commitment and change. Further, systems were more at the root of problems in organizations than the failure of individuals operating within the faulty systems. Deming and Juran began to question the incentives that had been built to motivate practices that were based on faulty premises. Great importance was placed on planning upstream, which would ultimately affect the output downstream. Finally, they recognized the need to understand process variation and the effect this was having on overall improvement.

MEASURING CHANGE

The "plan, do, check, act" (PDCA) cycle offers health care systems a simple yet effective way to measure and modify change based on the effect on the quality outcome of the change they are attempting to achieve. Sometimes it is referred to as the Deming cycle, after Deming introduced the concept in the 1950s. PDCA is an improvement cycle based on a scientific method of proposing a change in process, implementing the change, measuring the results, and taking appropriate action. It has four stages:

1. *Plan.* Determine goals for a process and changes needed to achieve them.

2. *Do.* Implement the changes.

3. *Check.* Evaluate the results in terms of performance.

4. *Act.* Standardize and stabilize the change or begin the cycle again, depending on the results.

Metrics

A metric is a standard used to measure and assess performance or a process. The new prospective patient safety measurements provide a robust set of measurements to assess the safety of an organization and guide improvement efforts.

Measurements typically used as part of patient safety work often embrace reactive and proactive measurements. Take patient falls data as an example. The patient falls rate (number of inpatients falling in a given time period divided by the total number of inpatient days) is often a retrospective measurement used to track the outcome of patient safety efforts. The patient falls rate tells leadership, risk management, and the patient safety staff whether process improvements are making a difference in reducing patient falls. Other types of measures often tracked in a patient falls prevention initiative include concurrent data, such as the percentage of patients that receive a falls risk assessment or the number of patients scored as high risk with an intervention in place to reduce the fall risk. These process measures indicate how well the nursing staff is addressing the issue of patient fall risk for the patient population and implementing appropriate care plans to reduce the risk of falls based on patients' risk profiles.

Another type of measure, called a **balancing measure**, is also used in prospective patient safety work. A balancing measure for the patient falls work would be the number of patients who receive a one-on-one attendant. This measure would help provide an assessment of whether the fall risk is decreasing because of the increased use of one-on-one attendants, rather than the more robust and less resource-draining prevention methods.

Good Catches and Near Misses

Beyond the typically reported safety events, hospitals have begun reporting events called "near misses" or "good catches." These events are not true events in the traditional risk management definition but rather are occurrences that are identified before they become events. The Joint Commission has used the term *near miss* in its sentinel event program to mean events that did not have a significant outcome but might have if the situation had been repeated. Similarly, *good catch* is a synonymous term used to describe an event caught before it harmed the patient. An example might be a nurse who prepared medications for two patients in separate rooms, walking into the first patient's room to administer the medication and almost giving the patient the wrong medications but catching the mistake before administering the medication in error.

Tracking these events and reporting on a monthly basis will do little for an organization except to demonstrate how staff members are reporting situations that could be acted on to prevent events before they happen. The underlying data on the events are most useful to guide organizational improvement efforts aimed at preventing significant events, rather than waiting until a major event occurs before action is taken. The best way to analyze such data is first to organize them into categories and then analyze the details to understand the processes leading to the near misses. Process review and improvement, using tools such as the PDCA model, enable the organization to monitor improvements and continually alter processes and measure results.

Accidents Waiting to Happen

In most health care organizations, potential accidents are rarely reported through traditional safety event or incident reporting systems. The "accident waiting to happen" is an event that most likely does not involve any specific patient but has the potential to cause harm to patients. For example, this might include the manner in which a medication is stored in a cabinet next to another medication with a similar name, potentially leading to error when the wrong medication is chosen. This type of situation is useful in guiding a health care organization to implement process improvements before adverse events occur. This information is important in leadership rounding programs, as an extra or external pair of eyes can pick up potential safety situations more easily than staff routinely working in the environment.

Comparative Data on Patient Safety

So many health care organizations established separate patient safety data collection processes following the 1999 IOM report that the National Quality Forum assigned a council to decide on a standard national patient safety taxonomy that will serve as the basic data collection taxonomy for future measurements. *Standardizing a Patient Safety Taxonomy*, released in 2006, is available at http://www.qualityforum.org/pdf/reports/taxonomy.pdf.

This taxonomy will be a guide for health care organizations in standardizing the data elements collected. This will allow for comparison of data across hospitals to determine trends of significant events and identify areas for improvement on a larger scale. Alignment with this taxonomy will be a key task for health care organizations over the next several years to permit reliable comparisons of data.

The most useful metrics support strategic goals of the health care organization and the risk management program and produce actionable information for use by the governing body, medical staff, risk management professional, or other stakeholders. Developing meaningful metrics that measure the factor desired requires time and thought. Sometimes mentally working backward from desired outcomes or the data needed to support decision making will lead to the needed process or outcome measure. Small-group brainstorming about the service or program that is being measured may also provide a focus for measurement and potential measures. Typically, developing good outcome measures poses the most difficult challenge, as outcomes may be delayed or under the influence of multiple factors outside the risk management program's control. Relying solely on process measures may be a prudent first step when devising a new measurement system or it might be possible to identify some measurable short-term or partial outcomes. It is more desirable to develop a few robust measures than to count multiple items for vague purposes.

DEVELOPING NEW METRICS

The following characteristics are associated with good measures:

▪ *Quantifiability.* Although this is an obvious characteristic, it is also a challenging one, as the broad goal in program evaluation is often to measure the "success" of a specific effort. The subjective term *success* must be measurable in ways such as fewer claims, reduced legal fees, or increased physician reporting, so that the data that must be collected can be identified. Qualitative information, such as comments from clinical staff, might provide some useful data when you cannot identify an objective quantifiable measure.

    ■   *Sensitivity or responsiveness.* The item to be measured is believed to change over time and to be responsive to risk management activities. The metric can capture or record these changes.

    ■   *Meaningfulness.* The metric addresses a key aspect of program operation or desired outcomes and is likely to be important as a basis for decision making. A meaningful measure will be understood both inside and outside the risk management department.

    ■   *Uniqueness.* The metric measures one item or factor or, if it measures more than one factor, is divided into subcomponents that each measure one item. For example, a metric regarding the number of adverse events and **near misses** reported in a quarter should have a separate indicator for counting adverse events and another for counting near misses.

    ■   *Realm of control.* Is the item being measured under the direct control of the risk management program or thought to be influenced by organizationwide risk management activities? If there are other internal or external factors affecting this measure, they need to be identified so that they can be factored into data analysis and reporting. Considering **realm of control** is particularly important when developing and reporting outcome measures. Jurisdiction, new state medical professional liability legislation, relative number, and expertise of the plaintiffs' bar are external factors that might affect the risk management program's ability to reduce aggregate claim settlement amounts.

    ■   *Feasibility.* Are the data needed for the measure readily available or easily derived from existing health information management systems? How often will data be needed: quarterly, monthly, weekly, or at some other frequency? Will data need to be pulled from various sources within the health system, such as from the medical record, incident reports, or audits? If the measure involves new data collection, how would this be accomplished, and what resources would be needed? Could data collection be piggybacked on an existing effort? Could the data collection process be automated through an electronic medical record system? If possible, do a rough cost-benefit analysis for implementing this measure. Reducing the burden of ongoing data collection should be a factor in the design of any new metric.

    ■   *Validity.* Does the metric actually measure what it is supposed to measure? Few risk management professionals routinely perform any statistical tests of **validity** of a measure. Most rely on face validity, which involves consensus by experts in the field that this is a reasonable measure of what is being measured or some dimension thereof. Seek some internal or external review of draft measures by professional colleagues or others knowledgeable in risk management, and try to improve the validity of new measures. If more assurance is needed regarding validity, get assistance from a statistician or health service researcher. One particular area of concern with relation to validity in risk and safety work is the underreporting associated with voluntarily reported safety events or incidents. When using trends or rates of voluntarily reported safety events, validity of the data is a concern if underreporting of events is a factor.

■ *Reliability.* Will the measure produce similar results in the hands of different users over time? If the measure involves considerable additional data collection, a simple test of interrater reliability (reliability among multiple raters) might be worthwhile before proceeding to full implementation. Interrater reliability indicates the consistency of data collection among separate individuals collecting the same data. For example, if two individuals are abstracting the same data elements and end up with the same results, there is high interrater **reliability**.

■ *Baseline.* It is important when selecting a metric to look for one that has a baseline period available to use as a comparison to the follow-up data once improvements have been put into place. A baseline is a measurement during a period of time before an intervention. It is collected to provide this comparison. Without a baseline measure, it is difficult to ascertain whether the current data indicate a change from the previous environment or if any improvement has been made.

■ *Multidimensionality.* Consider measuring different dimensions of the risk management program by using several structure, process, and outcome measures to develop a fuller picture of program functioning. In addition to these three standbys of measurement, many national evaluation programs, such as the Quality Improvement Organizations' *8th Scope of Work,*[9] include other types of measurements, such as patients' experience of care; infrastructure enhancements, such as use of health information technology; and cultural readiness for patient safety.

Using the right metrics helps create a **dashboard** or **scorecard** for risk management that directs leaders and board members to answer the question, Is the risk management program successful in its efforts?

A scorecard is an evaluation tool that specifies the criteria the health care facility's key stakeholders will use to rate risk management performance in relation to the requirements. By contrast, a dashboard is a tool used for collecting and reporting information about vital customer requirements or your business's performance for key customers. Dashboards provide a quick summary of process or performance outcomes.[10]

An effective performance metrics system does all of the following:[11]

■ Defines what is important from the customer's perspective

■ Builds measures that support the desired performance

■ Creates an environment of trust where real issues can be discussed openly and progress is celebrated

- Is routinely reviewed and analyzed

Effective metrics will have the following attributes:[12]

- They drive better decision making.

- They are objective and easily measured.

- They always result in action.

- Over time, they are predictive, not simply reactive.

- They are easily understood by multiple stakeholders.

- They drive improvements in efficiency and effectiveness, customer satisfaction, and employee satisfaction in an environment of mutual respect.

- They are owned and regularly reviewed by management and employees alike.

Performance metrics can be extremely useful to assess the effectiveness of a risk management program. Using predetermined goals that are measured against performance standards takes the subjectivity out of the effectiveness question. Further, by creating a team of people at the inception of the process to help define the measures and by monitoring the suitability and effectiveness of the measures, using predetermined goals permits the organization to stay focused on the risk management goals.

The **Institute for Healthcare Improvement (IHI)** (http://www.ihi.org) has defined measures for improvement as different from measures for research. It is important to differentiate the two. Measures for research have a purpose to discover new knowledge. The purpose of measurement for process improvement is to bring new knowledge into daily practice.

Research typically relies on one large blind test, whereas process improvement uses many sequential and observable tests of change. Volumes of data are gathered in research to ensure that all bases are covered. Just enough information is gathered to learn and complete another cycle of improvement, and research usually takes long periods of time to report on the results. **Performance improvement** relies on small tests of change to accelerate improvement.

SUMMARY

Connecting financial information with clinical risk information begins to paint a picture for the organization's leadership of the importance of risk management and patient safety to the viability of the health care organization. It is important to represent both components to relate the true picture of risk prevention and management in the organization.

Clinical risk measures focus on issues such as clinical and environmental risk assessments and on identifying gaps from regulatory standards to practices with strong links to patient outcomes and claims. Integrating the quality data and the risk management data not only provides the organization with a sense of continuity and teamwork between the disciplines but also begins to describe the various components of issues from a quality viewpoint, a patient safety vantage, and a risk management and prevention perspective.

Risk management, patient safety, and quality improvement are all vehicles currently used in health care to build a safe and reliable system of patient care. Past work has involved individual departments separately collecting data and analyzing that information to draw conclusions and direct the organization in setting plans and goals independent of each other. As risk management professionals continue to define and expand their professional discipline and assess their organizations' readiness to change, it is incumbent that past models be reevaluated. The disciplines of risk management, patient safety, and quality improvement need to integrate their approach to patient care. This integration will ultimately support the efficient use of organizational resources to improve outcomes.

KEY TERMS

Balancing measure
Benchmarking
Conformance to standards
Cycle time
Dashboard
Fitness for purpose
Frequency
Institute for Healthcare Improvement
Metric
Near miss

Performance improvement
Process cost
Realm of control
Reliability
Responsiveness
Risk analysis
Scorecard
Total cost of risk
Validity

ACRONYMS

APC
APQC
CT
CTS

FFP
IHI
PC
PDCA

NOTES

1. OIG Final Report: Risk Management at Health Centers (OEI-10-03-00050) Department of Health & Human Services, Office of Inspector General, Washington, D.C., February 17, 2005, p. 8. Available at: http://www.oig.hhs.gov/oei/reports/oei-01-03-00050.pdf (accessed November 10, 2008).

2. APQC. Glossary of Benchmarking Terms, page 1. Available online at: http://www.apqc.org/portal/apqc/ksn/GlossaryofBenchmarkingTerms.pdf?paf_gear_id=contentgearhome&paf_dm=full&pageselect=contentitem&docid=119519 (accessed November 11, 2008).

3. Productive Solutions Australia Pty. Ltd. "Benchmarking," 2001, http://www.pro
   ductivesolutions.com.au/Benchmarking.html.

4. Davis, R. I., and Davis, R. A. *How to Prepare for and Conduct a Benchmark
   Project.* Washington, D.C.: Department of Defense, 1994.

5. Productive Solutions, "Benchmarking."

6. Kohn, L. T., Corrigan, J. M., and Donaldson, M. S. (eds.). *To Err Is Human:
   Building a Safer Health System.* Washington, D.C.: National Academies Press,
   1999; Institute of Medicine. *Crossing the Quality Chasm: A New Health Care
   System for the 21st Century.* Washington, D.C.: National Academies Press, 2001.

7. Best, M., and Neuhauser, D. "Avedis Donabedian: Father of Quality Assurance
   and Poet." *Quality and Safety in Health Care,* 2004, *13,* 472–473.

8. Landesberg, P. "In the Beginning, There Were Deming and Juran." *Journal for
   Quality and Participation,* Nov.-Dec. 1999, pp. 59–61.

9. Harris, Y. *Quality Improvement Organizations: 8th Scope of Work: Transforming
   Nursing Home Quality,* 2007, http://www.ltcombudsman.org/uploads/NCCNHR8
   thscope0306.ppt.

10. Centers for Medicare and Medicaid Services. "Medicare Takes Major Step Toward
    Improving Quality of Care: Protecting Medicare Trust Fund Is Also Goal."
    Press release, Apr. 7, 2005, http://www.cms.hhs.gov/apps/media/press/release.asp
    ?Counter=1421.

11. Six Sigma. "Six Sigma and Quality Metrics," 2005, http://healthcare.isixsigma.com
    /me/metrics.

12. Romeu, M. *Developing a Performance Metrics System: An Introduction to
    Performance Management Tools.* Charleston, S.C.: MR Group, 2003, p. 1.

SUGGESTED READING

Donabedian, A. "Evaluating the Quality of Medical Care." *Milbank Memorial Fund
   Quarterly,* 1966, *44,* 166–206.

Juran, J. M. (ed.). *A History of Managing for Quality: The Evolution, Trends, and
   Future Directions of Managing for Quality.* Milwaukee: ASQC Quality Press,
   1995.

Juran, J. M. *Juran on Leadership for Quality: An Executive Handbook.* New York:
   Free Press, 1989.

Standards Australia. *Guidelines for Managing Risk in the Health Care Sector.* Canberra:
   Standards Australia, 2001.

CHAPTER

ACCREDITATION, LICENSURE, CERTIFICATION, AND SURVEYING BODIES

FREDERICK ROBINSON

LEARNING OBJECTIVES

- To be able to understand the type of atmosphere and culture of improvement that will lead management and governing bodies to research and implement voluntary accreditations

- To be able to identify necessary policies, procedures, protocols, and guidelines to monitor compliance with all applicable statutes, standards, and regulations

- To be able to identify resources and understand how to access them

- To be able to understand the various accreditation and licensing programs and related standards in order to identify deficiencies and improve the delivery of health care

This chapter acquaints the risk management professional with resources and information that will identify and explain the variety of organizations responsible for the licensure, accreditation, certification, and surveying of health care organizations.

It provides an overview of major bodies that oversee both mandatory and voluntary activities. It examines the rationales for participating in these activities and the role that the risk management professional may play. In some cases, states and local jurisdictions maintain the right to regulate health care through licensure of institutions and practitioners. In all states, prescriptive regulations and rules describe the compliance elements that must be in place before a health care enterprise can do business.

KEY CONCEPTS

- The consumer push to obtain better data about the quality of care and services that the medical community provides has led to increased attention to accreditation, licensure, and certification bodies.

- Failure to meet standards may adversely affect the health care organization's ability to operate, provide services, meet contract requirements, or receive funding from sources that require compliance with specific standards.

- The risk management professional who understands how to integrate risk management techniques for achieving compliance with standards and regulatory requirements adds value to the health care delivery system.

- Loss of funding due to any violation of regulatory or accreditation standards or public disclosure of a failure to meet established standards could result in an adverse effect on the health care organization's business operations or pending or future litigation.

- The health care industry will continue to be subject to increased demands for health care provider and payer accountability, including compliance with published standards and regulations.

THE CONSUMER ERA OF HEALTH CARE

The consumer movement in the United States has extended deep into the health care provider community. Health care organizations are subject to specific mandatory review and may also participate in voluntary accreditation and inspection programs that apply to either the organization as a whole or to specialized areas within the industry. Results are often posted in the community newspaper and on the Internet. The medical provider community must deal with the perceptions and expectations of increasingly concerned and inquiring public consumers.

The health care industry continues to experience transition in a consumer-focused marketplace. An aging population in the United States increasingly demands added information and accountability regarding the hospital and medical provider community. Furthermore, consumers believe they have the right to access certain information, statistics, and background details about the medical provider community and take personal responsibility for obtaining them. Internet access and friendly Web browser systems facilitate access to data and information that had previously not been accessed so easily.

The consumer push to obtain better data about the **quality of care** and services that the medical community provides has placed greater focus on the development of accreditation, licensure, and certification bodies. The medical provider community has been asked to be more accountable to the public to demonstrate its quality and commitment to providing health care services.

The medical provider community relies on meeting accreditation, licensure, and certification standards to demonstrate its quality and effectiveness. Customer service satisfaction surveys continue, but the pressing questions of the purchasing public revolve around the clinical expertise, training, and performance record of a medical provider or facility.

The American health care system has responded to the growing public demands for information by meeting evolving accreditation standards and licensure requirements. **Managed care** growth has been subject to regional ebb and flow as medical service providers have reacted to decreasing reimbursements and loss of control of the managed care environment. In some areas, there has been a significant shift of the population into integrated managed care delivery systems. With these changes, there has been an increased emphasis on measuring the quality of care. In addition, more public and private attention has been focused on the organizations assigned or related to health care organizational oversight.

WHAT THE HEALTH CARE RISK MANAGEMENT PROFESSIONAL NEEDS TO KNOW

Accrediting organizations and licensure, certification, and surveying bodies have continued their efforts to establish requirements and regulatory standards that are subject to review by federal, state, and private organizations. Although it might not be the risk management professional's job to manage or monitor compliance with published standards, the risk management professional should be familiar with the organizations responsible for oversight. Failure to meet standards may adversely affect the health care organization's ability to operate, provide services, meet contract requirements, or receive funding from sources that require compliance with specific standards.

Risk Management Responsibilities

Risk management program requirements have continued to expand. Note that nearly every single accreditation, certification, and regulatory requirement involves some form of risk management activity. At the same time, recognize that health care organizations must demonstrate a willingness to comply with published standards and regulations if they intend to succeed and remain in business.

The health care risk management professional must ensure collaboration with many professionals within the delivery system. There are too many issues and far too many details to expect that a single person can turn the tide of risk management events. The efforts must be championed by the top leadership of the organization and supported throughout the organization.

Patient safety, patient protection, and compliance with standards and regulations require management of outcomes data. The best-qualified health care organizations are focusing on how to demonstrate that they deliver safe, effective, and efficient care without compromising essential elements of control. One way to improve is to identify the inefficient areas of the system and to devote attention to the process of continuous improvement. This means that health care organizations must identify opportunities to improve and then design program infrastructures that support the design. Health care organizations that do not attend to this priority will suffer the consequences of increased risks, diminished financial return, and lack of public confidence.

The health care risk management professional is in a unique position to make a difference when knowledgeable and resourceful about the issues that the organization must address. The risk management professional who understands how to integrate risk management techniques for achieving compliance with standards and regulatory requirements adds true value to the health care delivery system.

Why Participate in Voluntary Accreditation Activities?

Given the staggering amount of mandated regulation in health care, it is reasonable to ask why organizations participate in additional programs, most of which are voluntary. There are significant reasons to participate voluntarily. First, demonstrating an organization's commitment to following established standards and regulations is the right thing to do. The principle of providing the best possible service and looking for ways to constantly improve that service is a core part of the medical ethic for individual caregivers and for provider organizations. Moreover, the public demands it. Public accountability is fulfilled through several different activities. Licensure, accreditation, and certification make up just one category but are important in ensuring that an organization meets or exceeds contemporary expectations of quality, safety, and performance.

Participation also makes good business sense. Although participation in many of the basic programs is necessary just to be in business, other programs enhance the organization in important ways. Through ongoing benchmarking and performance improvement programs, service quality and cost-effectiveness are addressed.

Participation in voluntary programs can also present marketing and recruiting advantages. From a risk management perspective, failure to meet licensure, accreditation, certification, and survey requirements might directly affect the health care organization's loss exposure.

Licensure, Accreditation, and Certification Activities

Licensure, accreditation, and certification activities can be characterized as mandatory and voluntary functions, although some, such as deemed status relationships, play a dual role. Mandatory functions include organizational licensure; individual health care professional licensure; specific licensure for activities such as handling radioactive materials or preparing and shipping blood or blood components; approval to participate in federal funding programs through either government inspection or deemed status; and compliance with broadly applicable regulatory programs such as workplace safety, equal rights, and the Americans with Disabilities Act.

Accreditation and certification programs make up the voluntary activities and are generally sponsored by the industry itself or by specialty organizations. Virtually all such entities are nongovernmental.

The Risk Management Professional's Role

The health care risk management professional should make it a priority to be aware of the multitude of organizations performing licensure, accreditation, certification, and surveying of health care organizations. The risk management program description may include participation in the processes associated with the oversight activities. Loss of funding due to any violation of regulatory or accreditation standards or public disclosure of a failure to meet established standards might result in an adverse effect on the health care organization's business operations or pending or future litigation.

It is critical for risk management professionals to understand the effect of compliance with regulatory, licensure, certification, and accrediting bodies. It is even more critical that health care risk management professionals understand their roles and responsibilities for working as team members in the framework of the organizational goals to meet standards and accreditation requirements.

MANDATORY SURVEYING BODIES

Mandatory surveying bodies are required for health care organizations to operate and obtain a license. This is a requirement in every state. The health care risk management professional must be acquainted with state requirements and have the ability to access the published standards criteria to fulfill certain job-related functions.

Department of Health and Human Services

The Department of Health and Human Services (**HHS**) is the United States government's principal agency for protecting the health of all Americans and providing essential human services, especially for the members of the population least able to help themselves.

HHS has more than three hundred programs that cover a wide spectrum of activities. The department works closely with all state and local governments, and many HHS-funded services are provided at the local level by state or county agencies. Eleven operating divisions report directly to the Secretary. Included in the eleven and represented by an asterisk (*) are components of the Public Health Service. The operating divisions are:

- Administration for Children and Families (ACF)

- Administration on Aging (AoA)

- Agency for Healthcare Research and Quality (AHRQ)

- Agency for Toxic Substances and Disease Registry (ATSDR)*

- Centers for Disease Control and Prevention (CDC)*

- Centers for Medicare & Medicaid Services (CMS)

- Food and Drug Administration (FDA)*

- Health Resources and Services Administration (HRSA)*

- Indian Health Service (IHS)*

- National Institutes of Health (NIH)*

- Substance Abuse and Mental Health Services Administration (SAMHSA)*

In the public sector, the most visible certification organization is the Centers for Medicare and Medicaid Services (CMS), which oversees payment for most of the health care covered by the federal government. This federal agency administers the Medicare, Medicaid, and State Children's Health Insurance programs. CMS provides health insurance for more than eighty-three million Americans.

In addition to providing health insurance, CMS performs several quality-focused activities, including regulation of laboratory testing, surveys, and certification of health care facilities (including nursing homes, home health agencies, intermediate care facilities for the mentally retarded, and hospitals), development of coverage policies, and improvement of quality of care.

CMS spends more than $519 billion a year buying health services for beneficiaries of Medicare, Medicaid, and the State Children's Health Insurance Program (SCHIP). It is responsible for ensuring that the Medicare, Medicaid, and SCHIP programs are properly run by its contractors and state agencies. CMS must establish policies for paying health care providers and must conduct research on the effectiveness of various health care management, treatment, and financial practices. CMS is also accountable to assess the quality of health care facility services and take enforcement actions as necessary.

CMS oversees payments that may comprise more than 50 percent of a health care organization's revenue. The onset of federal Medicare and Medicaid laws in the mid-1960s and federal **statutes** and **regulations** defined the requirements for health care organizations to participate in these programs. These requirements, known as conditions of participation (CoPs), define the organization structure and functional requirements, with particular focus on service quality and appropriateness.

Many of the requirements highlight documentation required in the clinical record to justify care and payment for care. CMS oversees these requirements by inspecting organizations directly, contracting with state health departments to inspect organizations, or relying on private accrediting organizations such as The Joint Commission, the American Osteopathic Association (**AOA**) or Det Norske Veritas Healthcare, Inc. (DNVHC).

To ensure public and expert involvement in its programs, CMS maintains standing committees. Committee meetings are open to the public and are used to provide advice or to make recommendations on several issues related to the health care organization's responsibilities. CMS also sponsors special projects and initiatives in response to national issues challenging the health care industry. The following standing committees have been established:

- Practicing Physicians Advisory Council

- Advisory Panel on Medicare Education

- Medicare Coverage Advisory Committee

- Advisory Panel on Ambulatory Payment Classification Groups

- Competitive Pricing Advisory Committee

- Emergency Medical Treatment and Labor Act Technical Advisory Group

- Advisory Board on the Demonstration of a Bundled Case-Mix Adjusted Payment System for End-Stage Renal Disease Services

- Medicaid Commission

- State Pharmaceutical Assistance Transition Commission

When CMS grants "deemed status" to private organizations, it reserves the right to assess their performance. It does this through an ongoing effort known as a validation survey, in which it conducts the inspection of a health care entity that has been privately accredited. CMS then compares its results with those of the deemed accrediting organization. CMS also monitors individual patient care through a series of contracted relationships with **quality improvement organizations** (**QIO**s) and through its own compliance programs, monitored by its inspector general.

On July 15, 2008, Congress voted to override President Bush's veto of the Medicare Improvements for Patients and Providers Act of 2008 which included a provision which changed the deeming authority status with CMS. The new law removes the "unique deeming authority" given to The Joint Commission via CMS since 1965, requiring instead that the accrediting body (as well as any other accrediting bodies seeking deeming status) to apply through CMS for that authority. In order to prevent any breaks in accreditation for Joint Commission-accredited hospitals, a two-year transition period has been included in the provision for The Joint Commission to apply for deeming authority through CMS. The Joint Commission expects to receive CMS's decision by July 15, 2010 for continuation of its Medicare recognition. Until then, the Joint Commission will continue to offer hospitals Medicare deemed status through its current statutory authority.

Health care organizations can be excluded from participation in Medicare if they fail to comply with any element of these activities. The CMS Web site (http://www .cms.hhs.gov) is a user-friendly tool to identify the correct regional office and to access specific program requirements. CMS regional offices are listed in Table 16.1.

TABLE 16.1. CMS Regional Offices

Region I CT, ME, MA, NH, RI, VT JFK Federal Building Room 2325 Boston, MA 02203 (617) 565-1188	Region II NJ, NY, PR, VI 26 Federal Plaza, 38th Floor New York, NY 10278 (212) 264-3657
Region III DE, DC, MD, PA, VA, WV Public Ledger Building Suite 216 150 South Independence Mall West Philadelphia, PA 19101 (215) 861-4140	Region IV AL, FL, GA, KY, MS, NC, SC, TN Atlanta Federal Center 61 Forsyth Street S.W., Suite 4T20 Atlanta, GA 30303 (404) 562-7500
Region V IL, IN, MI, OH, WI 233 North Michigan Avenue, Suite 600 Chicago, IL 60601 (312) 886-6432	Region VI AR, LA, NM, OK, TX 1301 Young Street, Suite 714 Dallas, TX 75202 (214) 767-6423
Region VII IA, KS, MO, NE Richard Bolling Federal Building 601 East 12th Street, Room 235 Kansas City, MO 64106 (816) 426-5233	Region VIII CO, MT, ND, SD, UT, WY Colorado State Bank Building 1600 Broadway, Suite 700 Denver, CO 80202 (303) 844-2111
Region IX AZ, CA, HI, NV, U.S. Pacific Islands 75 Hawthorne Street, Suite 408 San Francisco, CA 94105 (415) 744-3501	Region X AK, ID, OR, WA 2201 Sixth Avenue, Mail Stop RX-40 Seattle, WA 98121 (206) 615-2306

State Health Department

Another highly visible public entity is the state health department, which is the agency generally charged with overseeing health care organizations' right to do business. Not surprisingly, the approach taken by individual states varies tremendously and is often reflective of the culture of the state with respect to regulation. These activities include reviewing activities that are regularly scheduled, conducting independent inspections or surveys, forming deemed status relationships with private accrediting bodies, or simply reacting to tragic or highly publicized events.

In some states, the inspection is directed toward high-priority areas such as credentials review and privileging programs; others take a collaborative approach that might include The Joint Commission and state medical association as a part of the review process.

VOLUNTARY SURVEYING BODIES

To evaluate and improve their quality of care, health care organizations voluntarily request that outside agencies accredit them.

The Joint Commission

In 1951, the American College of Physicians, the American Hospital Association, the American Medical Association, and the Canadian Medical Association joined with the American College of Surgeons to create the Joint Commission on Accreditation for Healthcare Organizations (JCAHO), now known simply as The Joint Commission. This independent, not-for-profit organization was established for the primary purpose of providing voluntary accreditation.

The Joint Commission is a private nonprofit organization dedicated to improving the quality of care in organized health care settings. The organization provides evaluation, accreditation, and consultation and establishes standards for long-term care facilities, ambulatory health care organizations, home care agencies, hospices, hospitals, health care delivery networks, and organizations that offer major mental health services. The Joint Commission offers accreditation to more than seventeen thousand health care organizations throughout the United States.

On-site accreditation surveys are intended to assess the extent of the health care organization's compliance with applicable standards and to provide information and guidance to help the organization with continuing performance improvement. Surveys are conducted every three years and more frequently if a follow-up or revisit is required.

As new technologies and societal demands affect health care organizations, The Joint Commission may respond with the development of a standard that corresponds to identified needs.

Consumer demands for accountability have influenced standards revisions and the evolution of new standards. The Joint Commission is a major supplier of education and consultation to the health care industry, and it conducts educational programs for accredited organizations and those seeking accreditation.

The standards for each Joint Commission accreditation program are published in a separate manual. The Joint Commission also publishes reference manuals, guides to quality improvement, accreditation survey scoring guidelines, and periodicals. It also publishes an official monthly journal, the *Joint Commission Journal on Quality Improvement,* which is available from the organization's customer service office.

Joint Commission accreditation decisions are based on a survey and for a given organization will be one of the following types.[1]

Accreditation

This decision is awarded to a health care organization that is in compliance with all standards at the time of the on-site-survey or has successfully addressed requirements for improvement in an "evidence of standards compliance" (ESC) within forty-five days following the survey.

Provisional Accreditation

This is awarded when a health care organization (1) fails to address all requirements for improvement in an ESC within forty-five days following survey, (2) failed to achieve an appropriate level of sustained compliance as determined by a "measure of success" (MOS) result, or (3) fails to meet all requirements for the timely submission of data and information to The Joint Commission within thirty-one days of the date the information is due.

Conditional Accreditation

This accreditation results when a health care organization fails to be in substantial compliance with the standards, usually determined by the number of noncompliant standards that exceed established thresholds at the time of survey. The organization must remedy identified problem areas through preparation and submission of an ESC or MOS and a conditional follow-up survey. It may also be awarded if the organization fails to meet all requirements for the timely submission of data and information to The Joint Commission within sixty-one days of the due date.

Preliminary Denial of Accreditation

This results when there is justification to deny accreditation to the organization as usually determined by the number of noncompliant standards that exceed established thresholds at the time of survey. The decision is subject to appeal prior to the determination to deny accreditation; the appeal process may also result in a decision other than denial of accreditation.

Denial of Accreditation

This denial results when a health care organization does not permit the performance of any survey by The Joint Commission or fails to do one or more of the following: (1) meet requirements for the timely submission of data and information to The Joint Commission within ninety-one days of the due dates, (2) resolve a conditional accreditation status prior to withdrawing from the accreditation process, or (3) submit payment for survey fees or annual fees.

Preliminary Accreditation

This results when the organization demonstrates compliance with selected standards in the first of two surveys conducted under The Joint Commission's early survey policy option 1. The decision remains in effect until one of the other official accreditation categories is assigned, based on a complete survey against all applicable standards approximately six months later.

Accreditation Watch

Though not a separate accreditation decision, accreditation watch is a publicly disclosable attribute of an organization's existing accreditation status. An organization is placed on accreditation watch when a sentinel event has occurred and a thorough and credible root cause analysis of the sentinel event and an action plan have not been completed in a specified time frame. Following determination by The Joint Commission that the organization has conducted an acceptable root cause analysis and developed an acceptable action plan, the accreditation watch designation is removed from the organization's accreditation status.

Refer to The Joint Commission's accreditation manual for additional information on current accreditation decisions, policies, and procedures.

Benefits of Joint Commission accreditation for a health care organization may include the following:

- Improved patient care

- A demonstration of the organization's commitment to safety and quality

- A consultative and educational experience

- Enhanced safety and quality improvement efforts

- Strengthened recruitment and retention efforts

- Substitution for federal certification surveys for Medicare and Medicaid

- Secured managed care contracts

- Facilitation of the organization's business strategies

- Competitive advantage

- Enhanced image to the public, purchasers, and payers

- Fulfilling licensure requirements in many states

- Recognition by insurers and other third parties

- Strengthened community confidence

Standards and Performance Measurement

The Joint Commission's standards address the organization's level of performance in key functional areas, such as patient rights, patient treatment, and infection control.

The standards focus not simply on what the organization has but on what it does. Standards set forth performance expectations for activities that affect the safety and quality of patient care. If an organization does the right things and does them well, there is a strong likelihood that its patients will experience good outcomes. The Joint Commission develops its standards in consultation with health care experts, providers, measurement experts, purchasers, and consumers.

In February 1997, the commission launched ORYX, billed as "The Next Evolution in Accreditation," to integrate the use of outcomes and other performance measurement data into the accreditation process. It is intended to be a flexible and affordable approach for supporting quality improvement efforts in Joint Commission–accredited organizations and for increasing the value of the accreditation process.

A component of the ORYX initiative is the identification and use of "core measures"—standardized performance measures that can be applied across accredited health care organizations in a particular accreditation program. Sets of core performance measures for each accreditation program have been identified in a staggered approach.

In May 2001, the commission announced the four initial core measurements areas for hospitals: acute myocardial infarction, heart failure, community-acquired pneumonia, and pregnancy and related conditions. Hospitals began to collect core measure data for patient discharges beginning in July 2002 and for surgical infection prevention in July 2004. Also in 2004, the commission and CMS began working together to align measures common to both organizations. These standardized common measures, called "hospital quality measures," are in place for acute care myocardial infarction, heart failure, pneumonia, and the Surgical Care Improvement Project (surgical infection prevention measures). The commission also has core measures for pregnancy and related conditions and children's asthma care.[2]

Education and Information

Through its not-for-profit subsidiary, Joint Commission Resources (JCR), The Joint Commission sponsors several education programs, produces publications for health care professionals, and provides consultation to health care organizations. JCR is committed to offering standards-related educational support for the organizations that it accredits and to advancing provider understanding of current concepts in performance measurement and improvement.

On its Web site, The Joint Commission provides a comprehensive guide to help individuals learn more about the safety and quality of Joint Commission–accredited health care organizations and programs throughout the United States. Quality Check includes each organization's name, address, telephone number, accreditation decision, accreditation date, current accreditation status and effective date, and its most recent performance report. This report provides detailed information about an organization's performance and how it compares to similar organizations. Printed performance reports are available through the customer service center.[3]

American Osteopathic Association

The American Osteopathic Association has been accrediting health care facilities in the United States for more than fifty years. Since 1965, the AOA has had deemed status authority from CMS to survey hospitals under the Medicare CoPs. The AOA is one of only three voluntary accreditation programs in the United States authorized by CMS to survey hospitals under Medicare. The AOA conducts an on-site survey to verify compliance with published AOA standards. The AOA has also developed published accreditation requirements in the areas of ambulatory care and surgery, mental health, substance abuse, and physical rehabilitation medicine facilities.

Det Norske Veritas Healthcare, Inc. (DNVHC)

CMS, announced in the September 29, 2008 Federal Register that effective September 26, 2008 through September 26, 2012 they were recognizing DNVHC as an approved national accrediting program for hospitals seeking to participate in the Medicare and Medicaid programs. DNVHC's accreditation process combines CMS conditions of participation with ISO 9001:2000, a collection of standards for quality management systems. DNVHC's process is called the National Integrated Accreditation for Healthcare organizations and was designed to streamline the accreditation process, identifying ways to make continual improvements. Information of ISO 9001:2000 is offered below.

National Committee for Quality Assurance

The National Committee for Quality Assurance (**NCQA**) is a private, not-for-profit organization that assesses and reports on the quality of managed care plans. NCQA's mission is to provide information to purchasers and consumers of managed health care to distinguish the health plan's quality. NCQA has led national efforts to promote accountability for managed care health plans.

The managed care organization (**MCO**) accreditation program is voluntary. Currently, nearly half of the health maintenance organizations (**HMO**s) in the United States participate in the NCQA accreditation process. For an organization to become accredited by NCQA, it must go through a survey and meet standards that are designed to evaluate the health plan's administrative and clinical systems.

The health plan must also submit specific data as part of the accreditation process. During an accreditation survey, health plans must provide data on specific areas from the following five categories:

- Access and service to plan

- Qualified providers in plan

- Staying healthy: preventive health measures

- Getting better: effective treatments, drugs, and devices

- Living with illness: management of chronic illness

NCQA has expanded its accreditation programs in response to the demands for evaluation and accountability of sectors of the health care delivery system. In addition to accreditation of HMOs, NCQA also accredits managed behavioral health care organizations and preferred provider organizations (**PPO**s). The PPO accreditation program is designed to recognize and acknowledge health care PPO organizations that focus on access, network quality, and customer service.

NCQA also provides accreditation standards for disease management and new health plans and was awarded a contract to operate an accreditation program to ensure that the Veterans Administration medical centers are complying with the VA and other relevant federal regulations designed to protect human subjects of research.

Health Plan Employer Data and Information Set

NCQA has been viewed as a leader in health plan performance measurement since 1991. The Health Plan Employer Data and Information Set (**HEDIS**) was developed by NCQA as a group of specific standard measures for comparing health plans. The HEDIS data set includes more than fifty performance measures. A consumer survey and a survey to evaluate parents' experiences with their children's care are included in the survey process.

HEDIS evaluates the results that a health plan achieves in dozens of key areas of care and service, including immunization rates, cholesterol management, and member satisfaction. The results of HEDIS data are published and made available to prospective health plan purchasers and to the general public.[4]

ISO 9001:2000

The International Organization for Standardization (**ISO**) is composed of 149 member countries, with each country entitled to one vote. The United States' representative to the ISO is the American National Standards Institute (**ANSI**). The intent of the ISO is to create a universal approach to evaluating, managing, and directing quality based on global standards. ISO quality management standards were first published in 1987 as a quality management system. ISO publishes a set of standards that outlines procedures to establish performance standards, designate responsibilities, organize processes, and demand management accountability. The focus of ISO standards is to encourage continuous performance improvement and documentation of processes and procedures. ISO standards are intended to apply to a wide range of industries and are not industry-specific.

The intent of the standards is to help organizations achieve quality outcomes and results based on a consistent, reliable, and cost-efficient model. The ISO standards are used throughout the world by service industries, manufacturing, environmental industries, space and aviation industries, and their suppliers.

In recent years, the health care industry has recognized ISO standards as both an alternative and an adjunct to existing quality management systems. Perhaps the greatest influence of the ISO for the health care industry has been the growing movement for ISO-certified industry organizations to require ISO certification from suppliers, including health care providers. Health care providers and payers, viewed as major tier-one suppliers to organizations around the world, are responding accordingly to this requirement.

The ISO standards support business process improvement for all industries. The health care industry worldwide has increasingly embraced the ISO standards as an alternative to existing quality management systems.

Why Adopt ISO 9001:2000 in Health Care?

Health care organizations choose to adopt ISO 9001:2000 standards for several reasons. An organization's decision to do so might include the following considerations:

- To comply with customer requirements for ISO 9001:2000

- To compete in global and domestic markets

- To improve the existing quality management system

- To minimize repetitive auditing by accrediting organizations

- To improve subcontractor and vendor performance

  The benefits of ISO certification for health care organizations include the following:

- Enhanced understanding of quality management throughout the organization

- A mechanism to improve documentation of process and procedure

- A tool to strengthen and improve supplier and customer confidence

- Cost savings and improved profitability

- Improved organizational awareness of quality

- Strengthened continuous performance improvement

Complying with ISO 9001:2000 standards does not indicate that every product or service meets the customers' requirements, only that the quality system in use is capable of meeting them. Consistently measuring customer satisfaction and striving continually to improve processes are the keys to a successful quality management system.

What is the ISO 9001:2000 Series?

The core of the ISO 9001:2000 Quality Systems Standard is a series of international standards that provide guidance in developing and implementing an effective quality management system. Not specific to any particular product or service, these standards are applicable to both manufacturing and service industries. The ISO 9001 standard, directed at service industries, is the most common standard applied to health care organizations. This standard is a model with which organizations (both manufacturing and service) certify their quality systems, from initial design and development of a desired product or service through production, installation, and servicing.

What Do the ISO Standards Include?

ISO 9001 applies to the service industry, which includes all aspects of the health care delivery system. The ISO standards are a series of clauses that identify elements of performance required for ISO certification; however, the clauses do not stipulate how an organization must reach compliance thresholds. Table 16.2 summarizes the major requirements of the standard. A copy of the standards can be ordered from the American Society for Quality.

TABLE 16.2. **Major Requirements of ISO 9001 Standards**

4.	Quality management system
4.2.1	General
4.2	Documentation requirements
4.2.2	Quality manual
4.2.3	Control of documents
4.2.4	Control of records
5	Management responsibility
5.1	Management commitment
5.2	Customer focus
5.3	Quality policy
5.4	Planning
5.4.1	Quality objectives
5.4.2	QMS planning
5.5	Responsibility, authority, and communication
5.5.1	Responsibility and authority

5.5.2	Management representative
5.5.3	Internal communication
5.6	Management review
5.6.1	General
5.6.2	Review input
5.6.3	Review output
6	Resource management
6.1	Provision of resources
6.2	Human resources
6.2.1	General
6.2.2	Competence, awareness, and training
6.3	Infrastructure
6.4	Work environment
7	Product realization requirements
7.1	Planning of product realization
7.2	Customer-related processes
7.2.1	Determination of requirements related to the product
7.2.2	Review of requirements related to the product
7.2.3	Customer communication
7.3.1	Design and development planning

(Continued)

TABLE 16.2. *(Continued)*

7.3.2	Design and development inputs
7.3.3	Design and development outputs
7.3.4	Design and development review
7.3.5	Design and development verification
7.3.6	Design and development validation
7.3.7	Control of design and development changes
7.4	Purchasing
7.4.1	Purchasing process
7.4.2	Purchasing information
7.4.3	Verification of purchased product
7.5	Production and service provision
7.5.1	Control of production and service provision
7.5.2	Validation of processes for production and service provision
7.5.3	Identification and traceability
7.5.4	Customer property
7.5.5	Preservation of product
7.6	Control of monitoring and measuring devices

A quality management system refers to the activities carried out within an organization to satisfy the quality-related expectations of customers. To ensure that a quality management system is in place, customers or regulatory agencies may insist that the organization demonstrate that the quality management system conforms to ISO quality system models.

Auditing ISO Standards A "first-party" audit is performed by individuals in the organizations. "Second-party" audits are performed by the customer or an independent auditor. "Third-party" audits are performed by a registrar who comes into the organization to verify that a system is in place. When a third-party registrar finds that an organization fulfills the requirements of the ISO standards, the organization becomes "registered" and receives a certificate that indicates that registration is complete.

ISO registration requires annual audits to monitor continuing compliance. Overall, it has been well demonstrated that if a health care provider is ISO-qualified or registered, any other survey process is simpler and less costly regarding both preparation and compliance demonstration. Although ISO registration is not intended to replace Joint Commission or NCQA accreditation, it does make the compliance demonstration process appreciably less difficult, time-consuming, and costly.

Many health care organizations have turned to ISO registration as an efficient mechanism to demonstrate the presence and functioning capacity of a quality management system that is working throughout the organization.

Steps to ISO Registration The following is a generic process that health care organizations may follow to achieve ISO-quality system registration.

Phase I: Organizing for Registration
- Obtain management commitment.
- Establish a steering committee.
- Begin internal quality auditing.
- Select a registrar.

Phase II: Preparing for Registration
- Document existing processes with procedures and work instructions.
- Identify areas that need improvement.
- Adopt improved procedures and work instructions.
- Prepare the quality manual.
- Apply to your registrar for an assessment.
- Consider a preassessment.
- Conduct a "dress rehearsal" audit.
- Submit the revised manual to the registrar.
- Modify and finalize quality practices; train personnel.

Phase III: Experiencing the ISO Registration Audit

■ Arrange for your registrar to conduct the assessment and identify findings (discrepancies).

■ Respond to findings.

■ Submit to the registrar for review the corrective actions you will take.

■ Receive the registration certificate.

Phase IV: Continuing ISO Registration Through Surveillance Audits

■ Maintain quality practice to ensure continuing compliance.

■ Notify your registrar of major changes in practice.

■ Arrange for the registrar to conduct semiannual surveillance audits.

■ Continue to improve.

College of American Pathologists

The College of American Pathologists (**CAP**) is a medical society that serves more than fifteen thousand physician members and laboratories throughout the world. Established in 1922, CAP is the world's largest association composed exclusively of pathologists. It is widely considered the leader in providing laboratory quality improvement programs.

CAP published the first laboratory standards in 1951. In 1964, CAP performed the first laboratory accreditation, and by 1979, was designated as the official laboratory accreditation program.

CAP's mission is to represent the interests of patients, the public, and pathologists by fostering excellence in the practice of pathology and in laboratory medicine worldwide.

Clinical Laboratories Quality Standards—CLIA Program

The Centers for Medicare & Medicaid Services (CMS) regulates all laboratory testing (except research) performed on humans in the U.S. through the Clinical Laboratory Improvement Amendments (**CLIA**). The Division of Laboratory Services, within the Survey and Certification Group, under the Center for Medicaid and State Operations (CMSO) has the responsibility for implementing the CLIA Program.

The objective of the CLIA program is to ensure quality laboratory testing. They include specifications for quality control, quality assurance, patient test management, personnel, and proficiency testing. Although all clinical laboratories must be properly certified to receive Medicare or Medicaid payments, CLIA has no direct Medicare or Medicaid program responsibilities

The CLIA regulations establish minimum standards for laboratory practice and quality. These regulations concern all laboratory testing used for the assessment of human health or the diagnosis, prevention, or treatment of disease. CLIA applies to every laboratory and testing site in the United States, even if only a few basic tests are performed as part of physical examinations.

Some simple tests are waived from specific CLIA requirements. If a laboratory performs only these tests, the laboratory can obtain a certificate of waiver (CLIA waiver registration) to show that the laboratory is exempt from specific CLIA requirements. The following laboratory procedures are among the tests exempted from specific CLIA standards.[5]

- Dipstick or tablet urinalysis (nonautomated)

- Fecal occult blood

- Ovulation test using visual color comparison

- Urine pregnancy test using visual color comparison

- Erythrocyte sedimentation rate

- Hemoglobin by copper sulfate method

- Spun microhematocrit

- Blood glucose using certain devices cleared by the Food and Drug Administration (FDA) specifically for home use

- Whole blood hemoglobin assays

A laboratory with a certificate of waiver will not be inspected routinely. The laboratory may be inspected as part of complaint investigations and on a random basis to determine whether only the waived tests are being performed. CLIA registration certificates are valid for a maximum of two years or until such time as an inspection can be conducted to determine program compliance, whichever is shorter.

Certificates are issued to laboratories that comply with the CLIA standards. Certificates of accreditation are issued to those that comply with department-approved, private, nonprofit accreditation programs. In addition, in states with federally approved licensure programs, a laboratory may obtain a state license in lieu of a certificate or certificate of accreditation. If a laboratory is located in a state with an approved program and the laboratory obtains a state license, it is only necessary to comply with the state rules, not the federal CLIA regulations.

In choosing which type of certification to seek, you may consider factors such as cost, convenience, professional affiliations, and other considerations beyond the scope of this discussion. The major costs to all laboratories involve fees for certification and compliance and enrollment in proficiency testing programs. These costs will vary, depending on the amount of testing conducted in the laboratory and on the types of programs in which the laboratory enrolls.[6] (For more information, see Chapter 10.)

Commission on Accreditation of Rehabilitation Facilities

The Commission on Accreditation of Rehabilitation Facilities (**CARF**) is a private, not-for-profit organization that accredits programs and services in adult day services, behavioral health, employment, community services, and medical rehabilitation. CARF develops and maintains practical and relevant standards of quality for such programs.

The commission was formed in 1966 by two national organizations—the Association of Rehabilitation Centers and the National Association of Sheltered Workshops and Homebound Programs—who agreed to pool their interests to ensure quality in rehabilitation facilities.

CARF aims to promote the quality, value, and optimal outcomes of services through a consultative accreditation process that centers on enhancing the lives of the people who are served. Facilities accredited by CARF demonstrate that they have substantially met nationally recognized standards for quality of services, including customer service. The standards are developed by the field, which consists of the people served, rehabilitation professionals, and purchasers of services. The CARF standards are applied through a peer review process to determine how well an organization is serving its consumers.

Every year, the CARF standards are reviewed and new ones are developed to keep pace with changing conditions and current consumer needs. CARF's accreditation, research, and educational activities are conducted in accordance with the commission's core values and standards. In addition, CARF is committed to the following goals:

- The continuous improvement of both organizational management and service delivery

- Diversity and cultural competency in all CARF activities and associations

- Recognizing organizations that achieve accreditation through a consultative peer review process and demonstrating their commitment to the continuous improvement of their programs and services with a focus on the needs and outcomes of the people served

- Conducting accreditation research that emphasizes outcomes measurement and management and providing information on common program strengths and on areas that need improvement

- Providing consultation, education, training, and publications that support organizations in achieving and maintaining accreditation of their programs and services

In 1997, CARF and The Joint Commission initiated a combined accreditation survey process to freestanding rehabilitation hospitals. The CARF standards reflect the Standard Conformance Rating System. A standards manual and survey preparation guide are available directly from CARF.

In 2003, CARF acquired the Continuing Care Accreditation Commission (**CCAC**). The CCAC is the nation's only accrediting body for continuing care retirement communities and other types of aging services networks. CARF-CCAC implemented new standards in 2005 that are organized according to the ASPIRE to Excellence framework. The six basic categories of the framework are (1) assessing the environment; (2) strategy development; (3) person-served focus; (4) implementing the plan, processes, and programs for the person served; (5) reviewing results; and (6) evaluating results and progress of a strategy.

American Association for Accreditation of Ambulatory Surgery Facilities

The American Association for Accreditation of Ambulatory Surgery Facilities (**AAAASF**) is a voluntary program of accreditation in surgery facilities to ensure quality and excellence in care to patients. This organization originated from the field of office-based plastic surgery facilities. The focus of the AAAASF is identifying the practical matters surrounding office-based surgery. The AAAASF is unique in that it precludes physicians of different specialties from sharing a facility. The surveyors are often office-based surgical providers. The AAAASF has recently authorized anesthesiologists, nurses, and other specialties to serve as surveyors.

Regulations for the AAAASF survey are very specific. They include the following major areas of the office-based ambulatory surgery practice:

- Definition of facility classes

- General environment

- Operating room environment, policy, and procedures

- Recovery room environment, policy, and procedures

- General safety in the facility

- Blood and medications

- Medical records

- Quality assessment and improvement

- Personnel

- Governance

URAC

URAC is a nonprofit organization founded in 1990 to establish standards for the managed care industry. It was originally incorporated as the Utilization Review Accreditation Commission, but the name was shortened to URAC in 1996 when the commission began accrediting other types of organizations, such as health plans and PPOs. URAC sometimes uses an alternative corporate name, the American Accreditation HealthCare Commission, Inc. This name is sometimes used on URAC certificates and other written communications to help explain what URAC does.

URAC membership includes representation from a variety of constituencies affected by managed care: employers, consumers, regulators, health care providers, workers' compensation, and the managed care industries. Member organizations of URAC participate in the development of standards and are eligible to sit on the board of directors.

URAC offers twenty-two accreditation and certification programs for managed health care organizations:

- Case Management
- Claims Processing
- Consumer Education and Support
- Core Accreditation
- Credentials Support Certification
- Credentials Verification Organization (CVO)
- Disease Management
- Drug Therapy Management
- Health Call Center
- Health Content and Personal Health Management Providers Accreditation
- Health Network
- Health Plan
- Health Provider Credentialing
- Health Utilization Management
- Health Web Site
- HIPAA Privacy
- HIPPA Security
- Independent Review Organization
- Medicare Advantage Deeming Program
- Primary Benefit Management
- Vendor Certification
- Workers' Compensation Utilization Management

Any organization that meets URAC's survey eligibility criteria may apply for an accreditation survey. The following types of organizations have undergone URAC's survey for accreditation:

- Ambulatory health care clinics
- Multispeciality group practices
- Ambulatory surgery centers

- Occupational health services

- College and university health services

- Office surgery centers and practices

- Community health centers

- Oral and maxillofacial surgeons' offices

- Dental group practices

- Podiatrist offices

- Diagnostic imaging centers

- Radiation oncology centers

- Endoscopy centers

- Single-specialty group practices

- Health maintenance organizations

- Surgical recovery centers

- Indian health centers

- Urgent or immediate care centers

- Managed care organizations

Once a **managed care organization** decides to seek accreditation from URAC, it must obtain application materials from URAC and submit documentation of compliance with each standard. This documentation is reviewed by a member of the URAC accreditation staff who works with the applicant to resolve any issues that have been identified. The URAC staff follows up with a site visit to the applicant to ensure that operations are consistent with the documentation that was submitted. Finally, the application is reviewed by the accreditation committee and the executive committee, which are composed of representatives of URAC's member organizations.

To date, URAC has issued more than twelve hundred accreditation certificates to more than three hundred organizations doing business in all fifty states. In addition, regulators in more than half of the states recognize URAC's accreditation standards in the regulatory process. In addition to its commitment to evaluating and accrediting managed health care organizations, URAC participates in several research projects related to performance improvement in the health care system.

URAC has also published several books and reports to help people understand the many complex regulations, requirements, codes, and laws related to the health care delivery system, including *The Survey of State Health Utilization Review Laws and Regulations*, *The PPO Guide*, *Case Management State Laws: A 50-State Survey of Health and Insurance Statutory Codes*, and *Models of Care: Case Studies in Healthcare Delivery Innovation.*

To support its mission to educate the public about quality and best practices in health care, URAC conducts a variety of educational seminars throughout the country.

Accreditation Association for Ambulatory Health Care

The Accreditation Association for Ambulatory Health Care (AAAHC), incorporated in 1979, is a nonprofit corporation that serves as an advocate for the provision and documentation of high-quality health services in ambulatory health care organizations. AAAHC accreditation is a voluntary process that involves several steps. The core areas addressed by AAAHC are the following:

- Patient rights
- Governance
- Administration
- Quality of care
- Quality management and improvement
- Medical records
- Professional improvement
- Facilities and environment

Other adjunct standards may also apply, depending on the entity undergoing the accreditation.

Once an organization has decided to pursue AAAHC accreditation, it conducts a self-assessment using published AAAHC guidelines and standards. The next step is to participate in an on-site survey conducted by trained AAAHC surveyors. Following the on-site survey, the accreditation team makes an accreditation recommendation that is reviewed by the AAAHC board of directors. The board determines the final accreditation. AAAHC accreditation may be awarded for six months, one year, or three years, depending on the level of compliance with the published standards.

The AAAHC is dedicated to educating providers in both quality improvement and accreditation standards and procedures. Educational sessions are held throughout the year. To date, more than eighteen hundred organizations nationwide have been accredited by the AAAHC.

Accreditation offers quantitative and intangible benefits to an ambulatory surgery center beyond public recognition alone. The letter of accreditation can enhance a health care center's success by providing a process by which the organization examines its internal practices and controls. The added value of accreditation is in the ability to strengthen public confidence as the organization has voluntarily submitted to an external review and evaluation.

The AAAHC has worked collaboratively with health care accrediting organizations and has been approved by the American Medical Association's physician credentialing program to provide "environment of care" surveys.

Community Health Accreditation Program

The Community Health Accreditation Program (CHAP) provides accreditation services for the **home care** industry. CHAP accreditation is valued as a standard to determine the level of quality and excellence provided to home care patients. CHAP was the first home care accrediting organization in the nation to receive deeming authority from CMS. By approving CHAP for deeming authority in May 1992, CMS certified that the CHAP standards of excellence met or exceeded CMS's own standards for Medicare certification.

A home care agency that is accredited by CHAP is less likely to receive a routine inspection by the Medicare state survey agency. CHAP is also recognized by the state of New Jersey's Medicaid program.

CHAP accredits all home- and community-based health care organizations. CHAP is different from other accrediting organizations in that it specializes in home care and community health. The CHAP survey includes a site visit and review based on four key principles: (1) that an organization's structure and function consistently support its consumer-oriented philosophy and purpose; (2) that it consistently provides high-quality services and products; (3) that it has adequate human, financial, and physical resources effectively organized to accomplish its stated purpose; and (4) that it is positioned for long-term viability. These core standards are pertinent to all types of organizations.

Service-specific standards, also based on the four key principles, are used for each of the different services and programs. These service-specific standards cover the following areas:

- Adult day care services

- Community nursing centers

- Community rehabilitation centers

- Home care aide services

- Home dialysis services

- Home health services

- Home infusion therapy

- Home medical equipment

- Hospice care

- Pharmacy services

- Private-duty nursing

- Public health services

- Supplemental staffing

National Commission on Correctional Health Care

The health practitioners employed in correctional settings face unique challenges: strict security regulations, overcrowding in facilities, and the legal and public health issues related to providing health care to an incarcerated population.

The National Commission on Correctional Health Care (NCCHC) offers a voluntary health services accreditation program and a certification program to recognize the special knowledge and skills required to provide health care in the correctional setting. All correctional health care professionals are eligible to participate in the certification program. Eligible participants include physicians, nurses, mental health workers, dentists, and other professionals such as attorneys, administrators, and health information technicians. NCCHC offers continuing certification and advanced certification for participants that have exceeded the basic certification standards.

In 2004, NCCHC introduced an accreditation program for opioid treatment programs in correctional facilities. Accreditation by NCCHC enables these programs to obtain legally required certification from HHS's Substance Abuse and Mental Health Services Administration (SAMHSA). NCCHC is the only SAMHSA-authorized accrediting body that focuses on corrections.

Commission on Dental Accreditation

The Commission on Dental Accreditation (CODA) operates under the auspices of the American Dental Association. CODA serves the public by establishing, maintaining and applying standards that ensure the quality and continuous improvement of dental and dental-related education and reflect the evolving practice of dentistry. The scope of the Commission on Dental Accreditation encompasses dental, advanced dental and allied dental education programs.

The Commission on Dental Accreditation publishes standards for dental practice professionals and offers an accrediting program specifically for dental education programs and clinical training programs. An accreditation classification granted to a program provides evidence to the educational institution, a licensing body, the federal government, or other government agencies that at the time of evaluation, the developing education program appears to have the potential for meeting the standards set forth in the requirements for an accredited education program for that area.

The Commission of Dental Accreditation also publishes accreditation standards in the following areas:

- Dental public health
- Endodontics
- General dentistry
- General practice residency
- Oral and maxillofacial pathology
- Oral and maxillofacial radiology

- Oral and maxillofacial surgery

- Orthodontics and dentofacial orthopedics

- Pediatric dentistry

- Periodontics

- Prosthodontics

U.S. Food and Drug Administration

The Food and Drug Administration is one of the oldest U.S. consumer protection agencies. The agency is responsible for the manufacture, import, transport, storage, and sale of about $1 trillion worth of products each year. The FDA is a public health agency, charged with protecting American consumers by enforcing the federal Food, Drug, and Cosmetic Act and several related public health laws. The FDA is an agency in the Public Health Service, which is a part of HHS.

It is the responsibility of the FDA to manage the manufacturing, labeling, and distribution of the following products:

- Food

- Cosmetics

- Medicines

- Medical devices

- Blood supply

- Radiation-emitting products

- Animal feed

- Animal drugs

The FDA provides investigators and inspectors to visit more than sixteen thousand facilities a year. For any company found violating the laws that the FDA enforces, the FDA ensures the company will voluntarily correct the problem or recall a faulty product from the market. Recall is usually the fastest and most effective manner to protect the public from an unsafe product. This is also a very costly and time-consuming process. The FDA does not issue recalls unless it believes that the public safety is threatened.

If a company will not or cannot correct a threat to public safety, the FDA has jurisdiction to impose legal sanctions. The agency can go to court to force a company to stop selling a product and can issue a demand that products already produced and distributed be seized and destroyed. The FDA has authority to hold imported products if warranted. The agency can impose criminal penalties, including prison sentences, against manufacturers and distributors in violation of the laws enforced by the FDA.

In addition to its oversight authorities, the FDA provides scientific research and testing of products. The National Center for Toxicological Research, which investigates the biological effects of widely used chemicals, is operated by the FDA. Assessing risks and weighing risks against benefits is a primary focus of the FDA's pubic health protection duties. The FDA scrutiny of drugs and devices does not end once a product is on the market; the agency continues to collect and analyze reports on drugs and devices.

U.S. Equal Employment Opportunity Commission

The Equal Employment Opportunity Commission (**EEOC**) was established by Title VII of the Civil Rights Act of 1964 and began operating on July 2, 1965. The mission of the EEOC is to promote equal opportunity in employment through administrative and judicial enforcement of the federal civil rights laws and through education and technical assistance. The EEOC enforces the principal federal statutes prohibiting employment discrimination, which include the following:

- Title VII of the Civil Rights Act of 1964, as amended, which prohibits employment discrimination on the basis of race, color, religion, sex, or national origin

- The **Age Discrimination** in Employment Act of 1967 as amended (ADEA), which prohibits employment discrimination against individuals forty years of age and older

- The Equal Pay Act of 1963 (EPA), which prohibits discrimination on the basis of gender in compensation for substantially similar work under similar conditions

- Title I of the Americans with Disabilities Act of 1990 (ADA), which prohibits employment discrimination on the basis of disability in both the public and private sectors, excluding the federal government

- The Civil Rights Act of 1991, which includes provisions for monetary damages in cases of intentional discrimination and clarifies provisions regarding disparate impact actions

- Section 501 of the Rehabilitation Act of 1973 as amended, which prohibits employment discrimination against federal employees with disabilities

The EEOC maintains offices throughout the United States. Individuals who believe that they have been subject to discrimination in relation to their employment may file an administrative charge. Furthermore, individual EEOC commissioners may initiate charges that the discrimination laws have been violated. Once a claim is filed, the EEOC initiates an investigation to determine if there is "reasonable cause" to believe that discrimination has occurred. The EEOC must then seek to conciliate the charge to reach a voluntary resolution between the charging party and the respondent. In the event that conciliation is not successful, the EEOC may bring suit in federal court. Whenever the EEOC concludes its processing of a case, or earlier at the request of a charging party, it issues a "notice of right to sue," which enables the charging party to bring an individual action in court.

The EEOC also issues regulatory and other forms of guidance interpreting the laws that it enforces. The EEOC is responsible for the federal sector employment discrimination program, provides funding and support to state and local fair employment practices agencies (FEPAs), and conducts broad-based outreach and technical assistance programs.

In February 1996, the EEOC approved its National Enforcement Plan (NEP). This plan sets forth a framework for the EEOC's enforcement strategy as follows:

- Prevention of discrimination through education and outreach

- Voluntary resolution of disputes when possible

- Strong and fair enforcement when resolution fails

SUMMARY

Based on historical experience of the U.S. health care industry, it is likely that the future of health care will be subject to an even more highly regulated environment. Private organizations, ombudsmen organizations, and consumer watchdog organizations continue to demand information and accountability from the health care industry regarding patient safety issues, cost, reimbursement, and credentialing and peer review activities.

Many states are exploring the extent to which they may disclose specific health care provider information related to credentialing and event reporting in health care organizations. The rapid growth in health care costs has led government agencies and private organizations to begin rethinking their position on the release of actual data and statistics for hospitals, clinics, and practitioners. Internet access to information and data has driven consumers and health care professionals to explore how data can be retrieved and reviewed.

There is no easy way to maintain an understanding of the many standards and regulations facing the health care industry. It takes a great deal of time to identify the standards and understand how they affect a specific organization. It will behoove the health care risk management professional to know where to find standards information and to be viewed as a resource within the organization.

Given the trend for expanding government oversight in the health care industry, it is safe to anticipate that the health care industry will continue to be subject to increased demands for health care provider and payer accountability, including compliance with published standards and regulations.

It is also reasonable to expect government, regulatory, and accrediting bodies to expand requirements for the health care industry. Compliance program components will be crucial to the future of the health care delivery system. The primary areas of concern for risk management relate to patient safety, patient rights, governance, product safety, provider qualifications, and fiscal responsibility (of both payers and providers).

The movement toward increased managed care contracting and selection of providers will necessitate strong programs of compliance and formal quality management processes to identify, mediate, and reduce risks through the implementation of loss prevention programs.

Fraud and abuse have become focal points for the government, with both criminal and civil monetary penalties being assessed for violations. The threat of criminal charges, resulting in prison sentences, will result in growing fear and concern that health care programs are properly established and carried out under the direction and oversight of governing boards.

Accreditation and certification of health care programs are expected to develop in the areas of networks, independent contractors, and employer purchasing groups. Enhanced participation of consumer groups and public interest groups will also drive this process of ensuring that the industry is responsive to recognized areas of risk and loss.

New areas of risks for consideration will include health e-commerce, confidentiality of data, unauthorized access and disclosure of patient data, provider qualifications, and customer satisfaction. As the population ages, the health care industry will increasingly focus on resources directed at wellness rather than acute and episodic illness and treatment. This shift will result in both providers and payers being faced with decreasing financial resources to ensure compliance with administrative and clinical program requirements.

It is imperative that health care organizations identify efficient and effective methods for achieving compliance and satisfying the multitude of oversight requirements. In the future, there must be a continued focus on evaluation of existing risk management programs with an eye toward the development of policies, procedures, and programs to safeguard data and compliance efforts. Performance measures and tracking of risk-related data require sophisticated information systems. The health care organizations of the future must address the information requirements and respond accordingly.

Managing risks is an organizational responsibility. The shift to managing enterprise risks should prompt the health care risk management professional to focus on serving the organization as a reliable resource for a variety of compliance issues. Organizations working together as a team will obtain the best results.

KEY TERMS

Age discrimination	Quality Improvement Organization
Home health care	Quality of care
Managed care	Regulation
Managed care organization	Statute

ACRONYMS

AAAASF	FDA
AAAHC	HEDIS
ADA	HHS
ANSI	HMO
AOA	ISO
CAP	JCR
CARF	MCO
CCAC	NCCHC
CHAP	NCQA
CLIA	PPO
CMS	QIO
EEOC	SCHIP
EPA	URAC

NOTES

1. The Joint Commission. *Facts About Accreditation Decisions for 2008.* http://www.jointcommission.org/AboutUs/Fact_Sheets/08_accreditation_decisions.htm

2. The Joint Commission. *Facts About ORYX for Hospitals.* http://www.jointcommission.org/AccreditationPrograms/Hospitals/ORYX/oryx_facts.htm

3. The Joint Commission. *Contact Us: Quick Reference.* http://www.jointcommission.org/AboutUs/ContactUs/

4. National Committee for Quality Assurance. *HEDIS and Quality Measurement.* http://ncqa.org/tabid/59/Default.aspx

5. For a full listing of waived CLIA tests, see Centers for Medicare and Medicaid Services. *How to Obtain a CLIA Certificate of Waiver,* http://www.cms.hhs.gov/CLIA/downloads/HowObtainCertificateofWaiver.pdf

6. A copy of the *Federal Register* containing the CLIA standards for laboratories can be ordered for a fee from National Technical Information Services, 5285 Port Royal Road, Springfield, VA 22161; (800) 553-6847. Specify the date of the issue that you are requesting (February 28, 1992) and your choice of paper or microfiche format. Enclose a check or money order payable to the Superintendent of Documents. Credit card orders can also be placed by calling the order desk at (202) 783-3238 or by faxing to (202) 512-2250. In addition, you may view and photocopy or download the *Federal Register* document at most libraries designated as U.S. government depository libraries and at many other public and academic libraries throughout the country; see U.S. Food and Drug Administration. *CLIA: Clinical Laboratory Improvement Amendments,* http://www.fda.gov/cdrh/clia/

SUGGESTED READING

Crago, M. G. "Meeting Patient Expectations." *Quality Progress*, 2002, *35*(9), 41–43.

Dillon, L. R. "Healthcare and ISO 9000: An Interview with Dr. Michael Crago (Part II)." *Infusion,* 2002, *8*(5), 36–41.

Gross, S. *Of Foxes and Hen Houses.* Westport, Conn.: Quorum Books, 1984.

Institute of Medicine. *Crossing the Quality Chasm: A New Health System for the 21st Century.* Washington, D.C.: National Academies Press, 2001.

"Medicare Service Pushes Certification to ISO 9001." *Quality Progress,* 2002, *35*(3).

Pare, M. A. (ed.). *Certification and Accreditation Programs Directory: A Descriptive Guide to National Voluntary Certification and Accreditation Programs for Professionals.* Detroit: Gale Group, 1995.

APPENDIX 16.1

ACCREDITATION AND LICENSURE ORGANIZATIONS, SURVEYING BODIES, AND GOVERNMENT AGENCIES

Accreditation Association for Ambulatory Health Care, 3201 Old Glenview Road, Suite 300, Wilmette, IL 60091; (847) 853-6060; Fax: (847) 853-9028; http://www.aaahc.org

American Association for Accreditation of Ambulatory Surgery Facilities, 5101 Washington Street, Suite 2F, Gurnee, IL 60031; (888) 545-5222; Fax: (847) 775-1985; http://www.aaaasf.org/

American Dental Association–Commission of Dental Accreditation, 211 East Chicago Avenue, Chicago, IL 60611; (312) 440-2500; Fax: (312) 440-2800; http://www.ada.org

American Osteopathic Association, 142 East Ontario Street, Chicago, IL 60611; (800) 621-1773; Fax: (312) 202-8200; http://www.am-osteo-assn.org

American Society for Quality, 600 North Plankinton Avenue, Milwaukee, WI 53203; (800) 248-1946; Fax: (414) 272-1734; http://www.asq.org

Centers for Medicare and Medicaid Services, 7500 Security Boulevard, Baltimore, MD 21244; (877) 267-2323; TTY: (866) 226-1819; http://www.cms.hhs.gov

College of American Pathologists, 325 Waukegan Road, Northfield, IL 60093; (800) 323-4040; Fax: (847) 832-7000; http://www.cap.org

Commission on Accreditation of Rehabilitation Facilities, 4891 East Grant Road, Tucson, AZ 85712; (520) 325-1044; Fax: (520) 318-1129; http://www.carf.org

Community Health Accreditation Program, Inc., 39 Broadway, Suite 710, New York, NY 10006; (800) 656-9656; Fax: (212) 480-8832; http://www.chapinc.org

International Organization for Standardization, Central Secretariat, 1 rue de Varembe, Case Postale 56, CH-1211 Geneva 20, Switzerland; (141-22) 749-0111; http://www.iso.org

The Joint Commission, One Renaissance Boulevard, Oakbrook Terrace, IL 60181; (630) 792-5000; Fax: (630) 792-5005; http://jointcommission.org

National Commission on Correctional Health Care, 1145 West Diversey Parkway, Chicago, IL 60614; (773) 880-1460; Fax: (773) 880-2424; http://www.ncchc.org

National Committee for Quality Assurance, 2000 L Street N.W., Suite 500, Washington, DC 20036; (202) 955-3500; Fax: (202) 955-3599; http://www.ncqa.org

URAC, 1220 L Street N.W., Suite 400, Washington, DC 20005; (202) 216-9010; Fax: (202) 216-9006; http://www.urac.org

U.S. Equal Employment Opportunity Commission, 1801 L Street N.W., Washington, DC 20507; (202) 663-4900; http://www.eeoc.gov

U.S. Food and Drug Administration, 5600 Fishers Lane, Rockville, MD 20857; (888) 463-6332; http://www.fda.gov

CHAPTER

17

EMERGENCY MANAGEMENT

MICHAEL L. RAWSON, HARLAN Y. HAMMOND

LEARNING OBJECTIVES

- To be able to identify the four steps involved in emergency management
- To be able to describe the purpose for using a vulnerability analysis chart
- To be able to explain why written emergency plans are drafted
- To be able to identify the five major functions established by the health care facility in using the incident command system
- To be able to list and explain the postloss issues the risk management professional should consider when developing a response plan

It is Monday morning, and as you answer the phone in your Nashville office, you are told that the first floor of your flagship hospital in Houston is under three feet of water, thanks to tropical storm Dorothy and the resulting flooding. Your day has just begun, however, as the next call brings news that your system's long-term care center in Little Rock has been without water and sewer service for six hours due to Dorothy, with little hope that services will be restored soon. As you turn on the Weather Channel, you note that Dorothy is heading northeast and has remained stronger than was forecast by weather experts. Three additional facilities in your system are directly in its path, including the office building where you currently sit. You reach for your system emergency response plan wondering what direction it offers for this type of emergency.

Health care facilities (**HCF**s) face many scenarios that might require an emergency response. Some are internal conditions limited to the HCF itself, which are typically man-made. Examples include bomb threats, terrorism, hostage situations, release of hazardous materials, loss of medical gases, fires, loss of utilities, or communication system failures. Others faced are external to the HCF and can damage or destroy the infrastructure of the area around the facility. Weather disasters, landslides, floods, earthquakes, volcanic eruptions, infectious diseases, accidents involving mass transit, structural collapses, explosions, chemical spills, civil disobedience, and war are examples of external conditions that may require an emergency response. Both internal and external conditions can cause mass casualties and can also put the ongoing operations of the HCF in question. Since September 11, 2001, much has been published on emergency management, and more is being learned each day as scenarios are examined and reexamined. This chapter will address key basic elements of emergency management but will not cover all possibilities and contingencies. The goal is to offer sufficient information for HCF risk management professionals to assess whether their emergency management plan is comprehensive yet flexible enough to address any number of emergencies, regardless of type, size, or scope.

Besides not wanting to be caught unprepared when an emergency happens, there are other reasons for keeping response plans current. The HCF's commitment to comply with federal, state, community, and regulatory requirements for responding to emergencies is a compelling motivation to maintain an effective, up-to-date plan. The guidelines, requirements, and recommendations of organizations such as the Occupational Safety and Health Administration (**OSHA**), The Joint Commission, the National Fire Protection Agency (**NFPA**), and the Environmental Protection Agency (EPA) add complexity to designing an appropriate plan. Beyond compliance, however, is the risk management responsibility to prepare the HCF to manage and recover from emergencies that do occur. Clearly, this presents a risk management opportunity at its fullest.

KEY CONCEPTS

- Health care organizations have to be prepared to respond to both internal and external emergencies. Both types can affect operations through damage to or destruction of the infrastructure, mass casualties, and a decreased or inaccessible workforce.

- The best prevention starts with an assessment and understanding of the types of risks inherent in health care facilities that make them susceptible to emergencies.

- Prevention efforts will be meaningless unless human resources are available and trained to implement the right steps at the right time.

- Prevention or mitigation of financial loss to the health care facility from a disaster starts with a review of the risk financing program to uncover gaps in preloss coverage and allow time to discuss findings and evaluate financing options with senior leadership.

THE STEPS OF EMERGENCY MANAGEMENT

The foundation for preparing a workable plan is understanding what steps are involved in emergency management. There are several variations on how to describe these steps, but all seem to fit into the following four categories:[1]

- *Prevention.* Establish robust internal reporting systems to enable information about key risks to flow freely upward. Take warnings seriously. Foster a management culture that is open to hearing bad news and knows how to respond to it.

- *Planning and preparation.* Maintain an effective emergency response plan that addresses all key functions of response and recovery. Rehearse the plan. Ensure that management understands how roles may differ when the emergency plan is activated.

- *Implementation and response.* Know how to activate the emergency response plan and how to recognize the differing roles that people will assume when responding to the emergency. Ensure the readiness of your public information officer to manage media relations.

- *Recovery.* Get the HCF operational as quickly as possible. Initiate and manage the process of financial recovery. Minimize the effects on the workforce, which can be severe and long-lasting.

Attention to each of these steps, regardless of the size or configuration of the health care organization, can result in a plan that will provide a valued resource at the moment it is most needed. A more in-depth discussion of each of these steps follows.

PREVENTION

The best **prevention** starts with an assessment and understanding of the types of risk inherent in HCFs that make them susceptible to emergency situations. The Vulnerability Analysis Chart shown in Exhibit 17.1 can help HCFs identify where to focus preventive efforts to maximize the benefits from the resources invested. "Prevention is the cornerstone of public and occupational health."[2] By evaluating vulnerabilities and taking appropriate preventive action, loss can be minimized in an emergency. A framework for prevention planning is provided later in this chapter.

EXHIBIT 17.1.   Vulnerability Analysis Chart

	January	February	March	April	May	June	July	August	September	October	November	December
MANAGEMENT ORIENTATION/ REVIEW												
EMPLOYEE ORIENTATION/ REVIEW												
CONTRACTOR ORIENTATION/ REVIEW												
COMMUNITY/MEDIA ORIENTATION/ REVIEW												
MANAGEMENT TABLETOP EXERCISE												
RESPONSE TEAM TABLETOP EXERCISE												
WALKTHROUGH DRILL												
FUNCTIONAL DRILLS												
EVACUATION DRILL												
FULL-SCALE EXERCISE												

Source: Federal Emergency Management Agency. *Emergency Management Guide for Business and Industry: A Step-by-Step Approach to Emergency Planning, Response and Recovery for Companies of All Sizes.* Washington, D.C.: FEMA, 1993, p. 66

Design and Location

The location of the HCF has a direct relationship to its vulnerability to loss. Most HCFs cannot change locations easily, so mitigating vulnerabilities by implementing appropriate architectural design elements becomes critical. A few examples follow on how these two aspects work together.

Earthquake Unless your HCF was constructed after the most recent seismic code was enacted, your facility was most likely built to a lower (albeit approved at the time) construction standard, which might make it more susceptible to an earthquake. The costs of retrofitting a building to bring it into compliance with a higher seismic code are significant and often not affordable. Even so, each addition, upgrade, rehabilitation, or replacement to current standards will help the HCF survive an earthquake while meeting the goal of compliance with current building codes. Architects can advise how best to incorporate current seismic standards into any construction plans. Property insurers can also be helpful in identifying what can be done to mitigate the potential damage to the physical plant, short of replacing the HCF outright.

Another design element to consider is having sufficient space to store vital earthquake supplies, including food, water, drugs, and other medical supplies, for individuals at the HCF when an earthquake strikes or who might seek shelter after the earthquake.

Flood The location of your HCF may make it vulnerable to flooding. Again, assuming that it is not feasible to change location, the incorporation of design elements to prevent or mitigate loss should be considered; these include directing water flow away from the HCF using drainage channels, earth or concrete aqueducts and barriers, or other means, and using sandbags in strategic locations to impede and divert water flow. Keep equipment and materials on hand with the appropriate procedures in place to facilitate the sandbag operation. Also consider where in the HCF expensive equipment and supplies can be housed to protect them from potential water damage, such as moving them to a higher floor. The insurance company providing your flood damage coverage will also have loss prevention techniques to share.

Biological Terrorism The National Institute for Occupational Safety and Health (**NIOSH**), part of the Centers for Disease Control and Prevention (**CDC**), offers resource materials on protecting facilities from chemical, biological, and radiological attacks. There are no guarantees to prevent terrorist attacks; however, there are steps to minimize their effect. The NIOSH recommendations are multifaceted. They suggest starting with the simple step of knowing your building. This includes knowing the condition of your mechanical equipment, what filtration systems are in place and how well they work, whether the **HVAC** (heating, ventilation, and air conditioning) system responds to manual fire alarms, how the HVAC system is controlled, how air flows though the building, where the outdoor air louvers are located, and whether the roof is accessible from adjacent structures or landscaping. You can protect the outdoor air intakes where airborne agents can be introduced into your facility by relocating them, redesigning them to minimize public accessibility (the higher on the building the better), or establishing a security zone around the intakes. These steps, when accompanied by appropriate security surveillance (adding security lighting, surveillance cameras, and additional security patrols of the area), could deter harmful activity or detect its potential earlier to minimize resulting harm.[3]

Training

Preventive efforts will be meaningless unless human resources are available and trained to implement the right steps at the right time. For example, if HCF staff are trained to recognize and respond to clinical symptoms of biological agents introduced into the air system, lives can be saved. Training should include the steps necessary to protect not only themselves but also their patients from the harmful effects of those agents. Training on how to initiate the HCF's emergency response plan in case of an attack is critical. A tool developed to keep track of training is presented in Exhibit 17.2.

EXHIBIT 17.2. **Training Drills and Exercises Schedule**

TYPE OF EMERGENCY	Probability	Human Impact	Property Impact	Business Impact	Internal Resources	External Resources	Total
	High Low 5◄──►1	High Impact 5◄──►1 Low Impact			Weak Resources 5◄──►1 a		

[a]The lower the score, the better.

Source: Federal Emergency Management Agency. *Emergency Management Guide for Business and Industry: A Step-by-Step Approach to Emergency Planning, Response and Recovery for Companies of All Sizes.* Washington, D.C.: FEMA, 1993, p. 67.

Local Emergency Planning Councils

Some people mistakenly believe that a local hospital or HCF should take the lead in responding to community emergencies, when in reality the response is properly mounted by community leaders in a coordinated effort. Active participation by the HCF with local emergency planning councils (**LEPC**s) can help define the appropriate boundaries for the HCF's emergency response plan. By knowing what community resources will be available in an emergency, the HCF can avoid duplicating resources and focus on providing necessary assistance. Identifying what role each organization will play in a complementary response effort will thus avoid unnecessary competition and duplication. More information on working with LEPCs will be addressed later in the chapter.

Essential Service Providers

To ensure the continuation of essential services such as electricity, water, gas, oil, phone, garbage, and sewer for an HCF requires the ongoing commitment by local service providers in advance of the emergency. This commitment will necessitate an understanding by the service providers of the nature and types of emergency scenarios that can occur in the HCF, along with the HCF's role. HCFs should discuss and explain their need to be a priority when emergency service is needed. With this understanding and up-front commitment by local service providers, HCFs are being proactive in mitigating future losses. Essential service providers should be invited to visit the HCF as often as needed to become familiar with how utility services are configured and where main switches and other key components are located. Keep the relationship between the HCF and the service providers strong and productive so as to promote a quick and willing response when it becomes needed.

Insurance

A good start to prevent financial loss to the organization is to review what insurance is in place and identify coverage gaps that may exist pertaining to key vulnerabilities. If there are gaps in the insurance coverage, identify whether those gaps can be closed and at what price.

A local emergency could affect several types of insurance carried by the HCF, such as those noted here.

Property and Business Interruption These policies are most often written using an "**all risk**" form, which covers all physical damage perils other than those specifically excluded. Although the burden is on the insurance company to prove that the peril is not covered, several terrorism-related clauses have been added back to the core policy: electronic data processing, decontamination expenses, service interruption, ordinance or law coverage, civil authority, ingress and egress coverage, terrorism, and contingent business interruption. Typically, a sublimit—a coverage amount less than that provided for other claims under the policy—applies to these provisions. Other exclusions that can relate to terrorism are nuclear reaction or nuclear radiation, hostile or warlike action in time of peace or war, dishonest acts, and pollution.[4] It is important to review this coverage with the broker or insurance representative to learn the extent to which the policy contains sublimits and exclusions and what can be done to address any gaps they might create. See Chapter 13 for more information on basic principles and insurance coverage.

Directors' and Officers' Liability If the directors or officers are sued alleging negligence in overseeing the HCF's efforts to appropriately prepare for and respond to an emergency, this coverage would apply. A key issue would be to what extent the limits available to the directors or officers are eroded by other covered losses, such as D&O entity losses, employment practices liability, or fiduciary liability. Clearly, each HCF should procure limits sufficient to cover probable losses in all risk categories covered by the policy.

General, Professional, and Auto Liability Each of these insurance coverages likely contains exclusions specific to certain catastrophic exposures. In our current environment, though, one might see a suit claiming that an omission on the part of the HCF to plan appropriately for an emergency resulted in injury or death. Depending on policy language, legal fees may or may not be covered and reimbursed to the HCF.

Workers' Compensation In the September 11, 2001, World Trade Center attack, this coverage was very high profile. With so many people killed, injured, or emotionally scarred, the total loss to carriers was catastrophic.[5] Claims under this program are of three major types for those who witnessed and survived the disaster: (1) physical-mental claims, which typically involve a physical injury that precipitates a mental disability; (2) mental-physical claims, which involve mental stress that causes a physical disability; and (3) mental-mental claims, which involve psychiatric neuroses alleged to have developed without physical trauma.[6]

Aviation Since the September 11, 2001, terrorist attacks, terrorism exclusions in aviation policies have become commonplace. In some cases, however, limits for terrorism can still be purchased for an additional premium.

Closing Gaps Any gaps in the HCF's insurance coverage should be discussed with senior management. Part of this discussion should include options to close the gap in coverage, including the terms, conditions, and cost. All discussions regarding gaps in coverage (including decisions not to implement recommendations to cure gaps found) should be documented and preserved and revisited at the time of coverage renewal or if the HCF's vulnerability to loss increases or decreases during the year. Part of this documentation should be the rationale behind the decision to implement or not implement recommendations presented. To assist in this process, the risk management professional should prepare a cost-benefit analysis of the recommendation. This analysis will highlight possible reasons for not implementing an alternative, including high cost, limited coverage, reduced markets, or restrictive language.

Risk management professionals should also have a thorough understanding of the conditions contained in each insurance policy, such as reporting requirements (what to report, to whom, how, and when). This will avoid having a claim denied on the basis of a reporting technicality.

PLANNING AND PREPARATION

It has been said that emergency planners should "plan for the worst and hope for the best." Planning for the worst implies that planners review, evaluate, and develop contingencies for all possible emergencies. However, planning based on worst-case assumptions frequently results in written plans that are lengthy, detailed, cumbersome, and costly to produce and maintain. Lengthy plans are seldom read and rarely understood.

In this section, information, suggestions, and resources will be provided to allow planners to write emergency management plans that are easily read, quickly understood, and rapidly implemented.

Emergency Management Planning

HCF leaders must assume accountability for ensuring that **emergency management plans** are developed, written, and communicated to the organization. They should assign the development of the plan to one or more persons familiar with the facility and the organization who possess appropriate writing and communication skills. Once written, the plan should be reviewed, accepted, and approved by the organizational leaders, including executive leadership, board of directors, and the medical staff.

The plan writers must have access to a committee that represents departments critical to the success of the plan, such as the emergency department, nursing, medical staff, security, and those who are familiar with the building, operations and the environment. The plan will be accepted more quickly if the key stakeholders have had the opportunity to provide input during its development.

Hazard Vulnerability Analysis

An "all risk" hazard **vulnerability analysis** should be performed using available HCF and community resources. Emergency preparedness plans are unique, mainly because each HCF is in a specific community or neighborhood. A good plan for one HCF may be inadequate elsewhere. At a minimum, the plan should be updated annually (or whenever environmental or staffing changes make it necessary), communicated to all managers and employees, and thoroughly tested and evaluated.

The American Society for Healthcare Engineering (ASHE) has developed an effective tool for conducting a hazard vulnerability analysis, presented in Exhibit 17.3.

EXHIBIT 17.3. Hazard Vulnerability Analysis

INSTRUCTIONS:

Evaluate every potential event in each of the three categories of probability, risk, and preparedness. Add additional events as necessary.

Issues to consider for probability include, but are not limited to:

1. Known risk
2. Historical data
3. Manufacturer/vendor statistics

Issues to consider for risk include, but are not limited to:

1. Threat to life and/or health
2. Disruption of services
3. Damage/failure possibilities
4. Loss of community trust
5. Financial impact
6. Legal issues

Issues to consider for preparedness include, but are not limited to:

1. Status of current plans
2. Training status
3. Insurance
4. Availability of back-up systems
5. Community resources

Multiply the ratings for each event in the area of probability, risk, and preparedness. The total values, in descending order, will represent the events most in need of organization focus and resources for emergency planning. Determine a value below which no action is necessary. Acceptance of risk is at the discretion of the organization.

EVENT	PROBABILITY			RISK						PREPAREDNESS			TOTAL
				NONE	LIFE THREAT	HEALTH/ SAFETY	HIGH DISRUPTION	MOD DISRUPTION	LOW DISRUPTION				
	HIGH	MED	LOW	NONE	THREAT	SAFETY	DISRUPTION	DISRUPTION	DISRUPTION	POOR	FAIR	GOOD	
SCORE	3	2	1	0	5	4	3	2	1	3	2	1	
NATURAL EVENTS													
Hurricane													
Tornado													
Severe Thunderstorm													
Snow Fall													

NATURAL EVENTS														
Blizzard														
Ice Storm														
Earthquake														
Tidal Wave														
Temperature Extremes														
Drought														
Flood, External														
Wild Fire														
Landslide														
Volcano														
Epidemic														
TECHNOLOGICAL EVENTS														
Electrical Failure														
Generator Failure														
Transportation Failure														
Fuel Shortage														
Natural Gas Failure														
Water Failure														
Sewer Failure														
Steam Failure														
Fire Alarm Failure														
Communications Failure														
Medical Gas Failure														
Medical Vacuum Failure														
HVAC Failure														
Information Systems Failure														
Fire, Internal														
Flood, Internal														
Hazmat Exposure Internal														

(Continued)

EXHIBIT 17.3. *(Continued)*

EVENT	PROBABILITY			RISK						PREPAREDNESS			TOTAL
	HIGH	MED	LOW	NONE	LIFE THREAT	HEALTH/ SAFETY	HIGH DISRUPTION	MOD DISRUPTION	LOW DISRUPTION	POOR	FAIR	GOOD	
SCORE	3	2	1	0	5	4	3	2	1	3	2	1	
Unavailability of Supplies													
Structural Damage													
HUMAN EVENTS													
Mass Casualty Incident (trauma)													
Mass Casualty Incident (medical)													
Mass Casualty Incident (hazmat)													
Hazmat Exposure, External													
Terrorism, Chemical													
Terrorism, Biological													
VIP Situation													
Infant Abduction													
Hostage Situation													
Civil Disturbance													
Labor Action													
Forensic Admission													
Bomb Threat													

Reprinted with permission from the American Society for Healthcare Engineering of the American Hospital Association, *Hazard Vulnerability Analysis*, February 21, 2001, written by Susan B. McLaughlin, MBA, CHSP, MT(CASP) SC, Pages 10–13.

Developed by SBM Consulting, Ltd.

Community Planning

Health care facilities must participate in community planning efforts. The Joint Commission, under Environment of Care Standard EC 4.10,[7] requires Joint Commission–accredited organizations to use and coordinate with community emergency planning and management agencies when developing and testing their plans. In addition, the Centers for Medicare and Medicaid Services (**CMS**) require community coordination under 42 CFR 482:55(b) (2). To help meet the regulatory and accreditation standards and guidelines, each HCF should be represented on the local emergency planning council. Participating in the LEPC allows the facility to understand community expectations and to prepare for hazards and events identified by community and state agencies.

HCFs have traditionally prepared for a variety of disasters. Past events experienced by the HCF often dictate the direction of planning efforts. California prepares for earthquakes, Florida for hurricanes, and Montana for snowstorms. The Joint Commission now requires, under EC 4.10, planning based on a hazard vulnerability analysis performed by the HCF. This analysis will include many of the emergencies currently identified but might also reveal others that should be evaluated. The ASHE tool in Exhibit 17.3 can assist in this effort; although The Joint Commission does not require its use, the tool and its methodology meet the commission's requirements. Regardless of the form or tool used, HCFs should include in their analysis the elements of probability, risk, and preparedness.

The analysis must include natural, technological, and human events and internal and external vulnerabilities and risks. Once prioritized, the facility can then focus on the hazards with the highest probability of occurrence and the greatest financial impact.

Emergency planners are challenged to consider a variety of emergencies, including the threat of a bioterrorism attack. The CDC and local health departments have established reporting criteria and systems to assist in the early detection of such an attack. (Refer to the NIOSH recommendations mentioned earlier in this chapter on how buildings can be protected from a bioterrorism attack.) Insurance companies can assist by bringing experts in to help review and strengthen the planning process.

Community Resources

The importance of HCF participation in the LEPC cannot be overemphasized. HCF leaders should appoint one or more persons to represent the HCF on the LEPC. This appointment should be documented in the minutes and annual report of the **environment of care committee** (safety committee). The HCF representative to the LEPC should report regularly on LEPC developments to the environment of care committee and other committees as needed.

Typically, LEPCs are called together and chaired by a government official. On occasion, the HCF leader may be asked to chair the LEPC. This may require significant political sensitivity, as the HCF may be one of several competing HCFs participating on the LEPC. Whether in a leadership role or simply as an active participant, it will be key to the LEPC's success for the HCF leader to provide active input regarding what resources and capabilities the HCF has available to respond to a community emergency. In return, the HCF understands community expectations for its services and what community resources will be available to the HCF in time of an emergency. It also provides a forum for alerting community leaders if expectations for the HCF exceed its capability.

Community planning should include coordination between the health care facility and community resources such as the following:

- Emergency medical services

- Public safety agencies, such as law enforcement and fire

- Utilities (electric, gas, propane, telephone, cellular telephone, water, sewer, and garbage collection)

- Suppliers (food, medical supplies, office supplies, and so on)

- Contractors (maintenance, housekeeping, food service, and so on)

Agreement to restore essential services temporarily lost by the HCF was mentioned earlier in the chapter. For example, many cellular phone companies will routinely restrict or limit service for subscribers during an emergency to allow public service agencies to communicate. Has the HCF been granted priority as a public service customer? What phones are designated for priority service, meaning that they will not be turned off or restricted during an emergency?

A valuable community resource often overlooked is the amateur radio operators' network. Amateur radio operators are often members of volunteer emergency communication groups. One group organized in many communities is known as Amateur Radio Emergency Services (**ARES**). ARES makes use of amateur radio to provide disaster services. When phone service is interrupted by a disaster, amateur radios have the ability and means to communicate. HCF emergency planners should contact local amateur radio operating groups for assistance in establishing emergency communication networks between HCFs, public safety officers, and the community.

Other Resources

Other community, governmental, and private resources exist to help public and private organizations succeed with emergency management. Consider contacting all of the following:

- Local, county, and state departments of health

- Local building departments and inspectors

- Federal agencies including the Federal Emergency Management Agency (**FEMA**), Centers for Disease Control and Prevention, and the U.S. Army Corps of Engineers

- Insurance companies

- Risk management consulting firms

These organizations have valuable information that can assist in organizing an effective and comprehensive plan.

Incident Command System

The Joint Commission, governmental regulatory agencies, and other standard or code-writing organizations require (or recommend) that HCFs create written plans to address different emergencies (see Exhibit 17.4). Emergencies ranging from single-car accidents to large-scale disasters or terrorist activity require cooperation among several agencies, other HCFs, and health care providers.

EXHIBIT 17.4. **Emergency Management Planning—Standards and Regulations**

When developing an emergency management plan HCFs must take into account the requirements imposed by JCAHO and the Environmental Protection Agency (EPA). The Occupational Safety and Health Administration (OSHA) regulations and National Fire Protection Association (NFPA) codes and standards must also be taken into account, as well as the Centers for Disease Control and Prevention (CDC) Strategic Plan for Preparedness and Response to biological and chemical terrorism. The American Institute of Architects (AIA) has also issued certain guidelines for design and construction of facilities in locations where there is a recognized potential for certain natural disasters. These requirement include:

A. JCAHO Standards Environment of Care (EC)[1]

1. Provide processes to:

   a. Initiate a plan.

   b. Integrate the HCF's role with community-wide emergency response agencies, including who is in charge.

   c. Notify external authorities.

   d. Notify, identify, and assign personnel during emergencies.

   e. Manage the following:

     i. Patients, staff, and staff and family support activities

     ii. Logistics of critical supplies

     iii. Security

     iv. Interaction with media

   f. Evacuate entire HCF.

(Continued)

EXHIBIT 17.4. *(Continued)*

    g.   Establish alternative care sites, including processes to:

        i.   Manage patient necessities

        ii. Track patients

        iii. Communicate between HCF and alternate site

        iv. Transport patients, personnel, and equipment

    h.   Continue or reestablish operations after a disaster.

2.   Identify:

    a.   Alternative means of providing essential building utilities, including electricity, water, ventilation fuel, medical gas, and vacuum systems.

    b.   Back internal and external communications systems.

    c.   Nuclear, chemical, and biological decontamination facilities.

    d.   Alternate roles and responsibilities for personnel (such as non-clinical staff) during emergencies, including a command structure consistent with that used by the community (for example, an incident command system).

3.   Establish:

    a.   Education and training of personnel, including biannual drills.

    b.   Performance monitoring of personnel knowledge.

    c.   Annual plan evaluation.

B.   Environmental Protection Agency (EPA) Requirements.

EPA's Emergency Planning and Community Right-to-Know Act[2] relates to the release of hazardous substances, including biological and other disease-causing agents, which cause an emergency.

1.   Each state must establish an Emergency Response Commission.

2.   States divide into local emergency planning committees (LEPCs).

3.   Hospitals designated by the LEPC to handle victims of a hazardous substance emergency must have an emergency response plan.

C.   Occupational Safety and Health Administration (OSHA) Requirement

OSHA requires HCFs to prepare plans to deal with certain man-made disasters, including hazardous-substance emergencies, ethylene oxide releases, and fires. Plans must address, at a minimum, emergency escape procedures, procedures for employees who stay to perform critical operations, and procedures to account for all employees after an emergency.[3]

D. Centers for Disease Control and Prevention (CDC)

CDC's Bioterrorism Preparedness and Response Program coordinates implementation of the national preparedness and response plan for biological and chemical terrorism.[4] HCFs must coordinate with state and local public health agencies to ensure they are properly coordinating their own efforts with the national plan.

E. National Fire Protection Association (NFPA), American Institute of Architects (AIA)

The NFPA health care facilities standard states that HCFs should have a total program for responding to any disaster that could reasonably occur.[5]

AIA provides facility planning and design guidelines for disasters, whether they are natural, nuclear, biological, or chemical. The guidelines require:

1. Wind- and earthquake-resistant designs

2. Suitable location for new facilities

3. Adequate storage capacity, or a function program contingency plan, to ensure a day's supply of the following:

    a. Food

    b. Sterile supplies

    c. Pharmacy supplies

    d. Linens

    e. Water for sanitation

4. Emergency radio communication system that operates independently of the facility

[1]Joint Commission on Accreditation of Healthcare Organizations. "Emergency Preparedness Management Plan." In: *Comprehensive Accreditation Manual for Hospitals.* Oakbrook Terrace, Ill.: JCAHO, 2001, EC 1.4.

[2]42 U.S.C. 11001 et seq.

[3]29 C.F.R. 1910.38.

[4]Centers for Disease Control and Prevention. "Biological and Chemical Terrorism: Strategic Plan for Preparedness and Response." *MMWER,* April 21, 2000, 49(RR-4).

[5]National Fire Protection Association. *Standard for Healthcare Facilities.* Quincy, Mass.: NFPA, 2000.

Considering the number of hospitals, agencies, and organizations potentially involved in an event, a standard and common emergency management system was needed. This has resulted in adoption of the **Incident Command System (ICS)** by regulatory agencies and public response organizations alike.

ICS was originally developed by an interagency workgroup known as **FIRESCOPE** (Firefighting Resources of California Organized for Potential Emergencies) after several large wildfires in the early 1970s demonstrated the need for interagency cooperation. Since then, FEMA, the NFPA, and state and local public safety agencies have adopted ICS as a standard. NFPA Standard 99 states, "The emergency management committee shall model the emergency management plan on the incident command system (ICS) in coordination with local emergency response agencies."[8]

Although initially developed to respond to major wildfires, ICS principles apply to any emergency or mass casualty event. Emergencies occur without advance notice, develop rapidly, and grow in size and complexity. Often several agencies and organizations respond simultaneously, each with its own specialty or responsibility.

These and other factors make ICS an effective health care management tool in response to an emergency event. In 1991, Orange County, California, used ICS principles to develop the Hospital Emergency Incident Command System (**HEICS**). HEICS is the joint property of the State of California Emergency Medical Services Authority and the San Mateo County Health Services Agency Emergency Medical Services but is available free of charge to health care facilities at the Web site http://www.emsa.ca.gov. Also available is a smaller version, called the Medical Aid Station Incident Command System (MASICS), for freestanding clinics and medical complexes.

Many HCFs and organizations have taken the basic ICS system and adapted it to the health care emergency response environment. Although HEICS is the standard, other examples may be found on the Internet.

ICS in Health Care Facilities

The ICS command structure uses the existing HCF organization to establish five major functions: (1) command, (2) operations, (3) planning, (4) logistics, and (5) finance and administration.

These functions, or elements within each function, can flex to apply effectively to a minor emergency or manage response to a major disaster. While the HCF can adapt the ICS organization to meet its specific needs, several duties are common to each function and should be identifiable in all emergency responses.

■ *Command.* The command function is the hub of the ICS. It determines where the incident command is located. It provides direction, order, and control of the organization when the ICS becomes active. Because information flows into the ICS from multiple sources, the **incident commander (IC)** should have advisers designated to help formulate responses to issues brought to the ICS for resolution. These advisers may include the safety or security officer, the public information officer, the liaison officer, and others as needed.

■ *Planning.* The planning function is responsible for gathering and reporting information about the event, establishing a labor pool, providing staff support services, and monitoring recovery-planning activities. The planning function is typically a recordkeeper, providing an accurate account of activities and responses.

■ *Operations.* The operations function coordinates all patient care activities, directs emergency care operations, and supports evacuation procedures under the direction of the medical control officer.

■ *Logistics.* The logistics function supports facility operations by managing the utility systems and securing and distributing supplies needed for patient care operations. It coordinates meeting transportation requirements, oversees food service operations, and implements damage control activities as needed.

■ *Finance and administration.* This function provides financial resources for response needs, tracks expenses, and charges for cost recovery. It coordinates activities for liability control and claims management.

Large-scale events usually require that each function be established as a separate entity. Each of the five functions can be subdivided into several sections as needed. During a small event, not all functions or sections may be needed. One person may manage a number of functions or sections, whereas in a large-scale disaster, all functions or sections will require one or more persons.

Ideally, the CEO will assume the role of incident commander. Realistically, the CEO is often away from the facility when an emergency occurs. In the CEO's absence, the administrator on call, nursing supervisor, or another designated leader must temporarily assume ICS leadership. Upon arrival, the CEO should take over the IC role. This order of leadership should be documented in the written plan. All persons who might serve in the incident commander role must be regularly trained on the basics of incident command and must be familiar with the location and contents of the written plan.

The effectiveness of ICS is most frequently demonstrated by its ability to expand and contract based on the level of emergency and the number of resources required. Physicians and nurses are needed to treat patients; administrative and clerical personnel may be used in several functions as the emergency develops. Security personnel are generally kept in a staff position reporting to the incident commander and not used to fill ICS positions. This allows the security manager and officers to fulfill their role in building security, crowd control, and so on.

Emergency Operations Center

The emergency operations center (**EOC**) serves as the centralized management center for emergency operations. This is where ICS activities are coordinated and disseminated. Regardless of size, every facility should designate an EOC where decision makers can gather during an emergency.

The EOC should be located in an area of the HCF not likely to be involved in the incident but near enough to allow efficient communication with those responding to the emergency. An alternative location should be identified in the event that the primary location is not available.

Each facility must determine its requirements for an EOC based on the ICS functions needed and the number of people involved. The EOC should be equipped with communication equipment, reference materials, activity logs, and tools necessary to respond quickly and appropriately to an emergency.

Operational Issues

Planning for emergency events requires considering operational issues beyond the basic care and treatment of patients and the safety of patients, employees, and visitors. The emergency planner should consider the following points:

Employee Support Employees are the HCF's most valuable assets. Employees will respond more effectively if they know that their families are safe during the emergency. Health care facilities should write procedures to help employees contact and verify the well-being of family members. This process should include employees who are working at the time of the emergency and those called back to the HCF to assist.

Solutions include using on-site day care facilities to support families of employees. Arrangements might also be made in neighboring churches, schools, offices, or public facilities to gather employee family members. Employees called back to work might feel more inclined to respond if they know their family is welcome where health care, food, and shelter are available. Consider also how employees will communicate with their families to learn of their status and needs, assuming telephone communication is interrupted or limited due to increased patient care needs. Beyond employees, it is important to consider the families of physicians and volunteers. The ability to retain and call in essential patient care providers and support personnel may depend on the effectiveness of planning in this area.

Consider special services and accommodations the HCF could provide for employees and their families during an emergency, including cash advances, salary continuation, flexible or reduced work hours, crisis counseling, and care packages (including clothing, food, and personal items).

It is essential that all employees be accounted for when an emergency strikes, especially if there is damage to the HCF or if evacuation becomes necessary. Having a predetermined place to meet can help with this responsibility. Holding individual department leaders accountable to determine the location and well-being of each employee is essential. If there are employee injuries, they should be handled appropriately and compassionately by benefits and workers' compensation teams. If there are employee deaths, plan for surviving family members to be supported by HCF leaders, and assign responsibility for working with the employees' families in submitting appropriate claims for death benefits.

Mutual Aid Agreements To avoid confusion and conflict in an emergency, establish mutual aid agreements with local responders, HCFs, and businesses. These agreements should define or identify the type of assistance available, the chain of command for activating the agreement, and communication procedures. Include these agencies and facilities in training exercises whenever possible.

Security Emergency planners must consider the role of security during the event. Planning must include procedures for facility security, staffing, and resource allocation. Examples of specific areas where additional planning might be needed include the following:

- How will you lock down the facility with limited security resources available to lock the doors and monitor entrances?

- What effect will increased security have on your operations? Is it more difficult for employees, physicians, and visitors to access your HCF? How will it affect vendors who deliver essential supplies and materials? When limitations are put into place that change the daily routine, can you implement effective communication and directional signage to help minimize the inconvenience?

- If you close or evacuate buildings, how do you protect against vandalism?

- What staff are available to assist in crowd control, media activity, and vehicle and traffic control?

- Are employees and volunteers trained to perform security-related duties? Have you planned for increased security staffing for ongoing operations during emergencies?

Service Reduction Planners must consider what services the facility will continue to operate during an emergency. A multivehicle traffic accident will not limit range of services, but a major earthquake might overwhelm the facility due to structural damage or increased activity in the emergency room. Questions of whether day care centers, physician offices, clinics, and so on will continue to operate and who will make the decision to temporarily close specific sites must be considered as plans are written.

Training Training is vital to the success of emergency planning. Do employees, physicians, and volunteers understand their individual and department responsibilities once an emergency is declared? How are staff trained regarding their responsibilities? When is the training conducted and at what intervals? How are program and plan changes communicated to staff, physicians, and volunteers? Is your training program documented?

Integrated Delivery Systems Integrated delivery systems (IDSs) have a distinct opportunity to manage an emergency by shifting resources from one HCF to another. Aid in recovery can be promoted within the health system. Staff, supplies, and equipment can be moved to aid the facility most affected by the emergency. Following the Northridge, California, earthquake on January 17, 1994, staff at the central office of one IDS was heard to say, "We didn't know what to do or how to help, even though we knew one of our hospitals had been hit hard." In this case, resources were available but not organized in a manner sufficient to offer the hospital in crisis any assistance.

Multihospital systems should evaluate communication plans and identify how resources, including personnel, can be adjusted and relocated during times of emergency.

Drills and Practice Events

The plan is of little use if not tested before a real emergency occurs. Regulatory agencies require HCFs to periodically test and evaluate their emergency management plans. These requirements specify that each health care organization conduct an emergency preparedness drill twice each year. Currently, The Joint Commission specifies no less than four months and no more than eight months between drills. The Joint Commission further requires that one drill annually involve the influx of real or simulated patients.

Tabletop drills are an effective tool and can help evaluate planning effectiveness at minimal expense and inconvenience to the HCF staff. Tabletop drills can be organized using previous emergencies the HCF has experienced. Participants are given a designated scenario and then discuss how they and their teams will respond. Additional suggestions and options are given to each of the participants as the discussion takes place to provide them with more understanding of how their response affects other members of the emergency response team and the overall recovery success of the HCF. Under Joint Commission standards, tabletop drills do not fulfill the requirement for a biannual drill.

Evaluation As soon as possible after the drill, incident commanders, observers, and other HCF leaders should meet and evaluate the drill or actual event, looking for both successes and failures. Hospital leaders and others involved in the drill should be asked for observations and recommendations. Community responders (EMTs, police, fire department, and so on) should be involved in the critique.

Disaster drills should use observers familiar with the organization's plan and should be able to evaluate response accordingly. Observers should be briefed before the drill and provided with a checklist to help organize observations.

Good, Bad, and Ugly An effective critique will identify good, bad, and ugly circumstances or events. Those identified as "bad" and "ugly" should have a corresponding corrective action plan developed, completion date established, and responsible individuals identified. Corrective actions should be reviewed during the next drill to ensure that they have been implemented effectively. It is important to document the drill, the critique, and the resultant corrective actions. If it is not documented, change will seldom result.

Job Well Done In our haste to get through a drill, we often fail to recognize efforts of staff, physicians, and volunteers. Congratulate participants for a job well done. Health care workers are famous for expending extraordinary efforts in the most demanding circumstances, and yet they often receive little credit for such efforts. "**Well done**" and "**thank you**" go far to build support for the HCF's emergency response efforts.

IMPLEMENTATION AND RESPONSE

HCFs, clinics, and physician offices are routinely confronted by events that many might classify as disasters. Due to training and planning, most events involving multiple patients come and go as part of a normal day's work. Nevertheless, most health care workers know that the potential for a major event involving significant numbers of patients and damage to the HCF is very real—not if, but when!

Planning and training must establish the foundation on which each worker can offer a meaningful response. Although the plan cannot possibly anticipate or answer all potential emergency events, it does give the assurance that a plan exists with a starting point and a way to expand to meet unexpected circumstances that arise.

Command and Control

Typically, the incident commander will be the senior management person available. As additional personnel arrive, command will transfer based on who has primary authority for overall control of the incident. At transfer of command, the outgoing IC must give the incoming IC a full briefing and notify all staff of the change in command. As incidents grow, the IC may delegate authority for performing certain activities to others, as required. When expansion is required, the IC will establish the other staff positions as needed.

Safety

The IC's first priority is always the safety of patients, staff, and the public. Effective communication processes are essential to fulfill this priority. Early in the emergency management process, the IC should identify an individual to handle communications to both internal and external audiences.

Internal Communication Maintain a continual flow of updated information to medical staff, managers and employees, and trustees, governing boards, and volunteers.

External Communication To exercise media and community leadership, do the following:

- Identify one available spokesperson.

- Determine where your media briefing area will be.

- Encourage rapid approval of press releases through the command center. If you do not have the information requested or cannot answer a question, say so. You can always get back later with what has been requested. Do not let accuracy suffer in a rush to provide information. Inaccuracy and mixed messages can create misunderstandings that are difficult to correct.

- Conduct regular briefings.

- Coordinate with government agencies and organizations.

- Test media plans in practice drills.

RECOVERY

Much planning time and effort is spent organizing how to respond to the emergency event. Planners must also consider how the organization will recover from the event. As plans are written, consider the following issues:

- Who will inspect your HCF to determine whether it is structurally sound and safe to occupy? Who will inspect incoming utilities systems to ensure their safety? Local building inspectors can be very helpful in developing a plan for your HCF on what to check and whom to involve.

- Who will make the decision to close the incident command center? Who will take the logs and notes created and summarize the event to facilitate future improvement and media interaction?

- How will the financial impact of the event be documented? Is the finance department ready with a system to track the costs associated with providing emergency patient care? How will you prepare evidence to assert a business interruption claim? How will you document repairs made to your facility to assert a property damage claim? Should you have a third-party consultant retained to help with asserting insurance and governmental claims?

- How will the organization help its employees recover? Will additional counseling resources be brought in to help with the emotional trauma and grieving some people will experience? Will senior management provide continued updates on how the HCF is recovering to promote a feeling of job security among employees? Will recognition be given for the extraordinary efforts made by staff? Will staff members who have worked for extended hours have time off to rest and recover?

- If the HCF must be closed in whole or in part while repairs are made, how will management keep staff informed of progress? When ready to reopen, will the HCF have the labor pool needed to initiate operations? Does the business interruption policy provide salary continuation to keep essential staff paid during the HCF reconstruction?

- Is the public relations team prepared to keep media apprised on recovery progress?

Naturally, returning the HCF to its usual and customary service level is the objective, but this cannot be accomplished without addressing key safety, human resource, and financial issues.

SUMMARY

By carefully addressing prevention, planning and preparation, implementation and response, and recovery (the four steps of emergency management), the HCF will be better prepared to initiate an effective response to and recovery from an emergency. The challenge is to make this a dynamic process. Perhaps a rally cry of "Remember

9/11!" or "Remember the hurricanes of 2005" will help remind us that emergencies happen throughout the world and that we cannot lose our focus of being ready to respond. Develop and document the plan, train employees and leaders, rehearse the plan, and change it to incorporate what is learned along the way. Keep the plan as simple and flexible as possible, ensuring that each person knows his or her respective role to enable a successful response. By staying ready, our HCFs will be safe places for patients and employees, and they will be able to provide essential patient care in the face of emergencies. When the next tropical storm approaches, we won't be left wondering what to do but can instead follow the steps identified in our plan to respond appropriately.

KEY TERMS

Emergency management planning
Environment of care
Hospital Emergency Incident
  Command System
Implementation
Incident commander

Incident command system
Preparation
Prevention
Recovery
Response
Vulnerability analysis

ACRONYMS

ARES
CDC
CMS
EOC
FEMA
FIRESCOPE
HCF

HEICS
HVAC
IC
ICS
LEPC
NFPA
NIOSH
OSHA

NOTES

1. Bremer, L. P., III. "Corporate Governance and Crisis Management." *Directors and Boards*, Jan. 1, 2002, p. 16.

2. Department of Health and Human Services, Centers for Disease Control and Prevention, and National Institute for Occupational Safety and Health. *Protecting Building Environments from Airborne Chemical, Biological, or Radiological Attacks*. Washington, D.C.: U.S. Government Printing Office, 2002, p. 6.

3. Phillips, D. S. "Healthcare Insurance Issues and Terrorism." *HealthLine*, May 2002, pp. 3–6.

4. Ibid.

5. Ibid.

6. Ibid.

7. Available at http://www.jointcommission.org/NR/rdonlyres/266E870D-BEB4–48CC-9ABC-2EC3210C8291/0/BHC2008ECChapter.pdf

8. National Fire Protection Association. *NFPA 99: Standard for Health Care Facilities.* Quincy, Mass.: NFPA, 2005, §12.2.3.2.

RECOMMENDED WEB SITES

Amateur Radio Emergency Services (emergency communications): http://www.ares.org

Canadian Centre for Emergency Preparedness http://www.ccep.ca/cceppubl.html

DRI International (professional practices for business continuity planners): http://www.drii.org

Federal Emergency Management Agency (education, training, and planning materials): http://www.fema.org

HazMat for Healthcare (handling hazardous materials emergencies, including internal spills and contaminated patients, in a health care environment): http://www.hazmatforhealthcare.org

Institute for Biosecurity (center for the study of bioterrorism): http://www.bioterrorism.slu.edu

OSHA e-Tools and Electronic Products for Compliance Assistance (stand-alone, interactive, Web-based tools): http://www.osha.gov/dts/osta/oshasoft/index.html

CHAPTER

18

OCCUPATIONAL SAFETY, HEALTH, AND ENVIRONMENTAL IMPAIRMENT

A Brief Overview

JOHN C. WEST

LEARNING OBJECTIVES

- To be able to describe the rulemaking process followed by federal agencies
- To be able to explain the regulatory enforcement process
- To be able to discuss the mechanics of a regulatory inspection
- To be able to describe the steps an employer can take after an inspection to appeal the findings

Health care facilities are subject to intense levels of regulation as a result of both federal and state legislation regarding occupational safety and health and environmental impairment. However, legislation is rarely self-enacting or clear enough to allow for concrete interpretation in day-to-day practice. As a result, administrative agencies[1] typically use the legislation as a springboard for enacting rules and regulations to implement the legislature's intent in passing the statute. It is often informative to understand the processes by which administrative agencies perform their work, to appreciate the full effects of legislation.

As noted, many agencies at both the state and federal levels have rules and regulations that affect the operation of health care facilities. This discussion will focus on the agencies that have jurisdiction over worker safety and health and environmental impairment. However, the processes by which these agencies accomplish their missions are, overall, similar to the ways in which other agencies accomplish their missions. The chapter will also provide an overview of the safety and health concerns common to health care entities.

KEY CONCEPTS

- Legislation is rarely self-enacting or clear enough to allow for concrete interpretation in everyday practice. Administrative agencies therefore use legislation as a springboard for enacting rules and regulations to implement the legislature's intent.

- The Administrative Procedure Act governs the process of federal legislation.

- The act does not require public comment before enacting a final rule, but if the proposed rulemaking is particularly complex, an advanced notice of the proposed rule may be published by the agency in the *Federal Register,* allowing for public comment.

- Not all administrative agencies have enforcement powers. Enforcement powers include the ability to levy fines and impose sanctions.

ADMINISTRATIVE PROCEDURE ACT

There are specific processes for rulemaking and the enforcement of regulations. If the rules are promulgated at the federal level, the **Administrative Procedure Act** (**APA**; 5 USC 551 et seq.) governs the process. If the rulemaking is performed by state agencies, the process may vary according to state law, but it often follows the federal procedures. This chapter will use the federal approach as a model.

The APA was born out of the explosive growth of administrative agencies in the latter half of the nineteenth century and the early part of the twentieth but was given particular impetus by the growth of administrative agencies during President Franklin Roosevelt's New Deal years.[2] By and large, it was felt that administrative agencies were becoming a fourth branch of government, and their internal workings were largely unregulated.

Rulemaking Processes

The rulemaking process today is largely governed by the APA. On certain occasions, agencies may decide to publish an advance notice of proposed rulemaking, especially in situations where the rule may be complex and the agency would like public comment before enacting the final rule. This aspect of the procedure is not required by the APA.

The APA requires an agency to publish a general notice of proposed rulemaking in the *Federal Register,* unless another form of notice can be given. The agency then allows for public comment, which can normally be in writing or at a public hearing. The public also has the right to access the rulemaking record to determine the basis for the proposed rule. The agency is required to consider the public's comments before publishing its final rule. The comment period may vary, depending on the nature of the rule, but cannot be less than thirty days.

The final rule must also be published in the *Federal Register.* The agency normally addresses all of the comments received and discusses their effect on the proposed final rule. Sometimes final rules are remarkably similar to the proposed rules, but occasionally there are marked changes. On rare occasions, agencies may withdraw proposed rules altogether after considering the public comments. The agency must give an effective date for the final rule, which can range from months to years but cannot be less than thirty days.

Adjudicatory Process

Once the rules have been promulgated, the administrative agency will normally be charged with enforcing them. It may do this by permit approval or by adjudicative procedures, such as inspections and the assessment of fines and penalties. Adjudicative processes can be formal or informal. Formal processes involve hearings, a written record, and a final decision by an arbiter (ultimately the secretary of the department) within the agency, which is then subject to judicial review by the courts. Informal adjudicative procedures may involve inspections and negotiations to resolve disputed issues.

Hearings may be held for the purposes of adjudicating matters arising under the regulations that have been promulgated. These are often very similar to a judicial process, with specifications for notice, an opportunity to be heard, the submission of evidence, a written record or transcript, and a final decision. The **hearing** is normally before an employee of the agency, and levels of **appeal** may be available within the agency. The decision of the agency is subject to judicial review by a court.

Judicial review can be founded on any number of objections to the rule or the enforcement of the rule. For example, the decision of the agency may have been arbitrary or capricious, or it may have been unsupported by the record. It is sometimes argued that the rule exceeds the statutory authority granted to the agency by the **enabling legislation**. It is also sometimes argued that the proposed rule did not give adequate notice of the provisions of the final rule to allow for effective public comment.[3]

ADMINISTRATIVE ENFORCEMENT

Not all administrative agencies have enforcement powers. For example, neither the National Institute of Occupational Safety and Health (**NIOSH**) nor the Centers for Disease Control and Prevention (**CDC**) have enforcement powers. Their missions are to perform research and to educate the public and relevant industries. The Occupational Safety and Health Administration (**OSHA**) and the Environmental Protection Agency (**EPA**), on the other hand, have enforcement powers that include fines and penalties. This discussion will focus on the enforcement techniques employed by OSHA because OSHA's enforcement techniques are a major concern for health care entities.

Enforcement Process

OSHA has programs by which entities, industries, or associations can work cooperatively with it and remove some of the threat of enforcement action. OSHA's **Voluntary Protection Program (VPP)** allows entities to enter into a participation agreement and then, after a rigorous on-site evaluation if the entity qualifies, it can be admitted into the VPP.[4] If an employer participates in a VPP, the employer may be exempted from programmed inspections.

It is also possible to enter into a collaborative agreement with OSHA through its Strategic Partnership Program. In this program, an industry, association, or entity works with OSHA to solve a particular safety or health issue. OSHA acts as a technical resource and facilitator. It is also possible to bring in other interested parties, such as trade unions, insurance companies, or local or state governments. The idea is to create a synergy that any of the participants, working alone, may not have been able to achieve.[5]

For entities that do not participate in the voluntary programs, the inspection and enforcement processes, spelled out in the *OSHA Field Inspection Reference Manual CPL 2.103*, are as follows.[6]

Preinspection Processes Inspections can be unprogrammed (following reports or complaints of imminent dangers) or programmed (in industries with known high-hazard activities). Inspections follow a priority schedule, from highest to lowest: reports of imminent danger; investigations of fatalities or catastrophes; follow-up inspections of serious violations; investigation of complaints or referrals that are not felt to be serious; and programmed inspections. Unless a complainant allows it, disclosure of the identity of a complainant is prohibited. Under exigent circumstances, an inspector may obtain an inspection **warrant** or an administrative **subpoena** before making an inspection. Unless specifically authorized to do so, an inspector may not give advance notice of an inspection.

Inspection Procedures Inspections, whether unprogrammed or programmed, fall into one of two categories: comprehensive (a complete inspection of all of the high-hazard areas of the establishment) or partial (limited to certain potentially high-hazard areas or operations at the establishment).

The employer has the right to refuse admittance when the inspector appears on the premises. If the employer refuses admittance, the inspector must get an inspection warrant to enter the premises. There are exceptions to this rule, however. If the circumstances are exigent, for example, if there is a known high-hazard condition or operation on the premises that places employees at risk of harm, the inspector may enter without a warrant. There is also no need for a warrant if the operations are in plain view (the operations can be seen from a public way or other areas off the employer's premises). The employer always has the right to require a warrant; the employer's consent to an inspection merely acts as a waiver of the requirement that the inspector obtain a warrant. Furthermore, the consent of one employer on a multiemployer work site (as where a construction contractor is performing renovations in a hospital) operates as valid consent for entry for the inspector. If a warrant is obtained, the inspection must be in accordance with the provisions of the warrant.

OSHA inspectors are also permitted to obtain administrative subpoenas for the production of records, documents, or testimony to complete an inspection. Documents that may be sought could include illness and injury records, exposure records, the written hazard communication program, the lockout-tagout program, or other records relevant to the employer's safety and health program.

An inspection generally follows a set format. OSHA encourages the inspector and the facility to have an opening conference in which the inspector, the employer, and employees may participate. The inspector may be accompanied on the inspection by "walk-around representatives," who may be designated by the employer or employees (for example, union representatives or members of a safety committee). The inspector may collect samples (for example, air samples); take measurements, as for noise levels; or take photographs while inspecting the premises. Inspectors also have the right to interview employees in private, which may include interviews off the employer's premises. OSHA encourages inspectors to provide advice on the abatement of hazards during the inspection.

Postinspection Procedures There are specific procedures that must be followed after an inspection. If the inspector recommends that a citation be issued, the inspector must prescribe an abatement period, which must be a reasonable amount of time but does not usually exceed thirty days for safety violations. Abatement periods may be longer for health violations because these might require structural changes to the workplace. The employer may contest the issuance of the citation, the length of the abatement period, or both. A notice of contest must be filed within fifteen days of the receipt of the citation. The running of the abatement period is stayed during the period of a pending contest.

Employers may use several techniques to reduce the risk presented by the hazard. The most desirable abatement technique is to use engineering controls, which removes the hazard from the environment. These can be in the form of substitution, isolation, ventilation, or equipment modification, among others. Administrative controls constitute the second tier of abatement controls. These involve reducing exposure to the hazard through manipulation of the work schedule (for example, limiting the amount of time that someone can be in a high-noise environment). Work practice controls involve changes in the manner in which the work is performed, such as improvements in sanitation and hygiene practices. These should be implemented in the foregoing priority, if feasible. OSHA considers an abatement control "feasible" if it "can be accomplished by the employer." Personal protective equipment (**PPE**) is not considered an abatement procedure because its use does not reduce the risk of exposure to the hazard. PPE may be used only if there is no feasible abatement control.

Citations are issued in the same manner as for other forms of legal process. Certified mail with return receipt requested is preferred, but hand delivery is allowed. OSHA encourages a signed receipt for a citation whenever possible. As with other forms of legal process, entities must have a process in place to receive and handle citations in a timely manner.

OSHA has the authority to assess penalties for violations of its standards. For serious violations, the penalty may be up to $7,000. For willful violations, the penalty may not be more than $70,000 or less than $5,000. Penalties may be adjusted based on the gravity of the violation, on the good faith of the employer, on the employer's history and experience with respect to violations, and on the size of the business (certain reductions are available if the employer employs 250 or fewer employees).

Penalties may also be imposed for failure to maintain reporting or recordkeeping systems. For example, the employer may be cited for failing to maintain and post the OSHA logs that all employers are required to maintain. The employer may also be cited for failing to verbally report any occupationally related employee death or the hospitalization of three or more employees within eight hours of an occurrence. Compared to some of the other penalties, these penalties are somewhat nominal.

OSHA also has the power to impose criminal penalties. Criminal penalties may be imposed for the willful violation of a standard, rule, or order that causes the death of an employee. Criminal penalties can also be imposed for giving unauthorized advance notification of an inspection or for giving false information to an inspector. Criminal penalties may also be imposed, logically enough, for killing, assaulting, or hampering an inspector.

The employer may request an informal conference following the inspection. This will normally be performed within the fifteen-day period for providing the notice of contest. The informal conference requires the participation of an OSHA area director. Area directors have the authority to enter into settlement agreements with employers. If the matter is not resolved at this level, the notice of contest is forwarded to the

Occupational Safety and Health Review Commission (OSHRC) for adjudication. If the parties are not satisfied with the decision of the OSHRC, the matter can be appealed to federal court.

EPA's Enforcement Powers The **Environmental Protection Agency** has detailed its enforcement policies, procedures, and practices, all of which are a matter of public record. The structure of the EPA's enforcement practices is not markedly different than OSHA's, but the enforcement plan does differ in its details.[7]

SPECIFIC OCCUPATIONAL SAFETY AND HEALTH ISSUES

The primary regulatory agency with jurisdiction over occupational safety and health matters is, as noted previously, OSHA. OSHA has authority to promulgate standards pursuant to the Occupational Safety and Health Act of 1970 (29 USC 651 et seq.), which has a general-duty clause that requires that each employer furnish each employee with a job and a workplace that are free from recognized hazards that are causing or are likely to cause death or serious physical harm to employees. OSHA has full regulatory authority to enforce its standards and regulations.

NIOSH, by contrast, is an agency dedicated to research and education and has no regulatory authority. Unlike OSHA, which is part of the Department of Labor, NIOSH is a branch of the CDC within the Department of Health and Human Services.[8] NIOSH publishes the results of research and literature searches. Those publications often consist of recommendations to OSHA that a standard be developed to regulate exposure to a substance or abate the hazards associated with a given operation. These recommendations do not have the force of law, and OSHA must go through the rule-making process to enforce them. Sometimes these recommendations are taken up rapidly by OSHA, but in other cases, they might remain in the recommendation state for years.[9]

The CDC plays something of a tangential role in occupational safety and health, somewhat similar to that of NIOSH. OSHA has not hesitated to incorporate many of the guidance documents that the CDC has published on such topics as the prevention of transmission of bloodborne pathogens or the prevention of transmission of tuberculosis. The CDC's guidance has had a great impact in health care in preventing transmission of hospital-acquired infections and in the adoption of public health measures and availability of immunizations.[10]

The EPA has inspection and enforcement powers regarding air pollution, water pollution, solid waste disposal, hazardous waste disposal, cleanup of contaminated hazardous-waste dump sites, and many other matters. The EPA has allowed the states to provide most of the regulation of medical or infectious waste.[11] Most of its regulations deal with environmental impairment, but the EPA does provide guidance on some matters that involve occupational safety and health. For example, the EPA regulates exposure to asbestos during renovation or demolition. It also provides guidance materials on indoor air quality and remediation of mold.[12]

Specific Issues Regulated by OSHA

OSHA regulates several specific substances and practices. As noted previously, the general-duty clause in the OSHA Act requires that each employer provide employment and a working environment that are free from recognized hazards that are causing or are likely to cause death or serious physical harm to employees, but this does not really give OSHA free rein to cite an employer for any hazardous condition. OSHA must still go through the rulemaking process to set standards. The following substances or practices are areas of health care operations for which OSHA has set standards:[13]

Acetone

Alcohol, ethyl (widely used)

Alcohol, isopropyl (widely used)

Alcohol, methyl (methanol or wood alcohol, used in laboratories)

Asbestos (formerly used in insulation)

Benzene (sometimes encountered in laboratories)

Bloodborne pathogens (HIV, hepatitis B, hepatitis C, and so on)

Cadmium (sometimes used in radiology or plant operations)

Confined space entry

Ethylene oxide (used in central processing and central sterile)

Formaldehyde (used in the laboratory, surgery, and morgue)

Hazard communications (employees' "right to know")

Hazardous waste operations and emergency response (HAZWOPER) (spill training)

Hydrogen peroxide (used in central processing and central sterile)

Laboratory standard (hazard communications in the laboratory)

Lead (used in radiology and plant operations)

Lockout-tagout rule (control of hazardous energy)

Mercury (used in various kinds of instruments and devices)

Methyl methacrylate (a component of bone cement)

Noise (encountered in equipment areas near boilers and generators)

Personal protective equipment (PPE)

Toluene (used in laboratories)

Tuberculosis exposure (can occur in any clinical area)

Xylene (used in laboratories)

Other OSHA standards, primarily for safety, can be applied to health care, especially to nonclinical operations. These include standards that regulate such things as walking and working surfaces, wooden ladders, metal ladders, and welding, to name a few. These standards have wide applicability to any industry and are too numerous to mention in a treatise of this sort.[14]

Other Health Hazards Not Specifically Regulated by OSHA

Once outside the realm of OSHA regulation, trying to determine all safety and health hazards faced by health care workers becomes less straightforward. Some are known hazards, some are suspected hazards, and there are some that could be hazards, but we simply do not know enough about them at this time to make a determination.

These issues include the following:[15]

Compressed gases (used in surgery and laboratory)

Ergonomics and musculoskeletal disorders (an issue anywhere that lifting and transferring occurs)

Extremely low-frequency electric and magnetic fields (exist wherever electricity is present)

Flammable liquids (fire hazards due to bulk storage)

Glutaraldehyde (used for cold sterilization of certain equipment, such as endoscopes)

Hazardous drugs, such as chemotherapeutic drugs

Indoor air quality

Lasers (optical hazards)

Laser or electrocautery plume (smoke from surgical procedures)

Latex sensitivity (present in materials made from natural rubber)

Mold and fungus (an issue whenever materials can get and stay wet)

Radiation

Video display terminals

Waste anesthetic gases (WAG) (for example, nitrous oxide)

Workplace violence

OSHA has not promulgated standards on these issues, so they should not be the subject of an OSHA inspection. However, the risks associated with some of these substances or conditions are real, and employers would be well advised to manage the risks to the extent that it is feasible to do so.

Specific Issues Regulated by EPA

The EPA tends, as a general rule, to regulate materials and activities outside of buildings. For example, although OSHA regulates ethylene oxide exposure to employees inside a building, the EPA regulates its discharge into the atmosphere. OSHA is very much concerned about protection of human health at the individual level. The EPA is also concerned about the protection of human health, but it is more concerned about protection of populations by controlling environmental contamination.

The primary statutes by which EPA has been given the authority to regulate environmental impairment are as follows:

- *Resource Conservation and Recovery Act.* The **Resource Conservation and Recovery Act** (**RCRA**; 42 USC 6901 et seq.) gives the EPA the authority to regulate the dumping of solid and hazardous waste. It also provides the EPA with the authority to regulate **underground storage tanks** (**UST**s). It should be noted that the RCRA applies to currently active sites but not to abandoned sites.

- *Comprehensive Environmental Response, Compensation and Liability Act.* The **Comprehensive Environmental Response, Compensation and Liability Act** (**CERCLA**; 42 USC 9601 et seq.) is also known as the Superfund. It imposes liability on landowners and past landowners of contaminated waste sites for the costs of cleaning up the site. A current landowner can be liable for the costs of cleaning up a Superfund site unless the landowner can show that it did not dump materials on the site, that all dumping on the site has ceased, and that it took the land without knowledge of past dumping practices (the "innocent landowner" defense). Whenever land that has ever been used for commercial purposes is acquired, it is extremely important that an environmental assessment for past contamination be performed.

- *Clean Air Act.* The **Clean Air Act** (42 USC 7401 et seq.) was originally passed in 1970 and has been amended since then. It gives the EPA the power to implement the National Ambient Air Quality standards to address air pollution. The EPA regulates medical waste incineration under the Clean Air Act.

- *Toxic Substances Control Act.* The **Toxic Substances Control Act** (**TSCA**; 15 USC 2601 et seq.) gives the EPA the authority to track and control the toxic or potentially toxic chemicals used by industry.

Some of the specific areas that are regulated by the EPA that are or should be of concern to health care organizations include the following:[16]

Aboveground storage tanks

Asbestos release (during renovation or demolition)

Disposal of hazardous waste (any waste that readily ignites, is corrosive, is reactive, or is toxic)

Medical waste incineration

Superfund liability for environment contamination

USTs (if at least 10 percent of tank volume is below ground)

The EPA also has the power to regulate medical waste under the RCRA but has largely delegated the regulation of this material to the states.[17]

SUMMARY

As noted at the beginning of this chapter, this discussion is meant as an overview of the topic. If more detail is required, it can be easily found on the Internet at the Web sites identified in the endnotes.

Occupational safety and health can be a significant issue for health care entities. The failure to manage this risk can lead to increased workers' compensation costs, dissatisfaction among workers, property damage, and the potential for administrative fines and penalties. Managing these risks appropriately can lead to improved productivity, improved morale, and improved community relations.

Environmental impairment claims can be enormously expensive if not managed appropriately. For example, if a contaminant gets into sources of groundwater, it can take millions of dollars, or generations, for the hazard to be abated. Environmental impairment is important because this is the only planet that we have.

Finally, violations of any of the administrative regulations do not just carry fines and penalties. There are also potential criminal penalties that can be imposed. In today's environment, with CEOs going to jail for fraudulent accounting and other sins, this is not an exposure to be taken lightly.

KEY TERMS

Administrative agencies
Administrative Procedure Act
Appeal
Citation
Clean Air Act
Comprehensive Environmental
  Response
Compensation and Liability Act
Enabling legislation
Environmental Protection
  Agency
Hearing

Inspection
Occupational Safety and
  Health Review Commission
Resource Conservation and
  Recovery Act
Regulation
Subpoena
Toxic Substances Control Act
Underground storage tanks
Voluntary protection program
Warrant
Waste anesthetic gas

ACRONYMS

APA	OSHRC
CDC	PPE
CERCLA	RCRA
EPA	TSCA
HAZWOPER	UST
NIOSH	VPP
OSHA	WAG

NOTES

1. In this chapter, the term *administrative agency* should be understood to include departments of the federal executive branch of government, such as the Department of Health and Human Services, and subordinate agencies, such as the Food and Drug Administration or the Centers for Disease Control and Prevention. It also includes any nonjudicial governmental unit with the power to determine private rights and obligations by means of rulemaking or adjudication.

2. Shepard, G. "Fierce Compromise: The Administrative Procedure Emerges from New Deal Politics." *Northwestern University Law Review,* 1996, *90,* 1557.

3. Ibid.

4. More information is available on the OSHA Web site at http://www.osha.gov/dcsp/vpp/index.html

5. More information is available on the OSHA Web site at http://www.osha.gov/dcsp/partnerships/index.html

6. Detailed information is available on the OSHA Web site at http://www.osha.gov/Firm_osha_toc/Firm_toc_by_sect.html

7. Detailed information is available on the EPA Web site at http://www.epa.gov/ebtpages/complianceenforcement.html

8. More information is available on the NIOSH Web site at http://www.cdc.gov/niosh

9. For example, a NIOSH publication on waste anesthetic gases, "Criteria for a Recommended Standard: Occupational Exposure to Waste Anesthetic Gases and Vapors," was published in 1977, yet OSHA has never promulgated a standard for any of these gases.

10. More information is available on the CDC Web site at http://www.cdc.gov

11. Information on state programs for dealing with medical waste can be accessed on the EPA Web site at http://www.epa.gov/epaoswer/osw/stateweb.htm

12. Information on EPA policies regarding asbestos and mold is available on the EPA Web site at http://www.epa.gov

13. All under various parts of 29 CFR 1910.

14. Ibid.

15. Information compiled from publications available on the OSHA, NIOSH, and EPA Web sites.

16. Information compiled from publications available on the EPA Web site.

17. For links to the various state programs, go to http://www.epa.gov/epaoswer/osw/stateweb.htm

A RISK MANAGEMENT PROGRAM (EXAMPLE)

POLICY

Risk Management Program Plan

PURPOSE

The Risk Management Program is designed to protect the human and financial assets of the organization against the adverse effects of accidental losses, effectively managing losses that may occur, and to enhance continuous improvement of patient care services in a safe healthcare environment.

Risk Management is the process of creating and implementing strategies directed at minimizing the adverse effects of accidental loss on the (Entity's) human, physical, and financial assets through the identification and assessment of loss potential and selection of appropriate loss assumption, transfer, prevention, and control mechanisms.

AUTHORITY

The governing body has the ultimate responsibility to assure the provision of a safe environment. The governing body delegates authority for the establishment of a comprehensive, organization-wide risk management program to (Entity) administration.

SCOPE

The Risk Management Program is designed to identify, assess, prevent, and control losses that arise from employee work-related injury, liability, property, regulatory compliance and other loss exposures arising from operations.

The Risk Management Program involves loss prevention, control, and continuous quality improvement activities. Team effort to implement the risk management program will include physicians, administrators, management, supervisors, and line employees to identify, review, evaluate, and control risks that interfere with-quality patient care, safety and services rendered in the (Entity) and to take appropriate corrective and ¬preventive action as necessary.

PROGRAM ELEMENTS

The Risk Management Program at (Entity) will utilize a five-step process which includes:

1. Identification of potential loss exposures;
2. Assessing the feasibility of alternative techniques to treat the exposure identified;
3. Selecting the appropriate risk management technique;
4. Implementing the chosen technique; and
5. Monitoring the effectiveness of the action taken.

OBJECTIVES

The objectives of the Risk Management Program are to preserve the assets, reputation, and quality of care of (Entity) by utilizing a process to identify, reduce, or eliminate the risk of loss.

To meet these objectives, the Risk Management Program will undertake the following activities:

1. Administer all insurance or self-insurance programs so as to maximize coverage and minimize expenses;

2. Inspect all (Entity) premises to discover and correct potentially hazardous conditions which may present unnecessary risk to employees, patients, and others;

3. Review the performance of all persons providing care to patients to identify and correct practices which may present unnecessary risks to patients or deviate from acceptable practices;

4. Review policies and procedures to update, amend, edit, and revise to reflect appropriate care, legislative requirements, and minimize or prevent liability ramifications;

5. Investigate adverse occurrences to assess and determine how similar occurrences might be averted and to control the loss related to the adverse occurrence;

6. Handle complaints and grievances to resolve disputes and improve patient care and associated services;

7. Coordinate the local management of claims against (Entity) in a timely, organized, and cost effective manner as required by coverage documents; and

8. Organize educational programs on risk management topics to promote awareness of risk management issues and safer practices.

PROGRAM PLAN

1. GOVERNING BODY

   The Governing Body has the ultimate responsibility to assure that a Risk Management Program is established and implemented. The Governing Body will delegate the responsibility for the Risk Management Program to (Administrative Vice President or President).

   In discharging its responsibilities for the Risk Management Program, the Governing Body will:

   a. Assure that a comprehensive, ongoing and effective Risk Management Program is in place;

   b. Assure that significant deficiencies identified by the risk management process are corrected;

   c. Assure financial and administrative support necessary for the effective implementation of the Risk Management Program;

   d. Receive periodic reports on Risk Management Program activities as described in the plan.

2. ADMINISTRATION

   (Entity) administration actively supports the Risk Management Program. Administration is responsible for the general management of (Entity) and authorized to act on behalf of the Governing Body to assist with the implementation of the Risk Management Program and related activities. Administration/management

   a. Assigns accountability for Risk Management Program components within (Entity) as follows:

   Clinical Risk

   (Title): _____

   Essential functions:

   Quality assurance, utilization review, infection control, pharmacy and therapeutics, medical staff -credentialing and committees, and clinical practice guidelines or standards

Regulatory/Accreditation/Licensing Risks

(Title): _____

Essential functions:

Safety management and loss control, employee accidents, department hazard analysis, equipment management, plant safety and management including fire suppression, Safe Medical Device Act com¬pliance, EMTALA compliance, and OSHA compliance programs

Business Risk

(Title): _____

Essential functions:

Risk financing and insurance, employee benefits and workers' compensation, employment practices, contract review systems, administration and operational activities, disaster planning and preparedness, and security systems

b. Support the integration of the Risk Management Program into the overall management control system used to evaluate the delivery of quality care and services;

c. Participate in the review and evaluation of patient care and safety within (Entity);

d. Identify, implement, and support corrective action plans for (Entity) related to the Risk Management Program; and

e. Monitor results for effectiveness of techniques employed to manage risks for (Entity), and make any adjustments necessary to the corrective action plan.

3. PROFESSIONAL STAFF (Physicians, Nurses, and other licensed health care practitioners)

The professional staff are responsible for providing diagnostic and therapeutic medical care, and:

a. Actively participating in the functions of the Risk Management Program by monitoring, evaluating, and maintaining applicable standards of care within his/her licensure and position;

b. Report variances in care to responsible individuals in order to identify and resolve clinical risks;

c. Identify, recommend, and implement corrective action needed.

INTEGRATION WITH KEY ASPECTS OF OPERATIONS

The Risk Management Program interfaces with other key aspects of operations and shares pertinent information as appropriate with organizational functions/committees such as:

1. Quality Management

2. Medical Staff Services

3. Human Resources

4. Utilization Management

5. Performance Improvement

6. Safety

7. Infection Control

8. Medical Records

9. Patient Billing Office

10. Security

CONFIDENTIALITY

Risk management documents and records include information which relate to sensitive patient and provider information. It is the intent of this Risk Management Program to apply all existing legal standards and state or federal statutes to provide protection to the documents, proceedings and individuals involved in the program.

Any and all documents and records that are part of the internal Risk Management Program, as well as the proceedings, reports and records from any of the involved committees, shall be maintained in a confidential manner. Disclosure to any judicial or administrative proceeding will occur only under a court order or legal mandate. The Risk Management Program will ensure:

1. Documents/records generated as part of the organizational Risk Management Program, as well as the proceedings, reports/records are to be confidential and subject to the state and federal laws protecting such documents from discovery.

2. Copies of minutes, reports, worksheets, and other data summaries related to risk management are stored in a manner to maintain strict confidentiality.

3. Employees, volunteers, and physicians/medical staff are obligated to maintain complete confidentiality of all pertinent information to protect patient rights, as required by state and federal law.

EVALUATION OF THE RISK MANAGEMENT PROGRAM

The Risk Management Program and (Entity's) progress toward achieving objectives listed in this plan will be reviewed at least annually by the Governing Body of (Entity).

Approval:

_____   _____

Governing Body (Board Chair)   Date

_____   _____

President/CEO   Date

_____   _____

Medical Staff President   Date

_____

Adventist Health, 2005 Reprinted with permission

APPENDIX

REQUEST FOR RECORDS FORM (EXAMPLE)

North Broward Hospital District
Risk Management Department
REQUEST FOR RECORDS

☐ IPMC Region   ☐ NBMC Region   ☐ CSMC Region   ☐ BGMC Region   ☐ Western Region

TO: ☐ **Pathology**
        ☐ **Central Business Office**
        ☐ **Radiology**
        ☐ **QA/UR**
        ☐ **Medical Records**
        ☐ **Other**_____

FROM: Risk Management: _____
                                    Name   Telephone #   Location

RE: Patient: _____ Medical Record # _____

        Admitted: _____   Discharged: _____   DOB: _____

In anticipation that the above patient may file a claim against his/her health care providers:

☐ Secure all specimens, slides and blocks (itemize below)
☐ Secure all films, scans and x-rays (itemize below)
☐ Prepare   ☐ One   ☐ Two itemized copy(ies) of bill
                ☐ One   ☐ Two copy(ies) of Detailed Billing notes; forward all to Risk Management
☐ Forward a copy of the QA/UR review on this patient to the person identified above.
☐ Forward _____ copy(ies) of the medical records to: ☐ District   ☐ Regional Risk Management

        ☐ Number the pages of the original medical record prior to copying

DATE DONE	NUMBER	TYPE

Secured originals are not to be released out of your department or viewed without authorization by Risk Management.

Please complete and return to Risk Management within 5 days of receipt

APPENDIX

A GUIDE TO MEDICAL TERMINOLOGY

ELAINE RICHARD

LEARNING OBJECTIVES

- To identify the three basic terms used in the structure of medical terminology
- To define commonly used word roots, suffixes, and prefixes
- To analyze the formation of abbreviations and acronyms used in medical terminology
- To translate medical terminology used in a medical record

The field of medicine is no different from other professions in that it has a language all its own. However, in medicine, the ability to communicate effectively in any form, forum, or context is a critical component of delivering safe patient care. Miscommunication can cause patient harm. The press is replete with example of medical error, a primary and contributing cause of which is poor communication. Efforts abound in the industry to promote more effective and efficient means by which health care practitioners communicate, including the use of technology and revised systems and processes. Nevertheless, it all starts with understanding the words, symbols, abbreviations, and acronyms used in daily practice. This language may seem foreign until its mysterious components are unveiled, studied, and no longer act as impediments to understanding.

This guide to Medical Terminology is designed to introduce the concepts and structures of medical terms. It is recommended that a medical dictionary or glossary of medical terms be obtained as a resource in the practice of risk management.

HISTORY

Medical terminology derives primarily from the Greeks and Romans, in whose cultures modern medicine has its roots. In more recent centuries, research by the French and the Germans has influenced medical terms, and today, English, the de facto universal language, plays a prominent role as advances in medicine are made.

STRUCTURE OF MEDICAL TERMS

Most medical terms are composed of a root word and a suffix. Sometimes a prefix is also included. Thus nearly all medical words have a root and a suffix, but not all medical terms have a prefix. Let's begin with the word *medical:* the root word *medic* means "healing," and the suffix *-al* means "pertaining to." If we add a prefix, such as *pre-,* meaning "before," you have the word *premedical,* "preparing to enter the field of medicine."

pre / medic / al

Thus as you can see, learning the various suffixes and common root words will help you understand medical terminology.

Let's take another example. *Gastr* (root word for "stomach") and *-itis* (suffix for "inflammation") are combined to form *gastritis,* "inflammation of the stomach."

gastr / itis

The editor would like to acknowledge and thank Kathryn Hyer, PhD, MPP, associate professor in the School of Aging Studies at the University of South Florida, director of the Training Academy on Aging, and course director for the Healthcare Risk Management Online certificate course offered by the University of South Florida, for giving permission to publish this Guide to Medical Terminology in this book.

The suffix -logy means "the study of." If we wish to combine it with the root word *gastr*, however, the word would be unpronounceable. So when a suffix begins with a consonant, a "combining vowel" is inserted to facilitate pronunciation. In this case—as in most cases—it is an *o:* hence, *gastrology*, "study of the stomach."

gastr / o / logy

When examining a word, it is best to begin with the suffix, as it generally indicates the condition, procedure, disorder, or disease. Then look at the root word. In our examples of *gastritis* and *gastrology*, if you look first at the suffixes, you will know that the *-itis* word describes an inflammation and *-logy* word describes the study of something. Then you look at the root word, *gastr*, and see that both words refer to the stomach.

There you have the method of examining a medical term for its meaning.

Let's take a more complex example. If you know that the root word *cardi* means "heart" and you see the word *cardiology*, you recognize that it is "the study of the heart." Now look at the word *pericarditis*. You begin with *-itis*, then look at *card* (noting that if two vowels would fall together, one of them is dropped, so here *cardi* becomes *card*), and then see that there's also a prefix, *peri-*, which means "around" or "surrounding." And so you have figured out that the word *pericarditis* refers to "inflammation around the heart."

peri / card / itis

Learning the most common suffixes, root words, and prefixes requires study and frequent use. There are various approaches to this task, none of which will cover all the terms you will encounter. Therefore, it is helpful to have references readily available, such as a glossary of medical terminology or a medical dictionary. Many references are available online as well and are user-friendly.

SUFFIXES

As noted earlier, the suffix is the component of a medical term that gives precise meaning to the root. Table A.1 presents the most commonly used medical suffixes.

TABLE A.1. **Common Medical Suffixes**

Suffix	Meaning
-ac, -al, -ar, -eal, -ic, -ive, -ous	pertaining to
-algia	pain
-ectomy	excision, removal of
-emia	blood condition
-esis, -ion, -on, -tion, -y	process of
-gram	record

TABLE A.1. *(Continued)*

Suffix	Meaning
-graphy	process of recording
-ia	condition
-ist, -ologist	one who specializes in
-itis	inflammation
-logy	study of
-lysis	breakdown, separation, destruction
-oma	tumor, mass
-osis	abnormal condition
-plasty	repair
-porosis porosity	porosity
-rrhea	flow, discharge
-scopy	visual examination
-stasis	stopping, controlling
-tomy	incision

PREFIXES

Prefixes are parts of a word that precede the root part of a medical term. Not all medical terms have prefixes. Table A.2 presents the most common medical prefixes.

TABLE A.2. Common Medical Prefixes

Prefix	Meaning
a-, an-	no, not, without
ante-	before, forward
anti-	against
auto-	self
bi-	two, double, both
brady-	slow
con-	with
contra-	opposite
de-	from
di-, dia-	complete, through

dys-	painful, difficult, abnormal, bad
en-, endo-	within
epi-	on, over, outer, after
exo-	out, outside
hypo-	too little, deficient, below
hydr-	water
hyper-	too much, excessive, above
inter-	between
intra-	within
mal-	Bad
neo-	new
pan-	all
pre-, pro-	before
poly-	many
post-	after, behind
re-, retro-	back, behind
sub-	below, under
super-	above, upper
syn-	with, together
tachy-	rapid
trans-	across
tri-	three, triple
uni-	one

Note that the directional terms *anterior, posterior, inferior,* and *superior* are helpful in medicine and are often used when positioning patients, describing test results (such as X-rays and other scans), and rendering a diagnosis:

My face is on the ***anterior*** (forward) part of my body.
My back is on the ***posterior*** (behind) part of my body.
My feet are in the ***inferior*** (lower) region of my body.
My head is in the ***superior*** (upper) region of my body.

ROOT WORDS

The root part of a medical term provides the main concept of the word. For example, as previously discussed, *cardi* means "heart." Medical terms always contain one root word and can contain two root words connected by a vowel:

Gastr / o / enter / o / logy = study of the stomach and intestines

TABLE A.3. Musculoskeletal System Root Words and Meanings

Root	Meaning	Example
arthr, articul	joint	arthr / itis, "joint inflammation"
ceps	heads	bi / ceps, "two heads," a descriptive name for the muscle of the anterior upper arm
chondr	cartilage	chondr / oma, "tumor of the cartilage"
crani	skull	crani / al, "pertaining to the skull"
extens	straightening	hyper / extens / ion, "process of excessive straightening"
myel	bone marrow	myel / oma, "tumor of the bone marrow"
oste	bone	oste / oma, "tumor of the bone"

One way to become familiar with root words is to examine them within the context of body systems.

Musculoskeletal System

The musculoskeletal system consists of the musculature and the skeleton. The term *musculoskeletal* contains two roots words: *muscul* ("muscle") and *skelet* ("bones"):

muscul / o / skelet / al

Thus the musculoskeletal system is composed of muscles and bones. Table A.3 presents some examples of root words associated with the musculoskeletal system.

Nervous System

The nervous system is made up of the brain and spinal cord, nerves, ganglia, and parts of the receptor organs; it receives and interprets stimuli and transmits impulses to the effector organs. Table A.4 presents root words associated with the nervous system.

TABLE A.4. Nervous System Root Words and Meanings

Root	Meaning	Example
cerebr, ceph	brain, cerebrum	cerebr / al, "of the brain"
genit	birth	con / genit / al, "associated with birth"
lepsy	Seizure, attach	epi / lepsy, literally, "seizing on," a disorder of the central nervous system

lexia, phas	speech, word	dys / lexia, "speech disorder"
neur	nerve	neur / o / logy, "the study of nerves"
plegia	paralysis	hemi / plegia, "paralysis of half (one side) of the body"
psych	mind	psych/osis is an abnormal condition of the mind
spondyl vertebr	vertebra, spine	spondyl / osis, "spinal abnormality"
taxia	coordination	dys / taxia, "abnormal coordination"

Reproductive System

The reproductive system consists of the organs necessary for reproduction, consisting in the male of the testes, penis, seminal vesicles, prostate gland, and urethra and in the female of the ovaries, fallopian tubes, uterus, vagina, and vulva. Table A.5 presents common reproductive system root words.

TABLE A.5. **Reproductive System Root Words and Meanings**

Root	Meaning	Example
cele	swelling, hernia	hydr / o / cele, "water tumor of the testicle"
genit	reproduction	genit / alia, "reproductive organs
orch, orchi, orchid	testes	orchid / ectomy, "removal of a testicle"
prostat	prostate gland	prostat / itis, "inflammation of the prostate gland"
episi	vulva, perineum	episi / otomy, "incision in the perineum"
fet	fetus	fet / al, "pertaining to a fetus"
galact, lact	milk	lact / a / tion, "process of secreting milk from the breast"
gynec	woman, female	gynec / ologist, "physician specializing in female reproduction"
hyster	uterus	hyster / ectomy, "removal of the uterus"
mamm, mast	breast	mamm / o / gram, "record of the breast," as revealed through X-rays
men, menstru	month, menstruation	a / men / o / rrhea, "lack of menstruation"
obstetr	midwife	obstetr / ic / ian, "doctor who delivers babies"

TABLE A.6. Urinary System Root Words and Meanings

Root	Meaning	Example
cyst, vesid	bladder, cyst	cyst / itis, "inflammation of the (urinary) bladder"
diur	increased output of urine	diur / esis, "excessive output of urine"
lith	stone, calculus	lith / otomy, "an incision to remove stones"
neph, ren	kidney	ren / al, "pertaining to the kidney"
ur, urin	urine	ur / ology, "study of the urinary system"

Urinary System

The organs comprising the urinary system include the kidneys, ureters, urinary bladder, and urethra. Common root words associated with the urinary system are presented in Table A.6.

Cardiovascular System

The cardiovascular system involves the heart and blood vessels. Common root words associated with the cardiovascular system are presented in Table A.7.

Gastrointestinal System

The gastrointestinal tract functions as a unit and is comprised of the stomach and intestines. Table A.8 presents common root words associated with the gastrointestinal system.

TABLE A.7. Cardiovascular System Root Words and Meanings

Root	Meaning	Example
angi, vas, vascul	vessel	angio / plasty, "repair of a vessel"
arteri	artery	arteri/ o / scler / osis, "abnormal hardening and thickening of the artery wall"
card, cardi, coron	heart	cardi / ac, "pertaining to the heart"
megaly	enlargement	cardi / o / megaly, "enlargement of the heart"
phleb, ven	vein	phleb / itis, "inflammation of a vein"
thromb	clot	thromb / o / phleb / itis, "blood clot in a vein"

TABLE A.8. Gastrointestinal System Root Words and Meanings

Root	Meaning	Example
abdom, celi, lapar	abdomen	celi / ac, "pertaining to the abdomen"
bil, chol	bile, gall	chol / cyst /ectomy, "removal of the gallbladder"
col, colon	colon	colon / o / scopy, "examination of the colon"
enter	small intestine	gastr / o / enter / itis, "inflammation of the small intestine"
gastr	stomach	gastr / o / logy, "study of the stomach"
gluc, glyc	glucose, blood sugar	gluc / o / meter, "device for measuring blood sugar"
hepat	liver	hepat / itis, "inflammation of the liver"
phag	eating, digestion	dys / phag / ia, "difficulty eating"
proct, rect	rectum, anus	proct / oscopy, "examination of the rectum and anus"

Endocrine System

The endocrine system is comprised of glands that produce secretions that help integrate and control bodily metabolic activity. These include the pituitary and thyroid glands, parathyroids, adrenals, islets of Langerhans, and ovaries and testes. (The male and female reproductive systems were discussed earlier.) Table A.9 presents some root words commonly used in association with the endocrine system.

TABLE A.9. Endocrine System Root Words and Meanings

Root	Meaning	Example
aden	gland	aden / oma, "a tumor of glandular tissue"
crin	secreting, separate	endo / crin / e, system that "secretes within"
ket, keton	ketone bodies (substances that regulate metabolism)	ket / osis, "abnormal level of ketone bodies" (as in diabetes mellitus)
tox, toxic	poison, toxin	tox / emia, "condition resulting from toxins (such as bacteria) distributed via the bloodstream"
troph, trophy	growth, nourishment	hyper / trophy, "excessive growth"

TABLE A.10. Integumentary System Root Words and Meanings

Root	Meaning	Example
cutane, derm, dermat	skin	dermat / ology, "study of the skin"
erythem	redness	erythem / a, "abnormal redness"
melan	black	melan / oma, "a (black) tumor of the skin"
onych, ungu	nail	onych / o / phagia, "nail biting"
papul	pimple	papul / e, "a small elevated mass on the skin"
prurit, psor	itching	prurit / us, "severe itching of the skin"

Integumentary System

The word integument means a layer of skin, membrane, or husk enveloping an organism or one of its parts. In the human body, the integument is the skin, which is technically an organ. Table A.10 presents root words commonly associated with the human integumentary system.

Respiratory System

The respiratory system serves the function of respiration and consists of the nose, nasal passages, nasopharynx, larynx, trachea, bronchi, and lungs. Table A.11 presents roots commonly associated with the respiratory system.

TABLE A.11. Respiratory System Root Words and Meanings

Root	Meaning	Example
bronch	bronchus (airway)	bronch / oscopy, "visual examination of the bronchial tubes" with an endoscope
laryng	larynx (voice box)	laryng / itis, "inflammation of the larynx"
lob	lobe	lob / ectomy, "removal of a lobe of a lung"
ox, oxia	oxygen	hyp / oxia, "deficient amount of oxygen" in the tissue cells
pector, thorac	chest	pector / al, "of the chest"
phas, phasia	speech	a / phasia, "loss of the ability to speak"
pnea, respire, respirat	breath	respirat / ion, "the act of breathing"
pneu, pneumon, pulmon	lung, air	pulmon / ologist, "lung specialist"

TABLE A.12. **Singular and Plural Forms of English Words**

Singular	Plural	Possessive Of The Singular	Possessive Of A Plural Ending In S	Possessive Of A Plural Not Ending In S
hospital	hospitals	hospital's	hospitals'	—
child	children	child's	—	children's
woman	women	woman's	—	women's
physician	physicians	physician's	physicians'	—

SINGULAR AND PLURAL FORMS

In the English language, the addition of *s* or *es* to the end of a word usually turns a singular into a plural; some examples are presented in Table A.12. However, some words in the medical field derived from Greek and Latin form their plurals in other ways, as shown in Table A.13. If you are unsure of the correct plural of a particular term, consult a dictionary. Note that capitalized acronyms used to designate the plural always take s. (Abbreviations and acronyms are discussed in the following section.)

TABLE A.13. **Singular and Plural Forms of Certain Words Derived from Greek or Latin**

ENDING OF THE SINGULAR	ENDING OF THE PLURAL
a as in *vertebra*	*ae* as in *vertebrae*
is as in *diagnosis*	*es* as in *diagnoses*
on as *inganglion*	*a* as in *ganglia*
um as in *ovum*	*a* as in *ova*
us as in *bronchus*	*i* as in *bronchi*
ax as in *thorax*	*aces* as in *thoraces*
ex as in *apex*	*ices* as in *apices*
ix as in *appendix*	*ices* as in *appendices**
EXCEPTIONS	
sinus	sinuses
virus	viruses

*Many terms ending in ix can also form their plural as in English, by adding es.

TABLE A.14. Common Medical Abbreviations

Abbreviation	Meaning	Example
ac	before meals	"He was instructed to take his medicine ac meals."
bid	twice a day	"The prescription was for Protonix bid."
c̄	with	"Take 1 tablet c̄ meals."
g	gram*	"The physician ordered 400 g of the drug."
h	hour	"She took aspirin q4h." (See *q* below.)
Hx	history	"The physician took the patient's Hx."
lt	left	"Lt leg was put in a cast."
pc	after	"He was instructed to take his medicine pc meals."
pt	patient	"Pt was admitted at 9:12 a.m." REMOVE can be confused with prothrombin time, physical therapy and percussion therapy
q	every	"The antibiotic was administered q6h."
qid	four times a day	"Pt was given small meals qid." REMOVE this is on the do not use list by the Institute of Safe Medication Practices (ISMP)
prn	as needed	"Dr. Z ordered codeine for pain prn."
s̄	without	"She went s̄ treatment for 4 years."
stat	immediately	"The nurse called for CPR stat."

*Note that metric measurements are used in the medical field.

ABBREVIATIONS AND ACRONYMS

In the medical field, abbreviations (shortened words) and acronyms (also called *initialisms,* formed from the first letters of all important words in a name or phrase) are numerous and are used frequently, especially in medical records and prescriptions.

Some common medical abbreviations are presented in Table A.14, some common acronyms in Table A.15. Many short forms can also be found in the Glossary.

Be aware that certain abbreviations can be subject to misunderstanding and should be used with caution. In fact, The Institute for Safe Medication Practices has drawn up a list of "Error-Prone Abbreviations, Symbols, and Dose Designations" that are considered unacceptable and never to be used when communicating medical information. These can be found at http://www.ismp.org/Tools/errorproneabbreviations.pdf. In addition, The Joint Commission has a National Patient Safety Goal that addresses abbreviations to be avoided. Because the use of certain abbreviations has been linked

TABLE A.15. **Some Common Medical Acronyms**

AIDS	acquired immune deficiency syndrome
ASHD	arteriosclerotic heart disease
CBC	complete blood count
CC	chief complaint
CHF	congestive heart failure
COPD	chronic obstructive pulmonary disease
CVA	cebrovascular accident (stroke)
D/C	discontinue
DVT	deep-vein thrombosis (blood clot)
F/U	Follow-up
GERD	gastroesophageal reflux disease
H&P	history and physical
I&D	incision and drainage
LFT	Liver function test
LLQ	Left lower quadrant of abdomen
LUQ	left upper quadrant of abdomen
MI	myocardial infarction (heart attack)
NPO	nothing by mouth
NSAID	nonsteroidal anti-inflammatory drug
PERLA	pupils, equal, round, and react to light and accommodation
PET	positron emission tomography (scan)
RLQ	right lower quadrant of abdomen
RUQ	right upper quadrant of abdomen
R/O	rule out
SOB	shortness of breath
TPR	temperature, pulse, respirations
U/A	urinalysis
URI	upper respiratory infection
UTI	urinary tract infection

to misinterpretations leading to medication errors, the rule of thumb is "When in doubt, spell it out."

CONCLUSION

The use and understanding of medical terminology are vital to the practice of health care risk management. The risk management professional who masters medical terminology offers a necessary expertise to the organization in which he or she is employed.

GLOSSARY

A

AAAASF. American Association for Accreditation of Ambulatory Surgery Facilities, Inc.

AAAHC. Accreditation Association for Ambulatory Health Care, Inc.

AABB. American Association for Blood Banks.

AAFP. American Academy of Family Physicians: founded in 1947, the AAFP represents more than 93,000 physicians and medical students nationwide. It is the only medical society devoted solely to primary care.

AAHP. American Association of Health Plans.

AAHRPP. Association for the Accreditation of Human Research Protection Programs, Inc.

AAMC. Association of American Medical Colleges.

AANA. American Association of Nurse Anesthetists.

AAP. American Academy of Pediatrics.

AARP. Current name of the former American Association of Retired Persons.

Abd. Abdominal.

ABHR. Alcohol-based hand rubs: an alcohol-based preparation for hand use as a rub to reduce the number of microorganisms and thereby the potential for infection or disease. In the United States, most hand rubs contain ethanol or isopropanol in amounts from 60 to 95 percent.

ABMS. American Board of Medical Specialties.

Abuse. The willful infliction of injury, unreasonable confinement, intimidation, or punishment with resulting harm, pain, or mental anguish. "Fraud and abuse" describes practices that result in unnecessary costs to the Medicare or Medicaid program and other payer sources. "Patient abuse" is deliberate, nonaccidental contact or interaction that results in significant psychological harm, pain, or physical injury.

Academic medical center. Generally, a large inpatient teaching hospital with residency programs, faculty members, and research facilities and programs (see *Teaching hospitals*).

"Access" problem. Issues relating to impediments that restrict or limit persons in need of specific health care services from receiving them, such as lack of health insurance.

Accident (medical). An unintended occurrence resulting in injury or death that is not the result of willful action. Generally, an accident means that it resulted in some degree of injury or harm to the person or persons involved. In the medical field, the term *accident* is generally not used to describe an event associated with clinical care but refers to other types of events, such as one that involves damage to a defined system that disrupts the ongoing or future output of the system.

Accidental loss. A loss that occurs by chance and is unexpected, unintended, and fortuitous.

ACEP. American College of Emergency Physicians.

ACGME. Accreditation Council for Graduate Medical Education.

ACHE. American College of Healthcare Executives.

ACLS. Advanced cardiac life support.

ACO. Ambulatory care organization.

ACOG. American College of Obstetricians and Gynecologists.

ACP. American College of Physicians: a national organization of internists, physicians who specialize in the prevention, detection, and treatment of illnesses in adults. ACP is the largest medical-specialty organization and second-largest physician group in the United States.

Acquired immune deficiency syndrome (AIDS). A fatal, incurable disease caused by a virus (the human immunodeficiency virus) that can destroy the body's ability to fight off illness, resulting in recurrent opportunistic infections or secondary diseases afflicting multiple body systems.

Acquisition. A business transaction in which one corporation or entity purchases or otherwise acquires all of the assets or stock of another entity or organization.

ACR. American College of Radiology.

ACS. American Cancer Society.

ACS. American College of Surgeons.

Active error. An error that occurs at the level of the frontline operator, the effects of which are felt almost immediately and are readily apparent. This is sometimes called the "sharp end"; also called "active failure."

Active failure. A failure that results from an active error. Unsafe acts and deviation from expected and desired outcomes. Also called "active error" or "sharp end."

Actual cash value. Basis for insurance reimbursement: cost new minus depreciation.

Actuarial analysis. A study performed by a professional known as an actuary aimed at predicting the frequency and severity of claims for a specific line of insurance coverage for a future time period. Such an analysis includes both an estimation of the ultimate value of known claims and an estimation of the number and value of claims that have occurred but have not yet been reported.

Actuarial study. An analysis performed by an actuary that determines appropriate funding levels required for operation of a self-insurance trust.

Actuary. A person who uses statistics to compute loss probabilities to establish premiums for insurance companies and self-insurance trusts.

ACU. Ambulatory care unit.

Acuity. Degree or severity of illness.

Acute care hospital. Typically, a community hospital that has services designed to meet the needs of patients who require care for a period of less than thirty days.

ACV. Actual cash value.

ADA. American Dental Association; American Diabetes Association; Americans With Disabilities Act.

Additional insured. A person or entity added to an insurance policy by endorsement at the request of the named insured, often after the inception of the policy. Frequently required by contracts to give one contracting party the benefit of insurance coverage maintained by the other.

ADE. Adverse drug event.

ADEA. Age Discrimination in Employment Act.

Administrative agencies. Agencies within the executive branch of government. At the federal level, they generally fall under a cabinet official, such as, in the case of OSHA, the secretary of labor.

Administrative Procedure Act. Law that governs the ways in which administrative agencies can promulgate and enforce regulations.

Admission. An out-of-court statement made by a person who is a party to an action. Admissions are normally admissible as evidence at trial.

Admitted insurer. An insurance company that has applied to be financially qualified in every state in which it wishes to conduct business. Once admitted, a carrier must obey all state laws regulating the operation of insurance companies, including filing forms and rates.

ADR. Alternative dispute resolution.

Advance directive. Written instructions recognized under law relating to the provision of health care when an individual is incapacitated. An advance directive may take either of two forms: living will and durable power of attorney for health care.

Adverse drug event (ADE). An adverse event involving the use of medications; not necessarily related to error or poor quality of care. An adverse drug event may be the result of a medication error, but most are not.

Adverse drug reaction (ADR). Adverse effect produced by the use of a medication in the recommended manner.

Adverse event. Any injury (undesirable clinical outcome) caused by medical care and not an underlying disease process.

Adverse outcome. A clinical outcome that, while neither desirable nor necessarily anticipated, may have been a known possibility associated with a particular treatment or procedure. This definition does not imply that any provider was negligent or that any error in process or system factors contributed to the adverse outcome.

AED. Automatic external defibrillator.

AERS. Adverse event reporting system.

Affidavit. A written statement made under oath, without notice to the opposing party. A written or printed declaration or statement of facts, made voluntarily and confirmed by the oath or affirmation of the party making it, recorded before an officer having authority to administer such oath.

Age discrimination. Denial of privileges or other unfair treatment of employees because of their age. Age discrimination is prohibited by federal law under the Age Discrimination in Employment Act of 1978 to protect employees between the ages of forty and seventy years old.

Age Discrimination in Employment Act. The federal statute (29 USC 621 et seq) prohibiting certain types of employment discrimination on the basis of age.

Agency by estoppel. See *Ostensible agency doctrine*.

Aggregate limit. The maximum amount the insurer will pay during the policy period, irrespective of the policy's limit of liability.

AHA. American Heart Association; American Hospital Association.

AHACC. American Hospital Association Certification Center.

AHCA. American Health Care Association.

AHERA. Asbestos Hazard Emergency Response Act.

AHIMA. American Health Information Management Association.

AHRQ. Agency for Healthcare Research and Quality: a component of the Public Health Services responsible for research on quality, appropriateness, effectiveness, and cost of health care.

AIC. Associate in claims.

AICPCU. American Institute for Chartered Property Casualty Underwriters.

AIDS. Acquired immune deficiency syndrome.

ALAE. Allocated loss adjustment expense.

ALF. Assisted-living facility.

Allegation. In a pleading, the assertion, declaration, or statement of a person setting out what the party to an action expects to prove.

Allied health professional. A specially trained nonphysician health care provider. Allied health professionals include paramedics, physician assistants, certified nurse midwives, phlebotomists, social workers, nurse practitioners, and other caregivers who perform tasks that supplement physician services.

Allocated loss adjustment expense. Money paid in the claims resolution process. Includes defense attorney fees, court costs, expert witness fees, and photocopy costs attributed directly to an individual claim.

All-risk coverage. Insurance that covers all losses that are not explicitly excluded.

ALS. Advanced life support.

Alterations. To change the meaning or intent.

Alternative delivery systems. Health services provided in locations other than an inpatient, acute care hospital, such as skilled and nursing facilities, hospice programs, and home health care.

Alternative dispute resolution (ADR). A process or system to resolve disputes outside the formal judicial process. It can include mediation, arbitration, or both, and can be voluntary or mandatory, depending on jurisdiction.

Alternative risk financing. Any of a number of mechanisms other than traditional insurance programs employed by individuals or organizations to pay for claims, including various types of captive insurance companies, risk retention groups, and self-insurance trust funds.

Alternative risk transfer. See *Alternative risk financing.*

Alternative treatment plan. Provision in managed care arrangements for treatment usually outside a hospital.

AMA. American Medical Association: the AMA helps physicians help patients by uniting them nationwide to work on the most important professional, public health, and advocacy issues in medicine.

AMAP. American Medical Accreditation Program.

Ambulatory. Not confined to a bed; capable of walking.

Ambulatory care. Medical care provided on an outpatient basis.

Ambulatory care organization. A health care organization that includes multispecialty clinics, free-standing surgical centers, urgent care or walk-in medical clinics, and community health or public health facilities.

Americans With Disabilities Act. A federal statute (42 USC 12101 et seq) aimed at prohibiting discrimination in employment and public accommodation against individuals with certain mental and physical disabilities.

ANA. American Nurses Association.

Ancillary. Describing services that relate to a patient's care, such as lab work, X-rays, and anesthesia.

Annual aggregate limit. The maximum amount the insurer will pay during the policy period (usually one year), irrespective of the policy's limit of liability.

Annuity. A fixed sum payable periodically, subject to the limitations imposed by the grantor.

ANP. Advanced nurse practitioner.

ANSI. American National Standards Institute

Answer. A document filed with the court in response to a complaint or a petition. The answer must generally (1) admit that the plaintiff's allegations are true, (2) deny that the plaintiff's allegations are true, or (3) state that the defendant does not have information regarding the truth or falsity of the allegations.

Antikickback statutes. Medicare-Medicaid Antikickback Statute (42 USC 1320a-7b), outlawing "knowingly and willfully" seeking or receiving a bribe, rebate, or kickback for a referral (or the intent to induce a referral) for a program, reimbursable item, or service.

Antitrust laws. Laws designed to discourage or prohibit restraints of free trade, to unfairly reduce or eliminate competition, or to unfairly prevent entrance into a marketplace.

Any willing provider laws. Statutes in some jurisdictions prohibiting managed care organizations (MCOs) from discriminating among licensed providers of health care services and requiring that the MCO reimburse any licensed provider willing to accept the MCO's reimbursement schedule for the provision of covered services to a plan beneficiary.

AOA. American Osteopathic Association.

AONE. American Organizations of Nurse Executives.

AORN. Association of periOperative Registered Nurses.

APA. Administrative Procedure Act.

APC. Ambulatory patient classification.

Apparent agency. See *Ostensible agency doctrine*.

Appeal. An action that is taken after the trial of a matter or after a dispositive motion has been entered in a matter for the purpose of correcting an error made by the trial court or to obtain a new trial.

Appellate court. A court that is empowered to hear appeals. There are two tiers of appellate courts: an intermediate appellate court (such as the U.S. Circuit Courts of Appeal) and a supreme court (the U.S. Supreme Court, the New York Court of Appeals). Some states have only one appellate court tier.

APQC. American Productivity and Quality Center.

Arbiter. A neutral third party who issues a decision binding on the parties in a formal or informal hearing on a disagreement.

Arbitration. A method of dispute resolution used as an alternative to litigation where the hearing and determination of a case in controversy is by a person either chosen by the parties in opposition or appointed under statutory authority. May be binding (final) or nonbinding (aggrieved party may appeal or pursue conventional civil litigation).

Arbitration clause. A clause in a contract providing for arbitration of disputes arising under a contract. Arbitration clauses are treated as separable parts of the contract so that the illegality of another part of the contract does not nullify such agreements and a breach of repudiation of the contract does not preclude the right to arbitrate.

ARC. American Red Cross.

Archiving. Retaining and organizing expired insurance policies or revised policies and procedures to facilitate the determination of the provisions in place at a specific moment in the past.

ARES. Amateur Radio Emergency Services.

ARF. Alternative risk financing.

ARM. Associate in risk management.

ARM 54. Examination focusing on risk assessment; one of three required courses to obtain the designation as an associate in risk management (ARM) from the Insurance Institute of America.

ARM 55. Examination focusing on risk control; one of three required courses to obtain the designation as an associate in risk management (ARM) from the Insurance Institute of America.

ARM 56. Examination focusing on risk financing; one of three required courses to obtain the designation as an associate in risk management (ARM) from the Insurance Institute of America.

ARM-P. Associate in risk management for public entities.

ART. Accredited record technician.

ART. Alternative risk transfer.

ASA. American Society of Anesthesiologists.

ASC. Ambulatory surgery center.

ASCP. American Society of Clinical Pathologists.

ASHE. American Society for Healthcare Engineering.

ASHP. American Society of Health-System Pharmacists.

ASHRM. American Society for Healthcare Risk Management.

ASRS. Aviation Safety Reporting System.

Assault. An intentional act that is designed to make the victim fearful and produces reasonable apprehension of harm.

Assignment. The act of transferring to another party all or part of one's property, interest, or rights.

Assisted-living facility. Facility that provides supervision, assistance, or both, with the activities of daily living (ADL), facilitates the delivery of services by outside providers, and ensures resident safety, health, and well-being by monitoring activities.

Associate in claims. A designation conferred by the Insurance Institute of America.

Association. An unincorporated group of persons assembled for a specific purpose or to complete a specific project. Unless the state has a specific statute governing the liabilities of the members, each member may be liable for the debts and obligations of the association.

Association or group captive. Jointly owned by a number of companies that are affiliated through a trade, industry, or service group.

Assumption of risk. Understanding the risks associated with a particular course of action and agreeing to accept those risks. Also, in a negligence case, an affirmative defense that alleges that the plaintiff knew of the danger involved in what he was doing, did nothing to prevent his own injury, and hence must bear the consequences of the action and cannot ask for the defendant to pay for his injury.

ASTM. American Society for Testing and Materials.

ATLS. Advanced trauma life support.

Attorney-client privilege. A legal doctrine recognized by both common and statutory law protecting certain confidential communications between an attorney and his or her client from discovery in a legal proceeding unless the privilege is waived by the client.

Attorney work product privilege. A legal doctrine recognized by both common and statutory law protecting the documents generated, theories devised, and legal strategies formulated by an attorney on behalf of a client from discovery in a legal proceeding unless the privilege is waived by the client.

Authentication. Establishing or confirming that something is correct, accurate, or true.

Auto liability insurance. Insurance coverage for losses arising out of the ownership, maintenance, and use of automobiles and their equipment.

Automated dispensing cabinet. A cabinet that by its design has certain controls and documentation features that dispense medications pursuant to individualized patient drug profiles as ordered by a physician and confirmed by a pharmacist.

Autonomy. The right to self-govern or self-manage; capacity to make an informed, uncoerced decision.

Aviation coverage. Insurance coverage for losses arising from the use of helipads by life-flight operators or other emergency helicopter landings.

AWHONN. Association of Women's Health, Obstetric, and Neonatal Nurses.

B

BAA. Business associate agreement.

Back pay. In employment practices liability claims, a demand for or award of damages asking the defendant to pay the employee's wages from the time of the alleged improper act (such as wrongful termination) to the time of the settlement or judgment by the court in the employee's favor. In cases in which it is alleged that the employee was improperly denied a promotion or salary increase, back pay represents the difference in the wages actually earned by the employee and those that would have been earned had the promotion or salary increase not have been denied.

Bad outcome. Failure to achieve a desired outcome of care.

Balancing measure. Measure used to ensure that changes to improve a system or process do not create or cause problems in other areas.

Bar coding technology. A computer identification system that uses bar-stripe codes to identify specific items, medications, or patients. Most often used with a scanning device to read or verify each unique code.

Battery. The touching of one person by another without permission. See *Medical battery.*

BBA. Balanced Budget Act of 1997.

BBI. Basic building information.

BBRA. Balanced Budget Relief Act of 1999.

BCAA. Blue Cross Association of America.

Belmont Report. Report describing the basic ethical principles on which all biomedical and behavioral research should be based.

Benchmarking. A process that identifies best practices and performance standards to establish normative or comparative standards (benchmarks) for use as a measurement tool. By comparing an organization against a national or regional benchmark, providers are able to establish measurable goals as part of the strategic planning and total quality management processes.

Beneficence. The concept of doing good.

Benevolent gesture. Action taken to communicate a sense of compassion or compensation arising from humane feelings when there is no implication (direct or implied) as to "fault" for having contributed to or caused the outcome.

BI. Business interruption insurance coverage.

Bioethics activities. Activities associated with issues such as end of life (advance directives, withdrawal or withholding treatment, do-not-resuscitate orders, and so on) and human subject research.

BIPA. Benefits Improvement and Protection Act of 2000.

BLS. Basic life support.

BLS. Bureau of Labor Statistics.

Blunt end. See *Latent failure.*

Board certified. Officially acknowledged as a specialist in the physician's particular area of practice. To achieve board certification, a physician must meet specific standards of knowledge and clinical skills within a specific field or specialty. Usually, this means completion of a supervised program of clinical residency and passing both oral and written examinations administered by a medical specialty group.

Board eligible. Status of a physician who has graduated from a board-approved medical school, completed an accredited training program, practiced for a specified length of time, and is eligible to take a specialty board examination within a specific amount of time.

BME. Board of Medical Examiners.

Boiler and machinery coverage. Insurance that protects against the explosion of boilers and other pressure vessels and accidental damage to equipment. Covers resulting damage to other property, including property in your care for which you are liable as well as the cost of temporary repairs and any additional cost incurred to expedite repairs. Coverage is written on a "cost to repair or replace" basis and is not subject to depreciation.

Borrowed servant. A common law legal doctrine that stipulates that the employer of a borrowed employee, rather than the employee's regular employer, is liable for the employee's actions that occur while the employee is under the control of the temporary employer despite the lack of a permanent employee-employer relationship between the temporary employer and borrowed employee.

BP. Blood pressure

Brain death. Total irreversible cessation of cerebral function despite continued function of the respiratory and circulatory systems.

Breach of contract. Failure, without legal excuse, to perform any promise expressed in a contract. Also, hindrance by a party regarding the required performance of the rights and duties identified in the contract.

Breach of duty. One of the four elements necessary to prove negligence. The failure to fulfill (breach) an obligation or responsibility (duty).

Broker. A person who represents a buyer of insurance in negotiations with the underwriter and who serves as a consultant on various aspects of the buyer's insurance program.

BTLS. Basic trauma life support.

Builder's risk coverage. Insurance covering new construction.

BUN. Blood urea nitrogen.

Business interruption coverage. Insurance coverage typically provided as a part of a property insurance policy covering the lost revenues and extra operating expenses associated with a covered loss such as a fire.

C

CAA. Clean Air Act.

CAAS. Commission on Accreditation of Ambulance Services.

CABG. Coronary artery bypass graft.

CAH. Critical access hospital.

CAHPS. Consumer Assessment of Healthcare Providers and Systems. The CAHPS program is a public-private initiative to develop standardized surveys of patients' experiences with ambulatory and facility-level care.

CAMLTC. Comprehensive Accreditation Manual for Long-Term Care.

CAMTS. Commission on Accreditation of Medical Transport Systems.

CAP. College of American Pathologists.

Capitation. In managed care contracts, a payment method in which a provider is paid a set fee, often per member per month, to provide designated health care services to individuals covered by the managed care plan. The fee remains constant regardless of how much or how little health care service is actually provided.

CAPTA. Child Abuse Prevention and Treatment Act.

"Captain of the ship" doctrine. A doctrine that imposes liability on a surgeon in charge of an operation for the negligence of his or her assistants during the period when those individuals are under the surgeon's control, even though they are also employees of the health care entity.

Captive insurance company. An insurance company established to provide insurance coverage to a sponsoring entity as opposed to marketing and selling policies commercially to insureds. The sponsoring entity may be a parent corporation and its related subsidiaries, a professional association, or some other group.

Cardiac catheterization. A procedure used to diagnose disorders of the heart, lungs, and great vessels.

CARF. Commission on Accreditation of Rehabilitation Facilities.

CARME. Center for the Advancement of Risk Management Education.

Case management. A managed care technique in which a patient with a serious medical condition is assigned an individual who arranges for cost-effective treatment, often outside a hospital. See *Utilization management.*

CAT. Computerized axial tomography, a diagnostic technique that produces cross-sectional images of the head or body.

Catastrophic protection. Insurance that protects against the adverse effects of large losses from disasters of natural or human origin.

Cause of action. The facts that give the plaintiff the legal grounds to seek damages from another person. It is necessary to have a cause of action in order to bring and sustain a lawsuit.

CBC. Complete blood cell count.

CBRN. Chemical, biological, radiological, and nuclear (countermeasures).

CCAC. Continuing Care Accreditation Commission.

CCHSA. Canadian Council on Health Services Accreditation.

CCRC. Continuing care retirement community.

CCRN. Certification in critical care nursing.

CCU. Cardiac care unit.

CDC. Centers for Disease Control and Prevention.

CDRH. Center for Devices and Radiological Health, a division of the Food and Drug Administration.

Census. A count of the number of inpatients who receive hospital care each day, excluding newborns.

Centers for Disease Control and Prevention. An operating component of the Department of Health and Human Services whose mission is to promote health, prevent disease, injury, and disability and to prepare for new health threats.

Centers for Medicare and Medicaid Services. The federal agency responsible for administering Medicare, Medicaid, and the State Children's Health Insurance Program (SCHIP); formerly known as the Health Care Financing Administration (HCFA).

CEO. Chief executive officer.

CERCLA. Comprehensive Environmental Response, Compensation and Liability Act.

CERT. Centers for Education and Research in Therapeutics.

Certificate of insurance. A standardized form, usually produced by the insurance agent or broker who arranged for the coverage, evidencing specific insurance in place, the insurance carrier, policy period, policy number, and other particulars.

CfC. Conditions for coverage.

CFO. Chief financial officer.

CGL. Commercial general liability.

Chain of command. Communication route or hierarchy established by appropriate bodies (administration, medical staff and nursing) that allows staff members to air concerns and deal with difficult situations.

Chain of evidence. rocedure to ensure that the location and integrity of evidence (blood, clothing, weapons, and so on) collected from patients is accounted for, from the time it is collected until the time it is turned over to the police or court.

CHAP. Community Health Accreditation Program.

Charitable immunity doctrine. A doctrine that relieves a charity of liability in tort; most states have abrogated or restricted such immunity.

Chemotherapy. In the treatment of disease, the application of chemical reagents that have a specific and toxic effect on the disease-causing microorganism.

Chief executive officer. The corporate officer charged with responsibility for the financial and operational performance of the company. Often the CEO also carries the title of president.

Chief financial officer. The corporate officer charged with responsibility for overseeing the finance and accounting functions of the company, including reporting financial information to the public and to regulatory agencies, and interfacing with independent financial auditors.

Chief operating officer. The corporate officer charged with responsibility for the operations of the company.

Chief risk officer. The corporate officer charged with responsibility for identifying and managing a variety of financial, legal, strategic, and hazard risks faced by the organization. Distinguished from a traditional risk manager, whose role is generally confined to identifying and managing hazard risks.

Child Abuse Prevention and Treatment Act (CAPTA). One of the key pieces of legislation that guides child protection.

Child Protective Service agencies. A governmental agency in many of the states of the United States that responds to reports of child abuse and neglect. Many states change the name to reflect a more family-centered practice, such as the Department of Children and Family Services (DCFS).

CICU. Cardiac intensive care unit.

CISM. Critical incident stress management.

Citation. A writ that orders a person to appear and do something, such as defend or answer a charge made by a governmental agency.

Civil false claim. A claim that is submitted by a person or a person who knowingly causes someone else to submit a claim to the federal government for payment that is false or fraudulent.

Civil law. The system of laws by which one person may bring an action against another person seeking compensatory or punitive damages or injunctive relief. Also refers to the predominant theory of laws established by the governments of most western European countries (with the exception of the United Kingdom).

Civil monetary penalties (CMP). Any penalty, fine, or other sanction that is for a specific amount, or has a maximum amount, as provided by federal law, and is assessed or enforced by an agency in an administrative proceeding or by a federal court pursuant to federal law.

Civil Rights Act of 1964. A broad federal statute (42 USC 2000 et seq) prohibiting discrimination on the basis of race, color, creed, or national origin in a variety of settings, including employment.

Claim. The amount of damage for which an insured seeks reimbursement from an insurance company. Once the amount has been determined, it becomes a loss.

Claimant. Someone who brings a claim for alleged injuries.

Claims investigation. Process By which the necessary information to evaluate a claim is obtained. Information can be obtained through interviews, document review, visual inspection, and discovery requests.

Claims-made coverage. An insurance policy covering claims that are made during- the policy period and that occurred since the policy retroactive date. Although policy definitions vary somewhat, most claims-made insurance policies consider a claim to be made when it is first reported to the insurance company, subject to certain terms and conditions. Claims-made policies are common for professional liability and directors' and officers' liability insurance.

Claims management. A systemized approach to reducing the financial loss and negative community image of a health care organization in situations where prevention fails and injury occurs.

Class action. A lawsuit, frequently a liability lawsuit, including a number of similarly situated plaintiffs whose cases are factually almost identical. Joining all of the plaintiffs into a single lawsuit expedites pretrial discovery and prevents multiple trials on the same issues and can provide a forum for plaintiffs whose individual damages may be quite small. Seen most frequently in product liability and employment practices litigation.

Clean Air Act. Law that defines EPA responsibilities for protecting and improving the nation's air quality and the stratospheric ozone layer.

CLIA. Clinical Laboratory Improvement Amendments: these are certification standards for laboratories established to consolidate the requirements for Medicare participation with rules for laboratories engaged in interstate testing; standards contain quality control and quality assurance, proficiency testing, and personnel requirements.

Clinical practice guidelines. See *Critical paths.*

Clinical research trials. Use of experimental drugs, devices, or protocols on human subjects in a clinical setting under a set of prescribed procedures as part of the FDA approval process.

CMP. Civil monetary penalties.

CMS. Centers for Medicare and Medicaid Services.

CNM. Certified nurse-midwife.

CNS. Central nervous system.

COB. Coordination of benefits, an antiduplication provision under group health insurance to limit benefits where there is multiple coverage in a particular case to 100 percent of the expenses covered and to designate the order in which the multiple carriers are to pay benefits.

COBRA. Consolidated Omnibus Budget Reconciliation Act of 1986.

Code blue. Designation indicating that an emergency situation has occurred and mobilizes staff to respond.

Codefendant. A defendant who has been joined together with one or more other defendants in a single action.

COI. Certificate of insurance.

COLA. Commission of Office Laboratory Accreditation.

Collateral-source benefits. Amounts that a plaintiff recovers from sources other than the defendant, such as the plaintiff's own insurance.

Collective bargaining. Negotiations between an employer and a group of employees to determine the conditions of employment, resulting in a collective agreement. Employees are often represented in bargaining by a union or other labor organization.

Combined ratio. The sum of two ratios, one calculated by dividing incurred losses plus loss adjustment expense (LAE) by earned premiums (the calendar year loss ratio), and the other calculated by dividing all other expenses by written premiums. A combined ratio below 100 percent is indicative of an underwriting profit.

Commercial auto coverage. Insurance that protects against loss arising out of the ownership, maintenance, and use of automobiles and their equipment, both those a person owns, hires, or borrows and those a person doesn't own but may be responsible for, such as the personal car of an employee used to run a company errand.

Commercial general liability coverage. Insurance that protects against financial loss resulting from liability to third parties arising out of the premises a person owns or occupies, acts of independent contractors a person has hired, products a person sells when they leave the seller's premises, and liability a person assumes under contract, subject to exclusions of the policy. Coverage applies to bodily injury, property damage, and personal injury.

Commercial insurance. A distinction in property and liability coverage that is written for business or entrepreneurial interests as opposed to personal lines.

Commission error. Incorrect action performed or an intended action that was improperly performed.

Common cause. Factor that results from variation inherent in a process or system.

Common law. A legal system in which the elements of the substantive law must be gleaned from decided cases, as opposed to statutory law.

Compensatory damages. Damages sought or awarded to a plaintiff in a liability action to compensate for losses, such as lost wages or medical expenses, and for pain and suffering.

Complaint. One of the initial filings with a court to begin a lawsuit. The complaint normally recites all of the allegations against the defendant and theories on which the plaintiff seeks to recover damages. May be called a *petition* in some jurisdictions.

Complementary medicine. Any of a number of therapies and treatment modalities used alone or in combination to treat or alleviate specific symptoms or disease that fall outside of those traditionally employed by physicians, surgeons, and dentists, including acupuncture, massage therapy, and herbal medicine. Sometimes referred to as alternative medicine. Complementary medicine treatments often take a holistic approach to care and treatment and may include an emphasis on the spiritual dimensions of healing.

Complication. Undesired and unintended but often known negative clinical symptoms or physical injury that resulted from medical treatment.

Comprehensive Environmental Response, Compensation and Liability Act (CERLA). This law created a tax on the chemical and petroleum industries and provided broad federal authority to respond directly to releases or threatened releases of hazardous substances that could endanger public health or the environment; established prohibitions and requirements concerning closed and abandoned hazardous waste sites; provided for liability of persons responsible for releases of hazardous waste at these sites; and established a trust fund to provide for cleanup when no responsible party could be identified. Also known as the "Superfund."

Computed tomography scan. Technique for gathering anatomical information from a cross-sectional plane of the body, presented as an image generated by a computer synthesis of X-ray transmission data obtained in many different directions through a given plane.

Computer-aided decision support system. A computerized system that provides scientifically based diagnostic and patient care information.

Computerized physician/provider order entry. Computer system that allows direct entry of medical orders by the person with the licensure and privileges to do so.

CON. Certificate of need.

Conditions of participation. Requirements that hospitals must meet to participate in the Medicare and Medicaid programs; they are intended to protect patient health and safety and to ensure that high-quality care is provided to all patients.

Confidentiality. Parties to confidential communication cannot be compelled by law to disclose to any third party. Communication can be "confidential" in the sense that a person does not voluntarily disclose it to any other person. However, unless the law has defined a particular category of communications as confidential, anyone privy to that communication can be compelled to disclose it on penalty of law.

Confirmation bias. The human tendency to form a conclusion prematurely based on a preconceived expectation.

Consideration. In contract law, something of value exchanged for the promised performance of the other contracting party. Contracts frequently call for monetary consideration to be exchanged for the promise to provide specified goods or services.

Consolidated Omnibus Budget Reconciliation Act (COBRA). Federal law that provides for the continuation of health coverage applicable to group health plans. Employers with more than twenty employees must extend group health insurance coverage for at least eighteen months after employees leave their jobs. Employees must pay 100 percent of the premium.

Constitution. A relatively short document enacted by a state or federal government that specifies the essential nature of governance by the elected legislature and generally restrains the actions of military or police forces and the power exercised by regulatory agencies.

Constructive termination. In employment law, a situation in which, even though an employee is not formally terminated from a job, the conditions of employment become so manifestly untenable that the employee had no choice but to quit and hence are treated by the court as a termination.

Contingency fee. A fee for service, collectable only if the outcome is favorable to the payee.

Contract. An agreement, either written or oral, involving an offer, the acceptance of the offer, and an exchange of consideration.

Contributory negligence. Conduct on the part of a plaintiff that falls below the standard to which he or she should conform for his or her own protection. If the claimant is negligent and this negligence combines with that of the health care provider in causing the injury, the claimant cannot recover damages.

COO. Chief operating officer.

CoP. Condition of participation.

Copayment. A specified flat fee per unit of service or unit of time charged to an enrollee for a service or supply. Many HMOs charge their members a nominal fee for all nonemergent ambulatory patient visits or for prescription medications.

COR. Cost of risk.

CORF. Comprehensive outpatient rehabilitation facility.

Corporate compliance. As relates to health care fraud and abuse, any of a number of programs and initiatives undertaken by providers to avoid civil and criminal investigations and charges related to improper billing procedures, inappropriate referrals, kickbacks, and other prohibited activities under federal statutes such as the Antikickback Act and the Stark I and Stark II amendments to the Medicare Act. Many health care providers have taken corporate compliance programs beyond these specific legislative and regulatory requirements to encompass broader corporate business ethics concerns.

Corporate liability. The liability of the health care entity for the failure of administrators and staff to properly supervise the delivery of health care in that entity, including negligence in hiring, training, supervising, or monitoring.

Corporation. A legal entity that may be created by one or more persons or entities to carry out a business purpose. Corporations are persons in the eyes of the law and may sue and be sued. Except in extraordinary circumstances, the owners of the corporation—shareholders or members (in nonprofit corporations)—are shielded from the liabilities of the corporation.

Cost-benefit analysis. A method comparing the costs of a project to the resulting benefits, usually expressed in monetary value.

Cost containment. Control or reduction of inefficiencies in the consumption, allocation, or production of health care services.

Counterclaim. A claim presented by the defendant in opposition to the claim of the plaintiff.

Countersignatures. A second signature confirming and endorsing a document already signed.

Coverage determination. A process that companies use to decide if coverage is applicable.

CPA. Certified public accountant.

CPCU. Chartered property casualty underwriter.

CPG. Clinical practice guidelines.

CPHQ. Certified professional in health care quality.

CPHRM. Certified professional in health care risk management.

CPI. Consumer price index, an inflationary measure encompassing the cost of a basket of consumer goods and services.

CPOE. Computerized provider order entry.

CPR. Cardiopulmonary resuscitation.

CPS. Child Protective Service.

CPT. Current procedural terminology.

CQI. Continuous quality improvement, an approach to organizational management that emphasizes meeting (and exceeding) consumer needs and expectations, use of scientific methods to continually improve work processes, and the empowerment of all employees to engage in continuous improvement of their work processes.

Credentialing. The process of verifying and reviewing the education, training, experience, work history, and other qualifications of an applicant for clinical privileges conducted by a health care facility or managed care organization. Typically performed for independent contractors such as physicians and allied health practitioners who frequently are not employed by the credentialing entity but who are granted specific clinical privileges to practice.

Credentialing and privileging. Process by which hospitals determine the scope of practice of practitioners providing services in the hospital; criteria are determined by the hospital and include personal character, competency, training, experience, and judgment.

Crew (cockpit) resource management (CRM). A training concept originating at NASA, widely used in the aviation industry, and now adopted in health care to promote patient safety and enhance the efficiency of operations. Training elements include enhanced communications, situational awareness, problem solving, decision making, and teamwork.

Crime coverage. Insurance that provides coverage for losses arising out of employee or third-party theft or dishonesty.

Criminal false claim. Statute (18 USC 287) designed to "protect the government against those who would cheat or mislead it in the administration of its programs"; it has been employed to combat fraudulent claims filed under numerous federal programs, including Medicare and Medicaid.

Criminal law. The system of laws by which the state or federal government may bring suit against an individual, which suit may result in the loss of freedom or the person's life.

Critical access hospital. A small, limited-service, rural hospital that receives cost-based reimbursement for inpatient and outpatient care.

Critical paths. Any of a number of processes employed to define the generally accepted course of treatment for a specific medical condition or illness. Deviations from the prescribed critical paths must be explained by existing comorbidities, failure of prescribed treatments, and so on. Also known as *Clinical practice guidelines* or "care maps."

CRM. Crew resource management.

CRNA. Certified registered nurse-anesthetist.

CRO. Chief risk officer.

Cross-claim. A claim brought by a defendant against a plaintiff in the same action or against a codefendant concerning matters related to the original petition. Its purpose is to discover facts that will aid the defense.

C-section. Cesarean section, a procedure in which an incision is made through a mother's abdomen and uterus to deliver one or more infants.

CSO. Chief security officer.

CT. Cycle time, which records how responsive the process is. It is considered an efficiency measure.

CTS. Conformance to standard, which record how well the process is conforming to rules, regulations, standards, requirements, and specifications. These are quality measures.

CT scan. Computed tomography scan.

CVA. Cerebrovascular accident (stroke).

CWA. Clean Water Act.

Cycle time The time it takes to complete a defined process—for example, the length of stay for a patient in the emergency department from triage to final disposition (transfer to unit; discharge or transfer out).

D

D&C. Dilation and curettage.

D&O. Directors' and officers' (insurance coverage).

Damage cap. A legislatively imposed upper limit on the amount of a specific type of damages that may be awarded to a plaintiff in a specific type of lawsuit. State tort reform legislation frequently places a cap on the non-economic damages that may be awarded to a plaintiff in a medical malpractice action.

Damages. Monetary compensation for an injury. The injuries for which the plaintiff (claimant) seeks compensation from the defendant (health care provider). May include economic losses, emotional distress, pain and suffering, and disability.

Dashboard. Dashboards are a management tool used to distill extensive data into succinct results often offering result comparison. They focus on performance, use key indicators or best practice, and show results graphically.

Date of occurrence. Date when an event or loss occurred.

Date of report. The date an event or loss was reported. Specific reporting requirements are generally outlined in coverage documents. The date of report is a "heading" on many loss runs.

DBA. "Doing business as," the legally required phrase preceding the designation of an alternative business name under which a company wishes to operate.

DDS. Doctor of dental surgery.

DEA. Drug Enforcement Administration.

Declaration. A statement made out of court; an unsworn statement or narration of facts made by a party involved in a transaction or by someone who has an interest in the existence of the facts recounted. Recounts of statements made by a deceased person are admissible as evidence in some cases.

Declaration of Helsinki. International declaration setting forth ethical standards for human subject research.

DED. Dedicated emergency department: as defined under the Emergency Medical Treatment and Labor Act, it means any department or facility of the hospital, regardless of whether it is located on or off the main hospital campus, that meets at least one of the following requirements: (1) It is licensed by the state in which it is located under applicable state law as an emergency room or emergency department; (2) it is held out to the public (by name, posted signs, advertising, or other means) as a place that provides care for emergency medical conditions on an urgent basis without requiring a previously scheduled appointment; or (3) during the calendar year immediately preceding the calendar year in which a determination under this section is being made, based on a representative sample of patient visits that occurred during that calendar year, it provides at least one-third of all of its outpatient visits for the treatment of emergency medical conditions on an urgent basis without requiring a previously scheduled appointment.

Deductible. In insurance, the amount of loss that must be paid by the insured before the insurer starts to pay. The use of deductibles allows insured parties to avoid paying for coverage for smaller claims they are capable of paying themselves.

Deemed status. Status conferred when a health care organization is certified as complying with the conditions of participation (standards) set forth in federal regulations, which is a prerequisite for participating in and receiving payment from Medicare or Medicaid programs.

Deep pocket. In claims, an informal term for the defendant having the most assets or available insurance coverage, which becomes the target of the plaintiff. The "deep pocket" may have less responsibility for the plaintiff's injuries than other codefendants but may be pursued more aggressively because of its financial resources.

Default judgment. A judgment entered by the court in a civil case in favor of the plaintiff and against the defendant when the defendant has failed to file some appearance in response to a summons. A defendant's failure to so file is deemed to be an admission that the demands of the plaintiff's complaint are valid.

Defendant. The party against whom relief or recovery is sought in an action or suit.

Defense. A denial, answer, or plea opposing the truth or validity of the plaintiff's case. This may be accomplished by cross-examination or demurrer. It is more often done by introduction of testimony of the plaintiff's case.

Demurrer. Admission of the truth of the allegations asserted by a plaintiff accompanied by a request for their dismissal due to legal insufficiency to state a cause of action. This has largely been replaced in the federal court system and in jurisdictions following the federal court rules of civil procedure by the motion to dismiss.

Deposition. Testimony (under oath) of a witness taken on interrogatories reduced to writing and used to support or substantiate testimony offered at trial. The deposition is an important phase of the discovery process. It consists of a question-and-answer session in which the witness is interrogated under oath, after which the testimony is transcribed.

DFASHRM. Distinguished Fellow of the American Society for Healthcare Risk Management.

Diagnosis-related group. Any one of the various categories in a resource classification system that serves as the basis for reimbursing hospitals under federal Medicare programs, based on the medical diagnosis for each patient. Hospitals receive a set payment amount determined in advance, based on the length of time patients with a given diagnosis are likely to stay in the hospital. Is also used as the basis of the Medicare inpatient prospective payment system and has been adapted for use by some managed care plans.

DIC. Difference in conditions. Insurance coverage designed to close specific gaps in standard insurance policies; it allows coverage to be customized according to the insured's, needs extending coverage for exposures such as earthquake, landslide, flood, water damage, and collapse. Coverage may be provided by a separate insurance policy or it may be added by endorsement to the basic policy.

Diff. Differential blood cell count.

Direct insurance. A contractual arrangement involving the purchase of insurance by an insured from an insurer.

Direct liability. Liability imposed on a party as a result of the party's acts or omissions.

Directors' and officers' insurance coverage. Policies covering liability in connection with any actual or alleged error, misstatement, or misleading statement or act or omission or breach of duty by directors and officers while acting in their individual or collective capacities or any matter claimed against them solely by reason of their being directors or officers of the company.

Disclosure. Communication of information regarding the results of a diagnostic test, medical treatment, or surgical intervention.

Discovery. The process in litigation by which each party to the action seeks to learn all relevant facts that either support the plaintiff's cause of action or support the defendant's asserted defenses or denials.

Dismissal with prejudice. Dismissal of a defendant in a suit that bars any future action against the defendant by the plaintiff.

Dismissal without prejudice. A dismissal that has no effect on the plaintiff's future actions with regard to the dismissed party.

DMAT. Disaster medical assistance team.

DME. Durable medical equipment.

DNR. Department of Natural Resources.

DNR. Do not resuscitate.

DO. Doctor of osteopathy.

DOC. Date of closure: the date a file or claim was closed.

Doctor of osteopathy. A doctor who employs the diagnostic and therapeutic measures of ordinary medicine in addition to manipulative measures. This approach is based on the idea that the normal body when in "correct adjustment" is a vital machine capable of making its own remedies against infections and other toxic conditions.

Documentation. The recording of pertinent facts and observations about an individual's health history, including past and present illnesses, tests, treatments, and outcomes The legal evidence of professional accountability. See *Legal health record.*

DOD. U.S. Department of Defense.

DOE. U.S. Department of Education.

DOI. Date of incident.

DOJ. U.S. Department of Justice.

DOL. Date of loss; U.S. Department of Labor.

Do not resuscitate. A physician's order that resuscitation efforts should not be performed on a person should the person have a cardiac or respiratory arrest. This order can be generated by an advance directive, living will, health care proxy, or other legally recognizable document in which the person's wishes were identified as desiring no life-sustaining measure.

DOR. Date of report.

DOT. Department of Transportation.

DPM. Doctor of podiatric medicine.

DPT. Diphtheria, pertussis, tetanus: three illnesses for which vaccines are often administered in a single injection.

DRG. Diagnosis-related group.

DRS. Designated record set: a group of records maintained by or for a covered entity that is the medical and billing records about individuals maintained by or for a covered health care provider; the enrollment, payment, claims adjudication, and case or medical management record systems maintained by or for a health plan; or information used in whole or in part by or for the covered entity to make decisions about individuals

DSM-IV. The fourth edition of the American Psychiatric Association's *Diagnostic and Statistical Manual of Mental Disorders,* published in 1994.

Dual capacity. In employer's liability, an individual or entity serving as both an injured party's employer in a workers' compensation claim and in some other role in which it is alleged to have caused injury, such as the manufacturer of a defective piece of equipment involved in the injury or as the provider of improper medical treatment for the injury.

Due diligence. The review of an entity targeted for acquisition by the acquiring party to ascertain pertinent information about its financial and operating history and current status. Corporate staff are generally held to the legal standard of having performed the review with due diligence before making a recommendation to the board of directors as to whether to proceed with the acquisition.

Due process. A procedural requirement that may be met by providing the affected party with (1) adequate notice of the proceeding, (2) the right to be represented by counsel, (3) the opportunity to be heard, (4) the right to call and cross-examine witnesses, and (5) the right to a written transcript of the proceeding.

Durable power of attorney for health care. Also called a "health care power of attorney," it is a directive prepared by a person in advance of becoming incapacitated that empowers the attorney-in-fact (proxy) to make health care decisions for the person, up to and including terminating care and disconnecting machines that are keeping a critically and terminally ill patient alive. Health care decisions include the power to consent, refuse consent, or withdraw consent to any type of medical care, treatment, service, or procedure.

Duty. One person must be under a duty to another person (or to society) before negligence becomes an issue. In the context of professional liability, duty usually applies when the provider undertakes to care for a patient.

Duty of care. The duty to act in good faith, with the care that an ordinarily prudent person in a similar position would use under those circumstances and in the reasonable belief that the actions taken are in the best interest of the corporation. Courts call this the "reasonable person standard" because the action or any failure to act by the board is judged by what a reasonable person would do.

Duty of loyalty. The duty not to compete with the corporation, not to disclose confidential information obtained in the performance of one's duties as a board member, not to usurp corporate opportunity, and not to gain personal enrichment at the corporation's expense.

Duty to warn. A psychotherapist treating a mentally ill patient has a duty to use reasonable care to give threatened persons such warnings as are essential to avert foreseeable danger arising from the patient's condition or treatment. The protective privilege between psychotherapist and patient ends where the public peril begins. In some jurisdictions, this duty extends to other health care practitioners.

DVM. Doctor of veterinary medicine.

Dx. Diagnosis.

E

E&O. Errors and omissions (insurance).

EAP. Employee assistance program.

Early warning system. A systemized method for the early detection of adverse events, medical error, or situations that can give rise to medical error to facilitate loss mitigation or implement prevention techniques.

ECF. Extended care facility.

Economic damages. Damages sought by or awarded to a plaintiff to compensate for out-of-pocket expenses, such as medical treatment or housekeeping services and lost wages resulting from an injury, as distinguished from noneconomic damages, such as pain and suffering and loss of consortium, for which a dollar value is more speculative.

ECRI. Current name of the former Emergency Care Research Institute.

ED. Emergency department.

EDP. Electronic data processing.

EEG. Electroencephalogram.

EENT. Eye, ear, nose, and throat.

EEOC. Equal Employment Opportunity Commission.

EHR. Electronic health record.

EKG. Electrocardiogram.

Electronic data processing coverage. Insurance that provides coverage for loss of information stored on cards, disks, drums, or tapes.

Electronic health record. An electronic record of health-related information on an individual that conforms to nationally recognized interoperability standards and that can be created, managed, and consulted by authorized clinicians and staff across more than one health care organization.

Electronic incident reporting. The reporting and entering of relevant incident data into a computer.

EMC. Emergency medical condition: an acute illness, injury, or condition requiring immediate attention.

Emergency Medical Treatment and Active Labor Act. Federal statute (42 USC 1395 et seq) prohibiting the "dumping" of patients presenting to a hospital with an emergent medical condition or in active labor and limiting a hospital's ability to transfer them to other facilities. It also specifies when and how a patient may be refused treatment or transferred from one hospital to another when the patient is in an unstable medical condition.

EMF. Electromagnetic field.

EMG. Electromyogram.

Employee Polygraph Protection Act. Federal statute (29 USC 2001 et seq) limiting most employers' ability to use polygraph testing in the applicant screening process.

Employer's' liability. Any of a number of causes of action related to the employment relationship but falling outside of workers' compensation and employment practices liability insurance coverage, including dual capacity claims, spousal claims, and third-party-over claims.

Employment at will. Legal doctrine in most jurisdictions that an employer may discharge an employee for any reason, unless specifically prohibited by law.

Employment practices liability. Any of a number of violations by an employer, based on statute or common law, giving rise to damages outside of those covered by workers' compensation or similar statutes, including wrongful termination, discrimination, and sexual harassment.

Employment Retirement Income Security Act (ERISA). Federal statute (42 USC 1002 et seq.) that regulates retirement plans and health insurance plans. If a lawsuit is brought under ERISA against a health insurance plan, it may be removed to federal court, and damages will include the value of services wrongfully withheld.

EMS. Emergency medical service.

EMT. Emergency medical technician.

EMTALA. Emergency Medical Treatment and Labor Act.

Enabling legislation. A statute enacted by the legislature that permits an administrative agency to promulgate and enforce regulations.

Endorsement. A form attached to an insurance policy that either changes or adds to the provisions included in the policy. Endorsements may serve any number of functions, including broadening, limiting, or restricting the scope of coverage; clarifying coverage; adding other parties as insureds; or adding locations to the policy.

ENT. Ear, nose, and throat.

Enterprise liability. Liability to an organization or enterprise.

Enterprise risk management (ERM). An ongoing business decision-making *process* instituted and supported by a health care organization's board of directors, executive administration, and medical staff leadership. ERM recognizes the synergistic effect of risk across the continuum of care and aims to assist an organization to reduce uncertainty and process variability, promote patient safety, and maximize the return on investment through asset preservation and the recognition of actionable risk opportunities.

Environment of care. The environment in which patient care is received and delivered. A category of standards promulgated by the Joint Commission.

Environmental impairment liability. Negligent acts and/or omissions by individual(s) or organization(s) resulting in damage to the environment

Environmental Protection Agency. The EPA leads the nation's environmental science, research, education, and assessment efforts. EPA's mission is to protect human health and the environment.

EOB. Explanation of benefits.

EOC. Emergency operations center.

EOC. Environment of care.

EPA. Environmental Protection Agency.

EPA. Equal Pay Act.

EPL. Employment practices liability.

EPLI. Employment practices liability insurance.

EPO. Exclusive provider organization.

Equal Employment Opportunity Commission. Federal agency charged with enforcing several federal statutes prohibiting various types of employment discrimination. Under some statutes, administrative hearing procedures before the EEOC must be exhausted before an employee has access to the court system.

Equal Pay Act. Federal statute (29 USC 206 et seq) requiring equal pay for equal work without regard to the gender of the worker.

Equity. A system of justice that follows rules that differ and often override those of civil law and common law. In cases brought in equity, the court has the power, without a jury, to determine the facts of the matter and to make final determinations. Decisions are less affected by precedent than cases brought at law; they are generally based on principles of fairness to the parties. Examples of actions in equity include most domestic relations cases and cases for injunctive relief (restraining orders). Courts of equity have been merged with courts of law in the federal and most state systems.

Ergonomics. The scientific discipline concerned with design according to human needs and the profession that applies theory, principles, data, and methods to design to optimize human well-being and overall system performance.

ERISA. Employee Retirement Income Security Act.

ERISA preemption. A provision of ERISA that preempts state law governing qualified pension and benefit plans and makes the remedies provided for by ERISA exclusive. Generally interpreted as preempting malpractice actions against managed care plans that are governed by the act.

ERM. Enterprise risk management.

ERP. Extended reporting period.

Error. Failure of a planned action to be completed as intended or use of a wrong plan to achieve an aim. The accumulation of errors results in accidents.

Errors and omissions insurance. An insurance policy providing coverage for negligent advice or business services provided by individuals or entities not eligible for professional liability insurance coverage, such as medical billing companies, insurance brokers, and managed care organizations.

Essential job functions. Under the Americans With Disabilities Act, the tasks associated with a particular job that an applicant must be able to perform, either with or without accommodation, to do the job.

Ethics. A branch of philosophy, also called moral philosophy, that involves the systematizing, defending, and recommending of concepts of right and wrong behavior.

Ethics committee. A multidisciplinary group that convenes for the purpose of staff education and policy development in areas related to the use and limitation of aggressive medical technology and acts as a resource for patients, family, staff, physicians, and clergy regarding health care options surrounding terminal illness and assisting with living wills.

Event. An occurrence that is not part of the routine care of a particular patient or the routine operation of the health care entity.

Event reporting. A system in health care institutions by which employees use a standardized form to report any occurrence outside the routine so that the information can be used for loss prevention and claims management activities.

Evergreen clause. In contracts, a clause that makes the agreement perpetual unless terminated by one of the parties. Contracts with an evergreen clause have no set expiration date.

Evidence. Testimony, documents, objects, pictures, sound recordings, or other items that may prove that an occurrence did or did not occur. Such things may only be considered at trial if admitted into evidence by the court. Evidence may be excluded if it would unduly inflame the passions of the jury, if it is irrelevant, if it does not appear to be credible or probative, or for other reasons.

Evidence-based. Based on the best available scientific knowledge. Recommended evidence-based practices have generally gone through a rigorous review process by leading medical specialists.

Excess and surplus line carriers. Insurance companies that specialize in providing coverage above and beyond primary insurance policies or significant self-insured retentions. Under the insurance regulations of most states, such insurers may write coverage in the state according to certain specified conditions without going through the licensing provisions applicable to admitted insurance carriers.

Excess capacity. The difference between the number of hospital beds being used for patient care and the number of beds available.

Excess insurance policy. An insurance policy providing coverage above the limits provided by a primary insurer or a self-insurance program. Some insurance programs feature multiple layers of excess insurance policies.

Expense. Costs incurred associated with the generation of revenues.

Expenses within policy limits. A provision in some insurance policies that allocated- loss-adjusting expenses paid by the insurer are included when determining the applicable limits of coverage. For example, if $900,000 is paid to a claimant to settle a claim, expense costs come to $300,000, and the occurrence is covered by an insurance policy with a limit of $1 million that includes a provision for expenses within policy limits, the insurer will pay only $1 million. If the policy indicates that expenses are covered in addition to policy limits, the insurer will pay a total of $1.2 million. Expenses covered within policy limits are said to erode the limits.

Expert opinion. An opinion rendered by a person who by virtue of education, training, skill, or experience is believed to have knowledge in a particular subject beyond that of the average person, sufficient that others may officially (and legally) rely on that person's specialized (scientific evidence [law], technical or other) opinion about an evidence or fact issue within the scope of the person's expertise.

Exposure. Risk: the chance of loss and potential liability that is covered by insurance. Also, a percentage, calculated by the attorneys and claims adjusters, that estimates the likelihood of losing a trial.

Extended reporting endorsement. An endorsement to a claims-made policy that extends the reporting period for claims.

Extended reporting period. A designated period of time after a claims-made policy has expired during which a claim may be made and coverage triggered as if the claim had been made during the policy period.

Extra expense. Additional costs incurred in connection with to a covered loss.

F

FAA. Federal Aviation Administration.

Face value. A perception that the level of validity of a concept is high, even when there is no scientific evidence to support that hypothesis.

FACHE. Fellow of the American College of Healthcare Executives.

Factitious disorder by proxy. See *Munchausen syndrome by proxy.*

Facultative. Describing a single transaction handled directly with a reinsurer.

Failure mode. Ways in which a process or subprocess can fail to provide the anticipated result.

Failure mode cause. Reasons why a process or subprocess would fail to provide the anticipated result.

Failure mode effects analysis or criticality analysis. A proactive, systematic assessment used to identify the steps of a process that may be subject to failure in order to design measures to either prevent or control such failures. If a criticality phase is used in this process, the perceived level of criticality of each type of potential failure is identified, to aid in setting priorities for establishing control mechanisms.

Fair hearing plan. A document, either freestanding or part of the bylaws of a medical staff, describing the procedures applicable to denial, revocation, and suspension of clinical privileges and other medical staff disciplinary issues. Such plans specify due process requirements such as the right to notice, hearings, representation by counsel, and appeals.

Fair Labor Standards Act. Federal statute (29 USC 201 et seq) establishing the authority for the Department of Labor to promulgate wage and hour regulations and providing the framework for collective bargaining by employees.

False Claims Act. Two separate statutes defining false claims—18 USC 287 and 31 USC 3729(a), 3730(a)–(b). See *Civil false claims* and *Criminal false claims.*

Family Education Rights and Privacy Act. Federal legislation (20 USC 1232G; 34 CFR 99) designed to protect the privacy of student education records. It is applicable to all schools that receive funds under designated U.S. Department of Education programs.

Family Medical Leave Act. Federal statute (29 USC 2611 et seq.) requiring certain employers to provide a period of unpaid leave to employees meeting specified criteria in order for them to receive medical treatment or to provide care to designated family members.

FASHRM. Fellow of the American Society for Healthcare Risk Management.

Fatigue factors. Manifestations of a person's physical or mental fatigue that may have contributed to an adverse event or outcome.

Fault tree analysis. A total quality management technique in which a complex process is broken down into a series of simpler steps and then particular areas of vulnerability for system breakdown are identified in an effort to anticipate and thereby avoid problems.

FDA. Food and Drug Administration.

Federal Emergency Management Agency (FEMA). An independent response organization that reports directly to the president of the United States.

Federal Rules of Civil Procedure. Rules of practice and procedure and rules of evidence for cases in the U. S. district courts and courts of appeal.

Fee for service. A reimbursement mechanism that pays providers for each service or procedure they perform; opposite of *capitation.*

FEMA. Federal Emergency Management Agency.

FERPA. Family Educational Rights and Privacy Act.

FFP. Fitness for purpose, measures that record how well the process is satisfying stakeholders' interests, requirements, and desires. They define effectiveness measures.

Fiduciary duty. A duty to act for someone else's benefit while subordinating one's personal interests to those of the other person. It is the highest standard of duty implied by law (as in trustee and guardianship relationships).

Fiduciary liability. Liability of trustees, employers, fiduciaries, professional administrators, and the plan itself with respect to errors and omissions in the administration of employee benefit programs as imposed by ERISA.

Financial guarantees. A form of financial security posted by the applicant to ensure timely and proper completion of a project, warranty materials, workmanship of improvements, and design. Financial guarantees include assignments of funds, cash deposits, surety bonds, or other financial securities.

FIRESCOPE. Firefighting Resources of California Organized for Potential Emergencies, an interagency workgroup that developed the Incident Command System after several large wildfires in the early 1970s demonstrated the need for interagency cooperation.

First-dollar coverage. Commercial insurance providing protection against the entire loss covered by the policy, without requiring the insured to pay a deductible.

First-party coverage. Insurance that provides coverage for the insured's own property and person so that the insured will be restored to the financial position that existed before the loss.

Float staff. Hospital staff, generally assigned to a specific patient care unit or not, made available to work on other units as required to yield appropriate staffing levels for a given patient volume and acuity.

FLV. Full liability value.

FMEA. Failure mode and effects analysis.

FMLA. Family Medical Leave Act.

FOIA. Freedom of Information Act.

Force majeure. Occurrences or situations over which one has no control, exempted from coverage in certain contracts. Clauses governing force majeure often declare the contracts, or specific provisions thereof, inapplicable in the event of natural disasters, such as earthquakes or hurricanes and sometimes other crises, such as war, riot, and civil commotion.

Forcing function. A technological design feature that forces the user to conform to a certain process, usually for a safety reason (for example, a car is designed not to permit ignition if the gearshift is in reverse).

Forensic examination. The receiving, processing, documenting, analyzing, evaluating, and handling of evidence and work product for use in civil and criminal proceedings.

Formulary. A list of prescription medications that may be dispensed by participating pharmacies without health plan authorization. The formulary is based on effectiveness of the various drugs, as well as their cost. The physician is requested or required to use only formulary drugs unless there is a valid medical reason to use a nonformulary drug. Formularies may be open or closed. Closed formularies are restricted by the number and type of drugs included in the list.

Formulary system. A planned restriction on the inventory of medications stocked in a pharmacy, in order to limit the choice to essential drugs and promote safety by virtue of increasing staff familiarity with a more limited range of stocked medications.

For-profit hospital. A hospital operated for the purpose of making a profit for its owners. The initial source of funding is typically through the sale of stock, and profits are paid to stockholders in the form of dividends. Also referred to as a "proprietary hospital" or an "investor-owned hospital."

Forum non conveniens. A forum that is not convenient for the parties for some reason. Such a forum will normally have jurisdiction over the matter, and the venue of the action is appropriate, but hearing and deciding the matter there will work a hardship on the parties or the witnesses. Determining that a particular forum is not convenient is an exercise of the court's discretion.

FP. For profit.

FPO. Facility privacy official.

Fraud. Making false statements or representations of material facts in order to obtain some benefit or payment for which no entitlement would otherwise exist.

Fraud and abuse. Fraud is an intentional misrepresentation, deception, or act of deceit for the purpose of receiving greater reimbursement. Abuse is reckless disregard or conduct that goes against and is inconsistent with acceptable business, medical practices, or both, resulting in greater reimbursement. Terms are generally used together to refer to breach of federal statutes and regulations regarding inappropriate billing, kickbacks, referrals, related to the federal or state Medicare and Medicaid programs.

Free flow. The unrestricted flow of a fluid through an IV line.

Freestanding ambulatory surgery center. A medical facility that provides surgical treatment on an outpatient basis only.

Frequency. The likelihood (probability) that a loss will occur; refers to a number of times a loss occurs.

FTC. Federal Trade Commission.

FTE. Full-time equivalent.

Full liability value. An estimate of the jury award if the plaintiff prevails on all issues.

G

Gag rule. A provision found in some managed care contracts with physicians prohibiting the physicians from discussing treatment alternatives, such as experimental procedures, with managed care plan patients when such treatments are not covered by the plan.

GAO. Government Accountability Office.

Garage liability policy. Insurance that covers losses resulting from premises exposure of parking areas but excludes property in the care, custody, and control of the insured.

Gatekeeper. A primary care provider (PCP) who manages various components of a member's medical treatment, including all referrals for specialty care, ancillary services, durable medical equipment, and hospital services. The gatekeeper model is a popular cost-control component of many managed care plans because it requires a subscriber first to see the PCP and receive the PCP's approval before going to a specialist about a given medical condition (except for emergencies).

General liability. A business organization's liability for claims for bodily injury and property damage arising out of premises, operations, products, and completed operations; advertising and personal injury liability.

General liability insurance. A standard insurance policy issued to business organizations to protect them against liability claims for bodily injury and property damage arising out of premises, operations, products, and completed operations; advertising and personal injury liability.

GI. Gastrointestinal.

GL. General liability.

GMP. Good manufacturing practice.

Government Accountability Office. An independent, nonpartisan agency that works for Congress. Often called the "congressional watchdog," the GAO investigates how the federal government spends taxpayer dollars.

GP. General practitioner.

GU. Genitourinary.

Guarantee fund. A fund managed and controlled by the state to help pay the claims of financially impaired insurance companies. State laws specify the lines of insurance covered by these funds and the dollar limits payable. Coverage is usually for individual policyholders and their beneficiaries and not for values held in unallocated group contracts. Most states also restrict insurance agents and companies from advertising the funds' availability.

H

Hard insurance market. Insurance market conditions characterized by rising premiums and shrinking availability of coverage. Hard markets typically prompt insureds to accept larger deductibles or self-insured retentions, reduce coverage limits, or seek risk financing alternatives.

Hazard. A condition that increases the possibility of loss.

Hazard analysis. Collecting and evaluating information on hazards associated with a selected process so as to develop a list of hazards that are reasonably likely to cause injury or illness if not effectively controlled.

Hazard communication standard. To ensure chemical safety in the workplace, OSHA requires that standards are developed and information is disseminated about the identities and hazards of chemicals. Also known as the "employee right-to-know rule."

Hazardous condition. Any circumstance (beyond the disease or condition for which the patient is being treated) that significantly increases the likelihood of a serious adverse outcome.

Hazardous Waste Operations and Emergency Response standard. Applies to any person exposed or potentially exposed to hazardous substances, including hazardous waste, and who is engaged in one of five operations covered by HAZWOPER; certified by a qualified trainer.

HAZWOPER. Hazardous Waste Operations and Emergency Response.

HCCA. Health Care Compliance Association.

HCF. Health care facility.

HCFA. Health Care Financing Administration; currently known as the Centers for Medicare and Medicaid Services.

HCO. Health care organization.

HCQIA. Health Care Quality Improvement Act.

Health Care Compliance Association. The professional society for health care corporate com pliance officers.

Healthcare Facilities Accreditation Program. The AOA's Healthcare Facilities Accreditation Program (HFAP) has been providing medical facilities with an objective review of their services since 1945. The program is recognized nationally by the federal government, state governments, insurance carriers, and managed care organizations.

Healthcare Integrity and Protection Data Bank (HIPDB) (10). A flagging system that may serve to alert users that a comprehensive review of a practitioner's, provider's, or supplier's past actions may be prudent. The HIPDB is intended to augment, not replace, traditional forms of review and investigation, serving as an important supplement to a careful review of a practitioner's, provider's, or supplier's past actions. The secretary of the DHHS, acting through the OIG, was directed by the Health Insurance Portability and Accountability Act of 1996 to create HIPDB to combat fraud and abuse in health insurance and health care delivery. Health care organization. Entity that provides, coordinates, or ensures health and medical services for people.

Health Care Quality Improvement Act. Federal law (42 USC 11101et seq.) that requires reports to the National Practitioner Data Bank and protects the confidentiality of peer review materials.

Health Insurance Portability and Accountability Act. Amendments to ERISA (42 USC 201 et seq.) addressing a variety of health care–related issues, including fraud and abuse and the portability of group health insurance benefits, and mandating specific patient privacy protections.

Health maintenance organization. A health care payment and delivery system involving networks of doctors and hospitals. Members must receive all their care from providers within the network. In a "staff model HMO," physicians are on the staff of the HMO and are usually paid a salary. In a "group model HMO," the HMO rents the services of the physicians in a separate group practice and pays the group a per-patient rate. In a "network model HMO," the HMO contracts with two or more independent physician group practices to provide services and pays a fixed monthly fee per patient.

Hearing. A legal proceeding where an issue of law or fact is tried and evidence is presented to help determine the issue.

Hearsay. An out-of-court statement made by a person who is not a party to the action and is not available to testify that is offered to prove the truth of the matter asserted. Hearsay is normally not admissible as evidence.

HEDIS. Health Plan Employer Data and Information Set. A standard data reporting system developed in 1991 to measure the quality and performance of health plans. A main goal of HEDIS is to standardize health plan performance measures for consumers and payers. HEDIS concentrates on four aspects of health care: (1) quality, (2) access and patient satisfaction, (3) membership and utilization, and (4) finance. Within each focus area is a specific set of HEDIS data measures (for example, number of immunizations for pediatric enrollees). The National Committee for Quality Assurance (NCQA) is responsible for coordinating HEDIS and making changes each year.

HEICS. Hospital Emergency Incident Command System.

HFAP. Healthcare Facilities Accreditation Program.

HFE. Human factors engineering.

HFMA. Healthcare Financial Management Association.

Hgb. Hemoglobin.

HHC. Home health care organization.

HHS. The U.S. Department of Health and Human Services.

HIAA. Health Insurance Association of America.

Hierarchy effect (steep hierarchy). The effect that a perceived "pecking order" or relative differences in stature or status have on a lower person's level of willingness to question a higher person's actions or decisions.

High-alert medications. Medications that have the highest risk of causing injury when misused.

High-low agreement. An agreement made between the plaintiff and defendant whereby the plaintiff will be entitled to at least the low amount but no more than the high amount, and the defendant will be obligated to pay at least the low amount but no more than the high amount. If the jury returns a verdict between the low and high amounts, the case will settle for the amount of the verdict. A high-low agreement settles the case, and no appeal is permitted.

High-reliability organizations. Organizations with systems in place that are exceptionally consistent in accomplishing their goals and avoiding potentially catastrophic errors.

High-risk patients. Patients who are more susceptible to illness, injury, or disease or an exacerbation of an existing condition.

HIM. Health information management.

HIMSS. Health Information Management Systems Society.

Hindsight bias. The tendency for a reviewer to focus most heavily on facts learned after an event or only the most obvious contributing factors, thereby failing to consider other, more subtle contributing factors.

HIPAA. Health Insurance Portability and Accountability Act.

HIPDB. Health Integrity and Protection Data Bank.

HIV. Human immunodeficiency virus.

HMO. Health maintenance organization.

Hold-harmless agreement. A contractual clause providing that one party agrees not to pursue a tort claim for vicarious liability against the other. Hold-harmless provisions are usually accompanied by indemnification provisions and are usually mutual.

Home health care. Health care services are provided in a patient's home instead of a hospital or other institutional setting; services provided may include nursing care, social services, and physical, speech, or occupational therapy.

Hospice. An organization that provides medical care and support services (such as pain and symptom management, counseling, and bereavement services) to terminally ill patients and their families; may be a freestanding facility, a unit of a hospital or other institution, or a separate program of a hospital, agency, or institution.

Hospital-acquired infection. An infection acquired in a hospital. Also known as a *Nosocomial infection.*

Hospital Emergency Incident Command System. A flexible, customizable plan developed to assist in the operation of a medical facility in time of crisis. HEICS was developed in 1991 by the Orange County Emergency Medical Services from the Incident Command System (ICS), a standard operating procedure for use by fire departments throughout the United States.

Hospitalist. A physician whose practice is caring for patients while in the hospital. A primary care physician (PCP) turns patients over to a hospitalist, who becomes the physician of record and provides and directs the care of the patient while the patient is hospitalized and returns the patient to the PCP at the time of hospital discharge.

HPL. Hospital professional liability (insurance).

HR. Human resources (department).

HRSA. Health Resources and Services Administration.

Human factors. The interrelationship between humans, the tools they use, and the environment in which they live and work.

Human factors engineering. The discipline of applying what is known about human capabilities and limitations to the design of products, processes, systems, and work environments.

HVAC. Heating, ventilation, and air conditioning (system).

I

Iatrogenic. Adverse effects or complications caused by medical treatment or advice.

IBNR. Incurred but not reported.

IC. Incident commander.

ICD-9-CM. The International Classification of Diseases, Ninth Revision, Clinical Modification (ICD-9-CM), is based on the World Health Organization's Ninth Revision, International Classification of Diseases (ICD-9). ICD-9-CM is the official system of assigning codes to diagnoses and procedures associated with hospital utilization in the United States.

ICF/MR. Intermediate care facility for the mentally retarded.

ICS. Incident Command System.

ICU. Intensive care unit.

ICUSRS. Intensive Care Unit Safety Reporting System.

ID. Identification.

IDS. Integrated delivery system.

IHI. Institute for Healthcare Improvement.

IHO. Integrated health organization.

IIA. Insurance Institute of America.

IM. Information management.

IM. Intramuscular.

IME. Independent medical examination.

Immediate jeopardy. A situation in which the provider's noncompliance with one or more requirements of participation has caused or is likely to cause serious injury, harm, impairment, or death to a patient or resident.

Immigration Reform and Control Act. Federal legislation (8 USC 1324 et seq) requiring employers to verify the immigration status of prospective employees during the hiring process.

Impaired professional. A professional who is unable to practice his or her profession with reasonable skill and safety to patients because of mental or physical illness, including deterioration through the aging process, loss of motor skills, or excessive use or abuse of drugs or alcohol.

Implementation. Put into effect, carry out.

Improperly performed procedure or treatment. An appropriate procedure or treatment that is done incorrectly. Not to be confused with choosing the wrong procedure or treatment.

Inappropriate procedure or treatment. An incorrect procedure or treatment, usually as a result of poor medical judgment, skills, or techniques. Not to be confused with performing the correct procedure incorrectly.

Incident. Any occurrence not consistent with the routine operations of the facility or routine care of a particular patient; an unexpected event; an experience that leaves a patient, visitor, or other person feeling, rightly or wrongly, that he or she has been mistreated, neglected, or injured in some way.

Incident commander (IC). The individual responsible for the overall management of the response under HEICS.

Incident command system (ICS). A standardized, on-scene, all hazard incident management concept.

Incident report. The documentation of an accident or an occurrence that is not consistent with normal operating routine or expected outcomes.

Incident reporting. The filing of an incident report in an electronic, written, or verbal format.

Incident reporting system. Part of an early warning system intended to identify risk situations or adverse events in a timely manner to trigger prompt investigation from a claims management perspective as well as corrective action to prevent similar future events.

Incurred but not reported. Insurance and actuarial term applied to claims that have occurred but for which notification has not yet been received.

Indemnification. A contractual agreement in which one party agrees to accept the tort liability and legal defense of another. Indemnification provisions are usually accompanied by hold-harmless provisions and are usually mutual.

Indemnification provision. A clause in a contract or agreement that identifies the terms of indemnification.

Indemnify. To secure against loss, damage, or expenses that may occur in the future which another may suffer.

Indemnity. An assurance or contract by one party to compensate for the damage caused by another; shifting an economic loss to the person responsible for the loss; the right that the person suffering the loss or damage is entitled to a claim; compensation given to make a person whole from a loss already received; a settlement or award made directly to a plaintiff as a result of the claims resolution process.

Independent medical examination. Medical examination of a claimant by a practitioner other than the claimant's treating practitioner at the request of a defendant to verify the claimant's diagnosis and prognosis.

Independent practice association. A group of independent physicians who have formed an- association as a separate legal entity for contracting purposes. IPA physician providers retain their individual practices, work in separate offices, continue to see their non–managed care patients, and have the option to contract directly with managed care plans. A key advantage of the IPA arrangement is that it helps its members achieve some of the negotiating leverage of a large physician group practice with some degree of flexibility for each provider. Also referred to as an "independent physician association."

Indicator. In quality improvement, a quantifiable objective standard against which performance is measured. Designed to be indicative of whether other care processes are also meeting established standards.

Information technology. The study, design, development, implementation, support, or management of a computer-based information system, including software applications and computer hardware.

Informed consent. The legal doctrine that patients generally have a right to be informed regarding proposed medical and surgical treatments, including anticipated benefits, risks, and alternatives, and to accept or reject such proposed treatments.

Injunction. A court order prohibiting someone from doing some specified act or commanding someone to undo some wrong or injury.

INR. International normalized ratio.

Insolvent. Lacking the available financial resources to pay covered claims.

Inspection. A process in which an inspector (employed by an agency) comes onto the premises of an employer to interview employees, review documents, observe practices and conditions, take measurements or samples, and take photographs.

Institute for Safe Medication Practices (ISMP). The nation's only 501c (3) nonprofit organization devoted entirely to medication error prevention and safe medication use.

Institute of Medicine. A division of the National Academy of Sciences, a private nonprofit organization of scholars dedicated to research and publications related to engineering and the sciences. Noted for its 1999 publication *To Err Is Human: Building a Safer Health System*, which focused on medical errors.

Institutional review board. The body within a health care organization charged with establishing protocols for and overseeing clinical research trials and human experimentation.

Insurance. A contract to have internal losses paid for with funds external to the organization. A contractual relationship established when one party (the insurer), for consideration (the premium), agrees to reimburse another party (the insured) for loss to a specified subject (the risk) caused by designated contingencies (hazards or perils).

Insurance limits The total amount of losses to be paid expressed either on a per occurrence basis or on an aggregate basis, during an underwriting period. Limits vary by type of coverage, insurers, and insureds. Also referred to as "policy limits."

Insurance schedule. A document or graphic showing all of the insurance coverage in place for a given insured, usually including the names of insurers, policy limits, deductibles and retentions, policy numbers, and inception and expiration dates.

Insured versus insured exclusion. A provision common in insurance policies excluding coverage for claims in which one insured makes a claim against another.

Integrated care. A comprehensive spectrum of health services, from prevention through long-term care, provided via a single administrative entity and coordinated by a primary care "gatekeeper."

Integrated delivery system. A health care system made up of various types of providers, including hospitals, ambulatory care centers, surgery centers, home health agencies, and physician practices, and frequently a managed care organization, such as an HMO or a preferred provider organization (PPO).

Integrated health organization. An organization that requires a separate legal entity, such as a parent organization, with at least two subsidiaries, such as a hospital and a management services organization, and often a third subsidiary such as an educational or research foundation.

Intentional acts. Purposeful actions by an insured that result in harm or loss, ordinarily excluded from coverage in most insurance contracts.

Interrogatories. A written set of questions that is served on the other party in litigation. All questions must be answered under oath and returned to the party that served them.

Intravenous. In or through the veins.

Investigation. Detailed and careful examination to determine the facts surrounding an event, occurrence, or situation. The work of performing a thorough and systematic inquiry.

IOM. Institute of Medicine.

IP. Internet protocol.

IPA. Independent practice association.

IPPS. Inpatient Prospective Payment System.

IRB. Institutional review board.

IRMI. International Risk Management Institute.

IRS. Internal Revenue Service.

ISMP. Institute for Safe Medication Practices.

ISO. International Organization for Standardization.

IT. Information technology.

IV. Intravenously; also, an apparatus used for intravenous administration of a fluid.

IVP. Intravenous pyelogram (urogram).

J

JCR. Joint Commission Resources.

JD. Juris doctor (doctor of law).

Joint and several liability. Liability in which each liable party is individually responsible for the entire obligation. Under joint and several liability, a plaintiff may choose to seek full damages from all, some, or any one of the parties alleged to have committed the injury. In most cases, a defendant who pays damages may seek reimbursement from nonpaying parties.

The Joint Commission. A voluntary nonprofit accreditation body that sets standards for hospitals and other health care organizations and conducts education programs and a survey process to assess-organizational compliance. Formerly known as the Joint Commission on Accreditation of Healthcare Organizations (JCAHO).

Joint Commission Resources. A not-for-profit affiliate of The Joint Commission that provides quality and safety innovations to health care organizations worldwide.

Joint defense. A defense of all defendants (for example, physician and hospital) in an integrated response.

Joint venture. An organization formed by two or more entities for a single purpose or undertaking that makes each member liable for all the organization's debts.

JUA. Joint underwriting association: Nonprofit risk-pooling associations established by state legislatures in response to availability crises concerning certain kinds of insurance coverage.

Judgment. The official decision of a court that determines the relative legal rights and obligations of parties to a legal proceeding.

Jurisdiction. The power of a court or other tribunal to hear and decide a legal matter. Also, the physical location in which a particular court is permitted to hear and decide cases.

Jury. A group of persons impaneled to hear a legal matter and to render a verdict. The jury typically finds the facts of the matter, and the court applies the law to the facts. The number of jurors necessary to form a jury varies by jurisdiction and sometimes by type of case.

Justice. One of the three basic ethical concepts of the Belmont Report that refers to the fair distribution of the benefits and burdens of research.

L

LAE. Loss adjustment expenses.

LAN. Local area network.

Latent error. Errors removed from the direct control of the operator that include poor design, incorrect installation, faulty maintenance, bad management decisions, inadequate training, and poorly structured organizations whose effects typically lie dormant in the system for lengthy periods. Also called the *Blunt end.*

Latent failure. Weakness in an organization whose effects are usually delayed. Also called *Blunt end or Latent error.*

Law courts. Courts that have jurisdiction to hear most civil lawsuits (personal injury, breach of contract, and so on). For almost all practical purposes, law courts have been merged with courts of equity, but differences in actions based in law versus actions based in equity still remain.

LCF. Loss conversation factor: A factor that provides a charge to cover unallocated claims and the cost of an insurer's claim services. Used in formulas for retrospectively rated insurance programs.

LCL. Lower control limit.

LDF. Loss development factor, a common method of adjusting losses for the growth in claims and IBNR losses.

Leapfrog Group. A private business consortium for health care interests. A voluntary, member-supported program launched in 2000 aimed at mobilizing employer purchasing power to alert America's health industry that big leaps in health care safety, quality, and customer value will be recognized and rewarded.

Legal health record. Documentation of the health care services provided to an individual in any aspect of health care delivery by health care provider organizations. The legal health record is individually identifiable data, in any medium, collected and directly used in or documenting health care or health status. The term applies to records of care in any health-related setting used by health care professionals while providing patient care services, reviewing patient data, or documenting observations, actions, or instructions.

Legally cognizable injury. An injury for which the law can provide redress.

Legibility. Understandable or readable based on appearance.

Length of stay. The period of hospitalization, measured in days billed; determined by discharge days divided by discharges.

LEP. Limited English proficiency.

LEPC. Local emergency planning council.

Letter of intent. Formal notice to an organization that another organization is seeking to acquire or merge with it, setting due diligence in motion.

Libel. Defamatory language expressed in print, writing, pictures, or symbols intended to injure another's reputation, business. or means of livelihood.

Life Safety Code. A code promulgated by the National Fire Protection Association (NFPA) and that addresses construction, protection, and occupancy features necessary to minimize danger to life from the effects of fire, including smoke, heat, and toxic gases created during a fire.

Limited liability company (LLC). A company formed by one or more persons or entities to carry out a business purpose. The LLC shields its owners (members) from liability but enjoys certain tax advantages not available to corporations.

Limits (policy limits). In insurance, the maximum the insurer will pay, typically expressed either per occurrence or as an annual aggregate (the maximum the insurer will pay during the year for all claims covered under the policy).

Living will. Document generated by a person for the purpose of providing guidance about health care and medical decisions to be provided if the person is unable to articulate those decisions. A living will does not designate another to speak in the patient's stead; it only offers written documentation of the person's wishes.

LLC. Limited liability company.

Long tail. Lines of insurance coverage for which there is frequently an extended period between the time an incident giving rise to a claim occurs and the time the claim is reported. Medical professional liability is generally considered long-tail insurance business.

Long-term care A continuum of maintenance, custodial, and health services to the chronically ill, disabled, or mentally handicapped.

LOS. Length of stay.

Loss. The reduction in the value of an asset.

Loss adjustment expense. All costs and expenses allocable to a specific claim that are incurred in the investigation, appraisal, adjustment, settlement, litigation, defense, or appeal of a specific claim, including court costs, costs of bonds, and postjudgment interest.

Loss control. Any of a number of programs and initiatives undertaken to prevent losses from occurring (loss prevention) or to decrease the severity of losses that do occur (loss reduction), including education and training, policy and procedure development, equipment maintenance, use of personal protective equipment, and installation of sprinkler systems.

Loss frequency. A measure of how many times a particular loss occurs or can be expected to occur in a given period of time.

Loss of consortium. Claim for damages relating to the loss of companionship, advice, and sexual relationship with an injured party, typically filed by the injured party's spouse.

Loss prevention. Reducing an organization's losses by lowering their frequency of occurrence.

Loss reduction. Actions taken to decrease the severity of a loss.

Loss reserve. An estimate of the value of a claim or group of claims not yet paid.

Loss run. A listing, usually generated by computer, of claims brought against an insured for a specific line of insurance coverage; typically includes the name of the claimant, the date of occurrence, the date the claim was made, the status of claim (open or closed; suit, claim, or occurrence), amounts paid and reserved for both indemnity and loss adjustment expenses, and a description of the facts giving rise to the claim.

Loss severity. A measure of the size of an actual or expected loss; how much a loss will cost.

Lower control limit (LCL). A formula that will calculate a lowermost limit for samples to evaluate to. Used in charts of statistical process control.

LSC. Life Safety Code.

LPN. Licensed practical nurse.

LPT. Licensed physical therapist.

LTC. Long-term care.

LTD. Long-term disability.

LVN. Licensed vocational nurse.

M

M&A&D. Mergers, acquisitions, and divestitures.

M&M. Morbidity and mortality.

MA. Medical assistant.

Magnetic resonance imaging. Technology that uses radio and magnetic waves to create images of body tissue and monitor body chemistry.

Malfeasance. The wrongful or unjust doing of an act that the doer had no right to perform or had stipulated by contract not to do.

Malpractice. Improper professional actions or the failure to exercise proper professional skills by a professional adviser, such as a physician, dentist, or health care entity. Also, professional misconduct, improper discharge of professional duties, or failure to meet the standards of care of a professional, resulting in harm to another person.

Mammography Quality Standards Act. A law focused primarily on issues related to improving the diagnostic and technical standards of mammography. The act also calls for the proper reporting of study results to referring physicians and their patients.

Managed care. The integration of health care delivery and financing that includes arrangements with providers to supply health care services to members, criteria for the selection of health care providers, significant financial incentives for members to use providers in the plan, and formal programs to monitor the amount of care and quality of services.

Managed care organization. Any of a number of organizations, such as HMOs and PPOs, that arrange for the provision of and payment for health care services with an eye toward reducing costs through managing access to specific providers.

Managed care E&O liability. Insurance that covers allegations for wrongful acts in the design and administration of a managed care plan.

Management services organization. An organization that provides management services to medical practices, large physician groups, and hospitals.

Mandatory settlement conference. A court-ordered meeting of the plaintiff and defendant held under the judge's direction with the goal of resolving a claim. This meeting is not voluntary, and the opposing parties are required to participate.

Manufacturers and User Facility Device Experience database. A database of voluntary, user facility, distributor, and manufacturer reports of adverse events related to medical devices.

MAR. Medication administration record.

MAUDE. Manufacturers and User Facility Device Experience Database.

Maximum medical improvement (MMI). In workers' compensation, the point at which the injured employee has recovered to the maximum extent medically expected (also called "permanent and stationary" or P& S improvement). When an employee reaches MMI, any residual disability, pain, or injury is expected to be permanent.

MBWA. Management by walking around.

MCO. Managed care organization.

MD. Medical doctor.

MDR. Medical device reporting.

MedPAC. Medicare Payment Advisory Commission.

Mediation. Intervention between parties in conflict to promote reconciliation, settlement, or compromise.

Medicaid. A federal public assistance program enacted into law in 1966 under Title XIX of the Social Security Act, to provide medical benefits to eligible low-income persons needing health care regardless of age. The program is administered and operated by the states, which receive federal matching funds to cover the costs of the program. States are required to include certain minimal services as mandated by the federal government but may include any additional services at their own expense.

Medical battery. Traditionally, a battery that occurs during the administration of medical care and procedures. May also include actions against medical care providers for prolonging the lives of patients who had previously requested that no "heroic measures" be undertaken when faced with a medical emergency.

Medical Injury Compensation Reform Act (MICRA). Legislation passed in California in 1975 to curb the high cost of medical professional liability insurance and "runaway" verdicts. Often promoted as the model for state and federal liability reform efforts.

Medical malpractice review panel. A panel consisting of two lawyers, two health care providers, and a circuit court judge that at the request of any party passes nonbinding judgments on claims of alleged medical malpractice. The panel may conclude that there was negligence, no negligence, or a question of fact that must be decided by a jury.

Medical professional liability. Insurance coverage for losses arising from the rendering or failure to render health care services.

Medical screening exam. A screening examination to determine whether an emergency medical condition exists and to treat and stabilize any emergency condition. A requirement under EMTALA for all hospitals.

Medical services. The furnishing of professional health care services, including the provision of food, medications, or appliances; the postmortem handling of bodies; or service as a member of a formal accreditation review board.

Medical technology. Techniques, drugs, equipment, and procedures used by health care professionals in delivering medical care to individuals and the systems whereby such care is delivered.

Medicare. A federally administered health insurance program for persons aged sixty-five and older and certain disabled people under that age. Created in 1965 under Title XVIII of the Social Security Act, Medicare covers the cost of hospitalization, medical care, and some related services for eligible persons without regard to income. Medicare has two parts. Medicare Part A, the Hospital Insurance Program, is compulsory and covers inpatient hospitalization costs. Medicare Part B, the Supplementary Medical Insurance Program, is voluntary and covers medically necessary physicians' services, outpatient hospital services, and a number of other medical services and supplies not covered by Part A. Part A is funded by a mandatory payroll tax. Part B is supported by premiums paid by enrollees.

Medicare Modernization Act. Short name for the Medicare Prescription Drug Improvement and Modernization Act of 2003.

Medication administration record. The record of all medications ordered and when each was administered, maintained by the nursing staff.

Medication error. Any preventable event that may cause or lead to inappropriate medication use or patient harm while the medication is in the control of the healthcare professional, patient, or consumer.

Medical Error Reporting System–Transfusion Medicine (MERS-TM). Web-based medical event reporting system that documents, and allows for analysis of transfusion medicine-related events.

MedWatch. The FDA's information and adverse event reporting program.

MER. Medication Errors Reporting (program).

Merger. The union of two or more organizations by the transfer of all assets to one organization that continues to exist while the others are dissolved.

MERS-TM. Medical Event Reporting System-Transfusion Medicine,

Metric. Standard used to measure and assess performance or a process.

MGMA. Medical Group Management Association: The nation's principal voice for the medical group practice profession.

MHA. Master of health administration; master of hospital administration.

MHSA. Master of health services administration.

MI. Mental institution; mitral insufficiency; myocardial infarction.

MICRA. Medical Injury Compensation Reform Act.

Microsystem. Organizational unit built around the definition of repeatable core service competencies. Elements of a microsystem include (1) a core team of health care professionals, (2) a defined population of patients, (3) carefully designed work processes, and 4) an environment capable of linking information on all aspects of work and patient or population outcomes to support ongoing evaluation of performance.

Misrepresentation. Any untrue or intentionally deceptive statement presented as fact.

MMA. Medicare Modernization Act (official title: Medicare Prescription Drug Improvement and Modernization Act of 2003).

MOB. Medical office building.

Morbidity. Associated negative consequences relating to a clinical treatment or procedure; a complication. Also, the incidence and severity of illness and accidents in a well-defined class of individuals.

Mortality. Death rate; incidence of death in a well-defined class of individuals.

Motion. A filing with a court or other tribunal that requests that the court perform some function.

Motion for judgment notwithstanding the verdict. A filing that seeks to have a jury verdict set aside. In a trial process, the court normally enters judgment on a jury's verdict and thus gives effect to the verdict. This motion seeks to have the jury verdict set aside and judgment entered by the court that is not in accord with the verdict. Usually granted for the appearance of bias, prejudice, or possible jury misconduct.

Motion for new trial. A filing that seeks to invalidate the original trial and declare that the matter must be tried again. Usually granted when the verdict is contrary to the manifest weight of the evidence or when there is scant evidence to support the jury's verdict.

Motion for summary judgment. A filing that seeks to have a lawsuit decided because there are no genuine issues of material fact for the jury to decide.

Motion in limine. A filing to preclude the admission of certain facts, testimony, items, or proofs at trial. May be granted on the grounds that the evidence is not relevant, is redundant or duplicative of other evidence, will unduly arouse or inflame the jury, and so on.

Motion to dismiss. A filing that seeks to have a lawsuit rejected because the complaint or petition fails to state a cause of action on which relief may be granted. Such a filing often stays the period in which an answer must be filed.

Motion to strike. A filing to eliminate a cause of action in the complaint or petition or to preclude the defendant from mounting a defense based on a certain theory.

MPA. Master of public administration.

MPH. Master of public health.

MQSA. Mammography Quality Standards Act of 1992.

MQSRA. Mammography Quality Standards Reauthorization Acts of 1998 and 2004.

MRI. Magnetic resonance imaging.

MSE. Medical screening examination.

MSN. Master of science in nursing.

MSO. Management service organization.

MSW. Master of social work.

MT. Medical technologist.

Multihospital system. Two or more hospitals owned, leased, contract-managed, or sponsored by a central organization; they can be either not for profit or investor-owned.

Munchausen syndrome by proxy. A factitious disorder in which a person, usually a parent, exaggerates or feigns illness in a child or deliberately causes or exacerbates actual medical problems the patient is experiencing.

MVR. Motor vehicle records.

N

Named peril coverage. Insurance that covers only losses that fall under specific perils defined in the policy.

NASA. National Aeronautics and Space Administration.

National Center for Complementary and Alternative Medicine. An agency of the National Institutes of Health developed to study and provide information about complementary and alternative medicine treatments and therapies.

National Committee for Quality Assurance. A private nonprofit accrediting body for managed care organizations.

National Institute of Occupational Safety and Health. A research and education agency within the Department of Health and Human Services that has no enforcement powers.

National Labor Relations Act. The main body of law governing collective bargaining. It explicitly grants employees the right to bargain collectively and to join trade unions. Originally enacted by Congress in 1935 under its power to regulate interstate commerce.

National Organ Transplant Act. Legislation passed by the Congress in 1984 to address the nation's critical organ donation shortage and improve the organ placement and matching process. The act established the Organ Procurement and Transplantation Network (OPTN) to maintain a national registry for organ matching.

National Patient Safety Goals. Goals developed by The Joint Commission to promote specific improvements in patient safety. They highlight problematic areas in health care and describe evidence and expert-based consensus to solutions to these problems and are updated yearly.

National Practitioner Data Bank. A data bank maintained by the federal government containing reports on certain individual practitioners. A report must be made by any entity that pays money on behalf of a practitioner to settle a legal claim asserted against the practitioner. Reports must also be made by any hospital that restricts, suspends, or terminates a practitioner's privileges to examine or treat patients at the hospital.

NB. Newborn.

NBC emergencies. Disaster scenarios involving nuclear, bioterrorism, or chemical warfare agents.

NCCH. National Commission on Correctional Health Care.

NCC-MERP. National Coordinating Council for Medication Error Reporting and Prevention.

NCI. National Cancer Institute.

NCQA. National Committee for Quality Assurance.

NCVIA. National Childhood Vaccine Injury Act (42 USC 300); established the National Vaccine Injury Compensation Program.

NDS. National Disaster Medical System.

Near miss. Any variation in a procedure that did not affect the outcome but might have produced a serious adverse outcome. Also called a "good catch."

Neglect. Failure to provide goods and services necessary to avoid physical harm, mental anguish, or mental illness.

Negligence. A legal conclusion that is reached when it has been determined that (1) the defendant owed a duty of care to the plaintiff; (2) the defendant breached the duty of care; (3) the plaintiff was injured as a result of the breach of the duty of care; and (4) legally cognizable damages resulted from the injury. Less formally, carelessness: a failure to act as an ordinary prudent person would or action contrary to that of a reasonable party or the failure to use such care as a reasonably prudent and careful person would under similar circumstances.

Negligence per se. A legal doctrine whereby an act is considered negligent because it violates a statute or regulation.

Neonatal. Referring to the first twenty-eight days of an infant's life. The infant is referred to as a newborn during this period.

NESHAP. National Emission Standard for Hazardous Air Pollutants.

Network. A self-contained, fully integrated system of providers.

Never events. A list developed by the National Quality Forum of twenty-eight adverse events that are serious, largely preventable, and of concern to both the public and health care providers for the purpose of public accountability.

NF. Nursing facility.

NFP. Not for profit.

NFPA. National Fire Protection Agency.

NICU. Neonatal intensive care unit.

NIH. National Institutes of Health.

NIMH. National Institute of Mental Health.

NIOSH. National Institute of Occupational Safety and Health.

NLRA. National Labor Relations Act.

NLRB. National Labor Relations Board.

NMHPA. Newborns' and Mothers' Health Protection Act.

No-fault system. A system of compensation for injured parties that is not based on the fault or negligence of the party causing the injury. Examples include the workers' compensation system and the personal injury protection automobile insurance mandated or available in some jurisdictions.

Nomenclature. A naming classification system, such as the FDA's system for choosing new medication names.

Nonadmitted insurer. An insurance company that is exempt from rigorous state regulations. Because such companies do not file forms or rates and are not regulated by the state, they also do not participate in the state guaranty funds that protect insureds in case of insurance company failure.

Noneconomic damages (general damages). Damages asserted by or awarded to a claimant for pain and suffering, loss of consortium, loss of enjoyment of life, and so on, for which no objective dollar value exists. The term technically includes punitive damages, but those are typically discussed separately.

Noninsurance transfer. The transfer of the financial obligations to pay for defense, expenses, verdicts, awards, and settlements. It reduces the transferor's loss exposure by contractually shifting legal responsibility for a loss through leases, contracts, and agreements (known as "exculpatory clauses").

Nonmaleficence. Avoiding harm.

Nonsuit. A privilege granted to plaintiffs in Virginia that allows them to withdraw a civil lawsuit at any time before decision, without prejudice to their right or ability to bring it one more time.

NORA. National Occupational Research Agenda.

Nose coverage. Prior acts coverage.

Nosocomial infection. An infection acquired in a hospital.

NOTA. National Organ Transplant Act.

Notice of claim. A letter from or on behalf of a claimant that puts a health care provider on notice that a claim of alleged medical negligence is being made and triggers certain rights of the parties to request a medical malpractice review panel.

NPDB. National Practitioner Data Bank.

NPSF. National Patient Safety Foundation.

NPSG. National Patient Safety Goals.

NQF. National Quality Foundation.

NRC. Nuclear Regulatory Commission.

NTSB. National Transportation Safety Board.

Nuclear medicine. The use of radioisotopes to study and treat disease, especially in the diagnostic area.

Nuremberg Code. A ten-point statement delimiting permissible medical experimentation on human subjects. To some extent, the Nuremberg Code has been superceded by the Declaration of Helsinki as a guide for human experimentation.

Nurse practitioner. A licensed nurse who has completed a nurse practitioner program at the master's or certificate level and is trained in providing primary care services. NPs are qualified to conduct expanded health care evaluations and decision making regarding patient care, including diagnosis, treatment, and prescriptions, usually under a physician's supervision. NPs may also be trained in medical specialties, such as pediatrics, geriatrics, or midwifery. Legal regulations in some states prevent NPs from qualifying for direct Medicare and Medicaid reimbursement, writing prescriptions, and admitting patients to hospital. Also known as an "advanced practice nurse" (APN).

O

OASIS. Outcomes and assessment information set.

Oath of Hippocrates. An oath, dating from the fourth century B.C.E. and widely attributed to Hippocrates, that pertains to the ethical practice of medicine. The oath has been revised to reflect modern medical practice.

OBA. Office of Biotechnology Activities.

OBE. Occupied bed equivalent.

OB-GYN. (Specialist in) obstetrics and gynecology.

OBRA. Omnibus Budget Reconciliation Act.

OBS. Office-based surgery.

Obstetrics. The medical specialty concerned with the care of women during pregnancy and childbirth.

Occupational Safety and Health Act. Federal statute (29 USC 651 et seq) that created the Occupational Safety and Health Administration.

Occupational Safety and Health Administration (OSHA). Federal agency charged with responsibility for promulgating standards and enforcement mechanisms governing worker safety for most industries.

Occupational Safety and Health Review Commission. An independent federal agency created to decide contests of citations or penalties resulting from OSHA inspections of American workplaces. The review commission functions as an administrative court with established procedures for conducting hearings, receiving evidence, and rendering decisions by its administrative law judges (ALJs).

Occurrence insurance. Insurance providing coverage for claims that arise during the policy period, regardless of when the claim is reported.

Occurrence screening. A systematic review of medical records and cases (conducted either retrospectively or concurrently) using predetermined screening criteria to identify cases that may warrant closer review—for example, unplanned returns to the ED within seventy-two hours of admission or prior treatment for a similar condition.

OCR. Office of Civil Rights.

OD. Doctor of optometry.

OD. Right eye.

Office for Civil Rights. Promotes and ensures that people have equal access to and opportunity to participate in and receive services from all HHS programs without facing unlawful discrimination and that the privacy of their health information is protected while ensuring access to care.

Office for Human Research Protections. Protects the rights, welfare, and well-being of subjects involved in research conducted or supported by HHS and helps ensure that such research is carried out in accordance with the regulations described at 45 CFR part 46.

Office of Inspector General. Protects the integrity of HHS programs as well as the health and welfare of the beneficiaries of those programs.

Office of National Coordinator for Health Information Technology. Provides counsel to the secretary of HHS and departmental leadership for the development and nationwide implementation of an interoperable health information technology infrastructure.

OHRP. Office for Human Research Protections.

OIG. Office of the Inspector General.

Older Workers' Benefit Protection Act. Legislation (29 USC 621 et seq) amending the Age Discrimination in Employment Act restricting employers from making certain age-based distinctions in employee benefits plans.

OMB. Office of Management and Budget.

Omission error. Failure to carry out an intended action or to recognize that an action should have been carried out.

Omnibus Budget Reconciliation Act of 1987 (OBRA) (4). OBRA 1987 or Federal Nursing Home Reform Act created a set of national minimum standards of care and rights for people living in certified nursing facilities.

ONC. Office of the National Coordinator for Health Information Technology.

OPDRA. Office of Post-Marketing Drug Risk Assessment.

Operating margin. Net patient care revenues in excess of operating expenses.

Operating room. Locale where surgical interventions are performed.

OPO. Organ Procurement Organization.

OPPS. Outpatient Prospective Payment System.

OPTN. Organ Procurement Transplant Network.

OR. Operating room.

Ordinance. A law typically enacted by the elected legislative body of a city, town, county or other such minor political subdivision.

Organ Procurement Transplant Network. The unified transplant network established by the Congress under the National Organ Transplant Act of 1984.

Organizational culture. A set of values, guiding beliefs, or ways of thinking that are shared among members of an organization.

ORYX. The Joint Commission's program for integrating performance measures into the accreditation process. A key component is the use of standardized core measures.

OS. Left eye.

OSCAR. Online Survey Certification and Reporting Database.

OSHA. Occupational Safety and Health Administration.

OSHA general duty clause. OSHA's general requirement that employers maintain a safe work environment. OSHA inspectors may cite the general duty clause whenever an unsafe workplace condition or work practice is identified, but no specific OSHA regulation applies.

OSHRC. Occupational Safety and Health Review Commission.

Ostensible agency doctrine. The doctrine that permits a hospital to be held liable for the actions of an independent contractor. For example, in the absence of an employer-employee relationship, a managed care organization may still be held vicariously liable for the acts of provider physicians if the patient had a reasonable belief that the physician was the MCO's agent and that this belief was based on representations made by the MCO to that effect. The burden is on the plaintiff to prove that he or she relied on the fact that the MCO presented the physician as its agent.

OT. Occupational therapy.

OTC. Over the counter.

Outcome. The end result of medical care, as indicated by recovery, disability, functional status, mortality, morbidity, or patient satisfaction.

Outcomes measurement. The process of systematically tracking a patient's clinical treatment and responses to that treatment using generally accepted outcomes or quality indicators, such as mortality, morbidity, disability, functional status, recovery, and patient satisfaction. Such measures are considered by many health care researchers as the only valid way to determine the effectiveness of medical care.

Out-of-network (out-of-plan) services. In managed care, health care services required by a plan participant that are either not provided for by the plan (such as most experimental procedures) or must be provided for outside of the plan network (such as an emergency department visit for a participant who is traveling out of town).

Outpatient care. Treatment provided to a patient who is not confined in a health care facility. Includes services that do not require an overnight stay, such as emergency treatment, same-day surgery, outpatient diagnostic tests, and physician office visits. Also referred to as *Ambulatory care.*

Over-the-counter drugs. Medications that can be obtained without a written prescription from a physician.

Overuse. A health care quality problem involving the application or performance of unnecessary procedures or the provision of unnecessary services for patients.

P

P&P. Policy and procedure.

PA. Physician assistant; posterior-anterior.

PALS. Pediatric advanced life support.

Paradigm. A conceptual framework that aids in the explanation of a complex phenomenon or field of inquiry.

Parallel processes. Two or more processes being performed simultaneously.

Partnership. An entity formed by two or more persons to undertake a business purpose for profit. Each partner is liable for the obligations and liabilities of the partnership. Income to the partnership is considered income to the partners; there is no taxation at the level of the partnership.

Patient-controlled analgesia. A means for a patient to self-administer analgesics (pain medications) intravenously by a computerized pump, which introduces specific doses into an intravenous line.

Patient safety. Freedom from accidental injury. Ensuring patient safety involves the establishment of operational systems and processes that minimize the likelihood of errors and maximize the likelihood of intercepting them when they occur.

Patient Safety and Quality Improvement Act of 2005. Legislation signed into law in 2005 to improve patient safety by encouraging voluntary and confidential reporting of events that adversely affect patients. It creates patient safety organizations to collect, aggregate, and analyze confidential information reported by health care providers.

Patient safety evaluation system. The process of collecting, managing, or analyzing information the patient safety organization receives from health care providers.

Patient safety event taxonomy. A voluntary system for classifying patient safety incidents to enable different patient safety reporting systems to communicate with each other.

Patient safety work product. Data submitted by a health care provider to a listed patient safety organization; the data developed by the listed organization are privileged and confidential under the Patient Safety Act.

Patient Self-Determination Act of 1990. Federal statute (42 USC 1395 et seq.) requiring that certain health care organizations, including hospitals and HMOs, provide patients with information regarding advanced directives.

PC. Process cost: the fixed or investment costs associated with the process.

PC. Professional corporation.

PCA. Patient-controlled analgesia.

PCE. Potentially compensable event: any event that in the opinion of a risk management professional could give rise to a formal demand for compensation or an event that could generate an indemnity payment.

PDCA. The "plan, do, check, act" cycle offers health care systems a simple yet effective way to measure and modify change based on the effect on the quality outcome of the change they are attempting to achieve.

Peer review. A process whereby possible deviations from the standard of patient care are reviewed by an individual or committee from the same professional discipline to determine whether the standard of care was met and to make recommendations for improving patient care processes. Most jurisdictions provide at least a limited protection from discovery in civil actions for peer-review activities.

Per diem staff. Staff of a health care provider called in to work on an "as-needed" basis, depending on patient volume and acuity, as opposed to having their work schedules determined in advance.

Performance improvement. Analyzing a particular process or procedure, then modifying the process or procedure to increase the output, efficiency (economics), or effectiveness of the process or procedure.

Peril. The cause of a loss.

Perinatal care. The care of a woman before conception, of the woman and her fetus throughout pregnancy, and of the mother and her neonate until twenty-eight days after childbirth.

Personal health record. An electronic record of health-related information on an individual that conforms to nationally recognized interoperability standards and that can be drawn from multiple sources while being managed, shared, and controlled by the individual.

PET. Positron emission tomography.

Petition. See *Complaint.* Also used to denote the written instrument that initiates certain proceedings, such as bankruptcy.

Pharmacy patient profile. The specific record created for each patient in the pharmacy that typically notes the patient's name, diagnoses, weight, allergy history, and medications prescribed and dispensed.

PHI. Protected health information.

PHN. Public health nurse.

PHO. Physician-hospital organization.

PHR. Personal health record.

PHRP. Program for Human Research Protection.

PHS. Public Health Service.

Physician assistant. A specially trained and licensed allied health professional who performs certain medical procedures previously reserved to the physician. PAs practice under the supervision of a physician.

Physician-hospital organization. An integrated delivery system that links hospitals- and a group of physicians for the purpose of contracting directly with employers and managed care organizations. A PHO is a legal entity that allows physicians to continue to own their own practices and to see patients under the terms of a professional services agreement. This type of arrangement offers the opportunity to better market the services of both physicians and hospitals as a unified response to managed care.

PI. Performance improvement; process improvement.

PIAA. Physician Insurers Association of America.

PICU. Pediatric intensive care unit.

PIE. Problem, interventions, and evaluations of interventions.

PIP. Personal injury protection.

PL. Professional liability.

Plaintiff. A person who brings a civil lawsuit.

Pleadings. The formal allegations by the parties involved in a lawsuit that delineate the claims and defenses of each party and request judgment by the court prior to resolution.

PM. Preventive maintenance.

PMA. Premarket approval application.

PoC. Plan of correction.

Policy. A predetermined course of action established as a guide toward accepted business strategies and objectives.

POMR. Problem-oriented medical record.

POS. Point of service.

Positron emission tomography. An imaging technique that tracks metabolism and responses to therapy. Used in cardiology, neurology, and oncology; particularly effective in evaluating brain and nervous system disorders.

Postloss damage control. Any of a number of initiatives taken after a potentially compensable event to build rapport with the patient and family and to decrease the likelihood or severity of a subsequent claim.

Potentially compensable event. An occurrence for which a claim can be reasonably anticipated but for which no claim has yet been asserted.

PPE. Personal protective equipment.

PPO. Preferred provider organization.

PPS. Prospective payment system.

Practice guidelines. Formal procedures and techniques for the treatment of specific medical conditions that help physicians achieve optimal results. Practice guidelines are developed by medical societies and medical research organization such as the AMA and the Agency for Health Care Policy and Research, as well as many HMOs, insurers, and business coalitions. Practice guidelines serve as educational support for physicians and as quality assurance and accountability measures for managed care plans.

Precedent. A previously decided case that turned on the same facts, circumstances, or legal theory as the case under consideration. Lower courts are bound to follow precedents set by higher courts in the jurisdiction in which the lower court is located. Cases decided by courts in other jurisdictions may be considered "persuasive authority" by the court rendering judgment in a given case. In this event, the court may follow the decision of the other court, although it is not legally required to do so. The doctrine requiring the binding effect of precedent is called *stare decisis.*

Preemption. Doctrine adopted by the U.S. Supreme Court holding that certain matters are of such a national, as opposed to local, character that federal laws take precedence over state laws.

Preexisting condition. A physical or mental condition that an insured has prior to the effective date of coverage. Policies may exclude coverage for such condition for a specified period of time.

Preferred provider organization. A plan that contracts with independent providers at a discount for services. Generally, a PPO's network of providers is limited in size. Patients usually have free choice to select other providers but are given strong financial incentives to select one of the designated preferred providers. Unlike an HMO, a PPO is not a prepaid plan but does use some utilization management techniques. PPO arrangements can be either insured or self-funded. An "insurer-sponsored PPO" combines a large network of providers and utilization management programs; an "administrative-sponsored PPO" combines a large network of providers, utilization management programs, administrative services, and health care insurance. A "self-funded PPO" generally excludes administrative and insurance services from the plan package. However, employers can purchase these services separately.

Preparation. Readiness, to make ready.

Preventable adverse event. An adverse event that could have been avoided if actions were taken before the final step of the process.

Prevention. Action to make sure something does not happen; a risk control technique that decreases the probability of an event occurring.

Primary care. Basic health care, including initial diagnosis and treatment, preventive services, maintenance of chronic conditions, and referral to specialists.

Prior acts coverage. Insurance coverage that extends a claims-made policy to claims that occurred before the inception date of the policy but subsequent to a specified retroactive date for which a claim is made during the policy period. Sometimes referred to as *Nose coverage.*

Privileged communication. The exchange of information in an environment of confidentiality. A breach in privileged communication can result in a civil suit or tort.

Privileging (delineation of clinical privileges). The process of granting specific clinical privileges, based on training, experience, and competency, for individuals credentialed to provide health care services under medical staff bylaws.

Privity. A derivative interest founded on a contract or a connection between two parties; a mutuality of interest.

PRN. *Pro re nata,* Latin for "on an as-needed basis."

Procedure. A method by which a policy can be accomplished; it provides instructions necessary to carry out a policy statement.

Professional corporation. A corporation formed by individuals to practice their profession (as by physicians to practice medicine). The PC is typically licensed to practice the profession of the owners. Only members of the profession can be owners (shareholders) of the PC.

Professional liability insurance. Coverage for liability arising from the rendering of or failure to render professional services.

Promulgation. The process for creating rules or regulations. It typically involves announcement of a proposed regulation, allowance of a reasonable period for public comment, consideration of the comments received, and announcement of the final regulation.

Property coverage. Insurance on buildings, their contents, attached equipment, and equipment used for cleaning and maintenance.

Prospective payment system. A payment method in which the payment a hospital will receive for patient treatment is set up in advance; hospitals keep the difference if they incur costs less than the fixed price in treating the patient, and they absorb any loss if their costs exceed the fixed price. Also called "prospective pricing."

Protected concerted activity. A group activity that seeks to modify wages or working conditions.

Protected health information. Medical record information and other individually identifiable information for which privacy protection is afforded under HIPAA.

Provider-sponsored organization. A public or private entity established or organized and- operated by a health care provider or a group of affiliated health care providers that performs a substantial proportion of services under the Medicare+Choice contract and shares substantial financial risk.

Provider stop-loss coverage. Reimbursement to health care providers, subject to daily limitations and coinsurance requirements, for losses in excess of a stipulated amount per member per year.

PSA. Prostate-specific antigen.

PSDA. Patient Self-Determination Act.

PSES. Patient safety evaluation system.

PSET. Patient Safety Event Taxonomy.

PSO. Provider-sponsored organization.

PSQIA. Patient Safety and Quality Improvement Act of 2005.

PSRS. Patient Safety Reporting System.

PSWP. Patient safety work product.

PT. Physical therapy.

PTO. Paid time off.

Punitive damages. Damages sought or awarded to punish or deter a defendant or others from similar conduct rather than to compensate the injured party. The awarding of punitive damages generally requires a showing of gross negligence or willful and wanton misconduct. Such damages are not insurable in some jurisdictions and may be excluded by insurance policies. Also known as "exemplary damages."

Q

QA. Quality assurance.

QAPI. Quality assessment and performance improvement.

QI. Quality improvement.

QIO. Quality improvement organization.

QS. Quality system regulation for medical devices (21 CFR 820).

Quality assurance. Attempts by managed care organizations to measure and monitor the quality of care delivered.

Quality improvement organizations. QIOs are private contractor organizations working under the auspices of CMS to improve the effectiveness, efficiency, economy, and quality of services delivered to Medicare beneficiaries QIOs are required under sections 1152–1154 of the Social Security Act. CMS contracts with one QIO in each state, the District of Columbia, Puerto Rico, and the U.S. Virgin Islands to serve as that state or jurisdiction's QIO contractor. QIO contracts are three years in duration, with each three-year cycle referenced as an ordinal statement of work "SOW."[AU: WHAT IS "SOW"?]

Quality of care. The degree to which health services for individuals and populations increase the likelihood of desired health outcomes and are consistent with current professional knowledge.

Quid pro quo. Latin for "this for that": something received in exchange for something given.

Qui tam plaintiff. A plaintiff in an action under the False Claims Act that is brought on behalf of the federal government. The False Claims Act prohibits the presentation of false claims to the federal government. (*Qui tam* is the start of a Latin phrase meaning "Who sues on behalf of the king and himself.")

Qui tam relator. One who brings an action on behalf of the government (originally on behalf of the king).

R

RAC. Recombinant DNA Advisory Committee.

RAC. Rent-a-captive.

Radio-frequency identification. Technology that incorporates the use of electromagnetic or electrostatic coupling in the radio-frequency portion of the electromagnetic spectrum to uniquely identify an object, animal, or person.

RBC. Red blood cell count.

RCA. Root cause analysis.

RCRA. Resource Conservation and Recovery Act.

Realm of control. An area over which one exercises control; span of control.

Reasonable accommodation. Under the Americans With Disabilities Act, actions required by an employer to allow an otherwise qualified individual with a disability to perform a specific job. Reasonable accommodations include modifications to work processes and schedules and to physical facilities that are not "unduly burdensome."

Reconstruction Civil Rights Acts. Post-Civil War federal legislation (42 USC 1981, 1983) prohibiting certain types of racial discrimination.

Recovery. Postevent activities to restore an organization's operation to the same status as before an event.

Regulation. An enactment issued (promulgated) by a regulatory (nonelected) agency. Regulations must be promulgated pursuant to a statute that gives the agency the authority to do so and typically must go through a promulgation process.

Rehabilitation Act. Prohibits discrimination on the basis of disability in programs conducted by federal agencies, in programs receiving federal financial assistance, in federal employment, and in the employment practices of federal contractors.

Reimbursement. Compensating a person or entity for an expense; to pay back, refund, or pay.

Reinsurance. A contractual arrangement involving the purchase of insurance by an "insurer" from "another insurer" to protect against extraordinary losses.

Release. A document executed by the plaintiff, usually in exchange for a monetary settlement, that releases the defendant from any further obligation or threat of suit.

Reliability. Producing similar results with different users.

Rent-a-captive. A captive insurance company owned by investors rather than insureds and organized to insure or reinsure third-party risks.

Replacement cost. Basis for insurance reimbursement that is defined by the cost to repair or replace without any deduction for depreciation.

Reporting of claims. The process by which claims are reported to parties in an organization, such as the risk manager, and external to the organization, such as to the organization's insurance company.

Request for admission. A set of questions served on a party in litigation during discovery that asks that party to admit or deny the allegations presented.

Request for production. A written set of requests served on a party in litigation during discovery that asks the party to produce tangible things (records, photographs, equipment, and so on).

Request for proposal. A structured process by which an organization will invite external parties (vendors) to respond to their request for services.

Reservation of rights. An insurance carrier's attempt to preserve the rights to deny coverage at a later date even though the carrier may initially investigate and defend a claim.

Reserves. Money set aside, based on estimates of the amount that will ultimately be required to settle a claim or pay a judgment ("indemnity reserve") and to provide for a defense and pay other allocated expenses related to managing a claim ("expense reserve").

Res ipsa loquitur. Latin for "The thing speaks for itself"; a legal theory that applies in situations where the instrumentality was in the defendant's exclusive control and the accident was one that ordinarily could not happen in the absence of negligence.

Resource Conservation and Recovery Act. Authorizes the EPA to regulate the dumping of solid and hazardous waste. It also provides the EPA with the authority to regulate underground storage tanks.

Respondeat superior. Latin for "Let the master answer"; a doctrine of law under which the employer is responsible for the legal consequences of the acts and omissions of the employees who are acting within the scope of employment. While the employee is also generally liable for his or her own negligence, the employer remains vicariously liable.

Response. One of four categories in emergency management.

Responsiveness. One of the characteristic of a good measure. The item being measured is responsive or sensitive to risk management activities.

Restraint. Restriction of a person's freedom of movement. A "chemical restraint" is a medication used to control behavior or to restrict the patient's freedom of movement that is not a standard treatment for the patient's medical or psychiatric condition. A "physical restraint" is any manual method or physical or mechanical device, material, or equipment attached or adjacent to the patient's body that restricts freedom of movement or normal access to the' body.

Retrospective premium plan. An insurance policy for which an initial deposit premium is paid, -with the ultimate premium determined based on the loss experience of the insured. Some plans adjust the premium based on losses incurred (which include reserves for claims not yet settled), while others make adjustments based on paid losses only. Common in workers' compensation insurance programs.

Reuse. Using a single-use device more than once, as after reconditioning.

Reviewable sentinel event. An event that resulted in an unanticipated death or major permanent loss of function not related to the natural course of the patient's illness or underlying condition.

RFID. Radio-frequency identification.

RFP. Request for proposals.

Risk. The chance of loss. "Pure risk" is uncertainty as to whether loss will occur. "Speculative risk" is uncertainty about an event that could produce loss. Pure risk is insurable, but speculative risk usually is not.

Risk acceptance. The decision not to transfer an identified risk but instead to assume its financial consequences.

Risk-adjusted data. Data that have gone through the process of matching different groups in a manner that takes into account significant differences and equalizes them prior to performing comparisons. For example, prior to comparing mortality rates of different physicians, the patient population groups are "risk-adjusted" to equalize for age and other clinical status differences.

Risk analysis. The process used by the person or persons assigned risk management functions to determine the potential severity of the loss from an identified risk, the probability that the loss will happen, and alternatives for dealing with the risk.

Risk avoidance. The decision not to undertake a particular activity because the risk associated with the activity is unacceptably high. This is the only risk control technique that completely eliminates the possibility of loss from a given exposure.

Risk control techniques. Techniques designed to prevent the likelihood of an occurrence or reduce the frequency of occurrences that give rise to losses or to minimize at the least possible cost those losses that strike an organization.

Risk financing. Any of a number of programs implemented to pay for the costs associated with property and casualty claims and associated expenses, including insurance, self-insurance, and captive insurance companies.

Risk identification. The process of identifying problems or potential problems that can result in loss.

Risk management. The process of making and carrying out decisions that will help prevent adverse consequences and minimize the negative effects of accidental losses on an organization.

Risk management ethics. An articulated code of conduct to which a risk management professional must adhere if he or she is a member of the American Society for Healthcare Risk Management.

Risk management information system. Systems used to automate the gathering, reporting, storage, retrieval, analysis, evaluation, benchmarking, and display of risk information.

Risk purchasing group. Groups of policyholders with similar risks who may group together to purchase liability insurance authorized by the Federal Liability Risk Retention Act of 1986. Authorization under the federal statute allows a group to be incorporated in one state but to purchase insurance in all states, subject to specific restrictions.

Risk reduction. Reducing the severity of losses that other risk control techniques do not prevent.

Risk retention group. A liability-only domestic insurance captive for a group whose members are engaged in similar activities.

Risk transfer. The procedure of shifting risk of loss to another party who agrees to accept it.

RMIS. Risk management information system.

RN. Registered nurse.

Root-cause analysis. A multidisciplinary process of study or analysis that uses a detailed, structured process to examine factors contributing to a specific outcome (such as an adverse event).

RPG. Risk purchasing group.

RPLU. Registered professional liability underwriter.

RRG. Risk retention group.

R̄x. Prescription. (Originally the symbol ~Rx, standing for the first letter of the Latin word recipe, "take.")

S

Safe Medical Devices Act. Federal statute (21 USC 360 et seq.) governing the tracking of certain implantable medical devices and requiring reporting of patient deaths and serious injuries involving the use of medical devices or equipment.

Safety. Freedom from accidental harm.

Sarbanes-Oxley Act. The Public Company Accounting Reform and Investor Protection Act of 2002, also known as the Sarbanes-Oxley Act of 2002, introduced major changes to the regulation of financial practice and corporate governance. The legislation established new or enhanced standards for all U.S. public company boards, management, and public accounting firms. Named after Senator Paul Sarbanes and Representative Michael Oxley, who were its main architects.

SBAR. Situation, background, assessment, and recommendation.

SBS. Sick building syndrome.

SC. Subcutaneous.

SCCM. Society of Critical Care Medicine.

SCHIP. State Children's Health Insurance Program.

Scorecard. An evaluation tool that specifies the criteria a health care facility's key stakeholders will use to rate performance in relationship to the requirements.

SE. Sentinel event.

SEC. Securities and Exchange Commission.

Segregation. The separation of exposure units to reduce the uncertainty of losses by increasing the predictability of both loss frequency and severity.

Self-governing medical staff. The Joint Commission requirement that the hospital medical staff elect its own officers and approve its own bylaws and rules and regulations.

Self-insurance trust fund. A mechanism for funding claims and related expenses under a program of self-insurance whereby the insured establishes a segregated fund, administered by a trustee, that is replenished from time to time according to actuarially determined estimates of future loss costs.

Self-insured retention. The portion of a claim that the insured is required to pay before the insurer begins to pay. This is similar to a deductible but is frequently funded through a mechanism such as a self-insurance trust fund and is larger than a deductible. The insured generally manages claims falling entirely within the SIR (or contracts with a third party to do so) so that the insurer is involved only if the amount of the claim exceeds or is anticipated to exceed the amount of the retention. Common in hospital professional liability programs.

Sentinel event. An unexpected occurrence involving death or serious physical or psychological injury or the risk thereof, including loss of limb or function. The phrase "or risk thereof" includes any process variation for which a recurrence would carry a significant chance of a serious adverse outcome.

Sentinel event policy. A policy developed by The Joint Commission to encourage the self-reporting of medical errors to learn about the relative frequencies and underlying causes of sentinel events and to share lesions learned with other health care organizations, thereby reducing the risk of future sentinel events occurring.

Sentinel event reporting. The voluntary reporting of a sentinel event to The Joint Commission.

Settlement. An agreement between the parties in which consideration is paid and the matter is concluded with respect to those parties. Settlement may occur at any time.

Severance agreement. A contract between an employer and a terminated employee. Generally, severance agreements provide a lump sum payment or a period of salary continuation in return for the employee's agreement not to make certain claims against the employer.

Sexual harassment. Any of a number of statutorily prohibited kinds of unwanted sexual contact, remarks, or conditions of employment. In "quid pro quo sexual harassment", participation in sexual activity or performance of sexual favors is made an explicit or implicit condition of employment. A "hostile environment" exists when jokes, comments, cartoons, or touching of a sexual nature in the workplace interfere with an employee's ability to perform his or her job comfortably.

Sharp-end. See *Active failure*.

SICU. Surgical intensive care unit

SIDS. Sudden infant death syndrome.

Single-payer system. A financing system such as Canada's in which a single entity—usually the government—pays for all covered health care services.

Single-point weakness. A step in the process so critical that its failure would result in system failure or in an adverse event.

Single-use device. Devices manufactured for single use only.

SIR. Self-insured retention.

Skilled nursing facility. A facility, either freestanding or part of a hospital, that accepts patients in need of rehabilitation and medical care. To qualify for Medicare coverage, SNFs must be certified by Medicare and meet specific qualifications, including round-the-clock nursing coverage and availability of physical, occupational, and speech therapies.

Slander. A false and defamatory statement about a person.

Slip. Human error, usually occurring during an activity that the person is proficient in and is performing "automatically and hence somewhat inattentively."

SMDA. Safe Medical Devices Act.

SNF. Skilled nursing facility.

SOAP. Subjective, objective, assessment, plan: a popular problem-oriented model of documentation for use in progress notes.

SOAPIER. Subjective, objective, assessment, plan, interventions and evaluation, revision: a model of documentation that includes revision to the original plan of care.

SOB. Shortness of breath.

Special cause. A factor that intermittently and unpredictably causes a variation in a system.

SOM. State Operating Manual.

Specials. The elements of a plaintiff's damages that can be computed with relative precision, including lost wages, medical expenses, and future expenses.

SSA. Social Security Act.

SSI. Supplemental security income.

SSN. Social Security number.

Stair stepping. Periodic increases in the reserve by set amounts absent any circumstances that would support such an increase.

Standard. A minimum level or target range of acceptable performance or results. The American Society for Testing and Materials defines six types: (1) standard test methods: a procedure for identifying, measuring, and evaluating a material, product, or system; 2) standard specifications: a set of requirements to be satisfied and the procedures for determining whether each is satisfied; (3) standard practice: a recommended procedure for performing one or more specific operations or functions; (4) standard terminology: acceptable terms, definitions, descriptions, explanations, abbreviations, or acronyms; (5) standard guide: a series of options or instructions that suggest but do not dictate a specific course of action; and (6) standard classification: a systematic arrangement or division of products, systems, or services into groups based on similar characteristics.

Standard of care. As a measure of the competency of a medical professional, the typical level of skilled care and diligence exercised by members of the same professional or specialized field in light of the present state of medical and surgical science. In a legal proceeding, the degree to which the defendant' acted as an ordinary, prudent person with similar training and skill would have acted in a similar situation. If the defendant's conduct falls below this standard, the defendant may be determined to have acted negligently.

Standing. The right or authority by which a person may bring and sustain a legal proceeding. It is normally conferred on a person who has suffered an injury or that person's legal proxy.

Stat. Immediately.

Statement of fault. An acknowledgment of responsibility for a specific event or outcome.

Statute. A law enacted by the elected legislature of a state or the federal government.

Statute of limitations. The legal deadline by which a claimant must file a claim for damages or be barred from so doing. Most jurisdictions extend the deadline for individuals who are injured as minors, and many include a discovery rule extending the deadline for individuals whose injuries were not readily discoverable.

Statute of repose. A statute that sets a maximum period of time in which a suit may be brought. This statute is always longer than the statute of limitations and is generally subject to fewer, if any, exceptions or extension provisions.

STD. Sexually transmitted disease; short-term disability.

Stop loss. Insurance coverage for health care and managed care organizations that have agreed in advance to accept financial risk for the provision of health care services under capitated managed care contracts. Stop-loss policies limit the losses experienced by such entities when utilization of services exceeds estimates.

Subacute care. A level of care that is between acute care and long-term care.

Subpoena. A document issued by the court commanding a person to appear at a certain time and place to give testimony.

Subpoena duces tecum. A form of subpoena requiring not only the appearance of the subpoenaed party but also the production of books, papers, and other items.

Subrogation. The process of collecting from the person responsible for damages. It allows the insurer who is making a payment to the insured to assume the insured's right of recovery against the third party responsible for the loss.

SUD. Single-use device.

Summary judgment. A judgment rendered by the court before a verdict because no material issue of fact exists and one party or other is entitled to a judgment as a matter of law.

Summons. A brief (usually one-page) document commanding a defendant to appear and answer before a court.

Supreme court. The highest appellate court in most states and the federal government. Appeals entered after trial of a lawsuit are ultimately heard by this tribunal.

Surety. A party that guarantees the performance of another.

Surety bond. A three-part contract in which two parties, the surety and the principal (or obligor), agree to be bound by a promise to a third party, the obligee. If the principal defaults on the promise, the surety, for a premium paid in advance by the principal, steps in and fulfills the obligation. Surety bonds typical in the health care setting include patient trust fund bonds (to ensure that patient funds and valuables held by hospitals and nursing homes are appropriately safeguarded), performance bonds (to ensure that construction projects are completed as agreed), and various license bonds (to ensure appropriate performance of the licensee's duties). A surety who fulfills the obligations to the obligee may seek reimbursement from the principal.

Surge capacity. Reserve capacity in terms of staff, space, equipment, and supplies built into a health care provider's operations to accommodate emergency situations in which the demand for services may exceed normal levels.

Surgicenter. A health care facility that is physically separate from a hospital and provides prescheduled surgical services on an outpatient basis, generally at a lower cost than inpatient hospital care. Also called a *Freestanding ambulatory surgery center.*

Swing beds. Acute care hospital beds that can also be used for long-term care, depending on the needs of the patient and the community; only hospitals with fewer than one hundred beds located in a rural community, where long-term care may be inaccessible, are eligible to have swing beds.

System. A set of interdependent elements interacting to achieve a common aim. These elements may be both human and nonhuman (equipment, technologies, and so on).

Systemic or system-related issue. An issue that arises due to some design, process, or other operational aspect of a complex, multiple-entity "system" or multistep process.

T

T&A. Tonsillectomy and adenoidectomy.

Tail. The delay between an actual incident of malpractice or alleged action and the filing of a claim. An insurance company underwriting occurrence policies will be covering claims for many years after the policy has expired due to this long tail. In contrast, a claims-made policy covers only claims that are actually made during validity of the policy. Therefore, if you cancel your claims-made policy and wish to have continued coverage, you must purchase an extended reporting endorsement or tail coverage.

Tail coverage. Extended reporting endorsement.

TB. Tuberculosis.

Teaching hospital. A hospital that has an accredited medical residency training program and, typically, is affiliated with a medical school.

Telehealth. See *Telemedicine.*

Telemedicine. The use of telecommunications to provide medical information and services.

Tertiary care. Highly technical services for a patient who is in imminent danger of major disability or death.

Therapeutic privilege. A doctor's right to bar a patient's access to certain parts of the patient's medical records, out of a concern that the patient will not be able to cope with the information contained therein.

Third party. A party other than the insurer or the insured.

Third-party administrator. An independent organization that contracts to provide claims management services to a self-insured entity. Unlike insurance carriers, TPAs do not underwrite the insurance risk.

Third-party coverage. Insurance coverage for a party other than the insured to make that person whole for loss or injury caused by the insured.

Third-party-overclaim. A claim by an injured employee against a party other than his or her employer, such as the manufacturer of a machine involved in the injury, in which the third party brings the employer in as an additional defendant, as for failure to properly maintain the machine. Third-party overclaims fall outside workers' compensation coverage and are generally covered by employers' liability policies.

Threat envelope. In disaster planning, analysis of the types of occurrences most likely to occur, as well as those less likely but having particularly serious consequences for a community or organization for which it determines it must prepare.

Tight coupling. Dependence of each step of a process so closely on the preceding step that a variation in or adverse consequence resulting from the prior step affects the ensuing step and hence the entire desired outcome.

Title VII of the Civil Rights Act of 1964. Antidiscrimination legislation prohibiting harassment and discrimination of an employee based on that employee's race, gender, and national origin. Also prohibits sexual harassment.

Tomography. A diagnostic technique using X-ray photographs that do not show the shadows of structures before and behind the section under scrutiny.

Tort. A private or civil wrong or injury for which the court will provide a remedy in the form of an action for damages.

Tortfeasor. Party deemed liable as a result of the party's acts or omissions.

Total cost of risk. A report that captures a financial snapshot of the cost to an organization of a risk management program across all lines of coverage and operating units.

Total quality management. A systematic set of processes and tools designed to improve quality on an ongoing basis.

Toxic Substances Control Act. Federal statute that gives the Environmental Protection Agency the authority to track and control the toxic or potentially toxic chemicals used by industry.

TPA. Third-party administrator.

TPO. Treatment, payment, and operations.

TQI. Total quality improvement.

TQM. Total quality management.

Transitional duty. Altered working conditions put in place for an injured employee during the employee's period of recovery. Also known as "alternative duty," "light duty," and "modified duty."

Transparency. Full disclosure to the consumer or patient, as opposed to providing limited information or a policy of secrecy.

Treaty. A contract specifying that a reinsurer agrees in advance to accept certain classes of exposures. The insurer assumes underwriting authority on behalf of the reinsurer.

Triage. When multiple patients present for treatment, evaluating the urgency and seriousness of each patient's condition and establishing a priority list for their care to ensure that medical and nursing staff and facilities are used most efficiently.

Trial court. Usually, the lowest-level court in a given jurisdiction and the court in which the actual trial of the matter will be conducted.

Trust. A funding vehicle that, in its simplest terms, is a bank account administered by an independent third party (trustee); a common form of self-insurance for health care organizations.

Trustee. An individual or organization appointed to hold or manage and invest assets for the benefit of another.

TSCA. Toxic Substances Control Act.

Tx. Treatment.

U

UCL. Upper control limit.

Ultrasonography. An imaging technology for outlining various tissues and organs in the body.

UM. Utilization management.

Umbrella coverage. An insurance policy providing limits above those of a primary policy, such as for professional and general liability and auto liability. Umbrella policies may also include some specific coverage not found in the underlying policies.

Unanticipated outcome. A result of a treatment or procedure that differs significantly from what was anticipated.

Underground storage tank (UST). A tank that has at least ten percent of its volume underground. Generally referred to in terms of an "underground storage tank system," which includes the tank and any piping attached to the tank. USTs often house petroleum and other hazardous materials.

Underuse. Failure to provide a health care service or procedure for persons for whom it was clinically indicated or needed.

Underwriter. An insurance company employee who makes determinations regarding the acceptability of a given risk for insurance coverage and for specific terms, conditions, and pricing of such coverage.

Underwriting. The process of identifying, evaluating, and classifying the potential level of risk represented by a group seeking insurance coverage in order to determine appropriate pricing and administrative feasibility. The chief purpose of underwriting is to make sure that the potential for loss is within the range for which the premiums were established. Underwriting can also refer to the acceptance of risk.

United Network for Organ Sharing. A nonprofit scientific and educational organization that brings together medicine, technology, public policy, and science to facilitate every organ transplant performed in the United States. UNOS ensures that all organs are procured and distributed in a fair and timely manner.

United States Pharmacopeia. The U.S. Pharmacopeia is a nongovernmental, nonprofit public health organization whose independent volunteer experts work under strict conflict-of-interest rules to set scientific standards for all prescription and over–the–counter medicines and other health care products manufactured or sold in the

United States. They also set widely recognized standards for food ingredients and dietary supplements and for the quality, purity, strength, and consistency of these products critical to the public health.

Universal coverage. Making health care services available to all citizens.

UNOS. United Network for Organ Sharing.

Upper control limit. Used in quality control charts, it is a horizontal line representing the uppermost limit for samples to evaluate to. It is the upper limit of process capability in quality control for data points above the control (average) line. Opposite of LCL.

UR. Utilization review.

URAC. The former Utilization Review Accreditation Commission, also known as the American Accreditation HealthCare Commission.

Urgent care. Care for injury, illness, or another type of condition (usually not life-threatening) that should be treated within twenty-four hours. Also refers to after-hours care and to a health plan's classification of hospital admissions as urgent, semiurgent, or elective.

URL. Uniform resource locator, also known as a "Web address."

USA PATRIOT Act. Federal legislation (officially titled the Uniting and Strengthening America by Providing Appropriate Tools Required to Intercept and Obstruct Terrorism Act) that enhances the ability of law enforcement to deter and detect acts of terrorism, including cyberintelligence gathering, wiretapping, and other means of gathering information from designated private records.

USC. United States Code.

USERRA. Uniformed Services Employment and Reemployment Rights Act.

USP. United States Pharmacopeia.

USPHS. United States Public Health Service.

UST. Underground storage tank.

Utilization. Pattern of usage for a particular medical service such as hospital care or physician visits.

Utilization management. The function of monitoring the utilization of health care resources by individual patients (to verify that surgery was indeed required or that the length of a hospital stay is justified, for example). Also referred to as *Case management.*

Utilization review. An evolution of the care and services that patients receive, based on preestablished criteria and standards.

V

VAERS. Vaccine Adverse Event Reporting System: a program for vaccine safety of the CDC and the FDA. It collects, analyzes, and disseminates information about adverse events (possible side effects) that occur after the administration of U.S. licensed vaccines.

VAHRPAP. Veterans Administration Human Research Protection Accreditation Program.

Validity. The degree to which a test measures what it is designed to measure; support for the intended conclusion drawn from the results; one of the characteristic of a good measure.

VBAC. Vaginal birth after C-section.

VDRL. Venereal Disease Research Laboratory. VDRL is a screening test for syphilis that measures antibodies that can be produced by *Treponema pallidum,* the bacteria that causes syphilis.

Venue. The physical location, or the tribunal in that location, in which a legal proceeding may be brought. This is usually the place where the injury is alleged to have occurred.

Verdict. The formal decision or definitive answer of a jury impaneled to hear and decide the facts of a legal proceeding, which is reported to the court.

VHA. Veterans Health Administration.

Vicarious liability. The imposition of liability on one person for the actionable conduct of another, based solely on a relationship between the two persons, such as the liability of an employer for the acts of an employee.

VIP. Very important person.

Voir dire. The process of questioning jurors, prior to seating them, to determine if any jurors have knowledge of the case, personally know or know of the parties, or may otherwise have preconceptions that would prevent them from hearing and deciding the case impartially.

Volume-outcome relationship. The basis of a theory that for certain procedures, higher volume (by either a specific provider or a hospital) is associated with better health outcomes.

Voluntary protection program. A voluntary program created by OSHA in 1982 that recognizes businesses and work sites that show excellence in occupational safety and health and that are committed to effective employee protection beyond the requirements of OSHA standards.

Volunteer Protection Act of 1997. Signed into law by President Clinton in 1997, this law provides immunity from tort claims that might be filed against the volunteers of nonprofit organizations.

VPP (18). Voluntary protection program.

Vulnerability analysis. The process of identifying, quantifying, and prioritizing (or ranking) the vulnerabilities in a system.

W

WAG. Waste anesthetic gases.

Waiver of subrogation. A contractual provision in which one party agrees not to seek indemnification by the other in the event of a subsequent loss for which the second party may bear responsibility.

Warrant. A type of writ that is a formal written order issued by a body with administrative or judicial jurisdiction that commands or authorizes a person to do a particular thing. In modern usage, this public body is normally a court.

War risk exclusion. A exclusion found in many types of insurance policies excluding losses caused by acts of war or military action.

Waste anesthetic gas. Anesthetic gas and vapors that leak out into the surrounding room during medical and surgical procedures.

WBC. White blood cell count.

WC. Workers' compensation.

Whistleblower. An individual, frequently an employee or former employee, who reports unlawful activity, such as health care fraud and abuse or OSHA violations, to the government or an administrative agency. Some statutes provide for the whistleblower to receive a share of fines levied against the organization for making the report. Most statutes prohibit retaliatory discharge or other discriminatory actions against an employee who makes such a report.

WHO. World Health Organization.

WIC. Women and Infant Children Program.

Withholds. A provision in some managed care contracts withholding a portion of a health care provider's reimbursement until the end of a specific time period. If certain utilization targets are met for the period, the provider then receives the withheld reimbursement payments.

WMD. Weapons of mass destruction.

Workers' compensation. Statutory obligation requiring employers to provide compensation to employees for injuries arising out of and in the course of their employment.

Working memory. The concentrated short-term memory used by persons when learning any new task or process.

Worried well. Individuals who, in a disaster, contact health care providers for information or present at treatment sites for reassurance, even though they have no specific injuries or symptoms, inhibiting the provider's ability to assess and treat those truly in need of medical services.

INDEX

Page references followed by *fig* indicate an illustrated figure; followed by *t* indicate a table; followed by *e* indicate an exhibit

A